Climate Finance

Jian Chen

Climate Finance

A Comprehensive Guide to Financial Strategies in a Changing Climate

palgrave
macmillan

Jian Chen
Fudan University
Shanghai, China

ISBN 978-981-96-7974-4 ISBN 978-981-96-7975-1 (eBook)
https://doi.org/10.1007/978-981-96-7975-1

This Palgrave Macmillan imprint is published by the registered company Springer Nature Singapore Pte Ltd.
The registered company address is: 152 Beach Road, #21-01/04 Gateway East, Singapore 189721, Singapore

Preface

The world is at a crossroads. Climate change, once a distant threat, is now a stark reality, with its impacts felt from the melting glaciers of the Arctic to the rising sea levels threatening coastal communities. The science is unequivocal: human activities, primarily the burning of fossil fuels, are driving global warming at an unprecedented rate, with profound consequences for ecosystems, societies, and economies worldwide.

This is not just an environmental crisis, it's a financial crisis. The physical impacts of climate change are already causing billions of dollars in damages, disrupting businesses, and undermining economic stability. Moreover, the transition to a low-carbon economy, while essential, also presents financial risks for those who fail to adapt.

But amidst this challenge lies an unprecedented opportunity. We have the knowledge, the technology, and the resources to transition to a more sustainable and resilient future. A future powered by clean energy, built on climate-resilient infrastructure, and driven by a commitment to social equity and environmental stewardship.

To seize this opportunity, we need climate finance. Climate finance encompasses the flow of funds from public, private, and alternative sources to support the transition to a low-carbon and climate-resilient economy. It's about mobilizing the trillions of dollars needed to invest in renewable energy, energy efficiency, sustainable transportation, climate adaptation measures, and a host of other solutions that can mitigate climate change and build a more sustainable world.

This book provides a comprehensive guide to the complex and evolving landscape of climate finance. It is designed for a wide audience—students, investors, business leaders, policymakers, and anyone seeking to understand the crucial role of finance in addressing the climate crisis.

The book is structured in five parts:

Part I: Foundations of Climate Finance lays the groundwork for understanding the urgency and scale of the climate challenge, the financial risks it poses, and the essential role of financial institutions in mobilizing capital for climate solutions.

- Chapter 1: **The Imperative of Climate Finance** establishes the urgency of climate action, highlighting the scientific evidence, the economic impacts of climate change, and the potential for catastrophic consequences if we fail to act decisively. It introduces climate finance as a critical tool for addressing the crisis.
- Chapter 2: **Understanding Climate Risks** delves into the specific risks associated with climate change, exploring both the physical impacts of a changing climate and the economic and financial disruptions of the transition to a low-carbon economy.
- Chapter 3: **The Role of Financial Institutions** examines how banks, insurance companies, investors, and other financial institutions are exposed to climate risks, how they are mobilizing capital for climate solutions, and how they are navigating the evolving regulatory landscape of climate finance.

Part II: Climate Risk Modeling and Assessment explores the tools and techniques used to quantify and manage climate-related financial risks.

- Chapter 4: **Modeling the Climate** introduces the different types of climate models used to understand and project climate change, from weather prediction models to global climate models and risk assessment models.
- Chapter 5: **Climate Scenarios** dives into the world of climate scenarios, exploring how they are developed, the key frameworks used, and their applications in risk assessment, strategic planning, and decision-making.
- Chapter 6: **Physical Risk Modeling** examines the methodologies used to quantify the financial impacts of physical climate hazards, such as floods, droughts, and sea-level rise.
- Chapter 7: **Transition Risk Modeling** explores the tools and techniques for assessing the financial risks associated with the transition to a low-carbon economy, focusing on policy changes, technological advancements, and shifting market dynamics.
- Chapter 8: **The Challenge of Climate Risk Modeling** acknowledges the complexities and limitations of climate risk models, addressing issues related to data gaps, model uncertainty, and the importance of communication and expert judgment.

Part III: Climate Finance Investments examines the diverse landscape of climate-aligned investments, exploring the opportunities and challenges in various sectors and highlighting innovative financing mechanisms.

- Chapter 9: **Renewable Energy: Powering a Sustainable Future** delves into the world of renewable energy investments, exploring the technologies, the investment landscape, the challenges, and the financing mechanisms driving the transition to a clean energy future.
- Chapter 10: **Energy Storage: Enabling the Renewable Energy Transition** explores the crucial role of energy storage in supporting the integration of renewable energy, examining the different technologies, applications, and investment opportunities in this rapidly growing sector.
- Chapter 11: **Decarbonizing Hard-to-Abate Sectors** focuses on the challenges of reducing emissions from industries such as steel, cement, and aviation, exploring innovative technologies like CCUS and hydrogen, and examining the investment landscape.
- Chapter 12: **Investing in Nature-Based Solutions and Climate Adaptation** highlights the importance of nature-based solutions, such as reforestation and ecosystem restoration, and climate adaptation measures, exploring investment opportunities and financing mechanisms.
- Chapter 13: **Innovative Financing Mechanisms for Climate Action** explores a range of financial tools and strategies, including blended finance, green bonds, sustainability-linked loans, and impact investing.
- Chapter 14: **Navigating the Challenges: Greenwashing and Impact Measurement** addresses the crucial need for transparency and accountability in climate finance, discussing the risks of greenwashing and the importance of robust impact measurement.

Part IV: Climate Finance Tools and Applications provides a practical guide to the tools, frameworks, and strategies used to assess and manage climate risks, drive disclosure, and build climate-aligned investment portfolios.

- Chapter 15: **Climate Risk Assessment: Tools, Frameworks, and Applications** offers a comprehensive overview of climate risk assessment tools, discussing their applications, strengths and limitations, and key considerations for selecting and using these tools effectively.
- Chapter 16: **Climate-Related Disclosure: Standards, Best Practices, and Implementation** explores the key disclosure frameworks driving transparency and accountability in climate-related investments, providing guidance on how to implement disclosures and communicate effectively.
- Chapter 17: **Climate-Aligned Portfolio Management: Strategies and Tools** examines how investors can integrate climate considerations into their decision-making processes, setting climate-aligned investment

strategies and using tools to assess risks, identify opportunities, and manage their portfolios.
- Chapter 18: **Challenges of Integrating Climate Considerations** addresses the obstacles and complexities organizations face when implementing climate-related initiatives, offering guidance on overcoming data gaps, navigating model limitations, communicating effectively, and building organizational capacity.

Part V: Moving Forward: Shaping the Future of Climate Finance looks ahead to the emerging trends, opportunities, and challenges that are shaping the future of climate finance.

- Chapter 19: **The Role of Governments and Policy** examines the critical role of governments in creating an enabling environment for climate finance through policy instruments, international agreements, and multilateral finance mechanisms.
- Chapter 20: **International Climate Finance** explores the flows, challenges, and innovations in international climate finance, focusing on the need for increased ambition, greater transparency, and a more equitable distribution of funds.
- Chapter 21: **A Roadmap for Climate Finance** provides a practical guide for individuals and organizations seeking to integrate climate considerations into their financial decision-making, offering step-by-step guidance on setting objectives, assessing risks, selecting tools, engaging with stakeholders, and measuring impact.
- Chapter 22: **The Future of Climate Finance** explores the trends, opportunities, and challenges that will shape the future of climate finance, highlighting the role of technology, the evolving regulatory landscape, and the need for collective action to create a more sustainable and resilient world.

This book aims to equip readers with the knowledge, tools, and insights needed to navigate the complex world of climate finance and become active participants in the transition to a more sustainable future. We face an unprecedented challenge, but we also have an unprecedented opportunity. By harnessing the power of finance, we can create a world where economic prosperity and environmental sustainability go hand in hand.

Acknowledgments The completion of this Climate Finance textbook would not have been possible without the invaluable contributions and support of numerous individuals and groups. I would like to extend my deepest gratitude to my colleagues at the Fudan International School of Finance for their intellectual support, stimulating discussions, and collaborative spirit throughout this journey. Your expertise and insights have greatly enriched this work.

I am also thankful to the participants of the climate finance research seminars who shared their perspectives and provided constructive feedback during the development of this textbook, including Mr. Weng Haixiao, Co-founder and CEO of Carbon Baseline; Prof. Yuan Jiacan from Department of Atmospheric and Oceanic Sciences, Fudan University; Dr. Wang Rong from Department of Environmental Science and Engineering, Fudan University; Prof. Shan Rui from the Chinese University of Hong Kong, Shenzhen; Ms. Zhu Han from School of Pharmaceutical Sciences, Fudan University; Ms. Liu, Xiyue from Fudan University Press; Prof. Zhang Wenhong from the Department of Infectious Diseases at Huashan Hospital, Fudan University; Prof. Li Cheng, Director, Centre on Contemporary China and the World (CCCW) at the University of Hong Kong; Mr. Liao Shuanghui Chairman of the Shanghai Jinsinan Institute of Finance; Ms. Yan Danhong, Deputy Secretary-General of the Green Finance 60 Forum; Mr. Gao Erji, Executive President of Caixin Insight Group; Dr. Lin Su; Mr. Xiong Peng, Research Fellow at Fudan Western-China International Institute Of Finance, Chengdu. Your active engagement and thoughtful questions helped shape the content and ensure its relevance to the field of climate finance.

A special thank you goes to my research assistant, Julia Ju, for her tireless efforts in researching, organizing, and reviewing materials. Your dedication and meticulous attention to detail have been instrumental in bringing this project to fruition.

Finally, I would like to acknowledge the broader community of climate finance researchers, practitioners, and policymakers whose work has inspired and informed this textbook. Your contributions to advancing the field of climate finance are a cornerstone of this publication.

Thank you all for your support and collaboration.

Competing Interests The author has no competing interests to declare that are relevant to the content of this manuscript.

CONTENTS

Abbreviations

ADB	Asian Development Bank
A&E	Amend-and-Extend Transactions
AEO	Annual Energy Outlook
AFOLU	Agriculture, Forestry, and Other Land Uses
AI	Artificial Intelligence
AUM	Assets Under Management
BESS	Battery Energy Storage Systems
BEIR	Breakeven Inflation Rates
BIPV	Building-Integrated Photovoltaics
BIS	Bank for International Settlements
BM	Balancing Mechanism
BMD	Bangladesh Meteorological Department
BMS	Battery Management Systems
BNEF	Bloomberg New Energy Finance
BoE	Bank of England
BOS	Balance-of-System
BRT	Bus Rapid Transit
C&I	Commercial and Industrial
CAES	Compressed Air Energy Storage
CAPEX	Capital Expenditure
CAT	Catastrophe
CBES	Climate Biennial Exploratory Scenario
CBI	Climate Bonds Initiative
CCUS	Carbon Capture, Utilization, and Storage
CDR	Carbon Dioxide Removal
CESM	Community Earth System Model
CFRMs	Climate Finance Risk Models
CGFI	Centre for Greening Finance and Investment
CGT	Common Ground Taxonomy
CICERO	Center for International Climate and Environmental Research
CIF	Climate Investment Funds
CM	Capacity Market

CMIP6	Coupled Model Intercomparison Project Phase 6
CNCA	Carbon Neutral Cities Alliance
CONUS	Conterminous United States
COP	Conference of the Parties
CPI	Climate Policy Initiative
CFRMs	Climate Finance Risk Models
CPP	Cyclone Preparedness Program
CRA	Climate Risk Assessment
CSP	Concentrated Solar Power
CSRD	Corporate Sustainability Reporting Directive
CSWA	California Sustainable Winegrowing Alliance
DC	Dynamic Containment
DCF	Discounted Cash Flow
DERs	Distributed Energy Resources
DFI	Development Finance Institutions
DFR	Dynamic Frequency Response
DM	Dynamic Moderation
DNI	Direct Normal Irradiance
DR	Dynamic Regulation
DS3	Delivering a Secure, Sustainable Electricity System
DWR	Department of Water Resources
DWT	Discrete Wavelet Transform
EAD	Exposure at Default
EA Interest Rate	Euro Area Interest Rate
ECMWF	European Centre for Medium-Range Weather Forecasts
EGS	Enhanced Geothermal Systems
EIB	European Investment Bank
EJ	Exajoules
EMDEs	Emerging Markets and Developing Economies
EMS	Energy Management System
ENIAC	Electronic Numerical Integrator and Computer
EP	Exceedance Probability
EPC	Engineering, Procurement, Construction
ERM	Enterprise Risk Management
ESaaS	Energy Storage as a Service
ESG	Environmental, Social, and Governance
ESMValTool	Earth System Model Evaluation Tool
ESRS	European Sustainability Reporting Standards
ETS	Emissions Trading Schemes
EU	European Union
EV	Electric Vehicle
EVCI	Electric Vehicle Charging Infrastructure
FCDO	Foreign, Commonwealth & Development Office
FCAS	Frequency Control Ancillary Services
FCR	Facility for Rare Isotope Beams
FE	Fixed Effects
FERC	Federal Energy Regulatory Commission
FFR	Firm Frequency Response
FFSs	Fossil Fuel Subsidies

FID	Financial Investment Decision
FITs	Feed-in Tariffs
FTM	Front-of-the-Meter
GAR	Global Assessment Report
GCMs	Global Climate Models
GCF	Green Climate Fund
GEEREF	Global Energy Efficiency and Renewable Energy Fund
GHG	Greenhouse Gas
GIIN	Global Impact Investing Network
GIS	Geographic Information Systems
GP	Local Company
GBP	Green Bond Principles
GRI	Global Reporting Initiative
GSF	Gore Street Capital
GSI	Global Sustainable Investment
GSS+	Green, Social, Sustainability, and Sustainability-Linked
GT	Gigatonnes
HPC	High-Performance Computing
HPJ-FE	Half-Panel Jackknife Fixed Effects
HQLA	High-Quality Liquid Assets
IAD	Inland Air Defense
IAMs	Integrated Assessment Models
ICE	Internal Combustion Engine
ICMA	International Capital Market Association
IEA	International Energy Agency
IEEFA	Institute for Energy Economics and Financial Analysis
IFC	International Finance Corporation
IFRS	International Financial Reporting Standards
ILO	International Labour Organization
IMF	International Monetary Fund
IMO	International Maritime Organization
ING	Bank
IoT	Internet of Things
IPCC	Intergovernmental Panel on Climate Change
IRENA	International Renewable Energy Agency
IRR	Internal Rate of Return
ISIMIP2b	Inter-Sectoral Impact Model Intercomparison Project
ISSB	International Sustainability Standards Board
ITR	Implied Temperature Rise
IUGS	International Union of Geological Sciences
IWMI	International Water Management Institute
JICA	Japan International Cooperation Agency
kWh	Kilowatt-Hours
LCOE	Levelized Cost of Electricity
LDCs	Least Developed Countries
LGD	Loss Given Default
LISA	Local Indicators of Spatial Association
LMA	Loan Market Association
LNG	Liquefied Natural Gas

LSE	London School of Economics
MaaS	Mobility as a Service
MDBs	Multilateral Development Banks
ML	Machine Learning
MSR	Market Stability Reserve
MW	Megawatts
MWh	Megawatt-Hours
NAP	National Adaptation Programme
NASA	National Aeronautics and Space Administration
NbS	Nature-Based Solutions
NCEI	National Centers for Environmental Information
NCS	Natural Climate Solutions
NDC	Nationally Determined Contributions
NGFS	Network for Greening the Financial System
NHC	National Hurricane Center
NOAA	National Oceanic and Atmospheric Administration
NPPs	Nuclear power plants
NSU	Nova Southeastern University
NWP	Numerical Weather Prediction
NZAM	Net Zero Asset Managers
OECD	Organisation for Economic Co-operation and Development
OPEC	Organization of the Petroleum Exporting Countries
OPEX	Operational Costs
PACTA	Paris Agreement Capital Transition Assessment
PAYG	Pay-As-You-Go
PCAF	Partnership for Carbon Accounting Financials
PD	Probability of Default
PHS	Pumped Hydro Storage
pkm	passenger kilometre
PML	Probable Maximum Loss
PPAs	Power Purchase Agreements
PPPs	Public-Private Partnerships
PRI	Principles for Responsible Investment
PV	Photovoltaics
PwC	PricewaterhouseCoopers
QPF	Quantitative Precipitation Forecasts
R&D	Research and Development
RCPs	Representative Concentration Pathways
RCMs	Regional Climate Models
REITs	Real Estate Investment Trusts
RMI	Rocky Mountain Institute
RPS	Renewable Portfolio Standards
RRS	Retail and Reinsurance
SAF	Sustainable Aviation Fuels
SASB	Sustainability Accounting Standards Board
SBTi	Science Based Targets initiative
SCC	Social Cost of Carbon
SDGs	Sustainable Development Goals
SEC	Securities and Exchange Commission

SGIP	Self-Generation Incentive Program
SIDS	Small Island Developing States
SLLs	Sustainability-Linked Loans
SLBs	Sustainability-Linked Bonds
SMR	Steam Methane Reforming
SOEs	State-Owned Enterprises
SPTs	Sustainability Performance Targets
SSPs	Shared Socioeconomic Pathways
TA	Technical Assistance
TAS	Tasmania
TCFD	Task Force on Climate-Related Financial Disclosures
TIPS	Treasury Inflation Protected Securities
tkm	Tonne Kilometre
TMG	Tokyo Metropolitan Government
UAE	United Arab Emirates
UK	United Kingdom
UNEP FI	United Nations Environment Programme Finance Initiative
UNFCCC	United Nations Framework Convention on Climate Change
US	United States
USAID	US Agency for International Development
VaR	Value-at-Risk
VHF	Very High Frequency
VIC	Victoria
WEF	World Economic Forum
WMO	World Meteorological Organization
WRI	World Resource Institute
WT	Wavelet Transform

List of Figures

Chapter 1

Chapter 2

Chapter 3

Chapter 4

Chapter 5

Chapter 6

Chapter 7

Chapter 8

Chapter 9

Chapter 10

Chapter 11

Chapter 13

Chapter 17

Chapter 19

Chapter 20

Chapter 21

List of Tables

Chapter 11

Chapter 12

Chapter 15

PART I

Foundations of Climate Finance

Climate change is not just an environmental issue, it's a profound economic and social challenge that demands a global response. Finance plays a crucial role in addressing this crisis, providing the resources needed to mitigate greenhouse gas emissions, adapt to a changing climate, and build a more sustainable and resilient future.

This part lays the foundation for understanding the critical role of climate finance in navigating the complexities of a changing world. We'll explore the science behind climate change, examine the financial impacts it poses, and analyze the essential role of financial institutions in mobilizing capital for climate solutions.

Chapter 1: The Imperative of Climate Finance: A Call to Action
This chapter establishes the urgency of climate action, highlighting the overwhelming scientific consensus on climate change, the escalating risks of inaction, and the potential for catastrophic consequences if we fail to take decisive steps. We'll explore the financial impacts of climate change, both the tangible risks of physical impacts and the challenges of navigating the transition to a low-carbon economy. Finally, we'll introduce the concept of climate finance as a critical tool for mobilizing the capital needed to address this global challenge.

Chapter 2: Understanding Climate Risks: The Tangible Impacts of a Changing World
This chapter delves into the specific risks associated with climate change, exploring both the physical impacts of a changing climate and the economic and financial disruptions of the transition to a low-carbon economy. We'll examine the increasing frequency and intensity of extreme weather events, the

long-term consequences of gradual environmental changes, and the challenges of adapting to a more volatile and uncertain future.

Chapter 3: The Role of Financial Institutions: Navigating a Transformative Landscape
Financial institutions are at the heart of the climate finance landscape. This chapter examines the role of banks, insurance companies, investors, and other financial institutions in managing climate risks, mobilizing capital for climate solutions, and shaping the transition to a more sustainable and resilient financial system. We'll explore the increasing exposure of these institutions to climate-related risks, the innovative financial instruments they are using, and the evolving role of regulation and policy in driving climate finance.

By understanding the foundations of climate finance and the challenges we face, we can create a roadmap for action, harnessing the power of finance to build a more sustainable future for all.

CHAPTER 1

The Imperative of Climate Finance: A Call to Action

1 Introduction: A Defining Moment for Humanity

The world stands at a critical juncture. The climate crisis has transitioned from a distant threat to our current reality. From raging wildfires engulfing landscapes to increasingly powerful storms devastating coastlines, the effects of climate change demand global attention. The scientific consensus is irrefutable: human activities, primarily the combustion of fossil fuels, are driving global warming at an alarming rate, with far-reaching consequences for ecosystems, societies, and economies worldwide.

The below image provides clear evidence of global warming over the past 50 years. The warming trend is not uniform, with some regions experiencing significantly higher temperature increases than others. The accelerated warming in the Arctic is particularly concerning due to its potential impacts on sea ice, permafrost, and global climate systems (Fig. 1).

As shown below, while there are some minor differences between the datasets, global average temperature data from various scientific organizations show substantial agreement concerning the progress and extent of global warming. The most recent data points suggest that the global average temperature has increased by about 1.1 to 1.2 degrees Celsius above the pre-industrial level. This is approaching the 1.5 degree Celsius target set by the Paris Agreement to limit global warming (Fig. 2).

The Fourth National Climate Assessment includes the following chart, illustrating human activity is the dominant driver of recent global warming. The close alignment between the observed warming and the estimated human contribution underscores the significant impact of human-induced greenhouse gas emissions. Natural factors play a role but cannot explain the current

J. Chen, *Climate Finance*, https://doi.org/10.1007/978-981-96-7975-1_1

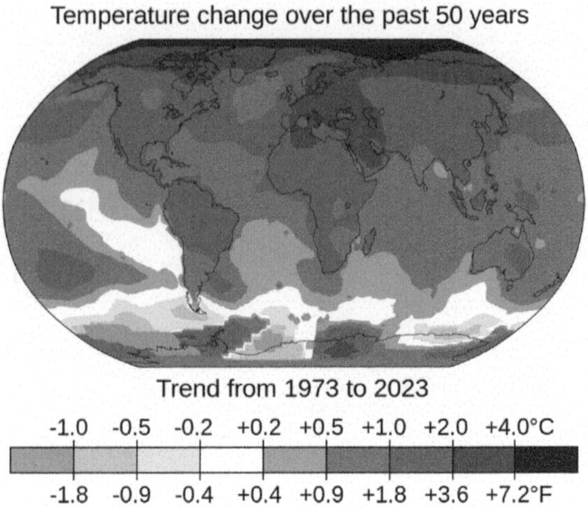

Fig. 1 Temperature change during the last 50 years (By NASA's Scientific Visualization Studio, CC BY-SA 4.0, https://commons.wikimedia.org/w/index.php?curid=113131169)

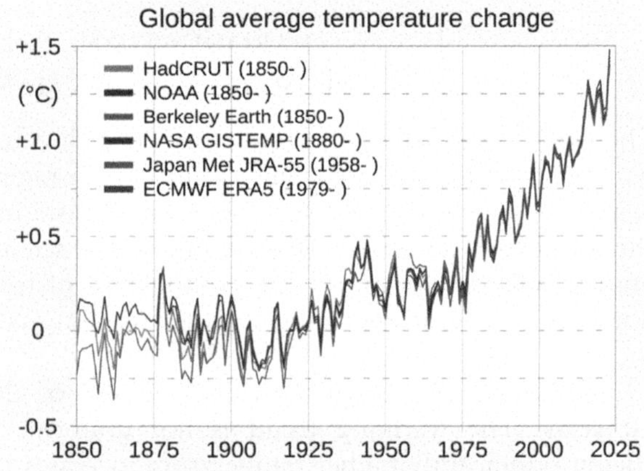

Fig. 2 Global average temperature change since 1850 (By RCraig09—Own work, CC BY-SA 4.0, https://commons.wikimedia.org/w/index.php?curid=88535596)

warming trend. Natural variability influences global temperature, but its overall impact is dwarfed by the human contribution in recent decades. The warming trend is accelerating. The steep rise in observed global temperature, particularly in the last few decades, highlights the urgency of addressing climate change (Fig. 3).

The above graph reflects the scientific consensus that human activities are the primary cause of the observed global warming. It serves as a visual reminder of the critical need to reduce greenhouse gas emissions to mitigate the impacts of climate change.

Among different human activities, **greenhouse gas emission is the dominant warming factor.** Carbon dioxide has the largest warming effect, followed by methane and nitrous oxide. Other greenhouse gases like halogenated gases

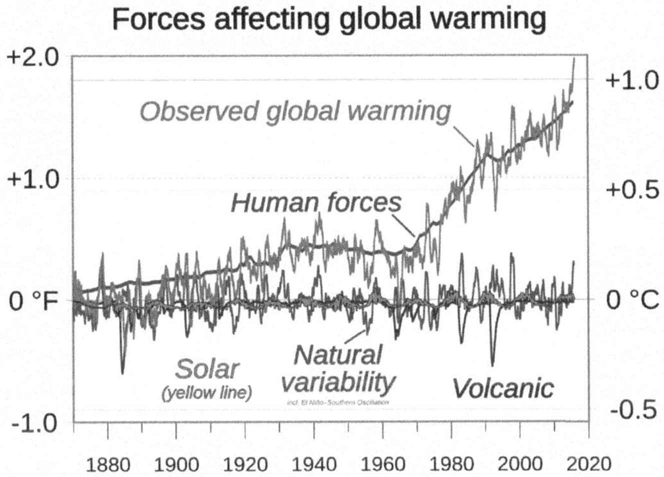

Fig. 3 Driving factors for global warming (By RCraig09—Own work, CC BY-SA 4.0, https://commons.wikimedia.org/w/index.php?curid=114309391)

and nitrogen oxides also contribute to warming, albeit to a lesser extent (Fig. 4).

According to the Copernicus Climate Change Service[1] (C3S) data, the Earth experienced its warmest days on record in July 2024. On July 22nd, the daily global average temperature reached a new record high of 17.16 °C, surpassing the previous records of 17.09 °C set on July 21, 2024, and 17.08 °C set on July 6, 2023. The difference between these temperatures

Fig. 4 Physical drivers of climate change (By Eric Fisk - Own work, CC BY-SA 4.0, https://commons.wikimedia.org/w/index.php?curid=81034563)

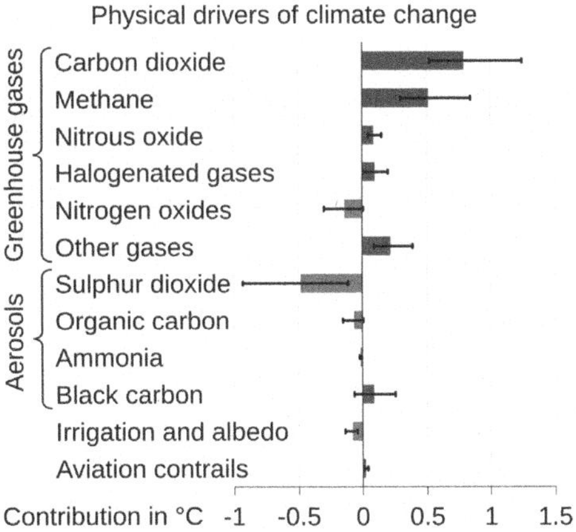

[1] https://climate.copernicus.eu/new-record-daily-global-average-temperature-reached-july-2024.

and the new record is larger than typical day-to-day variations. Moreover, the temperatures since July 2023 have been significantly higher than all previous years, indicating a concerning trend of global warming.

The records shouldn't come as a complete surprise. During 2021-2023, The IPCC[2] has conducted its Sixth Assessment Report,[3] the most comprehensive report on climate change until now. Its three Working Groups have generated three Special Reports and a Synthesis Report.

- The Working Group I contribution to the Sixth Assessment Report, Climate Change 2021: The Physical Science Basis was released on August 9, 2021.
- The Working Group II contribution, Climate Change 2022: Impacts, Adaptation and Vulnerability was released on February 28, 2022.
- The Working Group III contribution, Climate Change 2022: Mitigation of Climate Change was released on April 4, 2022.
- The Synthesis Report, Climate Change 2023: Synthesis Report was released on March 20, 2023 to inform the 2023 Global Stocktake under the United Nations Framework Convention on Climate Change.

The IPCC's "AR6 Synthesis Report, Climate Change 2023" provides a stark and comprehensive assessment of the state of the climate crisis, highlighting the urgency of immediate and ambitious action to avert catastrophic consequences. It builds upon the findings of three Working Group reports and three Special Reports from the IPCC's Sixth Assessment Cycle.

Key Findings:

- **Human-Induced Warming:** Human activities have unequivocally caused global warming, reaching 1.1 °C above pre-industrial levels in 2011–2020. Greenhouse gas emissions continue to rise, fueled by unsustainable energy use, land-use change, and consumption patterns.
- **Widespread and Intensifying Impacts:** Climate change is already impacting every region of the globe, causing widespread adverse effects on ecosystems, human health, food and water security, and economies. Vulnerable communities are disproportionately affected.
- **Escalating Risks:** The magnitude and rate of climate change and associated risks depend strongly on near-term actions. With every increment of warming, risks escalate, including more frequent and intense extreme

[2] The Intergovernmental Panel on Climate Change (IPCC) is the international body for assessing the science related to climate change. The IPCC was set up in 1988 by the World Meteorological Organization (WMO) and United Nations Environment Programme (UNEP) to provide policymakers with regular assessments of the scientific basis of climate change, its impacts and future risks, and options for adaptation and mitigation. https://www.ipcc.ch/site/assets/uploads/2024/04/IPCCFactSheet_WhatisIPCC.pdf.

[3] https://www.ipcc.ch/assessment-report/ar6/.

weather events, sea-level rise, biodiversity loss, and cascading impacts across sectors and regions.
- **Adaptation Limits:** While adaptation measures can effectively reduce risks, limits to adaptation are being reached in some sectors and regions, particularly at higher warming levels. Maladaptation is also increasing, exacerbating existing inequalities.
- **Mitigation Gaps:** Current policies and pledges are insufficient to limit warming to 1.5 °C or even 2 °C. Deep, rapid, and sustained reductions in greenhouse gas emissions across all sectors are essential.
- **Insufficient Finance:** Global climate finance flows have increased but fall short of the levels needed to achieve ambitious mitigation and adaptation goals, particularly in developing countries.
- **Urgent Need for Transformation:** Shifting development pathways toward sustainability is crucial to achieving climate-resilient development and securing a livable future. This requires integrating mitigation, adaptation, and sustainable development goals, with a strong focus on equity, justice, and inclusion.

The report emphasizes that there is a rapidly closing window of opportunity to secure a livable and sustainable future for all. Delaying action will result in irreversible and catastrophic consequences. It stresses the urgent need for transformative action at all levels of governance, involving governments, businesses, civil society, and individuals.

The WMO[4] (2024) "State of the Global Climate 2023" report also paints a bleak picture of a rapidly changing climate, highlighting that 2023 shattered numerous climate records, bringing humanity closer than ever to the critical 1.5 °C warming threshold set by the Paris Agreement.

Key Findings:

- **Record Warmest Year:** 2023 was the hottest year on record, with a global average temperature 1.45 °C above pre-industrial levels.
- **Greenhouse Gas Surge:** Concentrations of major greenhouse gases, including carbon dioxide, methane, and nitrous oxide, reached record observed highs.
- **Ocean at Record Heat:** Ocean heat content soared to its highest level in the 65-year observational record, contributing to rising sea levels and widespread marine heatwaves.
- **Shrinking Ice:** Antarctic sea-ice extent plummeted to record lows, and glaciers worldwide suffered significant mass loss, particularly in Switzerland and Western North America.

[4] World Meteorological Organization (WMO) is the United Nations system's authoritative voice on the state and behaviour of the Earth's atmosphere, its interaction with the land and oceans, the weather and climate it produces and the resulting distribution of water resources. https://wmo.int/about-wmo/overview.

- **Extreme Weather Impacts:** Heatwaves, floods, droughts, wildfires, and intense tropical cyclones wreaked havoc globally, causing substantial socioeconomic losses and exacerbating humanitarian crises.
- **Food Insecurity and Displacement:** Extreme weather further strained food security, leading to acute food insecurity for millions and displacing hundreds of thousands from their homes.

The WMO (2024) report underscores the urgent need to accelerate climate action on all fronts:

- **Scaling Up Mitigation:** Drastically reducing greenhouse gas emissions across all sectors, transitioning to renewable energy sources, and adopting sustainable land management practices are crucial.
- **Closing the Finance Gap:** Significantly increasing climate finance flows, particularly for adaptation, is essential to support vulnerable countries and communities.
- **Prioritizing Equity and Justice:** Ensuring that climate responses prioritize equity, climate justice, and inclusivity is crucial to address the disproportionate impacts on vulnerable populations.
- **Strengthening Early Warning Systems:** Expanding early warning systems is vital to protect lives and livelihoods from extreme weather events.

Another report by the WMO (2023), titled "Global Climate 2011–2020: A Decade of Accelerating Climate Change" offers a sobering analysis of the significant shifts in the Earth's climate system over the past decade, highlighting a disturbing trend of accelerating climate change and its impacts on human systems. Here are the key takeaways:

Accelerated Warming:

- The decade (2011–2020) was the warmest on record by a significant margin, with each decade since the 1990s being warmer than all preceding ones.
- This warming trend was observed across land and ocean, leading to record-high temperatures in numerous regions and countries.

Greenhouse Gas Surge:

- Atmospheric concentrations of major greenhouse gases (CO_2, methane, and nitrous oxide) continued to rise during the decade, accelerating the pace of climate change.
- CO_2 emissions from fossil fuels reached record highs, with the ocean and land sinks absorbing only about half of these emissions.

Impacts on the Climate System:

- Oceans are warming and acidifying at an alarming rate, leading to more frequent and intense marine heatwaves and threatening marine ecosystems.
- Global mean sea level is rising at an accelerated pace, primarily due to ocean warming and the melting of glaciers and ice sheets.
- Glaciers worldwide experienced unprecedented thinning, and the Greenland and Antarctic ice sheets lost mass at an accelerated rate.
- Arctic sea-ice extent continued its multi-decade decline, with record lows observed during the summer melt season.

Extreme Events and Impacts on Human Systems:

- The decade witnessed a high frequency of extreme events, including heatwaves, floods, droughts, wildfires, and tropical cyclones, with devastating impacts on human systems.
- Virtually every attribution study of extreme heat events during this period confirmed that anthropogenic climate change significantly increased their likelihood.
- Extreme heatwaves caused the highest number of casualties, while tropical cyclones resulted in the most significant economic damage.
- These events have had profound impacts on food security, causing widespread crop failures, livestock losses, and displacement, hindering progress toward Sustainable Development Goals (SDGs).

The WMO (2023) report also emphasizes the urgent need for ambitious climate action to mitigate greenhouse gas emissions and adapt to the increasingly severe impacts of climate change. It highlights the importance of:

- **Synergistic Action:** Integrating climate action with sustainable development policies to maximize co-benefits and address shared challenges.
- **Closing the Finance Gap:** Significantly increasing climate finance flows to support mitigation and adaptation efforts, especially in vulnerable developing countries.
- **Strengthening Early Warning Systems:** Expanding and improving early warning systems to protect lives and livelihoods from extreme events.

The report paints a clear picture: The climate crisis is accelerating, demanding immediate and transformative action to avert catastrophic consequences.

The WMO (2023) implications of climate change are profound. We are witnessing the melting of polar ice caps, rising sea levels that threaten coastal cities, and an increase in the frequency and intensity of extreme weather events, causing significant damage and displacing millions of people due to climate-related disasters. The World Bank estimates that by 2030, climate change could force over 100 million people into poverty, amplifying existing inequalities and creating new vulnerabilities.

Despite these challenges, a remarkable opportunity emerges. We possess the knowledge, technology, and resources to shift toward a sustainable and resilient future—one powered by clean energy, supported by climate-resilient infrastructure, and driven by a commitment to social equity and environmental stewardship. However, to capitalize on this opportunity, we must act decisively and with urgency. This is where climate finance plays a critical role.

Climate finance serves as a powerful tool for mobilizing the trillions of dollars required to address the climate crisis and transition to a low-carbon, climate-resilient future. It encompasses the flow of funds from public, private, and alternative sources to support both mitigation efforts—reducing greenhouse gas emissions—and adaptation measures—building resilience to the inevitable impacts of climate change.

This book delves into the imperative of climate finance, exploring its crucial role in shaping a sustainable future and highlighting the challenges and opportunities ahead.

2 The Financial Impact of Climate Change: A Looming Crisis

The climate crisis is not solely an environmental challenge; it poses a significant economic threat as well. The physical and transition risks associated with climate change are already having tangible financial impacts, projected to escalate dramatically in the coming decades. These impacts have the potential to destabilize markets, disrupt businesses, and undermine global economic growth.

The Financial Stability Oversight Council (FSOC, 2021) "Report on Climate-Related Financial Risk 2021" represents a landmark acknowledgment by US financial regulators of the systemic threat posed by climate change to the stability of the financial system and the broader economy.

Key Takeaways:

- **Climate Change as an Emerging Threat:** The report recognizes climate change as a significant and growing risk to financial stability, potentially affecting institutions, markets, and communities through both physical and transition risks.
- **Physical Risks:** The report highlights the increasing frequency and severity of climate-related events like hurricanes, wildfires, and floods, which can damage property, disrupt business activity, and lead to credit and market losses for financial institutions.

- **Transition Risks:** The report acknowledges the risks associated with the transition to a low-carbon economy, including potential policy changes, technological shifts, and investor preferences that could impact asset values and financial institutions' exposures.
- **Data and Methodological Gaps:** The report identifies significant data and methodological challenges in assessing climate-related financial risks, including the need for better data on climate impacts, exposures of non-financial and financial entities, and robust models to quantify these risks.

Disclosure Deficiencies:

- The report emphasizes the critical role of consistent, comparable, and decision-useful climate-related disclosures by companies and financial institutions. It acknowledges that existing disclosure requirements and voluntary frameworks fall short in providing investors and market participants with the information they need.
- **Scenario Analysis as a Key Tool:** The report recognizes scenario analysis as a valuable tool for assessing climate-related financial risks, both for individual firms and for regulators evaluating system-wide risks.
- **Prioritizing Vulnerable Communities:** The report acknowledges the disproportionate impact of climate change on financially vulnerable communities and the need for thoughtful policy responses that consider these impacts and potential trade-offs.

The FSOC (2021) report outlines a comprehensive set of recommendations for FSOC members and the Council itself, including:

- **Building Capacity:** Expanding internal expertise and resources at FSOC and its member agencies.
- **Improving Data and Methods:** Identifying and filling data gaps, standardizing definitions and metrics, and collaborating on data acquisition and sharing.
- **Enhancing Disclosures:** Reviewing and updating disclosure requirements for public issuers, banks, insurers, asset managers, and municipal securities, potentially leveraging the TCFD framework.
- **Assessing and Mitigating Risks to Financial Stability:** Conducting scenario analyses, reviewing and updating existing regulations and supervisory guidance, and clarifying expectations for regulated institutions.

This report marks a pivotal shift in the approach of US financial regulators to climate-related risks. It lays the groundwork for further action to strengthen the resilience of the financial system, mitigate systemic risks, and support an orderly transition to a low-carbon economy while prioritizing the needs of vulnerable communities.

2.1 *Physical Risks: The Economic Toll of Climate Impacts*

The physical impacts of climate change—from intensified extreme weather events to gradual changes like sea-level rise—are already imposing substantial costs on economies worldwide. These costs are manifested in various ways:

- **Damage to Infrastructure:** The WMO (2024) "State of the Global Climate 2023" report highlighted the devastating impacts of extreme weather events in 2023, including flooding from Mediterranean Cyclone Daniel that caused significant infrastructure damage and loss of life in Greece, Bulgaria, Türkiye, and Libya. Similarly, the IPCC AR6 Synthesis Report notes that projected increases in direct flood damages are estimated to be 1.4 to 2 times higher at 2 °C and 2.5 to 3.9 times higher at 3 °C of global warming compared to 1.5 °C, without adaptation. Hurricanes, floods, wildfires, and other extreme weather events cause billions of dollars in damage to buildings, roads, bridges, power grids, and other vital infrastructure. For example, the 2017 Atlantic hurricane season caused an estimated $265 billion in damage in the United States and the Caribbean (Fig. 5).

- **Business Disruptions:** Climate-related disasters can disrupt supply chains, force businesses to halt operations, and lead to productivity and revenue losses. The 2011 floods in Thailand, for instance, which inundated industrial estates, caused extensive disruptions to global supply

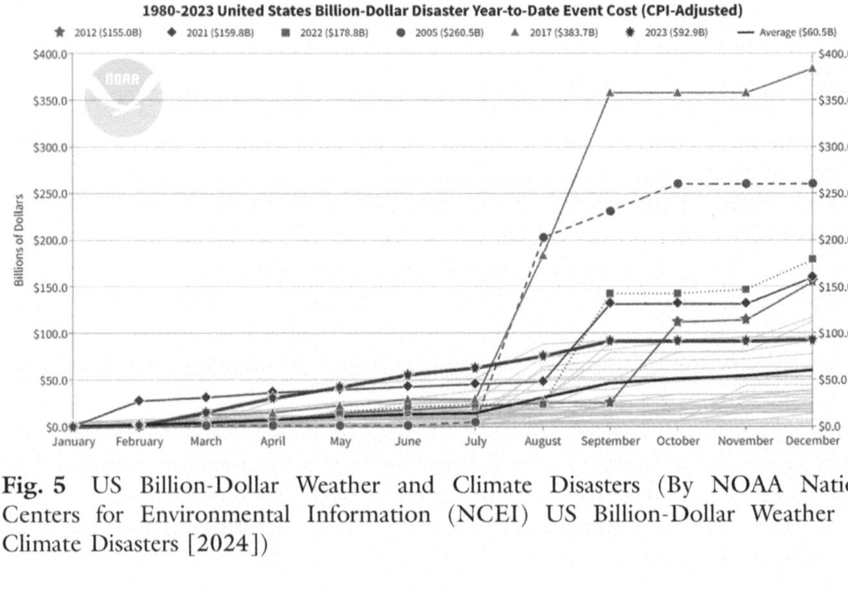

Fig. 5 US Billion-Dollar Weather and Climate Disasters (By NOAA National Centers for Environmental Information (NCEI) US Billion-Dollar Weather and Climate Disasters [2024])

chains for electronics, automotive, and other industries, resulting in billions of dollars in economic losses. The IPCC AR6 Synthesis Report highlights the increasing transboundary risks across food, energy, and water sectors as climate impacts propagate through supply chains, markets, and natural resource flows.

- **Reduced Agricultural Yields:** Changing precipitation patterns, more frequent droughts, and extreme heat can significantly diminish crop yields, affecting food security, increasing food prices, and undermining agricultural livelihoods. The World Bank estimates that climate change could reduce global agricultural productivity by up to 30% by 2050.
- **Health Impacts:** Climate change is contributing to an increase in heat-related illnesses, respiratory problems, and infectious diseases, leading to higher healthcare costs and reduced worker productivity. A 2019 report by the Global Commission on Adaptation found that climate change could reduce global GDP by up to 3% by 2100 due to health impacts alone.

2.2 *Transition Risks: The Challenges of Decarbonization*

While the transition to a low-carbon economy is crucial to mitigate climate change, it also presents financial risks for companies and investors who fail to adapt. As governments implement policies to curb greenhouse gas emissions, such as carbon pricing, renewable energy mandates, and stricter fuel efficiency standards, businesses operating in carbon-intensive sectors face a growing risk of:

- **Stranded Assets:** Fossil fuel reserves, coal-fired power plants, and other high-carbon assets may become "stranded"—meaning they lose value or become unusable—as the world transitions to cleaner energy sources. The Carbon Tracker Initiative estimates that up to $25 trillion in fossil fuel assets could be stranded by 2035 if governments take bold action to meet the Paris Agreement goals. The IPCC AR6 Synthesis Report also emphasizes that limiting warming to 2 °C or lower will inevitably result in stranded assets, with significant portions of coal, gas, and oil reserves becoming unburnable (Fig. 6).

- **Increased Compliance Costs:** Companies will need to invest in new technologies and processes to comply with stricter environmental regulations, potentially increasing operating costs and reducing profitability.
- **Reduced Competitiveness:** Companies that are slow to adapt to the low-carbon transition may find themselves at a competitive disadvantage as consumers and investors increasingly favor businesses with strong sustainability credentials.

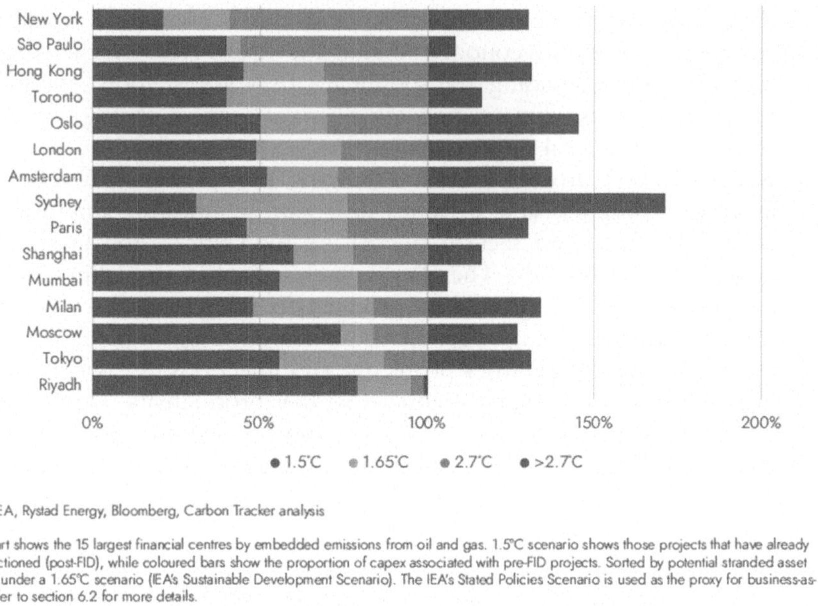

Fig. 6 Stranded asset exposure by financial center shown as upstream oil and gas capex by financial center, 2021–2030, as % of business-as-usual capex (2.7 °C). https://carbontracker.org/reports/unburnable-carbon-ten-years-on/

2.3 *Systemic Risks: The Threat to Financial Stability*

The financial impacts of climate change are not confined to individual companies or sectors; they pose systemic risks to the entire financial system. The interconnected nature of global financial markets means that climate-related losses in one area can rapidly spread and amplify, potentially leading to cascading failures and broader economic instability.

- **Cascading Effects:** A major hurricane, for example, could cause widespread property damage, resulting in substantial insurance payouts. This could strain the financial resources of insurance companies, potentially leading to insolvencies and triggering a chain reaction of losses throughout the financial system.
- **Asset Bubbles and Stranded Assets:** Climate change could also contribute to the formation of asset bubbles, where the value of certain assets—such as real estate in coastal areas or investments in fossil fuel companies—becomes artificially inflated. The eventual burst of these bubbles could trigger a sharp decline in asset values, causing financial losses for investors and potentially destabilizing the broader financial system.

The Bank for International Settlements (BIS), often called the central bank of central banks, has cautioned that climate change represents a "green swan" risk to the global financial system—a potentially catastrophic event that is difficult to predict but could have severe and widespread consequences. The BIS (2020) paper, "The Green Swan: Central Banking and Financial Stability in the Age of Climate Change," explicitly addresses the challenges climate change poses to central banks, regulators, and supervisors in maintaining financial stability. It highlights the limitations of traditional risk assessments due to the radical uncertainty and complex dynamics of climate-related risks, termed "green swan" risks, which could trigger systemic financial crises. The BIS (2020) paper advocates for **forward-looking scenario-based analyses** and coordinated action among governments, the private sector, and the international community, emphasizing the need for policy mixes, sustainable financial practices, and new international financial mechanisms.

Utilizing climate scenarios to assess the comprehensive systemic risks of financial systems has been widely adopted by central banks. For example, Bank of England (2022) examines three scenarios under Climate Biennial Exploratory Scenario (CBES), and assesses the financial risks posed by climate change to major UK banks and insurers, revealing that climate risks create a drag on profitability, but that early, well-managed action to reduce emissions minimizes overall costs. The Network for Greening the Financial System (NGFS, 2021) work report analyzes how 31 NGFS members are employing climate scenarios to assess and manage climate-related risks within their financial systems.

However, to understand the complexity of the systemic risks posed by climate change, the current scenario analysis methodology may not be bulletproof. Trust et al. (2023) critically examines the limitations and assumptions of commonly used climate change scenarios within financial services, highlighting a significant disconnect between climate science and economic models that leads to an underestimation of climate risks. It argues that current models often exclude crucial elements like tipping points and second-order impacts, resulting in overly benign or even implausible outcomes, especially in "hothouse world" scenarios. The document advocates for a new beginning that emphasizes education, the development of realistic qualitative and quantitative climate scenarios, and model enhancements to better capture risk drivers, uncertainties, and impacts, pushing for more informed decision-making and accelerated action toward decarbonization.

In addition to scenario analysis, financial disclosure is also important. The Taskforce on Nature-related Financial Disclosures (TNFD, 2023) presents a comprehensive framework to help companies and financial institutions integrate nature into their decision-making and reporting processes. The recommendations align with global sustainability goals, building upon the Task Force on Climate-related Financial Disclosures (TCFD) framework, the International Sustainability Standards Board (ISSB) standards, and the

Kunming-Montreal Global Biodiversity Framework (GBF). The TNFD framework encourages the disclosure of nature-related dependencies, impacts, risks, and opportunities, offering guidance and metrics to support the adoption of nature-positive practices, and the redirection of financial flows toward environmentally sustainable outcomes.

Apparently, addressing these systemic risks requires a proactive and coordinated approach from financial regulators, central banks, and governments. They must integrate climate change into their risk management frameworks, promote climate-aligned investments, and ensure a smooth transition to a low-carbon economy.

3 The Role of Climate Finance: Mobilizing Capital for Solutions

Amidst the potential financial crisis presented by climate change, climate finance offers a powerful instrument for positive change. It embodies a beacon of hope, providing a pathway to mitigate risks, build resilience, and unlock the economic opportunities of a sustainable future. By directing capital toward climate solutions, we can not only avert disaster but also fuel innovation, create jobs, and build a more equitable and prosperous world.

Climate finance is crucial for mitigating emissions and helping communities adapt to climate change, especially smallholders who receive a disproportionately small amount of funding despite producing a significant portion of food in developing countries. Meeting the Paris Agreement goals requires developed countries to provide substantial financial resources, including at least $100 billion annually, to developing countries for both mitigation and adaptation efforts, addressing the widening finance gaps. IFAD (2022) mobilizes climate finance through various programs and partnerships, channeling funds to vulnerable producers and aiming to increase private sector investment in climate-smart practices.

3.1 Defining Climate Finance

Climate finance encompasses the flow of funds from various sources—public, private, and alternative—to support both mitigation and adaptation efforts:

- **Mitigation Finance:** This type of finance supports projects and activities aimed at reducing greenhouse gas emissions, such as investing in renewable energy, improving energy efficiency, developing sustainable transportation systems, and protecting forests.
- **Adaptation Finance:** This finance focuses on building resilience to the impacts of climate change that are already happening or are unavoidable in the future. Examples include investing in early warning systems for extreme weather events, developing drought-resistant crops, building

seawalls to protect coastal communities, and strengthening healthcare systems to address climate-related health challenges.

Climate finance can be sourced from various channels:

- **Public Finance:** Governments play a crucial role in providing climate finance through grants, concessional loans, export credits, and other mechanisms.
- **Private Finance:** Private sector investors, including banks, institutional investors, corporations, and impact investors, are increasingly investing in climate-aligned projects and businesses, driven by both financial returns and a growing awareness of climate risks.
- **Alternative Finance:** Innovative financing mechanisms, such as crowdfunding, green bonds, and carbon markets, are also playing an increasingly important role in mobilizing capital for climate solutions.

3.2 *The Scale of the Challenge*

The magnitude of the climate challenge is immense. To limit global warming to well below 2 degrees Celsius, as outlined in the Paris Agreement, and achieve net-zero emissions by mid-century, trillions of dollars in investment will be needed in the coming decades. The Intergovernmental Panel on Climate Change (IPCC) estimates that achieving the 1.5-degree target requires increasing annual investments in clean energy alone to approximately $2.4 trillion by 2035.

Currently, global climate finance flows fall significantly short of these requirements. Although there has been some progress, with climate finance reaching $632 billion in 2019–2020, this remains a small fraction of what is needed. Closing this financing gap stands as one of the most critical challenges facing the global community. The IPCC AR6 Synthesis Report highlights that average annual investment requirements for 2020–2030 in scenarios limiting warming to 2 °C or 1.5 °C are three to six times greater than current levels, underscoring the urgent need to scale up climate finance flows.

3.3 *Key Areas of Investment*

To effectively address climate change, climate finance must be strategically directed toward areas that hold the greatest potential to reduce emissions, build resilience, and create a sustainable future:

- **Renewable Energy:** Scaling up investments in solar, wind, geothermal, and other renewable energy sources is paramount to decarbonize the electricity sector, reduce reliance on fossil fuels, and foster a cleaner, more secure energy future.

- **Energy Efficiency:** Improving energy efficiency in buildings, transportation, and industrial processes is one of the most cost-effective approaches to reducing energy consumption, lowering emissions, and saving money.
- **Sustainable Transportation:** Investing in electric vehicles, public transportation, cycling infrastructure, and other sustainable transportation solutions is essential to reduce emissions from the transport sector, improve air quality, and enhance urban livability.
- **Climate-Resilient Infrastructure:** Building infrastructure that can withstand the impacts of climate change, such as seawalls, drought-resistant roads, and resilient water systems, is crucial to protect communities, businesses, and economies from climate-related disasters.
- **Adaptation Measures:** Investing in adaptation measures, like early warning systems for extreme weather events, drought-resistant crops, and climate-resilient healthcare systems, is vital to reduce the vulnerability of communities and ecosystems to climate change impacts.

By prioritizing investments in these critical areas, we can accelerate the transition to a low-carbon and climate-resilient future, creating a more sustainable and prosperous world for all.

4 The Case for Action: Why Climate Finance Matters

The imperative of climate finance extends beyond averting a looming financial crisis. It is about recognizing that investing in climate solutions is not only an economic necessity but also a moral obligation and a pathway to a more just, equitable, and prosperous future for all.

4.1 Economic Benefits

Investing in climate solutions is not a drain on resources; it represents a powerful engine for economic growth and job creation. Such investments can:

- **Unlock New Markets:** The transition to a low-carbon economy is creating vast new markets for clean technologies, renewable energy, sustainable transportation, and climate-resilient infrastructure. The International Renewable Energy Agency (IRENA) estimates that the global renewable energy market could reach $23 trillion by 2030.
- **Drive Innovation:** Addressing climate change necessitates innovation across all sectors of the economy, from energy and transportation to agriculture and manufacturing. This innovation can lead to new technologies, products, and services, creating competitive advantages for businesses and stimulating economic growth.

- **Create Green Jobs:** The transition to a low-carbon economy will create millions of new jobs in sectors such as renewable energy, energy efficiency, sustainable transportation, and green building. The International Labour Organization (ILO) estimates that 24 million new jobs could be created globally by 2030 through climate action.

4.2 *Social Equity and Justice*

Climate change has a disproportionate impact on the most vulnerable populations, including those in developing countries, low-income communities, and marginalized groups. These communities often have the fewest resources to adapt to climate impacts and are frequently excluded from the benefits of economic growth.

Climate finance plays a critical role in addressing these inequalities by:

- **Supporting Adaptation:** Directing finance toward adaptation measures in vulnerable communities can help protect lives, livelihoods, and assets from the impacts of climate change.
- **Promoting a Just Transition:** As the world shifts to a low-carbon economy, it is crucial to ensure that workers and communities reliant on fossil fuel industries are supported in transitioning to new, sustainable livelihoods. Climate finance can facilitate this transition by providing retraining programs, creating green jobs, and investing in economic diversification in these regions.
- **Empowering Developing Countries:** Developed countries bear a historical responsibility for climate change and a moral obligation to support developing countries in their efforts to mitigate and adapt to its impacts. International climate finance is essential in enabling developing countries to leapfrog to cleaner technologies, build climate-resilient infrastructure, and achieve sustainable development goals.

4.3 *A Shared Responsibility*

Addressing the climate crisis requires a collective effort. Governments, businesses, investors, and civil society all have crucial roles to play in scaling up climate finance and driving the transition to a sustainable future.

- **Governments:** Must establish supportive policy environments, implement carbon pricing mechanisms, set ambitious targets for renewable energy and energy efficiency, and provide public finance to leverage private investment.

- **Businesses:** Need to incorporate climate considerations into their strategies, invest in low-carbon technologies, reduce their emissions, and transparently disclose their climate risks and opportunities.
- **Investors:** Should shift their portfolios toward climate-aligned investments, engage with companies on climate action, and support the development of green financial instruments.
- **Civil Society:** Plays a vital role in raising awareness, advocating for policy change, holding businesses and governments accountable, and mobilizing public support for climate action.

International cooperation is also essential. The Paris Agreement, a landmark global agreement adopted in 2015, provides a framework for collective action on climate change, including commitments from developed countries to mobilize climate finance for developing countries.

5 Conclusion: A Call to Action

The climate crisis confronts humanity with a defining challenge—and an unparalleled opportunity. The scientific evidence is undeniable, the financial stakes are immense, and the social and environmental consequences are far-reaching. Yet, we are not helpless in the face of this crisis. Climate finance offers a potent tool to mitigate risks, build resilience, and unlock the economic benefits of a sustainable future.

We have embarked on an initial exploration of the imperative of climate finance. We've examined the financial risks posed by climate change, the urgent need to mobilize trillions of dollars in investment, and the potential for climate finance to drive innovation, create jobs, and promote social equity.

The path forward is clear. We must act decisively and collaboratively to scale up climate finance, directing it toward the most impactful solutions, ensuring that it reaches those most vulnerable to climate impacts, and fostering a just transition to a low-carbon economy.

This journey necessitates leadership and action from all sectors of society:

- **Governments must:**
  - Adopt ambitious climate policies aligned with the latest scientific findings.
  - Implement effective carbon pricing mechanisms to internalize the cost of emissions.
  - Provide public finance to catalyze private investment in climate solutions.
  - Strengthen international cooperation to mobilize resources and share knowledge.
  - Prioritize a just transition, ensuring that workers and communities affected by the shift to a low-carbon economy are supported.

- **Businesses must:**
  - Integrate climate considerations into their core business strategies.
  - Invest in low-carbon technologies and processes to reduce their emissions.
  - Embrace transparency in disclosing their climate-related risks and opportunities.
  - Engage actively with stakeholders, including investors, customers, and employees, on climate action.
- **Investors must:**
  - Shift their portfolios toward climate-aligned investments, prioritizing renewable energy, energy efficiency, sustainable transportation, and climate-resilient infrastructure.
  - Engage actively with companies on their climate performance, advocating for stronger climate action and holding them accountable for their emissions.
  - Support the development and adoption of innovative green financial instruments, such as green bonds, sustainability-linked loans, and carbon markets.
- **Individuals can**:
  - Make informed consumer choices, opting for sustainable products and services, reducing energy consumption, and choosing low-carbon transportation options.
  - Make conscious investment decisions, directing their savings toward climate-aligned funds and companies committed to sustainability.
  - Engage actively in political and social movements demanding climate action from governments and businesses.

The chapters that follow will delve deeper into the complex and evolving landscape of climate finance. We will explore the various financial instruments and strategies being deployed, examine the role of financial institutions in driving the transition to a low-carbon economy, analyze the challenges and opportunities of climate risk management, and assess the emerging policy and regulatory frameworks shaping the future of climate finance.

The path ahead is not without obstacles, but the imperative is clear: climate finance is not merely an option; it is an absolute necessity. It is our collective responsibility—and our shared opportunity—to invest in a future where economic prosperity goes hand in hand with environmental sustainability and social justice. Let us rise to the challenge and build a world where all people have the chance to thrive on a healthy and resilient planet.

References

Bank of England (BoE). (2022). *Results of the 2021 Climate Biennial Exploratory Scenario*. https://www.bankofengland.co.uk/-/media/boe/files/stress-testing/2022/results-of-the-2021-cbes.pdf. Accessed 29 March 2025.

Bank for International Settlements (BIS). (2020). *The green swan: Central banking and financial stability in the age of climate change*. https://www.bis.org/publ/othp31.pdf

Financial Stability Oversight Council (FSOC). (2021). *Report on Climate-Related Financial Risk 2021*. https://home.treasury.gov/system/files/261/FSOC-Climate-Report.pdf. Accessed 25 January 2025.

International Fund for Agricultural Development (IFAD). (2022). *Why climate finance matters: your questions answered*. https://www.ifad.org/en/w/explainers/why-climate-finance-matters-your-questions-answered. Accessed 29 March 2025.

Network for Greening the Financial System (NGFS). (2021). *Network for Greening the Financial System Technical document Scenarios in Action A progress report on global supervisory and central bank climate scenario exercises*. https://www.regulationtomorrow.com/eu/ngfs-report-scenarios-in-action-a-progress-report-on-global-supervisory-and-central-bank-climate-scenario-exercises/

Taskforce on Nature-related Financial Disclosures (TNFD). (2023). *Recommendations of the Taskforce on Nature-related Financial Disclosures*. https://tnfd.global/wp-content/uploads/2023/08/Recommendations_of_the_Taskforce_on_Nature-related_Financial_Disclosures_September_2023.pdf. Accessed 25 January 2025.

Trust, S., et al. (2023). *The emperor's new climate scenarios limitations and assumptions of commonly used climate-change scenarios in financial services*.

WMO. (2024). *State of the global climate 2023. the World Meteorological Organization*. https://wmo.int/publication-series/state-of-global-climate-2023

World Meteorological Organization (WMO). (2023). *The Global Climate 2011–2020 A decade of accelerating climate change*. https://library.wmo.int/viewer/68585/download?file=1338_Decadal_State_Climate-HG_en.pdf. Accessed 25 January 2025.

CHAPTER 2

Understanding Climate Risks

1 Introduction

The world is waking up to a stark reality: climate change is no longer a distant threat but a present and escalating danger with profound implications for businesses, investors, and society as a whole. From the devastating wildfires ravaging entire landscapes to the increasing frequency of extreme floods and storms, the physical impacts of a changing climate are becoming impossible to ignore.

The scientific community has reached a strong consensus that the observed increases in the frequency and intensity of extreme weather events are primarily driven by the human-caused rise in greenhouse gas emissions. This conclusion is consistently supported by leading international and national scientific bodies, including the IPCC (2021, 2022a, 2022b), NASA (2025), and the WMO (2023, 2024). The alignment of these findings across multiple independent organizations lends significant weight to the assertion that anthropogenic climate change is the dominant factor influencing these escalating risks. This robust consensus provides a firm scientific basis for understanding and addressing the challenges posed by acute physical risks.

Several key mechanisms explain how climate change translates into more severe weather patterns. Rising global average temperatures lead to a warming of both the air and the oceans. Warmer air has a greater capacity to hold moisture, leading to more intense precipitation events in some regions. Simultaneously, warmer ocean temperatures provide more energy for storms like hurricanes, contributing to their intensification. Furthermore, the warming climate disrupts traditional weather patterns and can lead to prolonged periods of drought in some areas, increasing the risk and severity of wildfires. The melting of land-based ice, another consequence of rising global temperatures,

J. Chen, *Climate Finance*, https://doi.org/10.1007/978-981-96-7975-1_2

contributes to sea-level rise, which in turn exacerbates coastal flooding. These mechanisms are interconnected, forming a complex system where changes in one area can trigger cascading effects that amplify the overall impact of climate change on extreme weather. For instance, warmer temperatures increase atmospheric moisture, which can fuel stronger storms and lead to more intense rainfall, ultimately increasing the risk of flooding. The melting of glaciers and ice sheets directly contributes to rising sea levels, making coastal regions more vulnerable to inundation during high tides and storm surges. Understanding these intricate relationships is crucial for comprehending the systemic nature of climate change and its far-reaching consequences.

The NBER working paper "Long-Term Macroeconomic Effects of Climate Change: A Cross-Country Analysis" by Kahn et al. (2019) investigates the persistent impact of climate change on economic activity across 174 countries from 1960 to 2014. Here's a summary of the key findings and contributions:

Key Findings:

- **Persistent Temperature Deviations Harm Growth:** The study finds that persistent deviations of temperature above or below its historical norm negatively affect long-term real GDP per capita growth. A 0.01 °C annual increase above the norm reduces growth by 0.0543 percentage points per year.
- **Universal Impact:** Contrary to previous research, this study finds that these adverse growth effects are universal, impacting both rich and poor countries, as well as hot and cold regions.
- **Significant Economic Losses:** A counterfactual analysis projects significant economic losses due to climate change. An unmitigated scenario (RCP 8.5) with a persistent 0.04 °C annual temperature increase could reduce global GDP per capita by 7.22% by 2100.
- **Paris Agreement Mitigation:** Adhering to the Paris Agreement (RCP 2.6), limiting temperature increases to 0.01 °C per year, would significantly reduce the loss to 1.07% by 2100, highlighting the economic benefits of mitigation policies.
- **Adaptation Plays a Role:** The study acknowledges that adaptation can help mitigate these losses, but it is unlikely to offset them entirely. Faster adaptation leads to smaller losses, but even with rapid adaptation, the economic impact remains substantial.

US Case Study:

- **State-Level Analysis:** The paper includes a case study of the United States, analyzing 48 states from 1963 to 2016. It finds that climate change has a long-lasting negative impact on real output, labor productivity, and employment across various states and economic sectors.

- **Broad Sectoral Impact:** The study demonstrates that the impact of climate change on output growth is widespread, affecting all ten major economic sectors analyzed.

Methodological Contributions:

- **Focus on Long-Term Growth Effects:** The paper distinguishes between short-term and long-term effects of climate change on economic growth, addressing a gap in the existing literature.
- **Modeling Climate Deviations:** It uses deviations of climate variables (temperature and precipitation) from their historical norms, capturing the impact of persistent changes rather than focusing on trending levels.
- **Addressing Econometric Issues:** The study employs the Half-Panel Jackknife Fixed Effects (HPJ-FE) estimator to account for potential biases and size distortions in the commonly used Fixed Effects estimator when dealing with weakly exogenous regressors like temperature.

Policy Implications:

- The findings highlight the substantial economic benefits of mitigating climate change, particularly by adhering to the Paris Agreement targets.
- The study emphasizes the need for proactive adaptation policies to minimize the adverse impacts of climate change across various sectors and regions.

This NBER paper provides robust evidence for the long-term negative impact of climate change on economic growth, emphasizing the need for ambitious mitigation and adaptation strategies to ensure a sustainable and prosperous future.

Yet, the risks extend far beyond these visible consequences. As the global community grapples with the urgent need to transition to a low-carbon economy, a new set of challenges—transition risks—are coming to the forefront. These risks stem from the complex interplay of shifting policies, emerging technologies, evolving market dynamics, and changing societal expectations.

Understanding both the physical and transition risks associated with climate change is no longer a matter of choice but a necessity. This knowledge is paramount for making informed decisions, managing financial exposure, and seizing the opportunities that arise in a world undergoing a profound transformation.

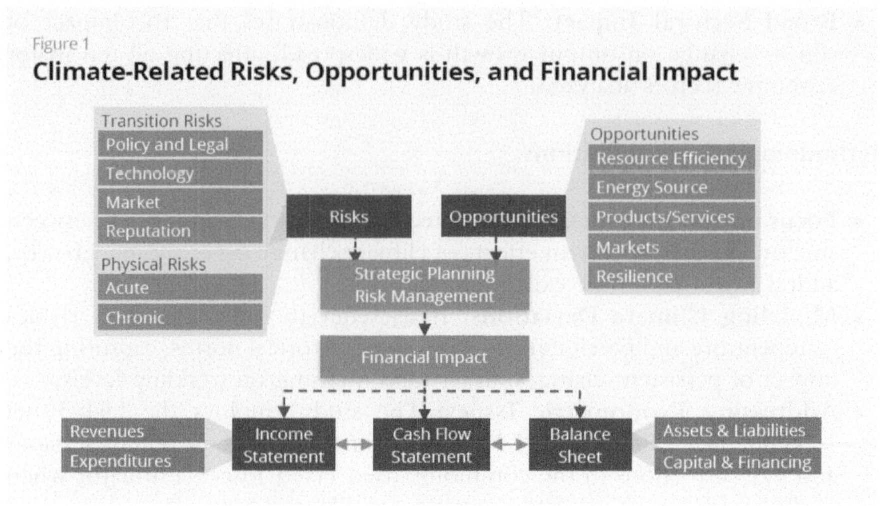

Source TCFD, Final Report, *Recommendations of the Task Force on Climate-related Financial Disclosures*, 2017

This chapter provides a comprehensive overview of the different types of climate risks, exploring their potential impact and emphasizing the interconnected nature of these challenges. By understanding the risks, we can begin to chart a more sustainable and resilient path forward.

2 Physical Risks: The Tangible Impacts of a Changing Climate

The physical risks of climate change are no longer theoretical projections for the distant future; they are already being felt in communities and economies worldwide. These risks manifest in two primary forms: acute and chronic, both with the potential to disrupt businesses, destabilize financial systems, and erode human well-being.

Physical Risks	Acute – Increased severity of extreme weather events such as cyclones and floods Chronic – Changes in precipitation patterns and extreme variability in weather patterns – Rising mean temperatures – Rising sea levels	– Reduced revenue from decreased production capacity (e.g., transport difficulties, supply chain interruptions) – Reduced revenue and higher costs from negative impacts on workforce (e.g., health, safety, absenteeism) – Write-offs and early retirement of existing assets (e.g., damage to property and assets in "high-risk" locations) – Increased operating costs (e.g., inadequate water supply for hydroelectric plants or to cool nuclear and fossil fuel plants) – Increased capital costs (e.g., damage to facilities) – Reduced revenues from lower sales/output – Increased insurance premiums and potential for reduced availability of insurance on assets in "high-risk" locations

Source TCFD, Final Report, *Recommendations of the Task Force on Climate-related Financial Disclosures*, 2017

2.1 Acute Physical Risks: Weather Extremes on the Rise

Acute physical risks encompass the immediate and often devastating impacts of extreme weather events, many of which are increasing in frequency and severity due to climate change. Hurricanes are gaining intensity, fuelled by warmer ocean temperatures, and causing unprecedented damage to coastal infrastructure and communities. In 2017 alone, Hurricanes Harvey, Irma, and Maria inflicted a combined estimated cost of $339.2 billion in damages in the United States and the Caribbean (NOAA, 2025).

Floods, exacerbated by changing precipitation patterns and sea-level rise, are inundating urban centers and agricultural lands alike. The 2011 floods in Thailand, for instance, caused an estimated $6.5 billion in economic losses (Strategic Risk, 2011), disrupting global supply chains for industries reliant on Thai manufacturing. Wildfires, amplified by prolonged droughts and hotter temperatures, are burning across vast areas, destroying homes and ecosystems, and releasing harmful pollutants into the atmosphere. The 2020 California wildfire season, the most destructive in the state's history, scorched over 4.3 million acres and caused billions of dollars in damages (Kerlin, 2022).

These are just a few examples of the escalating toll of acute physical risks. NOAA (2025) estimates that the total approximate cost of damages from weather and climate disasters in the United States from 1980 to February 2025 is $2.915 trillion, and the United States experienced 27 billion-dollar disasters in 2024 alone. The increasing frequency and intensity of these events pose a significant threat to businesses, investors, and communities worldwide, highlighting the urgent need for adaptation and resilience-building measures.

Case Study 1: Hurricane Maria and the Puerto Rican Debt Crisis

- Focus: Impact of hurricanes on critical infrastructure, economic disruption, and sovereign debt risk.
- Illustrate: How a major hurricane can exacerbate existing financial vulnerabilities and lead to a sovereign debt crisis.

- Discuss: The challenges of disaster recovery in a climate-vulnerable region, the role of climate resilience in financial planning, and the need for international support.

Hurricane Maria, which struck Puerto Rico in September 2017, was a devastating natural disaster that had profound impacts on the island's critical infrastructure, economy, and sovereign debt situation. This case study examines how a major hurricane can exacerbate existing financial vulnerabilities and lead to a sovereign debt crisis, highlighting the challenges of disaster recovery in a climate-vulnerable region and the importance of climate resilience in financial planning (Fig. 1).

Impact on Critical Infrastructure
Hurricane Maria caused unprecedented damage to Puerto Rico's infrastructure, including power grids, water systems, transportation networks, and telecommunications. The hurricane's 155 mph winds and torrential rains led to widespread power outages, with the entire island losing electricity. The power grid's fragility was exposed, and it took nearly a year to fully restore electricity to all residents. Water systems were also severely affected, with many communities lacking access to clean water for months. The destruction of roads and bridges hampered relief efforts and isolated communities, further complicating recovery efforts.

Fig. 1 Area with structural debris after Hurricane Maria (By Roosevelt Skerrit from Vieille Case, Dominica—Morning after Hurricane Maria, Public Domain, https://commons.wikimedia.org/w/index.php?curid=67208115)

Economic Disruption

The economic impact of Hurricane Maria was catastrophic. The hurricane caused an estimated $90 billion in damages, making it one of the costliest hurricanes in US history. The destruction of infrastructure and disruption of services led to a sharp decline in economic activity. Businesses were forced to close, tourism plummeted, and agricultural losses were substantial. The hurricane exacerbated Puerto Rico's already fragile economic situation, which was characterized by high unemployment, low labor force participation, and significant outmigration (Robles & Ferré-Sadurní, 2017).

Sovereign Debt Risk

Puerto Rico's financial vulnerabilities were significantly worsened by Hurricane Maria. Prior to the hurricane, Puerto Rico was already facing a severe debt crisis, with over $70 billion in outstanding debt and $49 billion in unfunded pension liabilities. The economic disruption caused by the hurricane further strained the government's finances, reducing its ability to generate revenue and meet debt obligations. The disaster highlighted the interconnectedness of natural disasters and financial stability, demonstrating how climate events can exacerbate sovereign debt risks.

Challenges of Disaster Recovery

The recovery process in Puerto Rico faced numerous challenges, including bureaucratic delays, insufficient funding, and logistical difficulties. The scale of the destruction overwhelmed local capacities, and the island's financial constraints limited its ability to invest in rebuilding efforts. Additionally, the lack of robust disaster preparedness and resilience planning exacerbated the recovery challenges. The slow and uneven recovery process underscored the need for comprehensive disaster risk management strategies and the importance of building climate resilience (Fischbach et al., 2020; Kishore et al., 2018).

Role of Climate Resilience in Financial Planning

Building climate resilience is crucial for mitigating the impacts of future disasters and ensuring financial stability. This involves investing in resilient infrastructure, improving emergency preparedness, and integrating climate risk into financial planning. Enhancing resilience can reduce the economic and social costs of disasters, protect critical infrastructure, and support long-term sustainable development. For Puerto Rico, this means not only rebuilding stronger but also addressing underlying vulnerabilities to create a more resilient and sustainable future.

Need for International Support

International support plays a vital role in disaster recovery and building climate resilience, especially for regions with limited financial resources. In the case of Puerto Rico, international aid, technical assistance, and financial support were critical in the immediate aftermath of Hurricane Maria and in the ongoing recovery efforts. Strengthening international cooperation and ensuring timely and effective support can significantly enhance the capacity of climate-vulnerable regions to recover and build resilience (Kishore et al., 2018).

This case study illustrates the complex interplay between natural disasters, economic disruption, and financial stability, highlighting the urgent need for comprehensive climate resilience strategies and international cooperation to support vulnerable regions.

2.2 *Chronic Physical Risks: Gradual Shifts with Long-Term Consequences*

Beyond the immediate devastation of extreme weather, climate change is driving gradual yet relentless environmental shifts that pose significant long-term risks. Sea-level rise, a consequence of melting glaciers and thermal expansion of ocean water, threatens to inundate low-lying coastal areas, displace millions of people, and cause trillions of dollars in damage to infrastructure and property. A 2019 study by the National Bureau of Economic Research estimated that by 2100, rising sea levels could reduce global GDP by 0.2% to 2%, with coastal regions in Asia and North America facing the most significant economic losses.

Ocean acidification, driven by the absorption of excess carbon dioxide from the atmosphere, is altering marine ecosystems, disrupting fisheries, and threatening the livelihoods of communities that depend on ocean resources. The warming of ocean waters is also contributing to coral bleaching events, which can devastate coral reefs, critical ecosystems that support marine biodiversity and provide tourism revenue and coastal protection.

Changes in precipitation patterns, resulting in more frequent and severe droughts in some regions and heavier rainfall in others, are disrupting agricultural yields, straining water resources, and increasing the risk of wildfires. These shifts can lead to food insecurity, economic instability, and social unrest, particularly in regions already facing resource constraints and political instability.

Addressing chronic physical risks requires a long-term perspective and proactive adaptation strategies. This includes investing in climate-resilient infrastructure, developing drought-resistant crops, and implementing water management strategies that ensure equitable access to this increasingly precious resource. Hallegatte et al. (2019) emphasize the need for resilient infrastructure to withstand extreme weather events, protecting communities and economies from long-term disruptions. The UN Office for Disaster Risk Reduction (McGlade, 2019) highlights the escalating global risks associated with natural disasters and the need for comprehensive disaster risk management strategies.

Case Study 2: The Mekong Delta and Sea-Level Rise

- Focus: Impact of sea-level rise on agricultural production, food security, and migration patterns in a densely populated delta region.
- Illustrate: The long-term economic and social consequences of sea-level rise, including potential disruptions to global food supply chains.
- Discuss: The need for adaptation measures such as seawalls, mangrove restoration, and drought-resistant crops, as well as the financial implications of these interventions.

The Mekong Delta in Vietnam is one of the most vulnerable regions to sea-level rise due to its low elevation, dense population, and reliance on agriculture. This case study examines the impact of rising sea levels on agricultural production, food security, and migration patterns, illustrating the long-term economic and social consequences and discussing necessary adaptation measures and their financial implications (Hanh & Furukawa, 2007; Smajgl, 2015; World Bank, 2010) (Fig. 2).

Impact on Agricultural Production
The Mekong Delta is a critical agricultural region, producing more than half of Vietnam's rice and a significant portion of its aquaculture. However, sea-level rise is causing increased salinity intrusion, which adversely affects rice paddies and freshwater aquaculture. The salinization of soil and water resources reduces crop yields, damages agricultural land, and decreases the productivity of fisheries (Wassmann et al., 2004).

Food Security
The Mekong Delta's agricultural output is vital for Vietnam's food security and export economy. The decline in rice and fish production due to salinity intrusion and flooding threatens local food supplies and livelihoods. Additionally, the reduction in agricultural productivity can lead to higher food prices and increased food insecurity, particularly for vulnerable populations (Chapman et al., 2016).

Migration Patterns
As agricultural livelihoods become unsustainable, many residents of the Mekong Delta are forced to migrate to urban areas in search of better opportunities. This migration can lead to overcrowded cities, increased pressure on urban infrastructure, and social challenges. Additionally, the loss of agricultural workers can further exacerbate the decline in agricultural productivity (Adger & Kelly, 1999).

Long-Term Economic and Social Consequences
The long-term economic consequences of sea-level rise in the Mekong Delta include reduced agricultural output, loss of income, and increased poverty. Socially, the displacement of communities and the disruption of traditional

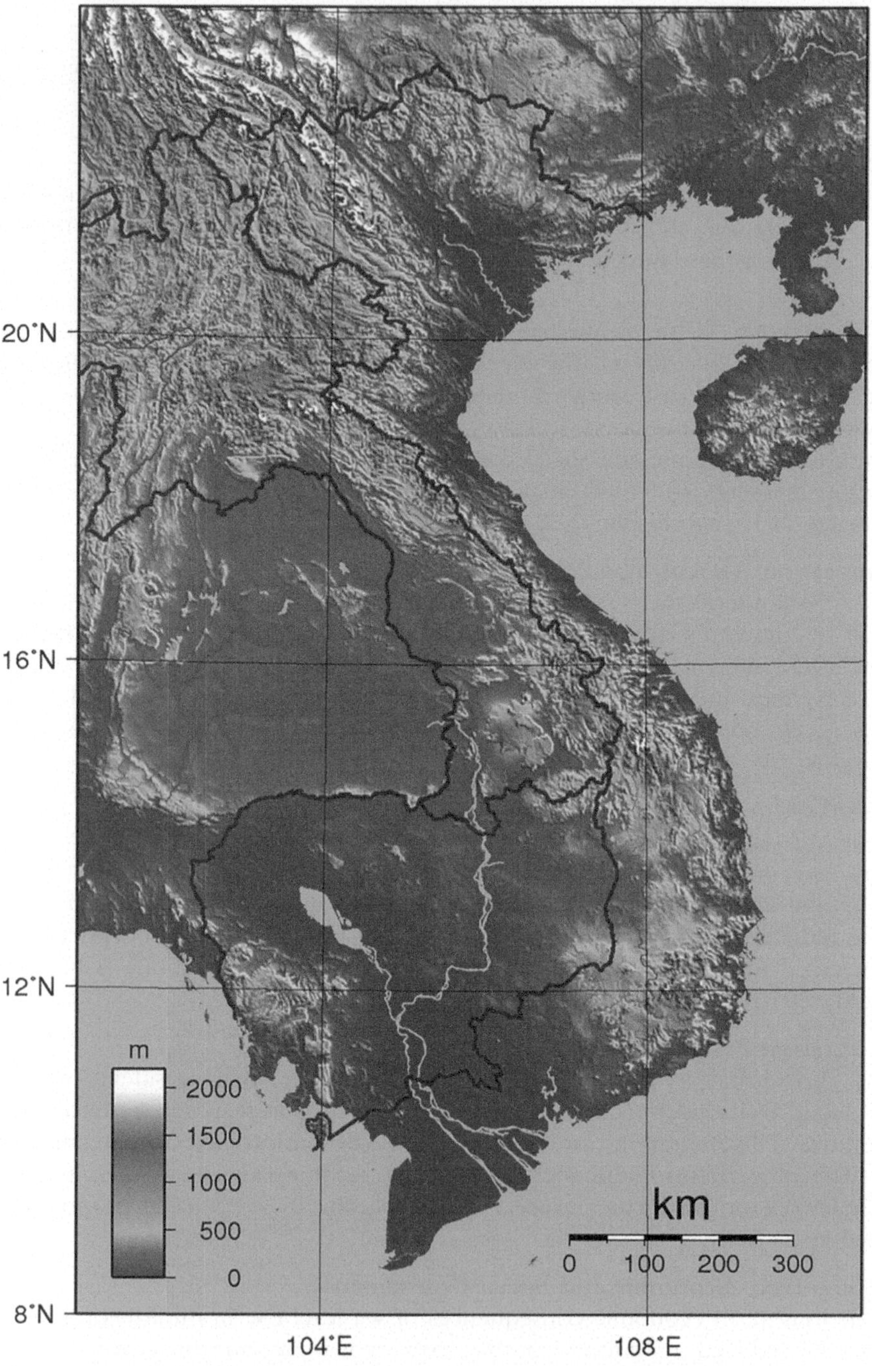

Fig. 2 Topographic map of Vietnam (By Sadalmelik—Own work, Public Domain, https://commons.wikimedia.org/w/index.php?curid=2221794)

ways of life can lead to social instability and increased vulnerability (Pham & Furukawa, 2007).

Adaptation Measures

To mitigate the impacts of sea-level rise, several adaptation measures are necessary (Schmitt et al., 2013):

- Seawalls and Dikes: Constructing and reinforcing seawalls and dikes can protect agricultural land and infrastructure from flooding and salinity intrusion.
- Mangrove Restoration: Restoring and expanding mangrove forests can provide natural barriers against storm surges and erosion, while also supporting biodiversity and fisheries.
- Drought-Resistant Crops: Developing and promoting the use of drought-resistant and salt-tolerant crop varieties can help maintain agricultural productivity in changing conditions.

Financial Implications of Adaptation

Implementing these adaptation measures requires significant financial investment. The costs of constructing and maintaining seawalls, restoring mangroves, and developing resilient agricultural practices can be substantial. However, these investments are crucial for protecting the livelihoods of millions of people and ensuring long-term food security and economic stability.

This case study highlights the urgent need for comprehensive adaptation strategies to address the multifaceted impacts of sea-level rise in the Mekong Delta. By investing in resilience-building measures, we can mitigate the economic and social consequences of climate change and support sustainable development in this vulnerable region.

3 Transition Risks: Navigating the Shift to a Low-Carbon Economy

While the physical risks of climate change pose a direct and tangible threat, the transition to a low-carbon economy also presents a unique set of challenges and uncertainties. These *transition risks* arise from the fundamental shifts occurring in policies, technologies, markets, and social expectations as the world moves away from fossil fuels and embraces a more sustainable future.

Understanding and effectively managing these transition risks is crucial for businesses and investors seeking to not only mitigate potential losses but also to capitalize on the emerging opportunities of a decarbonizing world.

Risk Category	*Description*	*Example*
Policy and Regulatory Risks	Uncertainty and volatility caused by government policies and regulations aimed at reducing greenhouse gas emissions	Introduction of carbon pricing mechanisms, stricter emissions standards for vehicles, phase-out of coal-fired power plants
Technological Risks	Risks and opportunities associated with the rapid development and adoption of low-carbon technologies	Disruptive innovation in renewable energy, battery storage, or carbon capture technologies leading to the obsolescence of existing technologies and assets
Market Risks	Shifts in supply and demand, consumer preferences, and investor sentiment driven by climate change awareness and the transition to a low-carbon economy	Increasing demand for electric vehicles leading to a decline in the market value of companies heavily invested in internal combustion engine technology
Reputation Risks	Potential damage to a company's reputation and brand value due to perceived inaction or inadequate efforts to address climate change	Consumer boycotts, negative media coverage, and difficulty attracting investors and employees for companies perceived as lagging in climate action

3.1 Policy and Regulatory Risks: The Changing Landscape

Governments around the world are increasingly enacting policies and regulations to curb greenhouse gas emissions and accelerate the transition to a low-carbon economy. While these measures are essential for mitigating climate change, they also create a complex and evolving landscape for businesses. Companies that fail to adapt to these policy shifts face a heightened risk of stranded assets, increased compliance costs, and diminished competitiveness.

For example, the introduction of carbon pricing mechanisms, such as carbon taxes or emissions trading schemes, can significantly impact industries with high-carbon footprints. Companies in sectors like energy production, transportation, and heavy manufacturing may face higher operating costs, reduced profitability, or even pressure to shut down facilities if they cannot adapt to a carbon-constrained world. As governments implement policies to transition to low-carbon economies, it is essential to ensure a just transition for workers and communities reliant on fossil fuel industries (ILO, 2016). This includes providing support for retraining, job placement, and economic diversification.

Similarly, stricter building codes and energy efficiency standards, while crucial for reducing emissions from the building sector, can increase construction costs and impact the value of existing buildings that do not meet the new standards.

To navigate policy and regulatory risks effectively, companies need to:

- **Stay Informed:** Closely monitor policy developments and anticipate future regulations.
- **Assess Exposure:** Analyze how different policy scenarios could impact operations, assets, and financial performance.
- **Engage in Advocacy:** Participate constructively in policy discussions to advocate for clear and predictable regulations that support a smooth transition.

By proactively addressing policy and regulatory risks, companies can minimize disruptions, adapt to the changing landscape, and potentially gain a competitive advantage.

3.2 Technological Risks: Innovation and Disruption

The transition to a low-carbon economy is driving rapid technological innovation across various sectors, from renewable energy generation and storage to energy efficiency and sustainable transportation. While these advancements offer significant opportunities for growth and efficiency, they also pose technological risks for companies unable to keep pace with the changing landscape.

One major risk is the **disruptive potential** of new technologies. For example, the rapid decline in the cost of solar and wind energy, coupled with advances in battery storage, is challenging the dominance of fossil fuels in the electricity sector. Companies heavily invested in traditional power generation and transmission infrastructure may face stranded assets and financial losses if they fail to adapt to the rise of distributed, renewable energy systems.

Similarly, the automotive industry is experiencing a seismic shift toward electric vehicles (EVs), driven by government incentives, falling battery costs, and growing consumer demand for sustainable transportation. Traditional automakers that are slow to embrace EV production risk falling behind competitors and losing market share.

To manage technological risks effectively, companies should:

- **Embrace Innovation:** Foster a culture of innovation within their organizations, invest in research and development, and actively explore new technologies.
- **Collaborate and Partner:** Seek partnerships with technology companies, start-ups, and research institutions to access cutting-edge knowledge and expertise.
- **Develop Workforce Skills:** Invest in training and retraining programs to equip employees with the skills needed to thrive in a low-carbon economy.

By actively engaging with technological advancements and fostering a forward-looking approach, companies can mitigate risks and position themselves to capitalize on the opportunities presented by the transition to a low-carbon future.

3.3 *Market Risks: Shifting Consumer Preferences and Investor Sentiment*

Market dynamics are increasingly influenced by climate change considerations as consumers become more environmentally conscious and investors seek to align their portfolios with sustainability goals. Companies that are slow to adapt to these evolving market preferences risk losing market share, facing increased financing costs, and experiencing a decline in their valuations.

Consumer demand for sustainable products and services is on the rise across various sectors. A 2021 global survey by Simon-Kucher & Partners found that 85% of consumers have shifted their purchase behavior toward sustainability in the past five years. This trend is particularly evident in industries like food and beverage, fashion, and consumer goods, where consumers are increasingly choosing products with lower environmental footprints and opting for brands with strong sustainability credentials.

At the same time, investors are increasingly incorporating climate change considerations into their investment decisions. A growing number of institutional investors, including pension funds, sovereign wealth funds, and asset managers, are divesting from fossil fuel companies and redirecting capital toward climate-aligned investments, such as renewable energy, energy efficiency, and sustainable agriculture.

To navigate market risks effectively, companies should:

- **Understand Evolving Consumer Preferences:** Conduct market research to understand how climate change is shaping consumer choices and tailor products and services accordingly.
- **Communicate Sustainability Efforts:** Clearly communicate sustainability initiatives and performance to consumers and investors through transparent reporting and engagement.
- **Develop Climate-Aligned Business Strategies:** Integrate climate considerations into core business strategies, including product development, supply chain management, and investment decisions.

By aligning with the evolving market landscape and demonstrating a commitment to sustainability, companies can mitigate market risks and position themselves for success in a low-carbon future.

3.4 Reputation Risks: Maintaining Public Trust in a Changing World

In an era of heightened awareness and scrutiny of corporate behavior, companies are increasingly held accountable for their environmental and social impacts. Those perceived as failing to address climate change adequately or engaging in "greenwashing"—making misleading claims about their sustainability practices—face significant reputational risks.

Negative perceptions of a company's climate actions can lead to:

- **Consumer Backlash:** Consumers are increasingly willing to boycott companies with poor environmental records or those perceived as contributing to climate change.
- **Investor Skepticism:** Investors, particularly those with ESG (environmental, social, and governance) mandates, are less likely to invest in companies with high-carbon footprints or weak climate risk management strategies.
- **Difficulty Attracting and Retaining Talent:** Top talent, particularly millennials and Gen Z, are increasingly drawn to companies with strong social and environmental values.

For example, in 2015, Volkswagen faced a significant reputational crisis when it was revealed that the company had cheated on emissions tests for its diesel vehicles. The scandal resulted in billions of dollars in fines, a decline in sales, and lasting damage to the company's reputation.

To manage reputation risks effectively, companies need to:

- **Develop Authentic Sustainability Strategies:** Move beyond superficial initiatives and implement comprehensive sustainability plans with measurable targets and transparent reporting.
- **Engage with Stakeholders:** Proactively engage with investors, customers, employees, and communities to understand their concerns and communicate the company's commitment to addressing climate change.
- **Walk the Talk:** Ensure that sustainability claims are backed by concrete actions and avoid any practices that could be perceived as greenwashing.

By taking a proactive and genuine approach to sustainability, companies can build trust with stakeholders, enhance their reputation, and mitigate the potentially damaging consequences of climate-related reputational risks.

Case Study 3: The Decline of Coal and the Stranded Asset Risk for Utilities

- Focus: Impact of policy shifts (e.g., carbon pricing, renewable energy mandates) on the value of coal-fired power plants and the financial risks for utilities heavily invested in coal assets.

- Illustrate: How the transition to a low-carbon economy can create stranded assets and financial losses for companies that fail to adapt.
- Discuss: The importance of scenario analysis in assessing transition risks, the need for utilities to diversify their energy mix, and the challenges of managing a just transition for workers in the coal industry.

The global energy landscape is undergoing a significant transformation as countries implement policies to mitigate climate change (International Energy Agency (IEA), 2020). These policy shifts, including carbon pricing and renewable energy mandates, are profoundly affecting the value of coal-fired power plants and the financial stability of utilities heavily invested in coal assets. This case study explores the impact of these policy changes, illustrating how the transition to a low-carbon economy can create stranded assets and financial losses for companies that fail to adapt. It also discusses the importance of scenario analysis in assessing transition risks, the need for utilities to diversify their energy mix, and the challenges of managing a just transition for workers in the coal industry.

Impact of Policy Shifts

Carbon Pricing: Carbon pricing mechanisms, such as carbon taxes and emissions trading systems, are designed to internalize the environmental costs of carbon emissions. These policies increase the operating costs of coal-fired power plants, making them less competitive compared to cleaner energy sources. For example, the European Union's Emissions Trading System (EU ETS) has significantly raised the cost of carbon emissions, leading to a decline in the profitability of coal plants (Fig. 3).

Renewable Energy Mandates: Governments worldwide are setting ambitious renewable energy targets to reduce greenhouse gas emissions. These mandates incentivize the development of renewable energy projects, further reducing the market share of coal. For instance, the United States has seen a significant increase in renewable energy capacity due to state-level Renewable Portfolio Standards (RPS).

Stranded Assets and Financial Losses

Stranded Assets: Stranded assets are investments that have become obsolete or non-performing due to changes in the market or regulatory environment. For utilities heavily invested in coal-fired power plants, the transition to a low-carbon economy can render these assets stranded. The decline in coal demand, coupled with increased regulatory costs, leads to reduced asset values and potential write-downs (Carbon Tracker Initiative, 2018).

Financial Losses: Utilities facing stranded assets may experience significant financial losses. These losses can stem from decreased revenues, higher operational costs, and the need to invest in decommissioning and site remediation. Additionally, utilities may face increased borrowing costs and reduced access to capital as investors shift their portfolios toward more sustainable

Fig. 3 Bełchatów power station in Bełchatów, Poland (By Morgre—Own work, CC BY-SA 3.0, https://commons.wikimedia.org/w/index.php?curid=19858375)

assets (Institute for Energy Economics and Financial Analysis (IEEFA), 2025) (Fig. 4).

Scenario Analysis and Transition Risks

Scenario Analysis: Scenario analysis is a critical tool for assessing transition risks. By modeling different policy, market, and technological scenarios, utilities can better understand the potential impacts on their assets and operations. This approach helps companies identify vulnerabilities, develop mitigation strategies, and make informed investment decisions (Task Force on Climate-related Financial Disclosures (TCFD), 2017).

Transition Risks: Transition risks encompass the financial and operational challenges associated with the shift to a low-carbon economy. These risks include policy and regulatory changes, technological advancements, market dynamics, and reputational considerations. Utilities must proactively manage these risks to ensure long-term financial stability.

Diversifying the Energy Mix

Importance of Diversification: Diversifying the energy mix is essential for utilities to mitigate the risks associated with the decline of coal. By investing in renewable energy, energy storage, and energy efficiency, utilities can reduce their reliance on coal and enhance their resilience to market and regulatory changes (IRENA, 2022).

Challenges: Transitioning to a diversified energy portfolio involves significant capital investment, technological innovation, and workforce retraining.

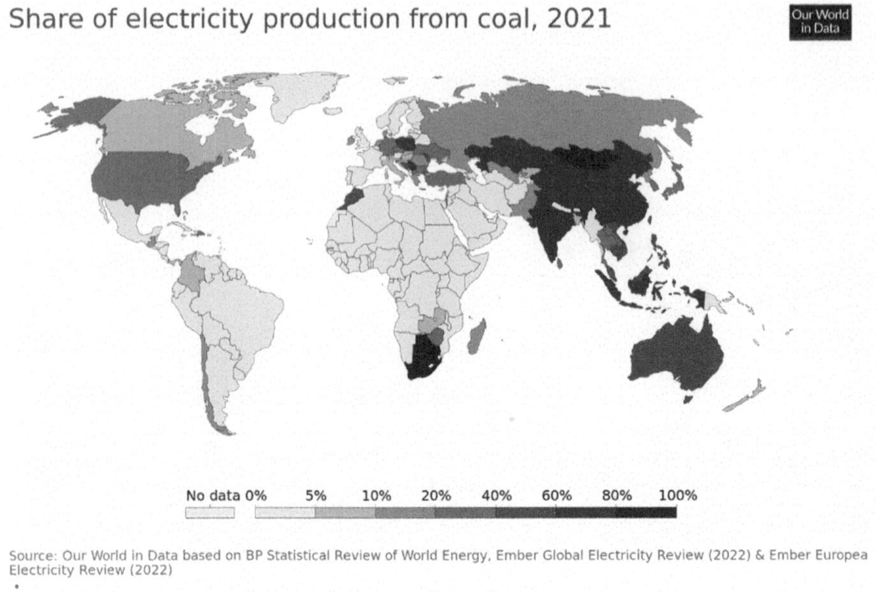

Fig. 4 Share of electricity production from coal (By Hannah Ritchie and Max Roser—https://ourworldindata.org/fossil-fuels, CC BY-SA 4.0, https://commons.wikimedia.org/w/index.php?curid=121265491)

Utilities must navigate these challenges while maintaining reliable and affordable energy supply (BloombergNEF, 2024).

Managing a Just Transition

Just Transition: A just transition ensures that the shift to a low-carbon economy is fair and inclusive, addressing the needs of workers and communities affected by the decline of coal. This involves providing support for retraining, job placement, and economic diversification in coal-dependent regions (International Labour Organization (ILO), 2016).

Challenges: Managing a just transition requires coordinated efforts from governments, industry, and civil society. It involves addressing social and economic disparities, ensuring access to new opportunities, and fostering community resilience.

This case study highlights the complex interplay between policy shifts, market dynamics, and financial risks in the context of the declining coal industry. By understanding these challenges and implementing proactive strategies, utilities can navigate the transition to a low-carbon economy while ensuring financial stability and social equity.

4 Climate Litigation Risk: The Legal Landscape

The legal landscape surrounding climate change is rapidly evolving, presenting a new and complex set of risks for companies, governments, and individuals. Climate litigation, once a niche area of law, has become a powerful tool for holding actors accountable for their role in contributing to climate change or failing to address its impacts.

4.1 *The Rise of Climate Litigation*

In recent years, there has been a surge in climate-related lawsuits filed across the globe. While the specific legal strategies vary, these cases generally fall into a few main categories:

- **Cases Against Governments:** Seeking to compel governments to take more ambitious action to reduce emissions or implement adaptation measures. For instance, in the landmark case of *Urgenda Foundation v. State of the Netherlands*, a Dutch court ruled that the government had a legal duty to protect its citizens from climate change and ordered it to reduce greenhouse gas emissions more aggressively.
- **Cases Against Corporations:** Holding companies accountable for their contributions to climate change, seeking damages for climate-related harms, or challenging misleading claims about climate action (greenwashing). A prominent example is the case of *Milieudefensie et al. v. Royal Dutch Shell*, in which a Dutch court ruled that Shell must significantly reduce its emissions to align with the Paris Agreement goals.
- **Cases Related to Climate Disclosures:** Focusing on the adequacy and accuracy of climate-related disclosures by companies and investors. For example, in 2021, the German Supreme Court ruled that the German government's climate action plans were insufficient to protect future generations, highlighting the increasing legal scrutiny of climate disclosures.

4.2 *Impacts and Implications*

The rise of climate litigation has significant implications:

- **Financial Liability:** Companies found liable for climate-related damages could face substantial financial penalties, legal costs, and insurance premium hikes.
- **Reputational Damage:** Even if lawsuits are ultimately unsuccessful, the negative publicity and public scrutiny associated with climate litigation can harm a company's reputation and brand value.

- **Increased Regulatory Scrutiny:** Climate lawsuits often put pressure on governments and regulatory bodies to strengthen climate policies and enforcement mechanisms.
- **Shifting Industry Standards:** Court rulings on climate change issues can establish new legal precedents and industry standards, shaping future behavior and investment decisions.

4.3 Strategies for Managing Litigation Risk

While the legal landscape remains complex and evolving, companies can take proactive steps to mitigate their climate litigation risk:

- **Robust Climate Risk Assessment:** Conduct comprehensive assessments of both physical and transition risks, considering how these risks might give rise to legal liability.
- **Transparent Climate Disclosures:** Provide accurate and detailed disclosures aligned with recognized frameworks like the Task Force on Climate-Related Financial Disclosures (TCFD) recommendations.
- **Ambitious Climate Action Plans:** Develop and implement credible and ambitious plans to reduce emissions, transition to cleaner technologies, and build resilience to climate impacts.
- **Stakeholder Engagement:** Engage openly and proactively with stakeholders, including investors, communities, and NGOs, to address concerns and build trust.

By taking a proactive and comprehensive approach to climate risk management, companies can not only mitigate their legal exposure but also position themselves as responsible corporate citizens in an era of increasing climate accountability.

Case Study 4: The People of the State of New York v. Exxon Mobil Corp. (2018)

- Focus: Allegations of misleading investors about climate risks, greenwashing, and the potential for financial liability for companies that misrepresent their climate actions.
- Illustrate: The legal and reputational risks associated with climate litigation, even if cases are ultimately dismissed.
- Discuss: The importance of transparent and accurate climate disclosures, the need for companies to align their actions with their climate pledges, and the role of investor activism in holding companies accountable.

In 2018, the New York Attorney General filed a lawsuit against Exxon Mobil Corp., alleging that the company had misled investors about the financial risks posed by climate change. The case centered on claims that Exxon had provided false and misleading information regarding how it accounted for climate risks in its business operations and financial disclosures. This case study examines the legal and reputational risks associated with climate litigation, even when cases are ultimately dismissed, and discusses the importance of transparent and accurate climate disclosures, the need for companies to align their actions with their climate pledges, and the role of investor activism in holding companies accountable (Fig. 5).

Legal and Reputational Risks

Allegations and Legal Proceedings: The lawsuit accused Exxon of using two sets of numbers to estimate the impact of future climate regulations on its business. One set was used internally for decision-making, while a more optimistic set was presented to investors. The New York Attorney General argued that this discrepancy misled investors about the true financial risks posed by climate change, constituting securities fraud.

Outcome: In December 2019, a New York state judge ruled in favor of Exxon, stating that the Attorney General had failed to prove that the company had committed fraud. However, the case highlighted the increasing scrutiny on how companies disclose climate risks and the potential for significant legal and reputational consequences.

Fig. 5 Protest in Washington, DC in 2015 (By Johnny Silvercloud—Exxon Knew, CC BY-SA 2.0, https://commons.wikimedia.org/w/index.php?curid=127196564)

Importance of Transparent and Accurate Climate Disclosures

Climate Disclosures: Transparent and accurate climate disclosures are essential for investors to understand the risks that climate change poses to a company's financial performance. The Task Force on Climate-related Financial Disclosures (TCFD) provides a framework for companies to disclose climate-related financial risks in a consistent and comparable manner (Task Force on Climate-related Financial Disclosures (TCFD), 2017).

Investor Expectations: Investors increasingly demand robust climate disclosures to assess the resilience of companies' business models to climate risks. Failure to provide transparent disclosures can lead to legal challenges, loss of investor confidence, and reputational damage.

Aligning Actions with Climate Pledges

Corporate Accountability: Companies must align their actions with their public climate pledges to maintain credibility and avoid accusations of greenwashing. Greenwashing occurs when a company exaggerates or misrepresents its environmental efforts, leading to potential legal and reputational risks.

Case Example: Exxon's case underscores the importance of consistency between internal practices and public statements. Companies must ensure that their climate strategies are reflected in their operational decisions and financial disclosures (Carbon Tracker Initiative, 2019).

Role of Investor Activism

Investor Activism: Investors play a crucial role in holding companies accountable for their climate actions. Activist investors use their influence to push for better climate risk management, improved disclosures, and alignment with global climate goals.

Examples: Shareholder resolutions, divestment campaigns, and engagement with company management are common strategies used by investors to drive corporate climate action. The Exxon case has galvanized investor activism, leading to increased scrutiny of corporate climate practices.

The People of the State of New York v. Exxon Mobil Corp. case illustrates the significant legal and reputational risks associated with misleading climate disclosures and greenwashing. It highlights the critical importance of transparent and accurate climate disclosures, the need for companies to align their actions with their climate pledges, and the influential role of investor activism in promoting corporate accountability. As climate litigation becomes more prevalent, companies must proactively manage their climate risks and ensure that their disclosures and actions are consistent with their stated commitments to sustainability.

By understanding the lessons from this case, companies can better navigate the complex landscape of climate-related financial risks and build trust with investors, regulators, and the public.

5 Conclusion: The Interconnected Nature of Climate Risks

As we've explored in this chapter, the risks associated with climate change are multifaceted and interconnected, weaving a complex web of challenges for businesses, investors, and society as a whole. It's not a matter of facing either physical or transition risks—it's about recognizing that these risks are intertwined and often amplify each other, creating a cascade of consequences that can be difficult to predict and manage.

For example, a company might face increased operational costs due to more frequent extreme weather events (physical risk), which could then impact its ability to invest in new, low-carbon technologies (transition risk). This, in turn, could lead to stranded assets and a decline in market value (market risk), potentially attracting negative attention from investors and the public (reputational risk) and increasing the likelihood of lawsuits (litigation risk).

The interconnectedness of climate risks underscores the need for a holistic and integrated approach to risk management. Companies and investors cannot afford to address these challenges in isolation. Instead, they must develop comprehensive strategies that account for the interplay of physical, transition, and litigation risks across their operations, investments, and value chains.

Moving forward, understanding climate risks is not merely an option but an imperative. It's the foundation for making informed decisions, developing resilient strategies, and seizing the opportunities that arise in a world transitioning toward a low-carbon future. By acknowledging the interconnectedness of these challenges, we can begin to chart a path that is not only sustainable for the planet but also resilient and prosperous for generations to come.

References

Hallegatte, S., Rentschler, J., & Rozenberg, J. (2019). *Lifelines: The resilient infrastructure opportunity*. World Bank Publications. https://hdl.handle.net/10986/31805

International Labour Organization (ILO). (2016). *Guidelines for a just transition towards environmentally sustainable economies and societies for all*. https://www.ilo.org/publications/guidelines-just-transition-towards-environmentally-sustainable-economies

Intergovernmental Panel on Climate Change (IPCC). (2021). *Assessment Report 6—Working Group I—Climate Change 2021: The Physical Science Basis*. https://www.ipcc.ch/report/ar6/wg1/

IPCC. (2022a). *Assessment Report 6—Working Group II—Climate Change 2022: Impacts, Adaptation and Vulnerability*. https://www.ipcc.ch/report/sixth-assessment-report-working-group-ii/

IPCC. (2022b). *Assessment Report 6—Working Group III—Climate Change 2022: Mitigation of Climate Change*. https://www.ipcc.ch/report/sixth-assessment-report-working-group-3/

Kahn, M. E., et al. (2019). *Long-term macroeconomic effects of climate change: A cross-country analysis*. https://doi.org/10.3386/w26167

Kerlin, K. (2022). *California's 2020 Wildfire Season*. https://www.ucdavis.edu/climate/news/californias-2020-wildfire-season-numbers

McGlade, J. (2019). *Global assessment report on disaster risk reduction 2019*. UN Office for Disaster Risk Reduction. https://www.undrr.org/publication/global-assessment-report-disaster-risk-reduction-2019

National Aeronautics and Space Administration (NASA). (2025). *Extreme Weather and Climate Change*. https://science.nasa.gov/climate-change/extreme-weather/

National Oceanic and Atmospheric Administration (NOAA). (2025). *Hurricane Costs*. https://coast.noaa.gov/states/fast-facts/hurricane-costs.html

Strategic Risk. (2011). *Thai floods cost $6.5bn and cripple supply chains*. https://www.strategic-risk-global.com/catastrophe-risk/thai-floods-cost-65bn-and-cripple-supply-chains/1393460.article

World Meteorological Organization (WMO). (2023). *The Global Climate 2011–2020 A decade of accelerating climate change*. https://library.wmo.int/viewer/68585/download?file=1338_Decadal_State_Climate-HG_en.pdf. Accessed 25 January 2025.

WMO. (2024). *State of the global climate 2023*. The World Meteorological Organization. https://wmo.int/publication-series/state-of-global-climate-2023

Case References

Adger, W. N., & Kelly, P. M. (1999). Social vulnerability to climate change and the architecture of entitlements. *Mitigation and Adaptation Strategies for Global Change, 4*(3/4), 253–266. https://doi.org/10.1023/a:1009601904210

Bloomberg New Energy Finance (BloombergNEF). (2024). *New energy outlook 2024*. https://about.bnef.com/new-energy-outlook/. Accessed 22 January 2025.

Carbon Tracker Initiative. (2018). *Powering down coal: Navigating the economic and financial risks in the last years of coal power*. https://carbontracker.org/reports/coal-portal/. Accessed 22 January 2025.

Carbon Tracker Initiative. (2019). *Balancing the budget: why deflating the carbon bubble requires oil & gas companies to shrink*. https://carbontracker.org/reports/balancing-the-budget/. Accessed 22 January 2025.

Chapman, A. D., et al. (2016). Adaptation and development trade-offs: Fluvial sediment deposition and the sustainability of rice-cropping in An Giang Province, Mekong Delta. *Climatic Change, 137*(3–4), 593–608. https://doi.org/10.1007/s10584-016-1684-3

Fischbach, J. R., Warren, M. L., Whipkey, K., et al. (2020). *After hurricane Maria: Predisaster conditions, hurricane damage, and recovery needs in Puerto Rico*. https://www.rand.org/pubs/research_reports/RR2595.html. Accessed 22 January 2025.

Hanh, P. T. T., & Furukawa, M. (2007). Impact of sea level rise on coastal zone of Vietnam. *Journal of Coastal Research, 84*, 45–59. http://hdl.handle.net/20.500.12000/5368

Institute for Energy Economics and Financial Analysis (IEEFA). (2025). *Accelerating the transition to a diverse, sustainable and profitable energy economy*. https://ieefa.org/. Accessed 22 January 2025.

International Energy Agency (IEA). (2020). *World Energy Outlook 2020*. https://www.iea.org/reports/world-energy-outlook-2020. Accessed 22 January 2025.

International Labour Organization (ILO). (2016). *Guidelines for a just transition towards environmentally sustainable economies and societies for all*. https://www.ilo.org/publications/guidelines-just-transition-towards-environmentally-sustainable-economies. Accessed 22 January 2025.

International Renewable Energy Agency (IRENA). (2022). *Climate action*. https://www.irena.org/Energy-Transition/Country-engagement/Climate-Action. Accessed 22 January 2025.

Kishore, N., et al. (2018). Mortality in Puerto Rico after hurricane Maria. *New England Journal of Medicine, 379*(2), 162–170. https://doi.org/10.1056/NEJMsa1803972

Pham, H., & Furukawa, M. (2007). Impact of sea level rise on coastal zone of Vietnam. *Faculty of Science, University of the Ryukyus, 84*, 45–59. https://www.researchgate.net/publication/238733023_Impact_of_Sea_Level_Rise_on_Coastal_Zone_of_Vietnam

Robles, F., & Ferré-Sadurní, L. (2017). Puerto Rico's agriculture and farmers decimated by maria. *The New York times*. https://www.nytimes.com/2017/09/24/us/puerto-rico-hurricane-maria-agriculture-.html. Accessed 22 January 2025.

Schmitt, K., Albers, T., Pham, T. T., & Dinh, S. C. (2013). Site-specific and integrated adaptation to climate change in the coastal mangrove zone of Soc Trang Province, Vietnam. *Journal of Coastal Conservation, 17*(3), 545–558. https://doi.org/10.1007/s11852-013-0253-4

Smajgl, A. (2015). Responding to rising sea levels in the Mekong Delta. *Nature Climate Change, 5*(2), 167–174. https://www.nature.com/articles/nclimate2469

Task Force on Climate-Related Financial Disclosures (TCFD). (2017). *Recommendations of the Task Force on Climate-related Financial Disclosures*. https://assets.bbhub.io/company/sites/60/2020/10/FINAL-2017-TCFD-Report-11052018.pdf

Wassmann, R., Hien, N. X., Hoanh, C. T., & Tuong, T. P. (2004). Sea level rise affecting the Vietnamese Mekong Delta: Water elevation in the flood season and implications for rice production. *Climatic Change, 66*(1/2), 89–107. https://doi.org/10.1023/b:clim.0000043144.69736.b7

World Bank. (2010). *Economics of adaptation to climate change: Vietnam*. https://openknowledge.worldbank.org/entities/publication/e3f28287-2665-5b3a-8c63-0d5247b21c83

CHAPTER 3

The Role of Financial Institutions

1 Introduction

The global financial system, a vast and complex network of institutions, markets, and instruments, stands at a crossroads. As the impacts of climate change escalate and the urgent need to transition to a low-carbon economy becomes undeniable, financial institutions find themselves on the frontlines of this unprecedented challenge. No longer merely passive actors in the global economy, they are increasingly recognized as pivotal agents of change, possessing both the responsibility and the capacity to reshape the trajectory of climate action.

The very nature of financial institutions—managing risk, allocating capital, and influencing corporate behavior—places them in a unique position to drive the transition to a more sustainable and resilient future. They control trillions of dollars in assets, making investment decisions that will shape the global economy for decades to come. Their lending practices can either support or hinder the growth of climate-friendly businesses and technologies. In the context of the United States (Federal Reserve, 2022), their risk management frameworks will determine the financial system's resilience to the shocks and disruptions of a changing climate.

This chapter delves into the multifaceted role of financial institutions in addressing climate change. We'll explore the risks they face, the opportunities that lie ahead, and the innovative financial instruments and strategies being deployed to mobilize capital toward climate solutions. We will also examine the evolving regulatory landscape and the crucial role of international cooperation in aligning the financial system with the goals of a net-zero and climate-resilient future.

J. Chen, *Climate Finance*, https://doi.org/10.1007/978-981-96-7975-1_3

2 Financial Institutions and Climate Risks

While financial institutions play a crucial role in mobilizing capital for climate solutions, they are not immune to the risks posed by climate change itself. In fact, they are uniquely exposed to both the physical and transition risks we explored in the previous chapter. This exposure arises from the very core of their business activities: lending, investing, and managing risk on behalf of their clients and stakeholders (Fig. 1).

2.1 *The Exposure of Financial Institutions*

The financial risks of climate change manifest across various dimensions of a financial institution's operations, potentially impacting their balance sheets, profitability, and long-term stability:

- **Credit Risk:** Banks and other lenders face increased credit risk as borrowers in climate-vulnerable sectors become more susceptible to physical and transition risks. For instance, a bank that provides loans to agricultural businesses in a drought-prone region could experience higher default rates as crop yields decline due to water scarcity. Similarly, a bank financing a coal-fired power plant might face losses if stricter emissions regulations or declining demand for coal-powered electricity render the asset unprofitable or "stranded."

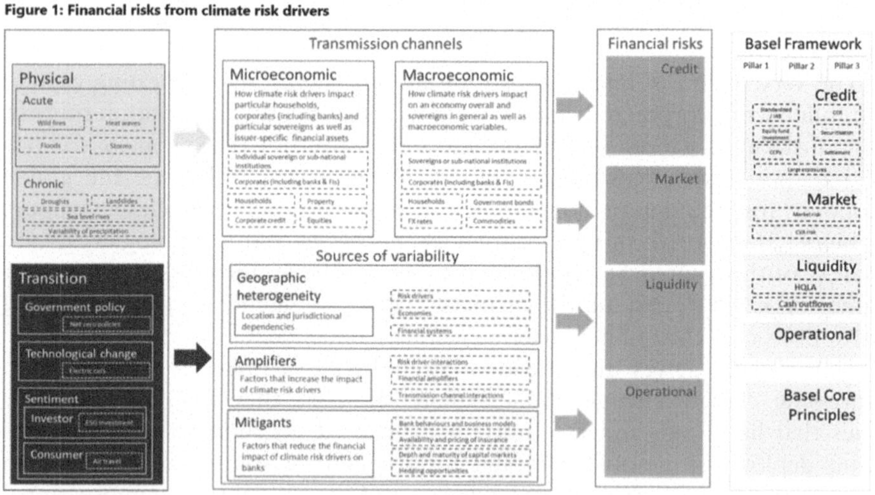

Fig. 1 Climate risk transmission channels (*Source* BIS, *Climate-related risk drivers and their transmission channels*, 2021)

- **Market Risk:** Climate change poses significant market risks for investors holding assets sensitive to climate impacts or the low-carbon transition. For example, real estate investments in coastal areas are increasingly vulnerable to sea-level rise and extreme weather events, potentially leading to property damage, reduced values, and higher insurance premiums. Similarly, investments in fossil fuel companies could decline in value as the world shifts toward cleaner energy sources and demand for fossil fuels diminishes.
- **Liquidity Risk:** Physical climate risks can disrupt operations, trigger unexpected cash outflows, and create systemic liquidity crunches, posing challenges for financial institutions' ability to meet their short-term obligations. The shift to a lower-carbon economy can create transition risks that impact financial institutions' liquidity by affecting asset valuations, investor behavior, and funding sources.
- **Operational Risk:** Financial institutions face operational risks from the direct impacts of climate change on their own infrastructure and operations. Extreme weather events such as hurricanes, floods, and wildfires can disrupt business operations, damage physical assets, and lead to financial losses. For instance, Hurricane Sandy in 2012 caused an estimated $71 billion in economic losses, including significant disruptions to financial institutions in the affected areas.
- **Reputational Risk:** Financial institutions are increasingly under scrutiny for their role in financing carbon-intensive activities. Investing in or lending to companies with high greenhouse gas emissions, engaging in deforestation, or lacking credible climate action plans can lead to reputational damage, loss of customers, and difficulty attracting and retaining talent. This is particularly relevant as public awareness of climate change grows and consumers and investors increasingly demand that their financial partners align with their values.
- **Litigation Risk:** As discussed in the previous chapter, the rise of climate litigation presents a growing risk for financial institutions. They could face lawsuits for financing projects that contribute to climate change, failing to disclose climate-related risks adequately, or engaging in greenwashing. These lawsuits can result in significant financial penalties, legal costs, and reputational damage.

Next, we will discuss in details of how climate risk can impact the clients of financial institutions, including households, corporates, sovereigns, and sub-national institutions, and affect traditional financial risks.

2.1.1 Credit Risk Induced by Physical Risk

Physical climate risk can impact the credit risk of various entities, including households, corporates, sovereigns, and sub-national institutions.

Households

Physical climate risks pose a direct threat to households' assets and income, directly impacting their ability to repay debts and thus increasing their credit risk.

Impact Pathways:

- **Property Damage:**
- Extreme weather events like floods, hurricanes, wildfires, and storms can cause significant damage to homes and personal property. This can lead to:
  - **Reduced Property Value:** Damaged properties lose value, reducing the collateral value for mortgages and increasing the loan-to-value ratio, making the loan riskier for lenders, as found by Bin and Polasky (2004) and Ortega and Taspinar (2018).
  - **Increased Debt Burden:** Households may need to take on additional debt to repair or rebuild their homes, increasing their overall debt burden and financial strain.
  - **Mortgage Delinquencies and Defaults:** Financial hardship from property damage can lead to missed mortgage payments and even foreclosures, increasing credit losses for lenders, as illustrated by Noth and Schüwer (2023).
- **Income Disruptions:** Physical climate events can disrupt employment, especially in industries like agriculture, tourism, and construction, leading to:
  - **Reduced Income and Cash Flow:** Households with reduced income or unemployment face difficulty in meeting their debt obligations, increasing the risk of loan defaults.
  - **Credit Downgrades:** Credit scoring models may downgrade borrowers with income instability, further restricting their access to credit.
- **Increased Living Expenses:** Climate change can lead to higher living expenses:
  - **Insurance Premiums:** Premiums for property, flood, and other types of insurance can rise significantly in areas prone to climate-related risks, increasing household expenses.
  - **Energy Costs:** Extreme weather can drive up energy costs for heating and cooling, adding to the financial burden.
  - **Water Costs:** Droughts and water scarcity can lead to increased water costs for households.

Specific Examples:

- **Hurricane Harvey, Irma, and Maria (HIM):** Caused extensive flooding in the Caribbean Islands, Puerto Rico, Texas and parts of western Florida, leading to widespread property damage, displacement, and financial hardship for households, resulting in increased mortgage delinquencies and foreclosures. The storms resulted in combined economic losses of USD 217 billion, and insured losses of USD 92 billion, estimated by Bevere (2018).
- **California Wildfires:** Recurring wildfires have destroyed homes, businesses, and infrastructure, causing significant losses for households, leading to insurance claims, increased debt, and financial instability.

Corporates

Physical climate risks can disrupt operations, damage assets, and impact supply chains, directly affecting corporate profitability, creditworthiness, and credit risk for lenders.

Impact Pathways:

- **Operational Disruptions:** Extreme weather events can force businesses to halt operations, leading to:
  - **Lost Productivity and Revenue:** Shutdowns and disruptions reduce productivity, disrupt sales, and lead to revenue losses, impacting a company's financial performance.
  - **Supply Chain Disruptions:** Climate events can disrupt supply chains, causing delays, shortages, and increased costs for businesses reliant on global supply networks.
  - **Increased Costs:** Companies may incur higher costs for repairs, insurance, and relocating operations to less risky areas.
- **Damage to Assets:** Physical damage to factories, warehouses, infrastructure, and other assets can:
  - **Reduce Asset Value:** Damaged assets lose value, reducing a company's collateral base and increasing the risk of loan defaults.
  - **Impair Operations:** Damaged infrastructure can disrupt production, transportation, and other critical business functions, affecting profitability and creditworthiness.
- **Market Disruptions:** Climate-related events can impact market dynamics, leading to:
  - **Reduced Demand:** Extreme weather can affect consumer demand for certain products and services, impacting sales and revenue.

   - **Price Volatility:** Climate change can increase price volatility for raw materials, energy, and other inputs, affecting business costs and profitability.

Specific Examples:

- **2011 Thailand Floods:** Floods inundated industrial estates, disrupting global supply chains for electronics, automotive, and other industries, causing significant losses for companies and impacting their creditworthiness.
- **Agricultural Impacts:** Droughts, floods, and extreme heat can severely affect agricultural production, leading to crop failures, reduced yields, and price volatility, impacting the profitability of agricultural businesses and their ability to repay loans.

Sovereigns

Physical climate risks pose challenges for sovereigns, potentially impacting their economies, fiscal positions, and creditworthiness.

Impact Pathways:

- **Economic Impacts:** Climate-related disasters and chronic climate change can have significant negative effects on national economies, leading to:
   - **Reduced GDP Growth:** Damage to infrastructure, disruptions to key industries, and reduced productivity can lower economic output and slow growth.
   - **Fiscal Strain:** Governments face higher costs for disaster relief, infrastructure repairs, and social safety net programs to support affected populations, straining public finances.
   - **Increased Debt Levels:** Governments may need to borrow more to cover disaster-related expenses or compensate for lower tax revenues, increasing their debt burden and potential risk of default.
- **Infrastructure Damage:** Extreme weather events can damage critical infrastructure, such as roads, bridges, power grids, and transportation systems, requiring costly repairs and potentially disrupting economic activity.
- **Reduced Tax Revenues:** Climate change can lower tax revenues as businesses and individuals face financial hardship, reducing the government's capacity to service its debt.

Specific Examples:

- **Small Island Developing States (SIDS):** These nations are particularly vulnerable to sea-level rise and extreme weather events. Damage to infrastructure, tourism, and agriculture can cripple their economies, increase debt levels, and threaten their ability to repay loans.
- **Droughts in Sub-Saharan Africa:** Prolonged droughts can devastate agricultural production, leading to food insecurity, economic decline, and increased reliance on foreign aid, potentially impacting sovereign creditworthiness.

Sub-National Institutions

Cities, states, and other sub-national entities are also exposed to physical climate risks, which can impact their finances, credit ratings, and ability to access capital markets.

Impact Pathways:

- **Damage to Public Infrastructure:** Extreme weather events can cause significant damage to local infrastructure, such as roads, bridges, schools, hospitals, and water systems, requiring costly repairs and potentially impacting the creditworthiness of the municipality.
- **Reduced Tax Base:** Climate-related damage can reduce property values and economic activity, leading to lower tax revenues for local governments, making it more challenging to service debt.
- **Increased Borrowing Costs:** Investors may demand higher interest rates on municipal bonds issued by entities perceived as vulnerable to climate risks, increasing borrowing costs.

Specific Examples:

- **Hurricane Katrina (2005):** The devastating hurricane caused widespread damage to New Orleans, Louisiana, requiring a massive federal bailout and significantly impacting the city's credit rating and financial stability.
- **California Drought:** The prolonged drought in California strained water resources, impacted agricultural production, and increased costs for local governments, highlighting the financial risks of climate change at the sub-national level.

Physical climate risks have a profound impact on the credit risk of households, corporates, sovereigns, and sub-national institutions. The increasing frequency and severity of extreme weather events and the gradual impacts of chronic climate change are creating new and complex financial challenges. It is essential for lenders, investors, and policymakers to understand these risks, assess exposures, and develop strategies to mitigate these risks and enhance resilience.

2.1.2 Credit Risk Induced by Transition Risk

The following is a detailed breakdown of how transition risk can affect the credit risk of various entities:

Households

Transition risks, driven by the shift to a lower-carbon economy, can impact households' finances and creditworthiness in several ways.

Impact Pathways:

- **Higher Energy Costs:** Transitioning away from fossil fuels can lead to higher energy prices in the short term, particularly if renewable energy and infrastructure investments haven't fully scaled up to meet demand. This can:
  - **Increase Household Expenses:** Elevated energy bills for heating, cooling, and transportation can strain household budgets, reducing disposable income and increasing the risk of loan defaults.
  - **Impact Affordability:** Higher energy costs can make it more challenging for households to afford essential services, potentially leading to utility bill delinquencies and reduced credit scores.
- **Changes in Housing Markets:** The transition to a low-carbon economy can affect housing markets:
  - **Reduced Value of Carbon-Intensive Homes:** Homes with poor energy efficiency ratings or reliance on fossil fuel heating systems may lose value as energy costs rise and consumer preferences shift toward sustainable housing. This can reduce the collateral value for mortgages and increase credit risk for lenders.
  - **Increased Renovation Costs:** Households may face higher costs to retrofit their homes with energy-efficient appliances, insulation, or renewable energy systems, potentially leading to increased debt and financial strain.
- **Job Disruptions:** The transition away from carbon-intensive industries can lead to job losses in sectors like fossil fuel extraction, manufacturing, and transportation, resulting in:
  - **Unemployment and Reduced Income:** Households facing unemployment or reduced income may struggle to meet their debt obligations, increasing the risk of loan defaults.

  - **Regional Economic Impacts:** Communities reliant on fossil fuel industries may experience economic downturns, further affecting employment and household finances.

Specific Examples:

- **Carbon Taxes:** The introduction of carbon taxes on fossil fuels can increase energy prices, directly impacting household budgets and potentially increasing the risk of loan defaults, particularly for low-income households.
- **Phasing Out Gas-Powered Vehicles:** Policies promoting electric vehicles and restricting the sale of gasoline or diesel cars can lead to:
  - **Higher Vehicle Costs:** EVs are currently more expensive than traditional vehicles, potentially making it more challenging for some households to afford new cars, impacting auto loan markets.
  - **Reduced Resale Value:** The value of gasoline-powered cars may decline as the transition progresses, reducing the value of collateral for auto loans.

Corporates

The transition to a low-carbon economy poses significant challenges and opportunities for corporations, affecting their profitability, competitiveness, and ultimately their credit risk.

Impact Pathways:

- **Stranded Assets:** Companies with significant investments in fossil fuel reserves, power plants, and other high-carbon assets face the risk of these assets becoming "stranded"—losing value or becoming unusable as the world shifts away from fossil fuels. This can:
  - **Impair Balance Sheets:** Stranded assets lead to write-downs and impairments on company balance sheets, reducing their financial strength and creditworthiness.
  - **Reduce Profitability:** Companies reliant on carbon-intensive activities may face declining revenues and profits as demand for their products or services decreases.
  - **Restrict Access to Capital:** Investors and lenders may be hesitant to provide financing to companies with high exposure to stranded assets, making it more challenging and costly for them to raise capital.
- **Increased Compliance Costs:** As governments implement stricter environmental regulations and carbon pricing mechanisms, companies will

need to invest in new technologies and processes to reduce their emissions, potentially leading to:

  - **Higher Operating Costs:** Compliance costs can significantly impact a company's profitability, reducing their ability to service debt.
  - **Reduced Competitiveness:** Companies that are slow to adapt to new regulations may find themselves at a competitive disadvantage.

- **Shifting Market Dynamics:** Consumer preferences for sustainable products and services are on the rise. Investors are also increasingly factoring in climate change considerations in their investment decisions. These shifts can:

  - **Impact Demand:** Companies that fail to develop low-carbon products or demonstrate a commitment to sustainability may see reduced demand for their offerings.
  - **Affect Investor Sentiment:** Companies with high-carbon footprints or weak climate strategies may face difficulty attracting investment, potentially leading to higher financing costs.

Specific Examples:

- **Fossil Fuel Companies:** Oil, gas, and coal companies face significant transition risks as the world shifts toward renewable energy. They are at risk of stranded assets, declining demand, and investor divestment, impacting their creditworthiness.
- **Automotive Industry:** The shift toward electric vehicles poses challenges for traditional automakers. They need to invest heavily in EV technology and adapt their production processes to remain competitive.
- **Energy-Intensive Industries:** Industries like steel, cement, and chemicals face higher compliance costs as carbon pricing is implemented and emissions regulations are tightened. Their ability to adapt and pass on these costs to consumers will impact their profitability and creditworthiness.

Sovereigns

Transition risks can impact sovereign creditworthiness through their effects on national economies, government revenues, and debt sustainability.

Impact Pathways:

- **Economic Dependence on Fossil Fuels:** Countries heavily reliant on fossil fuel exports for revenue face significant economic risks as global demand for fossil fuels declines. This can:

  - **Reduce Export Revenues:** Lower demand for fossil fuels will reduce export earnings, impacting government budgets and foreign exchange reserves.
  - **Impact Economic Growth:** Economic contraction in fossil fuel industries can have ripple effects on the broader economy, leading to slower growth, unemployment, and reduced tax revenues.
  - **Increase Debt Burden:** Governments may need to borrow more to compensate for lower revenues or to fund economic diversification efforts, increasing their debt burden.

- **Cost of Climate Action:** Governments face significant costs in implementing policies to achieve their emissions reduction targets, including:
  - **Investing in Renewable Energy:** Subsidies and investments in renewable energy infrastructure are costly, potentially impacting government finances.
  - **Supporting a Just Transition:** Programs to support workers and communities affected by the transition away from fossil fuel industries require substantial funding.

- **Potential for Social Unrest:** A disorderly or poorly managed transition can lead to:
  - **Job Losses and Economic Disruptions:** Significant job losses in carbon-intensive sectors can cause social unrest and political instability.
  - **Increased Inequality:** If the benefits and costs of the transition are not equitably distributed, it can exacerbate inequality and fuel social tensions.

Specific Examples:

- **Oil-Exporting Countries:** Nations like Saudi Arabia, Russia, and Venezuela face significant economic and fiscal challenges as the world transitions away from oil. They will need to diversify their economies and find new sources of revenue to maintain their creditworthiness.
- **Coal-Dependent Regions:** Countries and regions heavily reliant on coal mining and coal-fired power generation, such as parts of the United States, China, and India, face significant economic and social challenges as the coal industry declines.

Sub-National Institutions

Cities, states, and other sub-national entities are also vulnerable to transition risks, which can affect their budgets, credit ratings, and ability to access capital.

Impact Pathways:

- **Economic Impacts on Local Businesses:** The transition to a low-carbon economy can impact local businesses, leading to:
  - **Reduced Business Activity:** Companies in carbon-intensive sectors may face declining revenues and even closures, impacting local employment and tax revenues.
  - **Property Devaluation:**
  - Commercial properties in declining industries may lose value, impacting property tax revenues for municipalities.
- **Costs of Climate Action:** Local governments face costs in implementing climate policies, such as:
  - **Investing in Green Infrastructure:** Building renewable energy infrastructure, public transportation systems, and energy-efficient buildings requires significant investment.
  - **Providing Incentives:** Offering subsidies or tax breaks for households and businesses to adopt clean energy solutions can strain local budgets.

Specific Examples:

- **Cities with High Concentrations of Carbon-Intensive Industries:** Municipalities with a high concentration of businesses in declining sectors, such as fossil fuel extraction or manufacturing, may face economic downturns, job losses, and reduced tax revenues, potentially impacting their credit ratings.
- **Coastal Cities:** Adapting to sea-level rise and more frequent extreme weather events requires substantial investments in coastal protection and resilient infrastructure, posing significant financial challenges for many coastal cities.

Transition risks are increasingly impacting the creditworthiness of households, corporates, sovereigns, and sub-national institutions. The shift to a low-carbon economy is creating a complex and evolving landscape, presenting both financial challenges and opportunities. It is crucial for all stakeholders to understand these risks, assess their exposures, and develop proactive strategies to navigate the transition effectively and build a more sustainable and resilient future.

Here's a detailed discussion of how both physical and transition climate risks can significantly impact the market risk of financial institutions:

2.1.3 *Physical Risks and Market Risk*

Physical climate risks, stemming from the actual impacts of climate change, can lead to sudden, unpredictable, and potentially cascading effects on market valuations, volatility, and correlations, directly impacting the market risk of financial institutions.

Impact Pathways:

- **Asset Devaluation:** Extreme weather events and chronic climate change can damage or destroy physical assets, causing significant losses for investors.
  - **Real Estate:** Properties in areas prone to flooding, sea-level rise, wildfires, or hurricanes can experience severe devaluation, impacting the value of mortgages, real estate investment trusts (REITs), and other real estate-backed securities held by financial institutions.
  - **Infrastructure:** Damage to critical infrastructure, like power plants, transportation networks, and industrial facilities, can impact the value of infrastructure investments and bonds issued by companies operating in vulnerable regions.
  - **Commodities:** Climate change can disrupt agricultural production, affecting commodity prices and the value of agricultural futures, options, and other derivatives.
- **Increased Market Volatility:** The uncertainty surrounding the timing, location, and severity of climate events can lead to increased volatility in financial markets.
  - **Energy Prices:** Extreme weather can disrupt energy production and supply, leading to price spikes and volatility in oil, gas, and electricity markets, impacting energy companies and utilities, and their corresponding stock and bond prices.
  - **Insurance Stocks:** The stock prices of insurance companies can fluctuate dramatically in response to major climate-related disasters, as investors assess the potential impact of large insurance payouts on their profitability and capital adequacy.
- **Correlation Breakdowns:** Climate change can disrupt traditional market correlations, creating unexpected losses for investors using diversification strategies.
  - **Asset Class Correlations:** Correlations between historically uncorrelated asset classes, such as equities and bonds, can break down during periods of heightened climate-related uncertainty, reducing the effectiveness of diversification strategies.
  - **Geographic Correlations:** Climate impacts can affect different regions unevenly, leading to shifts in regional economic performance

and creating new correlations between investments across different geographies.

Specific Examples:

- **Hurricane Katrina (2005):** The devastating hurricane caused a significant decline in the value of real estate and insurance company stocks, highlighting the impact of extreme weather events on market valuations.
- **California Wildfires:** The increasing frequency and intensity of wildfires have led to volatility in the stock prices of utility companies operating in the affected areas and have impacted real estate values and insurance premiums.

2.1.4 *Transition Risks and Market Risk*

Transition risks, stemming from the shift to a low-carbon economy, can create significant market risks for financial institutions by impacting asset valuations, investor sentiment, and market dynamics.

Impact Pathways:

- **Stranded Assets and Asset Devaluation:**
- **Fossil Fuel Investments:** As the world transitions away from fossil fuels, companies in the oil, gas, and coal sectors face the risk of stranded assets, leading to a decline in their stock and bond values and impacting financial institutions holding these investments.
- **Carbon-Intensive Industries:** Companies in energy-intensive industries, like steel, cement, and chemicals, may face similar challenges as carbon pricing is implemented and emissions regulations are tightened.
- **Real Estate:** Buildings with poor energy efficiency ratings or reliance on fossil fuel heating systems could lose value as energy costs rise and demand for sustainable buildings increases.
- **Shifts in Investor Sentiment and Capital Flows:**
  - **Divestment from Fossil Fuels:** A growing number of institutional investors are divesting from fossil fuel companies and redirecting capital toward climate-aligned investments, potentially leading to a decline in the value of fossil fuel assets.
  - **ESG Investing:** The rise of ESG investing is driving capital flows toward companies with strong sustainability credentials, potentially leaving companies lagging in climate action with limited access to capital and facing higher financing costs.
- **Policy Uncertainty and Regulatory Risks:** The uncertainty surrounding government policies and regulations aimed at curbing emissions can create volatility and risks for investors.

  - **Carbon Pricing:** The introduction or strengthening of carbon pricing mechanisms can impact the profitability of carbon-intensive industries, affecting asset valuations.
  - **Regulatory Changes:** Sudden or unexpected regulatory changes, such as stricter emissions standards or bans on certain technologies, can create market disruptions and impact investment decisions.

- **Technological Disruption:** The rapid pace of innovation in clean technologies, such as renewable energy, battery storage, and electric vehicles, can disrupt existing industries and markets.
  - **New Entrants:** Emerging clean technology companies can challenge the market share of incumbents in carbon-intensive sectors, potentially leading to a shift in valuations.
  - **Technology Obsolescence:** Companies that fail to adapt to technological advancements risk their assets becoming obsolete and losing value.

Specific Examples:

- **Decline in Coal Industry:** The coal industry has faced a significant decline in recent years, with coal company stock prices plummeting as investors anticipate a continued shift away from coal-fired power generation.
- **Rise of Electric Vehicles:** The growing popularity of electric vehicles is impacting the valuations of traditional automakers and their suppliers as investors assess their ability to adapt to this transformative shift.

Key Considerations for Financial Institutions:

- **Scenario Analysis:** Conduct comprehensive scenario analyses that incorporate both physical and transition risks to assess the potential impact of different climate pathways on their portfolios.
- **Data and Analytics:** Invest in robust data and analytics capabilities to accurately measure climate risks, identify exposures, and make informed investment decisions.
- **Risk Management Frameworks:** Integrate climate risk considerations into their risk management frameworks, including credit risk, market risk, liquidity risk, and operational risk assessments.
- **Engagement with Clients and Policymakers:** Engage actively with clients on their climate strategies and advocate for clear and predictable climate policies that support a smooth transition to a low-carbon economy.
- **Transparency and Disclosure:** Provide transparent disclosures on their climate-related risks and opportunities to enhance investor confidence and support efficient capital allocation.

By proactively addressing climate-related market risks, financial institutions can mitigate their exposure to potential losses, capitalize on the opportunities presented by the low-carbon transition, and contribute to a more sustainable and resilient financial system.

2.1.5 *Climate Risks and Liquidity Risk*

Physical Risks and Liquidity Risk

Physical climate risks can disrupt operations, trigger unexpected cash outflows, and create systemic liquidity crunches, posing challenges for financial institutions' ability to meet their short-term obligations.

Impact Pathways:

- **Direct Operational Disruptions:** Extreme weather events can directly disrupt financial institutions' operations, leading to:
  - **Branch Closures:** Floods, hurricanes, wildfires, and other disasters can force branches to close temporarily, disrupting customer service and potentially limiting access to cash and financial services.
  - **Damage to Infrastructure:** Physical damage to data centers, communication networks, and other critical infrastructure can disrupt operations, delay transactions, and affect a financial institution's ability to function effectively.
- **Increased Demand for Liquidity from Clients:** In the aftermath of climate-related disasters, businesses and individuals may experience a surge in liquidity needs to:
  - **Cover Losses and Repairs:** Households and businesses may need to withdraw deposits or draw on credit lines to cover immediate expenses related to property damage, repairs, or business interruptions.
  - **Finance Reconstruction:** Reconstruction efforts following large-scale disasters can require substantial financing, leading to increased demand for loans and credit from financial institutions.
- **Insurance Payouts and Reinsurance Claims:** Insurers facing a surge in claims after catastrophic events may experience significant cash outflows, potentially impacting their liquidity.
  - **Reinsurance Dependencies:** Insurers rely heavily on reinsurance to manage their risk exposure. If reinsurers face their own liquidity challenges due to climate-related events, it can create a ripple effect through the insurance industry, impacting the liquidity of primary insurers.

- **Market Volatility and Asset Fire Sales:** Climate-related events can trigger volatility in financial markets, potentially leading to:
  - **Reduced Liquidity in Affected Markets:** Investors may become hesitant to trade assets exposed to climate risks, reducing market liquidity and making it more difficult for financial institutions to sell assets quickly to meet their own liquidity needs.
  - **Asset Fire Sales:** Forced selling of assets at distressed prices to raise cash can further exacerbate market volatility and potentially lead to cascading losses through the financial system.

Specific Examples:

- **Hurricane Katrina (2005):** The devastating hurricane caused significant operational disruptions for banks in the affected areas, leading to branch closures, limited access to ATMs, and difficulty processing transactions. It also triggered a surge in withdrawals and loan demand, straining banks' liquidity.
- **Japanese Earthquake and Tsunami (2011):** The disaster caused widespread damage to infrastructure and businesses, leading to a liquidity crunch in the Japanese financial system. The Bank of Japan had to inject trillions of yen into the market to stabilize the financial system and ensure liquidity for banks.

Transition Risks and Liquidity Risk

The shift to a lower-carbon economy can create transition risks that impact financial institutions' liquidity by affecting asset valuations, investor behavior, and funding sources.

Impact Pathways:

- **Devaluation of Carbon-Intensive Assets:** As the world transitions away from fossil fuels, companies in carbon-intensive industries may face a decline in the value of their assets. This can:
  - **Impact Collateral Value:** Financial institutions holding loans collateralized by fossil fuel reserves, power plants, or other carbon-intensive assets may experience a reduction in the value of this collateral, potentially increasing their liquidity risk if borrowers default.
  - **Reduce Asset Liquidity:** Investors may become less willing to buy assets perceived as "stranded," reducing market liquidity and making it more challenging for financial institutions to sell these assets quickly to raise cash.

- **Shifts in Investor Sentiment:**
  - **Divestment from Fossil Fuels:** The growing movement toward divestment from fossil fuel companies could lead to a decline in the value and liquidity of these companies' stock and bonds, impacting financial institutions holding these assets.
  - **Focus on ESG:** Investors increasingly prioritize ESG factors, potentially making it more challenging for companies with weak climate strategies to access capital, including from banks seeking to meet their own ESG commitments.
- **Policy Uncertainty and Regulatory Changes:**
  - **Carbon Pricing:** The introduction or strengthening of carbon pricing can impact the profitability of carbon-intensive industries, leading to uncertainty and potential volatility in their stock and bond prices.
  - **New Regulations:** Stringent emissions standards, technology bans, or other regulatory changes can create uncertainty and impact the financial viability of certain industries, potentially affecting banks' exposures and liquidity.
- **Changes in Funding Sources:**
  - **Reduced Access to Capital:** Banks heavily exposed to climate risks may face difficulty attracting investment or securing funding from other financial institutions that are integrating climate considerations into their lending practices.
  - **Higher Funding Costs:** Banks with high-carbon footprints or perceived as lagging in climate action may face higher borrowing costs as investors demand a premium for climate risk.

Specific Examples:

- **Divestment from Coal:** The decline in the coal industry has led to a reduction in the value and liquidity of coal company stocks and bonds, impacting investors holding these assets.
- **Stranded Asset Risk in Oil and Gas:** As the world shifts toward renewable energy, oil and gas companies face increasing scrutiny over the potential for stranded assets. This uncertainty can affect their access to capital and the liquidity of their assets.

Mitigating Liquidity Risks:

- **Stress Testing:** Financial institutions should conduct robust climate stress tests to assess their liquidity positions under various climate scenarios. The ECB (2022) further reinforces this point with its research highlighting the importance of robust risk management frameworks.

- **Portfolio Diversification:** Reduce exposure to sectors and assets vulnerable to climate change.
- **Data and Analytics:** Invest in data and analytics capabilities to identify climate risks and assess potential impacts on liquidity.
- **Contingency Planning:** Develop contingency plans to manage potential liquidity crunches arising from climate-related events.
- **Engagement with Regulators:** Collaborate with regulators to understand and adapt to evolving regulatory requirements and supervisory expectations for climate risk management.

By proactively addressing climate-related liquidity risks, financial institutions can enhance their resilience to potential shocks, maintain stability, and continue to fulfill their crucial role in supporting the global economy.

2.1.6 Climate Risks and Operational Risk, Reputational Risk

Here's a detailed breakdown of how climate change, through both physical and transition risks, can significantly impact the operational and reputational risks of financial institutions:

Physical Risks and Operational Risk:

Physical risks from climate change can directly disrupt financial institutions' operations, damage their assets, and increase compliance costs, creating substantial operational risk.

Impact Pathways:

- **Damage to Physical Assets and Infrastructure:**
  - **Branch and Office Damage:** Extreme weather events like floods, hurricanes, and wildfires can damage or destroy branches and offices, disrupting operations, causing data loss, and requiring costly repairs or relocation.
  - **Data Center Disruptions:** Data centers, crucial for processing transactions and storing sensitive information, are vulnerable to power outages, flooding, and extreme temperatures, potentially leading to service disruptions and financial losses.
  - **Disruption of Critical Infrastructure:** Damage to transportation networks, power grids, and communication systems can significantly impact financial institutions' ability to function, leading to delays in transactions, communication breakdowns, and operational inefficiencies.
- **Business Interruptions and Service Disruptions:**

  - **Customer Service Disruptions:** Natural disasters can make it challenging for banks to provide essential services to customers, such as account access, loan processing, and insurance claims settlements.
  - **Market Disruptions:** Extreme weather can disrupt financial markets, impacting trading activity and the settlement of transactions.

- **Increased Compliance Costs:** Financial institutions may face higher costs to adapt to climate change:
  - **Insurance Premiums:** Insurance premiums for property, business interruption, and other types of coverage can rise significantly in areas prone to climate risks, increasing operating expenses.
  - **Regulatory Compliance:** Governments may introduce new regulations requiring financial institutions to enhance their climate resilience, leading to additional compliance costs.

Specific Examples:

- **Hurricane Sandy (2012):** The superstorm caused significant damage to financial institutions in the northeastern United States, leading to branch closures, data center outages, and widespread service disruptions. It highlighted the vulnerability of critical infrastructure to extreme weather events.
- **Heatwaves and Droughts:** Prolonged heatwaves and droughts can impact the operations of data centers, requiring increased cooling and potentially leading to equipment failures and service disruptions. They can also affect the availability and cost of water, a critical resource for many financial institutions.

Transition Risks and Operational Risk:

Transition risks, arising from the shift to a low-carbon economy, can increase operational complexity, create new compliance burdens, and expose financial institutions to legal challenges.

Impact Pathways:

- **Adapting to New Regulations and Policies:**
  - **Climate-Related Regulations:** Financial institutions need to adapt to evolving climate-related regulations, such as mandatory climate risk disclosures, green finance taxonomies, and stricter environmental standards for lending and investment activities.

 - **Carbon Pricing:** The introduction of carbon pricing mechanisms can increase the cost of doing business for financial institutions with carbon-intensive operations or investments.

- **Integrating Climate Risk into Operations:**
  - **Updating Risk Management Frameworks:** Financial institutions must integrate climate risk assessments into their existing risk management frameworks, which requires developing new methodologies, acquiring data, and training staff.
  - **Adapting Business Models:** Shifting portfolios toward climate-aligned investments and developing new green finance products and services require significant operational adjustments.
- **Technological Changes:**
  - **Investing in New Technologies:** Financial institutions need to invest in new technologies and systems to support their climate risk management and sustainable finance activities, which can involve substantial costs and operational challenges.
  - **Cybersecurity Risks:** The transition to a more digital and interconnected financial system, accelerated by climate change considerations, can increase cybersecurity risks and require investments in robust cybersecurity measures.

Specific Examples:

- **EU Taxonomy and SFDR:** The EU Taxonomy and the Sustainable Finance Disclosure Regulation (SFDR) impose significant new reporting and compliance requirements on financial institutions operating in the EU, increasing their operational burden.
- **Shifting Investment Strategies:** Financial institutions divesting from fossil fuel companies or reallocating capital toward green investments need to adjust their investment processes, develop new expertise, and potentially restructure their portfolios, creating operational challenges.

Physical and Transition Risks and Reputational Risk:

Both physical and transition risks can significantly impact a financial institution's reputation, leading to a loss of trust, customer churn, and difficulty attracting investment and talent.

Impact Pathways:

- **Financing Carbon-Intensive Activities:** Financial institutions face reputational risk for:

  - **Fossil Fuel Financing:** Investing in or lending to fossil fuel companies, particularly those expanding oil and gas exploration and production, is increasingly seen as incompatible with climate goals and can attract negative attention from the public, NGOs, and investors.
  - **Deforestation:** Financing activities that contribute to deforestation, such as agriculture or logging in sensitive ecosystems, are highly controversial and can damage a financial institution's reputation.

- **Greenwashing:** Making misleading or exaggerated claims about sustainability practices and climate commitments can backfire:
  - **Misleading Disclosures:** Providing incomplete or inaccurate information about climate risks and opportunities in sustainability reports or financial filings can damage credibility and lead to accusations of greenwashing.
  - **Overstating Climate Actions:** Promoting investments as "green" or "sustainable" without rigorous due diligence or failing to meet stated environmental targets can lead to public criticism and reputational damage.

- **Inadequate Climate Risk Management:** Failing to demonstrate a comprehensive approach to managing climate risks can:
  - **Damage Investor Confidence:** Investors, particularly those with ESG mandates, may be less likely to invest in financial institutions perceived as lacking a credible climate strategy. Recent analyses like the European Investment Bank (2023) emphasizes that the key is to be as transparent as possible to draw in investors
  - **Reduce Customer Trust:** Consumers increasingly favor companies with strong environmental and social values. Banks and insurers seen as lagging in climate action may face customer churn.

Specific Examples:

- **Divestment Campaigns:** Several major banks have faced pressure from divestment campaigns targeting their financing of fossil fuel projects. Negative publicity and public protests can damage their reputations and attract negative media coverage.
- **Greenwashing Allegations:** Financial institutions have been accused of "greenwashing" for overstating their climate commitments or failing to deliver on their promises, leading to reputational damage.

Mitigating Operational and Reputational Risks:

- **Robust Climate Risk Management:** Develop and implement comprehensive climate risk management frameworks that encompass both physical and transition risks.
- **Transparency and Disclosure:** Provide accurate, transparent, and comparable disclosures on climate-related risks, opportunities, and actions, aligned with recognized frameworks like the TCFD.
- **Sustainable Finance Policies:** Develop clear and credible policies for sustainable finance, ensuring that investments align with climate goals and avoid greenwashing.
- **Engagement with Stakeholders:** Engage openly and proactively with investors, customers, NGOs, and other stakeholders on climate change and sustainability efforts.
- **Capacity Building:** Invest in training and education for staff on climate risks, sustainable finance, and ESG principles.
- **Reputational Risk Monitoring:** Actively monitor and address potential reputational risks related to climate change, responding promptly to criticism and demonstrating a commitment to continuous improvement.

By taking a proactive and transparent approach to managing climate-related operational and reputational risks, financial institutions can maintain trust with stakeholders, enhance their brand value, and ensure long-term sustainability in a world increasingly focused on climate action.

Case Study 1: The Impact of Hurricane Harvey on the Insurance Industry

Hurricane Harvey, which struck Texas in August 2017, was one of the most devastating hurricanes in US history. It caused widespread flooding, significant property damage, and substantial economic losses. This case study explores the impact of Hurricane Harvey on the insurance industry, focusing on physical and credit risks. It illustrates how a major hurricane event can lead to significant insurance payouts, impacting the profitability and capital adequacy of insurers. Additionally, it discusses the challenges of accurately pricing climate-related risks and the need for insurers to develop innovative risk transfer mechanisms, such as catastrophe bonds (Fig. 2).

Physical Risk: Impact on Insurance Payouts and Profitability

Insurance Payouts: Hurricane Harvey generated 765,000 claims with insured pay out reaching approximately $20 billion (TDI, 2019). The extensive flooding and property damage led to a surge in insurance claims, putting immense pressure on insurers to cover the losses. The high volume of claims strained the resources of insurance companies, impacting their profitability and capital reserves (Bevere, 2018).

Profitability and Capital Adequacy: The significant payouts required to cover the losses from Hurricane Harvey affected the profitability of many insurers. The financial strain was evident in the reduced earnings and weakened

Fig. 2 Flooding in Port Arthur, Texas, on August 31, 2017 (By SC National Guard—170831-Z-AH923-081, Public Domain, https://commons.wikimedia.org/w/index.php?curid=62096178)

capital positions of affected companies. Insurers had to reassess their risk exposure and capital adequacy to ensure they could withstand future catastrophic events (Moody's, 2025).

Credit Risk: Financial Stability and Market Implications

Credit Risk: The financial impact of Hurricane Harvey extended beyond immediate insurance payouts. Insurers faced increased credit risk as the event exposed vulnerabilities in their portfolios. The potential for downgraded credit ratings and reduced investor confidence posed additional challenges for the industry.

Challenges of Accurately Pricing Climate-Related Risks

Pricing Climate-Related Risks: Accurately pricing climate-related risks remains a significant challenge for insurers. Traditional risk models often fail to account for the increasing frequency and severity of extreme weather events driven by climate change. This underestimation can lead to inadequate premiums and insufficient reserves to cover catastrophic losses.

Innovative Risk Transfer Mechanisms

Catastrophe Bonds: To manage the financial risks associated with catastrophic events like Hurricane Harvey, insurers are increasingly turning to innovative risk transfer mechanisms such as catastrophe bonds. These bonds allow insurers to transfer a portion of their risk to capital markets, providing additional financial protection and diversifying their risk exposure.

Risk Pooling and Reinsurance: Risk pooling and reinsurance are other critical strategies for managing climate-related risks. By spreading risk across multiple insurers and reinsurers, companies can mitigate the financial impact of large-scale events and enhance their resilience to future disasters.

Conclusion

Hurricane Harvey underscored the significant financial risks that extreme weather events pose to the insurance industry. The event highlighted the challenges of accurately pricing climate-related risks and the need for innovative risk transfer mechanisms to manage these risks effectively. As climate change continues to drive the frequency and intensity of natural disasters, insurers must adapt their strategies to ensure financial stability and resilience. By leveraging tools such as catastrophe bonds, reinsurance, and advanced risk modeling, the industry can better navigate the complexities of climate-related risks and protect their profitability and capital adequacy. Artemis (2018) provides a detailed overview of the Catastrophe Bond and insurance-linked securities (ILS) market, highlighting its growing importance for risk transfer.

This case study provides valuable insights into the impact of major hurricanes on the insurance industry and underscores the importance of proactive risk management in the face of a changing climate.

2.2 *Systemic vs. Heterogeneous Nature of Climate Risks*

Climate change presents a complex challenge to financial institutions, posing risks that are simultaneously **systemic** and **heterogeneous**. Understanding this duality is crucial for effective risk management, regulation, and the stability of the entire financial system.

2.2.1 *Systemic Climate Risks*

Systemic climate risks refer to the broad, pervasive impacts of climate change that can affect the entire financial system. These risks are characterized by their potential to trigger widespread disruptions across multiple sectors and geographies simultaneously.

The interconnected nature of the global financial system means that climate risks faced by individual institutions can quickly escalate into broader systemic risks, potentially impacting the stability of entire markets and economies. This interconnectedness arises from the complex web of financial relationships, counterparty exposures, and dependencies within the financial system.

- **Cascading Failures:** Climate-related losses experienced by one financial institution, such as a major insurer facing a surge in claims after a severe hurricane season, can rapidly cascade through the system. These losses can trigger a domino effect, leading to counterparty defaults, liquidity crunches, and a loss of confidence in the market. For example, the failure of a large bank heavily exposed to fossil fuel investments could have ripple effects throughout the financial system, potentially triggering a broader financial crisis. A comprehensive analysis by Curcio et al. (2023) emphasizes the systemic connections.

- **Asset Bubbles and Stranded Assets:** Climate change has the potential to create asset bubbles and stranded assets on a massive scale. If investors fail to adequately price in climate risks, the value of certain assets, such as coastal properties or fossil fuel reserves, could become inflated, leading to a potential market bubble. When this bubble bursts, as it inevitably will, it could result in a rapid devaluation of assets and significant financial losses for investors, including banks, pension funds, and insurance companies.

Addressing the systemic risks posed by climate change requires a fundamental shift in how financial institutions assess, manage, and price climate-related risks. This includes integrating climate considerations into all aspects of their operations, from risk management frameworks and investment strategies to disclosure practices and engagement with clients and policymakers.

Key Characteristics of Systemic Climate Risks:

1. **Pervasive Impact:**

Systemic risks from climate change can lead to widespread financial instability. For instance, extreme weather events such as hurricanes and floods can cause significant physical damage, leading to large-scale insurance claims, asset devaluations, and increased loan defaults across various sectors (CEPII, 2016).

2. **Interconnectedness:**

The interconnected nature of the global financial system means that climate-related shocks in one region can propagate through financial markets, affecting institutions worldwide. This interconnectedness amplifies the potential for systemic crises.

3. **Aggregate Financial Impacts:**

Climate change can lead to aggregate financial impacts that are path-dependent. For example, a disorderly transition to a low-carbon economy can result in significant financial losses due to abrupt policy changes and technological shifts.

4. **Amplification Mechanisms:**

Financial institutions' overlapping portfolios and exposure concentrations can act as amplifiers of systemic risks. For instance, if multiple banks have significant exposure to high-carbon sectors, a regulatory crackdown on emissions could lead to simultaneous asset devaluations, exacerbating financial instability.

2.2.2 *Heterogeneous Climate Risks*

Heterogeneous climate risks, on the other hand, refer to the varied and uneven impacts of climate change on different financial institutions, sectors, and geographies. These risks are influenced by the specific characteristics and exposures of individual entities.

Key Characteristics of Heterogeneous Climate Risks:

1. **Diverse Exposures:**

Financial institutions have different levels of exposure to climate risks based on their portfolio compositions, geographical locations, and sectoral focuses. For example, banks with significant investments in coastal real estate are more vulnerable to sea-level rise and hurricanes.

2. **Sectoral Differences:**

Different sectors face distinct climate risks. High-emitting industries such as energy and manufacturing are more exposed to transition risks due to regulatory changes aimed at reducing carbon emissions. Conversely, sectors like agriculture are more susceptible to physical risks such as droughts and floods (Golnaraghi, 2018).

3. **Geographical Variability:**

Climate risks are not uniformly distributed across regions. Some areas may experience more severe physical impacts, such as increased frequency of extreme weather events, while others may face greater transition risks due to local policy measures. This geographical variability leads to heterogeneous risk profiles for financial institutions operating in different regions.

4. **Regulatory Fragmentation:**

The fragmented regulatory landscape across countries can result in heterogeneous climate risk exposures. Financial institutions operating in jurisdictions with stringent climate policies may face higher compliance costs and transition risks compared to those in regions with less aggressive climate regulations.

2.2.3 *Implications for Financial Institutions and Regulators*

The both systemic and heterogenous nature of climate risks has profound implications for Financial Institutions and Regulators:

- **Integrated Risk Management:** Financial institutions need to develop integrated risk management frameworks that consider both the systemic and heterogeneous nature of climate risks.
- **Scenario Analysis and Stress Testing:** Use scenario analysis and stress tests to assess the resilience of portfolios and the financial system to various climate pathways, recognizing the diversity of potential impacts.
- **Data and Analytics:** Invest in data and analytics capabilities to accurately measure and manage climate risks, considering granular data on exposures, vulnerabilities, and adaptation capacities.
- **Differentiated Regulation:** Regulators should adopt a differentiated approach to prudential regulation, considering the varying risks faced by different institutions and sectors.
- **International Cooperation:** Coordinate internationally to address the global and interconnected nature of climate risks, promote consistent standards, and facilitate cross-border climate finance.

Risk Management:

Financial institutions need to develop comprehensive risk management strategies that account for both systemic and heterogeneous climate risks. This includes enhancing data collection, improving climate risk modeling, and integrating climate considerations into strategic planning (European Central Bank, 2021).

Regulatory Frameworks:

Regulators play a crucial role in addressing climate risks. They must establish clear guidelines for climate risk disclosures, set standards for sustainable financial instruments, and implement macroprudential policies to mitigate systemic risks. Enhanced regulatory frameworks can help financial institutions better understand and manage their climate risk exposures (Carè et al., 2024).

Investment Strategies:

Financial institutions should diversify their portfolios to reduce exposure to high-risk sectors and regions. Investing in green technologies and sustainable projects can also help mitigate transition risks and capitalize on opportunities arising from the shift to a low-carbon economy.

The systemic and heterogeneous nature of climate risks presents significant challenges for financial institutions. Systemic risks can lead to widespread financial instability, while heterogeneous risks require tailored risk management approaches. By understanding and addressing these risks, financial institutions can enhance their resilience and contribute to a more sustainable financial system.

The complex interplay of systemic and heterogeneous climate risks demands a proactive, forward-looking, and adaptive approach from both financial institutions and regulators. By understanding the dual nature of these risks, we can work toward a more resilient and sustainable financial system that can effectively navigate the challenges and opportunities of a changing climate.

3 Mobilizing Capital for Climate Action

While acknowledging the significant risks posed by climate change is crucial, it's equally important to recognize the vast opportunities it presents for financial innovation and sustainable economic development. Financial institutions are uniquely positioned to play a leading role in mobilizing the trillions of dollars in capital needed to finance the transition to a low-carbon and climate-resilient future. By redirecting financial flows toward climate solutions, these institutions can not only mitigate climate risks but also unlock new markets, create jobs, and drive sustainable growth.

3.1 Green Finance Instruments

One of the most promising developments in climate finance has been the emergence of innovative financial instruments specifically designed to mobilize capital for green and climate-resilient projects. These instruments provide investors with opportunities to align their portfolios with their sustainability goals while also generating financial returns.

- **Green Bonds:** Green bonds are debt securities issued by governments, corporations, or financial institutions to raise capital specifically for projects with environmental benefits, such as renewable energy projects, energy-efficient buildings, or sustainable water management systems. The proceeds from green bond issuances are typically earmarked for specific green projects, enhancing transparency and accountability. Various agencies (CBI, 2014; Green Finance Portal, 2020; World Bank, 2015, 2020) have formulated guidelines and principles for green bond issuance. The green bond market has grown rapidly in recent years, exceeding \$5.4 trillion in total issuance (including green, social, sustainability and sustainability-linked bond) in 2024Q3, indicating strong investor appetite for climate-aligned investments (CBI, 2024).

- **Sustainability-Linked Loans:** These loans link a borrower's interest rate to their performance on predefined sustainability targets. This mechanism incentivizes companies to improve their environmental, social, and governance (ESG) performance to secure more favorable loan terms. For example, a company might receive a lower interest rate if it achieves a certain reduction in its greenhouse gas emissions or improves its water efficiency.
- **Green Equity Funds:** These investment funds focus specifically on companies and projects developing or deploying clean technologies, renewable energy solutions, or other climate-friendly products and services. By channeling capital toward these innovative companies, green equity funds are supporting the growth of the low-carbon economy.
- **Carbon Markets:** Carbon markets, including emissions trading schemes and carbon offset mechanisms, are designed to put a price on carbon emissions, creating economic incentives for companies to reduce their carbon footprints. While carbon markets have faced challenges in the past, they remain a potentially important tool for driving emissions reductions, particularly as governments work to implement the Paris Agreement goals.

Case Study 2: The World Bank's Green Bond Program

The World Bank has been a trailblazer in the issuance of green bonds, which are financial instruments designed to raise capital for climate-friendly projects. The World Bank launched its first green bond in 2008, responding to the demand from Scandinavian pension funds seeking investments that support climate-focused projects through fixed-income products. This initiative aligned with the World Bank's strategy to innovate in climate finance and raise awareness about the impact of climate change on developing countries (World Bank, 2015, 2020, 2023).

Key Elements of the World Bank's Green Bond Program

Project Selection and Eligibility: Projects funded by green bonds are selected based on stringent criteria that ensure they contribute to low-carbon and climate-resilient development. These criteria are reviewed by independent experts such as the Center for International Climate and Environmental Research (CICERO). Eligible projects include renewable energy installations, energy efficiency improvements, sustainable waste management, and reforestation efforts (World Bank, 2020).

Transparency and Reporting: The World Bank follows rigorous processes for project selection, fund allocation, and impact reporting. Proceeds from green bonds are credited to a special account and allocated to eligible projects, with regular updates provided to investors on the use of funds and environmental impacts (World Bank, 2015).

Market Impact: Since its inception, the World Bank has issued over 100 green bond transactions in multiple currencies, raising billions of dollars for climate projects (World Bank, 2015). This has set a precedent and encouraged other multilateral development banks to follow suit (Fig. 3).

Role of Multilateral Development Banks (MDBs) in Green Finance

Multilateral Development Banks (MDBs) like the World Bank play a crucial role in mobilizing green finance and setting standards for the market. Their involvement is pivotal in several ways. Recent analyses such as Council on Foreign Relations (2024) emphasizes that key is to be as transparent as possible to draw in investors.

Mobilizing Green Finance

Capital Raising: MDBs have the ability to raise substantial capital through green bonds, which are then used to fund large-scale climate projects in developing countries. This helps bridge the financing gap for sustainable development initiatives (The World Bank, 2015).

Fig. 3 The World Bank Group headquarters building in Washington, D.C. (By Shiny Things—Flickr, CC BY 2.0, https://commons.wikimedia.org/w/index.php?curid=2390362)

Investor Confidence: By adhering to high standards of transparency and accountability, MDBs instill confidence among investors, encouraging more participation in the green bond market (Green Bond Principles, 2020).

Setting Standards

Green Bond Principles: MDBs often align their green bond frameworks with internationally recognized guidelines such as the Green Bond Principles (GBP). These principles emphasize transparency, use of proceeds, project evaluation, and reporting.

Best Practices: MDBs contribute to the development of best practices in the green bond market. For example, the World Bank's rigorous project selection and reporting processes serve as a model for other issuers.

Preventing Greenwashing: By maintaining high standards for project eligibility and impact reporting, MDBs help prevent greenwashing, ensuring that funds are genuinely used for environmentally beneficial projects (Ministry of the Environment of Japan, 2024). The International Capital Market Association's Green Bond Principles (ICMA, 2022) offer guidelines for transparency and best practices in green bond issuance, preventing greenwashing and promoting investor confidence.

Conclusion

The World Bank's pioneering efforts in green bonds have significantly contributed to the growth of the green finance market. By setting high standards and demonstrating the viability of green bonds, the World Bank and other MDBs have mobilized substantial capital for climate-friendly projects, particularly in developing countries. Their role in establishing and maintaining best practices continues to be crucial for the integrity and expansion of the green bond market.

3.2 Sustainable Investment

Beyond these specialized green finance instruments, a broader shift toward sustainable investing is taking place across the financial industry. Sustainable investing, also known as responsible investing or ESG investing, considers environmental, social, and governance (ESG) factors alongside traditional financial metrics in making investment decisions.

- **ESG Integration:** This approach involves systematically integrating ESG factors into investment analysis and portfolio construction. Investors assess how a company manages environmental risks and opportunities, its social impact on stakeholders, and the strength of its corporate governance practices. By incorporating these non-financial factors, investors aim to identify companies that are better positioned for long-term success in a world grappling with sustainability challenges.

- **Impact Investing:** Impact investors seek to generate measurable, beneficial social or environmental impact alongside a financial return. They actively seek out investments in companies, organizations, and funds that are tackling social and environmental challenges, such as climate change, poverty, or lack of access to clean water.
- **Thematic Investing:** Thematic investors focus on specific investment themes or trends that are aligned with long-term structural changes in the global economy. Climate change is a major thematic investment theme, driving investments in renewable energy, energy efficiency, sustainable agriculture, and other sectors poised to benefit from the transition to a low-carbon economy.

3.3 Blended Finance and Concessional Capital

While private capital is essential for financing the transition to a low-carbon economy, many climate-friendly projects, particularly in developing countries, face higher perceived risks and lower expected returns, making it challenging to attract sufficient private investment. Blended finance and concessional capital are two mechanisms that can help bridge this financing gap and unlock private capital for climate action.

- **Blended Finance:** This approach involves strategically using public or philanthropic funds to de-risk climate projects and make them more attractive to private investors. For example, a development finance institution might provide a loan guarantee to a renewable energy project in a developing country, reducing the risk for commercial banks and encouraging them to provide financing.
- **Concessional Capital:** This type of funding, typically provided by governments or development finance institutions, offers more favorable terms than market-rate loans, such as lower interest rates, longer grace periods, or grant components. Concessional capital can be used to support climate projects in developing countries that might not be commercially viable without this support, such as adaptation projects, clean technology deployments, or capacity-building initiatives.

By leveraging blended finance and concessional capital effectively, financial institutions and governments can catalyze private investment in climate solutions, particularly in emerging markets where the need for climate action is most urgent and the potential for impact is significant.

4 The Role of Regulation and Policy

While financial innovation and voluntary action by financial institutions are essential for mobilizing capital for climate action, it is increasingly clear that regulation and policy play a critical role in shaping a financial system that is truly aligned with climate goals. Governments and regulators around the world are recognizing the need to establish clear rules, incentives, and supervisory frameworks to manage climate-related financial risks, prevent greenwashing, and ensure that capital flows toward sustainable and resilient investments.

4.1 Climate-Related Disclosure

Transparency is paramount in enabling informed decision-making and holding companies accountable for their climate impact. Mandatory climate-related disclosures are becoming increasingly common as regulators recognize the need for standardized and comparable information on climate-related risks and opportunities. The G7 leaders (2022) also emphasize the importance of disclosure in improving the decision-making on climate.

- **Key Frameworks:** Two leading frameworks are shaping global standards for climate disclosure:
  - **Task Force on Climate-Related Financial Disclosures (TCFD):** Established by the Financial Stability Board (FSB), the TCFD provides recommendations for climate-related disclosures across four key areas: governance, strategy, risk management, and metrics and targets. These recommendations are voluntary but widely adopted by companies and investors globally.
  - **Sustainability Accounting Standards Board (SASB):** SASB develops industry-specific sustainability accounting standards, including metrics for climate-related risks and opportunities. While initially focused on the United States, SASB standards are gaining international traction.
- **Emerging Regulations:** Several jurisdictions are moving beyond voluntary disclosure frameworks and implementing mandatory climate risk reporting requirements, particularly for publicly listed companies and financial institutions. The European Union, for example, has adopted the Corporate Sustainability Reporting Directive (CSRD), which will require companies to disclose a wider range of sustainability information, including climate-related data.

The move toward mandatory disclosure is crucial for several reasons:

- **Enhances Transparency and Comparability:** Standardized disclosures make it easier for investors and other stakeholders to assess climate-related risks and opportunities across different companies and sectors.
- **Informs Investment Decisions:** Accurate and comparable climate data enable investors to make more informed investment decisions, shifting capital toward companies with credible climate action plans.
- **Drives Accountability:** Mandatory disclosures increase accountability by requiring companies to publicly report on their climate performance and progress toward their stated goals.

4.2 *Central Banks and Financial Regulators*

Central banks and financial regulators are increasingly integrating climate change into their mandates, recognizing the potential systemic risks it poses to financial stability. They are taking proactive steps to assess and mitigate these risks, encourage climate-aligned investments, and promote a smooth transition to a low-carbon economy. As the ECB's (2024) report on climate-related risk emphasizes, climate risks require urgent and coordinated policy attention. Research, like the LSE's (2024) review of enhanced scenarios for climate stress test, provides guidance to central banks on how to increase their risk management. Battiston and Monasterolo (2024) introduces an enhanced methodological framework that incorporates investors' expectations, policy credibility, and risk materialization to improve climate stress tests.

- **Climate Stress Tests:** Climate stress tests are becoming an important tool for regulators to assess the resilience of financial institutions to various climate scenarios. As the ECB's (2021) report on climate-related risk and financial stability emphasizes, these stress tests are critical for identifying vulnerabilities and improving resilience. These tests involve modeling the potential impact of different climate pathways—such as a rapid transition to a low-carbon economy or a scenario with more severe physical climate impacts—on banks' and insurers' balance sheets, profitability, and capital adequacy. By identifying vulnerabilities, stress tests can help regulators and financial institutions take early action to mitigate risks and enhance resilience. The Federal Reserve Bank of New York (2023) offers practical insights into methodologies for climate stress testing. However, as pointed out by deRitis (2023), debate on whether central banks should address climate risk is intensifying, with the Federal Reserve's pilot climate scenario analysis exercise at the forefront.
- **Prudential Regulation:** Regulators are exploring ways to incorporate climate risks into existing prudential regulations, such as capital adequacy requirements. This could involve assigning higher risk weights to assets exposed to climate change, such as investments in fossil fuel companies or loans to businesses in climate-vulnerable sectors. By adjusting capital

requirements, regulators can incentivize financial institutions to reduce their exposure to climate risks and increase their lending and investment in climate-friendly activities.

- **Green Supporting Factors:** Central banks can use their monetary policy tools to promote green investments. By offering preferential refinancing rates for loans geared toward environmentally friendly projects or issuing their own green bonds, they can nudge the market in a sustainable direction.
- **The Network for Greening the Financial System (NGFS):** The NGFS, a global network of central banks and supervisors, is playing a leading role in developing and promoting best practices for greening the financial system. The NGFS conducts research, shares knowledge, and develops policy recommendations to help central banks and supervisors integrate climate risks into their mandates and mobilize capital for climate action.

Case Study 3: The Bank of England's Climate Stress Test

The Bank of England (BoE, 2022, 2023) has been at the forefront of integrating climate risk into financial stability assessments. In 2021, the BoE (2022) conducted its first comprehensive climate stress test, known as the Climate Biennial Exploratory Scenario (CBES). This exercise aimed to evaluate the resilience of the UK banking system to various climate scenarios over a 30-year horizon (Deloitte, 2021; Deloitte UK, 2021).

Key Aspects of the Bank of England's Climate Stress Test

Scenarios: The CBES included three different scenarios: *Early Action, Late Action, and No Additional Action*. These scenarios were designed to reflect varying degrees of policy response and physical risks associated with climate change. The *Early Action* scenario assumed immediate and orderly transition to a low-carbon economy, while the *Late Action* scenario anticipated delayed policy measures leading to a more disorderly transition. The *No Additional Action* scenario represented a future with minimal policy intervention, resulting in severe physical risks.

Methodology: The stress test incorporated both physical risks (e.g., extreme weather events) and transition risks (e.g., policy changes, technological advancements). Banks were required to model the impact of these scenarios on their balance sheets, including credit risk, market risk, and operational risk. The need for such various scenarios was highlighted by Fagan et al. (2022) during Bank of England's climate stress tests results.

Outcomes: The results highlighted significant potential losses for banks, especially under the No Additional Action scenario. These losses stemmed from increased defaults in high-carbon sectors and physical damage to assets. The exercise underscored the need for banks to enhance their risk management practices and integrate climate considerations into their strategic planning.

Role of Central Banks in Using Stress Tests

Central banks play a crucial role in utilizing stress tests to identify climate-related vulnerabilities and incentivize risk management practices within the financial sector.

Identifying Climate-Related Vulnerabilities

Risk Assessment: Climate stress tests allow central banks to assess the resilience of financial institutions to climate-related risks. By simulating adverse scenarios, central banks can identify potential weaknesses in banks' portfolios and business models. These tests help in understanding the exposure of banks to both physical risks (e.g., natural disasters) and transition risks (e.g., regulatory changes, shifts in market preferences).

Data and Transparency: Effective climate stress testing requires robust data on emissions, energy performance, and geographic exposure to physical risks. Central banks encourage financial institutions to improve data collection and transparency, which is essential for accurate risk assessment.

Incentivizing Risk Management Practices:

Regulatory Frameworks: Central banks use the insights from stress tests to inform regulatory and supervisory frameworks. This includes setting guidelines for climate risk management and encouraging banks to integrate climate risks into their Internal Capital Adequacy Assessment Process (ICAAP). By establishing clear expectations, central banks can drive the adoption of best practices in climate risk management across the financial sector.

Market Discipline: Stress tests also serve to enhance market discipline by providing stakeholders, including investors and policymakers, with information on the climate resilience of financial institutions. This transparency can incentivize banks to improve their risk management practices to maintain investor confidence and comply with regulatory requirements.

Capacity Building: Central banks support financial institutions in building the necessary capabilities to manage climate risks. This includes developing advanced modeling techniques, improving data governance, and fostering a culture of sustainability within the banking sector.

Conclusion

The Bank of England's climate stress test exemplifies how central banks can assess and manage climate-related financial risks. By identifying vulnerabilities and incentivizing robust risk management practices, central banks play a pivotal role in ensuring the stability and resilience of the financial system in the face of climate change. The lessons learned from such exercises are critical for developing effective regulatory frameworks and fostering a sustainable financial system.

4.3 *International Cooperation and Harmonization*

Given the global nature of climate change and the interconnectedness of the financial system, international cooperation and policy harmonization are essential for ensuring the effectiveness of climate finance regulations.

- **Aligning Taxonomies and Standards:** Aligning green finance definitions, taxonomies (classification systems for green activities), and disclosure standards across jurisdictions is crucial for preventing fragmentation and reducing the risk of greenwashing. Harmonized standards create a level playing field for businesses and investors, enhance transparency, and facilitate cross-border capital flows for climate solutions.
- **Mobilizing International Climate Finance:** Developed countries have pledged to mobilize $100 billion per year in climate finance by 2020 to support developing countries in their mitigation and adaptation efforts. While this target has not yet been met, scaling up international climate finance flows remains crucial for achieving global climate goals and ensuring a just transition. This requires continued international cooperation, innovative financing mechanisms, and stronger commitments from both public and private sectors.

By working together to establish a clear, consistent, and ambitious policy environment, governments and financial regulators can effectively manage climate-related financial risks, unlock trillions of dollars in climate-aligned investments, and accelerate the transition to a more sustainable and resilient financial system.

5 Conclusion: Charting a Sustainable Future

Financial institutions are at a pivotal juncture. The escalating risks of climate change, coupled with the urgent need to transition to a low-carbon economy, present both profound challenges and unprecedented opportunities. As we've explored in this chapter, financial institutions are not only exposed to climate risks but also uniquely positioned to play a leading role in driving the transition to a more sustainable and resilient future.

The task ahead is complex and multifaceted. Financial institutions must integrate climate risk considerations into all aspects of their operations, from credit assessments and investment strategies to risk management frameworks and disclosure practices. They must embrace innovation and develop new financial instruments and approaches to mobilize capital for climate solutions on a global scale. And they must work closely with policymakers and regulators to create a supportive policy environment that fosters transparency, accountability, and a level playing field for green finance.

Significant challenges remain. Data gaps, short-termism in financial markets, and the complexity of climate modeling pose ongoing obstacles to effective climate risk management and investment decision-making. Yet, the opportunities for positive impact and financial returns are equally significant. The transition to a low-carbon economy will create new markets, drive innovation, and generate trillions of dollars in investment opportunities across a wide range of sectors, from renewable energy and energy efficiency to sustainable agriculture and green infrastructure.

Financial institutions have a crucial responsibility—and a unique opportunity—to act as catalysts for change. By embracing their leadership role, they can not only safeguard their own institutions and the broader financial system from climate risks but also unlock the capital, innovation, and collaboration needed to chart a sustainable path forward for the global economy and ensure a more resilient and equitable future for all. The time to act is now.

References

Battiston, S., & Monasterolo, I. (2024). *Enhanced scenarios for climate stress-tests*. LSE. https://www.lse.ac.uk/granthaminstitute/publication/enhanced-scenarios-for-climate-stress-tests/. Accessed 22 January 2025.

Bevere, L. (2018). *Sigma 1/2018: Natural catastrophes and man-made disasters in 2017: Year of record-breaking losses*. Swiss Re. https://www.swissre.com/institute/research/sigma-research/sigma-2018-01.html

Bin, O., & Polasky, S. (2004). Effects of flood hazards on property values: Evidence before and after hurricane floyd, *Land Economics 80*(4). From https://le.uwpress.org/content/80/4/490

Carè, R., Fatima, R., & Boitan, I. A. (2024). Central banks and climate risks: Where we are and where we are going? *International Review of Economics & Finance, 92*, 1200–1229. https://doi.org/10.1016/j.iref.2024.01.057

CBI. (2024). Sustainable Debt Market Summary Q3 2024. From https://www.climatebonds.net/files/documents/publications/Sustainable-Debt-Market-Summary-Q3-2024.pdf

CEPII. (2016). *Climate and finance systemic risks*. http://www.cepii.fr/PDF_PUB/wp/2016/wp2016-10.pdf

Climate Bonds Initiative (CBI). (2014). *Green bond principles & climate bonds standard*. https://www.climatebonds.net/market/best-practice-guidelines

Curcio, D., Gianfrancesco, I., & Vioto, D. (2023). Climate change and financial systemic risk: Evidence from US banks and insurers. *Journal of Financial Stability, 66*, 101132. https://doi.org/10.1016/j.jfs.2023.101132

deRitis C. (2023). *Climate risk stress testing and the role of central banks*. https://www.garp.org/risk-intelligence/sustainability-climate/climate-risk-bank-020323. Accessed 22 January 2025.

ECB. (2022). *Climate-related risks to financial stability*. https://www.ecb.europa.eu/press/financial-stability-publications/fsr/special/html/ecb.fsrart202205_01~9d4ae00a92.en.html

ECB. (2024). *The role of the ECB in the face of climate and environmental risks*. https://www.ecb.europa.eu/press/key/date/2024/html/ecb.sp240607_1~faecc95713.en.html

European Central Bank (ECB). (2021). *Climate-related risk and financial stability*. https://www.ecb.europa.eu/pub/pdf/other/ecb.climateriskfinancialstability202107~87822fae81.en.pdf

European Investment Bank (EIB). (2023). *2022 joint report on multilateral development banks' climate finance*. https://thedocs.worldbank.org/en/doc/3258e1d4c1e84fd961b79fe54e7df85c-0020012023/original/2023-0128-MDB-Report-2022-NEW.pdf

Federal Reserve. (2022). *Climate-related financial stability risks for the United States*. https://www.federalreserve.gov/econres/feds/files/2022043pap.pdf

Federal Reserve Bank New York. (2023). *Climate stress testing*. https://www.newyorkfed.org/medialibrary/media/research/staff_reports/sr1059.pdf

Golnaraghi, M. (2018). *Climate change and the insurance industry: Taking action as risk managers and investors*. The Geneva Association. https://www.genevaassociation.org/sites/default/files/research-topics-document-type/pdf_public/climate_change_and_the_insurance_industry_-_taking_action_as_risk_managers_and_investors.pdf

Green Finance Portal. (2020). *Green bond and sustainability-linked bond guidelines: green bond and sustainability-linked bond guidelines*. Green Finance Portal. https://greenfinanceportal.env.go.jp/en/bond/guideline/guideline.html

International Financial Reporting Standards (IFRS). (2022). *G7 reiterates commitment to mandatory climate disclosures and welcomes the ISSB's work on global baseline*. https://www.ifrs.org/news-and-events/news/2022/10/g7-reiterates-commitment-to-mandatory-climate-disclosures-and-welcomes-the-issbs-work-on-global-baseline/

London School of Economics (LSE). (2024). *Enhanced scenarios for climate stress tests*. https://www.lse.ac.uk/granthaminstitute/publication/enhanced-scenarios-for-climate-stress-tests/

Ministry of the Environment, Japan. (2024). Green Bond and Sustainability-Linked Bond Guidelines 2024. From https://greenfinanceportal.env.go.jp/pdf/greenbond_guideline_eng.pdf

Noth, F., & Schüwer, U. (2023). *Natural Disaster and Bank Stability: Evidence from the U.S. Financial System*. SSRN Working Paper No. 2921000. From https://www.sciencedirect.com/science/article/abs/pii/S0095069623000104

Ortega, F., & Taşpınar, S. (2018). Rising Sea Levels and Sinking Property Values: Hurricane Sandy and New York's Housing Market. *Journal of Urban Economics, 106*(C), 81–100. From http://www.sciencedirect.com/science/article/pii/S0094119018300354

Texas Department of Insurance (TDI). (2019). *Final Compilation of Hurricane Harvey Data* (Data through December 31, 2018). https://www.tdi.texas.gov/reports/documents/harvey-dc-final-06302019.pdf

Case References

Artemis. (2018). *Catastrophe bond & ILS market report*. https://www.artemis.bm/wp-content/uploads/2019/01/q4-2018-cat-bond-ils-market-report.pdf

Bank of England (BoE). (2022). *Results of the 2021 climate biennial exploratory scenario (CBES)*. https://www.bankofengland.co.uk/stress-testing/2022/results-of-the-2021-climate-biennial-exploratory-scenario. Accessed 22 January 2025.

BoE. (2023). *Bank of England report on climate-related risks and the regulatory capital frameworks*. https://www.bankofengland.co.uk/prudential-regulation/publication/2023/report-on-climate-related-risks-and-the-regulatory-capital-frameworks. Accessed 22 January 2025.

Bevere, L. (2018). *Sigma 1/2018: Natural catastrophes and man-made disasters in 2017: Year of record-breaking losses*. Swiss Re. https://www.swissre.com/institute/research/sigma-research/sigma-2018-01.html

Council on Foreign Relations. (2024). *Mobilizing clean energy financing through the multilateral development banks*. https://www.cfr.org/blog/mobilizing-clean-energy-financing-through-multilateral-development-banks. Accessed 1 January 2024.

Deloitte. (2021). *Bank of England makes first steps towards stress-testing climate change risks*. https://www2.deloitte.com/ro/en/pages/risk/articles/Bank-of-England-makes-first-steps-towards-stress-testing-climate-change-risks.html. Accessed 22 January 2025.

Deloitte UK. (2021). *Comparing the ECB SSM Climate Change Stress Test and the Bank of England's CBES*. https://www.deloitte.com/uk/en/services/audit-assurance/blogs/comparing-the-ecb-ssm-climate-change-stress-and-the-bank-of-englands-cbes.html. Accessed 22 January 2025.

Fagan, P., et al. (2022). *Results of the bank of England's climate stress test*. https://sustainablefutures.linklaters.com//post/102hpru/results-of-the-bank-of-englands-climate-stress-test. Accessed 22 January 2025.

International Capital Market Association (ICMA). (2022). *Green Bond Principles (GBP)*. https://www.icmagroup.org/sustainable-finance/the-principles-guidelines-and-handbooks/green-bond-principles-gbp/

Moody's. (2025). *Moody's—Credit ratings, research, and data for global capital markets*. https://www.moodys.com/research/Moodys-Hurricane-Harvey-initial-thoughts-on-impact-on-US-property--PR_372076. Accessed 1 January 2024.

World Bank. (2015). *What are Green Bonds?* https://documents1.worldbank.org/curated/en/400251468187810398/pdf/99662-REVISED-WB-Green-Bond-Box393208B-PUBLIC.pdf. Accessed 22 January 2025.

World Bank. (2020). *The world bank green bond process implementation guidelines*. https://thedocs.worldbank.org/en/doc/217301525116707964-0340022018/original/GreenBondImplementationGuidelines.pdf

World Bank. (2023). *Sustainable development bonds*. World Bank. https://treasury.worldbank.org/en/about/unit/treasury/ibrd/ibrd-sustainable-development-bonds

PART II

Climate Risk Modeling and Assessment

Climate change presents a future filled with uncertainties. We cannot predict with absolute precision how the Earth's climate system will respond to rising greenhouse gas concentrations, how societies will adapt to the impacts, or what the precise economic and financial consequences will be. Yet, we cannot afford to be paralyzed by this uncertainty. To effectively manage climate risks and make informed decisions, we need tools to quantify these uncertainties, explore a range of possible futures, and assess the potential impacts on our businesses, investments, and communities.

This is where climate risk modeling and assessment come into play. This part delves into the world of climate models, scenarios, and risk assessment methodologies, providing a comprehensive overview of the tools and techniques used to understand, quantify, and manage climate-related financial risks.

Chapter 4: Modeling the Climate: From Weather Forecasts to Financial Risks
This chapter lays the groundwork for understanding climate modeling. We'll explore the different types of climate models used to understand and project climate change, from numerical weather prediction (NWP) models that provide short-term forecasts to global climate models (GCMs) that simulate long-term climate patterns and project future scenarios. We'll also introduce the specialized risk models used to assess the financial implications of climate change, including catastrophe (CAT) models and climate finance risk models (CFRMs).

Chapter 5: Climate Scenarios: Navigating a Range of Possible Futures
Climate scenarios are not about predicting a single definitive future; they"re about exploring a range of plausible pathways, acknowledging uncertainty, and

preparing for different possible outcomes. This chapter delves into the world of climate scenarios, explaining how they are developed, the key frameworks used (such as Representative Concentration Pathways (RCPs) and Shared Socioeconomic Pathways (SSPs)), and their applications in risk assessment, strategic planning, and decision-making.

Chapter 6: Physical Risk Modeling: Quantifying the Impacts of a Changing Climate
Physical risks from climate change, such as extreme weather events, sea-level rise, and changes in temperature and precipitation patterns, pose a direct threat to businesses, infrastructure, and communities. This chapter explores the methodologies used to model these physical risks, translating climate projections into tangible assessments of potential impacts. We'll delve into catastrophe (CAT) models, geospatial analysis techniques, and sector-specific models, examining their applications, strengths, and limitations.

Chapter 7: Transition Risk Modeling: Navigating the Shift to a Low-Carbon Economy
Transition risks arise from the economic and financial shifts associated with the move to a low-carbon economy. This chapter explores the drivers of transition risk, including policy changes, technological advancements, and evolving market dynamics. We'll examine the methodologies used to model these risks, such as scenario analysis, financial modeling, and sector-specific models, and highlight the challenges and opportunities of managing transition risks in a rapidly changing world.

Chapter 8: The Challenge of Climate Risk Modeling: Navigating Complexity and Uncertainty
Climate risk modeling is a complex and evolving field, fraught with challenges. This chapter confronts these challenges head-on, addressing issues related to data gaps, model limitations, and the difficulties of communicating uncertainty effectively. We'll also discuss the crucial role of expert judgment in interpreting model outputs and making informed decisions in the face of incomplete information.

By mastering the tools and concepts presented in this part, readers will gain a deeper understanding of how climate risks are assessed, modeled, and managed, providing a solid foundation for navigating the complexities of climate finance and making more informed and resilient decisions.

CHAPTER 4

Modeling the Climate: From Weather Forecasts to Financial Risks

1 Introduction: The Power and Limits of Climate Models

Imagine trying to predict the intricate dance of Earth's atmosphere, oceans, and land surfaces—a complex system driven by countless interacting factors, from solar radiation and volcanic eruptions to human activities and natural cycles. This is the daunting task of climate modeling, a scientific endeavor that seeks to understand and project the behavior of our planet's climate system.

Climate models are essential tools for comprehending the intricacies of climate change. They provide insights into past climate patterns, help us understand the drivers of current warming trends, and, most importantly, allow us to project potential future climate scenarios. These projections are not crystal balls; they are sophisticated simulations based on our best understanding of the physics, chemistry, and biology of the Earth system.

Climate models come in various forms, each with its own strengths and limitations: from numerical weather prediction (NWP) models that provide short-term weather forecasts to global climate models (GCMs) that simulate long-term climate patterns and project future scenarios. We also have regional climate models (RCMs) that offer higher-resolution projections for specific geographic areas and specialized risk models designed to assess the financial implications of climate change.

It's crucial to recognize that climate models, while powerful, are not perfect representations of reality. The climate system is immensely complex, and models must make simplifications and assumptions. They are also constrained by the availability and quality of data, as well as the computational power needed to run these sophisticated simulations.

J. Chen, *Climate Finance*, https://doi.org/10.1007/978-981-96-7975-1_4

Therefore, interpreting climate model outputs requires careful consideration of uncertainties and limitations. Model projections should be viewed as a range of possible futures, not as precise predictions. They are valuable tools for informing decision-making, but they should be used in conjunction with other sources of information and expert judgment.

This chapter provides an overview of the different types of climate models used to understand and project climate change, highlighting their strengths, limitations, and applications in assessing climate-related financial risks. By understanding the power and limits of these models, we can better utilize them to navigate the challenges and opportunities of a changing climate.

2 Technical Climate Models

Climate models are sophisticated computer programs that simulate the Earth's climate system, capturing the interactions of the atmosphere, oceans, land surfaces, and ice sheets. They are based on fundamental physical laws, such as the conservation of energy and momentum, and use mathematical equations to represent the complex processes that drive climate change. This section explores three key types of technical climate models.

2.1 Numerical Weather Prediction (NWP) Models

Numerical weather prediction (NWP), or numerical weather forecasting, numerical weather model, numerical forecast, is a method of weather forecasting based on mathematical models of the atmosphere, containing systems of partial differential, physical, and chemical equations, using current pressure, temperature, wind speed, and humidity as input data. It is the mainstream of modern weather forecasting. Although attempts were made as early as the 1920s (Richardson, 1922) and some results were achieved, it was not until the advent of computer simulations that numerical weather prediction became a practical method of real-time weather forecasting.

Theoretical Foundation of Numerical Weather Forecast

According to Friedman (1993), Vilhelm Bjerknes, a Norwegian physicist and meteorologist is the first to found the theoretical foundation of modern weather forecasting and his pioneering work laid the groundwork for the development of modern meteorology and weather forecasting.

Back in 1904, Bjerknes introduced the concept of using mathematical equations to describe atmospheric processes, which was revolutionary at the time. He emphasized the importance of understanding the dynamics of air movement and how different atmospheric conditions interact with one another. His work in the early twentieth century included the formulation of what is now known as the "Bjerknes Circulation Theorem," which describes how pressure differences in the atmosphere can lead to wind patterns and weather systems.

Later in early 1900s, the theory was put into practice to generate the first modern weather forecast, by an English mathematician and meteorologist, Lewis Fry Richardson.

Richardson's Vision and the "Forecast Factory"

In the early twentieth century, long before the advent of electronic computers, Richardson dared to imagine a future where weather forecasting would be transformed from an art based on experience and intuition into a rigorous science grounded in mathematical equations. He envisioned a vast "forecast factory," where a team of human "computers" would tirelessly perform calculations to solve the complex equations governing the atmosphere's behavior.

During World War I, while serving as an ambulance driver, Richardson meticulously gathered weather data and, using nothing more than a slide rule and logarithmic tables, embarked on a groundbreaking endeavor: to produce the world's first numerical weather forecast. He divided a region of Europe into a grid of squares, representing different atmospheric variables at each grid point. By painstakingly applying the equations of motion and thermodynamics, he attempted to predict how these variables would change over time.

Richardson's manual calculations, published in 1922 in his seminal work "Weather Prediction by Numerical Process," proved to be a monumental undertaking. His lone effort to produce a single six-hour forecast took months of tedious calculations. Even then, the results were far from accurate. The predicted changes in atmospheric pressure were unrealistically large, demonstrating the immense challenges of capturing the atmosphere's complexity.

Despite its apparent failure at the time, Richardson's work was a monumental achievement. It laid the conceptual foundation for modern numerical weather prediction. His "forecast factory" foreshadowed the powerful supercomputers that today run sophisticated NWP models. Moreover, his work highlighted the critical need for faster computing power, setting the stage for the digital revolution that would transform weather forecasting decades later.

From Slide Rule to Supercomputer

It wasn't until the 1950s, with the arrival of the first electronic computers, that Richardson's vision could be fully realized. Scientists at Princeton University, led by Jule Charney, used the ENIAC computer to produce the first successful numerical weather forecast. This breakthrough marked the dawn of a new era in meteorology, paving the way for the increasingly accurate and reliable NWP models we rely on today (Fig. 1).

Richardson's pioneering attempt, though computationally impractical at the time, stands as a testament to the power of human ingenuity and the enduring quest to unravel the mysteries of the natural world through the language of mathematics. His story serves as an inspiring reminder that even seemingly

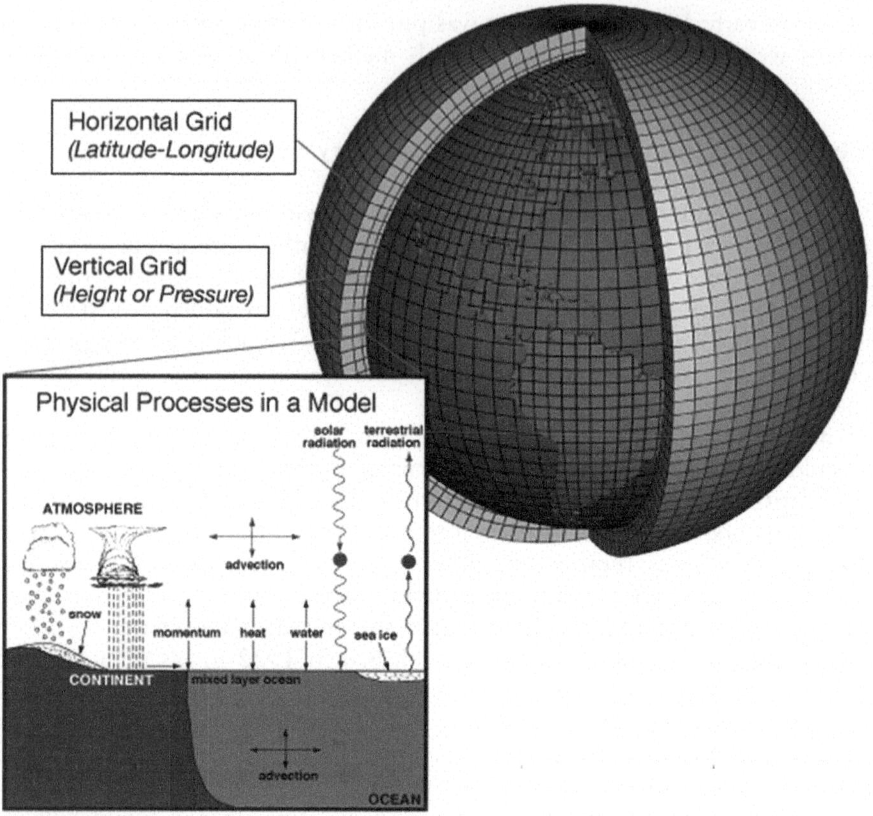

Fig. 1 Today's weather models still apply Richardson's original idea which divides the planet into a 3D grid (By NOAA—http://celebrating200years.noaa.gov/breakthroughs/climate_model/AtmosphericModelSchematic.png, Public Domain, https://commons.wikimedia.org/w/index.php?curid=7263986)

insurmountable challenges can be overcome with persistence, innovation, and a belief in the transformative power of science.

In order to obtain accurate forecast results, many countries around the world now use supercomputers to perform complex calculations. Many weather prediction models, whether global or regional in nature, contribute to global weather forecasting to a greater or lesser extent. Using these models together can reduce the uncertainty of weather forecasts and extend the predictable time horizon. Some models incorporate complex computational simulations such as the water cycle and carbon dioxide emissions of plants, or solar radiation taking into account the Milankovitch cycles,[1] and are combined with ocean models to form global climate models.

NWP models are the workhorses of modern weather forecasting. They use current weather observations, such as temperature, wind speed, humidity, and atmospheric pressure, as initial conditions and then apply mathematical equations to project how these conditions will evolve over time. NWP models are particularly adept at predicting short-term weather patterns, typically up to a few days or weeks in advance.

NWPs are designed for short-term weather forecasting, typically up to a week or two. They differ from climate models, which simulate long-term climate patterns over decades to centuries.

Bauer et al. (2015) serves as a comprehensive NWP review, highlighting the significant progress made in NWP over the past few decades, driven by advancements in computing power, data assimilation techniques, and model physics. It discusses how these improvements have led to more accurate and reliable weather forecasts, with significant societal benefits.

Key Features of NWP Models:

- **High Spatial Resolution:** NWP models divide the atmosphere into a grid of points, with a resolution ranging from a few kilometers to tens of kilometers, allowing for relatively detailed forecasts of local weather conditions.
- **Short-Term Forecasting:** They are optimized for predicting weather patterns over hours, days, or weeks, but their accuracy declines significantly beyond this timeframe.
- **Data Assimilation:** NWP models continuously incorporate new weather observations to improve their accuracy and adjust their predictions.

Examples of NWP Models:

- **The North American Mesoscale Forecast System (NAM)**: a weather forecasting model that produces grids of weather forecasts across North America. The NAM is one of the main models used by the National Centers for Environmental Prediction (NCEP). The NAM generates multiple grids of weather forecasts with different horizontal resolutions. Each grid contains data on many weather parameters, including precipitation, temperature, lightning, and turbulent kinetic energy. The NAM is run four times a day, at 00z, 06z, 12z, and 18z, and can provide

[1] Milankovitch cycles refer to the long-term variations in Earth's climate that are driven by changes in its orbital parameters. These cycles are named after the Serbian mathematician Milutin Milanković, who proposed that variations in Earth's orbit and axial tilt influence climate patterns over thousands of years. By understanding Milankovitch cycles, scientists can better comprehend past climate changes and improve predictions for future climate scenarios influenced by natural processes.

forecasts for up to 84 hours. The NAM has a 12 km horizontal resolution and a three-hour temporal resolution. The NAM can also be used to follow significant weather events, such as hurricanes, and to generate high-resolution forecasts for specific areas (Fig. 2).

- **European Centre for Medium-Range Weather Forecasts (ECMWF) Model:** The ECMWF model, developed by the European Centre for Medium-Range Weather Forecasts, is considered one of the most accurate global weather models, renowned for its skillful medium-range forecasts.

Limitations of NWP Models:

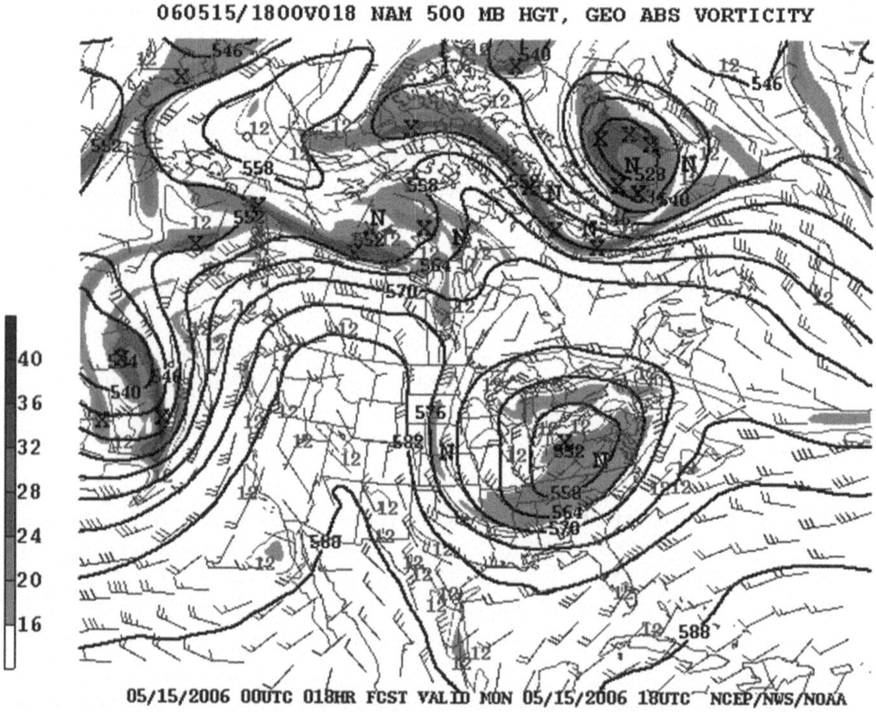

Fig. 2 500 mb geopotential height forecast by the US numerical weather prediction model NAM (By NWS, which is a branch of NOAA, a US government agency—National Weather Service website, http://www.nco.ncep.noaa.gov/pmb/nwprod/analysis/, Public Domain, https://commons.wikimedia.org/w/index.php?curid=958623)

- **Limited Predictability:** The chaotic nature of the atmosphere limits the predictability of weather patterns beyond a certain timeframe.
- **Computational Intensity:** Running NWP models requires significant computational resources, especially for high-resolution forecasts.

Case Study 1: Hurricane Harvey and the Role of NWP Models in Disaster Preparedness (2017)

Hurricane Harvey, which made landfall in Texas in August 2017, was one of the most devastating hurricanes in US history, primarily due to its unprecedented rainfall and resultant flooding. Numerical Weather Prediction (NWP) models played a crucial role in forecasting the storm's behavior, which was essential for issuing warnings, evacuating residents, and mobilizing emergency response efforts.

Key Contributions of NWP Models:

1. **Early Warnings:** NWP models provided early and accurate forecasts of Harvey's track and intensity. The National Hurricane Center (NHC) started issuing advisories for Harvey on August 23, 2017, three days before the most intense flooding began. These advisories included key messages about the likelihood of several days of heavy rainfall and potential life-threatening flooding in regions including Houston (Majumdar et al., 2021).
2. **Evacuation and Emergency Response:** The timely and precise forecasts enabled local authorities to issue evacuation orders and prepare emergency response measures. The National Weather Service (NWS) offices in Texas issued 372 warnings for tornadoes, flash floods, and other hazards, helping to mitigate the human impact of the storm (Majumdar et al., 2021).
3. **Quantitative Precipitation Forecasts (QPF):** High-resolution QPF products from operational NWP models were instrumental in predicting the extreme rainfall associated with Harvey. These forecasts helped in anticipating the scale of flooding and allowed for better preparedness and resource allocation (Chen et al., 2022).

Value of NWP Models in Mitigating Human and Economic Costs

NWP models have demonstrated significant value in mitigating the human and economic costs of extreme weather events like Hurricane Harvey.

1. **Improved Forecast Accuracy:** Advances in remote sensing, data assimilation, and computational power have enhanced the accuracy of hurricane track forecasts. For example, the track error for hurricanes has

been reduced by 64% since 2000, and intensity errors have been halved (Harvey, 2024).
2. **Economic Impact:** Accurate forecasts enable better planning and resource allocation, potentially saving billions in economic losses. For Hurricane Harvey, the accurate prediction of extreme rainfall and flooding allowed for timely interventions that likely reduced the overall damage and loss of life (Majumdar et al., 2021).
3. **Public Safety:** Effective communication of forecast information and uncertainties helps in making informed decisions about evacuations and other safety measures. This can significantly reduce the number of casualties and injuries during such events (Harvey, 2024).

Challenges in Predicting Hurricane Intensity and Track

Despite the advancements, predicting the intensity and track of hurricanes remains challenging due to several factors:

1. **Rapid Intensification:** One of the most difficult aspects of hurricane forecasting is predicting rapid intensification, where a storm's wind speeds increase dramatically in a short period. This phenomenon is influenced by complex, small-scale processes that are hard to capture accurately in models (NSU Florida, 2019).
2. **Forecast Uncertainty:** Communicating the inherent uncertainties in hurricane forecasts is crucial. Misunderstanding these uncertainties can lead to either complacency or unnecessary panic among the public. Effective communication strategies are needed to convey the range of possible outcomes and the associated risks (Harvey, 2024).
3. **Complex Interactions:** Hurricanes involve complex interactions between the atmosphere, ocean, and land. Accurate modeling of these interactions requires sophisticated coupled models and extensive data assimilation, which are areas of ongoing research and development (Chen et al., 2022; Majumdar et al., 2021).

Role of NWP Models in Informing Early Warning Systems

NWP models are central to the functioning of early warning systems for extreme weather events. They provide the data and forecasts that underpin these systems, enabling timely and effective responses.

1. **Data Integration:** NWP models integrate data from various sources, including satellites, radar, and in-situ observations, to produce comprehensive and accurate weather forecasts. This integration is vital for generating reliable early warnings (Chen et al., 2022).
2. **Scenario Planning:** These models allow for the simulation of different scenarios, helping emergency managers plan for various potential outcomes. This capability is crucial for preparing for the worst-case

scenarios and ensuring that response plans are robust and flexible (Majumdar et al., 2021).

3. **Continuous Improvement:** Ongoing advancements in NWP models, including better resolution, more accurate data assimilation techniques, and enhanced computational power, continue to improve the reliability and usefulness of early warning systems (Ko et al., 2020).

The accurate and timely forecasts provided by NWP models were instrumental in the disaster preparedness efforts for Hurricane Harvey. These models helped mitigate the human and economic costs by enabling early warnings, informed evacuations, and efficient emergency response. However, challenges remain in predicting hurricane intensity and communicating forecast uncertainties. Continued advancements in NWP models and effective communication strategies are essential for enhancing the resilience of communities to extreme weather events.

2.2 Global Climate Models (GCMs)

Global Climate Models (GCMs) are the primary tools for simulating long-term climate patterns and projecting future climate change scenarios. Unlike NWP models, which focus on short-term weather forecasting, GCMs simulate the climate system over decades, centuries, or even millennia. They incorporate a wide range of factors, including greenhouse gas concentrations, solar radiation, volcanic eruptions, and land-use changes, to project how the Earth's climate will respond to these influences.

GCMs are incredibly complex tools that require continuous improvement and scrutiny. This involves not only developing the models themselves but also creating robust methods for evaluating their performance and ensuring the accuracy of the data that feeds into them. We will introduce two papers to provide examples of these critical aspects of GCM development.

1. **ESMValTool: A Critical Tool for GCM Evaluation**

The paper by Schlund et al. (2023) introduces the Earth System Model Evaluation Tool (ESMValTool) v2.0, a significant advancement in our ability to assess the performance of GCMs.

- **The Need for Robust Evaluation:** GCMs are constantly being refined, with new versions released periodically. It's essential to have a standardized and comprehensive way to evaluate how well these models represent the real world, both in terms of their ability to simulate past climate and their projections of future change.

- **ESMValTool's Role:** ESMValTool provides a community-developed, open-source platform for evaluating GCMs using a wide range of observational datasets and metrics. This allows for consistent comparisons between different models and versions, helping to identify strengths, weaknesses, and areas for improvement. The tool also facilitates the analysis of large ensembles of model simulations, providing a more robust assessment of uncertainty.
- **Relevance to GCM Development:** By providing detailed diagnostics and performance metrics, ESMValTool helps model developers to pinpoint areas where their models might be deficient and better understand the models themselves (Schlund et al., 2023). This feedback is invaluable for guiding further research and development efforts aimed at improving the accuracy and reliability of GCM projections.
- **Black Carbon and Radiative Forcing: Refining Key Inputs for GCMs**

The paper by Wang et al. (2016) focuses on a specific but critical aspect of climate modeling: the accurate representation of black carbon aerosol and its impact on the climate system.

- **Black Carbon's Role in Climate Change:** Black carbon, a short-lived but potent climate forcer, warms the atmosphere by absorbing sunlight and reducing the reflectivity of snow and ice when deposited. Accurately representing black carbon in GCMs is crucial for making reliable projections of future climate change, especially on regional scales.
- **Improving Estimates of Black Carbon Forcing:** The study by Wang et al. (2016) uses a sophisticated modeling approach combined with observational data to provide improved estimates of black carbon's direct radiative forcing (its warming effect on the climate). By incorporating multiple datasets and accounting for uncertainties, they provide a more robust assessment of black carbon's impact.
- **Impact on GCM Accuracy:** More accurate estimates of black carbon forcing, like those provided by Wang et al. (2016), can be used to refine the representation of black carbon in GCMs. This, in turn, leads to more reliable projections of future temperature changes, particularly in regions sensitive to black carbon deposition, such as the Arctic.

The development and application of GCMs are ongoing processes that require continuous improvement and rigorous evaluation. Tools like ESMValTool provide essential benchmarks for assessing model performance, while studies like that by Wang et al. (2016) highlight the importance of refining key model inputs. Together, these efforts contribute to more accurate and reliable climate projections, providing policymakers and stakeholders with the best possible information for making informed decisions in the face of climate change (Fig. 3).

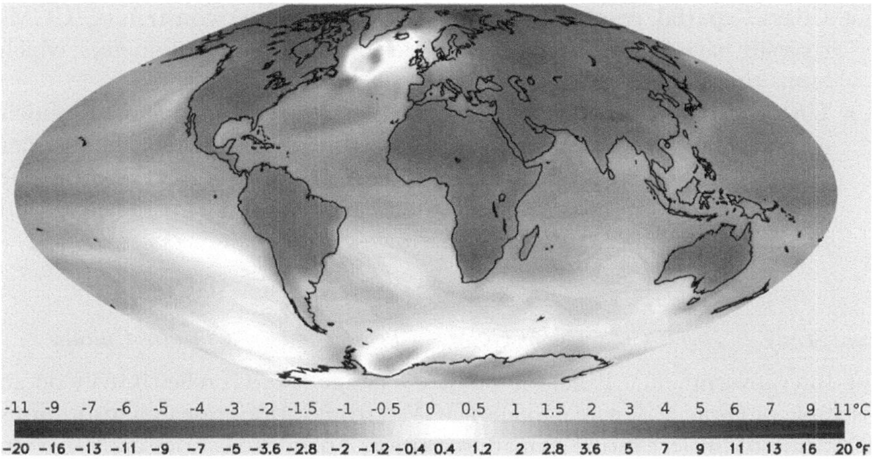

Fig. 3 Projected change in annual mean surface air temperature from the late twentieth century to the middle twenty-first century, based on SRES emissions scenario A1B (By NOAA Geophysical Fluid Dynamics Laboratory (GFDL), Public Domain, https://commons.wikimedia.org/w/index.php?curid=22038066)

Key Features of GCMs:

- **Global Coverage:** GCMs simulate the entire Earth system, representing the atmosphere, oceans, land surfaces, and ice sheets in a three-dimensional grid.
- **Long-Term Projections:** GCMs are designed to simulate climate change over long timeframes, allowing for the assessment of future climate scenarios.
- **Representative Concentration Pathways (RCPs):** GCMs use RCPs, which are scenarios of future greenhouse gas concentrations, to project different climate change pathways based on varying levels of mitigation efforts.

Examples of GCMs:

- **Community Earth System Model (CESM):** Developed by the National Center for Atmospheric Research (NCAR) in the United States, CESM is a widely used GCM for climate change research and projections.
- **HadCM3 Model:** Developed by the UK Met Office Hadley Centre, HadCM3 is a GCM that has been instrumental in past IPCC assessments.

Limitations of GCMs:

- **Coarse spatial resolution:** Due to computational constraints, GCMs typically have a spatial resolution of tens or hundreds of kilometers, which limits their ability to represent fine-scale climate features.
- **Uncertainty in projections:** Despite best efforts, some climate models can run "hot," thus there are limitations to climate models[2] (Hausfather et al., 2022). GCM projections are subject to uncertainties related to the complexity of the climate system, the accuracy of model parameters, and the choice of future emission scenarios.

Case Study 2: The IPCC's Use of GCMs to Project Future Climate Change

The Intergovernmental Panel on Climate Change (IPCC) relies heavily on an ensemble of Global Climate Models (GCMs) from various research institutions worldwide to project future climate scenarios. These projections are based on different greenhouse gas emission pathways, known as Representative Concentration Pathways (RCPs) and more recently, Shared Socioeconomic Pathways (SSPs).

Key aspects of the IPCC's approach

1. **Multi-Model Ensembles:** The IPCC uses results from multiple GCMs to create ensemble projections. This approach helps account for variations between models and provides a range of possible outcomes (Knutti et al., 2010).
2. **Scenario-Based Projections:** The IPCC considers various emission scenarios (e.g., SSPs) to project different possible climate futures. These scenarios range from low-emission, sustainable pathways to high-emission, fossil fuel-intensive futures (Knutti et al., 2010).
3. **Comprehensive Assessment:** The IPCC's assessment process involves analyzing vast amounts of data from GCMs, combining them with observational data, and synthesizing findings from peer-reviewed literature (Knutti et al., 2010).

Importance of Using Multiple GCMs

The use of multiple GCMs is crucial for several reasons:

1. **Uncertainty Quantification:** Different GCMs may produce varying results due to differences in their underlying assumptions, parameterizations, and computational methods. Using an ensemble of models helps quantify these uncertainties (Knutti et al., 2010).

[2] A subset of Coupled Model Intercomparison Project phase 6 (CMIP6) models, known as "hot models," project higher global warming than other evidence supports, potentially overestimating future climate impacts.

2. **Robust Assessments:** By considering outputs from multiple models, the IPCC can provide more robust assessments of potential climate change impacts. This approach helps identify consistent trends across models and highlight areas of high uncertainty (Knutti et al., 2010).
3. **Model Improvement:** Comparing results from different GCMs allows researchers to identify strengths and weaknesses in various models, contributing to ongoing model improvement efforts (Intergovernmental Panel on Climate Change, 2007).

Challenges in Communicating Climate Projections

Communicating complex climate projections to policymakers and the public presents several challenges (Painter et al., 2024; Torok et al., 2021):

1. **Complexity of Information:** GCM outputs often involve complex statistical analyses and multiple scenarios, which can be difficult to convey to non-expert audiences.
2. **Uncertainty Communication:** Effectively communicating the uncertainties inherent in climate projections without undermining their credibility is a significant challenge.
3. **Diverse Audience Needs:** Different stakeholders (e.g., policymakers, general public, specific sectors) may require different levels of detail and types of information from climate projections.
4. **Media Interpretation:** The media plays a crucial role in disseminating climate information, but may sometimes oversimplify or sensationalize findings, leading to misunderstandings.

Importance of Climate Scenarios in Long-Term Planning

Climate scenarios derived from GCMs are essential for long-term planning and decision-making (Knutti et al., 2010; Painter et al., 2024):

1. **Risk Assessment:** Climate scenarios help identify potential future risks and vulnerabilities across various sectors (e.g., agriculture, water resources, infrastructure).
2. **Adaptation Planning:** By providing insights into possible future climates, GCM-based scenarios inform the development of adaptation strategies at local, national, and global levels.
3. **Policy Development:** Climate projections guide the formulation of climate policies, including mitigation targets and adaptation measures.
4. **Economic Planning:** Long-term economic planning, especially in climate-sensitive sectors, relies on understanding potential future climate conditions.

Role of GCMs in Assessing Climate Mitigation Policies

GCMs play a crucial role in evaluating the effectiveness of climate mitigation policies:

1. **Policy Scenario Analysis:** GCMs can simulate the climate impacts of different policy scenarios, helping policymakers understand the potential outcomes of various mitigation strategies.
2. **Target Setting:** Climate model projections inform the setting of emission reduction targets by providing estimates of the climate response to different emission pathways.
3. **Feedback Assessment:** GCMs help in understanding climate system feedbacks, which is crucial for assessing the long-term effectiveness of mitigation efforts.
4. **Cost-Benefit Analysis:** By projecting potential climate impacts, GCMs contribute to cost-benefit analyses of different mitigation options (Painter et al., 2024).

In conclusion, the IPCC's use of GCM ensembles is fundamental to our understanding of potential future climate changes. While communicating these complex projections remains challenging, they are invaluable for informing long-term planning and assessing climate policies. As GCMs continue to improve, their role in guiding climate-related decision-making is likely to become even more critical.

2.3 Regional Climate Models (RCMs)

Regional Climate Models (RCMs) bridge the gap between the global scale of GCMs and the need for higher-resolution climate information at regional or local levels. RCMs focus on specific geographic areas, such as a country, a continent, or a watershed, and use the outputs of GCMs as boundary conditions to provide more detailed climate projections.

RCMs have become essential tools for translating the broad-scale projections of GCMs into more detailed and localized climate information. The papers by Giorgi (2019), Gutowski Jr et al. (2020), and Liang et al. (2012) highlight the evolution, ongoing need, and specific advancements in RCM development and application.

1. **Thirty Years of Progress and Future Directions**

Giorgi (2019) provides a comprehensive review of RCMs, tracing their history over the past three decades. The paper emphasizes the significant progress made in:

- **Increased Resolution:** Early RCMs had relatively coarse resolutions, limiting their ability to capture fine-scale climate features. Modern RCMs are now able to run at resolutions of a few kilometers, allowing for a more detailed representation of local topography, coastlines, and land-surface characteristics.

- **Improved Process Representation:** RCMs have also seen substantial improvements in their representation of key atmospheric and land-surface processes, such as cloud formation, convection, and vegetation-atmosphere interactions.
- **Expanded Applications:** RCMs were initially primarily used for downscaling GCM output. They are now used for a wider range of applications, including studying regional climate variability, assessing the impacts of climate change on specific sectors (e.g., water resources, agriculture), and informing adaptation strategies.

Giorgi also outlines future directions for RCM research, emphasizing:

- **Even Higher Resolution:** Pushing RCM resolutions even further will be crucial for capturing fine-scale processes and providing even more localized climate information.
- **Coupled Modeling:** Coupling RCMs with other models, such as ocean models, ice sheet models, and ecological models, will be essential for understanding the complex interactions within the Earth system.
- **Improved Communication:** Effectively communicating RCM results to stakeholders, including policymakers, resource managers, and the public, is crucial for ensuring that this information is used to inform decision-making.
- **The Enduring Need for High-Resolution Projections**

Gutowski Jr et al. (2020) argue persuasively for the ongoing need for high-resolution RCMs. The authors emphasize two key reasons why RCMs remain indispensable:

- **Process Understanding:** High-resolution simulations are essential for understanding the complex interplay of atmospheric processes that drive regional climate variability and change. This understanding is critical for improving the representation of these processes in both RCMs and GCMs.
- **Stakeholder Information:** Stakeholders need localized climate information to assess their vulnerability to climate change and to develop effective adaptation strategies. RCMs provide this crucial information at a scale relevant for decision-making.

The authors also highlight the importance of engaging stakeholders throughout the RCM development and application process to ensure that their needs are met.

3. An Example of RCM Advancements: The RegCM4

Liang et al. (2012) present the Regional Climate-Weather Research and Forecasting Model (RegCM4), a prime example of the advancements made in RCM development. RegCM4 incorporates several improvements over previous versions, including:

- **Updated Physics Packages:** The model includes updated parameterizations (simplified representations) of key atmospheric processes, such as cloud microphysics, convection, and radiation.
- **Flexible Configuration:** RegCM4 is highly configurable, allowing users to select from various options for representing different components of the climate system. This flexibility makes it suitable for a wide range of applications and regions.
- **Improved Computational Efficiency:** The model is designed to run efficiently on high-performance computing systems, allowing for simulations at higher resolutions and over larger domains.

RCMs have become indispensable tools for providing the detailed climate information needed to understand local impacts and inform adaptation strategies. The ongoing development and refinement of RCMs, as exemplified by RegCM4 and the research directions outlined by Giorgi (2019), will be essential for addressing the growing challenges posed by climate change in a changing world.

Key Features of RCMs:

- **Higher spatial resolution:** RCMs typically have a resolution of a few kilometers to tens of kilometers, allowing them to capture finer-scale climate features than GCMs.
- **Regional focus:** RCMs provide tailored climate projections for specific regions, accounting for local topography, land use, and other factors; this accounts for extreme events (Seneviratne et al., 2021).
- **Downscaling:** RCMs use downscaling techniques to translate the coarse-resolution outputs of GCMs into higher-resolution projections that are more relevant for local impact assessments.

Limitations of RCMs:

- **Dependence on GCMs:** The accuracy of RCM projections depends on the quality of the GCM outputs they use as boundary conditions.
- **Computational demands:** Running RCMs at high resolution requires significant computational resources.

Technical climate models, from NWP models used for weather forecasting to GCMs and RCMs that provide long-term climate projections, are essential tools for understanding and predicting climate change. While each model type has its own strengths and limitations, they collectively contribute to our understanding of the climate system and its potential future trajectory.

Comparison Between NWP, GCM, and RCM:

The following table illustrates the key features and limitations of NWP, GCM, and RCM. These are broad categories, and individual models within each type can vary.

Feature	*NWP Models (Numerical Weather Prediction)*	*GCMs (Global Climate Models)*	*RCMs (Regional Climate Models)*
Spatial Scale	Local to Global (at varying resolutions)	Global	Regional (a portion of the globe)
Temporal Scale	Hours to weeks	Decades to centuries	Typically years to decades, can be finer
Resolution	High (km-scale), varies by model	Coarse (100s of km)	Moderate to High (10s of km or finer)
Primary Focus	Short-term weather forecasting	Long-term climate projections	Downscaling global projections, regional climate variability
Key Strengths	High accuracy for short-range forecasts Data assimilation for continuous improvement	Represent global climate system interactions Simulate various climate scenarios	Higher resolution for regional detail Account for local geographic features
Key Limitations	Limited predictability beyond a few weeks Computationally intensive, especially at high resolution	Coarse resolution limits regional detail Uncertainties in projections due to model complexity	Dependence on GCM boundary conditions Computationally demanding, especially at high resolution

Additional Notes:

- **Data Assimilation:** NWPs heavily rely on data assimilation, where real-time observations are constantly integrated into the model to improve accuracy. This is less common in GCMs and RCMs, which are more focused on long-term simulations.

- **Computational Demands:** Higher resolution generally requires more computational resources. This is a significant factor in model development, particularly for RCMs, which strive for both high resolution and long simulations.
- **Model Complexity:** GCMs are inherently the most complex due to their representation of the entire global climate system. RCMs add further complexity by incorporating finer-scale regional processes.

Case Study 3: Using RCMs to Assess the Impact of Climate Change on Water Resources in the Colorado River Basin

Regional Climate Models (RCMs) are increasingly being used to project future changes in precipitation and temperature patterns in the Colorado River Basin, a critical water source for millions of people in the southwestern United States. These models provide higher-resolution climate projections that are essential for understanding the potential impacts on water availability, agriculture, and ecosystems in this region (Di Luca et al., 2015; Lukas & Payton, 2020).

Key aspects of RCM use in the Colorado River Basin

1. **Higher-Resolution Projections:** RCMs can simulate climate at much finer scales (typically 10–50 km) compared to Global Climate Models (GCMs), which usually have resolutions of 100–300 km. This higher resolution is crucial for capturing the complex topography and diverse microclimates of the Colorado River Basin.
2. **Incorporation of Local Factors:** RCMs can better account for local and regional factors that influence climate, such as topography, land-sea distribution, and land-use patterns. This is particularly important in the Colorado River Basin, where mountainous terrain plays a significant role in precipitation patterns.
3. **Improved Representation of Hydrological Processes:** RCMs can more accurately simulate orographic precipitation and snow accumulation, which are critical for understanding runoff from snowmelt in the Colorado River Basin.

Value of RCMs in Climate Impact Assessments

RCMs provide several advantages for assessing climate impacts in specific regions:

1. **Detailed Water Availability Projections:** The higher resolution of RCMs allows for more accurate projections of changes in precipitation patterns, snowpack, and runoff, which are crucial for water resource management in the Colorado River Basin.

2. **Agricultural Impact Assessment:** RCMs can provide more localized climate projections, enabling better assessment of potential impacts on agriculture, including changes in growing seasons, crop suitability, and irrigation needs.
3. **Ecosystem Impact Analysis:** The finer-scale projections from RCMs allow for more detailed analysis of potential impacts on ecosystems, including shifts in vegetation patterns and wildlife habitats.
4. **Extreme Event Simulation:** RCMs are better able to simulate extreme weather events, which is crucial for understanding potential changes in flood and drought frequencies in the basin.

Challenges and Considerations

Despite their advantages, using RCMs for climate impact assessment in the Colorado River Basin presents several challenges:

1. **Downscaling Complexities:** Downscaling from GCMs to RCMs involves various methodological choices that can influence the results. These include the choice of GCM boundary conditions, downscaling technique (dynamical or statistical), and the specific RCM used.
2. **Uncertainty Propagation:** While RCMs provide more detailed projections, they also inherit uncertainties from the parent GCMs and introduce new uncertainties related to regional-scale processes.
3. **Computational Demands:** RCM simulations are computationally intensive, which can limit the number of scenarios and time periods that can be simulated.
4. **Validation Challenges:** Validating RCM projections for future climates is inherently difficult, as there are no observations to compare against.

Incorporating Local Factors

The importance of incorporating local factors into RCMs for the Colorado River Basin cannot be overstated:

1. **Topography:** The complex terrain of the basin significantly influences local climate patterns. RCMs must accurately represent this topography to capture orographic effects on precipitation.
2. **Land-Use Changes:** Changes in land use and land cover can affect local climate. RCMs need to account for potential future changes in these factors to provide accurate projections.
3. **Snow Processes:** Given the importance of snowmelt for the basin's water supply, RCMs must accurately represent snow accumulation and melt processes.

Role in Water Resource Management and Adaptation

RCM projections play a crucial role in informing water resource management and adaptation strategies in the Colorado River Basin:

1. **Long-Term Planning:** Water managers use RCM projections to assess potential long-term changes in water availability and plan accordingly.
2. **Infrastructure Decisions:** Projections inform decisions about water infrastructure, such as reservoir management and potential new storage facilities.
3. **Adaptation Strategies:** RCM outputs help in developing adaptation strategies for agriculture, ecosystems, and urban water use in the face of changing climate conditions.
4. **Policy Development:** Climate projections from RCMs inform policy decisions related to water allocation, conservation measures, and interstate water agreements.

In conclusion, while RCMs provide valuable high-resolution climate projections for the Colorado River Basin, their effective use requires careful consideration of methodological choices, uncertainties, and local factors. Despite these challenges, RCM projections are essential tools for informing water resource management and adaptation strategies in this critical region.

3 Climate Risk Models

While technical climate models like NWP models, GCMs, and RCMs provide essential insights into climate change, specialized climate risk models are needed to translate these projections into tangible assessments of financial risks. This section explores two key types of climate risk models.

3.1 Catastrophe (CAT) Models

Catastrophe (CAT) models are widely used by insurance companies and reinsurers to quantify the financial risks associated with natural disasters. These models combine historical data on hazard events (e.g., hurricanes, earthquakes, floods), exposure data (e.g., building locations and values), and vulnerability data (e.g., building construction types and their resistance to hazards) to estimate the potential financial losses from future events.

Pita and Asce's (2022) "Foundation and Development of Natural Catastrophe Modeling" offers a fascinating exploration of the evolution of CAT models, providing valuable context for understanding their current state and future directions. This historical perspective allows us to appreciate the complex interplay of scientific advancements, technological innovation, and socioeconomic needs that shaped the field (Fig. 4).

From Humble Beginnings to Physics-Based Innovation

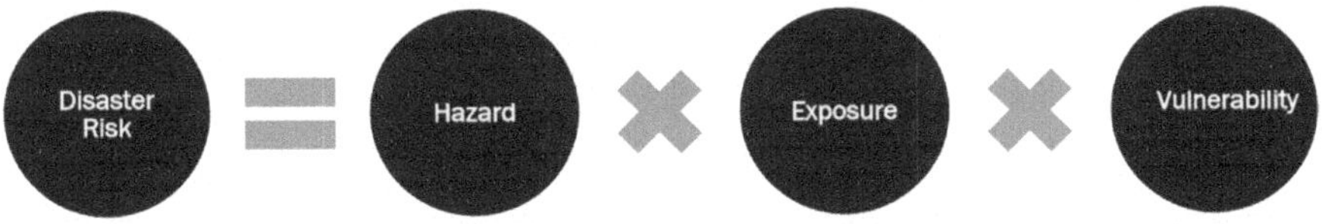

Fig. 4 The *risk equation* shows that climate risk is a product of hazard, exposure, and climate change vulnerability (where "x" represents interaction between the components) (By Gill, J.C. - Gill, J. C., Duncan, M., Ciurean, R., Smale, L., Stuparu, D., Schlumberger, J., de Ruiter M., Tiggeloven, T., Torresan, S., Gottardo, S., Mysiak, J., Harris, R., Petrescu, E. C., Girard, T., Khazai, B., Claassen, J., Dai, R., Champion, A., Daloz, A. S., ... Ward, P. 2022. MYRIAD-EU D1.2 Handbook of Multi-hazard, Multi-Risk Definitions and Concepts. H2020 MYRIAD-EU Project, grant agreement number 101003276, pp. 75, CC BY 4.0, https://commons.wikimedia.org/w/index.php?curid=138235132)

Pita meticulously traces the lineage of CAT modeling back to its rudimentary predecessors in the early twentieth century. These early attempts at quantifying risk relied heavily on empirical data and statistical averaging, often based on limited historical records of losses. As Pita notes:

> Fire insurers, on the other hand, began averaging annual loss claim data to conduct ratemaking around the 1890s, when sufficient consistent data was accumulated. The idea that underlined this approach was that a sufficiently long damage series could adequately characterize risk and remained as the main standard framework in the industry until the 1950s.

This approach, while providing a starting point, proved inadequate for capturing the true complexity of natural hazards and their potential for catastrophic losses.

The real breakthrough, as highlighted by Pita, came with the work of Don G. Friedman at the Travelers Weather Research Center in the mid-1950s. Friedman recognized the limitations of relying solely on historical loss data and championed a paradigm shift toward physics-based simulations. He envisioned a model that could:

- **Break down the damage-producing mechanism into its constituent parts:** This involved separately modeling the hazard process (e.g., hurricane wind fields) and the damage process (how these hazards interact with buildings).
- **Represent these processes using scientific principles and mathematical equations:** This move toward physics-based modeling allowed for a more nuanced and dynamic representation of risk.
- **Simulate thousands of potential disaster scenarios:** By simulating a wide range of possible events, Friedman's model could estimate the

probability of different levels of loss, moving beyond simple historical averages.

Key Drivers of CAT Model Evolution

Pita identifies several key factors that fueled the development and refinement of CAT models over the decades:

- **Exponential Growth in Computing Power:** The transition from slide rules and punch cards to powerful computers enabled increasingly complex simulations and data analysis.
- **Data Revolution:** The increasing availability of detailed historical data on natural disasters, exposure, and vulnerability, coupled with advancements in data collection and analysis techniques, provided the raw material for building more accurate models.
- **Scientific Progress:** Ongoing research in meteorology, seismology, engineering, and other fields has led to a deeper understanding of natural hazards, allowing for more realistic representations of these phenomena in CAT models.

Impact on Policy and Practice

Pita emphasizes the significant impact of CAT models on policy analysis and decision-making, particularly in the context of national insurance programs. The use of CAT models in the 1960s to assess the feasibility of flood and earthquake insurance programs marked a turning point in their acceptance and application.

The paper also discusses the increasing use of CAT models by the private sector, especially after Hurricane Andrew (also discussed by Clark [2022]), which exposed the limitations of traditional risk assessment methods and highlighted the need for more sophisticated tools.

Evolution Post-Hurricane Andrew

Clark (2022) details how Hurricane Andrew in 1992 served as a catalyst for the widespread adoption of CAT models within the insurance industry. The hurricane demonstrated that previous methods were inadequate for predicting actual losses, prompting a shift toward more sophisticated modeling techniques. CAT models now include components such as stochastic event sets that represent probabilities for different disaster magnitudes. This advancement enables insurers to calculate Exceedance Probability (EP) curves, which help in understanding the likelihood of various loss levels from catastrophic events.

Clark (2022) notes that these models have become standardized tools used globally by insurers to quantify risk across different perils—hurricanes, earthquakes, floods—allowing for more informed decision-making regarding reinsurance purchases and premium pricing.

Recent Advances and Climate Change Considerations

Davis (2024) discusses how recent advancements in modeling technology have incorporated climate change impacts into CAT models. Traditionally reliant on historical data, these models now adjust their projections to reflect current climate conditions, recognizing that climate change is increasing the frequency and intensity of extreme weather events. For instance, studies indicate that even a slight increase in global temperatures can significantly enhance hurricane wind speeds, leading to higher expected losses.

This integration of climate science into CAT modeling is crucial for accurately assessing future risks. As climate change continues to alter weather patterns, it becomes essential for catastrophe models to evolve beyond historical extrapolations to provide future-oriented risk assessments.

Key Features of CAT Models:

- **Probabilistic Approach:** CAT models simulate thousands of potential disaster scenarios to estimate the probability of different levels of financial loss.
- **Hazard, Exposure, and Vulnerability:** They integrate data on the frequency and severity of hazards, the location and value of assets at risk, and the vulnerability of those assets to specific hazards.
- **Financial Metrics:** CAT models produce a range of outputs, including:
  - **Probable Maximum Loss (PML):** The maximum loss that is likely to occur from a given event within a specific probability level (e.g., 1 in 100 years).
  - **Average Annual Loss (AAL):** The average expected loss per year from a particular hazard.

Applications in Climate Risk Assessment:

- **Assessing the Impact of Climate Change on Insurance Portfolios:** CAT models can be used to estimate how increasing climate-related hazards, such as more intense hurricanes or more frequent floods, will impact the losses experienced by insurance companies.
- **Pricing Insurance Premiums:** Insurers use CAT models to set premiums that reflect the level of risk associated with different locations and types of properties.

Limitations of CAT Models:

- **Reliance on Historical Data:** Traditional CAT models often rely heavily on historical data, which may not accurately reflect future climate conditions.
- **Challenges of Modeling Cascading Impacts:** CAT models may struggle to capture the cascading impacts of climate change, such as the interconnected risks of drought, wildfires, and flooding.

Case Study 4: The Role of CAT Models in Assessing Flood Risk in New York City

Insurance companies and city planners are increasingly relying on Catastrophe (CAT) models to assess flood risk in New York City, a coastal metropolis highly vulnerable to sea-level rise and storm surges. These models play a crucial role in understanding and quantifying the potential impacts of flooding events on the city's infrastructure, economy, and population.

Key Aspects of CAT Model Use in NYC

1. **Comprehensive Risk Assessment:** CAT models integrate various data sources, including topographical information, infrastructure details, and historical flood data, to provide a comprehensive assessment of flood risk across the city.
2. **Future Scenario Modeling:** These models can simulate various flood scenarios, incorporating projections of sea-level rise and changes in storm patterns due to climate change.
3. **Granular Analysis:** CAT models allow for detailed analysis at the borough, neighborhood, and even individual property level, providing nuanced insights into flood risk across the city.

Use of CAT Models in NYC

CAT models are being utilized in several ways to assess and manage flood risk in New York City:

1. **Financial Loss Estimation:** Insurance companies use CAT models to estimate potential financial losses from different flood scenarios. This helps in setting appropriate insurance premiums and managing their risk exposure. City planners use these loss estimates to justify investments in flood mitigation infrastructure and to allocate resources effectively.
2. **Identification of High-Risk Areas:** CAT models help identify areas of the city that are particularly vulnerable to flooding. According to the search results, an analysis using these models found that Brooklyn and Queens are the most vulnerable boroughs to flooding in NYC (Aerts

et al., 2013). This information is crucial for prioritizing flood protection measures and informing zoning decisions.

3. **Flood Mitigation Strategies:** The outputs from CAT models inform the development of flood mitigation strategies, such as the construction of sea walls, improvement of drainage systems, and implementation of building code changes. For instance, the NYC Department of Buildings uses flood risk information to enforce standards for flood-resistant construction in accordance with federal mandates (New York City Department of City Planning, 2022).
4. **Insurance Pricing Strategies:** CAT models help insurance companies develop more accurate and risk-based pricing strategies for flood insurance in different parts of the city. This can lead to more sustainable insurance practices and potentially incentivize property owners to invest in flood mitigation measures.

Challenges and Considerations

Despite their utility, the use of CAT models in assessing flood risk in NYC faces several challenges:

1. **Incorporating Climate Change Projections:** One of the major challenges is accurately incorporating climate change projections into CAT models. The uncertainty and variability in climate change scenarios make it difficult to predict future flood risks accurately. The New York City Panel on Climate Change (NPCC) provides projections that are used to inform flood risk assessments, but integrating these into CAT models remains complex(New York City Department of City Planning, 2022).
2. **Model Updating and Validation:** As new data becomes available and urban landscapes change, CAT models need regular updating to remain accurate. This is particularly challenging in a rapidly evolving urban environment like NYC. Validating model outputs against real-world flood events is crucial but can be difficult due to the infrequency of major flooding events.
3. **Data Quality and Availability:** The accuracy of CAT models heavily depends on the quality and comprehensiveness of input data. Ensuring up-to-date and accurate data on building characteristics, infrastructure, and local topography across NYC is an ongoing challenge.
4. **Communicating Uncertainty:** CAT models produce probabilistic outputs, which can be challenging to communicate effectively to policymakers and the public. Ensuring that the uncertainties inherent in these models are well understood is crucial for their appropriate use in decision-making.

Role in Resilient Urban Planning and Infrastructure Investment

CAT models play a significant role in informing resilient urban planning and infrastructure investment in NYC:

1. **Long-Term Planning:** City planners use CAT model outputs to develop long-term strategies for urban development, considering future flood risks under various climate change scenarios. This informs decisions about where to allow development, where to implement retreat strategies, and how to design resilient urban spaces.
2. **Infrastructure Prioritization:** CAT models help identify critical infrastructure at risk, allowing city officials to prioritize investments in flood protection measures. For example, the models might inform decisions about upgrading subway entrances, reinforcing coastal structures, or improving stormwater management systems.
3. **Building Code and Zoning Regulations:** Insights from CAT models contribute to the development and updating of building codes and zoning regulations in flood-prone areas (New York City Department of City Planning, 2022). This ensures that new developments and renovations are better equipped to withstand potential flood events.
4. **Public Awareness and Preparedness:** The risk assessments derived from CAT models are used to educate the public about flood risks and promote preparedness measures among residents and businesses in high-risk areas.

In conclusion, while CAT models are powerful tools for assessing flood risk in New York City, their effective use requires ongoing refinement, careful interpretation, and integration with other planning and decision-making processes. As climate change continues to alter the risk landscape, the role of these models in ensuring the resilience of NYC to flooding will likely become even more critical.

3.2 Climate Finance Risk Models (CFRMs)

Climate Finance Risk Models (CFRMs) represent an emerging field that aims to integrate climate change projections from GCMs and RCMs into financial risk assessments. These models are being developed to assess both the physical and transition risks of climate change and their potential impact on businesses, investors, and the financial system as a whole.

Types of CFRMs:

- **Transition Risk Models:** These models focus on the financial risks associated with the transition to a low-carbon economy. Examples include:

  - **Carbon Pricing Models:** Simulate the impact of carbon pricing policies (e.g., carbon taxes, emissions trading schemes) on company profits and asset valuations.
  - **Stranded Asset Models:** Assess the risk of assets becoming stranded due to policy changes, technological advancements, or shifting market dynamics.
- **Physical Risk Models:** These models assess the financial risks of climate-related hazards, such as sea-level rise, extreme weather events, and changes in temperature and precipitation patterns. They often build upon the methodologies of CAT models but incorporate climate change projections to account for future changes in hazard frequency and severity.

Applications of CFRMs:

- **Investment Decision-Making:** Investors can use CFRMs to assess the climate risks and opportunities associated with different investment options, helping them to make more informed and sustainable investment decisions.
- **Corporate Risk Management:** Companies can use CFRMs to identify and manage their climate-related risks, develop adaptation and mitigation strategies, and inform their business planning and capital allocation decisions.
- **Financial Regulation and Supervision:** Regulators can use CFRMs to assess the resilience of financial institutions to climate risks, design stress tests, and inform prudential regulations.

The works of Battiston et al. (2017) and the Network for Greening the Financial System (NGFS, 2021) report on bridging data gaps provide critical insights into how financial systems can better assess and manage climate-related risks.

Climate Stress Testing and Financial Vulnerability

Battiston et al. (2017) explore a network-based approach to understanding how climate risks, particularly those related to climate policy, can propagate through the financial system. They emphasize that both direct and indirect exposures to sectors affected by climate policies represent significant portions of investment portfolios, especially for institutional investors like pension funds.

The study highlights the importance of conducting stress tests that simulate different climate scenarios—referred to as "green" and "brown" scenarios—to assess potential impacts on financial stability. A key takeaway is that the timing of climate policy implementation is crucial; early and stable policies allow for smoother adjustments in asset values, while late or abrupt changes could lead to systemic risks within the financial system. This underscores the necessity for CFRMs to incorporate scenario analysis that reflects various policy timings and their potential impacts on financial assets.

Bridging Data Gaps for Effective Risk Assessment

The NGFS report on bridging data gaps further complements this understanding by identifying significant challenges in accessing high-quality, reliable climate-related data essential for effective CFRM development. The report outlines that persistent gaps in climate-related data hinder financial institutions' ability to assess risks accurately, manage exposures, and capitalize on opportunities arising from the transition to a low-carbon economy.

Key Recommendations from the NGFS Include:

- **Establishing Common Disclosure Standards**: A consistent set of global sustainability disclosure standards is necessary for improving the comparability and reliability of climate-related data across sectors and geographies. This would enhance stakeholders' ability to evaluate risks systematically.
- **Developing a Global Taxonomy**: A minimally accepted global taxonomy would help classify green investments and clarify what constitutes sustainable finance. This is vital for investors looking to align their portfolios with climate goals.
- **Creating Reliable Metrics**: The development of well-defined metrics and methodologies for assessing climate-related risks will enable better decision-making by organizations and individuals in the financial sector.

Challenges in CFRM Implementation

Both Battiston et al. (2017) and the NGFS (2021) report highlight several challenges in implementing effective CFRMs:

- **Data Availability**: There is a need for granular, forward-looking data that reflects current emissions pathways and transition targets. Many existing datasets are backward-looking, which limits their usefulness in predicting future risks.
- **Model Complexity**: CFRMs must navigate complex interactions between climate variables, economic systems, and regulatory frameworks, which introduces uncertainties into risk assessments.
- **Interdisciplinary Collaboration**: Effective CFRM development requires collaboration among climate scientists, financial experts, and data scientists to integrate diverse datasets and methodologies effectively.

Despite the challenges, the field of CFRMs is rapidly evolving, driven by the increasing recognition of climate-related financial risks and the need for sophisticated tools to assess and manage them. As data availability improves, models become more sophisticated, and interdisciplinary collaboration strengthens, CFRMs are poised to play an increasingly important role in informing climate-resilient decision-making across the financial system.

Case Study 5: Using CFRMs to Assess the Climate Risks of a Sovereign Bond Portfolio

Institutional investors, such as pension funds, are increasingly using Climate Finance Risk Models (CFRMs) to assess the climate risks associated with portfolios of sovereign bonds from different countries. These models help investors evaluate both physical and transition risks, providing insights into how these risks might impact bond yields and credit ratings. Bingler (2022) assesses climate risks and opportunities in sovereign bonds. PRI (2023) discusses climate risks in sovereign debt.

Application of CFRMs: Evaluating Physical and Transition Risks

1. **Physical Risks:**

Definition: Physical risks refer to the direct impacts of climate change, such as extreme weather events, rising sea levels, and prolonged droughts.

Assessment: CFRMs assess physical risks by integrating climate projections into financial models to estimate potential impacts on a country's infrastructure, economy, and overall stability. For example, countries highly vulnerable to hurricanes or floods might see increased costs for disaster recovery and infrastructure repair, which could affect their ability to service debt.

2. **Transition Risks:**

Definition: Transition risks arise from the shift to a low-carbon economy, including policy changes, technological advancements, and market shifts.

Assessment: CFRMs evaluate transition risks by analyzing a country's exposure to carbon-intensive industries, regulatory frameworks, and potential for economic transformation. Countries that rely heavily on fossil fuels may face higher transition risks as global policies shift toward renewable energy sources.

Impact on Bond Yields and Credit Ratings

Bond Yields: CFRMs help predict how climate risks might influence sovereign bond yields. Higher physical and transition risks can lead to increased yields as investors demand higher returns to compensate for the added risk.

Credit Ratings: CFRMs also inform credit rating agencies by providing data on how climate risks could affect a country's fiscal health and ability to repay debt. Countries with high climate risks might face downgrades, leading to higher borrowing costs.

Challenges in Developing CFRMs

Data Availability and Quality

Complexity: Accurate climate risk assessment requires high-quality data on climate projections, economic indicators, and country-specific vulnerabilities. However, data availability and quality can vary significantly between countries.

Integration: Integrating diverse data sources into a cohesive model is challenging. CFRMs must balance the need for detailed, localized data with the broader, systemic nature of climate risks.

Model Uncertainty

Scenario Analysis: Using a range of climate scenarios is crucial to account for uncertainties in climate projections and policy responses. CFRMs must be flexible enough to incorporate different scenarios and provide probabilistic outcomes.

Validation: Ensuring the robustness and reliability of CFRMs involves continuous validation against real-world events and updating models as new data becomes available. Cormack and Shrimali (2023) analyze challenges in climate risk modeling.

Importance of Using a Range of Climate Scenarios

1. Comprehensive Risk Assessment: Evaluating multiple scenarios helps capture the full spectrum of potential climate impacts, from best-case to worst-case outcomes.
2. Informed Decision-Making: Investors can make more informed decisions by understanding the range of possible futures, allowing for better risk management and strategic planning.
3. Policy Implications: Different scenarios can highlight the potential impacts of various policy measures, aiding in the development of effective climate policies and investment strategies.

Role of CFRMs in Informing Climate-Resilient Investment Strategies

Portfolio Optimization

Risk Mitigation: CFRMs help investors identify and mitigate climate risks within their portfolios, ensuring a more resilient investment strategy.

Diversification: By highlighting high-risk areas, CFRMs encourage diversification into less vulnerable assets and regions.

Sustainable Investment

Green Bonds: CFRMs support the issuance and investment in green bonds, which fund projects aimed at mitigating climate change and enhancing resilience. Climate Bonds Initiative (2024) promotes resilience investment.

Policy Alignment: Investors can align their portfolios with global climate goals, such as those outlined in the Paris Agreement, by using CFRMs to guide investment decisions.

Stakeholder Communication

Transparency: CFRMs provide a transparent framework for communicating climate risks to stakeholders, including investors, regulators, and the public.

Engagement: Informed by CFRMs, investors can engage with sovereign issuers on their climate policies and risk management practices, promoting greater accountability and action.

Climate Finance Risk Models (CFRMs) are essential tools for assessing the climate risks associated with sovereign bond portfolios. By evaluating both physical and transition risks, CFRMs provide valuable insights into potential impacts on bond yields and credit ratings. Despite challenges related to data quality and model uncertainty, the use of multiple climate scenarios and continuous model updates enhance the robustness of these assessments. Ultimately, CFRMs play a critical role in informing climate-resilient investment strategies, supporting sustainable finance, and promoting long-term economic stability in the face of climate change. Chakrabarty and Nag (2023) review climate finance risk models.

4 Conclusion: The Evolving Landscape of Climate Modeling

Climate modeling is a dynamic and rapidly advancing field. As our understanding of the climate system deepens, computational power increases, and new technologies emerge, climate models are becoming more sophisticated and capable of providing more detailed and reliable projections of future climate change.

One exciting development is the integration of artificial intelligence (AI) and machine learning (ML) into climate modeling. AI and ML algorithms can analyze vast datasets, identify patterns, and improve the accuracy of climate predictions. They can also be used to downscale global climate projections to regional or local levels, providing more relevant information for assessing climate risks.

Reichstein et al. (2019) and Huntingford et al. (2019) provide valuable insights into how these technologies enhance our understanding and forecasting capabilities regarding climate change.

Deep Learning and Process Understanding

Reichstein et al. (2019) highlight the potential of deep learning techniques to analyze complex datasets related to Earth systems. They argue that traditional climate models, while effective, often rely on simplified representations of physical processes. By incorporating deep learning, researchers can automatically extract spatial-temporal features from vast amounts of climate data, leading to improved understanding of underlying processes, including more accurate data-driven insights, enhanced simulations, and process discovery.

Machine Learning Applications in Climate Change Research

Huntingford et al. (2019) discuss how machine learning (ML) can be utilized to improve climate change research and preparedness strategies. Their work emphasizes that ML can significantly enhance our ability to analyze existing data and simulations, leading to better decision-making, including better predictive modeling, risk assessment, and resource optimization.

Another key trend is the increasing focus on interdisciplinary collaboration. Developing effective climate risk models requires expertise from climate scientists, financial experts, data scientists, economists, and social scientists. This collaboration is essential to ensure that models accurately capture the complex interactions between the climate system, human societies, and the financial system.

Despite these advancements, climate modeling remains a challenging endeavor. The climate system is inherently complex, and there will always be uncertainties associated with future projections. Data gaps, particularly in developing countries, can limit the accuracy of models, and the computational demands of running sophisticated simulations can be significant.

Nevertheless, climate models are indispensable tools for navigating the challenges of climate change. They provide valuable insights into potential future climate scenarios, allow us to assess climate-related financial risks, and inform decision-making across a wide range of sectors, from investment and insurance to infrastructure planning and policy development.

As climate models continue to evolve, their role in informing climate-resilient decisions will only become more critical. By embracing ongoing advancements in modeling techniques, fostering interdisciplinary collaboration, and acknowledging the inherent uncertainties involved, we can harness the power of climate models to build a more sustainable and resilient future.

References

Battiston, S., et al. (2017). A climate stress-test of the financial system. *Nature Climate Change, 7*(4), 283–288. https://doi.org/10.1038/nclimate3255

Bauer, P., Thorpe, A., & Brunet, G. (2015). The quiet revolution of numerical weather prediction. *Nature, 525*, 47–55. https://doi.org/10.1038/nature14956

Clark, K. (2022). The evolution of catastrophe modeling since Hurricane Andrew. *Insurance Journal*. https://www.insurancejournal.com/magazines/mag-features/2022/05/16/667461.htm. Accessed 25 January 2025.

Davis, C. (2024). *From disasters to data: The evolution of catastrophe modeling post-pandemic*. https://www.insurancebusinessmag.com/us/news/catastrophe/from-disasters-to-data-the-evolution-of-catastrophe-modeling-postpandemic-500142.aspx. Accessed 25 January 2025.

Giorgi, F. (2019). Thirty years of regional climate modeling: Where are we and where are we going next? *Journal of Geophysical Research: Atmospheres, 124*(11), 5696–5723. https://doi.org/10.1029/2018JD030094

Friedman, R. M. (1993). *Appropriating the Weather: Vilhelm Bjerknes and the Construction of a Modern Meteorology*. Ithaca, NY: Cornell University Press. https://doi.org/10.7591/9781501731105

Gutowski Jr, W. J., et al. (2020). The ongoing need for high-resolution regional climate models: Process understanding and stakeholder information. *Bulletin of the American Meteorological Society, 101*(5). https://journals.ametsoc.org/view/journals/bams/101/5/bams-d-19-0113.1.xml. Accessed 25 January 2025.

Hausfather, Z., et al. (2022). Climate simulations: Recognize the 'hot model' problem. *Nature, 605*(7908), 26–29. https://doi.org/10.1038/d41586-022-01192-2

Huntingford, C., et al. (2019). Machine learning and artificial intelligence to aid climate change research and preparedness. *Environmental Research Letters, 14*(12), 007–124. https://doi.org/10.1088/1748-9326/ab4e55

Liang, X.-Z., et al. (2012). Regional climate–weather research and forecasting model. *Bulletin of the American Meteorological Society, 93*(9), 1363–1387. https://doi.org/10.1175/BAMS-D-11-00180.1

Network for Greening the Financial System (NGFS). (2021). *Progress report on bridging data gaps*. https://www.ngfs.net/system/files/import/ngfs/medias/documents/progress_report_on_bridging_data_gaps.pdf. Accessed 25 January 2025.

Pita, G. L., & Asce, M. M. (2022). *Foundation and Development of Natural Catastrophe Modeling*. Natural Hazards Review. https://doi.org/10.1061/%28ASCE%29NH.1527-6996.0000567. Accessed 25 January 2025.

Reichstein, M., et al. (2019). Deep learning and process understanding for data-driven Earth system science. *Nature, 566*(7743), 195–204. https://www.nature.com/articles/s41586-019-0912-1

Richardson, L. F. (1922). *Weather Prediction by Numerical Process*. Cambridge: Cambridge University Press. https://doi.org/10.1002/qj.49704820311

Schlund, M., et al. (2023). Evaluation of native Earth system model output with ESMValTool v2.6.0. *Geoscientific Model Development, 16*(1), 315–333. https://doi.org/10.5194/gmd-16-315-2023

Seneviratne, S. I., Zhang, X., Adnan, M., Badi, W., Dereczynski, C., Di Luca, A., Ghosh, S., Iskandar, I., Kossin, J., Lewis, S., Otto, F., Pinto, I., Satoh, M., Vicente-Serrano, S. M., Wehner, M., & Zhou, B. (2021). Weather and climate extreme events in a changing climate. In V. Masson-Delmotte, P. Zhai, A. Pirani, S. L. Connors, C. Péan, S. Berger, N. Caud, Y. Chen, L. Goldfarb, M. I. Gomis, M. Huang, K. Leitzell, E. Lonnoy, J. B. R. Matthews, T. K. Maycock, T. Waterfield, O. Yelekçi, R. Yu, and B. Zhou (Eds.), *Climate Change 2021: The Physical Science Basis. Contribution of Working Group I to the Sixth Assessment Report of the Intergovernmental Panel on Climate Change* (pp. 1513–1766). Cambridge University Press. https://doi.org/10.1017/9781009157896.013

Wang, R., et al. (2016). Estimation of global black carbon direct radiative forcing and its uncertainty constrained by observations. *Journal of Geophysical Research: Atmospheres, 121*(10), 5948–5971. https://doi.org/10.1002/2015JD024326

Case References

Aerts, J., Lin, N., Botzen, W., Emanuel, K., & Moel, H. (2013). Low-probability flood risk modeling for New York City. *Risk Analysis, 33*(5), 772–788. https://doi.org/10.1111/risa.12008

Bingler, J. A. (2022). *Expect the worst, hope for the best: The valuation of climate risks and opportunities in sovereign bonds* (Economics Working Paper Series 22/371). https://doi.org/10.3929/ethz-b-000541138

Chakrabarty, S. P., & Nag, S. (2023). Risk measures and portfolio analysis in the paradigm of climate finance: A review. *SN Business & Economics, 3*(3), 69. https://doi.org/10.1007/s43546-023-00449-w

Chen, M., et al. (2022). A flood predictability study for hurricane Harvey with the CREST-iMAP model using high-resolution quantitative precipitation forecasts and U-net deep learning precipitation nowcasts. *Journal of Hydrology, 612*, 128–168. https://doi.org/10.1016/j.jhydrol.2022.128168

Climate Bonds Initiative. (2024). *Climate bonds resilience programme*. https://www.climatebonds.net/resilience. Accessed 3 September 2024

Cormack, C., & Shrimali, G. (2023). *The challenge of climate risk modelling in financial institutions*. UK Centre for Greening Finance and Investment (CGFI). https://www.cgfi.ac.uk/2023/12/the-challenge-of-climate-risk-modelling-in-financial-institutions-overview-critique-and-guidance/. Accessed 21 January 2025

Di Luca, A., de Elía, R., & Laprise, R. (2015). Challenges in the quest for added value of regional climate dynamical downscaling. *Current Climate Change Reports, 1*(1), 10–21. https://doi.org/10.1007/s40641-015-0003-9

Harvey, C. (2024). *Climate change adds new challenge to wild history of hurricane forecasts*. E&E News. https://www.eenews.net/articles/climate-change-adds-new-challenge-to-wild-history-of-hurricane-forecasts/. Accessed 2 September 2024

Intergovernmental Panel on Climate Change (IPCC). (2007). *1.5 examples of progress in modelling the climate—AR4 WGI chapter 1: Historical overview of climate change science*. https://archive.ipcc.ch/publications_and_data/ar4/wg1/en/ch1s1-5.html

Knutti, R., Abramowitz, G., Collins, M., Eyring, V., Gleckler, P. J., Hewitson, B., & Mearns, L. (2010). Good practice guidance paper on assessing and combining multi model climate projections. In T. F. Stocker, D. Qin, G.-K. Plattner, M. Tignor, & P.M. Midgley (Eds.), *Meeting Report of the Intergovernmental Panel on Climate Change Expert Meeting on Assessing and Combining Multi Model Climate Projections*. IPCC Working Group I Technical Support Unit, University of Bern, Bern, Switzerland. https://www.wcrp-climate.org/wgcm/references/IPCC_EM_MME_GoodPracticeGuidancePaper.pdf

Ko, M. C., Marks, F. D., Alaka, G. J., & Gopalakrishnan, S. G. (2020). Evaluation of hurricane Harvey (2017) rainfall in deterministic and probabilistic HWRF forecasts. *Atmosphere, 11*(6), 666. https://doi.org/10.3390/atmos11060666

Lukas, J., & Payton, E. (2020). *Colorado river basin climate and hydrology: state of the science*. West Water Assess. https://doi.org/10.25810/3HCV-W477

Majumdar, S. J., et al. (2021). *Multiscale forecasting of high-impact weather: current status and future challenges*. https://doi.org/10.1175/BAMS-D-20-0111.1

New York City Department of City Planning. (2022). *Flood risk in New York city*. https://www.nyc.gov/assets/planning/download/pdf/plans-studies/climate-resiliency/flood-risk-nyc-info-brief.pdf. Accessed 20 January 2025.

NSU Florida. (2019). *Predicting a hurricane's intensity can prove difficult—But very important*. NSU News. https://news.nova.edu/news-releases/predicting-a-hurricanes-intensity-can-prove-difficult/. Accessed 2 September 2024

Painter, J., Marshall, S., & Leitzell, K. (2024). Communicating climate futures: A multi-country study of how the media portray the IPCC scenarios in the 2021/2 working group reports. *Climatic Change, 177*(6), 82. https://doi.org/10.1007/s10584-024-03744-z

Principles for Responsible Investment (PRI). (2023). *Communicating climate risks in sovereign debt.* https://www.unpri.org/sovereign-debt/considering-climate-change-in-sovereign-debt/11894.article. Accessed 21 January 2025.

Torok, S., Goldie, J., & Ashcroft, L. (2021). Communicating climate change has never been so important, and this IPCC report pulls no punches. *The Conversation.* https://theconversation.com/communicating-climate-change-has-never-been-so-important-and-this-ipcc-report-pulls-no-punches-165252. Accessed 22 January 2025.

CHAPTER 5

Climate Scenarios: Navigating a Range of Possible Futures

1 Introduction: Why Scenarios Matter

The future is not a fixed destination, it's a landscape of possibilities shaped by the choices we make today. When it comes to climate change, this uncertainty is amplified by the complexity of the Earth system and the interplay of natural processes, human activities, and technological advancements.

In a world grappling with the escalating impacts of climate change, we cannot afford to rely on a single prediction of the future. Instead, we need a framework for exploring a range of plausible outcomes, understanding the risks and opportunities they present, and developing strategies that can adapt to a variety of potential conditions. This is where climate scenarios come into play.

Climate scenarios are not about predicting the future with certainty. Rather, they offer a structured way to explore alternative pathways, providing a glimpse into a range of possible futures shaped by different levels of greenhouse gas emissions, socioeconomic developments, and technological innovations. These scenarios are powerful tools that enable us to move beyond simplistic forecasts and embrace the inherent uncertainty of the future.

Climate scenarios are essential for:

- **Risk Assessment:** By exploring a range of possible futures, we can identify and quantify potential climate-related risks, such as the financial impact of extreme weather events, the risk of stranded assets, or the vulnerability of supply chains to climate disruptions.
- **Strategic Planning:** Climate scenarios provide a framework for developing robust strategies that can adapt to a variety of potential future conditions. Businesses can use scenarios to assess the resilience of their

J. Chen, *Climate Finance*, https://doi.org/10.1007/978-981-96-7975-1_5

operations, explore new market opportunities, and make investment decisions that align with a low-carbon future.
- **Decision-Making:** Climate scenarios inform choices about climate policies, adaptation measures, infrastructure investments, and technological innovation. By considering a range of potential outcomes, decision-makers can make more informed choices that are less likely to be blindsided by unexpected events.

In this chapter, we will delve into the world of climate scenarios, exploring their key elements, major frameworks, and applications in decision-making across various sectors. By understanding the power of scenarios, we can better navigate the uncertainties of a changing climate and shape a future that is more sustainable, resilient, and equitable for all. We will also illustrate the use of climate scenarios in decision-making, risk assessment via a few cases of different government agencies/financial institutions.

2 Key Elements of Climate Scenarios

Climate scenarios are not arbitrary predictions pulled from thin air; they are built upon a careful consideration of the factors that drive climate change and shape its impacts. Understanding these key elements is crucial for interpreting and utilizing climate scenarios effectively.

2.1 Emission Pathways

The future trajectory of the climate system is influenced by a complex interplay of factors:

- **Greenhouse Gas Emissions:** The most significant driver of climate change is the concentration of greenhouse gases (GHGs), primarily carbon dioxide, in the atmosphere. Different levels of future GHG emissions, driven by human activities such as fossil fuel combustion, deforestation, and agriculture, will lead to varying degrees of global warming and associated climate impacts.
- **Socioeconomic Factors:** Future emissions pathways are not solely determined by physical processes; they are heavily influenced by socioeconomic factors. Population growth, economic development, technological innovation, and policy choices all play a role in shaping the trajectory of GHG emissions. For example, rapid economic growth in developing countries could lead to a surge in energy demand, potentially driving up emissions if that demand is met primarily by fossil fuels. Conversely, policies promoting renewable energy deployment and energy efficiency could significantly curb emissions growth.

The following Fig. 1 shows projected pathways for global greenhouse gas emissions, measured in CO2-equivalent gigatons (Gt) per year, from 2000 to 2100. Each pathway represents a different scenario for future emissions and the resulting temperature increase.

- No Climate Policies (4.1–4.8 °C): This pathway, shown in dark pink, represents a scenario where no new climate policies are implemented beyond those already in place in 2020. It shows a continued increase in emissions throughout the twenty-first century, leading to a very high temperature increase of 4.1–4.8 °C above pre-industrial levels.
- Current Policies (2.5–2.9 °C): This pathway, in light orange/coral, reflects a scenario where current climate policies are maintained but not strengthened. Emissions peak around 2050 and then gradually decline, but not fast enough to prevent significant warming. The projected temperature increase is 2.5–2.9 °C.
- Pledges and Targets (2.1 °C): This teal pathway incorporates the climate pledges and targets made by countries as of 2021 (e.g., under the Paris

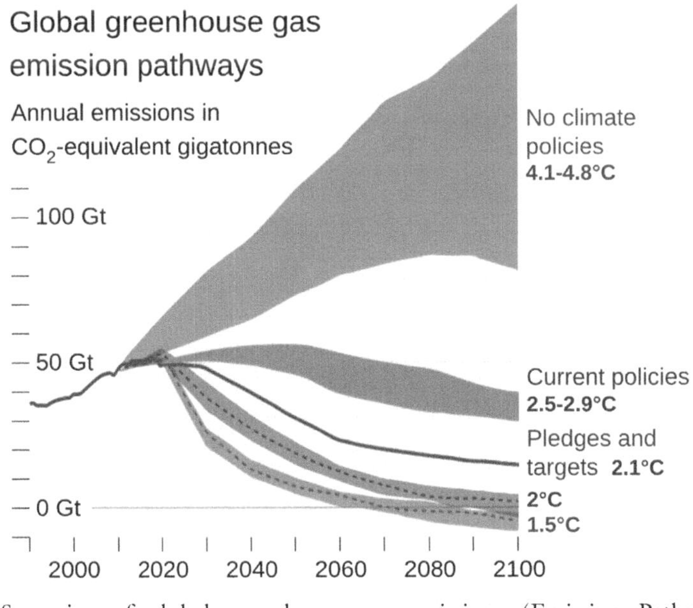

Fig. 1 Scenarios of global greenhouse gas emissions (Emission Pathways) (By Hannah Ritchie and Max Roser, adapted for svg and smartphone by Eric Fisk—Hannah Ritchie and Max Roser (2017)—"CO_2 and Greenhouse Gas Emissions." Published online at OurWorldInData.org. Retrieved from: https://ourworldindata.org/co2-and-other-greenhouse-gas-emissions#future-emissions, adapted for svg and smartphone by Eric Fisk, CC BY-SA 4.0, https://commons.wikimedia.org/w/index.php?curid=93453063)

Agreement). It shows emissions declining more rapidly than under the "current policies" scenario, limiting warming to approximately 2.1 °C.

- 2 °C and 1.5 °C: These dark blue and light green pathways, respectively, illustrate the emission reductions necessary to limit warming to 2 °C and 1.5 °C, the goals of the Paris Agreement. Both scenarios require a rapid and substantial decline in emissions, reaching net-zero emissions around or before mid-century.

2.2 *Representative Concentration Pathways (RCPs)*

To standardize climate projections, scientists have developed Representative Concentration Pathways (RCPs), which are scenarios of future GHG concentrations in the atmosphere. Each RCP represents a different pathway for radiative forcing—the change in the Earth's energy balance due to GHGs—leading to varying levels of warming.

The four main RCPs used in climate modeling are:

RCP	*Description*	*Approximate Warming by 2100 (Compared to Pre-Industrial Levels)*
RCP2.6	A "mitigation" scenario, assuming strong global efforts to reduce GHG emissions	0.3 °C to 1.7 °C
RCP4.5	An "intermediate" scenario, assuming moderate emissions reductions	1.1 °C to 2.6 °C
RCP6.0	Another intermediate scenario, with higher emissions than RCP4.5	1.4 °C to 3.1 °C
RCP8.5	A "business-as-usual" scenario, assuming continued high emissions growth	2.6 °C to 4.8 °C

These RCPs are not predictions of what will happen but rather provide a framework for exploring a range of possible futures based on different levels of mitigation efforts. There has been debate on the representativeness of these scenarios, e.g., Hausfather & Peters (2020) argue that the "business-as-usual" emissions scenario (often associated with RCP8.5) is misleading and overly pessimistic. Schwalm et al. (2020) contend that RCP8.5 accurately tracks cumulative CO2 emissions and remains a useful high-end scenario (Fig. 2).

The following Fig. 3 presents global climate forecasts under three different Representative Concentration Pathways (RCPs): RCP2.6, RCP4.5, and RCP6.0. It shows both the projected global mean temperature change and the spatial distribution of warming across the globe.

This figure reveals important forecasts on global mean temperature, sea-level rise, and spatial distribution of warming:

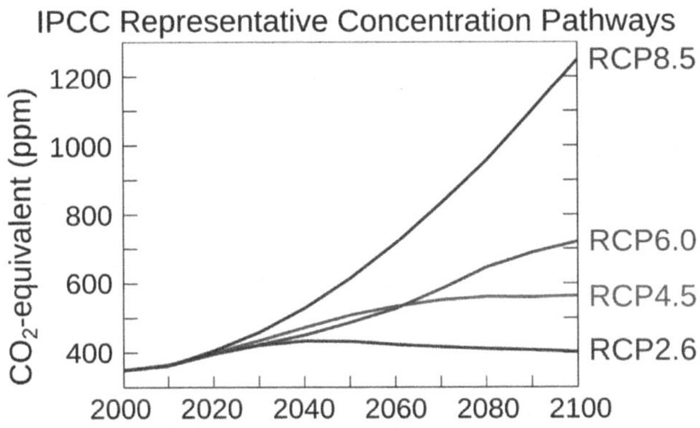

Fig. 2 Different RCP scenarios result in different predicted greenhouse gas concentrations in the atmosphere (By Efbrazil—Own work, CC BY-SA 4.0, https://commons.wikimedia.org/w/index.php?curid=87801257)

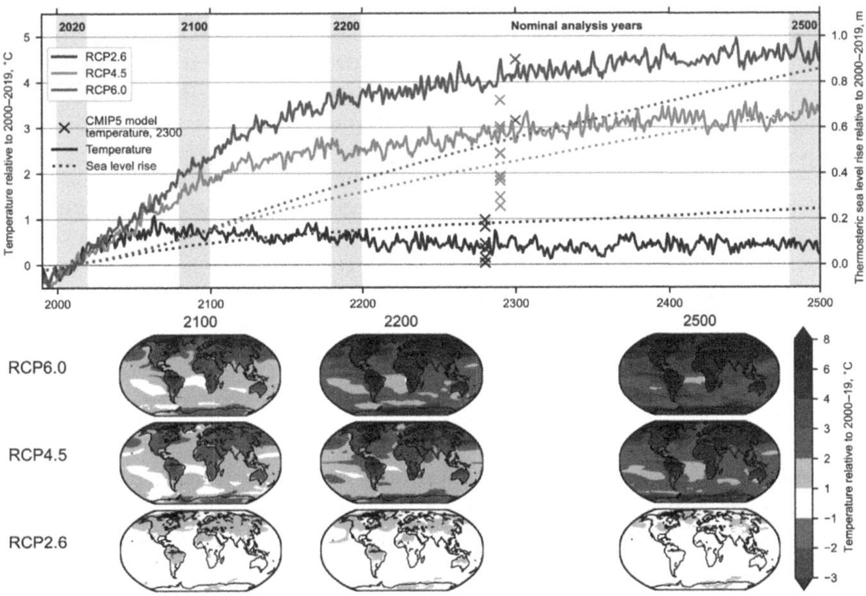

Fig. 3 Global mean near-surface air temperature and thermosteric sea-level rise anomalies relative to the 2000–2019 mean for RCP climate change scenarios (By Authors of the study: Christopher Lyon, Erin E. Saupe, Christopher J. Smith, Daniel J. Hill, Andrew P. Beckerman, Lindsay C. Stringer, Robert Marchant, James McKay, Ariane Burke, Paul O'Higgins, Alexander M. Dunhill, Bethany J. Allen, Julien Riel-Salvatore, Tracy Aze—https://onlinelibrary.wiley.com/doi/https://doi.org/10.1111/gcb.15871, CC BY 4.0, https://commons.wikimedia.org/w/index.php?curid=111204952)

- **Temperature Change:** The solid lines represent the projected change in global mean surface temperature from 2000 to 2500, relative to the 2000–2019 average:
  - **RCP2.6:** The lowest emission scenario. Temperature increases around 1 °C by 2100 and remains relatively stable after that. This pathway represents strong mitigation efforts.
  - **RCP4.5:** A moderate emission scenario. Temperature increases around 2 °C by 2100 and continues to rise slightly afterward. This pathway represents some mitigation but not as aggressive as RCP2.6.
  - **RCP6.0:** A higher emission scenario. Temperature rises around 3 °C by 2100 and continues to climb, approaching 4 °C by 2500. This pathway represents less stringent mitigation efforts.
- **Sea-Level Rise:** The dotted dark blue line shows the projected thermosteric sea level rise (rise due to thermal expansion of water) relative to the 2000–2019 average. The "x" markers show CMIP5 multi-model mean global average surface air temperature for the year 2300. The sea-level rise continues even if temperatures stabilize, reflecting the slow response time of ice sheets and glaciers to warming.
- **Spatial Patterns:** The maps reveal that:
  - Warming is not uniform across the globe. Land areas are generally warm more than oceans.
  - The Arctic experiences the most significant warming under all scenarios (polar amplification).
  - Higher emission scenarios (e.g., RCP6.0) result in more pronounced and widespread warming compared to lower-emission scenarios (e.g., RCP2.6).

This figure demonstrates that the magnitude and spatial distribution of future warming are strongly dependent on the emission pathway we follow. Lower-emission scenarios lead to substantially less warming and lower sea-level rise, highlighting the importance of reducing greenhouse gas emissions to limit the risks of climate change.

2.3 *Shared Socioeconomic Pathways (SSPs)*

To provide a more nuanced context for understanding climate impacts, scientists have developed Shared Socioeconomic Pathways (SSPs), which are scenarios of future socioeconomic development. SSPs consider factors like population growth, economic development, technological change, and governance, providing a framework for understanding how societies might evolve and adapt to climate change.

SSPs explore different narratives about the future:

- **SSP1–1.9: Sustainability:** A world characterized by low population growth, high levels of education and technological development, and a focus on sustainability and international cooperation.
- **SSP1–2.6: Middle of the Road:** A world that follows historical trends in terms of population growth, economic development, and technological progress.
- **SSP2–4.5: Regional Rivalry:** A world marked by high population growth, resource scarcity, nationalism, and conflict.
- **SSP3–7.0: Inequality:** A world with increasing inequalities within and between countries, with limited access to technology and resources for the poorest populations.
- **SSP5–8.5: Fossil-Fueled Development:** A world characterized by rapid economic growth, technological innovation, but heavy reliance on fossil fuels.

By combining RCPs with SSPs, climate scenarios can provide a more comprehensive picture of potential futures, taking into account both the physical impacts of climate change and the societal responses to those impacts. Riahi et al. (2017) gives an overview of the Shared Socioeconomic Pathways (SSPs) and their implications for energy use, land use, and greenhouse gas emissions. Riahi et al. (2021) examines the costs and feasibility of meeting stringent climate targets without overshoot using the SSP framework (Fig. 4).

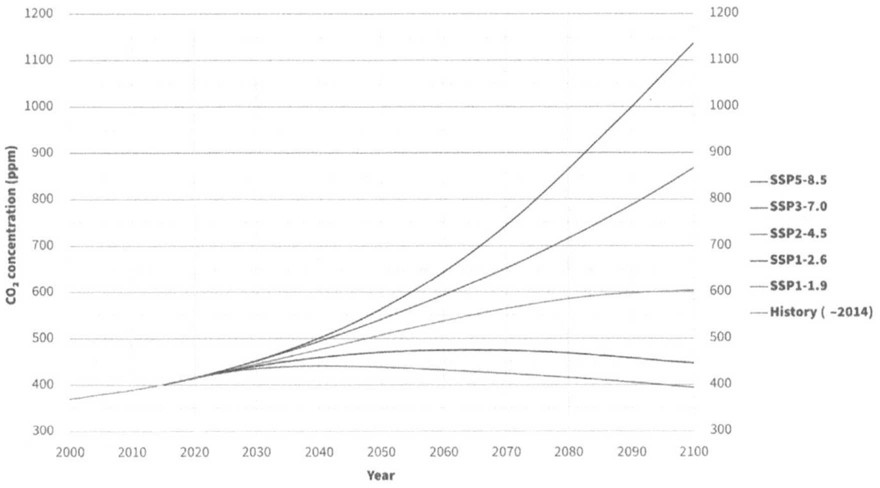

Fig. 4 Predicted atmospheric CO_2 concentrations for different shared socioeconomic pathways (SSPs) across the twenty-first century (projected by MAGICC7, a simple/reduced complexity climate model). Each data point represents an average of simulated values generated from five integrated assessment models (By Sfdiversity—Own work, CC BY-SA 4.0, https://commons.wikimedia.org/w/index.php?curid=86811464)

2.4 Climate Impacts and Risks

Climate scenarios are used to project a wide range of potential climate impacts, which can vary significantly depending on the chosen RCP and SSP. These impacts include:

- **Changes in Temperature:** Global average temperatures are projected to increase under all RCP scenarios, with the magnitude of warming depending on the level of GHG emissions. This warming will have cascading effects on regional and local climates, leading to changes in precipitation patterns, sea levels, and extreme weather events.
- **Extreme Weather Events:** Climate change is projected to increase the frequency and intensity of extreme weather events, such as heatwaves, droughts, floods, and storms. These events can cause widespread damage to infrastructure, disrupt agriculture and water resources, and pose significant threats to human health and safety.
- **Impacts on Ecosystems, Agriculture, and Water Resources:** Climate change will have profound impacts on ecosystems, shifting species distributions, disrupting biodiversity, and increasing the risk of forest fires. Agricultural yields will be affected by changes in temperature, precipitation, and extreme weather events, potentially leading to food shortages and price volatility. Water resources will also be strained, with some regions facing more severe droughts while others experience increased flooding.

Understanding these potential impacts is crucial for assessing climate risks, developing adaptation strategies, and making informed decisions about investments, policies, and long-term planning. Pedde et al. (2019) explores methods for bridging uncertainty concepts across narratives and simulations in environmental scenarios. Sillmann et al. (2019) discusses the implications of climate extremes for impact and risk assessment.

Case Study 1: Climate Scenarios: Navigating a Range of Possible Futures—The City of Rotterdam's Climate Adaptation Strategy

Rotterdam, a coastal city highly vulnerable to sea-level rise, flooding, and extreme heat, has developed a comprehensive climate adaptation strategy using a range of climate scenarios. The city's approach combines global Representative Concentration Pathways (RCPs) with localized climate projections to assess potential risks, identify vulnerable areas, and prioritize adaptation measures.

Rotterdam's Use of Climate Scenarios

1. **Risk Assessment:**

   Rotterdam utilized climate scenarios to project future sea-level rise, changes in precipitation patterns, and temperature increases. These projections helped identify areas at high risk of flooding and urban heat island effects.

The city considered both high-end and low-end scenarios to capture the full range of potential climate impacts, as illustrated by the development of "high-end climate change scenarios for flood protection" (KNMI, 2009).

2. **Vulnerability Mapping:**

   Using GIS and climate projections, Rotterdam created detailed vulnerability maps highlighting areas most at risk from various climate hazards. This allowed for targeted adaptation planning.
3. **Adaptation Measure Prioritization:**

   Based on the climate scenarios, Rotterdam prioritized key adaptation measures:

   (a) Upgrading flood defenses, including the Maeslant storm surge barrier (KNMI, 2009).
   (b) Developing innovative water storage systems, such as water squares and underground storage facilities (C40 Cities, 2015).
   (c) Creating green spaces to mitigate urban heat island effects, exemplified by projects like the Dakpark (Anastasopoulou, 2023).
4. **Scenario-Based Planning:**

   Rotterdam's adaptation strategy considers multiple future scenarios, allowing for flexible and robust planning that can adapt to changing conditions over time.

Challenges in Long-Term Climate Change Planning

1. **Uncertainty Management:**

   Dealing with the inherent uncertainty in long-term climate projections while making concrete planning decisions is a significant challenge.

   Rotterdam addresses this by using a range of scenarios and adopting flexible, adaptive measures.
2. **Integration with Urban Planning:**

   Incorporating climate adaptation into existing urban planning processes can be challenging due to institutional silos and short-term development agendas (Leonardsen et al., 2020).

   Rotterdam has worked to overcome this by developing an integrated approach that combines water management, climate-proofing infrastructure, and nature-based solutions (Anastasopoulou, 2023).
3. **Balancing Immediate Needs and Long-Term Risks:**

   The city faces the challenge of addressing current urban development needs while preparing for long-term climate risks.

   This is reflected in Rotterdam's approach of combining immediate actions with long-term strategic planning (van der Berg, 2023).

Importance of Integrating Climate Scenarios into Urban Planning

1. **Informed Decision-Making:**
   Climate scenarios provide a scientific basis for urban planning decisions, helping to justify investments in adaptation measures.
2. **Risk-Based Approach:**
   By integrating climate scenarios, Rotterdam has adopted a risk-based approach to urban planning, prioritizing areas and sectors most vulnerable to climate impacts.
3. **Multi-Functional Solutions:**
   The use of scenarios has led to the development of multi-functional adaptation measures, such as the Benthemplein Water Square, which serves as both a public space and a water retention facility (C40 Cities, 2015).

Role of Stakeholder Engagement in Developing Adaptation Strategies

1. **Community-Based Initiatives:**
   Rotterdam's adaptation strategy emphasizes community engagement, as seen in projects like the Dakpark, which was inspired and initiated by local communities (Anastasopoulou, 2023).
2. **Collaborative Governance:**
   The city has adopted a collaborative governance approach, involving various stakeholders in the planning and implementation of adaptation measures (van der Berg, 2023).
3. **Public Awareness and Support:**
   Engaging stakeholders has helped increase public awareness of climate risks and build support for adaptation measures, which is crucial for the long-term success of the strategy.
4. **Knowledge Sharing:**
   Stakeholder engagement facilitates knowledge sharing between experts, policymakers, and local communities, leading to more innovative and locally appropriate solutions.

Rotterdam's use of climate scenarios in developing its adaptation strategy demonstrates the value of this approach in navigating the complexities of long-term climate planning. By considering a range of possible futures, the city has been able to develop a robust, flexible, and comprehensive adaptation plan. The integration of these scenarios into urban planning processes, coupled with strong stakeholder engagement, has positioned Rotterdam as a leader in urban climate adaptation. However, challenges remain in managing uncertainties, overcoming institutional barriers, and balancing short-term needs with long-term risks. As cities worldwide grapple with similar challenges, Rotterdam's experience offers valuable lessons in using climate scenarios to enhance urban resilience and sustainability.

3 Major Scenario Frameworks

The development and assessment of climate scenarios are ongoing endeavors involving a global network of scientists, researchers, and institutions. This section explores three major scenario frameworks that are widely used to inform climate risk assessments, policy development, and strategic planning:

3.1 The Intergovernmental Panel on Climate Change (IPCC) Scenarios

The Intergovernmental Panel on Climate Change (IPCC) plays a pivotal role in assessing the science of climate change and providing policymakers with comprehensive reports on the current state of knowledge. The IPCC's scenario framework, updated with each major assessment report, serves as a benchmark for climate projections worldwide.

In its Sixth Assessment Report (AR6), the IPCC (2022) adopted a new scenario framework that integrates Representative Concentration Pathways (RCPs) with Shared Socioeconomic Pathways (SSPs). This integrated framework provides a more nuanced and comprehensive picture of potential future climates, considering both the physical drivers of climate change (GHGs) and the societal responses to those changes.

The IPCC's AR6 scenarios highlight a range of potential climate impacts, emphasizing that:

- **Global warming will continue under all scenarios:** Even under the most ambitious mitigation scenario (RCP2.6), global average temperatures are projected to increase by 1.5 °C to 2 °C above pre-industrial levels by the end of the century. Under higher emission scenarios, warming could exceed 4 °C, with potentially catastrophic consequences.
- **Climate impacts will intensify with increasing warming:** The severity of climate impacts, including sea-level rise, extreme weather events, and ecosystem disruptions, will increase with the magnitude of warming.
- **Socioeconomic choices play a critical role:** The choice of socioeconomic pathway (SSP) has a significant influence on the vulnerability of societies to climate change, even under the same RCP. For example, a world with high levels of inequality (SSP4) will be more vulnerable to climate impacts than a world characterized by sustainable development and international cooperation (SSP1).

Case Study 2: AXA's Use of Climate Scenarios in Investment Decision-Making

AXA, a major insurance company, has taken a leading role in incorporating climate scenarios into its investment portfolio management. This approach aims to mitigate climate risks and identify sustainable investment opportunities, demonstrating the company's commitment to addressing climate change through its financial strategies (AXA Group, 2022, 2023; Rajgopal, 2022).

How AXA Uses Climate Scenarios

1. **Combination of IPCC Scenarios and Internal Assessments:**

   AXA utilizes a range of climate scenarios, including those from the Intergovernmental Panel on Climate Change (IPCC) and internal climate risk assessments.

   The company considers multiple scenarios, such as the 1.5 °C, 2 °C, and 3 °C warming scenarios, to capture a range of possible future climate states.
2. **Warming Potential Methodology:**

   AXA has developed a "warming potential" methodology to assess the alignment of its investments with climate goals.

   As of 2021, AXA reported that its investment portfolio had a warming potential of 2.62 °C, compared to a benchmark of 2.96 °C, indicating progress toward alignment with lower-temperature scenarios (AXA Group, 2022).
3. **Climate Value-at-Risk (VaR) Analysis:**

   AXA employs a Climate VaR metric to quantify potential financial losses due to climate risks.

   In 2021, AXA estimated its climate VaR to be between 8 and 11% of the aggregate market value of its investment portfolio under various scenarios.
4. **Sector-Specific Strategies:**

   AXA has implemented strategies to reduce exposure to carbon-intensive sectors, such as coal, and increase investments in renewable energy and green infrastructure.

   The company has set targets for green investments, aiming for €26 billion by 2023.
5. **Integration with ESG Scoring:**

   AXA has developed comprehensive ESG scoring systems covering a large portion of its investment portfolio, including 93% of corporate equities, 87% of corporate debt, and 98% of sovereign debt (AXA Group, 2022).

Challenges and Considerations

1. **Long-Term vs. Short-Term Horizons:**

   One of the main challenges AXA faces is integrating long-term climate considerations into short-term investment horizons.

   The company acknowledges that climate trends manifest over decades, which can be at odds with the shorter-term focus of many investment strategies.
2. **Uncertainty in Climate Modeling:**

AXA recognizes the limitations and uncertainties in climate modeling, particularly when applied at the security level.

The company uses multiple approaches and metrics to triangulate their assessments and mitigate the impact of individual model uncertainties.

3. **Data Quality and Availability:**
   Obtaining reliable and comprehensive data for climate risk assessment remains a challenge, particularly for certain asset classes or regions.
4. **Balancing Climate Risk with Other Financial Considerations:**
   AXA must balance climate risk mitigation with other financial objectives and regulatory requirements, which can sometimes lead to competing priorities.

Role of Scenario Analysis in Asset Allocation

1. **Informing Strategic Decisions:**
   Climate scenario analysis plays a crucial role in informing AXA's strategic asset allocation decisions, helping to identify sectors and regions that may be more resilient to climate change (AXA Group, 2023).
2. **Risk Management:**
   Scenario analysis allows AXA to stress-test its portfolio against different climate futures, enabling better risk management and portfolio resilience.
3. **Opportunity Identification:**
   By analyzing various climate scenarios, AXA can identify investment opportunities in sectors that are likely to benefit from the transition to a low-carbon economy.

Growing Importance of Climate Risk Disclosure

1. **Regulatory Pressure:**
   AXA recognizes the increasing regulatory focus on climate risk disclosure and has been proactive in developing comprehensive reporting frameworks.
2. **Stakeholder Expectations:**
   Investors, customers, and other stakeholders are increasingly demanding transparent and detailed climate risk disclosures, driving AXA to continually improve its reporting practices.
3. **Industry Leadership:**
   Through its comprehensive climate risk disclosure and scenario analysis, AXA is positioning itself as a leader in sustainable finance, potentially influencing industry standards and practices.

AXA's use of climate scenarios in investment decision-making demonstrates a sophisticated approach to integrating climate considerations into financial strategy. By employing a range of scenarios and assessment methodologies, AXA is working to enhance the climate resilience of its portfolio while identifying sustainable investment opportunities. However, challenges remain in reconciling long-term climate projections with shorter-term investment horizons and in managing the uncertainties inherent in climate modeling. As climate risk disclosure becomes increasingly important, AXA's approach may serve as a model for other financial institutions seeking to navigate the complexities of climate change in their investment strategies.

3.2 The International Energy Agency (IEA) Scenarios

The International Energy Agency (IEA), an intergovernmental organization focused on energy security and sustainability, develops energy-focused scenarios that explore future energy demand, supply, and technological developments. These scenarios are widely used by governments, businesses, and investors to understand the implications of different energy choices for climate change, economic development, and energy security.

Key IEA scenarios include:

- **Net Zero Emissions by 2050 (NZE) Scenario:** This scenario outlines a pathway for achieving net-zero emissions by mid-century, requiring a rapid and transformative shift away from fossil fuels toward renewable energy, energy efficiency, and electrification.
- **Stated Policies Scenario (STEPS):** This scenario reflects current government policies and announced pledges related to energy and climate change. It serves as a baseline for understanding the likely trajectory of emissions and energy demand if current policies remain unchanged.
- **Announced Pledges Scenario (APS)**: This scenario assumes implementation of policies as in the STEPS, and also assumes fulfillment of looser pledges that are not yet backed by policy and legislation.

The IEA scenarios highlight the critical role of energy choices in shaping the future of climate change:

- **Urgent action is needed to achieve net-zero emissions:** The NZE scenario demonstrates that a rapid and ambitious transformation of the global energy system is necessary to limit warming to 1.5 °C and avert the worst impacts of climate change.
- **Current policies are insufficient:** The STEPS scenario indicates that current government policies and pledges are not enough to achieve the Paris Agreement goals and will lead to continued growth in emissions and warming.

3.3 The Network for Greening the Financial System (NGFS) Scenarios

The Network for Greening the Financial System (NGFS), a group of central banks and financial supervisors from around the world, develops climate scenarios specifically for financial risk assessment. These scenarios explore the implications of different climate pathways for the financial system, providing a framework for stress testing, risk management, and investment decision-making. The NGFS (2022) report presents climate scenarios for use by central banks and financial supervisors in assessing climate-related risks. The fifth vintage of the NGFS (2024) climate scenarios presents enhanced frameworks that adapt to ongoing global climate commitments while integrating new advances in climate science. Key updates include a new damage function that assesses physical risks more accurately, reflecting higher projected losses caused by climate change impacts. Additionally, the scenarios demonstrate that significant economic transformations are essential to achieving net-zero emissions by 2050, highlighting the importance of timely, coordinated policy action to mitigate risks and foster a resilient financial system.

These are the key features of the updated NGFS (2024) scenarios (Fig. 5):

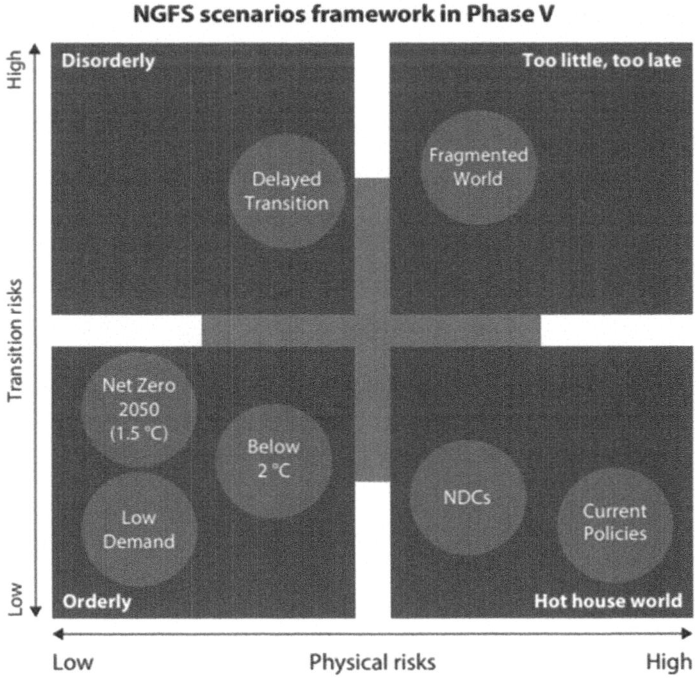

Fig. 5 Updated NGFS scenarios by physical and transition risk dimensions (NGFS, 2024)

- The NGFS scenarios have been updated to reflect new economic data, climate policies, and country commitments as of March 2024.
- A newly applied damage function incorporates the latest climate science, providing a more comprehensive understanding of the economic impacts of climate change.
- Limiting temperature rise to 1.5 °C requires intensified efforts, with most countries benefiting from early action on climate policies.
- Stagnation in climate policy implementation could lead to severe economic disruption, necessitating higher emissions in the short term.
- Physical risks now projected to cause significant GDP losses underscore the urgency of transitioning promptly to sustainable practices.
- The updated scenarios present a variety of future outcomes, emphasizing that transitioning to a green economy involves both physical and transition risks.
- Policy recommendations include adopting a shadow carbon price of approximately \$300/tCO_2 by 2035 to stimulate the shift to net-zero emissions.

The NGFS scenarios are categorized into four major narratives based on the level of climate policy ambition, timing, and coordination. Each scenario reflects different assumptions about how climate policies, emissions, and physical risks evolve.

1. **Orderly Scenarios**

   These scenarios assume that climate policies are introduced early and become gradually more stringent, leading to relatively subdued physical and transition risks. The key scenarios under this category include:

   - **Net Zero 2050**: Aims to limit global warming to 1.5 °C through stringent climate policies and innovation, achieving net-zero CO_2 emissions around 2050.
   - **Low Demand**: Incorporates significant behavioral changes that reduce energy demand, alongside a shadow carbon price and technological advancements, facilitating a transition to net-zero emissions by 2050.
   - **Below 2°C**: Gradually increases the stringency of climate policies, aiming for a 67% chance of limiting global warming to below 2 °C.

2. **Disorderly Scenario**

   This scenario explores higher transition risks due to delayed or divergent climate policies across countries and sectors. The scenarios in this category include:

   - **Delayed Transition**: Assumes The NGFS scenarios highlight the importance of considering climate risks in financial decision-making:

- **Climate change poses significant financial risks:** The scenarios demonstrate that climate change can lead to substantial financial losses for banks, insurers, and investors, particularly in scenarios with delayed or insufficient climate action.
- **Early action is essential to mitigate risks:** The Orderly Transition scenario shows that taking early and ambitious action to reduce emissions can significantly reduce financial risks and create opportunities for green investments.

By incorporating these diverse scenario frameworks into their assessments, financial institutions, policymakers, and other stakeholders can gain a more comprehensive understanding of the potential risks and opportunities presented by climate change and develop more robust and effective strategies for navigating an uncertain future (Fig. 6).

Comparison of Agency Scenarios

The following table compares climate scenarios from the IPCC, IEA, and NGFS across various dimensions:

Feature	*IPCC Scenarios*	*IEA Scenarios*	*NGFS Scenarios*
Overview	Focuses on a comprehensive view of climate change	Primarily energy-focused	Tailored for financial risk assessment
Scenarios	– RCPs (Representative Concentration Pathways): Define different GHG concentration trajectories – SSPs (Shared Socioeconomic Pathways): Explore diverse socioeconomic futures	– NZE (Net Zero Emissions by 2050): Pathway to net-zero emissions – STEPS (Stated Policies Scenario): Baseline based on current policies – Announced Pledges Scenario (APS):	– Orderly Transition: Early, ambitious climate action – Disorderly Transition: Delayed, disruptive action – Hot House World: Continued high emissions – Too-little-too-late: a late and uncoordinated transition fails to limit physical risks
Key Factors	– GHG emissions—Socioeconomic factors (population, economic growth, technology, governance)	– Energy demand and supply – Technological innovation in energy sector	– Climate impacts on physical and transition risks – Macroeconomic impacts (GDP, inflation, interest rates)

(continued)

(continued)

Feature	*IPCC Scenarios*	*IEA Scenarios*	*NGFS Scenarios*
Applicability	– Wide-ranging: climate science, impacts, adaptation, mitigation—Used by governments, researchers, businesses	– Primarily for energy policy analysis – Used by governments, energy companies, investors	– Financial risk assessment and management – Used by central banks, financial supervisors, investors
Strengths	– Comprehensive, integrates physical and socioeconomic factors – Scientific consensus, widely accepted	– Strong focus on energy sector dynamics – Useful for understanding energy transitions	– Tailored to financial system vulnerabilities—Incorporates macroeconomic impacts
Limitations	– Can be complex, multiple scenarios and storylines – Coarse resolution may limit regional detail	– Limited scope beyond the energy sector – Less emphasis on socioeconomic factors	– Primarily focused on financial risks – May not capture all climate-related impacts

Additional Points:

- **Time Horizons:** All three frameworks typically consider long-term horizons (to 2100 and beyond). However, NGFS scenarios often include shorter-term (e.g., 2030, 2050) time horizons relevant for financial planning.
- **Data and Modeling:** All rely on complex climate and economic models. The specific models used can vary, contributing to uncertainty in projections.
- **Evolving Frameworks:** These frameworks are continually being refined and updated as new data and scientific understanding become available.

O'Neill et al. (2020) describes a tool called the Scenario Model Intercomparison Project (ScenarioMIP) for Coupled Model Intercomparison Project Phase 6 (CMIP6), which provides a framework for comparing climate model projections. Here's how it can be used to compare different climate scenarios:

- **Why ScenarioMIP Matters:** In the past, different climate models often used slightly different methods for generating scenarios, making it challenging to compare projections across models and assess uncertainties consistently.

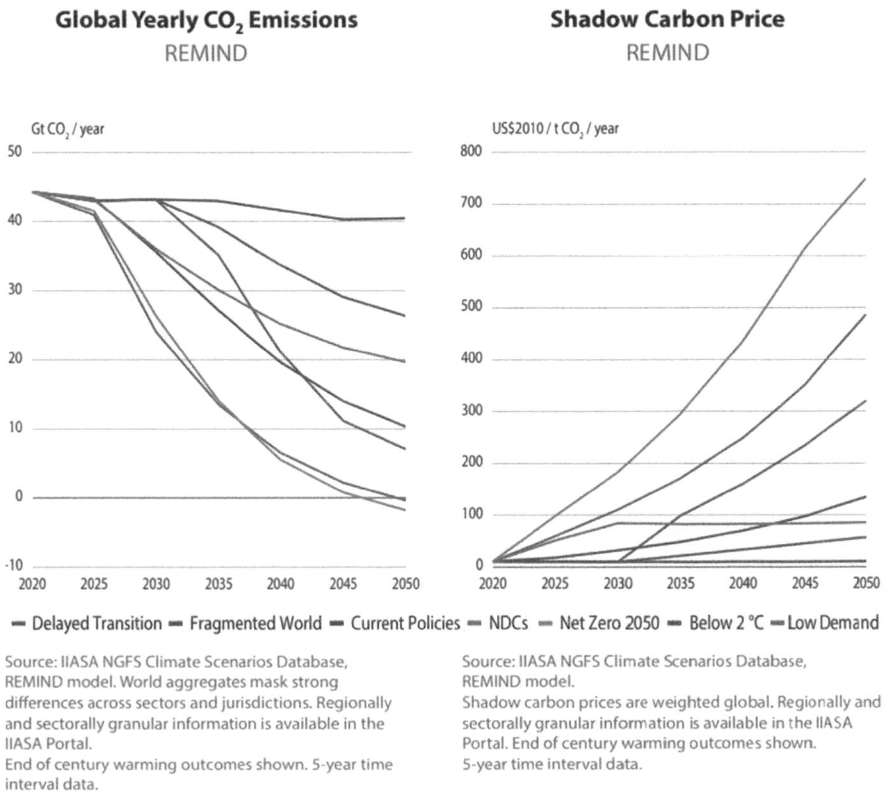

Fig. 6 Annual GHG emission and shadow carbon price in the various climate scenarios of the NGFS (2024) (By Source IIASA NGFS Climate Scenarios Database, REMIND model. Adapted from: NGFS Climate Scenarios for central banks and supervisors. September 2022. Public Domain, https://www.ngfs.net/system/files/import/ngfs/medias/documents/ngfs_scenarios_main_presentation.pdf)

- **What ScenarioMIP Does:** ScenarioMIP provides a coordinated framework for how different climate models should generate scenarios, based on standardized inputs for factors like greenhouse gas emissions, land use, and aerosols.
- **Benefits for Climate Scenario Development:** This standardization has several benefits:
  - **Improved Comparability:** Allows for more robust comparisons of climate projections across different models.
  - **More Robust Uncertainty Analysis:** Facilitates a more consistent and thorough assessment of uncertainty in future climate projections.

- **Facilitates Policy-Relevant Scenarios:** Helps to generate scenarios that are more directly relevant to policy questions (e.g., impacts of different emissions reduction targets).

4 Using Climate Scenarios in Decision-Making

Climate scenarios are not merely abstract projections; they are powerful tools that can inform and improve decision-making across a wide range of sectors. By considering a range of possible future climates, decision-makers can develop more robust strategies, identify emerging opportunities, and make more informed choices about investments, policies, and adaptation measures.

4.1 Scenario Planning

Scenario planning is a strategic planning methodology that uses a set of diverse and plausible scenarios to explore potential futures and develop strategies that are robust to a range of outcomes. Rather than trying to predict a single future, scenario planning encourages decision-makers to consider multiple possibilities, challenge their assumptions, and prepare for unexpected events. Hallegatte et al. (2019) explores opportunities for building resilient infrastructure in the face of climate change.

The scenario planning process typically involves:

1. **Defining the Scope:** Identifying the key decision or issue being addressed, the relevant timeframe, and the geographic scope.
2. **Identifying Key Drivers:** Determining the critical factors that are likely to shape the future, including both external factors (e.g., climate change, technological advancements, geopolitical trends) and internal factors (e.g., company strategies, competitor actions).
3. **Developing Scenarios:** Creating a set of plausible and diverse scenarios that capture a range of possible outcomes based on different combinations of key drivers. Scenarios should be internally consistent, plausible, and relevant to the decision at hand.
4. **Analyzing Impacts:** Assessing the potential impact of each scenario on the decision or issue being addressed.
5. **Developing Strategies:** Identifying robust strategies that can perform well across a range of scenarios or developing contingency plans for specific scenarios.
6. **Monitoring and Adapting:** Continuously monitoring the environment for changes in key drivers and adapting strategies as needed.

By embracing scenario planning, businesses and investors can move beyond linear forecasts and develop more flexible and adaptable strategies that are better equipped to navigate the uncertainties of a changing climate.

4.2 Stress Testing and Risk Management

Climate scenarios are increasingly being used by financial institutions and regulators to conduct stress tests and assess the resilience of the financial system to climate risks. Stress tests involve simulating the impact of different climate scenarios—such as a rapid transition to a low-carbon economy or a scenario with severe physical climate impacts—on the balance sheets, profitability, and capital adequacy of banks, insurers, and other financial institutions.

These stress tests help to identify:

- **Vulnerable Institutions:** Which institutions are most exposed to climate risks and may require additional capital buffers or risk management measures?
- **Systemic Risks:** How climate change could trigger cascading failures in the financial system and what steps can be taken to mitigate these risks?
- **Investment Opportunities:** Where are the opportunities for green investments that can help to decarbonize the economy and build resilience to climate impacts?

By incorporating climate scenarios into stress tests, regulators and financial institutions can proactively identify vulnerabilities, develop risk mitigation strategies, and ensure the stability of the financial system in the face of climate change.

4.2.1 Policy Development and Adaptation

Climate scenarios play a crucial role in informing the development of effective climate policies, adaptation plans, and long-term infrastructure investments. By providing insights into potential future climate impacts, scenarios help policymakers:

- **Set Emission Reduction Targets:** Climate scenarios can be used to assess the level of emissions reductions needed to achieve different climate goals, such as limiting warming to 1.5 °C or 2 °C.
- **Design Climate Policies:** Scenarios can inform the design of carbon pricing mechanisms, renewable energy policies, energy efficiency standards, and other policy instruments aimed at mitigating climate change.
- **Develop Adaptation Plans:** By projecting future climate impacts, such as sea-level rise, extreme weather events, and changes in water availability, scenarios can help policymakers identify vulnerable communities and ecosystems, prioritize adaptation measures, and allocate resources effectively.
- **Plan for Climate-Resilient Infrastructure:** Climate scenarios can inform the design and construction of infrastructure that can withstand future climate impacts, such as seawalls to protect coastal cities from flooding, drought-resistant roads, and resilient water systems.

By integrating climate scenarios into their planning processes, policymakers can make more informed decisions, develop more effective policies, and build a more resilient future for their communities and nations.

Case Study 3: The UK Government's Climate Change Risk Assessment

The UK government has employed climate scenarios to conduct a comprehensive national climate change risk assessment (CCRA). This process identifies key vulnerabilities and informs adaptation planning across various sectors, ensuring the country is prepared for future climate impacts.

How the UK Government Used Climate Scenarios

1. **Range of Climate Projections:**

   The UK government utilized a range of climate projections, including those from the UK Climate Projections 2018 (UKCP18), which provide detailed scenarios based on different Representative Concentration Pathways (RCPs).

   These scenarios helped assess potential risks from flooding, heatwaves, droughts, and other climate impacts on infrastructure, human health, and the economy.
2. **Risk Assessment Framework:**

   The CCRA framework involved evaluating the likelihood and potential impact of various climate hazards under different scenarios. This included both high-emission and low-emission pathways to capture a broad spectrum of possible futures.

   The assessment identified priority risks, such as increased flooding, water scarcity, and heat-related health issues, which require immediate and long-term adaptation measures.
3. **Sectoral Analysis:**

   The assessment covered multiple sectors, including infrastructure, agriculture, health, and biodiversity. For instance, it examined how increased rainfall and sea-level rise could exacerbate flooding risks and impact critical infrastructure like transportation and energy systems.

   It also looked at how rising temperatures could lead to more frequent and severe heatwaves, posing significant health risks, particularly to vulnerable populations.

Illustrating the Use of Climate Scenarios

1. **Flood Risk:**

   The CCRA used climate scenarios to project future flood risks, considering factors such as increased precipitation and sea-level rise. This informed the development of enhanced flood defenses and improved urban drainage systems.

For example, the Thames Estuary 2100 plan, which includes the Thames Barrier, was informed by these projections to protect London from future flood risks.

2. **Heatwaves and Health:**
   Climate scenarios indicated a higher frequency and intensity of heatwaves. This led to the implementation of public health strategies, such as the Heatwave Plan for England, which outlines measures to protect vulnerable populations during extreme heat events.
3. **Drought and Water Scarcity:**
   Projections of reduced summer rainfall and increased evaporation rates highlighted the risk of drought. This prompted investments in water efficiency measures, reservoir expansions, and the development of water transfer schemes to ensure a reliable water supply.
4. **Economic Impacts:**
   The assessment also considered the economic implications of climate impacts, such as damage to infrastructure, increased healthcare costs, and disruptions to agriculture. These insights helped prioritize investments in climate resilience to mitigate potential economic losses.

Challenges and Considerations in Long-term Climate Change Planning

1. **Uncertainty Management:**
   Planning for long-term climate change involves managing uncertainties inherent in climate projections. The UK government addressed this by using a range of scenarios and adopting a precautionary approach to ensure robustness in planning.
2. **Integration with Policy and Planning:**
   Integrating climate scenarios into national and local planning processes can be challenging due to the need for coordination across multiple sectors and governance levels. The UK government emphasized the importance of embedding climate risk assessments into all relevant policy areas.
3. **Resource Allocation:**
   Ensuring adequate funding and resources for adaptation measures is critical. The CCRA highlighted the need for sustained investment in climate resilience to protect communities and infrastructure from future risks.

Cross-Sectoral Collaboration

1. **Collaborative Approach:**
   Addressing climate risks requires collaboration across sectors, including government agencies, private sector entities, and civil society. The UK government facilitated this through multi-stakeholder engagement and partnerships.

For example, the National Adaptation Programme (NAP) involves collaboration between different government departments, local authorities, and industry stakeholders to implement adaptation measures.

2. **Knowledge Sharing:**

   Effective adaptation planning relies on the sharing of knowledge and best practices. The UK government promoted this through platforms like the UK Climate Resilience Programme, which supports research and knowledge exchange on climate adaptation.

Communicating Complex Climate Information

1. **Public Engagement:**

   Communicating complex climate information to the public is crucial for building awareness and support for adaptation measures (House of Commons Science and Technology Committee, 2014; UNFCCC, 2019). The UK government employed various strategies to enhance public understanding, such as using clear and relatable narratives, visual tools, and case studies. THECCC (2023) highlights the slow pace of Net Zero policy development and insufficient public engagement in the UK. Kumpu (2022) reviews climate communication research, emphasizing the need for a more sociological approach to public engagement.

   Reports like the THECCC (2023) Progress Report to Parliament emphasized the need for a coherent public engagement strategy to inform households and communities about climate risks and adaptation actions.

2. **Transparency and Trust:**

   Maintaining transparency in communicating climate risks and uncertainties is essential for building public trust. The government worked with trusted institutions like the Met Office and the Climate Change Committee (2023) to provide accurate and accessible climate information. Strachan (2018) stresses the importance of tailored, transparent climate communication for effective decision-making.

3. **Tailored Communication:**

   The government recognized the importance of tailoring communication to different audiences, considering factors such as local contexts, cultural values, and specific vulnerabilities. This approach helped ensure that climate information was relevant and actionable for various stakeholders.

   The UK government's use of climate scenarios in conducting a national climate change risk assessment highlights the importance of comprehensive and forward-looking planning to address climate risks. By employing a range of climate projections, the government was able to identify key vulnerabilities and prioritize adaptation measures across sectors. The challenges of integrating long-term climate considerations into policy, fostering cross-sectoral collaboration, and effectively communicating complex climate information underscore the need for a strategic and inclusive approach to climate adaptation. The insights gained from the CCRA process are instrumental in informing national adaptation policies, enhancing resilience, and safeguarding the United Kingdom's future in the face of climate change.

5 Conclusion: Embracing Uncertainty, Shaping the Future

The climate crisis confronts us with a future that is inherently uncertain. We cannot predict with absolute precision how the Earth's climate system will respond to rising greenhouse gas concentrations or how societies will adapt to the impacts of climate change. Yet, rather than succumbing to paralysis in the face of this uncertainty, we can embrace it as a call to action. Climate scenarios provide us with the tools to navigate a range of possible futures, assess risks, identify opportunities, and make more informed decisions. The IPCC (2022) report on "Climate Change 2022: Impacts, Adaptation and Vulnerability" provides the latest assessment of climate change impacts and adaptation options. Hausfather et al. (2022) highlights the "hot model" problem in climate simulations and its implications for scenario analysis. Lempert (2019) describes Robust Decision Making (RDM) as a method for decision-making under deep uncertainty.

Throughout this chapter, we've explored the key elements of climate scenarios, delving into Representative Concentration Pathways (RCPs) that outline different emissions trajectories and Shared Socioeconomic Pathways (SSPs) that capture a spectrum of potential societal responses. We've examined major scenario frameworks developed by the IPCC, IEA, and NGFS, highlighting their diverse perspectives and applications. And we've explored how climate scenarios are being used in decision-making, from strategic planning and risk management in the financial sector to policy development and adaptation planning at national and international levels.

The development and application of climate scenarios are ongoing endeavors. As our understanding of the climate system evolves, data availability improves, and modeling techniques advance, climate scenarios will continue to be refined and updated. This ongoing process requires collaboration between climate scientists, economists, social scientists, policymakers, and practitioners across various sectors.

The key takeaway is this: climate scenarios are not about predicting a single definitive future. They are about embracing uncertainty, exploring a range of possibilities, and making choices today that can lead to a more sustainable, resilient, and equitable future for all. By integrating climate scenarios into our planning processes, we can move beyond reactive responses and become active shapers of a future that we can be proud to leave for generations to come.

References

Hallegatte, S., Jun, R., & Julie, R. (2019). *Lifelines: The resilient infrastructure opportunity*. Sustainable Infrastructure Series. World Bank. https://doi.org/10.1596/978-1-4648-1430-3. License: Creative Commons Attribution CC BY 3.0 IGO. https://documents1.worldbank.org/curated/en/775891600098079887/pdf/Lifelines-The-Resilient-Infrastructure-Opportunity.pdf

Hausfather, Z., & Peters, G. P. (2020). Emissions–the 'business as usual' story is misleading. *Nature, 577*(7792), 618–620. https://doi.org/10.1038/d41586-020-00177-3

Hausfather, Z., et al. (2022). Climate simulations: recognize the 'hot model' problem. *Nature, 605*(7908), 26–29. https://doi.org/10.1038/d41586-022-01192-2

Intergovernmental Panel on Climate Change (IPCC). (2022). *Climate change 2022: Impacts, adaptation and vulnerability*. IPCC Sixth Assessment Report. https://www.ipcc.ch/report/ar6/wg2/

Lempert, R. J. (2019). Robust Decision Making (RDM). In: Marchau, V., Walker, W., Bloemen, P., Popper, S. (eds) *Decision Making under Deep Uncertainty*. Springer, Cham. https://doi.org/10.1007/978-3-030-05252-2_2

Network for Greening the Financial System (NGFS). (2022). *Network for greening the financial system (NGFS) report: Climate scenarios for central banks and supervisors*. https://www.ngfs.net/sites/default/files/medias/documents/ngfs_climate_scenarios_for_central_banks_and_supervisors_.pdf

O'Neill, B. C. et al. (2020). The scenario model intercomparison project (ScenariOMIP) for CMIP6. *Geoscientific Model Development, 9*, 3461–3482. https://gmd.copernicus.org/articles/9/3461/2016/

Pedde, S., et al. (2019). Bridging uncertainty concepts across narratives and simulations in environmental scenarios. *Regional Environmental Change, 19*, 655–666. https://doi.org/10.1007/s10113-018-1338-2

Riahi, K., et al. (2017). The shared socioeconomic pathways and their energy, land use, and greenhouse gas emissions implications: An overview. *Global Environmental Change, 42*, 153–168. https://www.sciencedirect.com/science/article/pii/S0959378021000662

Riahi, K., et al. (2021). Cost and attainability of meeting stringent climate targets without overshoot. *Nature Climate Change, 11*, 1063–1069. https://www.nature.com/articles/s41558-021-01215-2

Schwalm, C. R., Glendon, S., & Duffy, P. B. (2020). RCP8.5 tracks cumulative CO2 emissions. *Proceedings of the National Academy of Sciences, 117*(33), 19656–19657. https://doi.org/10.1073/pnas.2007117117

Sillmann, J., Sippel, S., & Russo, S. (2019). *Climate extremes and their implications for impact and risk assessment*. ScienceDirect. https://www.sciencedirect.com/book/9780128148952/climate-extremes-and-their-implications-for-impact-and-risk-assessment#book-info

Case Reference

Anastasopoulou, M. (2023). *Stakeholder engagement: A collaborative approach for climate adaptation at the urban environment*. Master thesis, University of Groningen. https://frw.studenttheses.ub.rug.nl/4353/1/Thesis_S4100077.pdf

AXA Group. (2022). *Climate and biodiversity report accelerating transition*. Accessed 21 Jan 2025. https://www-axa-com.cdn.axa-contento-118412.eu/www-axa-com/109c504e-bc3f-4e3a-bca0-5c3e1ccb65bb_AXA2022_Climate_and_Biodiversity-Report_Final_22_07_19.pdf

AXA Group. (2023). *Climate and biodiversity report*. Accessed 21 Jan 2025. https://www-axa-com.cdn.axa-contento-118412.eu/www-axa-com/6caad3e0-bf63-48b5-a3c4-78c904b26fbb_axa_climate_and_biodiversity_report_2023_va.pdf

C40 Cities. (2015). *Cities100: Rotterdam—Resilience and quality of life go hand in hand*. Accessed 22 Jan 2025. https://www.c40.org/case-studies/cities100-rotterdam-resilience-and-quality-of-life-go-hand-in-hand/

Climate Change Committee (CCC). (2023). *2023 progress report to parliament*. Climate Change Committee. Accessed 22 Jan 2025. https://www.theccc.org.uk/publication/2023-progress-report-to-parliament/

House of Commons Science and Technology Committee (HCSTC). (2014). *Communicating climate science*. https://publications.parliament.uk/pa/cm201314/cmselect/cmsctech/254/25403.htm

Koninklijk Nederlands Meteorologisch Instituut Ministerie van Infrastructuur en Waterstaat (KNMI). (2009). *High-end climate change scenarios for flood protection of the Netherlands*. https://www.knmi.nl/kennis-en-datacentrum/achtergrond/high-end-climate-change-scenarios-for-flood-protection-of-the-netherlands

Kumpu, V. (2022). What is public engagement and how does it help to address climate change? A review of climate communication research. *Environmental Communication, 16*(3), 304–316. https://doi.org/10.1080/17524032.2022.2055601

Leonardsen, J., Moens, E., & Parsons, G. (2020). *Planning for climate adaptation: Key actions for resilient and adaptive cities of the future*. Accessed 21 Jan 2025. https://www.swecogroup.com/wp-content/uploads/sites/2/2022/12/urban-insight-report_planning-for-climate-adoptation_a4.pdf

Rajgopal, S. (2022). A comparative analysis of incorporating climate risk in investment portfolios of AXA vs. Chubb, liberty mutual, and travelers. *Forbes*. https://www.forbes.com/sites/shivaramrajgopal/2022/11/18/a-comparative-analysis-of-incorporating-climate-risk-in-investment-portfolios-of-axa-vs-chubb-liberty-mutual-and-travelers/

Strachan, J. (2018). *Communicating long-term climate information*. https://www.metoffice.gov.uk/binaries/content/assets/metofficegovuk/pdf/business/international/communicating-climate_strachan.pdf

van der Berg, A. (2023). Climate adaptation planning for resilient and sustainable cities: Perspectives from the city of Rotterdam (Netherlands) and the city of Antwerp (Belgium). *European Journal of Risk Regulation, 14*(3), 564–582. https://doi.org/10.1017/err.2022.17

United Nations Climate Change Secretariat (UNFCCC). (2019). *Communicating climate change: A practitioner's guide*. https://unfccc.int/sites/default/files/resource/Communicating%20climate%20change_Insights%20from%20CDKNs%20experience.pdf

CHAPTER 6

Physical Risk Modeling: Quantifying the Impacts of a Changing Climate

1 Introduction: From Projections to Impacts

The images of wildfire-ravaged landscapes, flood-inundated cities, and parched, drought-stricken farmlands are stark reminders that climate change is no longer a distant threat; it's a present reality with tangible and escalating consequences. While climate projections provide crucial insights into potential future climates, understanding the specific impacts of these changes on human and natural systems is essential for effective risk management, adaptation planning, and investment decision-making.

This is where physical risk modeling comes in. It bridges the gap between abstract climate projections and the concrete impacts of a changing climate on the ground. Physical risk models translate scientific data on temperature changes, sea-level rise, and extreme weather events into quantifiable assessments of potential damages, financial losses, and disruptions to critical infrastructure, businesses, and ecosystems.

Why is physical risk modeling so crucial? Consider these compelling reasons:

- **Quantifying Impacts**: Models enable us to estimate the potential financial costs of climate-related damages, helping businesses, governments, and investors understand the magnitude of the risks they face.
- **Informing Adaptation**: By identifying vulnerable areas and assets, physical risk models guide the prioritization of adaptation measures, such as building seawalls to protect coastal communities, strengthening infrastructure to withstand extreme weather events, or developing drought-resistant crops.
- **Pricing Insurance**: As climate change alters the frequency and severity of hazards, insurance companies need to adjust premiums to reflect the

J. Chen, *Climate Finance*, https://doi.org/10.1007/978-981-96-7975-1_6

evolving risk landscape. Physical risk models provide the data needed to set premiums that accurately reflect the increasing risks of climate-related losses.

- **Guiding Investments**: Investors, developers, and infrastructure planners need to consider climate risks when making long-term investment decisions. Physical risk models can help assess the vulnerability of different locations and assets, guiding investments toward more resilient options.

In this chapter, we delve into the methodologies of physical risk modeling, exploring the diverse tools and techniques used to quantify the impacts of a changing climate. We'll examine the challenges of incorporating climate projections into risk assessments, discuss the importance of data availability and model accuracy, and highlight the emerging innovations that are advancing the field of physical risk modeling. By understanding these models and their applications, we can move from projections to action, building a more climate-resilient future for all.

2 Physical Risk Scenarios: Projecting Future Impacts

Assessing physical climate risks requires a forward-looking perspective. We need to understand not only the current impacts of climate change but also how these impacts are likely to evolve in the future as global temperatures continue to rise. This requires translating global climate projections into specific scenarios that capture the potential changes in physical hazards at regional and local scales.

2.1 Understanding Climate Projections

As discussed in Chapter 4, global climate models (GCMs) are sophisticated computer programs used to simulate the Earth's climate system and project future climate change based on different greenhouse gas emission scenarios. These scenarios are often represented by Representative Concentration Pathways (RCPs), which outline different trajectories for the concentration of greenhouse gases in the atmosphere.

Each RCP corresponds to a specific level of radiative forcing—the change in the Earth's energy balance due to GHGs—leading to varying degrees of warming. For example, RCP8.5 represents a high-emissions scenario with continued growth in GHG concentrations, leading to significant warming throughout the twenty-first century. In contrast, RCP2.6 represents a low-emissions scenario with ambitious mitigation efforts, limiting warming to well below 2 degrees Celsius above pre-industrial levels.

It's important to note that RCPs are not predictions of what *will* happen but rather represent a range of *possible* futures, depending on the choices we make about emissions reductions.

2.2 Downscaling Global Projections

While GCMs provide valuable insights into global climate trends, their spatial resolution is relatively coarse, typically representing climate conditions over grid cells that are tens or hundreds of kilometers in size. This coarse resolution limits their usefulness for assessing climate impacts at regional or local scales, where decisions about adaptation, infrastructure planning, and risk management are often made.

To address this limitation, climate scientists use downscaling techniques to translate the coarse-resolution outputs of GCMs into finer-scale projections that are more relevant for specific regions. Downscaling methods can be broadly categorized into two types:

- **Statistical Downscaling**: This approach uses statistical relationships between large-scale climate variables (e.g., temperature, precipitation from GCMs) and local-scale variables (e.g., rainfall at a specific weather station) to generate finer-scale projections. Maraun and Widmann (2018) provides a comprehensive overview of statistical downscaling and bias correction methods for climate research. These methods are crucial for translating coarse-resolution climate projections from Global Climate Models (GCMs) into finer-scale projections that are more relevant for regional and local risk assessments.
- **Dynamical Downscaling**: This approach uses Regional Climate Models (RCMs), which are similar to GCMs but focus on specific geographic regions at higher resolution. RCMs use the outputs of GCMs as boundary conditions, allowing them to simulate climate processes at a more local scale.

2.3 Key Physical Hazards

Climate change is projected to alter a range of physical hazards, with varying impacts depending on geographic location, emission scenarios, and local vulnerabilities. Key physical hazards can be categorized into two broad scopes: acute hazards and chronic hazards. Climate change is projected to alter a range of physical hazards, with varying impacts depending on emission scenarios (Eyring & Gillett, 2021). Table 1 from UNEP FI (2023) describes these major hazards and subtypes.

Acute hazards are characterized by their sudden onset and relatively short duration, unlike chronic hazards that unfold over longer periods. Acute hazards include:

Table 1 Key physical risk hazards

	Climate hazards	*Risk indicators*	*Secondary effects*
Acute	Hurricanes and typhoons	• Cumulative wind speed	Coastal regions and islands are the most vulnerable as they are affected not only by the direct impact of a storm but also by secondary hazards, such as storm surges and pounding waves
	Floods	• Flood frequency • Flood severity • Rainfall intensity • Very wet days (>95th p) • Wet days (>10 mm)	Disruption of services, health impacts such as famine and disease, and tertiary effects could change the position of river channels, leading to landslides
	Wildfire risk	• Change in days with high wildfire potential • Change in maximum wildfi re potential • Days with high wildfire potential • Maximum wildfire potential	Secondary effects, including erosion, landslides, impaired water quality, and smoke damage, often accompany fire events
Chronic	Sea level rise	• Absolute coastal flood frequency • Relative coastal flood exposure	Rising sea levels lead to multiple adverse effects like coastal erosion, inundations, storm floods, tidal waters encroachment into estuaries and river systems, and contamination of freshwater reserves
	Heat stress	• Energy demand • Extreme heat days • Extreme temperature	The health impacts of rising air temperature are compounded by increased atmospheric water vapor, which reduces humans' ability to dissipate heat

(continued)

Table 1 (continued)

Climate hazards	Risk indicators	Secondary effects
Drought stress	• Meteorological drought i.e. days per annum with precipitation below 1 mm	Increasing temperature, in addition to changes in precipitation patterns, can cause drier weather conditions and hence more intense and frequent drought events, which can have severe economic, environmental, and social impacts
Precipitation stress	• Current baseline water stress • Current inter-annual variability • Future water demand • Future water supply • Water demand change • Water supply change	The effects of adverse rain include flooding. Heavy rainfall effects in urban areas can be especially catastrophic, endangering lives and damaging infrastructure

Source UNEP FI (2023)

- **Hurricanes and Typhoons**:
  - **Risk Indicator**: Cumulative wind speed: The total wind energy experienced during the storm, which is a key factor in determining damage.
  - **Secondary Effects**: Coastal regions and islands are most vulnerable due to the combined effects of direct impacts from the storm (high winds, heavy rainfall) and secondary hazards like storm surges (rise in sea level caused by the storm) and pounding waves.
- **Floods**:
  - **Risk Indicators**:

    Flood frequency: How often floods occur.

    Flood severity: Magnitude of the flood, often measured by water depth or discharge.

    Rainfall intensity: The rate of rainfall, which can lead to flash floods.

    Very wet days (>95th p): Number of days with exceptionally high rainfall, exceeding the historical 95th percentile.

    Wet days (>10mm): Number of days with rainfall exceeding 10mm.
  - **Secondary Effects**: Disruption of services, health impacts (e.g., spread of waterborne diseases), famine and disease due to crop

damage and disruptions to food supplies, changes to river channels (e.g., erosion, landslides). Effective flood risk management can involve implementing nature-based solutions (van Wesenbeeck et al., 2017).

- **Wildfire Risk**:
  - **Risk Indicators**:
    Change in days with high wildfire potential: Increase in the number of days with weather conditions conducive to wildfires (e.g., high temperatures, low humidity, strong winds).
    Change in maximum wildfire potential: Increase in the maximum potential for severe wildfires.
    Days with high wildfire potential: Total number of days with conditions favorable for wildfires.
    Maximum wildfire potential: The highest level of wildfire risk expected.
  - **Secondary Effects**: Erosion, landslides, impaired water quality (e.g., ash and sediment runoff), smoke damage, and damage to property and infrastructure.

These acute hazards are becoming more frequent and intense in many regions due to climate change. Effective risk management requires monitoring these risk indicators, implementing early warning systems, and developing strategies for disaster preparedness and response.

Seneviratne et al. (2021) analyzes weather and climate extreme events in a changing climate as part of the IPCC's Sixth Assessment Report (AR6). This paper discusses the scientific findings of the AR6 on climate extreme events, focusing on changes in temperature and precipitation. It emphasizes the significant increase in the frequency and intensity of extreme climate events (e.g., heat waves and extreme precipitation) in response to global warming (especially under the 1.5 °C and 2 °C scenarios) and the role of human activities in these changes. By providing an integrated assessment of climate change in different regions, the report reveals the potential impacts of climate change on ecosystems and societies.

- Climate warming has led to a significant increase in the frequency and intensity of extreme temperature and precipitation events globally.
- Human activities are recognized as a major driver of changes in extreme weather events, especially greenhouse gas emissions.
- There are differences in the response and adaptive capacity of different regions to extreme weather changes.
- Climate models show significant trends in extreme weather events in the context of global warming at 1.5 °C and 2 °C.

- Statistical analyses of instrumental data and the past decade reveal sizable impacts of climate change, particularly in terms of drought and flood events.
- The increase in extreme weather events poses a serious threat to agriculture, ecosystems, and public health.
- Urgent measures are needed to address the impacts of climate change, including mitigation, adaptation, and prevention strategies for extreme events.

Chronic hazards, unlike acute events like hurricanes, unfold over longer time periods and often have cascading impacts. Chronic hazards include:

- **Sea-Level Rise**:
  - **Risk Indicators**:
    Absolute coastal flood frequency: How often coastal areas experience flooding.
    Relative coastal flood exposure: The extent to which coastal areas are exposed to flooding relative to other areas or over time.
  - **Secondary Effects**: Coastal erosion, inundations (flooding), storm floods (combination of storm surge and high tide), encroachment of tidal waters into estuaries and river systems, contamination of freshwater reserves.
- **Heat Stress**:
  - **Risk Indicators**:
    Energy demand: Increased energy demand for cooling during heatwaves.
    Extreme heat days: Number of days exceeding certain temperature thresholds.
    Extreme temperature: Maximum temperatures reached.
  - **Secondary Effects**: Increased atmospheric water vapor compounds the health impacts of rising air temperatures, reducing the human body's ability to dissipate heat.
- **Drought Stress**:
  - **Risk Indicators**: Meteorological drought: Measured as the number of days per year with very low or no precipitation (below 1mm).
  - **Secondary Effects**: Changes in precipitation patterns can lead to drier conditions, exacerbating the impacts of droughts. More frequent and intense droughts can cause economic, environmental, and social hardship.

- **Precipitation Stress**:
  - **Risk Indicators**:
    Current baseline water stress: Existing levels of water scarcity.
    Current inter-annual variability: Fluctuations in water availability from year to year.
    Future water demand: Projected future water needs.
    Future water supply: Projections of future water availability.
    Water demand change: Changes in water needs over time.
    Water supply change: Changes in water availability over time.
  - **Secondary effects**: Flooding due to heavy rainfall events, especially in urban areas, can be particularly damaging to infrastructure, endangering lives and having catastrophic effects.

In essence, these chronic hazards represent long-term, cumulative stresses on both human and natural systems. Their impacts are often multifaceted and can exacerbate the effects of acute events. Monitoring the risk indicators associated with these chronic hazards is critical for proactive adaptation planning and risk management.

Discussion on Chronic Hazard of Sea-Level Rise: As global temperatures rise, glaciers and ice sheets melt, and ocean water expands thermally, leading to rising sea levels. Coastal communities are particularly vulnerable to sea-level rise, facing increased risks of coastal erosion, flooding, and saltwater intrusion into freshwater aquifers. The IPCC projects that global mean sea level could rise by 0.28 to 0.98 meters by 2100 under RCP8.5, with even higher levels of rise possible in some regions. Oppenheimer et al. (2019) examines sea-level rise and its implications for low-lying areas in an IPCC Special Report. It discusses the drivers of sea-level rise, projects future changes, and outlines the implications for coastal communities, infrastructure, and ecosystems, making it highly relevant to coastal risk modeling. The chapter by Oppenheimer et al. addresses the critical issue of sea-level rise (SLR) as a significant physical hazard resulting from climate change. It highlights how rising sea levels threaten low-lying islands, coastal areas, and communities worldwide. The report outlines several key points:

- **Projected Sea-Level Rise**: The IPCC estimates that global mean sea level could rise by 0.28 to 0.98 meters by 2100 under high-emission scenarios (RCP8.5). This rise is attributed to thermal expansion of seawater and melting glaciers and ice sheets.
- **Vulnerability of Coastal Communities**: Coastal populations are particularly at risk due to their low elevation and proximity to the ocean. Increased flooding, coastal erosion, and saltwater intrusion into freshwater supplies pose significant threats to livelihoods, infrastructure, and ecosystems.

- **Adaptation Strategies**: The report emphasizes the need for adaptive measures such as building seawalls, restoring natural barriers like mangroves, and implementing managed retreat strategies in the most vulnerable areas.
- **Equity Considerations**: There is a focus on the disproportionate impacts of SLR on marginalized communities who often lack the resources to adapt effectively. This raises important questions about equity in climate adaptation efforts.

Gradual shifts in average temperature and precipitation patterns can have significant impacts on agriculture, water resources, ecosystems, and human health. For example, warming temperatures can shift plant and animal ranges, alter growing seasons, and increase the risk of heat stress for livestock. Changes in precipitation patterns can lead to water scarcity in some regions and increased flooding in others.

Understanding how these physical hazards are projected to change in the future is crucial for assessing climate risks, developing adaptation strategies, and making informed decisions about infrastructure investments, land-use planning, and disaster preparedness.

3 Physical Risk Modeling Methodologies

Modeling the physical risks of climate change requires a diverse toolkit of methods and approaches. This section explores some of the key methodologies used to translate climate projections into tangible assessments of potential impacts:

3.1 Catastrophe (CAT) Models

Catastrophe (CAT) models are sophisticated computer programs widely used by insurance and reinsurance companies to assess the financial risks associated with natural disasters. They combine historical data on hazard events (e.g., hurricanes, earthquakes, floods), exposure data (e.g., locations and values of insured properties), and vulnerability data (e.g., building construction types and their resistance to hazards) to estimate the potential financial losses from future events. Incorporating climate change into CAT models involves addressing uncertainties in projections and potential cascading impacts (Ranger et al., 2022). Foote (2017) provides a practitioner's guide to natural catastrophe risk management and modeling. This book is a comprehensive guide to catastrophe modeling, covering the theory, methodologies, and practical applications of these models. It's a valuable resource for practitioners involved in risk assessment, insurance pricing, and disaster management. Figure 1 shows the conceptual framework of CAT model under climate risk context.

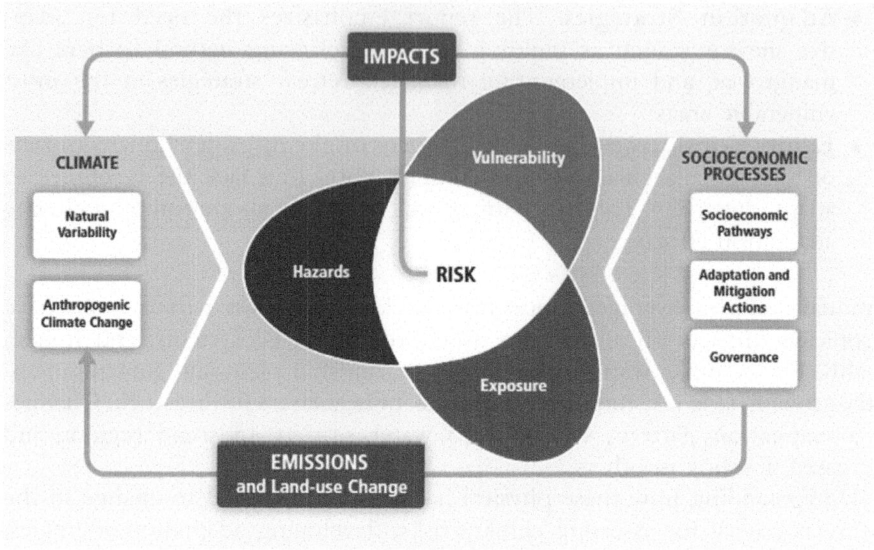

Fig. 1 The IPCC AR5 conceptual framework (*Source* IPCC [2014])

This figure illustrates the IPCC AR5 (Fifth Assessment Report) conceptual framework for understanding climate-related risk. It emphasizes that risk arises from the interplay of three core factors: **hazards, exposure, and vulnerability**.

- **Hazards**: These are the potential occurrences of natural or human-induced physical events or trends or physical impacts that may cause loss of life, injury, or other health impacts, as well as damage and loss to property, infrastructure, livelihoods, service provision, ecosystems, and environmental resources. In the context of climate change, hazards result from climate change itself (anthropogenic climate change) and also from natural variability in the climate system. Examples include heatwaves, floods, droughts, sea-level rise, and storms.
- **Exposure**: This refers to the presence of people, livelihoods, species or ecosystems, environmental functions and services, infrastructure, or economic, social, or cultural assets in places and settings that could be adversely affected. Essentially, it's *what* is at risk in a given location. For example, a coastal city is exposed to sea-level rise, while agricultural land is exposed to drought. Emissions and land-use change influence climate and therefore also influence hazards. Hazards, through impacts, influence exposure. Socioeconomic processes influence exposure.
- **Vulnerability**: This is the propensity or predisposition to be adversely affected. Vulnerability encompasses a variety of concepts and elements including sensitivity or susceptibility to harm and lack of capacity to cope and adapt. It describes how susceptible something is to harm from a given

hazard. For instance, a building constructed with weak materials is more vulnerable to earthquake damage than a building designed to withstand seismic activity. Similarly, a community with limited access to resources is more vulnerable to the impacts of a drought. Vulnerability is influenced by socioeconomic processes. Impacts also influence vulnerability.

The Interplay and Risk:
The intersection of these three factors defines **risk**. Risk is not simply the potential for a hazard to occur. It's the potential for *negative consequences* resulting from the combination of a hazard, exposure to that hazard, and vulnerability to its effects.

- **High risk** occurs when there's a significant hazard, high exposure, *and* high vulnerability. For example, a densely populated coastal city (high exposure) built on low-lying land (high vulnerability) facing the threat of a powerful hurricane (significant hazard) is at high risk.
- **Low risk** can result from a low hazard, low exposure, or low vulnerability, even if the other factors are high. For instance, a sparsely populated area (low exposure) might be at relatively low risk from a flood, even if the flood hazard is high and the area is inherently vulnerable to flooding.

Other Factors:
The framework also acknowledges that both climate (which leads to hazards) and socioeconomic processes (which influence vulnerability and exposure) contribute to risk and its outcomes (impacts). Adaptation and mitigation actions, as well as governance structures, can influence socioeconomic pathways and modify the level of risk. The impacts, in turn, can feed back into both climate and socioeconomic processes.

This framework highlights the interconnectedness of climate change and its impacts. It's not just about the physical hazards themselves but also how exposed and vulnerable societies are to these hazards. This understanding is crucial for developing effective climate risk management strategies.

We couldn't help noticing the similarity of the physical risk CAT model components with the Expected Credit Loss (ECL) calculation under IFRS 9. ECL is a crucial measure used by banks to estimate potential losses on their loans and advances. It's a forward-looking, probability-weighted estimate, meaning it considers a range of possible outcomes and their likelihoods. The formula and its components are as follows:

$$\begin{aligned}\textbf{ECL} &= \textbf{Exposure at Default (EAD)} \times \textbf{Probability of Default}(PD) \\ &\quad \times \textbf{Loss Given Default(LGD)}\end{aligned}$$

- **Exposure at Default (EAD)**: This represents the predicted amount of loss a lender would face if a borrower defaults. Under IFRS 9, it's generally taken as the current outstanding loan amount. In simpler terms, it's how much money the borrower currently owes.
- **Probability of Default (PD)**: This is the likelihood that a borrower will default on their loan obligations within a given timeframe, usually one year. IFRS 9 defines default as when a borrower is 90 days or more behind in making a repayment on their loan (e.g., mortgage). It is statistically determined using various factors like the borrower's credit history, financial situation, and economic conditions.
- **Loss Given Default (LGD)**: This is the percentage of the EAD that the lender expects to lose if a default occurs. It represents the portion of the loan that won't be recovered after accounting for the value of any collateral (e.g., the house in a mortgage). The formula is effectively: LGD = 1 − (Value of Collateral after Foreclosure/EAD). Foreclosure costs, typically around 20% of the collateral value, further reduce the recovery amount.

ECL is calculated by multiplying the amount owed (EAD) by the probability of the borrower not paying (PD), and the percentage of that amount the bank is likely to lose if the borrower defaults (LGD). This forward-looking and probability-weighted approach provides a more comprehensive view of credit risk than simply looking at historical losses.

Comparing the components of climate physical risk CAT model with the components of Expected Credit Loss (ECL) reveals interesting parallels and how climate change can exacerbate credit risk:

Climate physical risk component	*ECL component*	*Relationship and impact of climate change*
Hazard	Probability of Default (PD)	Climate hazards (e.g., floods, droughts, wildfires) directly increase the PD. More frequent and severe hazards, driven by climate change, heighten the likelihood of borrowers experiencing financial distress, leading to missed loan payments and defaults
Exposure	Exposure at Default (EAD)	While the EAD is typically the outstanding loan amount, climate change can *indirectly* impact it through two primary channels: (1) Increased loan demand for post-disaster reconstruction or relocation could lead to higher EADs. (2) Preemptive measures to mitigate risks (e.g., relocating or strengthening structures) can also influence lending and EAD if financed through loans
Vulnerability	Loss Given Default (LGD)	Climate change *significantly* impacts LGD. Damage or destruction of physical assets used as collateral (e.g., houses, farms) by climate hazards directly increases the LGD. Reduced property values in hazard-prone areas, even without direct damage, also contribute to a higher LGD

(continued)

(continued)

Climate physical risk component	*ECL component*	*Relationship and impact of climate change*

Further points of comparison and impact:

- **Chronic vs. Acute Hazards**: While acute hazards (e.g., hurricanes) can cause sudden spikes in PD and LGD, chronic hazards (e.g., sea-level rise) contribute to a gradual increase in risk over time, potentially affecting all three ECL components. This gradual impact is reflected in depreciating asset values and increasing insurance costs, which can make it challenging to assess the timing and magnitude of losses.
- **Sectoral Differences**: The impact of climate change on ECL components varies across sectors. For example, agriculture and real estate are particularly vulnerable to physical risks, which translate to higher PDs and LGDs for loans in these sectors compared to less climate-sensitive industries.
- **Geographic Concentration**: Areas with higher exposure to specific climate hazards, such as coastal regions or wildfire-prone areas, will see a more pronounced impact on ECL calculations for loans secured by assets in those regions. This geographic concentration of risk can amplify potential losses for lenders.
- **Data Challenges**: Accurate assessment of climate-related financial risks requires high-quality data on hazards, exposures, and vulnerabilities. Data gaps and limitations can hinder the accurate incorporation of climate change into ECL models.

By understanding the relationships between climate physical risk components and ECL components, banks can better assess and manage the growing financial risks associated with climate change. Integrating climate considerations into credit risk assessments is crucial for ensuring the stability of the financial system in the face of a changing climate.

Of course, climate physical risk not only exacerbates credit risk, but also impact other financial risks as well. Table 2 from BIS (2021) details the climate risk drivers impacting various common financial risks.

Adapting CAT Models for Climate Change:
Traditionally, CAT models have relied heavily on historical data to estimate the probability and severity of hazard events. However, as climate change alters the frequency and intensity of hazards, relying solely on historical data can lead to underestimation of future risks.

Table 2 Categories of climate risk drivers and their potential effects

Risk	*Primary drivers*	*Secondary drivers*
Credit risk	• Reduction in borrowers' ability to repay and service debt due to decreased income from climate-related impacts	• Decreased ability of banks to fully recover the value of a loan in the event of default, due to reduced asset values linked to climate risk
Market risk	• Reduction in financial asset values due to immediate climate risk factors not yet incorporated into prices	• Potential for large, sudden, and negative price adjustments • Breakdown in correlations between assets or changes in market liquidity for certain assets, undermining risk management assumptions
Liquidity risk	• Climate risk drivers causing counterparties to draw down deposits and credit lines, impacting banks' liquidity	• Reduced access to stable sources of funding as market conditions are affected by climate risk
Operational risk	• Direct damages to infrastructures from extreme weather events	• Secondary drivers are not distinctly separate for operational risk in this context, as the primary impact is the direct damage to infrastructure

Source BIS (2021)

To address this challenge, modelers are incorporating climate change projections into CAT models, using outputs from GCMs and RCMs to adjust hazard parameters, such as:

- **Frequency**: Adjusting the probability of occurrence of different hazard events based on projected changes in climate patterns. For example, if climate models project an increase in the frequency of intense hurricanes, CAT models can incorporate this information to estimate the likelihood of future hurricane-related losses.
- **Intensity**: Modifying the severity of hazard events based on projections of changes in climate variables. For example, if sea levels are projected to rise, CAT models can adjust the extent of flooding in coastal areas to reflect the higher sea levels.

Challenges of Incorporating Climate Change into CAT Models:

- **Non-Stationary Hazards**: Climate change is leading to hazards that are changing over time, making it difficult to rely solely on historical data. Modelers need to develop methods for incorporating projections of future hazard changes.

- **Uncertainty in Climate Projections**: Climate models provide a range of potential future scenarios, each with inherent uncertainties. CAT models need to account for this uncertainty and provide a range of possible loss estimates.
- **Cascading Impacts**: Climate change can trigger cascading impacts, such as a drought leading to increased wildfire risk, which then increases the risk of mudslides. CAT models need to be able to capture these complex interactions between different hazards.

Swiss Re Institute (2020) explores natural catastrophes in the context of economic accumulation and climate change. In this report, they analyze the interplay between economic growth, climate change, and natural catastrophes. The report provides insights into how these factors influence risk landscapes and insurance markets:

- **Economic Impact of Natural Disasters**: The authors present data indicating that global economic losses from natural catastrophes have been rising, with 2020 witnessing losses amounting to USD 190 billion. They highlight how economic accumulation increases vulnerability to disasters by concentrating assets in hazard-prone areas.
- **Changing Risk Dynamics**: The report emphasizes that climate change is altering the frequency and severity of natural disasters. This necessitates a shift in how CAT models are developed and utilized to reflect these changes accurately.
- **Focus on Secondary Perils**: The authors stress the importance of recognizing secondary peril events (e.g., severe convective storms) that have become significant contributors to insured losses. They argue that traditional CAT models often overlook these risks, leading to underestimations of potential losses.
- **Forward-Looking Risk Assessment**: The authors advocate for a forward-looking approach to risk assessment that integrates climate projections into CAT models. This includes adjusting historical data reliance to better reflect current conditions and future risks.

Open-Source CAT Risk Model: CLIMADA

CLIMADA is a state-of-the-art probabilistic modeling tool developed by ETH Zurich to assess the economic risks associated with climate change and extreme weather events. It provides high-resolution estimates of potential economic damages from hazards such as tropical cyclones, floods, and droughts, helping decision-makers understand the cost-effectiveness of various climate adaptation measures. The model is open-source, readily accessible, and supports transparency in understanding physical risks, setting an independent standard aligned with frameworks like the TCFD (Fig. 2).

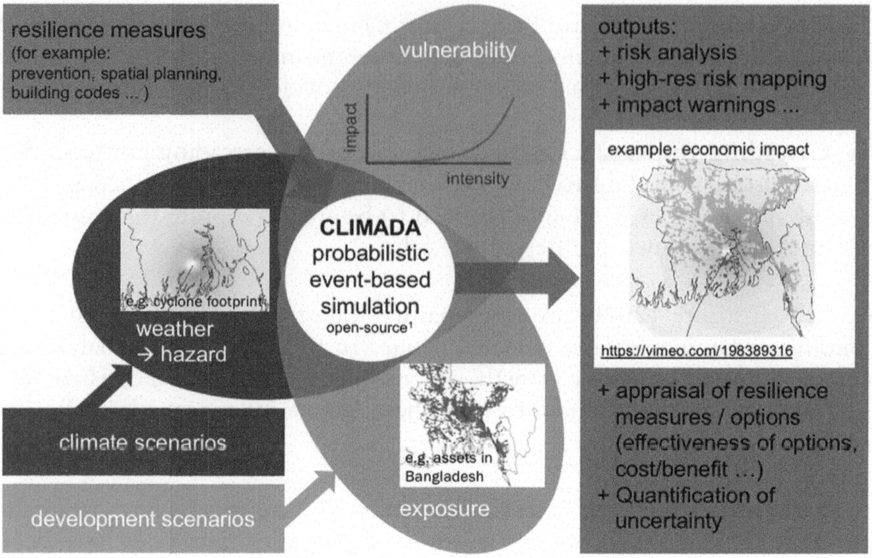

Fig. 2 CLIMADA Framework (*Source* https://wcr.ethz.ch/research/climada.html)

- CLIMADA uses advanced probabilistic modeling to estimate expected economic damage from climate-related risks.
- The platform helps decision-makers evaluate the economic impacts of extreme weather events and the benefits of risk reduction measures.
- Currently, CLIMADA offers global coverage of significant climate-related hazards with a high spatial resolution of 4 km.
- The model includes historical and probabilistic event sets, which are valuable for climate impact assessments at various future time horizons.
- CLIMADA is freely available as open-source software under the GNU GPL3 license and facilitates access to data via a comprehensive API.
- Key contributors to CLIMADA's development include Dr. Chahan Kropf, Dr. Lukas Riedel, and Emanuel Schmid from ETH Zurich.
- Extensive technical documentation and key publications related to CLIMADA are available online for users and researchers.

Case Study 1: The Zurich Flood Resilience Alliance

Focus: Using CAT models and vulnerability assessments to help communities in flood-prone regions build resilience to increasing flood risks.

The Zurich Flood Resilience Alliance is a multi-sector partnership focused on finding practical ways to help communities strengthen their resilience to floods globally. This case study examines how Zurich Insurance Group, in collaboration with NGOs and local communities, utilizes physical risk modeling to identify flood-prone areas, assess infrastructure vulnerability, and develop cost-effective flood mitigation and resilience measures.

Key Components:

1. Physical Risk Modeling and Vulnerability Assessments
   The Alliance employs sophisticated catastrophe (CAT) models and vulnerability assessments to (Zurich Climate Resilience Alliance, 2020):
   - Identify flood-prone areas with high-resolution mapping
   - Assess the vulnerability of buildings, infrastructure, and communities
   - Quantify potential economic and social impacts of flooding
2. Community-Based Approach
   The Alliance emphasizes community involvement in developing and implementing flood resilience strategies (Keating et al., 2017):
   - Engaging local stakeholders in risk assessment and planning
   - Incorporating local knowledge and practices into resilience measures
   - Building capacity within communities to manage and reduce flood risks
3. Cost-Effective Mitigation Measures
   The Alliance focuses on identifying and implementing cost-effective flood mitigation measures:
   - Nature-based solutions (e.g., wetland restoration, reforestation)
   - Structural interventions (e.g., flood barriers, improved drainage systems)
   - Non-structural measures (e.g., early warning systems, land-use planning)

Discussion Points:

1. Role of Insurance Companies in Promoting Climate Resilience
   Insurance companies play a crucial role in promoting climate resilience by (Brown, 2016):
   - Providing risk transfer mechanisms to protect against financial losses
   - Offering incentives for risk reduction through premium discounts
   - Sharing expertise in risk assessment and management with communities and policymakers
2. Importance of Community-Based Approaches to Adaptation
   Community-based approaches are essential for effective flood resilience (Pelling, 2007):
   - Ensuring local buy-in and ownership of resilience initiatives
   - Leveraging local knowledge and resources

   - Tailoring solutions to specific community needs and contexts
3. Potential for Public–Private Partnerships to Address Flood Risks
   Public–private partnerships offer significant potential in addressing flood risks (Pelling, 2007):
   - Combining public sector resources and authority with private sector expertise and innovation
   - Developing and implementing comprehensive flood risk management strategies
   - Scaling up successful interventions and sharing best practices

Conclusion:
The Zurich Flood Resilience Alliance demonstrates the power of collaborative, community-based approaches in building resilience to flood risks. By combining sophisticated risk modeling with local knowledge and engagement, the Alliance has developed effective strategies for flood mitigation and adaptation. This case study highlights the important role that insurance companies can play in promoting climate resilience, the value of community-based approaches, and the potential for public–private partnerships in addressing complex climate risks. As climate change continues to exacerbate flood risks globally, initiatives like the Zurich Flood Resilience Alliance offer valuable lessons and models for enhancing community resilience and reducing vulnerability to natural disasters.

3.2 Geospatial Analysis

Geographic Information Systems (GIS) and remote sensing data are powerful tools for mapping and assessing physical climate risks. GIS software allows users to combine and analyze spatial data from various sources, such as:

- **Hazard Maps**: Maps showing the probability or intensity of different climate hazards, such as flood zones, wildfire risk areas, or sea-level rise projections.
- **Exposure Data**: Data on the location and value of assets that are exposed to climate risks, such as buildings, infrastructure, agricultural lands, and population centers.
- **Vulnerability Data**: Data on the susceptibility of different assets to specific hazards, such as building construction types, elevation above sea level, or the presence of natural barriers (e.g., wetlands, forests).

By overlaying these different data layers in a GIS, analysts can identify areas where high hazard levels intersect with high exposure and vulnerability, highlighting "hotspots" of climate risk. This information can be used to:

- **Prioritize Adaptation Measures**: Targeting investments in flood defenses, drought-resistant infrastructure, or wildfire mitigation in areas that are most vulnerable.
- **Inform Land Use Planning**: Guiding decisions about where to develop new infrastructure, housing, or commercial areas to minimize exposure to climate risks.
- **Communicate Risks to Stakeholders**: Creating maps and visualizations that clearly convey the spatial distribution of climate risks to policymakers, businesses, and the public.

Tate et al. (2021) investigates flood exposure and social vulnerability in the United States. In this study, Tate and colleagues investigate the intersection of flood exposure and social vulnerability across the conterminous United States (CONUS). The research employs geospatial analysis techniques to map and understand how these two factors converge, highlighting significant findings:

- **Geographical Mapping**: The authors utilize advanced spatial analysis methods, including bivariate Local Indicators of Spatial Association (LISA), to identify hotspots where high flood exposure coincides with high social vulnerability. This approach allows for a nuanced understanding of the spatial dynamics at play, revealing that approximately 19 million people live in these vulnerable hotspots, predominantly located in rural areas of the US South.
- **Indicators of Vulnerability**: The study identifies key social vulnerability indicators, such as housing types (e.g., mobile homes) and demographic factors (e.g., racial minorities), that are overrepresented in flood-prone areas. This highlights how socioeconomic factors contribute to increased risk during flood events.
- **Policy Implications**: By mapping these vulnerabilities, the research provides critical insights for disaster management and mitigation strategies. It emphasizes the need for targeted interventions that address both physical flood risks and the social dimensions of vulnerability, suggesting that understanding who is most at risk can inform more equitable disaster response efforts.

Merkens (2018) presents gridded population projections for coastal zones under different socioeconomic pathways. Merkens and colleagues focus on projecting population changes along coastal zones under various socioeconomic scenarios, utilizing geospatial methodologies to enhance understanding of future population dynamics:

- **Shared Socioeconomic Pathways (SSPs)**: The study employs SSPs to create detailed gridded population projections for coastal areas, which are

crucial for assessing potential impacts from climate change, particularly sea-level rise and extreme weather events.
- **Spatial Resolution**: By providing high-resolution population data, this research aids in identifying vulnerable coastal communities that may face increased risks due to climate-related hazards. The projections help policymakers understand where population growth may exacerbate vulnerabilities related to flooding and other climate impacts.
- **Integration with Climate Models**: The gridded population data can be integrated with climate models to assess potential future risks more accurately. This integration is vital for effective planning and resource allocation in coastal regions facing climate change challenges.

Both studies underscore the importance of geospatial analysis in understanding the interplay between environmental hazards and social vulnerabilities. Tate et al.'s work highlights how spatial mapping can reveal critical insights into flood risks faced by marginalized communities, while Merkens et al. provide essential data for projecting future population trends in vulnerable coastal areas. Together, these studies emphasize the need for integrated approaches that consider both physical risks and social factors when developing effective adaptation strategies and policies in response to climate change.

3.3 Sector-Specific Models

In addition to general-purpose CAT models and geospatial analysis, specialized models are being developed to assess physical risks in different sectors, taking into account the unique vulnerabilities and characteristics of each sector.

Examples of sector-specific models include:

- **Infrastructure Models**: These models assess the vulnerability of roads, bridges, power grids, water systems, and other critical infrastructure to climate impacts, such as flooding, sea-level rise, extreme temperatures, and wildfires. They can be used to identify weak points in infrastructure networks, prioritize maintenance and upgrades, and design new infrastructure that is more resilient to future climate conditions.
- **Agricultural Models**: These models simulate the impacts of climate change on crop yields, livestock production, and food security, considering factors such as changes in temperature, precipitation, extreme weather events, and the availability of water resources. They can be used to assess the vulnerability of different agricultural regions, identify adaptation strategies (e.g., drought-resistant crops, irrigation systems), and inform agricultural policies and investment decisions. Luo and Zhang (2024) discusses the growing threats posed by climate change to rural financial institutions in China. To effectively identify and assess the climate-related physical risks associated with agricultural credit in

Guangxi, the Green Finance 60 Forum organized a team of experts to explore the establishment of a climate physical risk stress-testing framework. This was based on **over 13 million agricultural credit loans from 91 rural cooperative financial institutions** in Guangxi, China (including rural commercial banks, rural cooperative banks, and rural credit cooperatives, hereinafter referred to as cooperative institutions), quantifying and evaluating the climate physical risks faced by these institutions. They find that:

- Under adverse weather conditions and extreme climate events, the credit risk and operational pressure on rural financial institutions significantly increase. According to calculations, for each additional day of extreme low temperatures (below 5 °C) in a year, the non-performing loan rate of county-level agricultural cooperative institutions in Guangxi increases by an average of 0.24%, while the total profit decreases by an average of 0.94%. In scenarios of extreme drought with high temperatures (above 35 °C), the risk-bearing capacity based on financial indicators is projected to rise by 4.1% to 11.9%, with some calculations indicating that the risk level could increase by more than 60%.
- Also, under adverse weather conditions and extreme climate events, the repayment ability of clients of rural financial institutions significantly declines. Calculations focused on production loans to farmers indicate that for each additional day of extreme low or high temperatures, the overdue principal amount of farmer loans increases by 2% and 2.6%, respectively; for each additional day of extreme high temperatures, the balance of non-performing loans for farmers increases by 3%; and for each additional month of extreme flooding (when the standardized precipitation evapotranspiration index exceeds 2), both the balance and number of non-performing loans for farmers rise by approximately 18%.

- **Real Estate Models**: These models assess the impact of climate change on property values, considering factors such as sea-level rise, flooding, wildfire risk, and extreme heat. They can be used by investors, developers, and homeowners to evaluate the climate resilience of properties, assess the potential for property damage and insurance losses, and inform decisions about real estate development and investment.

Rosenzweig et al. (2020) advocates for a global food system approach to climate change responses. Rosenzweig and colleagues advocate for a holistic approach to climate change responses within the global food system. The authors emphasize that traditional sector-specific models often overlook the interconnectedness of food production, distribution, and consumption. Key points from the article include:

- **Integrated Food System Framework**: The authors propose a framework that breaks down silos between agriculture, nutrition, and environmental sustainability. This integrated perspective allows for more effective adaptation and mitigation strategies that consider the entire food supply chain.
- **Sector-Specific Vulnerabilities**: The article discusses how different sectors within the food system are uniquely vulnerable to climate impacts, such as changing precipitation patterns and increased frequency of extreme weather events. Understanding these vulnerabilities is crucial for developing targeted responses that enhance resilience.
- **Policy Implications**: By adopting a global food system approach, policymakers can better align agricultural practices with climate goals. This includes promoting sustainable farming techniques, reducing food waste, and improving supply chain efficiencies to minimize greenhouse gas emissions.
- **Collaboration Across Disciplines**: The authors highlight the importance of collaboration among various stakeholders—farmers, scientists, policymakers, and consumers—to create adaptive strategies that address both climate change and food security.

Koks et al. (2019) assesses the macroeconomic impacts of future river flooding in Europe. Koks and colleagues examine the potential macroeconomic impacts of river flooding in Europe using sector-specific models that assess both direct and indirect economic losses. These are the key findings from their research:

- **Projected Economic Losses**: The study estimates significant increases in economic losses due to future flooding events, projecting an increase of up to 350% under various climate scenarios. This highlights the need for robust models that can account for changing flood dynamics influenced by climate change.
- **Direct vs. Indirect Losses**: The authors differentiate between direct losses (e.g., damage to property and infrastructure) and indirect losses (e.g., disruptions to supply chains and economic activity). They find that indirect losses may rise by 65% more than direct asset damages, underscoring the cascading effects of flooding on broader economic systems.
- **Sector-Specific Vulnerabilities**: The model used in this study allows for an analysis of how different sectors—such as agriculture, manufacturing, and services—are affected by flooding. This sector-specific analysis is vital for understanding where vulnerabilities lie and where investments in resilience are most needed.
- **Policy Recommendations**: The findings suggest that policymakers should prioritize flood risk management strategies that consider both

direct and indirect economic impacts. This includes investing in infrastructure improvements, early warning systems, and community preparedness initiatives.

Rosenzweig (2020)'s work emphasizes an integrated approach to food systems that considers interdependencies across sectors, while Koks (2019) provide insights into the macroeconomic implications of flooding through detailed sectoral analyses. Together, these studies highlight the necessity for tailored modeling approaches that can inform effective adaptation strategies and policy decisions in response to climate risks.

Case Study 2: The California Wine Industry's Response to Climate Change

Focus: Using Agricultural Models and Climate Projections to Assess the Impact of Climate Change on Winegrape Production and Develop Adaptation Strategies for a Major Agricultural Sector

The California wine industry, a significant contributor to the state's economy, faces substantial challenges due to climate change. This case study explores how winegrowers in California use agricultural models and climate projections to assess the impacts of climate change on winegrape production and develop adaptation strategies. It highlights the industry's efforts to identify resilient grape varieties, implement water conservation measures, and adapt to changing growing seasons.

Illustration: Methodology and Implementation of Adaptation Strategies

1. **Agricultural Models and Climate Projections**:
   Winegrowers in California use advanced agricultural models and climate projections to understand the potential impacts of climate change on temperature, precipitation, and growing seasons. These models help predict how climate variables will affect grapevine phenology, yield, and quality (Jones et al., 2005).
2. **Identifying Resilient Grape Varieties**:
   To adapt to warmer conditions, winegrowers are identifying grape varieties that are more resilient to heat and drought. Research collaborations with universities and agricultural institutions are crucial in developing and testing these varieties (Hannah et al., 2013).
3. **Implementing Water Conservation Measures**:
   Water conservation is critical for the California wine industry, especially given the increasing frequency and severity of droughts. Winegrowers are adopting various water-saving techniques, such as drip irrigation, soil moisture monitoring, and the use of cover crops to reduce evaporation and improve soil health (CSWA, 2025).

Discussion: Challenges and Opportunities in Adapting Agriculture to Climate Change

1. Challenges of Adapting Agriculture to a Changing Climate:
   Adapting agriculture to climate change involves several challenges (Moser & Ekstrom, 2010), including:
   - **Uncertainty**: Climate projections involve uncertainties, making it difficult to plan long-term adaptation strategies.
   - **Costs**: Implementing adaptation measures, such as new irrigation systems or planting new grape varieties, can be costly.
   - **Knowledge Gaps**: There is a need for continuous research to understand the complex interactions between climate variables and agricultural systems.
2. **Importance of Research and Innovation**:
   Research and innovation are crucial for developing climate-resilient crops and farming practices. Collaborative efforts between winegrowers, researchers, and agricultural institutions are essential for advancing knowledge and implementing effective adaptation strategies (CalCAN, 2017).
3. **Role of Industry Collaboration**:
   Industry collaboration is vital for sharing knowledge and best practices. Organizations like the California Sustainable Winegrowing Alliance (CSWA) play a key role in promoting sustainable practices and facilitating information exchange among winegrowers (CSWA, 2025).

Conclusion

The California wine industry's response to climate change demonstrates the importance of using agricultural models and climate projections to assess impacts and develop adaptation strategies. By identifying resilient grape varieties, implementing water conservation measures, and fostering industry collaboration, winegrowers are enhancing their resilience to climate change. This case study highlights the challenges of adapting agriculture to a changing climate, the critical role of research and innovation in developing climate-resilient crops and farming practices, and the importance of industry collaboration in sharing knowledge and best practices.

Understanding the methodologies and strategies employed by the California wine industry can provide valuable insights for other agricultural sectors facing similar climate challenges, ensuring a more resilient and sustainable future for agriculture.

3.4 Agent-Based Models (ABMs)

Agent-Based Models (ABMs) represent a more complex approach to physical risk modeling that simulates the behavior of individual agents (e.g., households, businesses, governments) within a system. ABMs capture the interactions and feedback loops between agents and their environment, allowing for a more nuanced understanding of how societies might adapt to climate change and how these adaptation choices might influence the overall risk landscape.

ABMs are particularly useful for exploring:

- **Behavioral Responses**: How individual choices, such as migration decisions, changes in consumption patterns, or adoption of new technologies, can influence the overall vulnerability of a system to climate change.
- **Cascading Effects**: How climate impacts in one sector (e.g., agriculture) can ripple through other sectors (e.g., food prices, migration patterns, economic activity), leading to complex and interconnected risks.

While ABMs are computationally demanding and require detailed data on agent behavior, they offer valuable insights into the social and economic dimensions of climate risks and can help to identify potential unintended consequences of adaptation measures.

In this foundational paper, Patt and Siebenhüner (2005) explore the application of Agent-Based Models (ABMs) in understanding and facilitating adaptation to climate change. The authors emphasize several key advantages of ABMs, compared with previously mentioned models:

- **Individual Agent Behavior**: ABMs simulate the actions and interactions of individual agents (e.g., households, businesses, governments) within a defined environment. This allows researchers to capture the complexity of human behavior and decision-making processes in response to climate risks.
- **Adaptation Dynamics**: The paper discusses how ABMs can model various adaptation strategies employed by agents, such as changes in agricultural practices, migration decisions, or investments in infrastructure. By simulating these behaviors, ABMs provide insights into how collective adaptation can emerge from individual actions.
- **Feedback Loops**: One of the strengths of ABMs is their ability to illustrate feedback loops between agents and their environment. For instance, the decisions made by one agent can influence the behavior of others, leading to cascading effects that can either enhance or undermine overall resilience to climate change.
- **Policy Implications**: The authors argue that ABMs can inform policy design by identifying effective adaptation strategies and potential unintended consequences of different interventions. By understanding how

agents might respond to policy measures, decision-makers can tailor their approaches to foster more effective climate adaptation.

In this recent work, Taberna (2024) delves into the use of ABMs specifically for modeling climate-resilient economies. Key contributions from this research include:

- **Complex Systems Approach**: Taberna emphasizes that economies are complex adaptive systems influenced by multiple interacting factors, including environmental changes and socioeconomic dynamics. ABMs are well-suited for capturing these complexities by allowing for heterogeneous agents with diverse behaviors and objectives.
- **Simulation of Economic Responses**: The research showcases how ABMs can simulate economic responses to climate impacts, such as shifts in labor markets or changes in consumption patterns due to extreme weather events. This capability helps in understanding how different sectors may adapt or suffer under varying climate scenarios.
- **Resilience Assessment**: The study highlights the potential of ABMs to assess resilience at both micro (individual agent) and macro (system-wide) levels. By analyzing how agents adapt over time, researchers can identify vulnerabilities within the economy and propose targeted interventions to enhance resilience.
- **Interdisciplinary Collaboration**: Taberna calls for interdisciplinary collaboration in developing ABMs that incorporate insights from economics, environmental science, and social sciences. Such collaboration is crucial for creating robust models that reflect real-world complexities and inform effective policy responses.

While Patt and Siebenhüner's work provides foundational insights into how ABMs can simulate adaptation strategies and inform policy design, Taberna's research expands on these concepts by applying them within the context of economic resilience. Together, they illustrate the potential of ABMs as powerful tools for understanding complex adaptive systems in the face of climate change challenges, ultimately aiding in the development of more effective adaptation strategies and policies.

Agent-Based Model: EIRIN

Figure 3 outlines the EIRIN (European Institute for Research in Industrial Economics) agent-based stock-flow consistent model. It's designed to simulate an open economy with interconnected agents and markets, enabling analysis of macroeconomic impacts, including the effects of policies and shocks.

Key Features:

- **Agent-Based**: The model is built around individual agents (households, firms, banks, government) who interact with each other and with markets

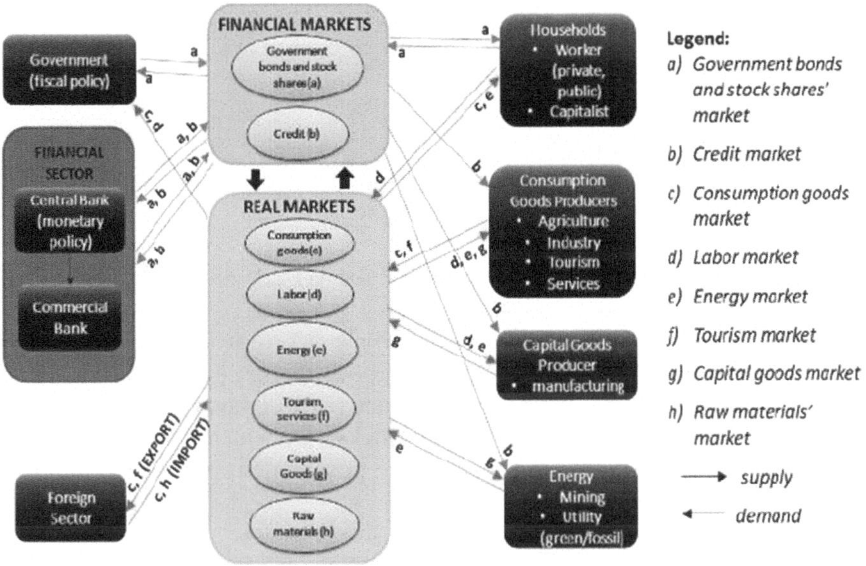

Fig. 3 Agents, sectors, and markets of the EIRIN economic model (*Source* World Bank and NGFS [2022])

according to specific behavioral rules. This allows for the modeling of complex system dynamics and feedback loops that are difficult to capture in traditional macroeconomic models.

- **Stock-Flow Consistent**: This means the model carefully tracks the stocks and flows of money and goods within the economy, ensuring that accounting identities are always satisfied. This makes it well-suited to analyzing financial issues and the impact of policies on balance sheets.
- **Open Economy**: The model includes a foreign sector, allowing for the simulation of international trade, capital flows, and exchange rate effects.

Structure and Interactions:
The model consists of two main market types:

- **Financial Markets (Light Blue)**: This block includes markets for government bonds and stocks, as well as credit. The government (fiscal policy) and the central bank (monetary policy) interact with these markets. Households (workers, capitalists), the foreign sector and the consumption goods producers also interact with financial markets.
- **Real Markets (Peach)**: This block includes markets for consumption goods, labor, energy, tourism services, capital goods, and raw materials. The various sectors of the economy (agriculture, industry, tourism, services, and capital goods manufacturing) interact with these markets,

as do households and the foreign sector. The energy sector (mining, utility—green/fossil) provides a supply of energy, while the other sectors exert demand.

Flow of Goods and Money:
The arrows in the diagram represent flows of either goods or money between the different agents and markets. For example:

- Households supply labor to the labor market (d) and receive wages in return.
- Firms demand labor (d) and raw materials (h) to produce goods, which they then supply to the consumption goods market (c).
- Households demand consumption goods (c) and pay for them.
- The government issues bonds and stocks (a), which are purchased by households and the foreign sector. The government uses this revenue to fund its spending.
- The central bank interacts with the credit market (b) to implement monetary policy.

Applications:
This type of agent-based model can be used to:

- **Assess Macroeconomic Impacts**: Simulate the effects of various policies (fiscal, monetary, financial) on economic variables like GDP, employment, inflation, and income distribution.
- **Analyze Transmission Channels**: Trace how shocks (e.g., climate change, pandemics) propagate through the economy, impacting different sectors and agents.
- **Test Policy Responses**: Evaluate the effectiveness of different policy interventions in mitigating the effects of shocks or achieving specific economic goals.

Example:
The description references the ability to analyze climate change impacts. A carbon tax policy could be modeled by adjusting the cost of energy for firms in the energy (green/fossil) sector and then observing the ripple effects on other sectors, consumption, investment, and government revenue.

By using an agent-based approach, the EIRIN model can capture the complex interplay of economic decisions, market dynamics, and policy interventions, providing a more realistic and nuanced understanding of the economy's behavior (Dunz, 2021; Monasterolo & Raberto, 2018).

4 Physical Climate Risk Assessment Process

World Bank and NGFS (2022) have proposed a six-step process for conducting a physical climate risk assessment. Each step builds upon the previous one, forming a structured approach to analyzing and understanding climate-related physical risks (Fig. 4).

1. **Define Needs and Objectives**: The first step is to clearly articulate the purpose of the risk assessment. What questions are you trying to answer? What decisions will this assessment inform? Defining clear objectives will guide the entire process and ensure that the assessment is relevant and useful. This might involve specifying the geographic area, timeframe, and types of hazards to be considered. For example, the objective might be to assess the risk of flooding to a coastal city's infrastructure over the next 50 years.
2. **Identify Available Data and Resources**: This step involves gathering all relevant data related to climate hazards, exposure, and vulnerability for the specified location and time horizon. It also includes assessing the resources available to conduct the analysis, such as expertise, software, and financial support. Examples of data include historical climate data, climate projections, maps of infrastructure and population density, and socioeconomic data on community vulnerability. Identifying data gaps is critical.
3. **Define the Scope and Approach**: With the objectives and data in hand, the next step is to define the specific scope and methodology of the assessment. This includes selecting the appropriate climate scenarios, risk assessment methods (e.g., qualitative vs. quantitative), and metrics for measuring risk (e.g., expected annual damage, number of people affected). The scope might focus on specific sectors (e.g., infrastructure, agriculture), specific hazards (e.g., flooding, heatwaves), or a combination of both. The specific risks addressed must be determined in this step.
4. **Generate the Scenarios**: This step involves creating a set of plausible future climate scenarios based on the chosen climate projections (e.g., RCPs) and downscaling techniques. These scenarios provide a range of potential future conditions (e.g., temperature, precipitation, sea level)

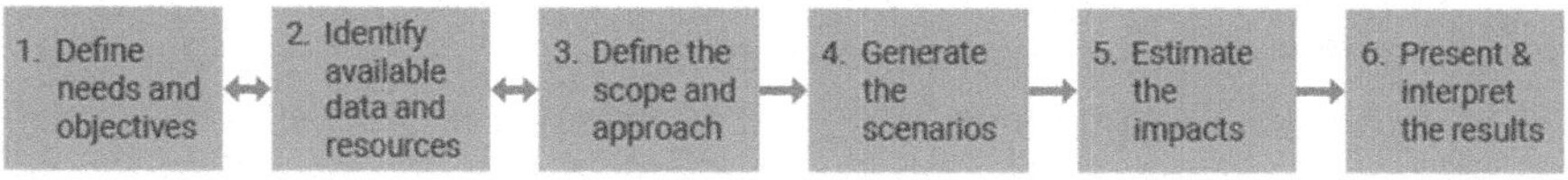

Fig. 4 Step-by-step process for physical climate risk assessment (*Source* UNEP FI [2023], World Bank)

that will be used to assess risks. Different emission scenarios or combinations of socioeconomic and physical climate pathways will likely be considered to account for uncertainty.

5. **Estimate the Impacts**: Using the generated scenarios, this step involves evaluating the potential impacts of climate change on the assets, systems, or populations within the defined scope. This can involve quantitative modeling (e.g., using CAT models, infrastructure models), qualitative assessments (e.g., expert judgment), or a combination of both. The output of this stage are measurable estimations of the potential impacts of each scenario, like expected economic losses or the number of people displaced.
6. **Present and Interpret the Results**: The final step is to present the results of the risk assessment in a clear and accessible way and to interpret their implications for decision-making. This might involve creating maps, charts, and reports that communicate the findings to stakeholders and decision-makers. It's also crucial to discuss the limitations and uncertainties associated with the assessment. Presenting a range of potential outcomes with associated probabilities (rather than a single deterministic prediction) is often preferred. The interpretations should directly link back to the objectives defined in Step 1 and should highlight opportunities for adaptation and mitigation.

4.1 Define Needs and Objectives

The World Bank and NGFS (2022) Physical Risk Assessment report emphasizes the crucial importance of the first step in conducting a climate risk assessment—defining needs and objectives. This step sets the foundation for the entire process, ensuring that the assessment is focused, relevant, and ultimately useful for decision-making. Here's a summary of the key aspects highlighted in the report concerning this initial step:

- **Understanding the Context**: Before diving into data collection and modeling, it's essential to grasp the specific context of the assessment. This includes understanding the country or region's unique climate risks, its economic structure, and the institutional capacity for risk management. For EMDEs (Emerging Markets and Developing Economies), this is particularly critical, as they often face distinct challenges related to data availability, technical expertise, and financial resources.
- **Stakeholder Engagement**: Early and continuous engagement with stakeholders is crucial. This includes not only government agencies (e.g., central banks, ministries) but also private sector actors (e.g., banks, insurers), civil society organizations, and local communities. Stakeholder input helps to ensure that the assessment addresses relevant needs and concerns and that the results are useful for decision-making across

different sectors. A questionnaire or interviews can be effective tools for gathering input and identifying priorities.

- **Identifying Information Gaps**: This step also involves assessing existing knowledge and identifying information gaps. What is already known about climate risks in the region? What data and information are lacking? Understanding these gaps helps to prioritize data collection efforts and ensures that the assessment adds value by providing new insights.
- **Defining Specific Objectives**: The objectives of the assessment should be clearly defined and measurable. Examples include:
  - Raising awareness of climate-related financial risks among stakeholders.
  - Identifying the most vulnerable sectors, regions, and populations.
  - Assessing the potential macroeconomic impacts of climate change.
  - Informing the development of climate adaptation and risk management strategies.
  - Supporting the design of climate-resilient financial products and services.
- **Iterative Approach**: The report highlights that defining needs and objectives should be an iterative process. Initial objectives may need to be revised as new data and information become available or as stakeholder priorities evolve. Flexibility is key to ensuring the assessment remains relevant and useful throughout the process. For instance, the initial scope might be narrowed if data limitations prevent a comprehensive analysis.
- **Examples from EMDEs**: The report provides examples of how this step has been approached in different EMDE contexts. In some cases, a qualitative assessment has been conducted as a first step due to data constraints, focusing on raising awareness and identifying priority areas for future quantitative assessments.

By carefully defining needs and objectives in this initial step, climate risk assessments can provide valuable insights to inform decision-making, enhance resilience, and support the transition to a more sustainable future. A well-defined first step sets the stage for a more robust, effective, and impactful assessment.

4.2 *Identify Available Data and Resources*

Step 2 is a critical stage in the physical climate risk assessment process, especially for emerging markets and developing economies (EMDEs) that often face data constraints. The Antoine (2022) report emphasizes a practical approach, leveraging existing resources and acknowledging limitations.

- **Data Needs**: Different data types are required to assess the various dimensions of physical climate risk. These include:
  - **Hazard data**: Information on the historical and projected frequency, intensity, and spatial distribution of climate hazards (e.g., floods, droughts, heatwaves).
  - **Exposure data**: Data on the location and value of assets exposed to these hazards (e.g., infrastructure, buildings, agricultural land, populations).
  - **Vulnerability data**: Information on the susceptibility of these assets and populations to harm from the hazards (e.g., building codes, flood defenses, socioeconomic factors).
  - **Financial and macroeconomic data**: Data needed to assess the potential economic and financial impacts of physical climate risks (e.g., GDP, national accounts, loan portfolios).
- **Data Sources and Tools**: The report highlights several publicly available data sources and tools that can be useful for physical climate risk assessments, particularly in EMDEs. These include:
  - **Global open-source hazard datasets and tools**: Examples include INFORM Risk Index, Aqueduct Floods, ThinkHazard!, and CLIMADA. These resources often provide global coverage and can be a valuable starting point, although their resolution and applicability may vary by region and peril.
  - **Publicly available risk metric datasets**: Resources like the Aqueduct Water Risk Atlas and the Climate Impact Explorer offer pre-calculated risk metrics combining hazard, exposure, and vulnerability. While convenient, these datasets may have limitations in terms of granularity and user-defined inputs.
  - **Academic literature and in-country expertise**: Research papers and local experts can provide valuable insights into specific regional climate risks and data availability.
- **Data Quality and Granularity**: Assessing data quality and granularity is essential. Factors to consider include:
  - **Coverage**: Does the data cover the relevant geographic area, time period, and sectors?
  - **Resolution**: Is the spatial and temporal resolution of the data sufficient for the assessment's objectives? For example, assessing flood risk requires high-resolution elevation data.
  - **Biases and anomalies**: Are there any known biases or anomalies in the data that could affect the results?
  - **Validation**: Has the data been validated against observations or other independent sources?

- **Data Gaps and Constraints**: The report acknowledges that data gaps are a common challenge in EMDEs. Strategies for addressing these gaps include:
  - **Using proxy data**: If direct data is unavailable, proxy data (e.g., satellite imagery, population density) can be used to estimate exposure or vulnerability.
  - **Leveraging statistical downscaling and bias correction**: Techniques to translate coarse-resolution global climate projections into finer-scale regional projections.
  - **Employing qualitative assessments**: When quantitative data is limited, qualitative methods like expert elicitation can be used to gain insights into potential risks.
  - **Building local capacity**: Investing in data collection and management infrastructure in EMDEs is crucial for long-term improvement in data availability and quality.
- **Prioritizing Data**: Given potential data limitations, prioritization is key. Focus on collecting the most relevant and impactful data first, based on the assessment's objectives and the specific risks being considered.
- **Iterative Process**: The data identification process is iterative. Initial data collection efforts may reveal new information gaps or limitations, requiring further investigation or adjustments to the scope and approach of the assessment.

The following list outlines some of the open-source hazard datasets and tools for acute physical climate risk assessment, as suggested by World Bank and NGFS (2022):

1. **INFORM Risk Index**: Combines hazard and exposure data. It uses the Global Human Settlement Layer (GHS-POP) for population data and various sources for hazard characterization (specifics not detailed in this table).
2. **Aqueduct Floods**: Uses flood maps from global hydrological models participating in the Inter-Sectoral Impact Model Intercomparison Project (ISIMIP2b).
3. **Notre Dame GAIN Index**: The University of Notre Dame's Global Adaptation Initiative (ND-GAIN) focuses on assisting governments and corporations in addressing climate change challenges through prioritizing climate adaptation strategies. It offers valuable tools, including the ND-GAIN Country Index and Global Urban Climate Assessment, which utilize extensive data to evaluate the vulnerability and readiness of various countries and urban areas. By delivering actionable insights, ND-GAIN aims to reduce risks associated with climate extremes and enhance adaptive capacity globally.

4. **ThinkHazard!**: Employs several underlying sources depending on the hazard:
    - **Storm surge**: Global Tide and Surge Reanalysis (GTSR) dataset (Muis et al., 2016)
    - **Cyclone**: Global Archive of Reanalysis and Forecast (GAR) 2015 cyclone wind intensity maps
    - **River flood**: GAR 2015 flood hazard maps.
    - **Wildfire**: 30-year fire weather climatology from CSIRO (Commonwealth Scientific and Industrial Research Organisation)
    - **Extreme heat**: Wet Bulb Globe Temperature dataset
    - **Landslide**: The Global Landslide Hazard Map
    - **Water scarcity**: European Space Agency's Metop AVHRR satellite data (Carrão et al., 2016); Global Precipitation Climatology Centre (GPCC) Full Data Reanalysis, version 6.0.
5. **Climate Impact Explorer**: Relies on several sources depending on the hazard:
    - **River flood**: Flood maps from hydrological models participating in ISIMIP2b.
    - **Wildfire**: No specific source indicated, likely model-based.
    - **Heat wave**: No specific source given, likely model-based or derived from temperature projections.
    - **Precipitation**: Monthly maximum consecutive 5-day precipitation data from Sillmann et al. (2013).
6. **FAO GIEWS Earth Observation**: Utilizes various satellite-based and ground-based data sources for agricultural drought monitoring (specifics not detailed in this table).
7. **UNCCD Drought Risk Assessment Visualization Tool**: Utilizes Global Precipitation Climatology Centre (GPCC) Full Data Reanalysis, version 6.0, for drought characterization.

By taking a practical and flexible approach to data identification and resource mobilization, while acknowledging data limitations, central banks and supervisors in EMDEs can conduct meaningful physical climate risk assessments that inform decision-making and strengthen financial resilience.

4.3 Define the Scope and Approach

Step 3, "Define the scope and approach," is where the practical considerations of the physical climate risk assessment take shape. Building upon the defined needs and objectives (Step 1) and the identified data and resources (Step 2), this step involves making key decisions about the focus, methodologies, and level of detail of the assessment. Here's a breakdown of the key aspects:

- **Tailoring the Scope**: There's no one-size-fits-all approach. The scope needs to be tailored to the specific context, objectives, and data availability. Key aspects of scope definition include:
  - **Geographic area**: Specify the region or area of interest. This could range from a national assessment to a focus on specific cities, river basins, or coastal zones.
  - **Time horizon**: Define the timeframe for the assessment. Short-term (e.g., 5–10 years), medium-term (e.g., 20–30 years), and long-term (e.g., to 2100) horizons may be relevant depending on the objectives.
  - **Perils**: Select the specific climate hazards to be assessed, based on the region's vulnerability and data availability. This could include floods, droughts, heatwaves, sea-level rise, wildfires, or storms.
  - **Sectors**: Identify the sectors to be included in the assessment. This could range from a broad analysis covering multiple sectors (e.g., agriculture, infrastructure, finance) to a more focused assessment of a specific sector (e.g., the impact of drought on agriculture).
- **Choosing the Approach**: The approach should align with the scope, objectives, and data/resource constraints. Key decisions include:
  - **Qualitative vs. Quantitative**: If data is limited or the objective is primarily awareness-raising, a qualitative approach might be sufficient. This could involve expert elicitation, literature reviews, or scenario narratives. As data and capacity improve, the assessment can be progressively refined to incorporate more quantitative methods.
  - **Level of Sophistication**: The level of model complexity and analytical detail should be appropriate for the available data and resources. Simpler methods might be more suitable in data-scarce environments, while more sophisticated models can be employed when data is readily available.
  - **Peril- and Sector-Specific Methodologies**: A generic approach may not always be ideal. In some cases, using peril-specific (e.g., flood risk models) or sector-specific (e.g., agricultural impact models) methodologies can provide more accurate and relevant insights.
- **Considering Systemic Impacts**: When appropriate, the assessment should consider:
  - **Systemic risks**: Large-scale disruptions to entire economic sectors or systems.
  - **Distributional impacts**: Uneven distribution of impacts across different regions, sectors, or populations.
  - **Compound impacts**: The combined effects of multiple hazards or the interplay of climate change with other risks (e.g., pandemics, economic crises).

- **Tailoring Scenarios**: Climate scenarios (generated in Step 4) need to be tailored to the specific scope of the assessment. This includes selecting appropriate:
  - **RCPs (Representative Concentration Pathways)**: These represent different greenhouse gas emission trajectories.
  - **SSPs (Shared Socioeconomic Pathways)**: Explore different narratives of future socioeconomic development.
  - **Time horizons and return periods**: Aligned with the assessment's timeframe and the need to assess both chronic and acute risks.
- **Iterative Refinement**: Defining the scope and approach is not a one-time activity. It's an iterative process that may require adjustments as new data becomes available, understanding of risks evolves, or stakeholder priorities change.

By carefully defining the scope and approach in this step, ensuring it aligns with the needs and objectives, available data and resources, and specific characteristics of the region or sector, climate risk assessments can provide more valuable and targeted insights, leading to better risk management and adaptation decisions.

4.4 *Generate Climate Scenarios*

Step 4, "Generate the scenarios," is crucial for translating climate projections into a format suitable for assessing physical climate risks. It involves creating plausible representations of future climate conditions that can be used to evaluate potential impacts. The World Bank and NGFS (2022) report emphasizes the importance of using scenarios that are not just scientifically sound but also relevant to the specific needs of the risk assessment and the decision-making context. Key considerations for generating scenarios, as outlined in the report, include:

- **Scenario Characteristics**: Effective scenarios should be:
  - **Plausible**: Representing realistic potential futures based on current understanding of the climate system and socioeconomic trends.
  - **Distinctive**: Exploring a range of different possible outcomes, including both optimistic and pessimistic scenarios, to capture uncertainty and avoid tunnel vision.
  - **Consistent**: Internally coherent and aligned with underlying assumptions about emissions pathways, socioeconomic development, and technological change.
  - **Relevant**: Providing information that is useful for answering the specific questions posed by the risk assessment and informing decision-making.

  - **Challenging**: Pushing the boundaries of current thinking and exploring potential "tail risks" or low-probability, high-impact events that could have significant consequences.

- **Translating Climate Projections**: Raw climate model output is often not directly usable for risk assessment. Scenarios need to translate this output into peril-specific information that is relevant for the region and sector of interest. This might involve:
  - **Downscaling**: Using techniques to translate coarse-resolution global climate projections into finer-scale regional or local projections.
  - **Bias correction**: Adjusting model outputs to account for known biases or systematic errors.
  - **Generating hazard indicators**: Converting climate variables (e.g., temperature, precipitation) into specific hazard indicators (e.g., flood depths, drought indices, heatwave duration) that are more relevant for assessing impacts.

- **Minimum Requirements**: The report recommends developing at least two scenarios:
  - **Baseline scenario**: Represents current conditions or a historical baseline. This allows for comparison with future scenarios and helps to understand the incremental risk due to climate change.
  - **Alternative scenario(s)**: Integrate climate change projections, exploring potential future changes in hazards. Multiple alternative scenarios, representing different levels of warming or socioeconomic development pathways (SSPs), can be used to capture uncertainty.

- **Key Inputs and Considerations**:
  - **Climate models (GCMs and RCMs)**: Provide projections of future climate change under different emission scenarios (RCPs).
  - **Socioeconomic factors (SSPs)**: Influence both future emissions and vulnerability to climate change.
  - **Time horizons and return periods**: The length of time into the future the analysis considers (e.g., 2030, 2050, 2100) and how often different magnitude events happen (e.g., 1 in 10 year flood event). Longer time horizons and rare, high-impact events (low-probability, high-consequence scenarios) are essential for capturing long-term risks.
  - **Perils**: The specific hazards being assessed.
  - **Regional and local context**: Specific climate vulnerabilities, exposure characteristics, and adaptation capacity of the area.

- **Examples and Tools**: The report provides examples of scenario generation approaches used in different risk assessments, including those

conducted in Morocco, Indonesia, and the Philippines. It also highlights the use of various tools, including the NGFS scenarios database and open-source catastrophe models like CLIMADA.
- **Addressing Uncertainty**: Given the inherent uncertainties in climate projections, using a range of scenarios is essential. This allows for exploring different possible futures and understanding the sensitivity of results to different assumptions.

By carefully considering these factors and using a structured approach to scenario generation, climate risk assessments can provide more robust and insightful information for decision-making, supporting adaptation planning and building resilience to the potential impacts of climate change.

4.5 *Estimate the Impacts*

Step 5, "Estimate the impacts," is where the potential consequences of climate change are quantified. This step uses the climate scenarios generated in Step 4 to assess how different hazards might affect assets, systems, or populations within the defined scope. Key aspects of this step include:

- **Direct and Indirect Impacts**: The assessment should consider both:
  - **Direct impacts (first-order damages)**: The immediate physical consequences of a hazard event, such as damage to buildings, infrastructure, and crops. These are typically estimated using catastrophe models or other quantitative methods.
  - **Indirect impacts (second-order damages)**: The broader economic, social, and financial consequences that cascade from the direct impacts. These can include disruptions to supply chains, business interruption, displacement of populations, and impacts on public health. Macroeconomic models can be particularly useful for assessing these broader consequences.
- **Methods for Estimating Impacts**: A range of methods can be used, depending on the data availability, resources, and the specific objectives of the assessment. These include:
  - **Catastrophe (CAT) models**: Sophisticated computer models that estimate potential losses from natural disasters. They combine hazard data with information on exposure and vulnerability to produce probabilistic loss estimates. While valuable, CAT models can be data-intensive and may not be readily available for all perils or regions in EMDEs.
  - **Financial and economic models**: Used to assess the broader economic and financial impacts of physical climate risks. These

  models can range from simple sectoral impact assessments to complex macroeconomic models.
  - **Sector-specific models**: Designed to evaluate the impacts of climate change on specific sectors, such as agriculture, infrastructure, or tourism.
  - **Qualitative methods**: When quantitative data is scarce, expert elicitation, literature reviews, or case studies can provide valuable insights into potential impacts.

- **Transmission Channels**: Analyzing how climate impacts transmit through the economy and financial system is crucial for understanding the full range of potential consequences. Key transmission channels include:

  - **Direct damage to assets and infrastructure**: Leads to economic losses and disruptions to services.
  - **Impacts on productivity and economic activity**: Reduced agricultural yields, disruptions to businesses, and health impacts can all affect economic output.
  - **Impacts on public finances**: Increased government spending on disaster relief and reconstruction, reduced tax revenue, and increased debt can strain public finances.
  - **Impacts on financial stability**: Losses to banks and insurers, changes in asset valuations, and increased financial distress can affect the stability of the financial system.

- **Scenarios and Time Horizons**: Impacts should be estimated for each climate scenario developed in Step 4. This allows for comparing the potential consequences of different emission pathways and adaptation strategies. Both short-term and long-term impacts should be considered, as the timing of climate change impacts can be crucial for decision-making.
- **Data and Resource Constraints**: The report acknowledges that data limitations in EMDEs can pose challenges for estimating impacts. Strategies for addressing these limitations include:

  - **Using proxy data and making simplifying assumptions.**
  - **Focusing on order-of-magnitude estimates rather than precise quantification.**
  - **Prioritizing the assessment of the most critical sectors and perils.**
  - **Conducting sensitivity analyses to understand the influence of data gaps and uncertainties on results.**

- **Communicating Uncertainties**: Clearly communicating the uncertainties associated with the impact estimates is essential. This can involve

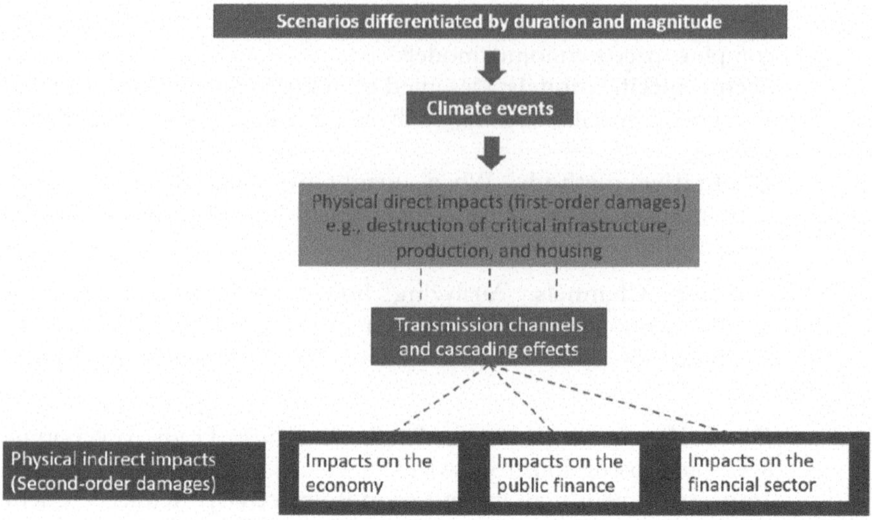

Fig. 5 Estimate the climate event impacts (*Source* World Bank and NGFS [2022])

using ranges, confidence intervals, or qualitative descriptions of uncertainty.

Figure 5 from the World Bank and NGFS (2022) illustrates the direct and indirect impacts of extreme weather events, highlighting how initial physical damage can cascade through various channels to affect the broader economy and financial system. The framework emphasizes the importance of looking beyond immediate, localized damage to understand the full scope of climate-related risks.

By using a combination of quantitative and qualitative methods, and by explicitly addressing data limitations and uncertainties, climate risk assessments can provide valuable insights into the potential impacts of climate change, even in data-scarce environments. This information can then be used to inform adaptation planning, risk management, and policy development.

4.6 *Present and Interpret the Results*

Step 6 is the crucial final step in a physical climate risk assessment. It's not enough to simply generate numbers; the results must be effectively communicated to stakeholders and decision-makers to inform action. The NGFS report stresses the importance of clear, accessible communication that acknowledges uncertainties and limitations, particularly in the context of EMDEs. Here's a breakdown of the key aspects of this step:

- **Target Audience**: Consider the specific needs and level of understanding of the target audience. Different stakeholders will have different priorities and levels of technical expertise. Tailor the presentation and interpretation accordingly. This may include policymakers, financial regulators, investors, business leaders, and the general public.
- **Key Messages**: Focus on the most relevant and impactful findings. What are the key takeaways for decision-making? What are the most significant risks and opportunities? Prioritize clarity and conciseness, avoiding technical jargon and using plain language whenever possible.
- **Visualizations**: Use charts, graphs, maps, and other visuals to effectively communicate complex information. Visualizations can make the results more engaging and easier to understand, particularly for non-technical audiences. For example, maps showing areas at high risk of flooding or drought can be powerful tools for communicating the spatial distribution of climate risks.
- **Order of Magnitude and Trends**: In EMDEs, where data limitations and uncertainties can be substantial, it's often more appropriate to focus on the order of magnitude of the estimated impacts and on identifying key trends rather than on precise quantification. Clearly communicate the level of confidence in the results and avoid presenting overly precise estimates that might be misleading.
- **Uncertainties and Limitations**: Transparency is paramount. Openly acknowledge the limitations of the assessment, including data gaps, model uncertainties, and assumptions made. Explain how these uncertainties might affect the results and discuss the implications for decision-making. Presenting a range of potential outcomes, rather than a single deterministic prediction, is a good practice for conveying uncertainty.
- **Sensitivity Analysis**: If conducted, present the results of sensitivity analyses. This shows how the results change when key input parameters are varied, providing insights into the robustness of the findings and the influence of uncertainties.
- **Recommendations and Implications**: Link the results back to the needs and objectives defined in Step 1. What are the implications for policy development, risk management, investment decisions, or adaptation planning? Offer concrete recommendations for action, based on the assessment's findings. These recommendations should be tailored to the specific context and consider the capacity of different stakeholders to implement them.
- **Engagement and Dialogue**: Presenting the results is not a one-way communication exercise. Facilitate dialogue with stakeholders to discuss the findings, address their questions and concerns, and ensure that the results are understood and used effectively. This can involve workshops, webinars, or other forms of interactive communication. Ongoing engagement can build trust, foster collaboration, and ensure that the assessment leads to meaningful action.

By presenting and interpreting the results in a clear, transparent, and accessible way, climate risk assessments can empower stakeholders to make informed decisions, strengthen financial resilience, and promote effective adaptation to the growing challenges of a changing climate.

5 Challenges and Opportunities in Physical Risk Modeling

While physical risk modeling is a rapidly advancing field, it faces several challenges that must be addressed to enhance its accuracy, relevance, and usefulness for decision-making. However, these challenges also present opportunities for innovation and collaboration, leading to more sophisticated and impactful models. Deloitte (2023) highlights the key challenges in physical risk modeling include data availability, granularity, and the lack of standardization.

5.1 Data Gaps and Uncertainties

One of the biggest challenges in physical risk modeling is the lack of comprehensive, high-quality data on climate hazards, asset exposures, and vulnerabilities. This data gap is particularly acute in developing countries, where resources for data collection and monitoring are often limited.

Key data gaps include the following:

- **Hazard Data**: Accurate and high-resolution data on the frequency, intensity, and spatial distribution of climate hazards, such as sea-level rise, extreme precipitation events, and heat waves, is essential for reliable risk assessments. However, such data is often lacking, particularly for localized projections.
- **Exposure Data**: Detailed information on the location and value of assets at risk, such as infrastructure, buildings, agricultural lands, and population centers, is crucial for quantifying potential losses. However, obtaining this data can be challenging, especially for assets that are privately owned or located in informal settlements.
- **Vulnerability Data**: Understanding how different assets and populations are likely to be affected by specific hazards requires detailed vulnerability data. This includes information on building construction types, elevation above sea level, the presence of natural protective barriers, and the adaptive capacity of communities.

Modelers employ several strategies to address data gaps:

- **Assumptions and Expert Judgment**: When data is unavailable, modelers may rely on assumptions or expert judgment to estimate hazard parameters, exposure levels, or vulnerability factors.

- **Proxy Data**: In some cases, modelers use proxy data, such as satellite imagery or population density maps, to infer information about exposure or vulnerability.
- **Sensitivity Analysis**: Modelers conduct sensitivity analysis to assess how model outputs change when key input parameters are varied, providing insights into the impact of data gaps and uncertainties on the results.

The paper by Otto et al. (2020) highlights the significant challenges in understanding how climate change is influencing extreme weather events in lower-income countries. These challenges are particularly acute when it comes to attributing the role of climate change in specific high-impact events, such as droughts, floods, and tropical cyclones that have caused major loss of life and economic damages in developing regions. The authors identify several key reasons why event attribution studies have been lacking for the most deadly extreme weather events:

1. **Lack of Historical Observations**: Many regions, especially in the developing world, lack long-term, high-quality observational data on weather and climate variables. This makes it difficult to quantify the severity of an event and put it in the context of the historical record.
2. **Inadequate Model Evaluation**: Without sufficient observational data, it is challenging to thoroughly evaluate climate models to ensure they reliably represent the real-world climate in a given region. Models often struggle to capture important tropical climate processes.
3. **Biases in Climate Models**: Most climate models are developed and tuned in the Global North, leading to biases in their representation of tropical climates and weather phenomena in the developing world.
4. **Lack of Local Expertise**: There is a significant shortage of scientists with the necessary skills and knowledge to conduct attribution studies in many lower-income countries. Studies by foreign researchers may lack the proper framing and context.

These factors, combined with the inherent uncertainties in attributing complex weather events to climate change, result in a systematic bias in attribution research toward regions with better data availability and modeling capabilities—often the wealthier nations in the Global North. The authors argue that this mismatch between where attribution studies are conducted and where the most devastating impacts occur is problematic from a climate justice perspective. It means that for the places that need the most urgent information on how climate change is altering extreme weather risks, robust attribution assessments are often lacking. To address these challenges, Otto et al. propose several strategies:

- Utilizing alternative data sources like satellite observations and reanalysis products to supplement sparse in-situ observations
- Employing storyline approaches that explore plausible scenarios of how climate change may have influenced an event, even without a full probabilistic attribution
- Developing standardized protocols for attribution studies to improve transparency and robustness
- Prioritizing efforts to rescue historical weather data and make it publicly available
- Building capacity of local researchers in the developing world to conduct attribution studies
- Integrating assessments of vulnerability and exposure alongside the hazard component when framing attribution questions

The authors emphasize that while these challenges are significant, it is crucial to find ways to provide useful information on the changing risks of extreme weather in the most vulnerable regions. Focusing attribution research solely on the Global North would be a disservice to those most impacted by climate change. Innovative approaches and concerted efforts are needed to fill these critical data and knowledge gaps.

5.2 Communicating Risk

Effectively communicating physical risk assessments is crucial for translating model outputs into actionable insights and informing decision-making. However, communicating complex climate risk information to diverse audiences, including policymakers, business leaders, and the public, presents significant challenges.

Key Challenges:

- **Technical Jargon**: Climate models often rely on specialized terminology and complex statistical concepts that can be difficult for non-experts to understand.
- **Uncertainty and Probabilities**: Climate projections and risk assessments involve inherent uncertainties, which need to be communicated clearly without undermining the credibility of the information.
- **Psychological Barriers**: People often struggle to grasp the magnitude and immediacy of climate risks, particularly if the impacts are perceived as distant in time or space.

Effective Risk Communication Strategies:

- **Clear and Concise Language**: Avoid technical jargon and use plain language that is accessible to a broad audience.

- **Visualizations and Maps**: Use maps, charts, graphs, and other visual aids to present complex information in a clear and engaging way.
- **Storytelling and Narrative**: Frame risk assessments within relatable stories or narratives that connect with people's values and experiences.
- **Tailored Communication**: Adapt communication styles and messages to different audiences, considering their level of understanding, interests, and concerns.

Sutton (2019) argues for a more robust integration of risk assessment into climate science, particularly within the framework of the Intergovernmental Panel on Climate Change (IPCC) assessments. The author emphasizes that effective communication of climate risks is essential for informing decision-making in government, business, and civil society. Key points from the article include:

- **Risk Assessment as a Central Concern**: Sutton posits that climate change should be viewed primarily as a problem of risk assessment and management. This perspective shifts the focus from merely projecting future climate scenarios to understanding the implications of those scenarios for human and ecological systems.
- **Principles of Risk Assessment**: The article outlines fundamental principles of risk assessment, which include identifying possible events, their likelihood, and potential impacts. Sutton emphasizes that a comprehensive risk assessment must consider both likelihood and impact together, rather than sequentially.
- **Siloing of Expertise**: One of the major challenges identified is the "siloing" of expertise within the IPCC's working groups. This separation has led to insufficient integration of knowledge across disciplines, particularly between physical climate science (Working Group I) and impact assessments (Working Group II). Sutton argues that this siloing has resulted in a neglect of risk assessment needs in climate science.
- **High-Impact, Low-Likelihood Events**: The author highlights the importance of considering high-impact but low-likelihood events in risk assessments. Decision-makers are often more concerned with understanding the worst-case scenarios that could have catastrophic consequences, even if they are deemed unlikely.
- **Need for Scenarios**: Sutton advocates for the development of climate scenarios that can inform risk assessments. Unlike traditional projections that focus on likelihoods, these scenarios should explore a range of plausible futures and their potential impacts. This approach would provide decision-makers with valuable insights into possible outcomes under different climate conditions.

- **Quantifying Current Risks**: The article calls for more attention to quantifying current risks associated with extreme weather events. Understanding how climate change is altering the likelihood and severity of these events is crucial for effective contingency planning and resilience building.
- **Collaboration Across Disciplines**: Finally, Sutton stresses the need for collaboration between physical climate scientists and other disciplines (e.g., social sciences, economics) to develop comprehensive risk assessments that address both the scientific and societal dimensions of climate change.

Sutton's article underscores the critical need for climate science to prioritize risk assessment in its research and communication efforts. By integrating risk assessment principles into climate modeling and scenario development, scientists can provide more relevant information to decision-makers, ultimately enhancing society's ability to prepare for and respond to climate-related risks. Effective communication strategies that convey complex risk information in accessible ways are essential for fostering informed decision-making and promoting resilience in the face of climate change challenges.

5.3 Advancements in Modeling Techniques

The field of physical risk modeling is constantly evolving, driven by advances in technology, data availability, and our understanding of climate change. These advancements are leading to more sophisticated and accurate models that can better capture the complexity of climate risks.

Key Advancements:

- **Artificial Intelligence (AI) and Machine Learning (ML)**: AI and ML algorithms are being used to analyze vast datasets, identify patterns in climate data, and improve the accuracy of risk predictions.
- **High-Performance Computing (HPC)**: HPC allows modelers to run complex climate simulations and risk assessments at higher resolutions and with greater speed, enabling more detailed and localized projections.
- **Integration of Multiple Models**: Modelers are increasingly using ensembles of multiple climate models and risk assessment frameworks to account for model uncertainties and provide a more robust assessment of potential impacts.

Reichstein (2019) examines deep learning and process understanding for data-driven Earth system science. In this influential paper, Reichstein and colleagues explore the integration of deep learning techniques into Earth system modeling, highlighting how these advancements can enhance our understanding of complex climate processes. Key points from the article include:

- **Hybrid Modeling Approaches**: The authors propose a hybrid modeling framework that combines traditional mechanistic models with machine learning techniques. This approach aims to leverage the strengths of both methods—mechanistic models provide a solid physical basis, while machine learning can identify patterns and relationships within large datasets that may not be easily captured by traditional models.
- **Data-Driven Insights**: By utilizing vast amounts of observational data, deep learning algorithms can extract spatiotemporal features that help improve model accuracy. This capability is particularly valuable in understanding nonlinear processes in the Earth system, such as carbon cycling and climate feedback mechanisms.
- **Parameterization Improvements**: The paper discusses how deep learning can enhance parameterization schemes in climate models. By learning from global observations, models can adapt their parameters dynamically to reflect real-world conditions better, leading to improved predictions of climate variables.
- **Challenges and Opportunities**: While the integration of deep learning into Earth system science presents exciting opportunities, the authors also acknowledge challenges such as data quality, model interpretability, and the need for interdisciplinary collaboration to ensure effective implementation.

Schneider et al. (2017) proposes a blueprint for Earth system models that learn from observations and targeted high-resolution simulations. In this article, Schneider et al. (2017) present a forward-looking vision for the next generation of Earth system models (ESMs), termed "Earth System Modeling 2.0." The authors outline several key advancements:

- **Learning from Observations**: The blueprint emphasizes the importance of developing ESMs that can learn from observational data rather than relying solely on predefined parameterizations. This approach aims to create more adaptive models that can adjust based on real-time data inputs.
- **High-Resolution Simulations**: The authors advocate for targeted high-resolution simulations that capture local processes more accurately. By integrating these simulations into the modeling framework, researchers can better understand regional climate impacts and improve predictive capabilities.
- **Interdisciplinary Integration**: Schneider et al. (2017) stress the need for collaboration across disciplines—combining insights from climate

science, machine learning, and computational modeling—to develop robust ESMs that address complex climate challenges.
- **Framework for Implementation**: The article provides a detailed framework for implementing these advancements in ESMs, including guidelines for model development, testing, and validation against observational data.

Both Reichstein (2019) and Schneider et al. (2017) highlight significant advancements in modeling techniques that leverage machine learning and observational data to enhance our understanding of Earth systems. The integration of deep learning into traditional modeling frameworks allows for improved parameterization and adaptability to changing conditions, while the vision for Earth System Modeling 2.0 emphasizes the importance of interdisciplinary collaboration and high-resolution simulations. Together, these advancements represent a transformative shift in how climate models are developed and utilized, ultimately leading to more accurate predictions and informed decision-making in response to climate change challenges.

These advancements are creating exciting opportunities to enhance the effectiveness of physical risk modeling, enabling more informed decision-making and supporting efforts to build a more climate-resilient future.

6 Conclusion: From Models to Action

Physical risk modeling is not an end in itself, it's a means to an end. The ultimate goal is to translate the insights gained from these models into concrete actions that reduce climate risks, enhance resilience, and protect lives, livelihoods, and assets.

In this chapter, we've explored the diverse methodologies used to model the physical risks of climate change, from adapting catastrophe models to incorporate climate projections to using geospatial analysis to map vulnerable areas and developing sector-specific models to assess risks in critical industries. We've also examined the challenges of data gaps, uncertainty, and risk communication, as well as the exciting opportunities presented by advances in modeling techniques.

The key message is this: physical risk models are essential tools for understanding and managing the tangible impacts of climate change. They provide the data and insights needed to:

- **Inform Adaptation Strategies**: By identifying vulnerable areas, assets, and populations, models can guide the prioritization of adaptation measures, such as strengthening infrastructure, investing in early warning systems, and developing drought-resistant crops.
- **Guide Investment Decisions**: Investors, developers, and infrastructure planners can use physical risk models to assess the climate resilience of

different projects and locations, guiding capital toward more sustainable and resilient options.

- **Shape Policy Development**: Policymakers can use risk assessments to inform the design of climate adaptation policies, land-use regulations, building codes, and disaster preparedness plans.
- **Empower Communities**: By communicating risks clearly and effectively, we can empower communities to take action to protect themselves, their homes, and their livelihoods from climate impacts.

The journey from models to action requires collaboration, innovation, and a commitment to using the best available science to inform decision-making. By working together, we can harness the power of physical risk modeling to build a more climate-resilient future for all.

References

Antoine, B., et al. (2022). *Physical climate risk assessment: Practical lessons for the development of climate scenarios with extreme weather events from emerging markets and developing economies*. World Bank & NGFS. https://documents.worldbank.org/en/publication/documents-reports/documentdetail/099657511082325958/idu0004b1eec0d7f304e7c0967305183f75f92a2

Bank for International Settlements (BIS) (2021). *Climate-related Risk Drivers and Their Transmission Channels*. https://www.bis.org/bcbs/publ/d517.pdf.

Deloitte. (2023). *Physical risk modeling: A deep dive into climate risk management*. https://www2.deloitte.com/content/dam/Deloitte/us/Documents/financial-services/us-physical-risk-modeling-a-deep-dive-into-climate-risk-management-may23.pdf

Dunz, N., et al. (2021). *Macroeconomic and financial impacts of compounding pandemics and climate risks*. https://www.cascades.eu/wp-content/uploads/2021/05/SSRN-id3827853.pdf

Eyring, V., & Gillett, N. P. (2021). Human influence on the climate system. In *Climate change 2021: The physical science basis*. Contribution of working group I to the sixth assessment report of the IPCC. https://www.ipcc.ch/report/ar6/wg1/downloads/report/IPCC_AR6_WGI_Chapter03.pdf

Foote, M. (2017). *Natural catastrophe risk management and modelling: A practitioner's guide*. https://onlinelibrary.wiley.com/doi/book/10.1002/9781118906057

Intergovernmental Panel on Climate Change (IPCC). (2014). *Climate change 2014 synthesis report*. http://ipcc.ch/site/assets/uploads/2018/02/SYR_AR5_FINAL_full.pdf

Koks, E. E. (2019). The macroeconomic impacts of future river flooding in Europe. *Environmental Research Letters, 14*(8), 042–084. https://doi.org/10.1088/1748-9326/ab3306

Luo, J., & Zhang, J. (2024). *Rural financial institutions need to be proactive in addressing the physical risks of climate*. Accessed 27 Jan 2025. http://www.cnfinance.cn/magzi/2024-10/09-33730.html

Maraun, D., & Widmann, M. (2018). *Statistical downscaling and bias correction for climate research*. Cambridge University Press. https://www.cambridge.org/core/books/statistical-downscaling-and-bias-correction-for-climate-research/4ED479BAA8309C7ECBE61362 36E3960F

Merkens, J. L. (2018). Gridded population projections for the coastal zone under the Shared Socioeconomic Pathways. *Global and Planetary Change, 169*, 245–260. https://www.sciencedirect.com/science/article/pii/S0921818116301473

Monasterolo, I., & Raberto, M. (2018). The EIRIN flow-of-funds behavioural model of green fiscal policies and green sovereign bonds. *Ecological Economics, 144*, 228–243. https://doi.org/10.1016/j.ecolecon.2017.07.029

Oppenheimer, M., et al. (2019). Sea Level Rise and Implications for Low-Lying Islands, Coasts and Communities. In: IPCC Special Report on the Ocean and Cryosphere in a Changing Climate [H.-O. Pörtner, D. C. Roberts, V. Masson-Delmotte, P. Zhai, M. Tignor, E. Poloczanska, K. Mintenbeck, A. Alegría, M. Nicolai, A. Okem, J. Petzold, B. Rama, N. M. Weyer (eds.)]. Cambridge University Press, Cambridge, UK and New York, NY, USA, pp. 321–445. https://doi.org/10.1017/9781009157964.006.

Otto, F. E. L., et al. (2020). *Challenges to understanding extreme weather changes in lower income countries*. Bulletin of the American Meteorological Society, 1851–1860. https://journals.ametsoc.org/view/journals/bams/101/10/bamsD190317.xml

Ranger, N., Mahul, O., & Monasterolo, I. (2022). *Assessing financial risks from physical climate shocks: A framework for scenario generation*. https://climateimpact.edhec.edu/publications/assessing-financial-risks-physical-climate

Reichstein, M., et al. (2019). Deep learning and process understanding for data-driven Earth system science. *Nature, 566*(7743), 195–204. https://www.nature.com/articles/s41586-019-0912-1

Rosenzweig, C., et al. (2020). Climate change responses benefit from a global food system approach. *Nature Food, 1*(2), 94–97. https://www.researchgate.net/publication/339347598_Climate_change_responses_benefit_from_a_global_food_system_approach

Schneider, T., et al. (2017). Earth system modeling 2.0: A blueprint for models that learn from observations and targeted high-resolution simulations. *Geophysical Research Letters, 44*, 12, 396–12, 417. https://doi.org/10.1002/2017GL076101

Seneviratne, S. I., Zhang, X., Adnan, M., Badi, W., Dereczynski, C., Di Luca, A., Ghosh, S., Iskandar, I., Kossin, J., Lewis, S., Otto, F., Pinto, I., Satoh, M., Vicente-Serrano, S. M., Wehner, M., & Zhou, B. (2021). Weather and climate extreme events in a changing climate. In *Climate c2021: The physical science basis*. Contribution of Working Group I to the Sixth Assessment Report of the Intergovernmental Panel on Climate Change [Masson-Delmotte, V., Zhai, P., Pirani, A., Connors, S. L., Péan, C., Berger, S., Caud, N., Chen, Y., Goldfarb, L., Gomis, M. I., Huang, M., Leitzell, K., Lonnoy, E., Matthews, J. B. R., Maycock, T. K., Waterfield, T., Yelekçi, O., Yu, R., & Zhou, B. (Eds.)]. Cambridge University Press, Cambridge, United Kingdom and New York, NY, USA (pp. 1513–1766). https://doi.org/10.1017/9781009157896.013

Sutton, R. T. (2019). Climate science needs to take risk assessment much more seriously. *Bulletin of the American Meteorological Society, 1637–1642*. https://journals.ametsoc.org/view/journals/bams/100/9/bams-d-18-0280.1.xml

Swiss Re Institute. (2020). *Natural catastrophes in times of economic accumulation and climate change*. https://www.swissre.com/dam/jcr:85598d6e-b5b5-4d4b-971e-5fc9eee143fb/sigma-2-2020-en.pdf

Taberna, A. (2024). *Navigating complexity: Agent-based simulations for climate-resilient economies*. Delft University of Technology. https://research.tudelft.nl/en/publications/navigating-complexity-agent-based-simulations-for-climate-resilie

Tate, E., et al. (2021). Flood exposure and social vulnerability in the United States. *Natural Hazards, 106*(1), 435–457. https://doi.org/10.1007/s11069-020-04470-2

United Nations Environment Programme Finance Initiative (UNEP FI). (2023). *The 2023 climate risk landscape*. https://www.unepfi.org/themes/climate-change/2023-climate-risk-landscape/

van Wesenbeeck, B. K., et al. (2017). *Implementing nature based flood protection: Principles and implementation guidance*. World Bank. Accessed 22 Jan 2025. https://documents.worldbank.org/en/publication/documents-reports/documentdetail/739421509427698706/Implementing-nature-based-flood-protection-principles-and-implementation-guidance

World Bank and NGFS. (2022). *Physical Climate Risk Assessment: Practical Lessons for the Development of Climate Scenarios with Extreme Weather Events from Emerging Markets and Developing Economies*. https://www.ngfs.net/system/files/import/ngfs/media/2022/09/02/ngfs_physical_climate_risk_assessment.pdf

Case References

Brown, A. (2016). Agricultural management. *Nature Climate Change, 6*(2), 127–127. https://doi.org/10.1038/nclimate2928

California Climate & Agriculture Network (CalCAN). (2017). *Climate solutions in California agriculture*. Accessed 23 Jan 2025. https://calclimateag.org/

California Sustainable Winegrowing Alliance (CSWA). (2025). *Sustainable winegrowing report*. Accessed 23 Jan 2025. https://sustainablewinegrowing.org/

Carrão, H., Naumann, G., & Barbosa, P. (2016). Mapping global patterns of drought risk: An empirical framework based on sub-national estimates of hazard, exposure and vulnerability. *Global Environmental Change 39*, 108–124. https://0.1016/j.gloenvcha.2016.04.012

Hannah, L., et al. (2013). Climate change, wine, and conservation. *Proceedings of the National Academy of Sciences, 110*(17), 6907–6912. https://doi.org/10.1073/pnas.1210127110

Intergovernmental Panel on Climate Change (IPCC). The Ocean and Cryosphere in a Changing Climate Special Report of the Intergovernmental Panel on Climate Change

Sea Level Rise and Implications for Low-Lying Islands Coasts and Communities. Cambridge University Press. 321–446

Jones, G. V., et al. (2005). Climate change and global wine quality. *Climatic Change, 73*(3), 319–343. https://doi.org/10.1007/s10584-005-4704-2

Keating, A., et al. (2017). Development and testing of a community flood resilience measurement tool. *Natural Hazards and Earth System Sciences, 17*(1), 77–101. https://doi.org/10.5194/nhess-17-77-2017

Moser, S. C., & Ekstrom, J. A. (2010). A framework to diagnose barriers to climate change adaptation. *Proceedings of the National Academy of Sciences, 107*(51), 22026–22031. https://doi.org/10.1073/pnas.1007887107

Muis, S., Verlaan, M., Winsemius, H. C., Aerts, J. C., & Ward, P. J. (2016). A global reanalysis of storm surges and extreme sea levels. *Nature communications, 7*(1), 11969. https://10.1038/ncomms11969

Patt, A., & Siebenhüner, B. (2005). Agent based modeling and adaptation to climate change. *Vierteljahrshefte zur Wirtschaftsforschung, 74*(2), 310–320. https://doi.org/10.3790/vjh.74.2.310

Pelling, M. (2007). Learning from others: The scope and challenges for participatory disaster risk assessment. *Disasters, 31*(4), 373–385. https://doi.org/10.1111/j.1467-7717.2007.01014.x

Sillmann, J., Kharin, V. V., Zhang, X., Zwiers, F. W., & Bronaugh, D. (2013). Climate extremes indices in the CMIP5 multimodel ensemble: Part 1. Model evaluation in the present climate. *Journal of geophysical research: atmospheres, 118*(4), 1716–1733. https://10.1002/jgrd.v118.4.10.1002/jgrd.50203

Zurich Climate Resilience Alliance (ZCRA). (2020). *Flood resilience measurement for communities (FRMC) exercises: Facilitation guide*. Accessed 22 Jan 2025. https://floodresilience.net/resources/item/flood-resilience-measurement-for-communities/

CHAPTER 7

Transition Risk Modeling: Navigating the Shift to a Low-Carbon Economy

1 Introduction: The Risks and Opportunities of Transformation

The global energy system is undergoing a profound transformation. Driven by the urgent need to address climate change, governments, businesses, and investors are shifting away from fossil fuels and embracing a future powered by renewable energy, energy efficiency, and sustainable technologies. This transition to a low-carbon economy is not just an environmental imperative, it's a financial reality that is reshaping markets, disrupting industries, and creating both risks and opportunities for those who are unprepared or fail to adapt. The transition is not a straightforward process and is characterized by deep uncertainty. Christian et al. (2023) discuss this uncertainty and its implications for navigating this transformative period.

Transition risks are distinct from the physical impacts of climate change, such as extreme weather events or sea-level rise. The International Monetary Fund (IMF) (2023) has analyzed the broader global economic impacts of these physical climate risks. Transition risks stem from the economic and financial disruptions associated with the decarbonization process itself. These risks can arise from policy changes, technological advancements, shifting market dynamics, and evolving social expectations.

For example, the introduction of carbon pricing policies can increase the cost of fossil fuels, impacting the profitability of carbon-intensive industries. Rapid advancements in renewable energy technologies can disrupt traditional energy markets, leading to stranded assets and shifting investment patterns. And growing consumer demand for sustainable products can create both opportunities for companies that embrace sustainability and risks for those that lag behind. Managing the impacts of the low-carbon transition requires

J. Chen, *Climate Finance*, https://doi.org/10.1007/978-981-96-7975-1_7

specific frameworks, especially for long-term investments like infrastructure. The Sustainability Leadership CI (2019) has developed a transition risk framework focused on managing these impacts on infrastructure investments.

Understanding and effectively managing transition risks is crucial for businesses, investors, and policymakers. Understanding and effectively managing these transition risks is where climate risk modeling becomes essential. PwC (2023) offers an introductory guide on what businesses need to know to begin with climate risk modeling. These transition risk models provide a framework for assessing the potential financial impacts of the low-carbon transition, informing investment decisions, guiding corporate strategies, and shaping effective climate policies. The significance of effectively managing transition risks has led to the development of a market for climate risk modeling solutions. According to a report by Chartis Research (Bassett et al., 2023), the landscape of vendors offering these solutions is continuously evolving.

This chapter will explore the key drivers of transition risk, delve into the methodologies used to model these risks, and examine the challenges and opportunities associated with this evolving field. By understanding transition risks and utilizing appropriate modeling tools, we can navigate this transformative era, mitigating potential losses and seizing the opportunities of a more sustainable future.

2 Drivers of Transition Risk

Transition risks arise from a complex interplay of factors that are reshaping the global economic landscape, as indicated by the following Table 1.

The above table outlines the risk drivers associated with four key categories of transition risk: **Policy and Legal, Technology, Markets,** and **Reputation**. These drivers represent the forces that can create financial risks for companies and sectors as the world transitions to a lower-carbon economy.

- **Policy and Legal:** This category focuses on risks stemming from government regulations and legal actions. Drivers include:
  - Increased pricing of greenhouse gas (GHG) emissions (e.g., through carbon taxes or emissions trading schemes).
  - Enhanced emissions-reporting obligations, requiring companies to disclose their GHG emissions.
  - Mandates and regulations on existing products and services, pushing for lower-emission alternatives.
  - Exposure to litigation related to climate change impacts or a company's contribution to emissions.
- **Technology:** This category covers risks associated with technological changes and innovation in the low-carbon transition. Key drivers are:

Table 1 Transition risk drivers

Transition risks	*Risk drivers*
Policy and legal	• Increased pricing of GHG emissions, carbon footprint scope 1–3 • Enhanced emissions-reporting obligations • Mandates on and regulation of existing products and services • Exposure to litigation
Technology	• Substitution of existing products and services with lower-emission options (within lifetime = stranding assets; after lifetime = replacement investment) • Unsuccessful investment in new technologies • Stranding new investments • Upfront costs to transition to lower-emission technologies • Higher operating costs from high-emission technologies
Markets	• Changing customer behavior • Shift in consumer preferences • Uncertainty in market signals • Increased cost of raw materials • Shift in financial and balance-sheet asset values • Failure to capture new market opportunities and technologies via clean technology research and development and clean technology export activities
Reputation	• Stigmatisation of sector • Increased stakeholder concern or negative stakeholder feedback • Brown share assessment

Source UNEP FI (2023)

- Substitution of existing products and services with lower-emission options. This can lead to stranded assets if existing technologies become obsolete before the end of their useful life. After their lifetime, they might require costly replacements.
- Unsuccessful or stranded investments in new technologies that don't become commercially viable.
- Upfront costs associated with transitioning to lower-emission technologies (e.g., investing in new equipment).
- Higher operating costs from high-emission technologies as carbon prices rise or regulations become stricter.

• **Markets:** This category encompasses risks related to shifts in market dynamics, consumer preferences, and investor behavior. Drivers include:

- Changing customer behavior and shifts in consumer preferences toward sustainable products and services.
- Uncertainty in market signals regarding the direction and pace of the low-carbon transition.

- Increased cost of raw materials used in lower-emission technologies or due to disruptions caused by climate change.
- Shifts in financial and balance-sheet asset values as investors re-evaluate companies based on their climate risk exposure.
- Failure to capture new market opportunities associated with the low-carbon transition (e.g., in renewable energy or green technologies).
- Missed R&D and export opportunities in clean technologies.

- **Reputation:** This category focuses on risks to a company's reputation and brand image. Drivers include:
  - Stigmatization of sectors or companies perceived as having a negative environmental impact.
  - Increased stakeholder concern (from investors, consumers, or communities) about climate change and corporate actions.
  - Negative stakeholder feedback and activist pressure related to environmental performance.
  - "Brown Share Assessment," reflecting the portion of a company's activities or investments tied to high-emission assets or industries.

These transition risk drivers, while posing challenges, also create opportunities for companies that proactively adapt to the changing landscape. By understanding these drivers and incorporating them into risk management strategies, businesses can better navigate the low-carbon transition and position themselves for success in a more sustainable future. We will discuss the transition risk drivers in the following sections in detail.

2.1 Policy and Regulatory Changes

Governments worldwide are increasingly implementing policies and regulations aimed at reducing greenhouse gas emissions and accelerating the transition to a low-carbon economy. While these measures are essential for addressing climate change, they can create significant financial risks for companies and investors that fail to adapt.

Key policy instruments that drive transition risks include carbon pricing, and energy policy initiatives, including renewable energy mandates and incentives, energy efficiency standards, and fossil fuel subsidy reforms.

2.1.1 Carbon Pricing

Carbon taxes and emissions trading schemes (ETS) put a price on carbon emissions, incentivizing companies to reduce their emissions and invest in cleaner technologies. However, carbon pricing can also increase costs for carbon-intensive industries, potentially impacting their profitability and competitiveness. The stringency and pace of carbon pricing implementation can significantly influence the level of transition risk. A gradual increase in carbon prices may allow companies time to adapt, while a sudden and steep price hike could lead to more abrupt disruptions.

Aldy and Stavins (2012) explores the theoretical foundations and practical experiences of various carbon pricing mechanisms, including carbon taxes and cap-and-trade systems. The authors believe carbon pricing is a vital tool for reducing greenhouse gas emissions. But challenges remain, such as political resistance, economic impacts on vulnerable sectors, and the risk of "leakage," where emissions may shift to jurisdictions with less stringent regulations. They suggest effective carbon pricing requires careful design to address equity concerns, ensure competitiveness, and provide revenue for public investments in clean technology. Burke et al. (2016) also highlight the need for more research on the optimal design of carbon pricing policies, including how to address distributional impacts and international coordination challenges. Goulder and Schein (2013) provides a detailed comparison of two main carbon pricing approaches: carbon taxes and cap-and-trade systems. The authors analyze the relative merits of each approach in terms of efficiency, cost certainty, ability to address distributional concerns, and political feasibility. Klenert et al. (2018) focuses on the political economy of carbon pricing, emphasizing the importance of public acceptance for successful implementation. The authors discuss strategies for designing carbon pricing policies that are both effective in reducing emissions and politically sustainable, including approaches to revenue recycling that can address equity concerns.

2.1.2 Renewable Energy Mandates and Incentives

Policies that require a certain percentage of electricity to come from renewable sources, such as solar or wind power, create opportunities for renewable energy companies but can also disrupt traditional energy markets. Utilities heavily invested in fossil fuel-based power generation may face stranded assets and financial losses if they are slow to transition to renewables.

Carley et al. (2017) provides a comprehensive analysis of policy instruments used globally to promote renewable energy generation. The authors examine the effectiveness of various policies, including renewable portfolio standards (RPS), feed-in tariffs (FITs), tax incentives, and other mechanisms. They use a large dataset covering 164 countries over the period 1990–2013 to assess which policies have been most effective in driving renewable energy adoption.

The authors made the following key findings:

- Feed-in tariffs and investment incentives have been particularly effective in promoting renewable energy deployment.
- The effectiveness of policies varies depending on the type of renewable energy and the country's level of development.
- Policy design and implementation details matter significantly for effectiveness.

In the context of transition risk, this paper highlights the importance of understanding the specific renewable energy policies in place in different jurisdictions. The effectiveness of these policies in driving the transition to renewable energy can significantly impact the risks and opportunities faced by both traditional energy companies and new entrants in the renewable sector. For transition risk modeling, this suggests the need to consider not just the presence of renewable energy policies, but also their specific design features and likely effectiveness based on the local context.

2.1.3 Energy Efficiency Standards

Standards that mandate minimum levels of energy efficiency for buildings, appliances, and vehicles can drive innovation and reduce energy consumption. However, they can also increase costs for manufacturers and consumers in the short term.

Gillingham et al. (2009) provides a comprehensive overview of the economics behind energy efficiency standards (EES) and their role in reducing energy consumption. The authors discuss various market failures that can lead to suboptimal levels of energy efficiency investment, including information problems, principal-agent issues, and behavioral factors. They then examine the effectiveness of different policy approaches to address these market failures, including energy efficiency standards, information programs, and financial incentives.

They found that:

- Energy efficiency policies can be justified by various market failures, but their optimal level is often difficult to determine.
- Energy efficiency standards can be effective in reducing energy consumption, but may have unintended consequences and can be less flexible than market-based approaches.
- The "energy efficiency gap" (the difference between optimal and actual energy efficiency levels) may be smaller than sometimes claimed when all costs are properly accounted for.

For transition risk modeling, this paper underscores the complexity of assessing the impacts of energy efficiency policies. While such policies can drive significant changes in energy consumption patterns and technology adoption, their effects can be difficult to predict precisely. Models need to account for both the direct impacts of standards on affected industries (e.g., appliance manufacturers, building sector) and the broader effects on energy demand and prices.

2.1.4 Fossil Fuel Subsidy Reforms

Phasing out subsidies for fossil fuels can level the playing field for renewable energy and reduce carbon emissions. However, it can also lead to higher energy prices and potentially impact industries that rely heavily on subsidized fossil fuels.

Rentschler and Bazilian (2017) examines fossil fuel subsidies (FFSs) and presents principles for designing effective reforms. The authors identify key principles for effective reform, drawing on case studies and economic theory. They discuss the potential benefits of subsidy reform, including reduced fiscal burdens, improved energy efficiency, and lower greenhouse gas emissions, as well as the potential negative impacts, particularly on vulnerable populations.

Key principles for effective reform:

- Gradual implementation to allow for adjustment
- Comprehensive approach addressing multiple fuel types
- Transparent communication of reform plans and rationale
- Compensatory measures to protect vulnerable groups
- Complementary policies to support economic diversification

In terms of transition risk, this paper highlights the potentially significant impacts of fossil fuel subsidy reforms on both energy markets and the broader economy. For companies in fossil fuel-intensive industries, the removal of subsidies could substantially increase costs and reduce demand for their products. However, the paper also emphasizes that the specific impacts depend greatly on how reforms are designed and implemented.

For transition risk modeling, this suggests the need to consider various scenarios for subsidy reform, including different timelines, scopes, and accompanying policies. Models should account for both the direct effects on energy prices and the potential broader economic impacts, including possible changes in energy consumption patterns, industrial competitiveness, and social welfare.

Not only do policy and regulatory changes pose transition risk, advancements in technology can also have significant impact on financial institutions' transition finance portfolio as well. In the next section, we will discuss the transition risk factor of technology changes.

2.2 *Technological Advancements*

Rapid innovation in low-carbon technologies is a major driver of transition risks. As cleaner and more efficient technologies become commercially viable and costs decline, they can disrupt existing markets, creating both opportunities for innovators and challenges for incumbents.

The concept of "disruptive innovation" is particularly relevant in the context of transition risks. Disruptive technologies often start out as being less performant or more expensive than existing technologies but improve rapidly, eventually overtaking incumbents and transforming markets. Examples of disruptive technologies driving the low-carbon transition include:

- **Renewable Energy:** The falling cost of solar photovoltaics, wind turbines, and battery storage is making renewable energy increasingly competitive with fossil fuels, disrupting the electricity sector and creating opportunities for new market entrants.
- **Electric Vehicles (EVs):** Advances in battery technology, declining battery costs, and supportive government policies are driving the rapid growth of the electric vehicle market, challenging the dominance of internal combustion engine vehicles.
- **Carbon Capture and Storage (CCS):** While still in its early stages of development, CCS technology has the potential to capture carbon dioxide emissions from power plants and industrial facilities and store them underground, mitigating the climate impact of fossil fuel use.

The transition to a low-carbon economy is significantly influenced by technological advancements, particularly in renewable energy and electric vehicles. The following papers provide insights into the cost reductions associated with photovoltaic (PV) modules and battery packs for electric vehicles, highlighting their implications for transition risks.

Kavlak et al. (2018) investigates the factors contributing to the declining costs of photovoltaic modules, which are critical for the expansion of solar energy. The authors identify several key drivers:

- **Technological Innovation**: Advances in manufacturing processes and materials have led to significant improvements in efficiency and reductions in production costs. The study emphasizes that innovations such as improved cell designs and automated production techniques have played a crucial role.
- **Economies of Scale**: As production volumes increase, manufacturers benefit from economies of scale, further driving down costs. The authors note that global demand for solar PV has surged, incentivizing larger-scale production.
- **Market Competition**: Increased competition among manufacturers has spurred innovation and cost reduction. The authors argue that competitive pressures lead to continuous improvements in technology and efficiency.

The implications of these cost reductions are profound for transition risks. As solar energy becomes more economically viable, it disrupts traditional fossil fuel markets, potentially leading to stranded assets for companies heavily invested in carbon-intensive technologies. This shift necessitates that investors and businesses reassess their portfolios and strategies to mitigate risks associated with technological obsolescence.

Another similar paper, Nykvist and Nilsson (2015) focuses on the dramatic decline in costs of lithium-ion battery packs, a key component for electric vehicles (EVs). The authors present several findings:

- **Cost Trends**: Between 2007 and 2014, the average cost of battery packs fell from over $1,000 per kWh to around $410 per kWh, with market leaders achieving even lower costs at approximately $300 per kWh. This represents an annual decline of about 14%.
- **Learning Rates**: The study identifies learning rates (the percentage reduction in costs associated with a doubling of cumulative production) ranging from 6 to 9%. This indicates that as more batteries are produced, the costs continue to decrease due to improved manufacturing efficiencies and technological advancements.
- **Market Implications**: The falling battery costs enhance the competitiveness of electric vehicles against internal combustion engine vehicles, accelerating the transition toward low-carbon transportation solutions.

The rapid decline in battery costs poses both opportunities and risks. While it enables wider adoption of EVs, traditional automotive manufacturers face significant transition risks as consumer preferences shift toward electric models. Companies that fail to adapt may experience diminished market share and financial performance.

Both papers illustrate how technological advancements are pivotal in driving down costs associated with renewable energy and electric vehicles, thereby influencing transition risks:

- **Disruption of Traditional Markets**: As technologies become cheaper and more efficient, they disrupt existing markets reliant on fossil fuels, leading to potential stranded assets for companies slow to adapt.
- **Investment Reassessment**: Investors must consider the implications of these technological changes on asset valuations and future profitability. Companies that embrace these advancements may gain competitive advantages, while those that do not may face significant financial risks.
- **Policy Implications**: Policymakers should recognize the importance of fostering innovation through supportive policies and incentives that promote research and development in clean technologies. This can help mitigate transition risks by ensuring a smoother transition toward a low-carbon economy.

Understanding the dynamics of technological advancements is crucial for managing transition risks effectively as the world shifts toward sustainable energy solutions.

Case Study 1: Tesla's Disruption of the Automotive Industry

Focus: Analyzing How a Disruptive Technology, Electric Vehicles (EVs), is Transforming the Automotive Industry and Creating Transition Risks for Traditional Automakers

Tesla, Inc. has been a pioneer in the electric vehicle (EV) market, driving significant changes in the automotive industry. This case study explores how Tesla's innovation in EVs, combined with supportive government policies and declining battery costs, has accelerated the shift toward electric mobility. It examines the challenges and opportunities this shift creates for traditional automakers, highlighting the transition risks and the need for adaptation.

Illustration: Methodology and Implementation of Tesla's Disruption

1. **Tesla's Innovation in Electric Vehicles:**

Tesla has revolutionized the automotive industry with its advanced EV technology, including high-performance electric drivetrains, long-range batteries, and over-the-air software updates. The company's focus on innovation has set new standards for vehicle performance, safety, and user experience (IEA, 2020; Tesla Inc., 2023).

2. **Supportive Government Policies and Declining Battery Costs:**

Government policies, such as subsidies, tax incentives, and emissions regulations, have played a crucial role in promoting EV adoption. Additionally, advancements in battery technology have led to significant cost reductions, making EVs more competitive with internal combustion engine (ICE) vehicles (BloombergNEF, 2023).

3. **Accelerating the Shift Toward Electric Mobility:**

Tesla's success has accelerated the transition toward electric mobility, challenging the dominance of ICE vehicles. Traditional automakers are now investing heavily in EV technology to remain competitive, leading to a rapid expansion of the EV market.

Discussion: Adapting to Technological Disruption and the Role of Policies

1. **Importance of Adapting to Technological Disruption:**

Traditional automakers face significant transition risks as the industry shifts toward electric mobility. Companies that fail to adapt may experience declining market share, stranded assets, and reduced profitability. Adapting to technological disruption requires substantial investment in R&D, retooling manufacturing facilities, and developing new business models.

2. **Role of Government Policies in Shaping Market Transitions:**

Government policies are crucial in shaping market transitions toward low-carbon transportation. Policies such as emissions standards, fuel economy regulations, and incentives for EV purchases can accelerate the adoption of clean energy technologies and support the development of necessary infrastructure.

3. **Potential for New Business Models in a Low-Carbon Transportation Sector:**

The transition to electric mobility opens up opportunities for new business models, such as mobility as a service (MaaS). These models focus on providing transportation solutions that are flexible, efficient, and environmentally friendly, leveraging digital platforms and shared mobility services (World Economic Forum, 2020).

Conclusion

Tesla's disruption of the automotive industry exemplifies the transformative impact of electric vehicles on traditional automakers. By driving innovation in EV technology, benefiting from supportive government policies, and leveraging declining battery costs, Tesla has accelerated the shift toward electric mobility. This case study highlights the importance of adapting to technological disruption, the critical role of government policies in shaping market transitions, and the potential for new business models to emerge in a low-carbon transportation sector.

Understanding the methodologies and strategies employed by Tesla can provide valuable insights for traditional automakers and policymakers seeking to navigate the challenges and opportunities of the transition to electric mobility.

2.3 *Shifting Market Dynamics*

The transition to a low-carbon economy is also influencing market dynamics, shifting consumer preferences, investor sentiment, and creating new markets for sustainable products and services. The shifting market dynamics are also reflected in the growing attention toward climate finance. Stroebel and Wurgler (2021) explore the perspectives and considerations within this evolving field.

Key market shifts driving transition risks include:

- **Consumer Demand for Sustainable Products:** Consumers are increasingly demanding products and services with lower environmental footprints, leading to growth in markets for organic food, sustainable fashion, and energy-efficient appliances. Companies that fail to respond to this shift in consumer preferences risk losing market share.
- **Investor Pressure for Climate Action:** Investors are increasingly integrating climate change considerations into their investment decisions, seeking out companies with strong sustainability performance and divesting from those with high-carbon footprints or weak climate risk management practices. This shift in investor sentiment can impact a company's access to capital and its valuation.
- **Emergence of New Low-Carbon Markets:** The transition is creating new markets for green technologies, renewable energy, and climate-related services. Companies that position themselves to capitalize on these emerging markets can gain a competitive advantage.

The transition to a low-carbon economy is reshaping market dynamics, particularly in how institutional investors perceive and respond to climate risks. The following papers delve into the implications of these shifting market dynamics for investment strategies and asset valuations. The transition is also significantly influencing how financial institutions perceive and respond to climate risks. The Bank for International Settlements (BIS) (2020) has highlighted these concerns in their seminal "Green Swan" report, emphasizing the implications for central banking and financial stability.

Krueger et al. (2020) highlights the growing recognition among institutional investors of the financial risks posed by climate change. The authors present several key findings:

- **Integration of Climate Risks**: Institutional investors are increasingly integrating climate-related risks into their investment decisions. The paper emphasizes that these risks can significantly affect asset valuations, particularly for companies with high-carbon footprints.
- **Materiality of Climate Risks**: The authors argue that climate risks are material to financial performance, affecting both short-term returns and long-term sustainability. They highlight that investors are beginning to demand greater transparency regarding companies' exposure to climate risks and their strategies for mitigation.
- **Impact on Investment Strategies**: The paper discusses how shifting market dynamics, driven by heightened awareness of climate risks, are leading investors to re-evaluate their portfolios. This includes divesting from high-carbon assets and increasing allocations to sustainable investments.

These findings underscore the transition risk associated with shifting market dynamics, as companies that fail to adapt to the changing landscape may face declining investor confidence and reduced access to capital.

Bolton and Kacperczyk (2021)'s paper, "Do Investors Care About Carbon Risk?" investigates whether investors are responsive to carbon risk when making investment decisions. Key insights include:

- **Investor Behavior**: The authors find that investors do care about carbon risk, as evidenced by the negative impact on stock prices for firms with high-carbon emissions during periods of heightened climate concern. This suggests that market participants are increasingly factoring in carbon risk when evaluating potential investments.
- **Market Reactions**: The study highlights that market reactions to carbon risk are more pronounced in sectors directly exposed to regulatory changes or public scrutiny regarding environmental performance. This indicates that shifting market dynamics can lead to significant valuation adjustments based on perceived carbon risks.
- **Implications for Corporate Strategy**: Companies with higher carbon footprints may find it challenging to attract investment as investor preferences shift toward sustainability. This creates a transition risk for firms that do not proactively manage their carbon emissions or communicate their sustainability strategies effectively.

This paper illustrates how investor sentiment is evolving in response to climate risks, creating pressures for companies to align their operations with sustainable practices.

Schlenker and Taylor (2021) examines how market expectations regarding climate change influence asset prices and investment decisions. Key points include:

- **Price Adjustments**: The authors demonstrate that markets are beginning to incorporate expectations of future climate impacts into asset valuations. This includes adjustments based on anticipated regulatory changes, shifts in consumer preferences, and physical impacts from climate change.
- **Long-Term Implications**: The study suggests that as awareness of climate risks increases, there will be a growing divergence in asset prices based on companies' exposure to climate-related vulnerabilities. Firms perceived as resilient may benefit from higher valuations, while those considered at risk may see declines.
- **Transition Risk Management**: Investors need to consider how shifting market dynamics will affect long-term returns. Companies must develop robust strategies for managing transition risks associated with changing market expectations and regulatory landscapes.

Schlenker and Taylor's research highlights the importance of understanding how market expectations shape investment behavior and asset pricing in the context of climate change.

All three papers collectively illustrate the significant transition risks posed by shifting market dynamics in response to climate change:

- **Investor Behavior**: There is a clear trend among institutional investors toward incorporating climate risks into their decision-making processes, leading to potential capital reallocation away from high-carbon assets.
- **Corporate Strategy**: Companies must adapt their strategies to align with evolving investor expectations regarding sustainability. Failure to do so could result in diminished access to capital and lower valuations.
- **Market Valuation Adjustments**: As markets begin to price in climate-related risks, firms with higher emissions or inadequate sustainability strategies may face significant valuation penalties.

Overall, understanding these shifting dynamics is crucial for both investors and corporations as they navigate the challenges and opportunities presented by the transition to a low-carbon economy. Effective management of transition risks will be essential for sustaining financial performance in this evolving landscape.

2.4 *Social and Reputational Factors*

Growing public awareness of climate change and the increasing scrutiny of corporate behavior are also shaping transition risks. Companies with high-carbon footprints, weak climate policies, or a history of environmental controversies can face reputational damage, consumer boycotts, and difficulty attracting and retaining employees.

Conversely, companies that demonstrate leadership in climate action can enhance their brand image, attract investors, and gain a competitive advantage in a market increasingly valuing sustainability. Flammer (2021) examines the role of corporate green bonds as a tool for financing environmentally friendly projects. They find that companies issuing green bonds can enhance their reputation among investors and consumers by signaling commitment to sustainability. This can lead to a "greenium," where green bonds trade at lower yields compared to traditional bonds due to increased demand from environmentally conscious investors. The study highlights that the issuance of green bonds can positively influence a company's stock price, reflecting growing investor interest in sustainable practices. This trend underscores the importance of social and reputational factors in investment decisions. On the contrary, companies that fail to align with sustainability expectations may face reputational damage, reduced access to capital, and potential declines in market value. This creates a transition risk for firms that do not proactively engage in sustainable practices.

3 Transition Risk Modeling Methodologies

Modeling transition risks requires a multifaceted approach that integrates diverse data sources, analytical tools, and expert judgment. This section explores some of the key methodologies used to assess the potential financial impacts of the low-carbon transition.

3.1 Scenario Analysis

Scenario analysis is a fundamental tool for assessing transition risks, providing a structured way to explore a range of possible future outcomes based on different assumptions about policy changes, technological advancements, market dynamics, and other key drivers. Various institutions are actively involved in modeling low-carbon transitions to understand the associated financial implications. For example, the Agence Française de Développement (AFD) (2024) has conducted research on modeling low-carbon transitions in Colombia, focusing on the macrofinancial opportunities and risks involved.

As discussed in Chapter 5, IPCC's Sixth Assessment Cycle and the IEA's World Energy Outlook (WEO), and NGFS scenarios all offer insights into the challenges and potential pathways associated with the global transition to a low-carbon economy. UNEP FI (2023) has compared their corresponding scenarios with the following conclusion:

IPCC (International Panel on Climate Change):

The IPCC highlights four conclusions relevant to transition risk:

1. **GHG emissions have risen globally:** Despite increasing awareness and policy efforts, global greenhouse gas emissions continue to rise. This underscores the scale of the challenge and the urgency of accelerating the transition. While unit costs and policies enabling low-emissions technologies have dramatically accelerated deployment since AR5's release in 2014, it hasn't been enough to reverse the overall emissions trend.
2. **Transition to global net zero by 2050 will require an all-encompassing system transformation:** Achieving net-zero emissions by mid-century requires a fundamental shift across all sectors of the economy, including energy, transportation, industry, and agriculture. This transformation needs a portfolio approach involving a combination of mitigation technologies, energy efficiency improvements, building retrofits, carbon dioxide removal (CDR), and demand-side measures (reducing energy consumption).

3. **Linking mitigation and adaptation:** Effective climate action requires integrating mitigation (reducing emissions) and adaptation (adjusting to the impacts of climate change). These two strategies are not mutually exclusive but rather complementary and essential for achieving sustainable development.
4. **Strengthened global response is crucial:** Improving governance, regulations, and economic instruments (e.g., carbon pricing) are necessary to remove barriers to mitigation in the near term. This includes international cooperation, policy coordination, and financial support for developing countries.

IEA (International Energy Agency):

The IEA's WEO focuses on the energy sector and its role in the low-carbon transition. Key assumptions underlying the IEA's transition risk scenarios include:

1. **Global energy demand will increase significantly:** Energy demand is projected to grow substantially, driven primarily by emerging and developing economies. This highlights the need for a rapid expansion of clean energy sources to meet this growing demand while reducing reliance on fossil fuels.
2. **Clean energy investments are below requirements:** Despite increased investment in clean energy technologies, current levels are still well below what's needed to achieve net-zero emissions by 2050. This "underinvestment" poses a major barrier to a successful energy transition. The field of energy transition modeling is rapidly evolving, with new economic models emerging to better capture the complexities of the low-carbon shift. Hafner et al. (2020) provide a comprehensive review of these emerging models.
3. **Enabling policies can rapidly increase renewable investments:** Supportive government policies can accelerate investments in renewable energy technologies and drive the transition away from fossil fuels. This includes policies like carbon pricing, renewable energy mandates, and incentives for clean energy innovation.
4. **No new unabated coal investments and declining demand:** To achieve net-zero emissions, no new investments in unabated coal-fired power plants or mines should be made after 2030. Global coal demand is projected to decline under all scenarios, albeit faster in developed economies. This reflects the increasing competitiveness of renewable energy and the growing recognition of coal's contribution to climate change.

NGFS (Network for Greening the Financial System)

1. **Higher carbon price is needed:** The NGFS (2020) scenarios suggest that a higher carbon price is required to achieve a net-zero transition by 2050. This is reflected in the inclusion of a "shadow carbon price" in the scenarios, which represents the economic cost of carbon emissions not yet fully reflected in market prices. The shadow carbon price accounts for the expected increasing stringency of climate policies, technological advancements that make low-carbon solutions more cost-competitive, and changes in consumer preferences that drive demand for sustainable products and services. It reflects the growing consensus that strong policy action is necessary.
2. **Low to medium availability of CDR technologies:** The NGFS scenarios assume limited or moderate deployment of Carbon Dioxide Removal (CDR) technologies. These technologies aim to remove carbon dioxide from the atmosphere, but their large-scale deployment faces technological, economic, and environmental challenges. The NGFS acknowledges that CDR might play some role but doesn't assume its widespread availability to drive emissions reductions. The scenarios consider different cost assumptions, geographic distributions of CDR projects (countries), and variations in the availability of different CDR options (reflecting uncertainties around their future development and deployment).
3. **Net-zero transition requires massive investments in green electricity and storage:** Achieving net-zero will necessitate significant investment in renewable energy sources (like solar and wind), green electricity infrastructure, and energy storage technologies (like batteries and pumped hydro). The scenarios project a substantial decline in coal use, approaching zero by 2050, with renewables and biomass providing about two-thirds of global energy needs. This shift to renewables and storage will be a key driver of the transition and a major focus for investment.

In summary, both the IPCC and IEA emphasize the urgent need for accelerated action to mitigate climate change and manage transition risks. The IPCC highlights the need for a system-wide transformation and a strengthened global response, while the IEA focuses on the crucial role of increased clean energy investments and enabling policies in driving the energy transition. The NGFS scenarios emphasize strong policy action on carbon pricing, CDR, and massive investment in green energy and storage.

The IPCC, IEA, and NGFS all develop scenarios related to the low-carbon transition, but they differ in their scope, focus, and intended use. Here's a comparison:

Feature	*IPCC*	*IEA*	*NGFS*
Scope	Broad, covering the entire climate system	Primarily focused on the energy sector	Specifically designed for financial risk assessment
Focus	Physical science, impacts, mitigation, and adaptation	Energy supply and demand, technology developments	Financial risks and opportunities of the transition
Time Horizon	Long-term (to 2100 and beyond)	Typically to 2050, sometimes further out	Short, medium, and long-term (often to 2100)
Scenarios	RCPs (emissions pathways), SSPs (socioeconomic pathways)	NZE (net-zero), STEPS (stated policies), etc	Orderly/Disorderly Transition, Hot House World, etc
Key Assumptions/ Conclusions (Examples)	– GHG emissions are still rising – Net-zero requires system transformation – Linking mitigation and adaptation is crucial – Stronger global response needed	– Global energy demand will increase – Clean energy investment is insufficient – Enabling policies boost renewables – No new unabated coal investments	– Higher carbon price needed – Limited CDR availability – Massive green investment needed
Primary Users	Scientists, policymakers, researchers	Governments, energy companies, investors	Central banks, supervisors, financial institutions, investors
Strengths	Comprehensive, scientific consensus	Detailed energy sector analysis	Tailored to financial sector, integrates macroeconomic factors
Limitations	Can be complex, coarse resolution	Limited scope beyond energy	Primarily focused on financial risks

Key Differences and Overlap:

- **Breadth:** IPCC is the broadest, providing a holistic view of climate change. IEA focuses specifically on energy, while NGFS is tailored for financial risks.
- **Emphasis:** IPCC emphasizes the physical science and impacts of climate change. IEA emphasizes energy market dynamics and technology. NGFS emphasizes financial stability and the economic implications for the financial sector.

- **Scenario Design:** IPCC scenarios (RCPs and SSPs) are widely used as inputs by other organizations, including the IEA and NGFS. The IEA scenarios often align with the RCPs, while the NGFS scenarios typically incorporate elements from both RCPs and SSPs, adjusting them to be more relevant to financial risk assessment.

By using these different scenario sets in conjunction, decision-makers can gain a more comprehensive understanding of the risks and opportunities associated with the low-carbon transition. For instance, a financial institution might use IPCC projections to understand the potential physical impacts of climate change, IEA scenarios to analyze energy sector trends, and NGFS scenarios to assess the financial implications for their portfolio.

By considering multiple scenarios, such as an "orderly transition" with ambitious climate policies and rapid technological progress, a "disorderly transition" with delayed action and abrupt policy changes, or a "failed transition" with insufficient action and severe climate impacts, businesses and investors can assess their vulnerability to different pathways and develop more robust strategies.

For example, an energy company could use scenario analysis to evaluate the impact of different carbon pricing policies on the profitability of its fossil fuel assets, explore the potential for investing in renewable energy, and assess the financial implications of various transition pathways for its overall business model.

Case Study 2: The REmap Scenario Analysis by the International Renewable Energy Agency (IRENA)

Focus: Using an Energy System Model to Explore Different Scenarios for Achieving a Rapid Transition to Renewable Energy

The International Renewable Energy Agency (IRENA) developed the Renewable Energy Roadmap (REmap) scenario analysis to explore pathways for achieving a rapid transition to renewable energy. This case study examines how IRENA uses the REmap model to simulate the deployment of renewable energy technologies, energy efficiency measures, and policy changes needed to achieve various levels of decarbonization in the energy sector.

Illustration: Methodology and Implementation of the REmap Model

1. **Development of the REmap Model:**

IRENA's REmap model is designed to evaluate the potential for renewable energy deployment and energy efficiency improvements across different regions and sectors. The model integrates data on energy demand, technology costs, and policy frameworks to simulate various decarbonization scenarios (IRENA, 2016; IRENA, 2019a).

2. **Simulating Renewable Energy Deployment and Energy Efficiency Measures:**

The REmap model simulates the deployment of renewable energy technologies, such as solar, wind, hydro, and bioenergy, as well as energy efficiency measures. It assesses the potential contributions of these technologies to reducing greenhouse gas emissions and achieving energy transition goals (IRENA, 2018, 2020a).

3. **Assessing Policy Changes and Decarbonization Pathways:**

The REmap model evaluates the impact of various policy changes, such as carbon pricing, subsidies for renewable energy, and regulatory measures, on the energy transition. It provides insights into the necessary policy actions to achieve different levels of decarbonization (IRENA, 2019b).

Discussion: Potential for Renewable Energy, Challenges, and Policy Incentives

1. **Potential for Renewable Energy to Drive Economic Growth and Job Creation:**

Renewable energy has significant potential to drive economic growth and create jobs. The deployment of renewable energy technologies can stimulate investment, enhance energy security, and reduce greenhouse gas emissions, contributing to sustainable development (IRENA, 2021).

2. **Challenges of Integrating Variable Renewable Energy Sources into Electricity Grids:**

Integrating variable renewable energy sources, such as solar and wind, into electricity grids presents challenges related to grid stability, energy storage, and demand management. Addressing these challenges requires investments in grid infrastructure, advanced energy storage solutions, and smart grid technologies (IRENA, 2017).

3. **Role of Policy Incentives in Accelerating the Deployment of Clean Energy Technologies:**

Policy incentives play a crucial role in accelerating the deployment of clean energy technologies. Measures such as feed-in tariffs, tax credits, and renewable energy mandates can provide the necessary support to overcome market barriers and drive investment in renewable energy (IRENA, 2020b).

Conclusion

The REmap scenario analysis by the International Renewable Energy Agency (IRENA) provides a comprehensive framework for exploring different pathways to achieve a rapid transition to renewable energy. By using an energy system model to simulate the deployment of renewable energy technologies, energy efficiency measures, and policy changes, IRENA's REmap model offers valuable insights into the potential for renewable energy to drive economic growth and job creation. This case study highlights the challenges of integrating variable renewable energy sources into electricity grids, the importance of policy incentives in accelerating the deployment of clean energy technologies, and the critical role of research and innovation in advancing the energy transition.

Understanding the methodologies and findings of IRENA's REmap scenario analysis can provide valuable guidance for policymakers, investors, and stakeholders seeking to achieve a sustainable and decarbonized energy future.

3.2 *Financial Modeling*

Financial models are essential for quantifying the potential financial impacts of transition risks on companies, projects, and investment portfolios. These models use a variety of techniques to assess how changes in key variables, such as carbon prices, energy demand, technology costs, and regulatory policies, could affect financial performance.

UNEP FI (2023) report discusses different methodologies for assessing transition risk, contrasting top-down and bottom-up approaches and highlighting hybrid methodologies.

Top-Down Approach:

The top-down approach focuses on assessing transition risk at a macroeconomic or national level, often starting with global emissions budgets or scenarios.

- **Methodology:** It uses aggregate data, such as national-level emissions data or projected changes in energy demand, to estimate the overall impact of the low-carbon transition on the economy or specific sectors. For example, it could model how a carbon tax would ripple through the economy. Top-down assessments often use Integrated Assessment Models (IAMs) to simulate the interactions between the energy system, the economy, and the climate.
- **Strengths:**
  - Can provide a broad overview of systemic risks.
  - Often relies on readily available national-level data, making it suitable for initial assessments or when company-level data is scarce.

  - Can capture the interconnectedness of different sectors and the economy-wide effects of policy changes.
- **Weaknesses:**
  - May not capture the specific risks and opportunities faced by individual companies.
  - Can lack granularity, especially regarding variations in transition risks within a country, sector or portfolio.
  - Simplifying assumptions at the macro level can mask important nuances and heterogeneities at the firm level.

The report cites Ortec Finance's *ClimateMAPS* and Entelligent's *SmartClimate Technologies* as examples of tools employing a top-down approach. They measure emissions against global carbon budgets, arguing that country-level emissions data is often more reliable and consistent than firm-level data.

Bottom-Up Approach:

The bottom-up approach focuses on assessing the financial impact of transition risk at the individual company level, which is particularly pertinent for credit risk analysis. This information can then be aggregated to generate a portfolio-level assessment.

- **Methodology:** This approach analyzes how specific transition drivers (e.g., policy changes, technological shifts, market changes) will impact a company's financial statements (income statement, balance sheet, cash flow statement). The adjusted financial statements feed into credit risk models to estimate impacts on key metrics like probability of default (PD) or loss given default (LGD).
- **Strengths:**
  - Provides more granular insights into company-specific risks.
  - Can be linked directly to financial performance and creditworthiness.
  - Allows for more detailed analysis of specific adaptation and mitigation strategies at the firm level.
- **Weaknesses:**
  - Requires granular company-level data, which can be challenging to obtain, especially for non-public companies.
  - Can be resource-intensive, requiring detailed financial modeling for each company.
  - May not fully capture systemic risks or broader market dynamics.

Hybrid Approach:

Recognizing the strengths and weaknesses of both top-down and bottom-up approaches, some providers use a hybrid methodology.

- **Methodology:** This typically involves combining macro-level analysis (e.g., carbon pricing scenarios, technology forecasts) with company-level data and financial modeling. For instance, a hybrid approach might use a top-down analysis to project future carbon prices and then incorporate these prices into a bottom-up assessment of the financial impact on individual companies.
- **Strengths:**
  - Can offer a more comprehensive view of transition risk, capturing both macro-level trends and company-specific vulnerabilities.
  - Can be tailored to different levels of data availability and resources.
- **Weaknesses:**
  - Requires careful integration of different models and datasets, which can be complex.

The report mentions MSCI and ISS ESG as examples of providers using hybrid methodologies. They often combine macroeconomic projections with firm-level financial data to assess transition risks.

Example of Bottom-up Approach: Oliver Wyman/S&P Global

The below Fig. 1 outlines a bottom-up, company-level transition risk modeling approach, as described by UNEP FI (2023) as the Oliver Wyman and S&P Global approach. This approach focuses on assessing the financial impact of climate change scenarios on individual companies, ultimately affecting their creditworthiness. Here's a step-by-step breakdown:

1. **Input: Industry and Market Data and Company Financials:**
   - **Industry and Market Data:** The process begins with gathering industry and market data from sources like S&P Global Market Intelligence and S&P Global Trucost. This data provides context on industry trends, peer comparisons, and potential market shifts related to the low-carbon transition.
   - **Company Financials:** Company-specific financial information is also crucial. This includes historical data on:
     - Price of products/services
     - Sales volume
     - Unit cost of production
     - Capital expenditure (capex)
     - Asset value

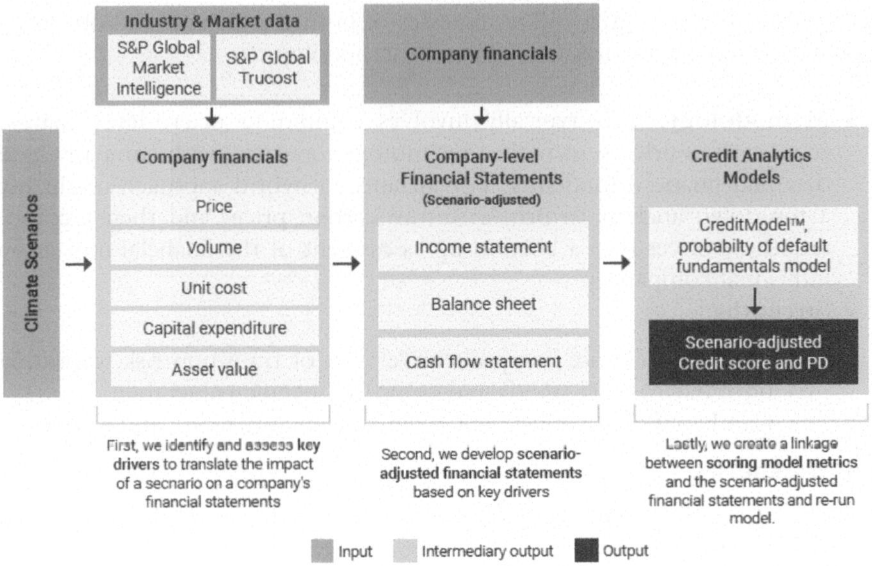

Fig. 1 Bottom-up transition risk model (*Source* Oliver Wyman/S&P Global, UNEP FI [2023])

2. **First Step: Identifying Key Drivers:** The first step in the analysis involves identifying and assessing the key drivers that translate the impact of a climate scenario onto a company's financial statements. This helps pinpoint how specific climate-related changes (e.g., carbon pricing, shifts in consumer demand) will affect the company's financial performance. It links the broad climate scenarios to company-specific variables.
3. **Second Step: Developing Scenario-Adjusted Financials:** Next, scenario-adjusted financial statements are developed. This means incorporating the key drivers identified in the previous step into the company's financial statements to create projected financials under different climate scenarios. This provides a forward-looking view of the company's financial health under various potential futures. The outputs of this stage include adjusted:

    - Income statement
    - Balance sheet
    - Cash flow statement

4. **Third Step: Linking to Credit Analytics Models:** Finally, the scenario-adjusted financial statements are linked to credit analytics models, specifically a probability of default (PD) model like CreditModel™. This model uses the adjusted financial information to generate a scenario-adjusted credit score and estimate the company's probability of default under each

climate scenario. This step quantifies the credit risk associated with each scenario.

By understanding the different methodologies, their strengths and limitations, financial institutions can choose the most appropriate approach for their specific needs and context. The UNEP FI (2023) report implicitly favors hybrid models when feasible, as they offer the most holistic view of transition risk. However, data constraints in EMDEs often necessitate simpler approaches, at least initially.

Other commonly used financial models for transition risk assessment include:

- **Discounted Cash Flow (DCF) Models:** DCF models estimate the present value of future cash flows, incorporating adjustments for the impact of transition risks. For example, a DCF model for a coal-fired power plant could incorporate a carbon price, leading to higher operating costs and potentially reducing the plant's profitability.
- **Valuation Models:** These models assess the impact of transition risks on the value of companies or assets. For example, a valuation model for an oil and gas company could incorporate the risk of stranded assets, leading to a lower valuation if a significant portion of the company's reserves are deemed unburnable under stricter climate policies.

Key financial metrics that can be used to assess transition risks include:

- **Carbon Intensity:** Measures a company's emissions relative to its revenue or output, providing an indicator of its exposure to carbon pricing policies.
- **Emissions Reduction Targets:** Companies are increasingly setting targets for reducing their greenhouse gas emissions. The ambition and credibility of these targets can be an indicator of their commitment to the low-carbon transition.
- **Stranded Asset Exposure:** The value of assets at risk of becoming stranded due to policy changes, technological advancements, or shifting market dynamics.

Giglio et al. (2021) reviews various approaches for integrating climate risk into financial modeling. The authors discuss how climate risks can be incorporated into asset pricing models across different asset classes, including real estate, equities, and fixed-income securities. They suggest that investors can construct portfolios that hedge against climate risks by considering the exposure of assets to these risks.

Bernstein et al. (2019) analyzes how rising sea levels impact property values. The authors find that anticipated sea-level rise leads to significant declines in property prices in vulnerable areas, reflecting shifting market dynamics influenced by physical climate risks. The findings highlight the need for financial models to account for the long-term impacts of climate change on asset valuations, emphasizing the importance of integrating environmental factors into financial decision-making.

3.3 Sector-Specific Models

Specialized models are being developed to assess transition risks in specific sectors, taking into account the unique characteristics and vulnerabilities of each industry.

For example:

- **Energy Sector Models:** These models simulate the impact of renewable energy deployment, carbon pricing policies, and energy efficiency measures on electricity generation, transmission, and distribution. They can be used to assess the financial viability of different power plants, evaluate the impact of policy changes on electricity prices, and guide investments in grid modernization and energy storage.
- **Transportation Sector Models:** These models assess the shift toward electric vehicles, the impact of fuel efficiency standards, and the potential for disruptions in the automotive industry. They can be used to project the growth of the EV market, evaluate the impact of policy incentives on EV adoption, and assess the financial implications for traditional automakers.
- **Agriculture Sector Models:** These models evaluate the impact of climate-smart agriculture practices, changes in land use, and the potential for carbon sequestration in the agricultural sector. They can be used to assess the economic viability of different farming practices, project the impact of climate change on crop yields, and evaluate the potential for agriculture to contribute to climate change mitigation.

Vermeulen et al. (2021) presents a framework for assessing transition risks in the energy sector, focusing on the potential financial impacts of a disruptive energy transition. While Battiston et al. (2017) does not exclusively focused on a single sector, this paper presents a methodology for assessing climate-related financial risks across various sectors, including fossil fuels, utilities, transportation, and housing. Monasterolo and De Angelis (2020) examines the stock market reaction to the Paris Agreement, providing insights into how investors perceive transition risks across different sectors.

Sen and von Schickfus (2020) focuses on the fossil fuel sector, examining how climate policies affect investors' expectations and asset valuations. Semieniuk et al. (2021) discusses transition risks across various sectors, including energy, transportation, and agriculture. Kruttli et al. (2024) provides insights into sector-specific climate risk modeling that could be applied to transition risks. Cahen-Fourot et al. (2021) models the potential for stranded assets across interconnected economic sectors due to decarbonization policies.

These papers collectively highlight several key aspects of sector-specific transition risk modeling:

1. Interconnectedness: Many studies emphasize the importance of considering interconnections between sectors. Transition risks in one sector (e.g., fossil fuels) can have cascading effects on others (e.g., transportation, utilities).
2. Policy Sensitivity: Different sectors show varying levels of sensitivity to climate policies. Models need to account for these differences in policy exposure and adaptive capacity.
3. Investor Perceptions: Several papers examine how investors perceive and price transition risks across different sectors, highlighting the importance of market dynamics in transition risk assessment.
4. Stranded Assets: The concept of stranded assets is particularly relevant for sector-specific transition risk models, especially in carbon-intensive industries.
5. Temporal Dynamics: Transition risks can evolve differently across sectors over time. Models need to capture both short-term shocks and long-term structural changes.
6. Data Challenges: Sector-specific modeling often requires detailed, sector-specific data, which can be challenging to obtain consistently across different industries and regions.
7. Scenario Importance: Many studies emphasize the importance of considering multiple transition scenarios, as the impacts can vary significantly across sectors depending on the speed and nature of the transition.

For practitioners developing sector-specific transition risk models, these papers suggest the need for:

- Detailed sector-specific data and expertise
- Consideration of inter-sector dependencies and cascading effects
- Integration of policy scenarios and market dynamics
- Attention to both short-term and long-term risk factors
- Transparency about model assumptions and limitations

The literature indicates that while sector-specific transition risk modeling is complex, it's crucial for understanding the nuanced impacts of the low-carbon transition across different parts of the economy.

3.4 Integrated Assessment Models (IAMs)

Integrated Assessment Models (IAMs) are complex models that combine economic, energy, and climate systems to explore the long-term interactions between these systems. They are used to assess the macroeconomic impacts of climate policies, the potential for different transition pathways, and the costs and benefits of various mitigation and adaptation strategies.

Nordhaus, W.D. (2017) discusses IAMs as tools for evaluating the economic impacts of climate change policies. Nordhaus emphasizes the importance of accurately estimating the social cost of carbon (SCC) as a basis for effective policy-making. IAMs provide insights into long-term interactions between economic growth, energy use, and climate change impacts, helping policymakers understand potential future scenarios.

While IAMs are valuable tools for exploring long-term scenarios, they are computationally demanding and require extensive data inputs. Their outputs should be interpreted with caution, recognizing the inherent uncertainties associated with modeling complex systems over long timeframes.

Case Study 3: The 2° Investing Initiative's PACTA Tool (Paris Agreement Capital Transition Assessment)

Focus: Using a Transition Risk Model to Assess the Alignment of Investment Portfolios with the Paris Agreement Goals

The 2° Investing Initiative (2°ii) developed the Paris Agreement Capital Transition Assessment (PACTA) tool to help investors analyze the alignment of their investment portfolios with the goals of the Paris Agreement. This case study explores how the PACTA tool uses transition risk models to assess the carbon intensity of portfolios, evaluate exposure to transition risks, and identify opportunities to shift investments toward a low-carbon trajectory.

Illustration: Development and Implementation of the PACTA Tool

1. **Development of the PACTA Tool:**

The PACTA tool was developed by the 2° Investing Initiative to provide investors with a robust methodology for assessing the alignment of their portfolios with the Paris Agreement's climate goals. The tool leverages a range of data sources, including company-level emissions data, sectoral decarbonization pathways, and climate scenarios, to evaluate the carbon intensity and transition risks of investment portfolios (2° Investing Initiative, 2021).

2. **Analyzing Carbon Intensity and Transition Risks:**

The PACTA tool allows investors to analyze the carbon intensity of their portfolios by comparing the emissions profiles of their investments to sector-specific decarbonization pathways. The tool assesses exposure to transition risks, such as regulatory changes, market shifts, and technological advancements, that could impact the financial performance of high-carbon assets (Battiston et al., 2017; Dietz et al., 2016).

3. **Identifying Opportunities for Low-Carbon Investments:**

The PACTA tool helps investors identify opportunities to shift their investments toward low-carbon technologies and sectors. By aligning their portfolios with the Paris Agreement goals, investors can reduce their exposure to transition risks and contribute to the global effort to mitigate climate change (TCFD, 2017; UNEP FI, 2019).

Discussion: Role of Investor-Led Initiatives, Challenges, and Importance of Transparency

1. **Role of Investor-Led Initiatives in Promoting Climate Action:**

Investor-led initiatives like the PACTA tool play a crucial role in promoting climate action by encouraging investors to align their portfolios with climate goals. These initiatives provide the tools and frameworks needed to assess and manage climate risks, driving the financial sector toward more sustainable practices.

2. **Challenges of Standardizing Climate Risk Assessments for Investment Portfolios:**

Standardizing climate risk assessments for investment portfolios presents several challenges, including:

- **Data Availability:** Access to consistent and reliable emissions data across companies and sectors is limited.
- **Methodological Differences:** Variations in climate risk assessment methodologies can lead to inconsistent results.
- **Scenario Uncertainty:** Different climate scenarios and assumptions can yield divergent risk assessments.

3. **Importance of Transparency in Methodology and Data:**

Transparency in the methodology and data used for climate risk assessments is essential for building trust and credibility. Investors need clear and consistent information to make informed decisions and ensure that their portfolios are aligned with climate goals (CDSB, 2022; GRI, 2021).

Conclusion

The 2° Investing Initiative's PACTA tool exemplifies the use of transition risk models to assess the alignment of investment portfolios with the Paris Agreement goals. By analyzing the carbon intensity of portfolios, evaluating exposure to transition risks, and identifying opportunities for low-carbon investments, the PACTA tool supports investors in managing climate risks and promoting climate action. This case study highlights the role of investor-led initiatives in driving sustainable finance, the challenges of standardizing climate risk assessments, and the importance of transparency in methodology and data.

Understanding the methodologies and strategies employed by the PACTA tool can provide valuable insights for investors seeking to align their portfolios with climate goals and contribute to a sustainable future.

4 Challenges and Opportunities in Transition Risk Modeling

Transition risk modeling is a rapidly evolving field facing ongoing challenges and exciting opportunities. Addressing these challenges and seizing the opportunities will be crucial for enhancing the accuracy, relevance, and usefulness of transition risk models in supporting informed decision-making.

4.1 Data Gaps and Uncertainties

A major challenge in transition risk modeling is the lack of reliable and comprehensive data on key drivers of transition risk, such as:

- **Policy Trajectories:** Predicting future policy changes, such as the stringency of carbon pricing mechanisms or the pace of renewable energy deployment, is inherently uncertain.
- **Technological Advancements:** The pace and direction of technological innovation, particularly in areas like renewable energy, battery storage, and carbon capture, are difficult to forecast with precision.
- **Market Dynamics:** Predicting shifts in consumer preferences, investor sentiment, and the emergence of new markets can be challenging.

Addressing these uncertainties requires:

- **Sensitivity Analysis:** Testing how model outputs change when key input parameters are varied, providing insights into the impact of uncertainty on the results.

- **Scenario Planning:** Developing a range of plausible scenarios based on different assumptions about key drivers, enabling decision-makers to explore a spectrum of possible outcomes and prepare for different eventualities.
- **Expert Judgment:** Incorporating insights and perspectives from experts in relevant fields, such as climate policy, technology, and market analysis, to supplement data-driven models.

4.2 Model Complexity and Assumptions

Transition risk models can be complex, involving numerous variables, assumptions, and interdependencies. This complexity can make it challenging to understand the underlying logic of the models, interpret the results, and communicate the findings to decision-makers.

To enhance transparency and credibility:

- **Clearly Document Assumptions:** Modelers should clearly document the assumptions made about future policy developments, technological progress, economic growth, and other key factors.
- **Conduct Validation and Peer Review:** Models should be rigorously validated against historical data, and the results should be subject to peer review to ensure quality and accuracy.
- **Develop User-Friendly Interfaces:** Creating user-friendly interfaces for models can make them more accessible to non-experts, allowing decision-makers to explore different scenarios, test assumptions, and understand the implications of model outputs.

Farmer et al. (2015) argues for a "third wave" in the economics of climate change, advocating for more complex and realistic models that incorporate insights from complexity science, behavioral economics, and other fields. The authors suggest that traditional economic models (the "first wave") and integrated assessment models (the "second wave") are insufficient to capture the full complexity of climate-economy interactions. The authors propose models that can capture nonlinear dynamics, tipping points, and heterogeneous agent behavior. They emphasize the importance of considering technological innovation, institutional change, and social dynamics in climate-economy models. The paper argues for a more interdisciplinary approach, integrating insights from climate science, ecology, and other relevant fields.

Dietz et al., (2016) examines whether economic models of climate change accurately represent key climate dynamics. The authors focus on three specific aspects of climate dynamics: the carbon cycle, the role of non-CO_2 greenhouse gases, and the relationship between warming and economic damages. They find that many economic models oversimplify climate processes, potentially leading to underestimation of climate damages and optimal carbon prices. The paper finds that more accurately representing climate dynamics can significantly affect policy recommendations, such as the optimal carbon price. The authors emphasize the importance of collaboration between economists and climate scientists to improve the representation of climate processes in economic models.

4.3 Integrating Social and Governance Factors

Many transition risk models focus primarily on environmental factors, such as greenhouse gas emissions, energy consumption, and carbon pricing. However, social and governance factors (the "S" and "G" in ESG) are also playing an increasingly important role in shaping the low-carbon transition.

These factors include:

- **Social Equity and Justice:** The transition to a low-carbon economy must be fair and equitable, ensuring that workers and communities dependent on fossil fuel industries are not left behind.
- **Consumer Behavior:** Shifts in consumer preferences toward sustainable products and services are driving market demand for low-carbon solutions.
- **Corporate Governance:** Strong corporate governance practices, including transparency in climate-related disclosures and accountability for climate commitments, are becoming increasingly important for investors and consumers.

Integrating these social and governance factors into transition risk models is essential for capturing the full complexity of the low-carbon transition and providing a more comprehensive assessment of risks and opportunities.

5 Conclusion: Navigating a Transformative Era

The transition to a low-carbon economy is a defining challenge of our time, presenting both significant risks and unprecedented opportunities. Transition risk modeling provides essential tools for navigating this transformative era, helping us understand the potential financial impacts of decarbonization, identify emerging opportunities, and make more informed decisions.

By embracing scenario planning, utilizing robust financial models, developing sector-specific tools, and integrating social and governance considerations, we can enhance the accuracy and relevance of transition risk assessments. This knowledge can empower investors, guide corporate strategies, and inform policy decisions that support a smooth and equitable transition to a low-carbon and climate-resilient economy.

The journey toward a sustainable future is complex, but by utilizing the power of transition risk modeling, we can navigate the challenges, seize the opportunities, and shape a world where economic prosperity and environmental sustainability go hand in hand.

References

Aldy, J. E., & Stavins, R. N. (2012). The promise and problems of pricing carbon: Theory and experience. *The Journal of Environment & Development, 21*(2), 152–180. https://journals.sagepub.com/doi/10.1177/1070496512442508

Bank for International Settlements (BIS). (2020). *The green swan: Central banking and financial stability in the age of climate change*. https://www.bis.org/publ/othp31.pdf

Bassett, D., Crum, T., & Hoskins, J. (2023). *Climate risk modeling solutions, 2023: Market and vendor landscape*. Chartis Research. https://www.chartis-research.com/esg/7947050/climate-risk-modeling-solutions-2023-market-and-vendor-landscape

Bernstein, A., Gustafson, M. T., & Lewis, R. (2019). Disaster on the horizon: The price effect of sea level rise. *Journal of Financial Economics, 134*(2), 253–272. https://doi.org/10.1016/j.jfineco.2019.03.013

Bolton, P., & Kacperczyk, M. (2021). Do investors care about carbon risk? *Journal of Financial Economics, 142*(2), 517–549. https://www.sciencedirect.com/science/article/pii/S0304405X21001902

Burke, M., Craxton, M., Kolstad, C. D., Onda, C., Allcott, H., Baker, E., Barrage, L., Carson, R., Gillingham, K., Graff-Zivin, J., & Greenstone, M. (2016). Opportunities for advances in climate change economics. *Science, 352*(6283), 292–293. https://science.sciencemag.org/content/352/6283/292

Cahen-Fourot, L., Campiglio, E., Godin, A., Kemp-Benedict, E., & Trsek, S. (2021). Capital stranding cascades: The impact of decarbonisation on productive asset utilization. *Energy Economics, 103*, 105581. https://doi.org/10.1016/j.eneco.2021.105581

Carley, S., Baldwin, E., MacLean, L. M., & Brass, J. N. (2017). Global expansion of renewable energy generation: An analysis of policy instruments. *Environmental and Resource Economics, 68*(2), 397–440. https://10.1007/s10640-016-0025-3

Christian, H., Jahns, H., Kempa, K., & Moslener, U. (2023). Deep uncertainty and the transition to a low-carbon economy. *Environmental Science & Policy, 133*, 1–12. https://doi.org/10.1016/j.envsci.2023.05.002

Dietz, S., Bowen, A., Dixon, C., & Gradwell, P. (2016). 'climate value at risk' of global financial assets. *Nature Climate Change, 6*(7), 676–679. https://doi.org/10.1038/nclimate2972

Farmer, J. D., Hepburn, C., Mealy, P., & Teytelboym, A. (2015). A third wave in the economics of climate change. *Environmental and Resource Economics, 62*(2), 329–357. https://doi.org/10.1007/s10640-015-9965-2

Flammer, C. (2021). Corporate green bonds. *Journal of Financial Economics, 142*(2), 499–516. https://www.sciencedirect.com/science/article/abs/pii/S0304405X21000337

Giglio, S., Kelly, B., & Stroebel, J. (2021). Climate finance. *Annual Review of Financial Economics, 13*, 15–36. https://doi.org/10.1146/annurev-financial-102620-103311

Gillingham, K., Newell, R. G., & Palmer, K. (2009). Energy efficiency economics and policy. *Annual Review of Resource Economics, 1*(1), 597–620. https://www.annualreviews.org/doi/abs/10.1146/annurev.resource.102308.124234

Goulder, L. H., & Schein, A. R. (2013). Carbon taxes versus cap and trade: a critical review. *Climate Change Economics, 4*(03), 1350010. https://doi.org/10.1142/S2010007813500103

Hafner, S. Anger-Kraavi, A. Monasterolo, I., & Jones, A. (2020). Emergence of new economics energy transition models: A review. *Ecological Economics, 177*, 106–779, ISSN 0921–8009. https://doi.org/10.1016/j.ecolecon.2020.106779

International Monetary Fund (IMF). (2023). *Global economic impacts of physical climate risks*. https://www.imf.org/en/Publications/WP/Issues/2023/05/01/Global-Economic-Impacts-of-Physical-Climate-Risks-460989

Kavlak, G., McNerney, J., & Trancik, J. E. (2018). Evaluating the causes of cost reduction in photovoltaic modules. *Energy policy, 123*, 700–710. https://doi.org/10.1016/j.enpol.2018.08.015

Klenert, D., Mattauch, L., Combet, E., Edenhofer, O., Hepburn, C., Rafaty, R., & Stern, N. (2018). Making carbon pricing work for citizens. *Nature Climate Change, 8*(8), 669–677. https://www.nature.com/articles/s41558-018-0201-2

Kruttli, M. S., Tran, B. R., & Watugala, S. W. (2024). Pricing Poseidon: Extreme weather uncertainty and firm return dynamics. *The Journal of Finance, 80*(2), 783–832. https://doi.org/10.2139/ssrn.3284517

Krueger, P., Sautner, Z., & Starks, L. T. (2020). The importance of climate risks for institutional investors. *The Review of Financial Studies, 33*(3), 1067–1111. https://doi.org/10.1093/rfs/hhz137

Monasterolo, I., & de Angelis, L. (2020). Blind to carbon risk? An analysis of stock market reaction to the Paris agreement. *Ecological Economics, 170*, 106–571. https://www.sciencedirect.com/science/article/abs/pii/S0921800919309607

Network for Greening the Financial System (NGFS). (2020). *Guide to climate scenario analysis for central banks and supervisors*. https://www.ngfs.net/sites/default/files/medias/documents/ngfs_guide_scenario_analysis_final.pdf

Nordhaus, W. D. (2017). Revisiting the social cost of carbon. *Proceedings of the National Academy of Sciences, 114*(7), 1518–1523. https://doi.org/10.1073/pnas.1609244114

Nykvist, B., & Nilsson, M. (2015). Rapidly falling costs of battery packs for electric vehicles. *Nature Climate Change, 5*(4), 329–332. https://doi.org/10.1038/nclimate2564

PwC. (2023). *Climate risk modeling: What you need to know to get started*. https://www.pwc.com/us/en/services/esg/library/climate-risk-modeling.html

Rentschler, J., & Bazilian, M. (2017). Policy monitor—principles for designing effective fossil fuel subsidy reforms. *Review of Environmental Economics and Policy. 11*(1). 138–155 https://doi.org/10.1093/reep/rew016

Schlenker, W., & Christian A. Taylor. (2021). Market expectations of a warming climate. *Journal of Financial Economics, 142*(2), 627–640. https://www.sciencedirect.com/science/article/abs/pii/S0304405X21001495?via%3Dihub

Semieniuk, G., Campiglio, E., Mercure, J. F., Volz, U., & Edwards, N. R. (2021). Low-carbon transition risks for finance. *Wiley Interdisciplinary Reviews: Climate Change, 12*(1), 678. https://doi.org/10.1002/wcc.678

Sen, S., & Von Schickfus, M. T. (2020). Climate policy, stranded assets, and investors' expectations. *Journal of Environmental Economics and Management, 100*, 102277. https://doi.org/10.1016/j.jeem.2019.102277

Stroebel, J., & Wurgler, J. (2021). What do you think about climate finance? *Journal of Financial Economics, 142*(2), 487–498. https://doi.org/10.1016/j.jfineco.2021.08.004

Sustainability Leadership CI. (2019). *Transition risk framework: Managing the impacts of the low carbon transition on infrastructure investments*. https://www.cisl.cam.ac.uk/system/files/documents/cisl-climate-wise-transition-risk-framework-report.pdf

The Agence Française de Développement (AFD). (2024). *Modelling low-carbon transitions in Colombia: Macrofinancial opportunities and risks*. https://www.afd.fr/en/ressources/modelling-low-carbon-transitions-colombia-macrofinancial-opportunities-and-risks

United Nations Environment Programme Finance Initiative (UNEP FI). (2023). *The 2023 climate risk landscape*. https://www.unepfi.org/themes/climate-change/2023-climate-risk-landscape/

Vermeulen, R., Schets, E., Lohuis, M., Kölbl, B., Jansen, D. J., & Heeringa, W. (2021). The heat is on: A framework for measuring financial stress under disruptive energy transition scenarios. *Ecological Economics, 190*, 107205. https://doi.org/10.1016/j.ecolecon.2021.107205

Case References

° Investing Initiative. (2021). *PACTA/climate scenario analysis program*. https://2degrees-investing.org/resource/pacta/

Battiston, S., Mandel, A., Monasterolo, I., Schütze, F., & Visentin, G. (2017). A climate stress-test of the financial system. *Nature Climate Change, 7*(4), 283–288. https://doi.org/10.1038/nclimate3255

Bloomberg New Energy Finance (BloombergNEF). (2023). *Electric vehicle outlook 2024*. https://about.bnef.com/electric-vehicle-outlook/

Climate Disclosure Standards Board (CDSB). (2022). *CDSB Framework for reporting environmental and climate change information*. Accessed 23 January 2025. https://www.cdsb.net/what-we-do/reporting-frameworks

Dietz, S., Bowen, A., Dixon, C., & Gradwell, P. (2016). 'Climate value at risk' of global financial assets. *Nature Climate Change, 6*(7), 676–679. https://doi.org/10.1038/nclimate2972

Global Reporting Initiative (GRI). (2021). *GRI standards: Sustainability reporting guidelines*. Accessed 9 September 2024. https://www.globalreporting.org/standards/

International Energy Agency. (IEA). (2020). *Global EV outlook 2020*. https://www.iea.org/reports/global-ev-outlook-2020

International Renewable Energy Agency (IRENA). (2016). *REmap: Roadmap for a renewable energy future (2016 edition)*. Accessed 1 January 2020. https://www.irena.org/publications/2016/Mar/REmap-Roadmap-for-A-Renewable-Energy-Future-2016-Edition

IRENA. (2017). *Electricity storage and renewables: Costs and markets to 2030*. Accessed 23 January 2025. https://www.irena.org/publications/2017/Oct/Electricity-storage-and-renewables-costs-and-markets

IRENA. (2018). *Renewable energy prospects for the European Union*. https://www.irena.org/publications/2018/Feb/Renewable-energy-prospects-for-the-EU

IRENA. (2019a). *Global energy transformation: A roadmap to 2050 (2019 edition)*. https://www.irena.org/publications/2019/Apr/Global-energy-transformation-A-roadmap-to-2050-2019Edition

IRENA. (2019b). *Innovation landscape for a renewable-powered future*. Accessed 23 January 2025. https://www.irena.org/publications/2019/Feb/Innovation-landscape-for-a-renewable-powered-future

IRENA. (2020a). *Renewable energy policies in a time of transition: Heating and cooling*. Accessed 23 January 2025. https://www.irena.org/publications/2020/Nov/Renewable-energy-policies-in-a-time-of-transition-Heating-and-cooling

IRENA. (2020b). *Renewable energy and jobs—Annual review 2020*. https://www.irena.org/publications/2020/Sep/Renewable-Energy-and-Jobs-Annual-Review-2020

IRENA. (2021). *World energy transitions outlook: 1.5°C pathway*. Accessed 23 January 2025. https://www.irena.org/publications/2021/Jun/World-Energy-Transitions-Outlook

Task Force on Climate-Related Financial Disclosures. (TCFD). (2017). *Final report: Recommendations of the task force on climate-related financial disclosures*. https://www.fsb-tcfd.org/publications/final-recommendations-report/

Tesla, Inc. (2023). *Impact report 2023*. https://www.tesla.com/ns_videos/2023-tesla-impact-report-highlights.pdf

United Nations Environment Programme Finance Initiative (UNEP FI). (2019). *Changing course: A comprehensive investor guide to scenario-based methods for climate risk assessment, in response to the TCFD*. Accessed 1 January 2024. https://www.unepfi.org/publications/investment-publications/changing-course-a-comprehensive-investor-guide-to-scenario-based-methods-for-climate-risk-assessment-in-response-to-the-tcfd/

World Economic Forum (WEF). (2020). *The future of the last-mile ecosystem*. Accessed 27 January 2025. https://www.weforum.org/publications/the-future-of-the-last-mile-ecosystem/

CHAPTER 8

The Challenge of Climate Risk Modeling: Navigating Complexity and Uncertainty

1 Introduction: The Imperfect Crystal Ball

Climate risk models are powerful tools, but they are not crystal balls. While they provide valuable insights into the potential impacts of climate change, they are inherently limited by the complexity of the Earth system, the availability of data, and the assumptions built into the models themselves. Recognizing these limitations is crucial for interpreting model outputs appropriately, identifying areas for improvement, and making informed decisions in the face of uncertainty.

The quest to quantify the risks of climate change is a daunting endeavor. We are attempting to model a complex system with countless interacting variables, from atmospheric circulation patterns and ocean currents to human behavior and technological advancements. Moreover, we are trying to project these complex interactions into the future, a future shaped by choices we have yet to make about greenhouse gas emissions, economic development, and technological innovation.

While acknowledging these challenges might seem discouraging, it is essential for advancing the science of climate risk modeling and ensuring that these models are used responsibly and effectively. By understanding the limitations of climate models, we can:

- **Interpret Results with Caution:** Avoid overconfidence in model outputs and recognize that projections represent a range of possible futures, not precise predictions.
- **Improve Models:** Identify areas where data gaps exist, assumptions need to be refined, or modeling techniques can be enhanced, leading to more accurate and robust risk assessments.

J. Chen, *Climate Finance*, https://doi.org/10.1007/978-981-96-7975-1_8

- **Make Informed Decisions:** Use model outputs as one input among many when making decisions, incorporating expert judgment, considering a range of possible outcomes, and developing strategies that are flexible and adaptable to changing conditions.

This chapter will explore the key challenges of climate risk modeling, examining issues related to data limitations, model complexity, uncertainty communication, and the integration of expert judgment. By confronting these challenges head-on, we can strengthen the science of climate risk modeling and enhance its ability to support informed decision-making in a world facing the growing impacts of a changing climate (Fig. 1).

The UNEP FI (2023) report presents survey results of important factors financial institutions (FIs) consider when choosing or collaborating with a vendor for climate risk assessment tools. In the context of the challenges of climate risk modeling—navigating complexity and uncertainty—this figure highlights several key themes:

- **Transparency Is Paramount:** The most important factor, by a significant margin, is *transparency*. This underscores the "black box" problem often associated with climate risk models. FIs recognize that to trust and effectively use these tools, they need to understand the underlying methodologies, data sources, and assumptions. Lack of transparency can create mistrust and hinder the integration of climate risk assessments into decision-making processes.
- **Data Scope/Coverage Is Crucial:** The second most important factor is *data scope/coverage*. This highlights the critical role of data availability, quality, and relevance in climate risk modeling. FIs need tools that cover

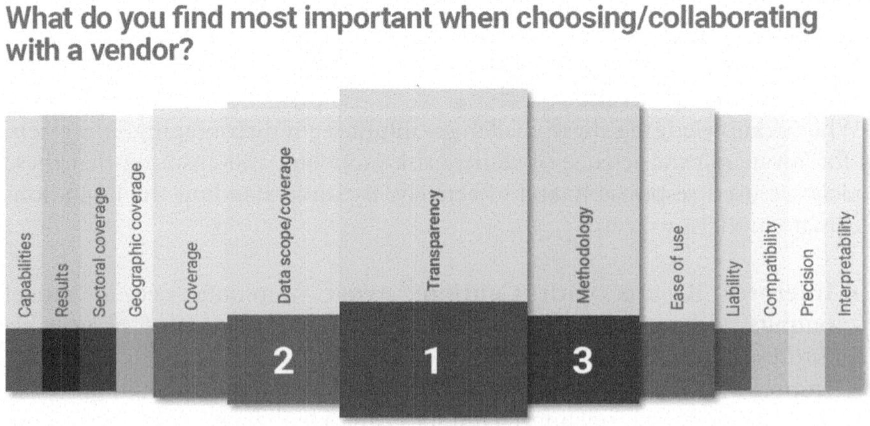

Fig. 1 Survey results of important factors when choosing a vendor (*Source* UNEP FI [2023])

the relevant geographies, sectors, and hazards for their specific portfolios and investments. Data gaps and limitations are a major challenge in climate risk modeling, particularly for physical risk assessments, and FIs prioritize vendors that can address these challenges effectively.
- **Methodology Matters:** The third most important factor is *methodology*. This emphasizes that FIs recognize the complexity of climate risk modeling and the importance of choosing appropriate methodologies. Different approaches (e.g., top-down vs. bottom-up, probabilistic vs. deterministic) have different strengths and weaknesses, and FIs need to ensure that the chosen methodology aligns with their objectives and the available data.
- **Other Factors:** While less critical than the top three, other factors also play a role in vendor selection:
  - **Capabilities and results:** FIs consider the vendor's overall expertise and track record in providing reliable and useful climate risk assessments.
  - **Sectoral and geographic coverage:** Reflects the need for tools that cover the specific sectors and regions relevant to the FI's activities.
  - **Ease of use, liability, compatibility, precision, and interpretability:** These factors are related to the practical application and integration of climate risk tools into existing workflows and decision-making processes.

The survey results directly address several key challenges of climate risk modeling:

- **Data limitations:** The emphasis on data scope/coverage underscores the need for high-quality, relevant data, which is often a limiting factor in climate risk assessments, particularly in emerging markets.
- **Model complexity:** The importance of methodology highlights the need for transparent and appropriate modeling approaches. Complex models can be difficult to understand and interpret, which can hinder their effective use in decision-making.
- **Uncertainty:** While not explicitly mentioned, the focus on transparency and methodology is implicitly linked to the challenge of communicating and managing uncertainty. Transparent methodologies and clear communication of limitations and assumptions are crucial for building trust and enabling informed decision-making in the face of uncertainty.

By prioritizing transparency, data, and methodology, FIs demonstrate their understanding of the key challenges in climate risk modeling and their commitment to using these tools effectively to manage the growing financial risks associated with climate change.

2 Data Challenges

Data is the lifeblood of climate risk modeling. The accuracy, reliability, and completeness of data inputs directly influence the quality and usefulness of model outputs. However, obtaining high-quality data for climate risk assessments is a persistent challenge, particularly when it comes to capturing the localized impacts of climate change and accounting for future uncertainties.

2.1 Data Availability and Quality

Climate risk models rely on a wide range of data, including:

- **Climate Hazard Data:** Information on the historical frequency, intensity, and spatial distribution of climate hazards, such as temperature extremes, precipitation events, sea-level rise, and wildfires.
- **Asset Exposure Data:** Data on the location and value of assets that are exposed to climate risks, including infrastructure, buildings, agricultural lands, and population centers.
- **Vulnerability Data:** Information on the susceptibility of different assets and populations to specific climate hazards, such as building construction types, elevation above sea level, and the adaptive capacity of communities.

While significant progress has been made in collecting and disseminating climate data, data gaps and quality issues remain persistent challenges, particularly for:

- **Historical Data Limitations:** Climate change is altering the frequency and intensity of hazards, making the past an imperfect guide to the future. Historical data may not fully capture the risks associated with more extreme events or gradual shifts in climate patterns. Nissan et al. (2019) highlight the limitations of long-term climate projections for local adaptation.
- **Regional and Local Data Scarcity:** Global climate models (GCMs), which provide projections of future climate change, often have a coarse spatial resolution, making it difficult to assess risks at the local scales where adaptation decisions are made. Downscaling techniques can help to translate global projections to regional scales, but data limitations at local levels can still hinder accurate risk assessments. Reichstein et al. (2019) suggest deep learning can improve Earth system models and predictions of long-range spatial connections.
- **Data Quality Issues:** Inconsistent data collection methods, incomplete datasets, errors in data entry, and a lack of standardized data formats can all compromise the quality of climate risk assessments.

For example, assessing the risk of flooding in a coastal city requires detailed data on local sea-level rise projections, elevation data for coastal areas, building codes and construction types, and the capacity of drainage systems to handle extreme rainfall events. Gaps or inaccuracies in any of these data sources can significantly affect the reliability of the risk assessment.

2.2 Data Standardization and Accessibility

Even when data is available, ensuring its consistency and accessibility across different sectors, regions, and organizations is crucial for effective climate risk modeling. The lack of standardized data formats, inconsistent data collection methods, and limited data sharing can hinder collaboration and impede the development of comprehensive risk assessments. Wilkinson et al. (2016) propose FAIR principles for scientific data.

Efforts are underway to address these challenges:

- **Standardized Data Formats:** Organizations like the Open Geospatial Consortium (OGC) are developing standardized data formats for climate-related information, making it easier to share and integrate data from different sources.
- **Open Data Platforms:** Platforms like the Climate Data Factory and the World Bank's Climate Change Knowledge Portal are making climate data more accessible to researchers, policymakers, and practitioners worldwide.
- **Data Sharing Initiatives:** Collaborations like the Coalition for Climate Resilient Investment are promoting data sharing and standardization to facilitate more robust and comparable climate risk assessments. Sherbinin et al. (2015) use remote sensing for climate vulnerability mapping, highlighting data integration challenges.

However, much work remains to be done to create a truly integrated and accessible global climate data infrastructure that supports effective risk modeling and decision-making.

Case Study 1: The World Bank's Climate Change Knowledge Portal (CCKP) and Data Gaps in Developing Countries

Focus: Highlight the Challenges of Accessing Reliable Climate Data in Developing Countries, Hindering Their Ability to Assess Climate Risks and Plan for Adaptation

Access to reliable climate data is crucial for assessing climate risks and planning for adaptation. However, developing countries often face significant challenges in accessing such data, which hinders their ability to develop effective climate policies and adaptation strategies. This case study explores the World Bank's Climate Change Knowledge Portal (CCKP) and its efforts to provide open and accessible climate data for developing countries, while also addressing the persistent data gaps.

Illustration: Methodology and Implementation of the CCKP.

1. The World Bank's Climate Change Knowledge Portal (CCKP):

The CCKP is an online platform designed to provide comprehensive global, regional, and country-level climate data and information. It aims to support decision-making by offering accessible climate data, including historical climate conditions, future climate projections, and vulnerability assessments (Climate ADAPT, 2016; World Bank, 2021a).

2. Addressing Data Gaps:

Despite the comprehensive data available on the CCKP, significant data gaps remain, particularly for localized climate projections, socioeconomic data, and vulnerability assessments. These gaps make it challenging for developing countries to accurately assess climate risks and plan for adaptation (Dinku, 2019; Dupraz-Dobias, 2022).

3. Efforts to Improve Data Collection:

The World Bank is actively working to improve data collection and address these gaps. This includes partnerships with national governments and research institutions, as well as the use of innovative technologies such as satellite imagery and crowdsourcing to gather more comprehensive and accurate climate data (World Bank, 2022, 2023a).

Discussion: Role of the World Bank, Challenges, and Potential Solutions

1. Role of the World Bank in Improving Climate Data:

The World Bank plays a crucial role in improving climate data availability and quality in developing countries. Through initiatives like the CCKP, the World Bank provides essential data and tools to help countries better understand and manage climate risks (World Bank, 2023b, 2024).

2. Challenges of Implementing the CCKP and Addressing Data Gaps:

Several challenges hinder the effective implementation of the CCKP and the collection of reliable climate data in developing countries (Bonnisseau, 2022), including:

- Inadequate Funding: Limited financial resources for data collection and infrastructure development.
- Poor Data-Sharing Practices: Lack of collaboration and data-sharing between countries and institutions.
- Technological Barriers: Insufficient access to advanced technologies and expertise for data processing and analysis.

3. Potential Solutions and Innovations:

To address these challenges, the World Bank and its partners are exploring various solutions (World Bank, 2021b; UNDP, 2024), including:

- Satellite Imagery and Remote Sensing: Utilizing satellite technology to gather climate data in remote and underserved regions.
- Crowdsourcing: Engaging local communities in data collection efforts to improve data coverage and accuracy.
- Capacity Building: Providing training and resources to national meteorological services and research institutions to enhance their data collection and analysis capabilities.

Conclusion

The World Bank's Climate Change Knowledge Portal (CCKP) is a valuable resource for providing open and accessible climate data to developing countries. However, significant data gaps remain, particularly for localized climate projections, socioeconomic data, and vulnerability assessments. These gaps hinder the ability of developing countries to accurately assess climate risks and plan for adaptation.

The World Bank's efforts to improve data collection, through partnerships with national governments and research institutions, and the use of innovative technologies such as satellite imagery and crowdsourcing, are crucial steps toward addressing these challenges. By enhancing the availability and quality of climate data, the World Bank can help developing countries build resilience to climate change and develop effective adaptation strategies.

Understanding the methodologies and strategies employed by the World Bank can provide valuable insights for other organizations and stakeholders seeking to improve climate data collection and support climate resilience in developing countries.

3 Model Limitations

While data quality and accessibility are fundamental to climate risk modeling, the models themselves also face inherent limitations. These limitations stem from the complexity of the climate system, the need to make assumptions about future conditions, and the challenges of communicating complex model outputs to decision-makers.

3.1 *Model Complexity and Assumptions*

Climate risk models, particularly those that integrate both physical and transition risks, can be highly complex, involving numerous variables, assumptions, and interdependencies. This complexity can create challenges for:

- **Understanding Model Logic:** Decision-makers need to understand how the models work and what assumptions underpin the results to interpret the outputs appropriately. Lack of transparency in model methodologies can lead to mistrust and hinder the use of models in decision-making. Saltelli et al. (2020) propose five principles for responsible modeling, emphasizing transparency, appropriate complexity, and clear communication.
- **Validating Models:** Models should be rigorously validated against historical data to assess their accuracy and predictive power. However, validating complex models with multiple interconnected components can be challenging, especially when dealing with uncertain future conditions. Smith and Stern (2011) highlight the importance of understanding and communicating scientific uncertainty in climate policy-making.
- **Communicating Complexity:** Explaining complex model outputs to non-expert audiences can be difficult. Modelers need to find ways to communicate key findings and insights clearly and concisely, avoiding technical jargon and using visualizations and narratives that make the information more accessible.

For example, a model that assesses the risk of stranded assets in the fossil fuel sector might incorporate assumptions about future carbon pricing policies, technological advancements in renewable energy, and shifts in consumer demand. Clearly communicating these assumptions and the potential impact of different scenarios on asset valuations is crucial for investors and policymakers to understand the model's results and use them to inform their decisions.

3.2 *Uncertainty in Climate Projections*

Climate change is a complex process with inherent uncertainties. Climate models, while sophisticated, provide a range of possible future scenarios, not precise predictions. This uncertainty arises from:

- **Natural Variability:** The climate system exhibits natural fluctuations and cycles that are difficult to predict precisely.

- **Model Limitations:** Climate models are simplifications of reality and cannot capture every aspect of the climate system. Stainforth (2007) discuss the limitations of climate models for long-term predictions and the importance of communicating uncertainties.
- **Emission Scenarios:** Future greenhouse gas emissions depend on human choices and behaviors, which are inherently uncertain.

This uncertainty creates challenges for:

- **Quantifying Uncertainty:** Expressing uncertainty in model outputs in a meaningful way, such as using confidence intervals or probability distributions, is essential for conveying the range of possible outcomes.
- **Communicating Uncertainty:** Presenting uncertainty clearly and avoiding overconfidence in any single scenario is crucial for avoiding misleading decision-makers.
- **Making Decisions Under Uncertainty:** Decision-makers need to recognize that climate risk assessments are not about predicting the future with certainty but rather about providing a framework for understanding potential risks and opportunities and making informed choices in the face of uncertainty. Hawkins and Sutton (2009) explore reducing uncertainty in regional climate predictions.

For example, a model that projects future sea-level rise might provide a range of possible outcomes, from a relatively modest increase to a more extreme scenario. Communicating this range of possibilities, along with the associated probabilities, is crucial for coastal communities planning adaptation measures.

Case Study 2: The Insurance Industry's Struggle to Model Wildfire Risk in California

Focus: Examine the Challenges Faced by the Insurance Industry in Accurately Modeling and Pricing Wildfire Risk in a Region Experiencing More Frequent and Severe Wildfires Due to Climate Change.

The insurance industry in California is grappling with the increasing frequency and severity of wildfires, driven by climate change. This case study explores the challenges insurers face in accurately modeling and pricing wildfire risk, highlighting the complex interplay of factors such as climate change, drought, forest management practices, and human development patterns.

Illustration: Methodology and Implementation of Wildfire Risk Modeling.

1. Challenges of Traditional Models:

Traditional insurance models rely heavily on historical data to assess risk. However, the rapidly changing climate has rendered these models less reliable, as past wildfire patterns no longer accurately predict future occurrences. The increasing frequency and intensity of wildfires in California have outpaced the assumptions built into these models (Insurance Information Institute, 2025).

2. Complex Interplay of Factors:

Wildfire risk is influenced by a combination of factors, including climate change, prolonged droughts, forest management practices, and human development patterns. These factors interact in complex ways, making it difficult to predict the frequency, intensity, and location of future fires (U.S. Forest Service, 2025).

3. Incorporating Climate Projections:

To address the limitations of traditional models, the insurance industry is incorporating climate projections into their risk assessments. This involves using advanced climate models to predict future wildfire risks based on various climate scenarios, including changes in temperature, precipitation, and vegetation (IPCC, 2019).

4. New Data Sources and Technologies:

Insurance companies are leveraging new data sources and technologies to improve wildfire risk modeling. Satellite imagery, remote sensing, and fire behavior simulations provide real-time data and predictive insights that enhance the accuracy of risk assessments (National Aeronautics and Space Administration (NASA), 2023).

Discussion: Efforts, Challenges, and Potential Solutions.

1. Efforts to Improve Wildfire Risk Modeling:

The insurance industry is making concerted efforts to improve wildfire risk modeling by integrating climate projections and utilizing advanced technologies. These efforts aim to provide more accurate risk assessments and enable better pricing of insurance policies (Bevere & Gloor, 2020).

2. Challenges of Balancing Affordability with Risk-Based Pricing:

One of the significant challenges for insurers is balancing affordability with risk-based pricing. As wildfire risks increase, so do insurance premiums, making it difficult for homeowners to afford coverage. Insurers must find ways to offer affordable policies while accurately reflecting the heightened risk.

3. Potential Solutions and Innovations:

To address these challenges, the insurance industry is exploring various solutions and innovations, including:

- Parametric Insurance: Policies that pay out based on predefined triggers, such as the occurrence of a wildfire, rather than actual losses.
- Public-Private Partnerships: Collaborations between insurers, governments, and communities to improve wildfire resilience and risk mitigation.
- Community-Based Fire Management: Engaging local communities in fire prevention and management efforts to reduce overall risk.

Conclusion

The insurance industry's struggle to model wildfire risk in California highlights the significant challenges posed by climate change. Traditional models based on historical data are no longer sufficient to predict future wildfire risks, necessitating the incorporation of climate projections and the use of advanced technologies. Despite these efforts, balancing affordability with risk-based pricing remains a critical challenge.

The industry's ongoing efforts to improve data collection, leverage new technologies, and explore innovative solutions are crucial steps toward more accurate wildfire risk modeling. By enhancing their ability to predict and price wildfire risks, insurers can better protect homeowners, support community resilience, and contribute to a more sustainable future.

Understanding the methodologies and strategies employed by the insurance industry can provide valuable insights for other sectors facing similar challenges in adapting to the impacts of climate change.

4 Bridging the Gap Between Science and Decision-Making

Climate risk models are ultimately tools for informing human decisions. However, bridging the gap between complex scientific projections and actionable insights for decision-makers in business, finance, and government is an ongoing challenge (Fig. 2).

The above figure from UNEP FI (2023) report shows survey results of the biggest challenges financial institutions (FIs) face when using vendor-provided climate risk assessment tools, *excluding* data availability and modeling certainty. These are additional challenges that hinder practical use. This figure directly relates to the challenge of bridging the gap between climate science and decision-making within the financial sector.

Fig. 2 Survey results of challenges FIs are facing with vendors outputs (*Source* UNEP FI [2023])

- **Interpretation of Outputs Is the Biggest Hurdle:** The most significant challenge is *interpreting the outputs* of these tools. This highlights the difficulty of translating complex, technical model results into actionable insights for financial decision-making. Even if the models are robust and the data is sound, if FIs cannot understand and interpret the results, they won't be able to use them effectively.
- **Understanding the Tools Is Essential:** The second biggest challenge is *understanding the tools* themselves. This includes understanding the underlying methodologies, assumptions, and limitations of the models. The "black box" nature of some climate risk assessment tools can make it difficult for FIs to trust and effectively use them. This also relates to the broader issue of capacity building within the financial sector—FIs need the expertise to critically evaluate and apply these tools.
- **Model Validation Is Important:** The third biggest challenge is *model validation*. FIs recognize the importance of ensuring that the models they use are accurate and reliable. Validating climate risk models can be complex, particularly given the long time horizons and uncertain nature of climate change, but it's essential for building trust and ensuring the credibility of the results.
- **Other Challenges:** Other challenges include:
  - **Handling big datasets:** Managing and processing the large datasets often required for climate risk modeling can be a logistical hurdle.
  - **Scalability of use:** Adapting the use of tools and data across a business's lending and investing portfolios can prove difficult when scaling from initial use cases.
  - **End-to-end use:** This refers to the integration of climate risk assessments into all relevant business processes, which often requires

significant changes to existing workflows and decision-making frameworks.
  - **Stability:** Ensuring that the platform and models are technically robust, which is essential for reliability and practical application.

The survey results highlight the critical challenges in bridging the gap between climate science (as embedded in these tools) and practical decision-making within financial institutions. Even if the science is sound, several barriers prevent its effective translation into action:

- **Communication and interpretability:** Complex model outputs need to be translated into clear, concise, and actionable insights for financial professionals.
- **Capacity building:** FIs need the expertise to understand and critically evaluate the tools and methodologies used in climate risk assessment.
- **Integration with existing processes:** Climate risk information needs to be integrated into existing financial decision-making frameworks, such as credit risk assessment and portfolio management.

Addressing these challenges requires a collaborative effort between climate scientists, model developers, financial institutions, and regulators. Improved communication, training, and the development of more user-friendly tools are crucial steps toward bridging the science-action gap and enabling FIs to effectively manage the growing financial risks associated with climate change.

4.1 Translating Science into Action

Several factors can hinder the effective translation of climate science into action:

- **Communication Barriers:** Technical jargon, complex statistical concepts, and a lack of clear communication can make it difficult for decision-makers to understand the relevance and implications of climate risk assessments.
- **Information Overload:** The sheer volume of climate data and research can be overwhelming, making it challenging for decision-makers to sift through the information and identify the most relevant insights.
- **Misaligned Timeframes:** Climate models often focus on long-term projections, while many business and policy decisions are made on shorter timeframes. Bridging this gap between long-term risks and short-term priorities requires careful communication and framing of the issues.

To bridge the science-action gap, it's crucial to:

- **Communicate Effectively:** Use clear language, avoid technical jargon, and employ visuals, narratives, and metaphors to make complex information more accessible and engaging. Cvitanovic and Hobday (2018) suggest studying "bright spots" in science-policy interaction to foster optimism and improve knowledge exchange.
- **Tailor Information:** Provide decision-makers with information that is relevant to their specific needs, contexts, and decision-making timeframes. Cash et al. (2003) highlight the importance of managing boundaries between knowledge producers and users for effective knowledge systems in sustainable development.
- **Engage Stakeholders:** Involve stakeholders throughout the modeling process, from identifying data needs to interpreting model outputs, to ensure that the assessments address their concerns and provide relevant information for their decision-making processes.

4.2 *The Role of Expert Judgment*

While climate risk models provide valuable quantitative insights, they cannot replace human judgment. Expert knowledge, experience, and understanding of local context are essential for interpreting model outputs, assessing the limitations of the models, and making informed decisions. Morgan (2014) discusses the effective use of expert elicitation in policy decisions, emphasizing careful protocol and bias mitigation.

For example, a model that projects the impact of climate change on agricultural yields in a specific region might not capture the full complexity of local farming practices, soil conditions, or adaptation strategies. Local agricultural experts can provide valuable insights that supplement the model outputs and inform more effective adaptation planning.

5 Conclusion: Embracing the Challenge, Advancing the Science

Climate risk modeling is a complex and challenging endeavor, but it is an essential tool for navigating the uncertainties of a changing climate. Knutti (2018) advocates for broader use of climate scenarios beyond modeling. Weaver et al. (2013) call for integrating climate models into robust decision frameworks. By acknowledging the limitations of models, embracing transparency in methodologies and assumptions, communicating uncertainties effectively, and integrating expert judgment, we can enhance the credibility, relevance, and usefulness of climate risk assessments.

The quest to improve climate risk modeling is an ongoing journey. As our understanding of the climate system evolves, data availability expands, and computing power increases, we can expect to see continued advancements in modeling techniques, leading to more sophisticated and accurate assessments of climate-related financial risks.

Despite the challenges, there is cause for optimism. The field of climate risk modeling is rapidly advancing, providing increasingly valuable tools for informing decision-making, managing risks, and building a more resilient future. By embracing the challenges, we can advance the science and contribute to a world that is better prepared to face the impacts of climate change.

References

Cash, D. W., Clark, W. C., Alcock, F., Dickson, N. M., Eckley, N., Guston, D. H., Jäger, J., & Mitchell, R. B. (2003). Knowledge systems for sustainable development. *Proceedings of the National Academy of Sciences, 100*(14), 8086–8091. https://www.pnas.org/content/100/14/8086

Cvitanovic, C., & Hobday, A. J. (2018). Building optimism at the environmental science-policy-practice interface through the study of bright spots. *Nature Communications, 9*(1), 1–5. https://www.nature.com/articles/s41467-018-05977-w

Hawkins, E., & Sutton, R. (2009). The potential to narrow uncertainty in regional climate predictions. *Bulletin of the American Meteorological Society, 90*(8), 1095–1108. https://doi.org/10.1175/2009BAMS2607.1

Knutti, R. (2018). A wider role for climate scenarios. *Nature Sustainability, 1*(5), 214–215. https://www.nature.com/articles/s41893-018-0067-3

Morgan, G. (2014). Use (and abuse) of expert elicitation in support of decision making for public policy. *Proceedings of the National Academy of Sciences, 111*(20), 7176–7184. https://www.pnas.org/content/111/20/7176

Nissan, H., Goddard, L., de Perez, E. C., Furlow, J., Baethgen, W., Thomson, M. C., & Mason, S. J. (2019). On the use and misuse of climate change projections in international development. *Wiley Interdisciplinary Reviews: Climate Change, 10*(3), Article e579. https://doi.org/10.1002/wcc.579

Reichstein, M., Camps-Valls, G., Stevens, B., Jung, M., Denzler, J., Carvalhais, N., & Prabhat, F. (2019). Deep learning and process understanding for data-driven earth system science. *Nature, 566*(7743), 195–204. https://www.nature.com/articles/s41586-019-0912-1

Saltelli, A., Bammer, G., Bruno, I., Charters, E., Di Fiore, M., Didier, E., Nelson Espeland, W., Kay, J., Lo Piano, S., Mayo, D., & Pielke Jr, R. (2020). Five ways to ensure that models serve society: A manifesto. *Nature, 582*(7813), 482–484. https://www.nature.com/articles/d41586-020-01812-9

De Sherbinin, A., Chai-Onn, T., Jaiteh, M., Mara, V., Pistolesi, L., Schnarr, E., & Trzaska, S. (2015). Data integration for climate vulnerability mapping in west Africa. *ISPRS International Journal of Geo-Information, 4*(4), 2561–2582. https://www.mdpi.com/2220-9964/4/4/2561

Smith, L. A., & Stern, N. (2011). Uncertainty in science and its role in climate policy. *Philosophical Transactions of the Royal Society A: Mathematical, Physical and Engineering Sciences, 369*(1956), 4818–4841. https://doi.org/10.1098/rsta.2011.0149

Stainforth, D. A. (2007). Confidence, uncertainty and decision-support relevance in climate predictions. *Philosophical Transactions of the Royal Society A: Mathematical, Physical and Engineering Sciences, 365*(1857), 2145–2161. https://doi.org/10.1098/rsta.2007.2074

United Nations Environment Programme Finance Initiative (UNEP FI). (2023). *The 2023 climate risk landscape*. https://www.unepfi.org/themes/climate-change/2023-climate-risk-landscape/

Weaver, C. P., Lempert, R. J., Brown, C., Hall, J. A., Revell, D., & Sarewitz, D. (2013). (2013). Improving the contribution of climate model information to decision making: The value and demands of robust decision frameworks. *Wiley Interdisciplinary Reviews: Climate Change, 4*(1), 39–60. https://doi.org/10.1002/wcc.202

Wilkinson, D. M. et al. (2016). The FAIR guiding principles for scientific data management and stewardship. *Scientific Data, 3*(1), 1–9. https://www.nature.com/articles/sdata201618

Case References

Bevere, L., & Gloor, M. (2020). *Natural catastrophes and man-made disasters in 2019: A year of many records*. Swiss Re. Accessed 23 January 2025. https://www.swissre.com/institute/research/sigma-research/sigma-2020-02.html

Bonnisseau, N. (2022). *The implications of data gaps in climate science*. Plan A Academy. Accessed 23 January 2025. https://plana.earth/academy/data-gaps-climate-science

Climate ADAPT. (2016). *Climate change knowledge portal of the world bank (CCKP)*. Accessed 23 January 2025. https://climate-adapt.eea.europa.eu/en/metadata/portals/climate-change-knowledge-portal-of-the-world-bank-cckp-year-of-launch

Dinku, T. (2019). *Challenges with availability and quality of climate data in Africa* (pp. 71–80). Elsevier. https://doi.org/10.1016/B978-0-12-815998-9.00007-5

Dupraz-Dobias, P. (2022). *How climate data scarcity costs lives*. The New Humanitarian. https://www.thenewhumanitarian.org/news-feature/2022/03/01/how-climate-data-scarcity-costs-lives

Insurance Information Institute (III). (2025). *Facts + statistics: Wildfires*. https://www.iii.org/fact-statistic/facts-statistics-wildfires

Intergovernmental Panel on Climate Change (IPCC). (2019). *Climate change and land*. Accessed 23 January 2025. https://www.ipcc.ch/srccl/

National Aeronautics and Space Administration (NASA). (2023). *Fire Information for Resource Management System (FIRMS)*. Accessed 23 January 2025. https://firms.modaps.eosdis.nasa.gov/map/

United Nations Development Programme (UNDP). (2024). *What is climate change adaptation and why is it crucial?* Accessed 23 January 2025. https://climatepromise.undp.org/news-and-stories/what-climate-change-adaptation-and-why-it-crucial

U.S. Forest Service. (2025). *Wildfire risk to communities*. Accessed 27 January 2025. https://wildfirerisk.org/

World Bank. (2021a). *Climate change knowledge portal metadata*. Accessed 27 January 2025. https://climateknowledgeportal.worldbank.org/sites/default/files/2021-09/CCKP_Metadata_Final_January2021.pdf

World Bank. (2021b). *Climate change knowledge portal*. https://climateknowledgeportal.worldbank.org

World Bank. (2022). *Closing the weather and climate data gap for effective economic decision-making*. https://www.worldbank.org/en/events/2022/11/03/closing-the-weather-and-climate-data-gap-for-effective-economic-decision-making

World Bank. (2023a). *Leveraging data and artificial intelligence for climate-smart decision-making in government*. https://blogs.worldbank.org/en/governance/leveraging-data-and-artificial-intelligence-climate-smart-decision-making-government

World Bank. (2023b). *Development projects : Improving climate data and information management*. https://projects.worldbank.org/en/projects-operations/project-detail/P129633

World Bank. (2024). *Climate change*. Accessed 23 January 2025. https://www.worldbank.org/en/topic/climatechange

PART III

Climate Finance Investments: Mobilizing Capital for a Sustainable Future

The global financial system holds the key to unlocking the trillions of dollars needed to address climate change. Redirecting capital toward climate solutions is not just a moral imperative, it's an economic opportunity. This part explores the diverse landscape of climate finance investments, examining how capital is being mobilized to power the transition to a low-carbon and climate-resilient future.

We'll navigate the investment landscape, highlighting both the challenges and the opportunities presented by climate-aligned investments. From renewable energy and energy storage to innovative financing mechanisms and strategies for decarbonizing hard-to-abate sectors, this part provides a comprehensive overview of the financial tools and strategies driving a sustainable transformation.

Chapter 9: Renewable Energy: Powering a Sustainable Future
This chapter delves into the world of renewable energy investments, exploring the rapid growth of this sector, the diverse technologies involved, and the key drivers behind its success. We'll examine the investment landscape, highlighting both the opportunities and the challenges, and discuss the innovative financing mechanisms used to fund renewable energy projects.

Chapter 10: Energy Storage: Enabling the Renewable Energy Transition
Energy storage is a crucial technology for unlocking the full potential of renewable energy. This chapter explores the different types of energy storage, their applications across diverse scales, and the factors driving investment in this sector. We'll analyze the key business models and investment opportunities in energy storage, from grid-scale projects to commercial and industrial applications.

Chapter 11: Decarbonizing Hard-to-Abate Sectors
Some sectors of the economy, such as steel, cement, and aviation, are particularly challenging to decarbonize. This chapter explores the technologies and solutions being developed to address these challenges, focusing on carbon capture, utilization, and storage (CCUS) as a promising option. We'll examine the investment landscape, the opportunities, and the challenges associated with scaling up these technologies.

Chapter 12: Investing in Nature-Based Solutions and Climate Adaptation
Nature-based solutions offer a powerful and cost-effective approach to addressing climate change. This chapter examines investments in reforestation, mangrove restoration, sustainable land management, and other natural climate solutions. We'll also explore investments in climate adaptation, focusing on projects that build resilience to the impacts of climate change.

Chapter 13: Innovative Financing Mechanisms for Climate Action
Climate finance requires innovative and flexible financing mechanisms to attract investors and scale up climate action. This chapter explores a range of instruments and approaches, including blended finance, concessional capital, green bonds, sustainability-linked loans, and impact investing.

Chapter 14: Navigating the Challenges: Greenwashing and Impact Measurement
The burgeoning world of climate finance is not without its challenges. This chapter addresses the issue of greenwashing—making misleading claims about sustainability performance—and explores the crucial need for robust impact measurement to ensure that investments deliver genuine environmental and social benefits.

By understanding the diverse landscape of climate finance investments, the challenges they face, and the innovative solutions emerging to address them, readers will gain a deeper appreciation for the critical role of finance in shaping a sustainable future.

CHAPTER 9

Renewable Energy: Powering a Sustainable Future

1 Introduction: The Rise of Renewable Energy

Renewable energy is no longer a niche sector, it's a global powerhouse driving the transition to a sustainable future. From solar panels glinting on rooftops to wind turbines gracefully turning across landscapes, renewable energy technologies are rapidly transforming the way we generate and consume power. This revolution is fueled by a confluence of factors, creating unprecedented investment opportunities and reshaping the global energy landscape.

The traditional dominance of fossil fuels is waning as renewable energy sources claim an increasingly larger share of the global energy mix. This shift is evident in the exponential growth of renewable energy capacity installations worldwide. In 2022 alone, a record 295 gigawatts (GW) of new renewable power capacity was added globally, with solar and wind power leading the charge. This remarkable growth is projected to continue, with the International Energy Agency (IEA) forecasting that renewables will account for nearly 95% of the increase in global power capacity through 2025. IRENA (2023, 2024a, 2024b) provides comprehensive statistics on global renewable energy capacity, generation, and investments. BloombergNEF (2023) analyzes global investment trends in the energy transition, including renewables and other clean energy sectors (Fig. 1).

Several key drivers are propelling this renewable energy revolution:

- **Falling Costs:** The cost of renewable energy technologies, particularly solar photovoltaics (PV) and wind power, has plummeted in recent years, making them increasingly competitive with fossil fuels. For example, the cost of solar PV modules has fallen by more than 90% since 2010

J. Chen, *Climate Finance*, https://doi.org/10.1007/978-981-96-7975-1_9

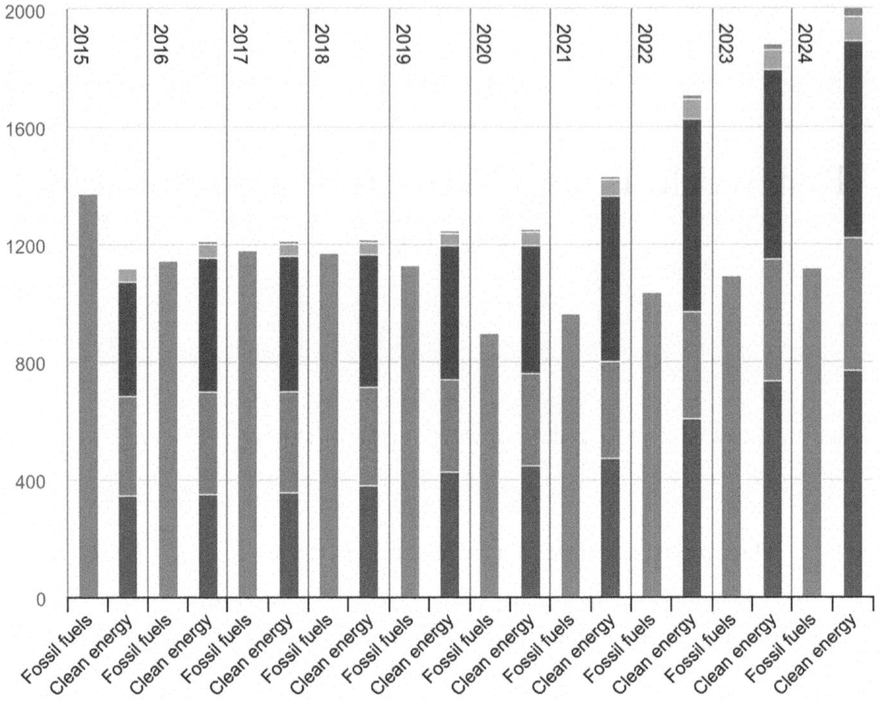

Fig. 1 Global investment in clean energy and fossil fuels ($USD Billions), 2015–2024 (*Source* IEA [2024a], Licence: CC BY 4.0

(IRENA, 2024c), making solar energy the cheapest source of electricity in history for many regions.

- **Climate Change Concerns:** Growing awareness of the urgent need to address climate change is driving governments, businesses, and investors to shift away from fossil fuels and embrace cleaner energy solutions. International agreements like the Paris Agreement, national climate policies, and corporate sustainability commitments are all contributing to this momentum.
- **Technological Advancements:** Continued innovation in renewable energy technologies, energy storage, and grid integration is further accelerating the adoption of renewables. Advancements in battery technology, for example, are addressing the intermittency challenges of solar and wind power, making them more reliable and dispatchable sources of electricity.
- **Energy Security and Independence:** Renewable energy sources provide countries with greater energy independence, reducing reliance on volatile fossil fuel markets and enhancing energy security. This is particularly attractive for countries that import a significant portion of their energy supply (Fig. 2).

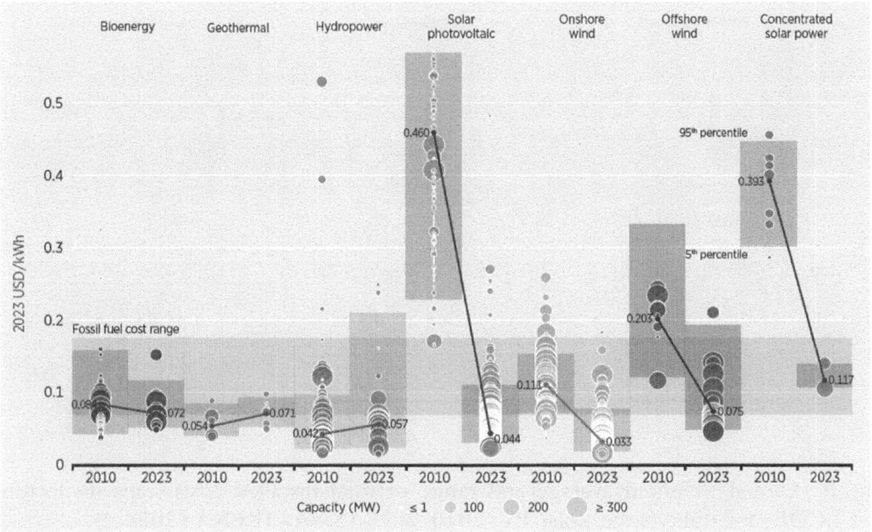

Fig. 2 Global weighted average LCOE from newly commissioned, utility-scale renewable power generation technologies, 2010–2023 (*Source* IRENA [2024c])

The growth of renewable energy presents vast investment opportunities across a range of sectors, from utility-scale solar and wind farms to distributed rooftop solar systems, corporate renewable energy procurement, and off-grid solutions for remote communities. This chapter will explore these opportunities, delve into the challenges and risks associated with renewable energy investments, and examine the financing mechanisms that are driving the transition to a cleaner, more sustainable energy future.

2 Types of Renewable Energy Technologies

Renewable energy technologies harness various natural resources to generate electricity and heat, offering a diverse portfolio of solutions to meet our energy needs sustainably.

2.1 Solar Energy

Solar energy harnesses the power of the sun to generate electricity through photovoltaic (PV) panels or heat through concentrated solar power (CSP) systems.

Photovoltaic (PV): PV technology converts sunlight directly into electricity using semiconductor materials. Solar PV systems range from small rooftop installations on homes and businesses to large-scale solar farms that can generate hundreds of megawatts (MW) of electricity. Haegel et al. (2019)

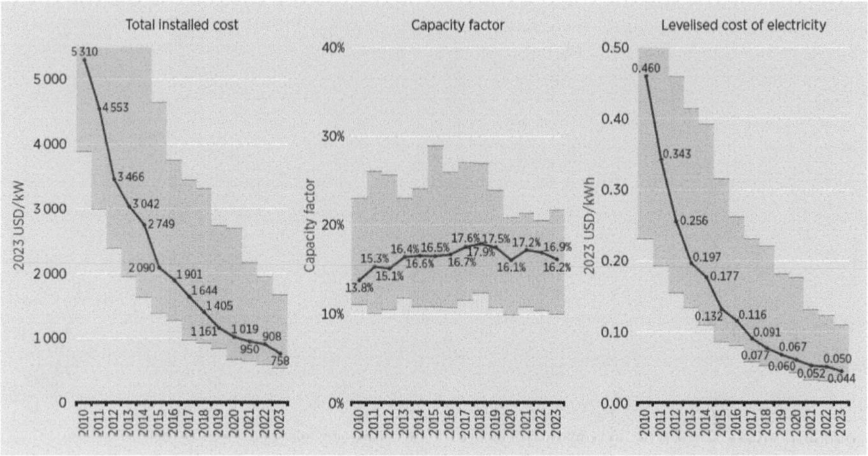

Fig. 3 Global weighted average and range of total installed costs, capacity factors and LCOEs for utility-scale, solar PV, 2010–2023 (*Source* IRENA [2024c])

discuss terawatt-scale photovoltaics transforming global energy. Polman et al. (2016) review photovoltaic materials, efficiencies, and future challenges (Fig. 3).

The solar PV market has experienced remarkable growth and cost reductions over the past decade, solidifying its position as a leading renewable energy technology. Key trends include:

- **Dramatic LCOE Decline:** The levelized cost of electricity (LCOE) for utility-scale solar PV has plummeted by 90% between 2010 and 2023, reaching USD 0.044/kWh. This dramatic cost reduction makes solar PV increasingly competitive with conventional fossil fuel-based power generation. The year-on-year reduction in 2023 alone was 12%, indicating continued progress in cost competitiveness. This trend is also reflected at the individual country level, with LCOE declines between 76 and 93% observed since 2010. This demonstrates the global nature of solar PV's cost competitiveness.
- **Significant Capacity Growth:** Solar PV capacity has expanded dramatically, growing 35-fold between 2010 and 2023, with over 1,412 GW installed globally by the end of 2023. This explosive growth is a testament to the declining costs, supportive policies, and increasing investor confidence in the technology.
- **Improved Capacity Factors:** The global weighted average capacity factor for new, utility-scale solar PV has increased from 13.8% in 2010 to 16.2% in 2023. This improvement is attributed to several factors:

- **Evolving Inverter Load Ratios:** Modern inverters can handle higher loads, allowing solar PV systems to operate more efficiently and produce more electricity.
- **Shift in Average Market Irradiance:** The average amount of sunlight reaching solar panels in key markets has likely increased or become more predictable, contributing to higher capacity factors.
- **Expanded Use of Trackers:** Solar tracking systems, which follow the sun throughout the day, increase energy capture and improve capacity factors.
- **Increased Adoption of Bifacial Technologies:** Bifacial solar panels, which capture light from both sides, enhance energy generation and improve performance in various latitudes and weather conditions.

- **Declining Installed Costs:** The global capacity-weighted average total installed cost of utility-scale solar PV projects commissioned in 2023 was USD 758/kW. This represents an 86% decrease compared to 2010 and a 17% decrease compared to 2022. This trend of declining installed costs further strengthens the economic case for solar PV. In 2023, balance-of-system (BOS) costs comprised about 61% of total installed costs for utility-scale PV projects, illustrating the significant contribution of BOS components to the overall project cost.
- **Declining Module Costs:** The cost of crystalline silicon PV modules sold in Europe declined by an impressive 93% between December 2009 and December 2023. This significant decrease in module costs is a major contributor to the overall decline in solar PV system costs.

These trends indicate a robust and dynamic solar PV market with continued growth potential. However, challenges remain, including supply chain constraints, permitting delays, and the need for supportive policies and financing mechanisms to ensure equitable access to solar PV technology globally. Addressing these challenges is essential to unlock the full potential of solar PV in the transition to a clean energy future.

An alternative solar energy power generation approach to solar PV is **Concentrated Solar Power (CSP)**. CSP systems use mirrors to concentrate sunlight onto a receiver, generating heat that can be used to produce steam and drive turbines for electricity generation. CSP plants often incorporate thermal energy storage, allowing them to dispatch electricity even when the sun is not shining (Fig. 4).

The Concentrated Solar Power (CSP) market, while demonstrating progress in cost reduction and efficiency, has experienced slower growth and faces distinct challenges compared to the rapidly expanding photovoltaic (PV) solar market. Here's a breakdown of the key trends:

- **LCOE Reduction, but with Caveats:** The global weighted average levelized cost of electricity (LCOE) for CSP has decreased by 70%

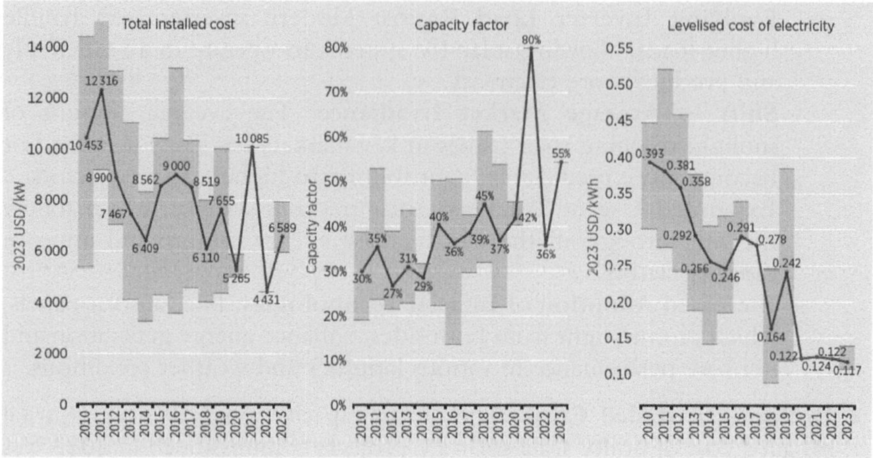

Fig. 4 Global weighted average and range of total installed costs, capacity factors and LCOEs for CSP, 2010–2023 (*Source* IRENA [2024c])

between 2010 and 2023, falling from USD 0.393/kWh to USD 0.117/kWh. This is significant progress, but it's important to note that only one new CSP plant was commissioned each in 2022 and 2023. This limited deployment makes it difficult to draw definitive conclusions about long-term cost trends. Furthermore, total installed costs actually *increased* by 49% in 2023 compared to 2022, largely due to the single project coming online that year in the United Arab Emirates. Another single project was commissioned in China in 2022 at a significantly lower cost, illustrating the variability in project costs. The Chinese project's lower cost was attributed to being 56% smaller than the 2021 CSP facility that was commissioned; notably, the project's total installed costs were 58% less expensive than CSP projects completed in 2010. This variation underscores the influence of project size, location, and technology on overall costs.

- **Improved Capacity Factors:** The globally weighted average capacity factor for CSP has increased significantly, from 30% in 2010 to 55% in 2023. This substantial improvement is primarily due to advancements in thermal energy storage technology. CSP plants with thermal storage can continue generating electricity even when sunlight is not available, leading to higher capacity factors and more reliable power output. The average number of hours of storage for commissioned projects has also increased, contributing to the improved capacity factors.
- **Declining Total Installed Costs (Overall Trend):** Despite the 49% increase in 2023, the overall trend between 2010 and 2023 shows a 37% decline in global average total installed costs for CSP, reaching USD 6,589/kW in 2023. This cost reduction is being achieved in a context

of increasing project energy storage capacities, which is a positive sign for the technology's long-term viability. This indicates that despite year-on-year fluctuations, driven mainly by smaller sample sizes and one-off events, the long-term trajectory is positive when analyzing a large dataset spanning several years.

- **Challenges and Opportunities:** The limited deployment of new CSP plants in recent years highlights some of the key challenges facing the technology. These include higher upfront capital costs compared to solar PV, competition from other renewable energy sources, and the need for suitable locations with high direct normal irradiance (DNI). However, CSP also offers unique advantages, such as its ability to provide dispatchable power (thanks to thermal storage) and its potential for integration with industrial processes that require heat.

The CSP market is demonstrating technological progress, particularly in terms of cost reductions and increased capacity factors. However, the slow pace of deployment raises concerns about the technology's ability to compete with solar PV and other renewable energy sources in the near term. Continued innovation in thermal storage, cost reductions, and supportive policies will be crucial for unlocking the full potential of CSP and enabling it to play a larger role in the global energy transition.

Case Study 1: The Mohammed bin Rashid Al Maktoum Solar Park in Dubai, UAE

Focus: Highlight the Ambition and Scale of Utility-Scale Solar Projects in Driving a Transition to Clean Energy in Regions with High Solar Potential

The Mohammed bin Rashid Al Maktoum Solar Park in Dubai, UAE, is one of the largest and most ambitious solar projects in the world. This case study explores how this massive solar park is driving the transition to clean energy in a region with high solar potential. It highlights the park's use of a combination of photovoltaic (PV) and concentrated solar power (CSP) technologies to generate electricity and reduce Dubai's reliance on natural gas.

Illustration: Methodology and Implementation of the Solar Park

1. **The Project:**

The Mohammed bin Rashid Al Maktoum Solar Park is the largest single-site solar park in the world, with a planned production capacity of 5,000 MW by 2030. The project, developed by the Dubai Electricity and Water Authority (DEWA), involves an investment of AED 50 billion and aims to reduce over 6.5 million tons of carbon emissions annually (C40 Cities, 2019; DEWA, 2024).

2. **Combination of PV and CSP Technologies:**

The solar park uses a combination of photovoltaic (PV) and concentrated solar power (CSP) technologies to generate electricity. The PV technology involves solar panels that convert sunlight directly into electricity, while CSP technology uses mirrors to concentrate sunlight and generate thermal energy, which is then used to produce electricity (SolarPACES, 2023).

3. **Rapid Response and Grid Stabilization:**

The solar park has demonstrated its ability to respond rapidly to fluctuations in solar power generation, stabilizing the grid and preventing blackouts. The combination of PV and CSP technologies allows for continuous power generation, even during periods of low sunlight (DEWA, 2024; Global Energy Monitor, 2024).

Discussion: Government Vision, Economic Benefits, and Challenges

1. **Role of Government Vision and Investment:**

The success of the Mohammed bin Rashid Al Maktoum Solar Park is largely attributed to the visionary leadership and investment by the UAE government. The Dubai Clean Energy Strategy 2050 and the Dubai Net Zero Emissions Strategy 2050 aim to provide 100% of Dubai's power production capacity from clean energy sources by 2050 (DEWA, 2024; UAE Embassy in Washington, 2023).

2. **Economic Benefits of Solar Energy:**

The solar park provides significant economic benefits by reducing reliance on natural gas, lowering energy costs, and creating job opportunities. It also enhances energy security and contributes to the UAE's economic diversification efforts (AtkinsRéalis, 2025; Obaideen et al., 2021).

3. **Challenges of Financing and Managing Complex Mega-Projects:**

Financing and managing large-scale renewable energy projects like the Mohammed bin Rashid Al Maktoum Solar Park present several challenges. These include securing sufficient investment, coordinating multiple stakeholders, and ensuring timely project completion. The use of the Independent Power Producer (IPP) model has been crucial in attracting private investment and sharing risks (Insights, 2023).

Conclusion

The Mohammed bin Rashid Al Maktoum Solar Park in Dubai exemplifies the transformative potential of large-scale solar projects in driving the transition to clean energy. By leveraging a combination of photovoltaic (PV) and concentrated solar power (CSP) technologies, the solar park enhances grid stability, reduces reliance on natural gas, and provides significant economic and environmental benefits.

The visionary leadership and investment by the UAE government have been instrumental in the success of this project. The solar park demonstrates the potential for solar energy to transform energy systems in sunny regions and highlights the importance of government policies in incentivizing renewable energy development.

Understanding the methodologies and strategies employed by the Mohammed bin Rashid Al Maktoum Solar Park can provide valuable insights for other regions and stakeholders seeking to enhance renewable energy deployment and achieve sustainable energy goals.

2.2 *Wind Energy*

Wind energy harnesses the kinetic energy of wind to generate electricity using wind turbines. Veers et al. (2019) outline three grand challenges in wind energy science: understanding atmospheric physics, advancing turbine technology, and optimizing grid integration.

Onshore Wind: Onshore wind farms are located on land, often in areas with strong and consistent wind resources. Onshore wind technology is mature and cost-effective, making it a major contributor to renewable energy capacity growth worldwide (Fig. 5).

The onshore wind market is experiencing a period of growth and cost declines, but faces headwinds related to supply chain constraints, permitting challenges, and rising interest rates in some markets.

- **LCOE Decline:** The global weighted average levelized cost of electricity (LCOE) for onshore wind has fallen by 70% between 2010 and 2023, decreasing from USD 0.111/kWh to USD 0.033/kWh. This substantial cost reduction demonstrates the increasing competitiveness of onshore wind power. A 3% year-on-year decline was observed in 2023. Every onshore wind project commissioned in 2023 had electricity costs below the weighted average LCOE for fossil fuel-fired power plants by country/region. This further underscores the economic attractiveness of wind power compared to traditional fossil fuel sources.
- **Increased Capacity:** The global cumulative capacity of onshore wind has increased more than fourfold between 2010 and 2023, growing from 178 to 944 GW. This significant capacity expansion highlights the continued growth and adoption of onshore wind technology. China's contribution

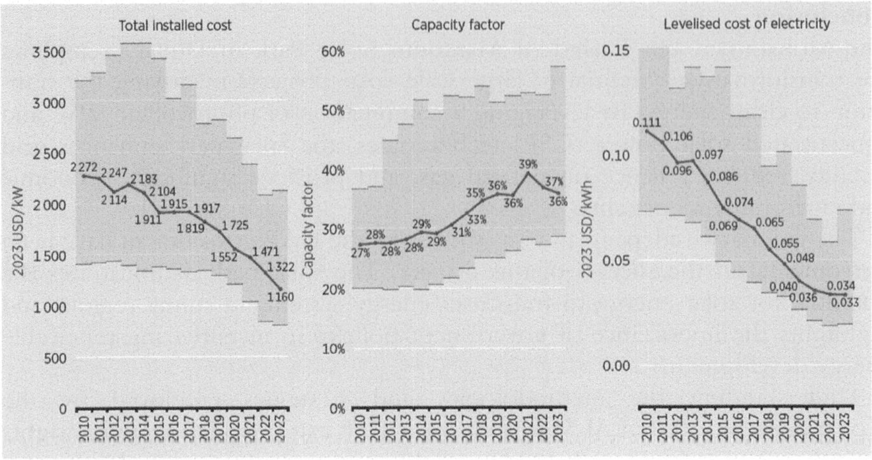

Fig. 5 Global weighted average and range of total installed costs, capacity factors and LCOEs for onshore wind, 2010–2023 (*Source* IRENA [2024c])

to this growth is substantial, with its new capacity additions accounting for 63% of the global annual increase in 2023. This reinforces China's leading role in the global wind market.

- **Declining Installed Costs:** The global weighted average total installed cost of onshore wind fell by 49% between 2010 and 2023, reaching USD 1,160/kW. A 12% decline was observed in 2023 compared to the previous year. This continued cost reduction is a key driver of onshore wind's increasing affordability. In China, significant cost declines have been achieved, with installed costs falling below USD 1000/kW, reaching USD 986/kW. This cost leadership in China is contributing to the downward pressure on global wind turbine prices. Conversely, smaller markets experienced cost increases in 2023 due to higher turbine prices outside of China, impacting project costs. IRENA data on 15 markets indicated a range of installed costs between USD 986/kW and USD 1,746/kW, with Japan being an outlier at USD 2,384/kW. These regional variations highlight the influence of local market conditions and policy landscapes on project economics.
- **Falling Turbine Prices:** Average onshore wind turbine prices (excluding China) ranged between USD 706/kW and USD 1,040/kW in 2023. This is significantly lower than the USD 1471/kW cost in 2010, as noted in Fig. 2.3. Prices have fallen by between 41 and 64% from 2010 values in most regions (excluding China). In China, turbine prices have experienced a remarkable 73% decrease since 2010, reaching an average of USD 233/kW. This dramatic cost reduction in China is a significant driver of the global decline in turbine prices and is increasing China's dominance in the wind turbine manufacturing market.

- **Improved Capacity Factors:** Technological advancements have led to a more than one-third improvement in the global weighted average capacity factor for onshore wind, which rose from 27% in 2010 to 36% in 2023. This improvement reflects the development of more efficient turbines and better siting practices, resulting in higher energy capture and improved project economics.

While onshore wind shows positive long-term trends, challenges remain. The rising cost of capital poses significant financing challenges, especially for projects in emerging markets and developing economies. Furthermore, supply chain bottlenecks and permitting delays in some regions continue to hinder deployment. Addressing these challenges through policy support, streamlining permitting processes, and innovative financing mechanisms will be critical for unlocking the full potential of onshore wind power.

Offshore Wind: Offshore wind farms are located in bodies of water, typically in shallow coastal areas. Offshore wind offers several advantages, including higher wind speeds, less turbulence, and the potential for larger-scale projects. However, offshore wind projects are also more complex and expensive to develop due to the challenges of constructing and maintaining turbines in marine environments (Fig. 6).

The offshore wind market is showing strong growth and significant cost reductions, driven by technological advancements and increasing deployment, particularly in China and Europe. However, like onshore wind, it also faces challenges related to supply chains and rising interest rates.

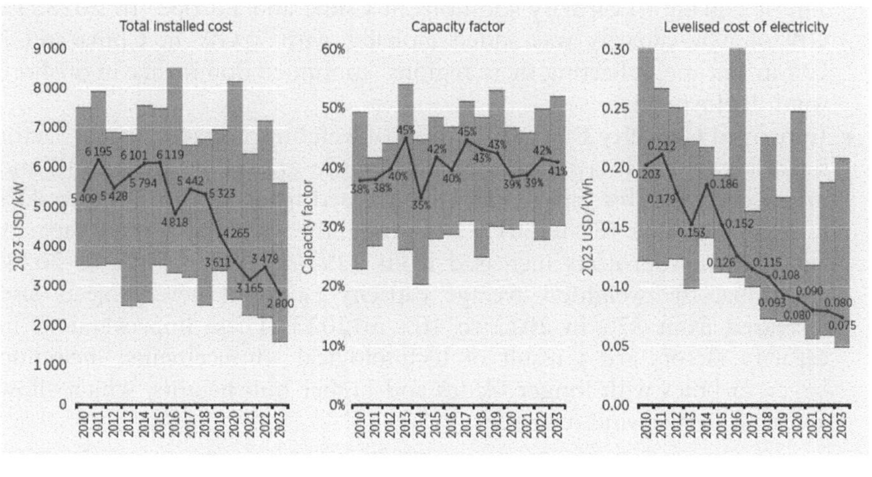

Fig. 6 Global weighted average and range of total installed costs, capacity factors and LCOE for offshore wind, 2010–2023 (*Source* IRENA [2024c])

- **LCOE Decline:** The global weighted average LCOE for offshore wind has decreased by 63% between 2010 and 2023, falling from USD 0.203/kWh to USD 0.075/kWh. A 7% year-on-year reduction was observed in 2023, indicating continued improvement in cost competitiveness. In Europe, between 2022 and 2023, the projected average LCOE of newly commissioned projects decreased by 8%, from USD 0.073/kWh to USD 0.067/kWh. In China, the weighted average LCOE of newly commissioned projects saw a steeper decline of 9% between 2022 and 2023, reaching USD 0.070/kWh. These regional differences in LCOE trends reflect varying market conditions, policy support, and technology deployment.
- **Decreased Installed Costs:** Global weighted average total installed costs have decreased by 48% from 2010 to 2023, falling from USD 5,409/kW to USD 2,800/kW. The peak cost was observed in 2011 at USD 6,195/kW, 2.2 times higher than the 2023 value. This underscores the significant progress made in reducing the cost of offshore wind projects. In 2023, a 16% year-on-year decrease in total installed costs was observed. This continued cost reduction is a positive indicator for the future growth of the offshore wind market. In Europe, 2023 saw a 21% decrease in total installed costs, a notable improvement compared to the previous year. These cost reductions are being driven by both technological improvements, such as larger turbines and longer blades, and growing competitiveness in the supply chain.
- **Increased Capacity:** Global cumulative installed capacity of offshore wind has grown more than twenty-threefold between 2010 and 2023, increasing from 3 to 73 GW. This significant expansion is attributed almost equally to capacity additions in China and Europe. In 2023, 11 GW of new capacity was added globally, with 7 GW in China and 3 GW in Europe, reflecting these regions' continued dominance in offshore wind deployment.
- **Improved Capacity Factors:** The global weighted average capacity factor for offshore wind has increased, albeit more gradually than LCOE and installed costs. This capacity factor increased from 38% in 2010 to 41% in 2023, reaching 45% in 2017. In Europe, the weighted average capacity factor of new projects increased from 42% in 2022 to 48% in 2023. In China, the weighted average capacity factor of new projects also increased from 37% in 2022 to 40% in 2023. These improvements in capacity factors are a result of technological advancements, including larger turbines with longer blades and higher hub heights, which allow access to better wind resources.

The offshore wind industry is demonstrating substantial progress and holds considerable potential for future growth. However, it still faces challenges such as complex and lengthy permitting processes, supply chain constraints, and the need for significant grid infrastructure upgrades to accommodate the increasing capacity. The rising cost of capital also poses a financing challenge, especially for projects in developing economies. Continued technological advancements, supportive policies, and innovative financing mechanisms will be essential for overcoming these challenges and accelerating the deployment of offshore wind power.

2.3 *Hydropower*

Hydropower harnesses the energy of moving water to generate electricity, typically through dams that create reservoirs and channel water through turbines.

- **Conventional Hydropower:** Large-scale hydroelectric dams are a major source of renewable energy, providing baseload power—meaning they can generate electricity consistently over long periods.
- **Run-of-River Hydropower:** This approach uses the natural flow of rivers to generate electricity without the need for large dams or reservoirs. Run-of-river hydropower has a lower environmental impact than conventional hydropower but often has a lower energy output capacity.

While hydropower is a significant source of renewable energy, it's essential to consider its potential environmental and social impacts, such as altering river flows, affecting fish migration, and displacing communities. Sustainable hydropower development requires careful planning, environmental impact assessments, and mitigation measures (Fig. 7).

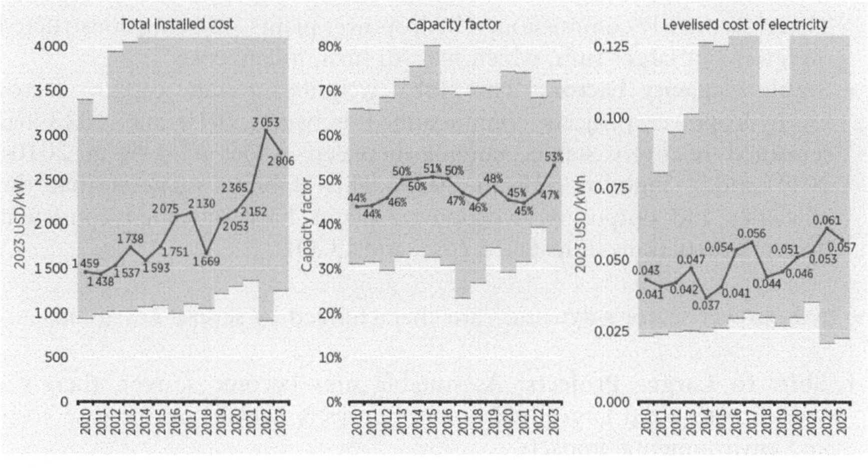

Fig. 7 Global weighted average and range of total installed costs, capacity factors and LCOE for hydropower, 2010–2023 (*Source* IRENA [2024c])

The hydropower market presents a complex picture. While LCOE has generally increased and total installed costs have fluctuated, capacity factors remain relatively stable. There's a clear trend of increasing project sizes and a geographical shift in new capacity additions.

- **Increased LCOE:** The global weighted average LCOE of newly commissioned hydropower projects was USD 0.057/kWh in 2023. This represents a 7% decrease compared to 2022, but a 33% *increase* compared to the USD 0.043/kWh recorded for projects commissioned in 2010. This rise in LCOE since 2010 is primarily attributed to rising installed costs, particularly in Asia, where many projects face challenging site conditions and recent supply chain inflation. Importantly, in 2023, all newly deployed hydropower capacity had an LCOE lower than the country- or region-specific weighted average cost of newly commissioned fossil fuel-fired capacity. This indicates that despite the rise in LCOE, hydropower remains competitive with fossil fuels in many regions.
- **Fluctuating Total Installed Costs:** The global weighted average total installed cost for newly commissioned hydropower projects decreased to USD 2,806/kW in 2023, lower than the 2022 figure of USD 3,053/kW. However, this cost has fluctuated over the 2010–2023 period, achieving its highest recorded value in 2022. These variations are primarily due to shifts in the location and size of projects. For example, in 2022 there were a number of large hydropower projects, notably in Canada and the Lao People's Democratic Republic, which contributed to higher average installed costs. Smaller projects tend to have lower total installed costs, as seen in 2023. The increase in hydropower project size is likely due to challenging site conditions and the need for greater energy capacity. Therefore, newly commissioned hydropower plants are being constructed on fewer but larger sites, which may, in turn, inflate costs.
- **Stable Capacity Factors:** The global weighted average capacity factor for hydropower projects commissioned between 2010 and 2023 has remained relatively stable, ranging between a low of 44% in 2010–2011 and a high of 53% in 2023. This stability suggests that the efficiency and output of hydropower plants have remained consistent despite fluctuations in installed costs and LCOE.

The hydropower sector's dynamics are characterized by several key trends:

1. **Shift to Larger Projects:** As suitable sites become scarcer, there's a tendency to build larger hydropower projects, which can increase costs and environmental impacts.
2. **Geographical Shift:** New hydropower capacity is increasingly concentrated in specific regions, particularly Asia, where demand for electricity is growing rapidly.

3. **Sustainability Concerns:** Growing concerns about the environmental and social impacts of large hydropower projects, including displacement of communities and alteration of river ecosystems, are leading to increased scrutiny and opposition to new projects in some regions.
4. **Focus on Modernization:** There's a growing emphasis on modernizing existing hydropower plants to improve efficiency and reduce environmental impacts, rather than building entirely new dams.
5. **Role in Grid Stability:** Hydropower, with its ability to provide dispatchable power, plays an important role in maintaining grid stability and supporting the integration of variable renewable energy sources like solar and wind.

Overall, the future of the hydropower market will depend on balancing the need for increased energy capacity with environmental and social considerations. Modernization of existing plants, exploration of alternative hydropower technologies (such as pumped hydro storage), and careful assessment of the environmental and social impacts of new projects will be crucial for ensuring the sustainable development of the sector.

2.4 Geothermal Energy

Geothermal energy taps into the heat contained within the Earth's interior to generate electricity or provide direct heat for buildings and industrial processes.

Geothermal power plants use steam or hot water from geothermal reservoirs to drive turbines and generate electricity. Geothermal heat pumps can be used for heating and cooling buildings, using the relatively constant temperature of the ground as a heat source or heat sink (Fig. 8).

The geothermal market, while presenting a stable LCOE and high capacity factors, is characterized by slow growth due to its unique deployment challenges. The relatively small number of newly commissioned plants each year makes it difficult to establish clear cost trends.

- **Stable LCOE:** The global weighted average LCOE for geothermal projects commissioned in 2023 was USD 0.071/kWh. This is similar to the global average in 2021 and suggests a relatively stable cost of electricity generation from geothermal sources. However, the report acknowledges that the low deployment rate for geothermal—meaning a small number of new plants commissioned annually—results in weighted average costs and performance being based on a limited sample size, making it challenging to identify robust long-term cost trends. This makes year-on-year comparisons less reliable than for technologies with larger deployment numbers.

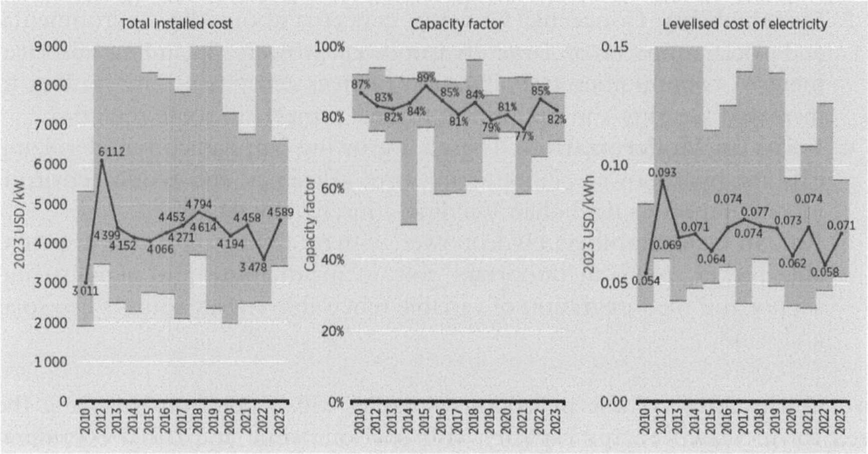

Fig. 8 Global weighted average and range of total installed costs, capacity factors and LCOE for geothermal, 2010–2023 (*Source* IRENA [2024c])

- **Fluctuating Installed Costs:** In 2023, the global weighted average total installed cost for the seven geothermal plants in IRENA's database was USD 4,589/kW. This represents a decrease compared to the higher costs observed in recent years, particularly the USD 4,589/kW recorded in 2022. However, the range of total installed costs for projects commissioned in 2023 was quite wide, from a low of USD 3,413/kW to a high of USD 6,595/kW. This variability reflects differences in project size, location-specific factors (such as resource quality and site conditions), and technology choices.
- **High and Relatively Stable Capacity Factors:** Geothermal plants are designed to run as often as possible to maintain constant flows from the reservoir and provide baseload power. In 2023, the global weighted average capacity factor for newly commissioned geothermal plants was 82%. This high capacity factor is a key advantage of geothermal energy, as it ensures a reliable and consistent supply of electricity. Capacity factors have remained relatively high and stable over the past decade, fluctuating between 77 and 89%. This consistency underscores the reliability of geothermal technology.
- **Limited Deployment:** A key challenge for the geothermal market is the slow pace of deployment. Only 203 MW of new geothermal power generation capacity were commissioned worldwide in 2023, slightly higher than the 181 MW added in 2022. This slow growth is due to several factors:
  - **High Upfront Costs:** Geothermal projects require significant upfront investment in exploration and drilling, which can be a barrier to entry.

- **Resource Availability:** Geothermal resources are not evenly distributed geographically, limiting the potential for development in some regions.
- **Technological Challenges:** Harnessing geothermal energy can be technically complex, particularly for enhanced geothermal systems (EGS) which require fracturing rock to access heat resources.
- **Long Lead Times:** Geothermal projects can have long lead times from exploration to commissioning, further slowing down deployment.

Despite the challenges, geothermal energy offers several advantages:

- **Baseload Power:** Geothermal can provide a consistent and reliable source of baseload power, unlike intermittent renewable sources like solar and wind.
- **Small Footprint:** Geothermal power plants have a relatively small land footprint compared to other energy sources.
- **Low Emissions:** Geothermal energy is a low-carbon source of electricity, contributing to climate change mitigation.

The future of the geothermal market hinges on addressing the key challenges related to cost and deployment. Technological advancements, such as improved drilling techniques and EGS technologies, along with supportive policies and innovative financing mechanisms, could help unlock the full potential of geothermal energy and enable it to play a larger role in the global energy transition. However, the inherent limitations related to resource availability and geological suitability will likely continue to constrain its widespread adoption compared to more geographically versatile renewables like solar and wind.

2.5 Biomass Energy

Biomass energy utilizes organic matter, such as wood, crops, and agricultural waste, as a fuel source.

- **Biofuels:** Liquid biofuels, such as ethanol and biodiesel, can be blended with gasoline or diesel fuel to reduce reliance on fossil fuels in the transportation sector.
- **Biogas:** Biogas, primarily composed of methane, can be produced from the anaerobic digestion of organic waste, providing a renewable source of fuel for electricity generation or heating.
- **Wood Pellets:** Wood pellets, made from compressed wood waste, can be used as a fuel source for heating or electricity generation.

The sustainability of biomass energy depends on the sourcing of feedstocks. Sustainable biomass production requires using waste materials, sustainably managed forests, or dedicated energy crops that do not compete with food production or contribute to deforestation. EU renewable energy policy incentivizes wood burning, threatening forests (Searchinger et al., 2018) (Fig. 9).

The bioenergy market presents a complex picture with declining LCOE and relatively high capacity factors, but fluctuating installed costs and a dependence on feedstock availability and cost. Its future role in the broader energy transition remains a subject of ongoing debate.

- **Declining LCOE:** The global weighted average LCOE for bioenergy power projects has generally decreased between 2010 and 2023, falling from USD 0.084/kWh to USD 0.072/kWh. However, the LCOE in 2023 was higher than the 2022 value of USD 0.063/kWh. Despite this slight uptick, bioenergy's LCOE remains at the lower end of the cost spectrum for new fossil fuel-fired projects, suggesting its continued competitiveness in the electricity market. In 2023, variations in LCOE across different countries and regions were observed, ranging from a low of USD 0.063/kWh in India and USD 0.066/kWh in China to highs of USD 0.097/kWh in Europe and USD 0.107/kWh in North America. These regional variations reflect differences in feedstock availability, technology choices, and policy landscapes.
- **Fluctuating Total Installed Costs:** For newly commissioned bioenergy projects, the global weighted average total installed cost was USD 2,730/kW in 2023. This represents an increase compared to the 2022 figure of USD 2,242/kW. Total installed costs have fluctuated significantly over

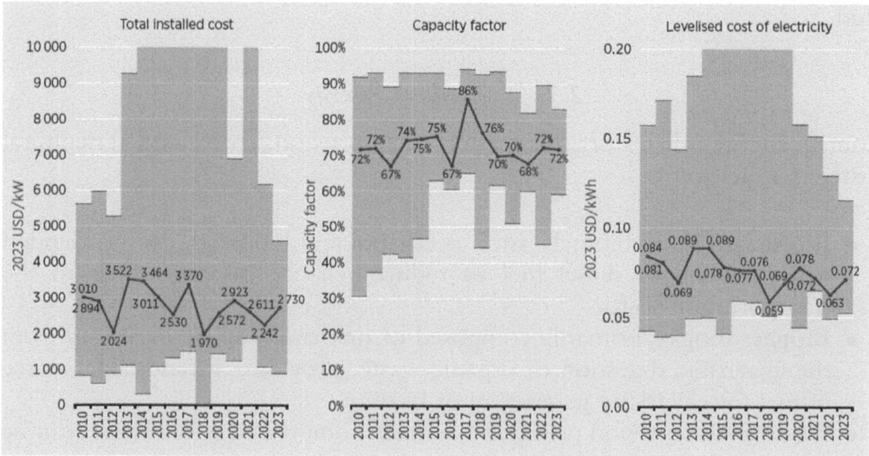

Fig. 9 Global weighted average and range of total installed costs, capacity factors and LCOE for bioenergy, 2010–2023 (*Source* IRENA [2024c])

the 2010–2023 period, with values ranging from around USD 2,000/kW to over USD 3,500/kW. These variations likely reflect differences in the scale and complexity of bioenergy projects, as well as changes in the cost of equipment and materials.

- **High Capacity Factors:** Capacity factors for bioenergy plants can vary depending on the specific technology employed and the availability and consistency of feedstock. Between 2010 and 2023, the global weighted average capacity factor for bioenergy projects ranged from a low of 67% in 2012 and 2016 to a high of 86% in 2017. The capacity factor in 2023 was 72%, indicating a relatively high and stable level of utilization for bioenergy plants. This high capacity factor is a key advantage of bioenergy, as it enables a consistent and predictable supply of electricity.
- **Diversity of Options:** Bioenergy for electricity generation encompasses a wide range of feedstocks and technologies, offering flexibility and adaptability to different contexts. Where low-cost feedstocks from agricultural or forestry by-products are available, bioenergy can provide highly competitive, dispatchable electricity. This flexibility is an important advantage of bioenergy, as it allows the technology to be deployed in various regions and utilize diverse resources. However, reliance on feedstocks also presents challenges, as feedstock availability and cost can fluctuate significantly, impacting the overall economics of bioenergy projects.

Overall, the future of bioenergy will depend on several factors:

1. **Sustainable Feedstock Sourcing:** Ensuring a sustainable and reliable supply of feedstocks is crucial for the long-term viability of the bioenergy sector. This requires careful consideration of land use, environmental impacts, and potential competition with food production.
2. **Technological Advancements:** Continued innovation in bioenergy technologies, particularly in areas such as gasification and pyrolysis, can improve efficiency and reduce costs.
3. **Policy Support:** Supportive policies and incentives are essential for promoting the development and deployment of sustainable bioenergy projects. These policies can include renewable portfolio standards, carbon pricing mechanisms, and feed-in tariffs.
4. **Addressing Environmental Concerns:** Careful assessment and mitigation of the potential environmental impacts of bioenergy, such as air emissions and land-use change, are necessary for ensuring its sustainable development.
5. **Competition with Other Renewables:** The competitiveness of bioenergy in the electricity market will depend on its ability to compete with other renewable energy sources, such as solar and wind, which have experienced significant cost reductions in recent years.

6. **Integration with Other Sectors:** Bioenergy can play a role in decarbonizing other sectors, such as heating and transportation, through the production of biofuels and biogas. Exploring these opportunities can enhance the overall value and impact of bioenergy.

The continued role of bioenergy in the future energy mix remains subject to debate, given the challenges and concerns surrounding sustainability and land use. However, with careful planning and sustainable practices, bioenergy can contribute to a diversified renewable energy portfolio and offer solutions for decarbonizing specific sectors and regions.

3 Investment Landscape and Opportunities

The renewable energy sector is a dynamic and rapidly growing market, attracting substantial investment and offering a wide range of opportunities for investors, developers, and businesses.

3.1 Global Market Overview

The global renewable energy market has experienced remarkable growth in recent years. In 2023, global investments in renewable energy reached a record $622.5 billion, driven by strong policy support, falling technology costs, and increasing investor interest in sustainable assets (REN21, 2024). In addition to the Increased Investment, there are many other positive trends in 2023 as well:

- **Record Growth in Capacity:** In 2023, a record-breaking 473 gigawatts (GW) of renewable power capacity were added globally. This signifies a substantial 36% increase from the previous year, demonstrating the accelerating adoption of renewable energy sources.
- **Global Policy Support:** A significant development is the pledge by 130 countries at the 2023 United Nations Climate Change Conference to triple renewable energy capacity and double the annual rate of energy efficiency improvement by 2030. This signals a strong political will to drive the transition toward cleaner energy sources.
- **Job Creation:** The renewable energy sector is proving to be a significant source of employment opportunities, with an 8% increase in jobs in 2022, bringing the total to 13.7 million. This highlights the potential for renewable energy to contribute to economic growth and development.
- **Increased Access to Electricity:** While still a challenge, the number of people without access to electricity globally decreased from 756 million in 2022 to 745 million in 2023. This suggests that renewable energy is playing a role in expanding energy access, particularly in remote and underserved areas.

However, the reports from three major energy agencies, REN21 (2024), IRENA (2024a), and IEA (2024a, 2024b, 2024c) paint a complex picture of the renewable energy market, characterized by record growth in certain sectors, persistent challenges, and an urgent need for accelerated action to meet global climate goals.

I. **Record Growth and Positive Trends:**

- **Renewables Dominate New Capacity:** All three reports concur that renewables constituted the vast majority of new power capacity additions in 2023, driven primarily by solar PV and wind power (IEA, 2024b; IRENA, 2024a; REN21, 2024).
- **Solar PV Leading the Charge:** Solar PV additions set new records, surpassing all other generation technologies combined in terms of investment (IEA, 2024b). Costs continue to decline rapidly, making solar PV increasingly competitive (IEA, 2024b; IRENA, 2024a).
- **Clean Energy Investment Surge:** Investment in clean energy technologies and infrastructure has grown substantially, now exceeding fossil fuel investment by a significant margin. (IEA, 2024b)
- **Wind Power Expansion:** Onshore and offshore wind capacity continued to expand, with notable contributions from China and Europe (IEA, 2024b; IRENA, 2024a). Turbine prices have decreased significantly, particularly in China (IEA, 2024b).
- **Grid and Storage Investment Increasing:** Investment in grids and storage is recovering, spurred by the need to integrate growing renewable energy capacity (IEA, 2024b).

II. **Persistent Challenges and Gaps:**

- **Insufficient Pace of Transition:** Despite the record growth, the overall pace of the renewable energy transition is still too slow to achieve the Paris Agreement targets (IRENA, 2024a; REN21, 2024). Targets set for tripling renewables by 2030 will require continued significant growth rates (IEA, 2024b; IRENA, 2024a), in all renewable technologies, not just Solar PV (IRENA, 2024a).
- **Geographical Disparities:** Renewable energy investment and deployment remain geographically concentrated, with China, the United States, and Europe dominating. Emerging markets and developing economies (EMDEs) receive a disproportionately small share of investment, despite having significant needs and potential (IEA, 2024b; IRENA, 2024a).
- **Grid Infrastructure Bottleneck:** Grid infrastructure is not keeping pace with the rapid expansion of renewable energy,

creating a bottleneck for further growth and increasing curtailment in some regions (IEA, 2024b, REN21, 2024). Intermittency challenges related to VRE are pushing the development and implementation of flexibility solutions, including storage capacity and sector coupling (IRENA, 2024a), but face difficulties for wide-scale application (IRENA, 2024a).

- **Financing Challenges:** The rising cost of capital, driven by increased interest rates, poses a significant challenge for financing energy projects, especially in EMDEs (IEA, 2024b, REN21, 2024). This financial challenge also hampers start-ups looking to deploy innovative solutions (IEA, 2024b). Access to finance is an issue for low-income countries and those in the Global South, highlighting the need for increased international collaboration on wealth taxation and/or philanthropy (IRENA, 2024a).
- **Policy Gaps:** While many countries have set ambitious renewable energy targets, the policy landscape remains fragmented, and implementation often lags behind ambition. Stronger and more consistent policies are needed to accelerate the transition (REN21, 2024). Supportive policies have led to growth in investment in some regions, like India and Brazil (IEA, 2024b).
- **Energy Access Deficit:** Progress on achieving universal access to affordable, reliable, sustainable, and modern energy (SDG7) is insufficient. Hundreds of millions still lack access to electricity and clean cooking, primarily in sub-Saharan Africa. Renewables offer cost-effective solutions, but access to finance and technology remains a barrier (IRENA, 2024a).
- **Data Gaps and Transparency:** Challenges remain in tracking and reporting climate and renewable energy finance flows, particularly in certain sectors (like energy storage and adaptation) and in developing countries. Improved data quality and transparency are crucial for effective monitoring and decision-making. (CPI) REN21 (2024) also emphasizes their crowd-sourced data approach, relying on a global network to compile data, but notes the importance of transparency and validation.

III. **Key Opportunities and Priorities:**

- **COP28 and NDC Commitments:** The pledges made at COP28 to triple renewable energy capacity and double energy efficiency by 2030 provide a strong political impetus for accelerated action. The upcoming round of Nationally Determined Contributions (NDCs) provides an opportunity for countries to strengthen their commitments and translate them into concrete plans (IEA, 2024b; IRENA, 2024a).
- **Declining Technology Costs:** The continued decline in the cost of renewable energy technologies, particularly solar PV and wind,

makes them increasingly competitive with fossil fuels and creates favorable investment opportunities (IEA, 2024b; IRENA, 2024a).

- **Innovative Financing and De-Risking:** Innovative financing mechanisms, such as blended finance and green bonds, along with public finance support for de-risking investments, are crucial for mobilizing capital, particularly in EMDEs (IEA, 2024b). There is also significant potential for philanthropy to play a role in early stage or "unbankable" projects (IRENA, 2024a).
- **Grid Modernization and Flexibility:** Investments in grid modernization, expansion, and flexibility solutions, including storage and sector coupling, are essential for integrating growing renewable energy capacity and ensuring reliable power systems (IEA, 2024b; IRENA, 2024a).
- **Focus on Hard-to-Abate Sectors:** Increased attention and investment are needed to decarbonize hard-to-abate sectors, such as industry, heavy transport, and buildings (IEA, 2024b; IRENA, 2024a).
- **International Collaboration:** Enhanced international collaboration, including financial and technical assistance from developed to developing countries, is essential for achieving a just and inclusive energy transition and meeting global climate goals (IEA, 2024b; IRENA, 2024a). This includes a focus on establishing a New Collective Quantified Goal (NCQG) for climate finance (IRENA, 2024a).
- **Sustainable Supply Chains:** Diversification and strengthening of clean energy technology supply chains, including for critical minerals, are crucial for reducing reliance on single suppliers and mitigating geopolitical risks (IEA, 2024b).

The reports collectively emphasize that a successful energy transition requires a coordinated and multifaceted approach that goes beyond focusing solely on renewable power generation. Addressing the challenges related to finance, grids, policy, and international cooperation is essential for accelerating the transition, unlocking the full potential of renewable energy, and achieving a sustainable energy future.

3.2 Investment Opportunities Across Sectors

Based on various recent reports from REN21 (2024), IRENA (2024a), and IEA (2024b), renewable energy investment opportunities span various sectors, offering diverse avenues for deploying capital and driving the energy transition.

1. **Power Sector:**

    - **Solar PV:** Remains the most attractive investment opportunity due to its rapidly declining costs, versatile applications (utility-scale, distributed generation, rooftop solar), and strong growth trajectory. Investment opportunities exist across the entire value chain, from manufacturing to project development and financing (IEA, 2024b; IRENA, 2024a). Innovative approaches like agrivoltaics and building-integrated photovoltaics offer further opportunities (REN21, 2024).

- **Wind Power:** Onshore and offshore wind offer significant potential, particularly in regions with favorable wind resources. Investment opportunities include turbine manufacturing, project development, and grid infrastructure upgrades to accommodate new wind farms (IEA, 2024b). Offshore wind, while requiring higher upfront investment, offers advantages in terms of capacity factors and access to stronger wind resources. Floating offshore wind presents an emerging opportunity, although it is still at an early stage of development (IEA, 2024b).
- **Hydropower:** Opportunities exist primarily in modernizing existing hydropower plants to improve efficiency and reduce environmental impact, rather than building new large-scale dams. Pumped hydro storage, offering grid flexibility and energy storage, presents another investment opportunity (IEA, 2024b; IRENA, 2024a).
- **Geothermal:** Although facing deployment challenges, geothermal offers a stable and reliable source of baseload power. Investment in exploration, drilling technologies, and enhanced geothermal systems (EGS) could unlock greater potential (IRENA, 2024a).
- **Bioenergy:** While facing sustainability concerns and feedstock limitations, bioenergy offers diverse options for electricity generation, heating, and transportation fuels. Investment opportunities include sustainable feedstock production, advanced bioenergy technologies (such as gasification and pyrolysis), and biofuel production (IRENA, 2024a).

2. **Transport Sector:**

- **Electric Vehicles (EVs):** The EV market is expanding rapidly, driven by declining battery costs and supportive policies. Investment opportunities include EV manufacturing, charging infrastructure deployment, battery production, and battery materials (IEA, 2024b). Growth in the commercial fleet segment and the emergence of new business models (such as battery swapping and vehicle-to-grid technologies) offer further opportunities (IEA, 2024b).
- **Electric Buses:** The market for electric buses is growing, particularly in China and Europe. Investment opportunities include bus manufacturing, charging infrastructure, and fleet management solutions (IEA, 2024b). Concessional financing and support from

multilateral development banks can play a role in accelerating deployment in developing countries (IEA, 2024b).
- **Sustainable Aviation Fuels (SAFs):** SAFs offer a pathway to decarbonize aviation. Investment opportunities include SAF production technologies, feedstock supply, and infrastructure for blending and distribution (IEA, 2024b).
- **Hydrogen in Transport:** Hydrogen, especially green hydrogen, has potential for use in heavy-duty transport, including trucks, buses, and shipping. Investment opportunities include electrolyzer manufacturing, hydrogen production, refueling infrastructure, and fuel cell technologies (IEA, 2024b).

3. **Buildings Sector:**
    - **Energy Efficiency Retrofits:** Improving the energy efficiency of existing buildings offers a significant investment opportunity. This includes investments in insulation, windows, heating and cooling systems, and building management systems (IEA, 2024b). Financing mechanisms, such as green mortgages and property-assessed clean energy (PACE) programs, can facilitate these investments (IEA, 2024b).
    - **Heat Pumps:** Heat pumps offer a highly efficient and low-carbon solution for heating and cooling. Investment opportunities include heat pump manufacturing, installation, and integration with renewable energy sources (IEA, 2024b).
    - **Building-Integrated Photovoltaics (BIPV):** BIPV integrates solar PV into building materials, offering both energy generation and building material functionality. Investment opportunities include BIPV product development, manufacturing, and installation (REN21, 2024).

4. **Industry Sector:**
    - **Energy Efficiency Improvements:** Investing in energy efficiency measures in industrial processes, such as process optimization, waste heat recovery, and electrification of industrial heat, can offer significant cost savings and emissions reductions (IEA, 2024b).
    - **Electrification of Industrial Heat:** Replacing fossil fuel-based heat with electric heating powered by renewable energy can decarbonize industrial processes. Investment opportunities include electric heating technologies, such as heat pumps and electric boilers, and associated infrastructure (IEA, 2024b).
    - **Green Hydrogen in Industry:** Green hydrogen can be used as a feedstock and fuel in various industrial processes, such as steelmaking and chemical production. Investment opportunities include electrolyzer manufacturing, hydrogen production, and industrial applications of hydrogen (IEA, 2024b).

- **Carbon Capture, Utilization, and Storage (CCUS):** CCUS can play a role in decarbonizing industrial processes by capturing CO_2 emissions. Investment opportunities include CCUS technologies, transport and storage infrastructure, and utilization pathways for captured CO_2 (IEA, 2024b).

5. **Cross-Sectoral Opportunities:**
    - **Grid Modernization and Expansion:** Investments in grid infrastructure, including transmission and distribution networks, smart grids, and microgrids, are crucial for accommodating the growing share of renewable energy in all sectors (IEA, 2024b).
    - **Energy Storage:** Energy storage technologies, such as batteries, pumped hydro, and thermal storage, are essential for ensuring grid stability and reliability as renewable energy penetration increases. Investment opportunities exist across a range of storage technologies, from short-duration to long-duration storage (IEA, 2024b; IRENA, 2024a).
    - **Critical Minerals:** The increasing demand for clean energy technologies is driving demand for critical minerals, such as lithium, cobalt, and nickel. Investment opportunities exist in mining, processing, and recycling of these minerals (IEA, 2024b).
    - **Hydrogen Production and Infrastructure:** Green hydrogen, produced from renewable energy, offers significant potential for decarbonizing various sectors, including transport, industry, and buildings. Investment opportunities include electrolyzer manufacturing, hydrogen production facilities, transport and storage infrastructure, and end-use applications (IEA, 2024b).

These investment opportunities highlight the diverse and dynamic nature of the renewable energy market. Realizing the full potential of these opportunities will require supportive policies, innovative financing mechanisms, and continued technological advancements. It will also be crucial to address the challenges related to geographical disparities in investment, grid infrastructure limitations, and the sustainable sourcing of critical materials. Furthermore, focusing on a just and inclusive energy transition, ensuring that the benefits of renewable energy are shared equitably, will be essential for building public support and achieving long-term sustainability.

3.3 *Emerging Technologies and Innovations*

Continued innovation in renewable energy technologies is further expanding investment opportunities and creating new avenues for growth. Promising advancements include:

- **Perovskite Solar Cells:** Perovskite solar cells are a next-generation solar technology with the potential to significantly increase energy conversion efficiency and reduce costs.
- **Floating Solar:** Floating solar farms, installed on water bodies such as reservoirs or lakes, offer several advantages, including reduced land-use requirements, improved panel efficiency due to water cooling, and the potential for co-location with hydropower projects.
- **Airborne Wind Energy:** This emerging technology harnesses wind energy at higher altitudes, where wind speeds are stronger and more consistent, using tethered kites or drones to generate electricity.

4 Challenges and Risks in Renewable Energy Investments

While the renewable energy sector offers significant investment potential, it also faces challenges and risks that investors need to carefully consider.

4.1 Intermittency and Grid Integration

One of the primary challenges associated with variable renewable energy sources, such as solar and wind power, is their intermittency—meaning their output fluctuates depending on weather conditions. Integrating these variable sources into electricity grids requires careful planning and investment in grid infrastructure and flexibility solutions. Grid stability in high renewable systems is achievable with current technologies (Brown et al., 2018).

Key solutions for addressing intermittency include:

- **Energy Storage:** Energy storage technologies, such as batteries, pumped hydro storage, and compressed air energy storage, can store excess renewable energy when generation is high and release it when demand exceeds supply, smoothing out fluctuations and enhancing grid stability.
- **Grid Modernization:** Upgrading electricity grids with advanced monitoring systems, smart meters, and flexible transmission lines can enable better integration of renewable energy, allowing grid operators to manage variations in supply and demand more effectively.
- **Demand Response:** Demand response programs encourage consumers to shift their electricity usage to times when renewable energy generation is abundant or to reduce their consumption during peak demand periods. This helps to balance supply and demand and reduce the need for fossil fuel-based “peaker” power plants.

4.2 Policy and Regulatory Uncertainty

Government policies, subsidies, and regulations play a crucial role in supporting the development of renewable energy markets. However, changes in policies, particularly retroactive changes, can create uncertainty for investors and impact the financial viability of renewable energy projects.

For example, sudden reductions in feed-in tariffs—guaranteed prices paid to renewable energy producers—or changes in net metering policies—which allow homeowners with solar panels to sell excess electricity back to the grid—can negatively impact the returns on renewable energy investments.

4.3 Financing Challenges

Financing renewable energy projects, particularly large-scale projects, can be challenging due to:

- **High Upfront Costs:** Renewable energy projects often require significant upfront capital investments, particularly for equipment and infrastructure.
- **Long Payback Periods:** While operating costs for renewable energy are typically low, the payback periods for these projects can be relatively long, especially for large-scale projects.
- **Technology Risks:** Investing in new or emerging renewable energy technologies can carry higher risks due to uncertainties about technology performance, cost reductions, and market adoption.

Case Study 2: M-KOPA Solar: Pay-As-You-Go Solar in Africa

Focus: Demonstrate How Off-Grid Solar Solutions Are Providing Access to Clean and Affordable Energy for Millions of People in Developing Countries

M-KOPA Solar is a leading provider of off-grid solar solutions in Africa, leveraging a pay-as-you-go (PAYG) model to provide clean and affordable energy to millions of people who lack access to traditional electricity grids. This case study explores how M-KOPA Solar uses this innovative business model to empower customers in Kenya, Uganda, and other African countries, enabling them to pay for solar home systems in small, incremental installments using mobile money.

Illustration: How M-KOPA Solar's Pay-As-You-Go Model Works

1. **The Pay-As-You-Go (PAYG) Model:**

M-KOPA Solar's PAYG model allows customers to purchase solar home systems on a pay-as-you-go basis. Customers make an initial deposit and then pay for the systems in small, manageable installments using mobile money platforms like M-PESA. This model makes solar energy accessible to low-income households by spreading the cost over time (International Renewable Energy Agency (IRENA, 2020).

2. **Providing Solar Home Systems:**

M-KOPA Solar offers a range of solar home systems that include solar panels, batteries, LED lights, phone chargers, and radios. These systems provide reliable and clean energy for lighting, mobile phone charging, and other basic needs, improving the quality of life for off-grid households (Ashiru, 2023; ICMR India, 2018).

3. **Leveraging Mobile Money:**

The PAYG model relies heavily on mobile money platforms, which enable customers to make payments conveniently and securely. This integration of mobile technology facilitates financial inclusion by allowing unbanked populations to access energy services and build a credit history (Lighting Global, 2025; Waldron, 2016).

Discussion: Social and Economic Impact, Innovative Business Models, and Mobile Technology

1. **Social and Economic Impact of Off-Grid Solar:**

Off-grid solar solutions like those provided by M-KOPA Solar have significant social and economic impacts. They improve living conditions by providing reliable lighting, reducing reliance on kerosene lamps, and enabling children to study at night. Additionally, they create economic opportunities by allowing small businesses to operate longer hours and increasing household savings on energy costs (Ireri et al., 2022; Radley & Lehmann-Grube, 2022).

2. **Role of Innovative Business Models in Expanding Energy Access:**

M-KOPA Solar's PAYG model is an example of an innovative business model that addresses the financial barriers to energy access. By allowing customers to pay in small installments, M-KOPA makes solar energy affordable for low-income households. This model also includes features like remote monitoring and control, which ensure that systems are maintained and payments are collected efficiently (KPMG, 2014; Vanadzina et al., 2019).

3. **Potential for Mobile Technology to Drive Financial Inclusion and Sustainable Development:**

Mobile technology plays a crucial role in the success of PAYG solar models. It enables secure and convenient payment processing, supports remote monitoring and control of solar systems, and facilitates financial inclusion by providing unbanked populations with access to energy services and credit. This integration of mobile technology with renewable energy solutions drives sustainable development by improving energy access and economic opportunities (Ahiase et al., 2024; Chopra, 2023).

Conclusion

M-KOPA Solar's pay-as-you-go model demonstrates how off-grid solar solutions can provide access to clean and affordable energy for millions of people in developing countries. By leveraging mobile money and innovative business models, M-KOPA Solar enables low-income households to access solar home systems and improve their quality of life. The social and economic impacts of off-grid solar are significant, including improved living conditions, increased economic opportunities, and enhanced energy security.

The success of M-KOPA Solar highlights the potential for mobile technology to drive financial inclusion and sustainable development. By addressing the financial barriers to energy access and integrating mobile payment systems, M-KOPA Solar and similar initiatives can play a crucial role in achieving universal energy access and promoting sustainable development in underserved regions.

Understanding the methodologies and strategies employed by M-KOPA Solar can provide valuable insights for other organizations and stakeholders seeking to expand energy access and drive sustainable development through innovative business models and mobile technology.

5 Financing Renewable Energy Projects

5.1 Investment Mechanisms

To overcome the financing challenges and attract the capital needed to scale up renewable energy deployment, a variety of financing mechanisms are being used:

Project Finance

Project finance is a specialized financing structure commonly used to fund large-scale infrastructure projects, including renewable energy projects. In project finance, the project itself is used as collateral for the loan, and the lender's repayment is primarily dependent on the project's future cash flows.

Key considerations in project finance include:

- **Risk Allocation:** Carefully allocating risks between the project developer, lenders, and other stakeholders is crucial to ensure project viability.
- **Debt Structuring:** Structuring the debt financing in a way that aligns with the project's cash flow profile and risk profile is essential to attract investors.
- **Financial Modeling:** Detailed financial models are used to project the project's revenues, expenses, and cash flows, demonstrating its financial viability to potential lenders.

Equity Investments

Equity investors, such as venture capital firms and private equity funds, provide capital in exchange for ownership stakes in renewable energy companies or projects. Equity investments are particularly important for financing early-stage companies and technologies that may not yet have the track record or cash flow to secure debt financing.

Green Bonds

Green bonds are debt securities issued to raise capital specifically for projects with environmental benefits, such as renewable energy projects, energy efficiency upgrades, or sustainable transportation initiatives.

The green bond market has grown rapidly in recent years, providing a significant source of funding for renewable energy projects. Investors are attracted to green bonds due to their potential to generate both financial returns and positive environmental impact.

Public-Private Partnerships (PPPs)

PPPs leverage public funding to attract private investment in infrastructure projects, including renewable energy projects. In a PPP, the government typically provides some form of financial support, such as grants, loans, or guarantees, to de-risk the project and make it more attractive to private investors.

5.2 A Step-by-Step Guide for Renewable Energy Investment Analysis

In a series of column articles, Chen et al. (2024a, 2024b, 2024c, 2024d) have proposed a step-by-step guide for renewable energy investment analysis. By determining the long-term financing costs, revenue models, electricity price expectations and operating costs, we can make a more reasonable and reliable analysis of the investment in renewable energy projects.

Chen et al. (2024b) emphasizes the critical importance of stabilizing long-term expectations for renewable energy investments, as they significantly influence project financing costs, income models, and operational expenses. It discusses how stable expectations reduce perceived risk, thereby attracting long-term investors, and outlines key income models employed in renewable projects, including Power Purchase Agreements and capacity markets. Lastly, it underscores the need for accurate long-term electricity price forecasts to maximize profitability and reduce operational costs through effective management strategies.

Key Points

- Stable long-term expectations lower perceived risks and financing costs, making renewable energy projects more appealing to investors.
- A comprehensive analysis of global capital markets reveals that long-term risk-free rates and investment return requirements for renewable energy vary significantly across countries.
- Income models for renewable energy projects include long-term Power Purchase Agreements (PPAs), government subsidies, and various market-based strategies for securing revenue streams.
- Understanding the volatility of electricity prices is essential for project developers to forecast income and optimize operational efficiency effectively.
- Long-term electricity price forecasts show different trends across major economies, impacting overall profitability for renewable energy investments.
- Predictive models for electricity prices vary significantly in approach, reflecting the complexities of market dynamics, technological advancements, and consumer behavior.
- The cost of long-term operations, including equipment maintenance and upgrades, can be anticipated through careful planning and management strategies, ensuring project sustainability.

5.2.1 *Establishing Long-Term Financing Costs*

When investors and lending institutions evaluate renewable energy projects, stable long-term expectations can reduce perceived risk, thereby lowering financing costs. If market expectations are unstable, lenders may raise interest rates to compensate for the increased risk. Stable long-term expectations can attract more long-term investors, such as pension funds and insurance companies.

After analyzing the bond and stock markets of major global economies, our main conclusions are:

- Except for China and Japan, the long-term risk-free interest rates of major global economies have continued to rise since the end of 2022, with a slight decrease by the end of 2023;

- In the bond market, the interest rates on the lowest-rated (Baa) corporate bonds in the United States have also increased, although the risk premium has decreased;
- In the real estate market, the capitalization rates for commercial properties in the United States have also risen;
- In the stock market, the beta values of the renewable energy sector currently range from approximately 0.5 to 1.38;

From this, we derive the required IRR for investing in renewable energy projects in the capital market (excluding the project's specific risk premium/idiosyncratic risk premium):

The following discusses how we arrived at these conclusions from four aspects.

1. **Risk-Free Rate**

The risk-free rate typically refers to the yield on the safest investments, such as government bonds, and is considered a rate without credit risk. Below are the changes in the long-term (10-year) risk-free rates for the United States, United Kingdom, Germany, and the Eurozone.

Except for China and Japan, the long-term risk-free rates of major global economies have continued to rise since the end of 2022, with a slight decline by the end of 2023 (Fig. 10).

2. **Cost of Debt Financing**

From the perspective of the US debt market, the long-term yield on the lowest investment-grade (Baa) corporate bonds remains high, but the risk premium has decreased (Fig. 11).

3. **Cost of Equity Financing**

The cost of equity financing refers to the cost a company must pay to raise equity, which is the expected return rate for investors. A common forecasting method is the Capital Asset Pricing Model (CAPM), which calculates the expected return using the risk-free rate, the beta coefficient of the stock (market risk exposure), and the market risk premium. The most critical elements are estimating the beta value and calculating the market risk premium.

We estimated the beta values for several representative new energy stocks and funds, with the beta values for the new energy sector currently ranging from approximately 0.5 to 1.15:

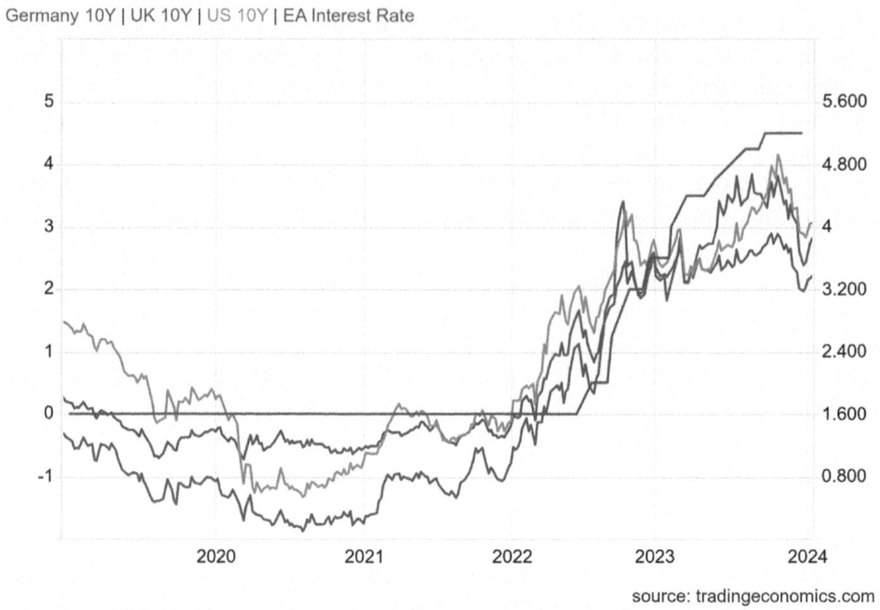

Fig. 10 Risk free rates of Germany, the United Kingdom, the United States, and Euro Area (*Source* TradingEconomics.com, Chen et al. [2024b])

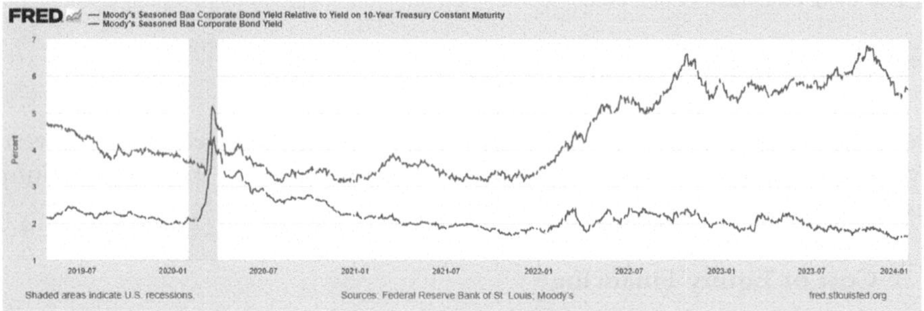

Fig. 11 Baa Bond Yield and Spread (*Source* Federal Reserve Bank of St. Louis, Moody's, Chen et al. [2024b])

- S&P Global Clean Energy Index beta = 0.959
- Nasdaq CleanEdge Green Energy Index beta = 1.376
- Huaxia CSI New Energy Vehicle ETF beta = 1.09
- Southern CSI New Energy ETF beta = 1.04
- Ping An CSI New Energy Vehicle Industry ETF beta = 1.08
- Energy Storage Closed Fund GSF.L beta = 0.622

Table 1 US Capital Market Long-Term Risk-Free Rate

20-yr	*30-yr*	*50-yr*
2003–08-01	1992–06-30	1972–01-03
2022–08-31	2022–06-30	2021/12/31
2.87	3.96	6.10

Source Chen et al. (2024b)

- Energy Storage Closed Fund GRID beta = 0.462

For the market risk premium, we primarily calculated the long-term performance of the US market over 20, 30, and 50 years, with the steps and results as follows (Table 1).

(1) Calculate the average return rate of long-term risk-free government bonds Rf:
(2) Calculate the average return rate of the long-term market portfolio (S&P 500) RM, and the market risk premium RP:
    - Over the 20-year period (2003/08–2022/08), the average return rate of the S&P 500 Index was 11.25%. RM = 11.25%, Rf = 2.87%, RP = RM − Rf = 8.38%;
    - Over the 30-year period (1992–2022), the average return rate of the S&P 500 Index was 9.9%. RM = 9.9%, RP = RM − Rf = 5.94%;
    - Over the 50-year period (1972–2021), the average return rate of the S&P 500 Index was 12.58%. RM = 12.58%, RP = RM − Rf = 6.48%;

Therefore, the range of long-term market risk premiums derived from the US market is between 6.5% and 8.4%.

4. **Comprehensive Financing Costs for Projects**

Based on the data above, the internal rate of return (IRR) requirements for investing in new energy projects should fall within the following ranges, depending on the ratio of debt to equity financing:

- United States, United Kingdom, Italy, Canada, Australia: 6.5%–13%;
- Germany, France: 5%–10%;
- Brazil, Russia, South Africa: 13%–22%;
- Japan: 2%–8%.

It is important to note that these are average results or expectations derived from capital market data and do not account for the specific risks of the projects themselves (idiosyncratic risk). Therefore, when evaluating specific projects, adjustments for their inherent risks are also necessary.

5.2.2 Long-Term Revenue Models

Stable long-term expectations make the revenue models of renewable energy projects more predictable, which helps ensure the continuous profitability of the projects. This is particularly important for investments based on revenue returns. When the revenue model is stable, projects are more likely to attract investors and partners, especially institutional investors seeking long-term stable returns.

1. **Power Contracts**

Long-term Power Purchase Agreements (PPAs): This is one of the most common revenue models in renewable energy projects. By signing long-term power purchase agreements with electricity users (such as utility companies or large industrial and commercial users), renewable energy projects can secure electricity revenue for a fixed period. PPAs typically specify the purchase price and quantity of electricity, providing stable cash flow for the projects.

Government subsidies and incentives: In some cases, the government may support renewable energy projects through subsidies or incentives, such as providing a fixed feed-in tariff for electricity fed into the grid.

2. **Price Arbitrage**

Exploiting market price fluctuations: Renewable energy projects (particularly those equipped with energy storage facilities) can take advantage of market electricity price fluctuations for arbitrage opportunities. For example, selling electricity when prices are high and storing electricity when prices are low. The following chart shows the hourly average electricity price in Spain's Day-Ahead Market for 2023. Operators or industrial and commercial users equipped with energy storage can charge during low price periods in the early morning and noon and discharge during peak usage times in the morning and evening to save on electricity costs or engage in arbitrage trading (Fig. 12).

Optimizing energy usage: Through intelligent software and market data analysis, renewable energy projects can optimize electricity generation and usage, thereby maximizing profits.

3. **Grid Ancillary Services**

Frequency regulation and backup services: Renewable energy projects, especially those with storage capabilities, can provide ancillary services to the grid, such as frequency regulation, voltage support, and emergency backup services.

Enhancing grid stability: By participating in these services, renewable energy projects not only help improve the reliability and stability of the grid but can also generate additional income from these activities.

Fig. 12 Hourly Average Electricity Price in Spain's Day-Ahead Market for 2023 (*Source* Red Eléctrica de España, Chen et al. [2024b])

4. **Capacity Markets**

Ensuring electricity supply: In capacity markets, renewable energy projects earn revenue by providing a certain amount of generation capacity or backup capacity. These markets are designed to ensure that there is enough electricity supply during peak demand periods.

Additional sources of income: Capacity markets provide renewable energy projects with revenue sources beyond electricity sales, helping them maintain economic viability in the competitive electricity market.

The revenue models for renewable energy projects are diverse, covering various aspects from electricity sales to providing ancillary services. Choosing the appropriate revenue model is crucial for ensuring the economic feasibility and long-term profitability of the projects. As market conditions evolve and new technologies develop, these revenue models may continue to evolve, offering more profit opportunities for renewable energy projects.

5.2.3 Long-Term Electricity Price Expectations

In renewable energy projects, electricity prices are the primary source of revenue. Stable expectations for future electricity prices help in more accurately assessing the long-term profitability potential of projects. Understanding long-term electricity price trends aids project operators in optimizing their operation and maintenance strategies to maximize revenue and reduce operational costs. Stable long-term expectations allow project developers to utilize various financial instruments to hedge against electricity price volatility risks, such as futures contracts and long-term Power Purchase Agreements (PPAs).

1. **Relationship Between Renewable Energy Revenue and Electricity Prices**

Taking the day-ahead market in Spain for 2023 as an example, the following chart shows the daily peak and trough price differences over the course of a year (Fig. 13).

The peak and trough price differences appear very random and irregular; however, regression analysis of the daily average electricity prices, as shown in the following chart, indicates a high correlation with the average electricity price. Once the average electricity price can be determined, it becomes possible to predict the daily peak and trough price differences with reasonable accuracy and obtain revenue forecasts for renewable energy projects (Fig. 14).

Electricity price forecasts can be categorized into short-term (hours or days), medium-term (months or years), and long-term (over 20 years). Below are commonly used models for these three types of electricity price forecasts:

Modeling for Hours or Days

- Data-driven models
- Artificial Neural Networks (ANNs)
- Wavelet Transform (WT)
- SARIMA/ARIMA
- Quantile Regressions
- Discrete Wavelet Transform (DWT)
- Fourier Analysis
- Empirical Mode Decomposition

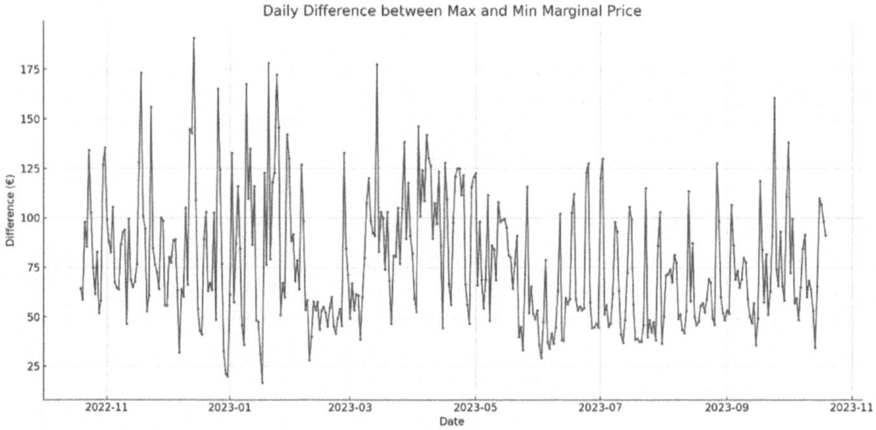

Fig. 13 Daily peak and trough price differences over the course of 2023 (*Source* Red Eléctrica de España, Chen et al. [2024b])

Fig. 14 Regression results of daily peak-trough price differences vs. daily average prices over the course of 2023 (*Source* Red Eléctrica de España, Chen et al. [2024b])

Modeling for Months or Years

- Support Vector Machines
- Probabilistic Forecasting Methods
- Market-based Models
- Data-Driven Models

Longer-Term Forecasts

- Fundamental (Supply-Demand-Substitution) Models
- Market (Derivative) Forecast Models
- Time Series Models
- Stochastic Models (Drift with Volatility-Jump)

We are particularly interested in long-term electricity price forecasts that extend beyond 20 years. The following analysis of long-term electricity price forecast models provides a comprehensive comparison of the electricity markets in China, the United States, Germany, and Switzerland:

Fundamental Models

- US EIA Long-Term Electricity Price Forecast (AEO2023): Decline in US electricity prices from 2022 to 2050 (US EIA, 2023)
- EY Power Price Forecasts (PPF): German electricity prices decline from 2022 to 2050 (EY, 2023)
- ETHZ Nexus-e: Increase in Swiss electricity prices from 2020 to 2050 (Gjorgiev et al., 2021)

Investment Cycle Method+ Cost-Benefit Models

- State Grid Energy Research Institute Long-Term Electricity Price Forecast: Increase in Chinese electricity prices from 2020 to 2060 (Sun et al., 2023).

We will provide detailed introductions to these four models in the following sections.

2. US Long-Term Electricity Price Forecast

The most authoritative long-term electricity price forecast in the United States is provided by the US Energy Information Administration (US EIA, 2023) through its annual Energy Outlook (AEO), with the latest edition being AEO2023. Below are the key forecast results for various electricity prices from 2022 to 2050: initially declining, then rising, and stabilizing.

In the "2023 Annual Energy Outlook" (AEO, 2023), the main conclusions are (Fig. 15):

- From 2022 to 2050, the consumption of various forms of energy in the United States will grow by 0% to 15%.

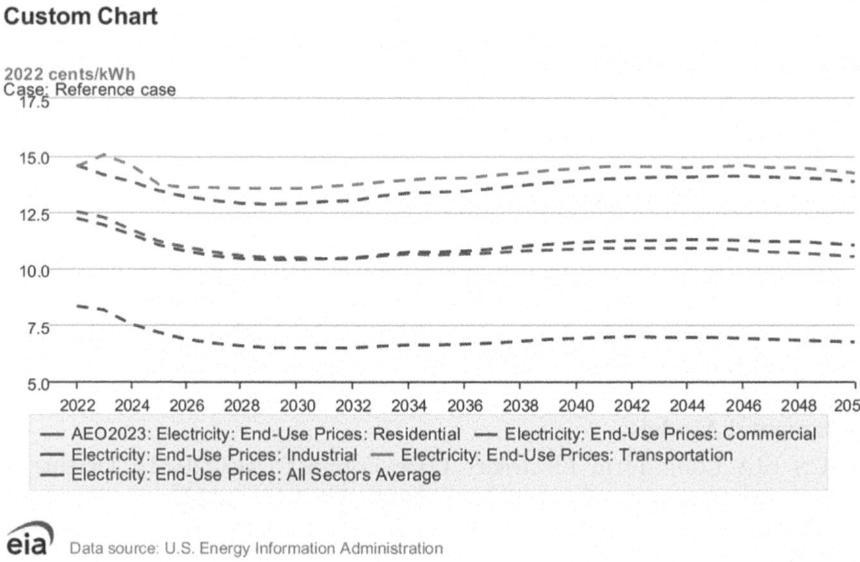

Fig. 15 Long-term electricity price forecast by EIA (*Source* US EIA [2023], Chen et al. [2024b])

- The forecast for growth in US energy consumption reflects the offsetting effects of economic growth, population growth, and increased travel against continuous improvements in energy efficiency.
- The total energy consumption of the four end-use sectors in the United States (industrial, transportation, residential, and commercial) includes primary energy consumption, electricity use, and electricity-related losses. The energy consumption in the industrial and transportation sectors is most sensitive to changes in assumptions under different scenarios, expressed as a percentage: in the industrial sector, energy consumption is expected to increase by 5% to 32% from 2022 to 2050; in the transportation sector, energy consumption is projected to range from a decline of 10% to an increase of 8% during the same period. Both sectors are significantly influenced by economic growth assumptions, consuming more energy as the economy grows.
- The increase in energy consumption, improvements in technology and efficiency in end-use and electricity sectors, and the declining costs of zero-carbon generation technologies lead to cheaper electricity, driving an increase in electrification in the end-use sectors across all scenarios in the AEO2023 reference case.
- Although the total energy consumption in the residential and commercial sectors shows slight growth, the average energy intensity in all scenarios is expected to decline by 2050 due to the increase in the number of households and the expansion of commercial building space. The efficiency of building envelopes is improved as states and localities adopt new building energy codes, and some existing homes and commercial spaces undergo additional insulation, air sealing, and other weatherization upgrades.

3. **China Long-Term Electricity Price Forecast**

For China's long-term electricity price forecast, we refer to the State Grid Energy Research Institute's forecast from 2020 to 2060:

The main conclusions are:

- The volatility of renewable energy requires reliance on other power sources to smooth output fluctuations, leading to increased costs for other sources.
- The intermittency of renewable energy necessitates reliable backup power sources for the electricity system, reducing the efficiency of other sources and increasing overall system costs.
- The actual utilization hours of renewable energy are far lower than traditional sources like coal power, and as penetration increases, the efficiency of the grid will decline, pushing up grid costs to some extent.

- The study constructs a cost forecasting model that combines changes in power source structure, generation costs, fuel costs, and grid investment to measure cost trends across various segments of the electricity system.
- The results indicate that the future costs of the electricity system are on an upward trend, with significant increases in costs on the power source side and smaller increases on the grid side.
- The terminal cost of electricity per kilowatt-hour is expected to rise by 12.1–19.3% and 15.7–30.9% by 2030 and 2060, respectively, compared to 2020.

4. **Germany Long-Term Electricity Price Forecast**

Germany, as the largest economy in the European Union, has a high correlation of long-term electricity prices with countries such as the United Kingdom, France, Italy, the Netherlands, and Belgium, as well as a significant correlation with Spain and Portugal (Fig. 16).

Therefore, for EU countries, we primarily focus on Germany's long-term electricity price forecast. We examined EY's Power Price Forecast (EY PPF) service, which predicts a decline in long-term electricity prices similar to the forecasts for the United States.

5. **Switzerland Long-Term Electricity Price Forecast**

Switzerland is not a member of the European Union; however, it has close economic and trade relations with the EU and has chosen not to join. Switzerland maintains a series of bilateral agreements with the EU to access the internal market and promote economic cooperation. This model, known as the "Swiss Model," allows Switzerland to collaborate with the EU while maintaining its national independence.

According to the ETHZ Nexus-e model from ETH Zurich, despite ambitious renewable energy targets, net electricity imports in winter are expected to increase for three main reasons:

- The currently highest annual installation rate of rooftop photovoltaic (PV) systems only generates 20–30% of its annual output in winter.
- Nuclear power plants (NPPs) that currently meet winter electricity demand are being decommissioned.
- The demand for electricity is continuously increasing, especially in winter.

Considering the long construction times for nuclear power plants in Europe and the challenges faced during the COVID-19 pandemic, this model discusses scenarios for Switzerland's future electricity supply, focusing on nuclear power and its impact on winter net imports and electricity prices. The

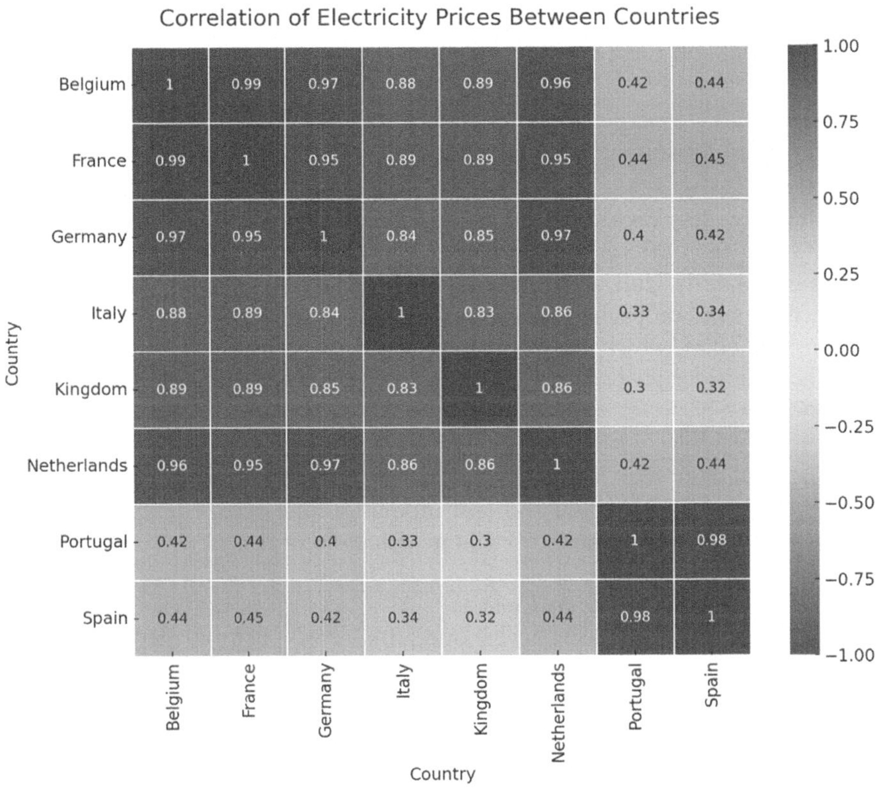

Fig. 16 Correlation of electricity prices between major EU countries (*Source* US EIA [2023], Chen et al. [2024b])

cost of electricity supply largely depends on the assumed investment costs for new nuclear power plants (NPPs). Its long-term (2020–2050) electricity price forecast is projected to continue rising.

6. Comparison of Long-Term Electricity Price Forecast Models

The characteristics of these four long-term electricity price forecast models are compared below:

Both EIA AEO2023 and EY PPF consider the impact of supply and demand on long-term electricity prices:

- The energy efficiency of households and businesses has significantly improved, leading to a decrease in per-household energy demand.
- Although total energy demand shows slight increases, the combination of supply growth and declining renewable energy costs results in a downward trend in overall electricity prices (as per the Swiss model).

- They also take into account factors such as macroeconomic growth rates, oil prices, and carbon reduction costs.

The State Grid Energy Research Institute and ETHZ Nexus-e models primarily consider supply-side impacts:

- They give less consideration to changes in energy efficiency at the user end and their effects on demand.
- The volatility and intermittency of renewable energy lead to faster increases in comprehensive generation costs and moderate rises in transmission costs, which are ultimately passed on to user costs.
- They consider fewer factors such as macroeconomic growth rates and oil prices.

Thus, it is evident that long-term electricity price forecasting is quite challenging. Beyond fundamental and cost models, a long-term energy derivatives market may also be necessary to facilitate price discovery.

5.2.4 Long-Term Operating Costs

Stable expectations for long-term operating costs help project managers plan and manage maintenance costs, technology upgrades, and equipment replacements more effectively.

1. **Equipment Replacement**

The costs of equipment replacement include the following three aspects of forecasting and estimation:

Lifetime Prediction:

- The expected lifespan of equipment is a key factor affecting long-term operating costs. This includes the lifespan of power generation equipment (such as wind turbines and solar panels), energy storage devices (such as batteries), and other critical components;
- The impact of technological advancements on equipment lifespan needs to be considered, as new technologies may enhance durability and efficiency.

Cost Estimation:

- When forecasting equipment replacement costs, it is important to consider the cost of purchasing new equipment, as well as potential price changes due to technological advancements;
- Costs related to the dismantling and installation of equipment should also be included.

Preventive Replacement:

- Adopting a preventive replacement strategy can reduce the risk and costs of unexpected failures, although this may require replacement before the equipment is completely worn out.

According to predictions from the State Grid Energy Research Institute, the costs of long-term wind energy, photovoltaics, solar thermal energy, and electrochemical energy storage are expected to continue to decline between 2020 and 2050.

2. **Operating and Maintenance Costs**

Operating and maintenance costs include the following two aspects.

Regular Maintenance:

- Regular maintenance is essential for ensuring stable equipment operation. Maintenance costs include routine inspections, parts replacements, and fault repairs;
- When forecasting maintenance costs, it is necessary to consider the intensity of equipment use, environmental factors (such as extreme weather conditions), and their impact on equipment wear.

Labor and Management Costs:

- Labor costs include the wages and training expenses of operators;
- Management costs encompass project management, safety supervision, and compliance inspections.

Currently, operating and maintenance costs can be estimated based on long-term inflation expectations, and we will conduct empirical discussions on specific calculations in Chapter 10.

Once we have determined the long-term financing costs, revenue models, electricity price expectations, and operating costs, we can conduct a reasonably sound and reliable analysis of investments in renewable energy projects.

Case Study 3: RE100: The Global Corporate Renewable Energy Initiative

Focus: Highlight the Role of Collaborative Initiatives in Driving Corporate Action on Renewable Energy

RE100 is a global initiative that brings together over 300 companies committed to sourcing 100% renewable electricity. This case study explores how RE100 is accelerating the transition to a clean energy future by demonstrating corporate demand for renewables and influencing policy changes. It highlights the power of corporate leadership in driving market transformation, the importance of setting ambitious targets, and the role of collaborative platforms in sharing knowledge and best practices.

Illustration: How RE100 Drives Corporate Action on Renewable Energy

1. **The RE100 Initiative:**

RE100, led by the Climate Group in partnership with CDP, is a collaborative initiative that unites influential businesses committed to 100% renewable electricity. Since its launch at Climate Week NYC in 2014, RE100 has grown to include over 300 companies from various industries, including telecommunications, retail, cement, and automobile manufacturing.

2. **Corporate Power Purchase Agreements (PPAs):**

Many RE100 members use power purchase agreements (PPAs) to source renewable energy at scale. PPAs are long-term contracts between corporations and renewable energy developers, providing financial certainty for new renewable energy projects. Companies like Google and IKEA have signed significant PPAs, driving the development of new renewable energy capacity (RE100, 2019, 2023).

3. **Demonstrating Corporate Demand for Renewables:**

RE100 members collectively drive significant demand for renewable electricity. If RE100 were a country, it would be the world's 10th largest in terms of electricity demand. This collective demand sends a powerful signal to markets and governments about the importance and feasibility of transitioning to renewable energy (Egli et al., 2023; Envizi, 2022).

Discussion: Benefits, Challenges, and Future Potential

1. **Power of Corporate Leadership in Driving Market Transformation:**

Corporate leadership is crucial in driving market transformation toward renewable energy. By committing to 100% renewable electricity, RE100 members set ambitious targets that inspire other companies and influence market dynamics. Their leadership helps create a more favorable environment for renewable energy investments and policy changes (Ishida, 2022; World Economic Forum, 2022).

2. **Importance of Setting Ambitious Targets:**

Setting ambitious targets is a critical component of RE100's success. Companies that commit to 100% renewable electricity by a specific date demonstrate their commitment to sustainability and drive the adoption of renewable energy. These targets also help companies align their operations with global climate goals (Climate Group, 2025; Fransen, 2024).

3. **Role of Collaborative Platforms in Sharing Knowledge and Best Practices:**

Collaborative platforms like RE100 facilitate the sharing of knowledge and best practices among members. Through peer-learning, policy support, and local market insights, RE100 helps companies navigate the complexities of renewable energy procurement and accelerate their transition to clean energy (European Commission, 2019; RE100, 2018).

4. **Challenges and Future Potential:**

While RE100 has made significant progress, challenges remain, including regulatory and market barriers in certain regions. However, the initiative's continued growth and the increasing number of companies committing to 100% renewable electricity highlight its potential to drive global change. By setting interim targets and expanding membership, RE100 can further accelerate the energy transition (Egli et al., 2023; RE100, 2023).

Conclusion

RE100 exemplifies the power of collaborative initiatives in driving corporate action on renewable energy. By bringing together over 300 companies committed to 100% renewable electricity, RE100 accelerates the transition to a clean energy future. The initiative demonstrates the importance of corporate leadership, ambitious targets, and collaborative platforms in influencing market dynamics and policy changes.

Understanding the methodologies and strategies employed by RE100 can provide valuable insights for other corporations and initiatives seeking to enhance their sustainability efforts and contribute to a clean energy future.

6 Conclusion: A Brighter, More Sustainable Future

The renewable energy revolution is underway, transforming the global energy landscape and offering unprecedented opportunities for investment, innovation, and job creation. Falling technology costs, supportive government policies, and growing public awareness of climate change are driving a rapid shift toward a future powered by clean, sustainable energy sources.

While challenges remain, such as the need to address intermittency issues and ensure grid stability, the momentum behind renewable energy is undeniable. By continuing to invest in renewable energy technologies, developing innovative financing mechanisms, and implementing smart policies, we can accelerate the transition to a brighter, more sustainable energy future for all.

References

Bloomberg New Energy Finance (BloombergNEF). (2023). *Energy transition investment trends 2023.* https://about.bnef.com/energy-transition-investment/

Brown, T. W., Bischof-Niemz, T., Blok, K., Breyer, C., Lund, H., & Mathiesen, B. V. (2018). Response to burden of proof: A comprehensive review of the feasibility of 100. *Renewable and Sustainable Energy Reviews, 92,* 834–847. https://www.sciencedirect.com/science/article/pii/S1364032118303307

Chen, J. et al. (2024a). *Why the performance of new energy assets is dismal: Breaking new ground in new energy investment (Part I).* Caixin Column Article. https://opinion.caixin.com/2024-01-12/102155632.html

Chen, J. et al. (2024b). *Stabilizing long-term expectations: Breaking new ground in new energy investment (Part II).* Caixin Column Article. https://opinion.caixin.com/2024-01-15/102156495.html

Chen, J. et al. (2024c). *Exploring commercial and industrial energy storage models: Breaking new ground in new energy investment (Part III).* Caixin Column Article. https://opinion.caixin.com/2024-01-23/102159486.html

Chen, J. et al. (2024d). *How to invest in large-scale energy storage systems: Breaking new ground in new energy investment (Part IV).* Caixin Column Article. https://opinion.caixin.com/2024-01-30/102161886.html

Earnest & Young (EY). (2023). *Why EY power price forecasts is important for your organization.* https://www.ey.com/en_gl/media/webcasts/2023/11/why-ey-power-price-forecasts-is-important-for-your-organization

Gjorgiev, B., Garrison, J. B., Han, X., Landis, F., van Nieuwkoop, R., Raycheva, E., Schwarz, M., Yan, X., Demiray, T., Hug, G., & Sansavini, G. (2021). Nexus-e: A platform of interfaced high-resolution models for energy-economic assessments of future electricity systems. *Applied Energy, 177,* 118–193. From https://doi.org/10.1016/j.apenergy.2021.118193

Haegel, N. M., Atwater Jr, H., Barnes, T., Breyer, C., Burrell, A., Chiang, Y. M., De Wolf, S., Dimmler, B., Feldman, D., Glunz, S., & Goldschmidt, J. C. (2019). Terawatt-scale photovoltaics: Transform global energy. *Science, 364*(6443), 836–838. https://science.sciencemag.org/content/364/6443/836

International Energy Agency (IEA). (2024a). *Global investment in clean energy and fossil fuels, 2015–2024.* Paris. https://www.iea.org/data-and-statistics/charts/global-investment-in-clean-energy-and-fossil-fuels-2015-2024

IEA. (2024b). *World energy outlook 2024.* Paris. https://www.iea.org/reports/world-energy-outlook-2024

IEA. (2024c). *World energy investment 2024.* Paris. https://www.iea.org/reports/world-energy-investment-2024

International Renewable Energy Agency (IRENA). (2023). *Renewable energy statistics 2023.* https://www.irena.org/Publications/2023/Jul/Renewable-energy-statistics-2023

IRENA. (2024a). *World energy transitions outlook 2024: 1.5°C pathway.* International Renewable Energy Agency, Abu Dhabi. https://www.irena.org/-/media/Files/IRENA/Agency/Publication/2024/Nov/IRENA_World_energy_transitions_outlook_2024.pdf

IRENA. (2024b). *Renewable capacity statistics 2024.* International Renewable Energy Agency, Abu Dhabi. https://www.irena.org/-/media/Files/IRENA/Agency/Publication/2024/Mar/IRENA_RE_Capacity_Statistics_2024.pdf

IRENA. (2024c). *Renewable power generation costs in 2023.* International Renewable Energy Agency, Abu Dhabi. https://www.irena.org/-/media/Files/IRENA/Agency/Publication/2024/Sep/IRENA_Renewable_power_generation_costs_in_2023.pdf

Polman, A., Knight, M., Garnett, E. C., Ehrler, B., & Sinke, W. (2016). Photovoltaic materials: Present efficiencies and future challenges. *Science, 352*(6283). https://science.sciencemag.org/content/352/6283/aad4424

Renewable Energy Policy Network for the 21st Century (REN21). (2024). *Renewables 2024 global status report collection.* https://www.ren21.net/gsr-2024/annex/downloads/

Searchinger, T. D., Beringer, T., Holtsmark, B., Kammen, D. M., Lambin, E. F., Lucht, W., Raven, P., & van Ypersele, J. P. (2018). Europe's renewable energy directive poised to harm global forests. *Nature Communications, 9*(1), 37–41. https://www.nature.com/articles/s41467-018-06175-4

Sun, Q. X. Zhang, C., LI, C., You, P., GAO, X., ZHAO, Q., XU, Z., LIU, S., & LI, Y. (2023). Prediction of power system cost and price level under the goal of "Carbon peak and carbon neutralization". *Electric Power, 56*(1), 9–16. https://doi.org/10.11930/j.issn.1004-9649.202208069

US Energy Information Administration (US EIA). (2023). *Annual energy outlook 2023.* https://www.eia.gov/outlooks/aeo/

Veers, P. Dykes, K., Lantz, E., Barth, S., Bottasso, C. L., Carlson, O., Clifton, A., Green, J., Green, P., Holttinen, H., & Laird, D. (2019). (2019). Grand challenges in the science of wind energy. *Science,* 366(6464), 20–27. From https://science.sciencemag.org/content/366/6464/eaau2027

Case References

Ahiase, G., Nugraha, N., Andriana, D., & Sari, M. (2024). Digital financial inclusion and environmental sustainability in Africa: The moderating effect of income inequality. *Management of Environmental Quality: An International Journal, 35*(7), 1671–1690. https://doi.org/10.1108/MEQ-11-2023-0382

Ashiru, G. (2023). *M-KOPA launches pay-As-you-go solar solutions in South Africa.* Tech In Africa. https://www.techinafrica.com/m-kopa-launches-pay-as-you-go-solar-solutions-in-south-africa/

AtkinsRéalis. (2025). *Everything about the UAE's Solar Park*. Accessed 23 January 2025. https://careers.atkinsrealis.com/blogs/2022-10/everything-about-mohammed-bin-rashid-al-maktoum-solar-park

C40 Cities Climate Leadership Group (C40 Cities). (2019). *Dubai's "Mohammed Bin Rashid Al Maktoum" 5,000MW Solar Park*. Accessed 23 January 2025. https://www.c40.org/case-studies/dubai-s-mohammed-bin-rashid-al-maktoum-5-000mw-solar-park-aims-to-save-6-5-million-tco2e-annually/

Chopra, N. (2023). Powering the future: How renewable energy is revolutionising the mobile sector. *Economic Times*. Accessed 23 January 2025. https://economictimes.indiatimes.com/industry/renewables/powering-the-future-how-renewable-energy-is-revolutionising-the-mobile-sector/articleshow/102109014.cms

Climate Group. (2025). *We are committed to 100% renewable power*. https://www.theclimategroup.org/about_re100

Dubai Electricity and Water Authority (DEWA). (2024). *Mohammed bin rashid Al maktoum solar park*. Accessed 23 January 2025. https://www.dewa.gov.ae/en/about-us/strategic-initiatives/mbr-solar-park

Egli, F., Zhang, R., Hopo, V., Schmidt, T., & Steffen, B. (2023). The contribution of corporate initiatives to global renewable electricity deployment. *Nature Communications, 14*(1). https://doi.org/10.1038/s41467-023-40356-0

Envizi. (2022). *RE100 initiative explained*. IBM. From https://www.ibm.com/blog/re100-initiative-explained/

European Commission. (2019). *A collaborative approach to renewable energy*. https://projects.research-and-innovation.ec.europa.eu/en/projects/success-stories/all/collaborative-approach-renewable-energy

Fransen, B. (2024). *Green leadership: driving sustainable practices in an organisation*. EcoMatcher. https://www.ecomatcher.com/green-leadership-driving-sustainable-practices-in-an-organisation/

Global Energy Monitor. (2024). *Mohammed Bin Rashid Al Maktoum Solar Park*. https://www.gem.wiki/Mohammed_Bin_Rashid_Al_Maktoum_Solar_Park

Lighting Global. (2025). *Pay-As-You-Go (PAYGo)*. Accessed 27 January 2025. https://www.lightingglobal.org/paygo/

Indian Council of Medical Research (ICMR India). (2018). *M-KOPA solar: "solarpreneur" with a unique business model|leadership and entrepreneurship|case study|case studies*. Icmrindia.org. https://www.icmrindia.org/casestudies/catalogue/Leadership%20and%20Entrepreneurship/LDEN131.htm

IRENA. (2020). *Pay-as-you-go models: Innovation landscape brief*. https://www.irena.org/-/media/Files/IRENA/Agency/Publication/2020/Jul/IRENA_Pay-as-you-go_models_2020.pdf

Ireri, M., Tonui, P. T., Gallery, B., Elahi, R., & Dohrenbusch, H. (2022). *How off-grid solar solutions are key to climate adaptation and resilience*. World Bank. Accessed 1 January 2024. https://blogs.worldbank.org/en/energy/how-grid-solar-solutions-are-key-climate-adaptation-and-resilience

Ishida, M. (2022). *RE100 revised the technical criteria, adding 15-year commissioning date limit*. Renewable Energy Institute. Accessed 1 January 2024. https://www.renewable-ei.org/en/activities/column/REupdate/20221026.php

KPMG. (2014). *PAYGO: Solar distribution through pay as you go business models in east Africa*. https://assets.kpmg.com/content/dam/kpmg/ke/pdf/idas/thought-leaderships/paygo-development-in-practice-a.pdf

Obaideen, K., AlMallahi, M. N., Alami, A. H., Ramadan, M., Abdelkareem, M. A., Shehata, N., & Olabi, A. G. (2021). On the contribution of solar energy to sustainable developments goals: Case study on mohammed bin rashid Al maktoum solar park. *International Journal of Thermofluids, 12*, 100–123. https://doi.org/10.1016/j.ijft.2021.100123

Radley, B., & Lehmann-Grube, P. (2022). Off-grid solar expansion and economic development in the global south: A critical review and research agenda. *Energy Research & Social Science, 89*, 102–673. https://doi.org/10.1016/j.erss.2022.102673

Renewable Energy 100 (RE100). (2018). *Business leadership in the transition to renewable electricity*. https://www.there100.org/sites/re100/files/2020-09/RE100%20Leadership%20report.pdf

RE100. (2019). *Going 100% renewable: How committed companies are driving the transition*. https://www.there100.org/sites/re100/files/2020-09/RE100ProgressandInsightsAnnualReport2019.pdf

RE100. (2023). *Driving renewables in a time of change*. https://www.there100.org/sites/re100/files/2023-01/CDP_RE100_Report_2023%20%282%29.pdf

SolarPACES. (2023). *DEWA inaugurates its 700 MW trough and tower CSP project for Dubai*. Accessed 23 January 2025. From https://www.solarpaces.org/dewa-inaugurates-its-700-mw-trough-and-tower-csp-project-for-dubai/

UAE Embassy in Washington. (2023). *UAE energy diversification*. Accessed 23 January 2025. https://www.uae-embassy.org/discover-uae/climate-and-energy/uae-energy-diversification

Vanadzina, E., Pinomaa, A., Honkapuro, S., & Mendes, G. (2019). An innovative business model for rural sub-saharan Africa electrification. *Energy Procedia, 159*, 364–369. https://doi.org/10.1016/j.egypro.2019.01.001

Waldron, D. (2016). *Financial inclusion and off-grid solar: Three takeaways*. CGAP. Accessed 1 January 2024. From https://www.cgap.org/blog/financial-inclusion-and-grid-solar-three-takeaways

World Economic Forum (WEF). (2022). *Cross-sector partnerships are enabling a clean energy transition*. https://www.weforum.org/agenda/2022/08/how-cross-sector-partnerships-enabling-clean-energy-transition/

CHAPTER 10

The Role of Energy Storage: Enabling the Renewable Energy Transition

1 Introduction: The Power of Energy Storage

Renewable energy sources like solar and wind power are abundant, clean, and increasingly cost-effective. However, their intermittent nature—the fact that their output fluctuates depending on the availability of sunlight or wind—presents a significant challenge for integrating them into the electricity grid and achieving a truly sustainable energy system. Energy storage is the key to unlocking the full potential of renewable energy, providing the flexibility and reliability needed to create a cleaner, more resilient, and affordable grid.

Imagine a world where solar panels capture abundant energy during the day, but that energy can be stored for use in the evening when the sun sets. Or a wind farm harnessing the power of strong gusts, storing that energy to provide a steady supply of electricity even when the wind dies down. This is the transformative power of energy storage.

Energy storage technologies act as a bridge between the variable nature of renewable energy generation and the constant demand for electricity, allowing us to:

- **Smooth out Fluctuations:** Energy storage systems can absorb excess renewable energy when generation exceeds demand, storing it for later use when demand is higher.
- **Enhance Grid Reliability:** Storage can provide backup power during outages, ensuring a more reliable and resilient electricity supply.
- **Enable Greater Renewable Energy Penetration:** By addressing the intermittency challenge, energy storage enables a higher penetration of renewable energy sources into the grid, reducing our reliance on fossil fuels.

J. Chen, *Climate Finance*,
https://doi.org/10.1007/978-981-96-7975-1_10

This chapter will explore the various types of energy storage technologies, their diverse applications across different scales, the key drivers of investment in this rapidly growing sector, and the challenges and opportunities that lie ahead. By understanding the power of energy storage, we can unlock the full potential of renewable energy and accelerate the transition to a sustainable energy future.

2 Types of Energy Storage Technologies

Energy storage technologies come in various forms, each with its unique characteristics, advantages, and limitations. This section explores some of the most prominent and promising energy storage solutions. IRENA (2020) provides a framework for valuing electricity storage, emphasizing its role in renewable energy integration and revenue stacking opportunities.

2.1 Pumped Hydro Storage

Pumped hydro storage (PHS) is the most mature and widely deployed energy storage technology globally, accounting for the vast majority of grid-scale energy storage capacity. It works by using excess electricity to pump water uphill from a lower reservoir to a higher reservoir. When energy is needed, the water is released downhill through turbines, generating electricity.

Advantages:

- **Large-Scale Storage Capacity:** PHS plants can store large amounts of energy, typically in the range of hundreds of megawatt-hours (MWh) to gigawatt-hours (GWh), making them suitable for grid-scale applications.
- **Long Lifespan:** PHS plants can operate for decades with proper maintenance.
- **Mature Technology:** PHS technology is well understood and proven, with a long history of operation.

Limitations:

- **Geographic Constraints:** PHS requires specific geographic features, such as two reservoirs at different elevations, limiting its deployment to suitable locations.
- **Environmental Impacts:** Construction of dams and reservoirs can have significant environmental impacts, altering river flows and affecting aquatic ecosystems.
- **High Capital Costs:** PHS projects require substantial upfront capital investments, although operating costs are relatively low.

2.2 *Battery Storage*

Battery storage is rapidly gaining prominence as a versatile and scalable energy storage solution. Batteries store chemical energy that can be converted into electricity when needed. Various battery technologies are used for energy storage, each with its own characteristics. BloombergNEF (2021) reports Li-ion battery pack prices dropped to $137/kWh in 2020, with some reaching below $100/kWh, and projects $101/kWh by 2023.

- **Lithium-Ion Batteries:** Lithium-ion batteries are the most common type of battery used for energy storage due to their high energy density, relatively long lifespan, and declining costs. They are used in a wide range of applications, from electric vehicles and portable electronics to grid-scale energy storage systems.
- **Flow Batteries:** Flow batteries store energy in liquid electrolytes that are pumped through a cell stack. They are well-suited for large-scale, long-duration storage applications, but their energy density is lower than that of lithium-ion batteries. Flow batteries using abundant, low-cost materials show promise for achieving the needed cost targets (Ziegler et al., 2019).
- **Sodium-Sulfur Batteries:** Sodium-sulfur batteries use molten sodium and sulfur as electrodes and a solid ceramic electrolyte. They have a high energy density and long lifespan, making them suitable for grid-scale storage (Fig. 1).

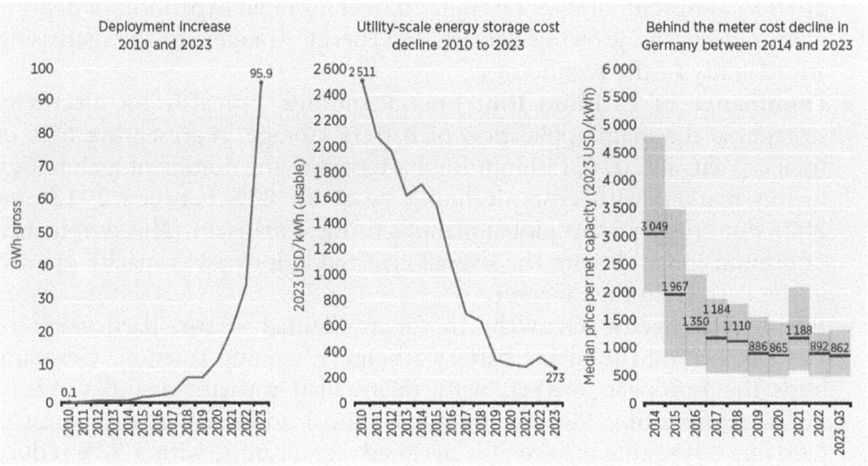

Fig. 1 Global deployment increase and utility-scale energy cost decline, 2010–2023, and behind-the-meter cost decline in Germany, 2014-Q1 2023 (*Source* IRENA [2024])

Battery technology	*Advantages*	*Disadvantages*	*Applications*
Lithium-ion	High energy density, long lifespan, declining costs	Safety concerns, limited lifespan at high temperatures, potential for thermal runaway	EVs, portable electronics, grid-scale storage
Flow Batteries	Scalable, long duration, safe, long lifespan	Lower energy density, higher cost	Grid-scale storage, renewable energy integration
Sodium-Sulfur	High energy density, long lifespan, high efficiency	High operating temperatures, safety concerns	Grid-scale storage, industrial applications

The battery storage market is experiencing rapid growth, driven by declining costs, expanding manufacturing capacity, and the increasing need for energy storage to support the integration of renewable energy sources into the power grid.

- **Declining Costs:** The cost of battery storage projects has decreased significantly. Between 2010 and 2023, costs fell by 89%, from USD 2511/kWh to USD 273/kWh. This dramatic cost reduction has been driven by economies of scale in manufacturing, improved materials efficiency, and advancements in manufacturing processes. These cost improvements are making battery storage an increasingly viable solution for a wide range of applications.
- **Increased Capacity Additions:** Annual capacity additions for battery storage have seen tremendous growth, increasing from just 0.1 GWh in 2010 to a substantial 95.9 GWh in 2023. This rapid expansion of deployment reflects the growing demand for energy storage and the increasing affordability of the technology.
- **Dominance of Lithium-Ion:** Energy shifting, primarily for electricity storage, is the main application of battery storage, representing 67% of total capacity in 2023. Lithium-ion batteries are the dominant technology in this market, with costs declining by about 82% between 2013 and 2023 due to significant global manufacturing expansion. This dominance of lithium-ion is driving the overall cost reductions and capacity growth in the battery storage market.
- **Residential Sector Growth:** In the residential sector, particularly in Europe, behind-the-meter battery storage is gaining traction. Germany leads the European market, with an installed capacity of 5.6 GWh in 2023, representing 93% of the total annual additions in the country. Costs in this segment have also declined significantly, with a 72% reduction observed in Germany between 2014 and Q1 2023. This growth in the residential sector is driven by increasing consumer interest in

self-consumption of solar power, backup power solutions, and energy independence.

- **Geographical Distribution:** China leads the world in new battery storage capacity additions, installing 46.5 GWh in 2023, nearly half of the global total. The United States is the second largest market, adding 22 GWh in 2023, almost a quarter of the global total. This concentration of deployment in China and the United States reflects supportive government policies, growing demand for energy storage, and the presence of major battery manufacturers in these countries. However, it also highlights the need for increased deployment in other regions to ensure a more equitable distribution of the benefits of energy storage.

The battery storage market is poised for continued growth as costs decline and technology improves. The increasing penetration of renewable energy sources will further drive demand for energy storage solutions to address intermittency challenges and ensure grid stability. Further advancements in battery chemistries, manufacturing processes, and system integration will be key to unlocking the full potential of battery storage and its contribution to the global energy transition. However, challenges remain, including supply chain security for critical minerals, the need for supportive regulatory frameworks, and ensuring the responsible sourcing and recycling of battery materials. Addressing these challenges will be crucial for the sustainable growth and development of the battery storage market.

2.3 Compressed Air Energy Storage

Compressed air energy storage (CAES) systems store energy by compressing air and storing it in underground caverns, salt domes, or other suitable geological formations. When electricity is needed, the compressed air is released and heated, driving turbines to generate electricity.

Advantages:

- **Large-Scale Storage Potential:** CAES can store large amounts of energy for long durations.
- **Long Lifespan:** CAES systems can operate for decades with proper maintenance.
- **Use of Existing Infrastructure:** Existing underground caverns or salt domes can be repurposed for CAES, potentially reducing development costs.

Limitations:

- **Geographic Constraints:** CAES requires specific geological formations for air storage, limiting its deployment to suitable locations.

- **Energy Losses:** The compression and heating processes in CAES systems result in energy losses, reducing overall efficiency.

2.4 *Other Energy Storage Technologies*

- **Thermal Energy Storage:** This approach stores heat or cold in materials for later use. Examples include molten salt storage in concentrated solar power plants, ice storage for cooling buildings, and phase-change materials that store energy during phase transitions (e.g., melting and freezing).
- **Flywheels:** Flywheels store kinetic energy in rotating rotors. They can release energy quickly, making them suitable for short-duration grid stabilization applications.
- **Hydrogen Storage:** Hydrogen can be produced from renewable energy sources through electrolysis and stored as a gas or liquid. When energy is needed, the hydrogen can be used in fuel cells to generate electricity or burned as a fuel source.

3 Energy Storage Applications

Energy storage technologies are being deployed across a range of applications, from grid-scale systems that enhance the reliability and flexibility of the electricity grid to commercial and industrial systems that reduce energy costs for businesses and residential systems that provide backup power for homes.

Introduction to Energy Storage Systems.

Energy storage systems play a critical role in modern power systems. They can be installed on the generation side, grid side, or user side, each with different functions and advantages. Below is a brief introduction to these three energy storage modes:

1. **Generation Side Storage**

Definition: Generation side storage is typically installed at power generation sites, such as wind farms or solar power plants.

Functions:

- Peak shaving and valley filling: Balancing generation and demand to reduce energy waste.
- Increasing renewable energy utilization: Storing excess energy when wind or sunlight is abundant for use during calm or cloudy periods.
- Frequency regulation and grid stability: Responding to changes in grid frequency and providing rapid adjustments.

Advantages:

- Enhancing generation efficiency and reliability.
- Reducing dependence on traditional peaking power plants (such as gas-fired power plants).

2. **Grid Side Storage**

Definition: Grid side storage systems are installed at key nodes in the power transmission and distribution network.

Functions:

- Enhancing grid resilience: Providing support during grid failures or peak demand periods.
- Optimizing grid operation: Reducing grid losses by adjusting grid loads.
- Load balancing: Helping the grid cope with demand fluctuations and improving overall grid efficiency.

Advantages:

- Reducing the need for large-scale grid upgrades.
- Providing emergency backup power, enhancing the reliability and safety of the grid.

3. **User Side Storage**

Definition: User side storage is installed at the premises of end users, such as residences, commercial buildings, or industrial facilities.

Functions:

- Reducing electricity bills: Charging and discharging based on price differences to lower electricity expenses.
- Backup power: Providing backup electricity during grid outages.
- Enhancing self-sufficiency: For users with solar panels, storing self-generated electricity for use at night or on cloudy days.

Advantages:

- Providing energy independence and reducing reliance on the grid.
- Enabling users to utilize their self-generated renewable energy more effectively.

These three energy storage modes each have unique application scenarios and advantages. Generation side storage primarily aims to improve generation efficiency and reliability, grid side storage focuses on enhancing the flexibility and stability of grid operations, while user side storage offers users energy autonomy and economic benefits. With the continuous development of renewable energy and the modernization of power systems, these storage modes are playing an increasingly important role in achieving a cleaner and more efficient energy system.

Based on whether they are installed in front of or behind the meter, battery storage systems can also be classified into the following three categories:

- Front-of-the-meter (FTM) utility-scale storage systems (including generation side and grid side), typically greater than 10 megawatt-hours (MWh);
- Behind-the-meter (BTM) commercial and industrial storage systems, typically ranging from 30 kilowatt-hours (kWh) to 10 megawatt-hours;
- Behind-the-meter residential storage, typically less than 30 kWh.

In the next section, we will discuss in detail the FTM energy storage system, grid-scale storage.

3.1 Grid-Scale Storage

Grid-scale energy storage systems, typically ranging in size from megawatts to gigawatts, play a vital role in enhancing the stability, reliability, and resilience of electricity grids. DOE (2020) outlines a roadmap for US leadership in energy storage by 2030.

Key applications of grid-scale storage include:

- **Frequency Regulation:** The frequency of the electricity grid must be maintained within a narrow range to ensure the stable operation of electrical equipment. Energy storage systems can respond rapidly to fluctuations in frequency, injecting or absorbing power as needed to maintain a stable grid frequency.
- **Peak Shaving:** Energy storage can reduce peak demand for electricity by storing energy during off-peak hours and releasing it during periods of high demand. This helps to avoid the need to build expensive "peaker" power plants, which are only used during peak demand periods and often rely on fossil fuels.
- **Energy Arbitrage:** Energy storage systems can be used to buy electricity when prices are low (e.g., during periods of high renewable energy generation) and sell it when prices are high (e.g., during peak demand periods), enabling energy traders to profit from price fluctuations.

Case Study 1: The Hornsdale Power Reserve (Tesla Big Battery) in South Australia

Focus: Showcase How a Large-Scale Battery Project Enabled Greater Integration of Wind Energy into the Grid, Improving Reliability and Demonstrating the Crucial Role of Storage in Maximizing Renewable Energy Deployment.

The Hornsdale Power Reserve, commonly known as the Tesla Big Battery, is a pioneering large-scale battery storage project in South Australia. This case study explores how the 100 MW/129 MWh battery system, paired with the Hornsdale Wind Farm, has enabled greater integration of wind energy into the grid, improved reliability, and demonstrated the crucial role of storage in maximizing renewable energy deployment.

Illustration: Methodology and Implementation of the Hornsdale Power Reserve

1. **The Project:**

The Hornsdale Power Reserve was commissioned in 2017 and is one of the world's largest lithium-ion batteries. It was developed by Tesla in partnership with Neoen, a French renewable energy company, and is co-located with the Hornsdale Wind Farm. The battery system provides grid stability by storing excess wind energy and releasing it during periods of high demand or low wind generation.

2. **Responding to Fluctuations in Wind Power Generation:**

The Hornsdale Power Reserve has demonstrated its ability to respond rapidly to fluctuations in wind power generation. The battery system can provide fast frequency response and grid stabilization services, helping to prevent blackouts and ensure a reliable power supply. For example, during a major power outage in South Australia in 2017, the battery responded within milliseconds to stabilize the grid.

3. **Economic Benefits of Grid Stability:**

The Hornsdale Power Reserve has provided significant economic benefits by enhancing grid stability and reducing the need for expensive fossil fuel "peaker" plants. The battery has saved millions of dollars in grid stabilization costs and has demonstrated the potential for battery storage to provide cost-effective and reliable energy solutions.

Discussion: Government Policies, Economic Benefits, and Future Potential

1. **Importance of Government Policies in Incentivizing Battery Storage:**

Government policies have played a crucial role in incentivizing the development of battery storage projects like the Hornsdale Power Reserve. Supportive policies, such as subsidies, tax incentives, and regulatory frameworks, have encouraged investment in renewable energy and storage technologies.

2. **Economic Benefits of Grid Stability:**

The economic benefits of grid stability provided by battery storage are substantial. By reducing the reliance on fossil fuel "peaker" plants, batteries can lower energy costs for consumers and enhance the overall efficiency of the energy system. This contributes to a more resilient and sustainable energy infrastructure (International Renewable Energy Agency).

3. **Potential for Batteries to Replace Traditional Fossil Fuel "Peaker" Plants:**

Battery storage has the potential to replace traditional fossil fuel "peaker" plants, which are used to meet peak electricity demand. Batteries can provide fast and flexible response to grid needs, reducing greenhouse gas emissions and supporting the transition to a low-carbon energy system (Rocky Mountain Institute (RMI), 2015).

Conclusion

The Hornsdale Power Reserve (Tesla Big Battery) in South Australia exemplifies the transformative potential of large-scale battery storage in enhancing the integration of renewable energy into the grid. By providing rapid response to fluctuations in wind power generation, stabilizing the grid, and preventing blackouts, the project has demonstrated the crucial role of storage in maximizing renewable energy deployment.

Government policies have been instrumental in incentivizing battery storage, and the economic benefits of grid stability are clear. As battery costs continue to decline and technology advances, the potential for batteries to replace traditional fossil fuel "peaker" plants becomes increasingly viable, supporting the transition to a low-carbon energy system.

Understanding the methodologies and strategies employed by the Hornsdale Power Reserve can provide valuable insights for other regions and stakeholders seeking to enhance grid stability and maximize the deployment of renewable energy through battery storage.

3.2 Commercial and Industrial (C&I) Storage

Businesses are increasingly adopting energy storage systems to reduce their energy costs, improve reliability, and enhance their sustainability.

Key applications of C&I storage include:

- **Reduce Energy Costs:** By storing electricity during off-peak hours when prices are lower and using it during peak demand periods when prices are higher, businesses can significantly reduce their electricity bills. Jülch (2016) compares electricity storage costs using LCOS, finding PSH as currently cheapest and batteries promising in the future.
- **Improve Reliability:** Energy storage systems can provide backup power during outages, ensuring continuity of operations and reducing financial losses due to downtime.
- **Increase Efficiency:** By optimizing energy usage and reducing peak demand, businesses can improve their energy efficiency, lowering their overall energy consumption and environmental footprint.

McKinsey (2023) believes that industrial and commercial energy storage systems can be further divided into the following four areas:

- Electric Vehicle Charging Infrastructure (EVCI)
- Critical Infrastructure
- Public Infrastructure, Commercial Buildings, and Factories
- Harsh Environments and Outdoor Activities

Electric Vehicle Charging Infrastructure (EVCI): According to data from McKinsey's Center for Future Mobility, the share of electric vehicles in global car sales is expected to leap from around 23% in 2025 to 45% by 2030. This growth will necessitate a rapid expansion of conventional charging stations and supercharging stations, putting pressure on the current grid infrastructure and requiring costly and time-consuming upgrades. To avoid this, charging station companies and property owners may choose to install Battery Energy Storage Systems (BESS) on their properties. Partnerships have already been established between BESS participants and electric vehicle manufacturers to build more EVCI, including in remote areas.

Critical Infrastructure, such as telecom towers, data centers, and hospitals: In this segment, lead-acid batteries are typically used to provide temporary backup power through uninterruptible power supplies during outages until power is restored or diesel generators are started. In addition to replacing lead-acid batteries, lithium-ion BESS products can reduce reliance on less environmentally friendly diesel generators and can be integrated with renewable energy sources such as rooftop solar. In some cases, excess energy stored in batteries can allow organizations to generate revenue through grid services.

Some telecom operators and data center owners have already turned to BESS as their uninterruptible power supply solution, along with the additional benefits provided by BESS.

Public Infrastructure, Commercial Buildings, and Factories: This segment will primarily use energy storage systems to assist with peak shaving, integrate with on-site renewable energy, optimize self-consumption, provide backup applications, and offer grid services. BESS has the potential to reduce energy costs in these areas by up to 80%. In countries like Germany, North America, and the United Kingdom, where demand charges are frequently implemented, the argument for supporting BESS is particularly strong.

Harsh Environments—applications in mining, construction, oil and gas exploration, and outdoor festivals: The source of growth will be customers moving away from diesel or gas generators in favor of low-emission solutions such as BESS and hybrid generators. A major driver for adoption in this field is the upcoming regulations, including the EU Commission's large buyer initiative focused on sustainability and the Oslo net-zero emissions plan for construction sites by 2025. Many companies undergoing transformation will first turn to hybrid generator solutions rather than immediately transitioning fully to BESS.

Case Study 2: Stem Inc.'s AI-Powered Energy Storage Solutions for Businesses

Focus: Highlight the Use of Artificial Intelligence (AI) to Optimize Energy Storage Systems for C&I Customers

Stem Inc. is a leader in providing AI-powered energy storage solutions, particularly for commercial and industrial (C&I) customers. This case study explores how Stem's Athena platform uses AI to predict energy demand, optimize battery charging and discharging, and provide customers with cost savings and demand response services. It highlights the role of software and intelligent controls in enhancing the value of energy storage, the potential for AI to reduce energy costs and improve efficiency, and the emergence of energy storage as a service (ESaaS) business models.

Illustration: How Stem Inc.'s Athena Platform Works

1. **The Athena Platform:**

Stem Inc.'s Athena platform is an AI-driven energy storage management software that optimizes and monetizes clean energy solutions. It integrates distributed energy resources (DERs), utility, and grid controls to maximize energy asset performance and investments. Athena uses real-time data and predictive analytics to manage energy storage systems effectively (Business Wire, 2023).

2. **Predicting Energy Demand and Optimizing Battery Operations:**

Athena uses AI to predict energy demand by analyzing historical data, weather forecasts, market prices, and utility rates. It optimizes battery charging and discharging to reduce energy costs, avoid peak demand charges, and participate in demand response programs. This intelligent control helps businesses save on energy bills and improve operational efficiency (Bizeray, 2024; Podorozhko, 2025).

3. **Providing Cost Savings and Demand Response Services:**

Athena enables businesses to achieve significant cost savings by optimizing energy usage and participating in demand response programs. By responding to grid signals and market conditions, Athena helps businesses reduce their energy costs and earn revenue through demand response incentives (Murray, 2023).

Discussion: Benefits, Challenges, and Future Potential

1. **Role of Software and Intelligent Controls in Enhancing the Value of Energy Storage:**

Software and intelligent controls like Athena are crucial in maximizing the value of energy storage systems. By using AI to manage energy storage, businesses can optimize their energy usage, reduce costs, and enhance grid reliability. Intelligent controls also enable the integration of renewable energy sources, making energy systems more sustainable (Bizeray, 2024; Whitney, 2023).

2. **Potential for AI to Reduce Energy Costs and Improve Efficiency:**

AI has the potential to significantly reduce energy costs and improve efficiency by optimizing energy storage operations. Predictive analytics and real-time data processing enable precise control of energy resources, leading to cost savings and enhanced performance. AI can also facilitate energy arbitrage, where energy is stored during low-cost periods and used or sold during high-cost periods (Murray, 2023; Podorozhko, 2025).

3. **Emergence of Energy Storage as a Service (ESaaS) Business Models:**

The ESaaS business model is gaining traction, where companies like Stem Inc. offer energy storage solutions as a service. This model allows businesses to benefit from energy storage without the need for significant upfront investment. Instead, they pay for the service based on usage, making it more accessible and financially viable (Bizeray, 2024).

Conclusion

Stem Inc.'s AI-powered energy storage solutions, particularly through the Athena platform, demonstrate the transformative potential of artificial intelligence in optimizing energy storage systems for commercial and industrial customers. By predicting energy demand, optimizing battery operations, and providing cost savings and demand response services, Athena enhances the value of energy storage and supports the integration of renewable energy.

The role of software and intelligent controls is crucial in maximizing the benefits of energy storage, reducing energy costs, and improving efficiency. The emergence of energy storage as a service (ESaaS) business models further expands access to these technologies, making them more financially viable for businesses.

Understanding the methodologies and strategies employed by Stem Inc. can provide valuable insights for other companies and stakeholders seeking to leverage AI and energy storage solutions to achieve sustainability goals and enhance energy management.

3.3 Residential Storage

Home battery storage systems are becoming increasingly popular, especially for homeowners with rooftop solar panels.

Key benefits of residential storage include:

- **Backup Power:** During power outages, home battery systems can provide electricity for essential appliances, lighting, and other devices, enhancing household resilience and safety.
- **Reduce Reliance on the Grid:** Homeowners with solar panels and battery storage can reduce their reliance on the grid, using stored solar energy to power their homes in the evening or during periods of high electricity prices. RMI (2015) discusses the economics of battery energy storage.
- **Enable Greater Solar Adoption:** Battery storage can address the limitations of rooftop solar systems, which only generate electricity during daylight hours, making solar a more viable option for homeowners who want to maximize their use of clean energy. Gudmunds et al. (2020) find

EVs can achieve similar self-consumption as stationary batteries, aided by V2H.

Case Study 3: The Tesla Powerwall: Enabling Home Energy Independence

Focus: Demonstrate the Growing Popularity of Home Battery Systems for Backup Power, Solar Self-Consumption, and Grid Independence

The Tesla Powerwall is a lithium-ion battery system designed for residential use, enabling homeowners to store solar energy generated during the day and use it at night. This case study explores how the Tesla Powerwall allows homeowners to reduce their reliance on the grid, provide backup power during outages, and lower their energy expenses. It highlights the benefits of home battery systems, the role of government incentives and financing options in driving adoption, and the potential for networked home batteries to provide grid services.

Illustration: How the Tesla Powerwall Works

1. **The Tesla Powerwall System:**

The Tesla Powerwall is a rechargeable lithium-ion battery designed for home energy storage. It stores energy generated by solar panels during the day and makes it available for use at night or during power outages. The system can be installed indoors or outdoors and integrates seamlessly with solar PV systems (Tesla, 2025).

2. **Reducing Reliance on the Grid:**

By storing solar energy, the Tesla Powerwall allows homeowners to reduce their reliance on the grid. During the day, excess solar energy that is not immediately used is stored in the Powerwall. This stored energy can then be used during the evening or night, reducing the need to draw electricity from the grid.

3. **Providing Backup Power During Outages:**

The Tesla Powerwall provides backup power during grid outages, ensuring that essential appliances and systems continue to operate. This feature is particularly valuable in areas prone to power outages due to extreme weather events or grid instability.

Discussion: Benefits, Government Incentives, and Grid Services

1. Benefits of Home Battery Systems for Homeowners:

Home battery systems like the Tesla Powerwall offer several benefits for homeowners:

- **Energy Independence:** By storing solar energy, homeowners can reduce their reliance on the grid and increase their energy independence.
- **Cost Savings:** Homeowners can save on electricity bills by using stored solar energy during peak demand periods when electricity rates are higher.
- **Backup Power:** The Powerwall provides reliable backup power during outages, ensuring that essential appliances and systems remain operational.

2. Role of Government Incentives and Financing Options:

Government incentives and financing options play a crucial role in driving the adoption of home battery systems. Incentives such as tax credits, rebates, and grants can reduce the upfront costs of installing battery storage systems, making them more accessible to homeowners. Financing options, such as solar loans and leases, also help spread the cost over time.

3. Potential for Networked Home Batteries to Provide Grid Services:

Networked home batteries, also known as virtual power plants (VPPs), have the potential to provide valuable grid services. By aggregating the stored energy from multiple home batteries, utilities can use this distributed energy resource to balance supply and demand, provide frequency regulation, and support grid stability (Tesla, 2025).

Conclusion

The Tesla Powerwall exemplifies the growing popularity of home battery systems for backup power, solar self-consumption, and grid independence. By storing solar energy generated during the day and using it at night, the Powerwall allows homeowners to reduce their reliance on the grid, provide backup power during outages, and lower their energy expenses.

Home battery systems offer significant benefits for homeowners, including increased energy independence, cost savings, and reliable backup power. Government incentives and financing options play a critical role in making these systems more accessible and financially viable. Additionally, the potential for networked home batteries to provide grid services highlights the broader impact of home energy storage on the stability and efficiency of the electricity grid.

Understanding the methodologies and strategies employed by Tesla Powerwall can provide valuable insights for homeowners, policymakers, and energy providers seeking to enhance energy reliability, reduce costs, and improve sustainability through the adoption of home battery systems and on-site renewable energy solutions.

4 Energy Storage Investment Analysis

4.1 Key Drivers of Energy Storage Investment

Several factors are driving the rapid growth of the energy storage market and attracting increasing investment from a range of players, including utilities, businesses, governments, and venture capitalists.

Renewable Energy Integration

The single most significant driver of energy storage investment is the need to integrate increasing amounts of variable renewable energy sources like solar and wind power into the grid. As the share of renewables in the electricity mix grows, energy storage becomes essential to balance supply and demand, ensure grid stability, and enable a smooth transition to a cleaner energy future.

Grid Stability and Resilience

Energy storage plays a crucial role in enhancing grid stability and resilience, mitigating the risks of blackouts and ensuring the reliable delivery of electricity. Storage systems can respond rapidly to fluctuations in supply or demand, helping to maintain a stable grid frequency and prevent outages. They can also provide backup power during emergencies, enhancing the resilience of critical infrastructure and supporting disaster recovery efforts.

Peak Shaving and Demand Response

Energy storage can contribute to peak shaving—reducing peak demand for electricity—by storing energy during off-peak hours and releasing it during peak periods. This helps to reduce stress on the grid, avoid the need to build new power plants, and lower electricity prices for consumers.

Energy storage can also enable demand response programs, which encourage consumers to shift their electricity usage to times when renewable energy generation is abundant or to reduce their consumption during peak demand periods.

Electric Vehicle Charging Infrastructure

The rapid growth of the electric vehicle (EV) market is creating a surge in demand for charging infrastructure. Energy storage is playing a key role in supporting the expansion of EV charging, particularly fast-charging stations, which can place a significant strain on the grid.

Storage systems can store energy during off-peak hours and release it quickly to power fast chargers, reducing the impact on the grid and making it possible to install more charging stations without requiring costly grid upgrades.

In the renewable energy investment analysis series of column articles, Chen et al. (2024a, 2024b, 2024c, 2024d) have also discussed in details, the analysis steps of BESS investment projects, including C&I and utility-scale BESS projects, which will be explored in the next two sections.

4.2 C&I BESS Investment Analysis

Compared to traditional renewable energy projects such as photovoltaics and wind power, energy storage systems, particularly battery energy storage systems (BESS), have become a hotspot for investment in the renewable energy sector over the past two years. According to a report by McCarthy, investments in BESS exceeded $5 billion in 2022, nearly tripling compared to the previous year. It is expected that by 2030, the global BESS market size will reach between $120 billion and $150 billion, more than double its current size. However, this remains a fragmented market where many suppliers need to understand which submarkets to compete in and how to compete. In this section, we will discuss one of these submarkets—commercial and industrial energy storage; the next section in this chapter will focus on the large-scale energy storage market.

While becoming an investment hotspot, battery storage has also turned into an investment challenge. Unlike the generation side of solar and wind energy, which is dependent on weather conditions, energy storage applications are very diverse and can be installed at various points in the power grid to provide different services. Additionally, the technology is more complex; in addition to storage batteries, it requires inverters (PCS), grid connection services, and software management systems, including battery management systems (BMS). It can even be integrated with other power systems of users into a comprehensive energy management system (EMS).

The revenue models for energy storage systems are also more complicated, including price arbitrage, frequency regulation services, and capacity markets. Therefore, investment analysis for energy storage systems is more challenging than for traditional renewable energy projects. In this section, we will take relatively mature commercial and industrial energy storage systems both domestically and internationally as examples to discuss investment analysis for such projects.

4.2.1 Recent Day-Ahead Market Electricity Pricing Model

Currently, the profit model for commercial and industrial energy storage primarily revolves around electricity price arbitrage: charging when prices are low and discharging when prices are high (for self-use or sale), essentially buying low and selling high. Due to the differences in electricity markets across countries, the strategies for charging and discharging may vary, but the underlying principle remains largely the same. Below, we discuss several representative electricity markets: Australia, Europe, and mainland China.

1. **Australia (Various States)**

Australia's electricity market is divided into three systems: southeastern, western (Western Australia), and northern (Northern Territory). The National Electricity Market (NEM), which covers the southeastern part of Australia and includes a majority of the population (excluding Western Australia and the Northern Territory), has been operational since 1999. After more than 20 years of operation and refinement, it encompasses five major states: Queensland (QLD), New South Wales (NSW), Victoria (VIC), South Australia (SA), and Tasmania (TAS). Western Australia and the Northern Territory are not connected to the NEM, primarily due to their significant distances from the other states.

The NEM employs two pricing methods: Day-Ahead and Spot Market. Pricing is conducted in groups, potentially including more than ten price intervals, and must occur within 288 trading intervals on a trading day (one price every five minutes for 24 hours). Pricing consists of day-ahead pricing schemes and real-time adjustments to generation plans. Day-ahead pricing refers to the pricing proposals submitted before 12:30 PM for the next trading day (from 4:00 AM the next day to 4:00 AM the day after). Each pricing proposal includes two components: the generation plan for the units and the corresponding prices at ten different generation loads. The following chart displays the average day-ahead electricity prices over 24 hours for these five states in 2023 (Fig. 2).

Based on this pricing model, if we assume two charge and discharge cycles per day, with each charging session lasting one hour, the maximum revenue can be calculated as shown in the table below. Queensland has the highest revenue at AUD 354.33 per megawatt-hour, while Tasmania has the lowest at AUD 56.25 per megawatt-hour. Therefore, for investments in commercial and industrial energy storage projects in Australia, Queensland should be prioritized under equivalent conditions (Table 1).

If we assume two charge and discharge cycles per day, with each charging session lasting two hours, this could increase battery utilization efficiency and electricity price arbitrage income (Table 2).

Assuming the scenario in the table, if the first two-hour charging occurs at midnight, followed by discharging during the morning peak; a second

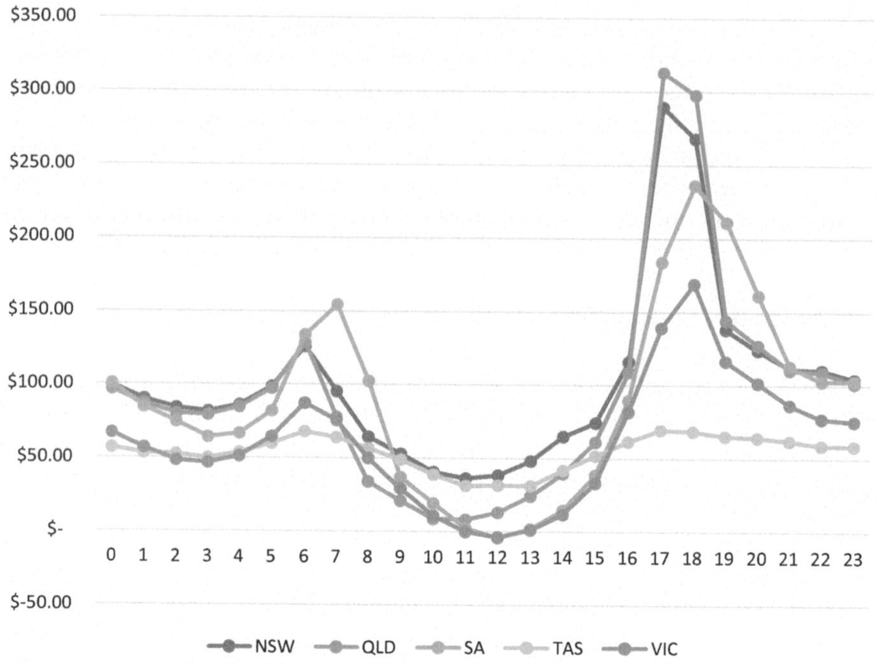

Fig. 2 Australia Regional Hourly Average Power Price in 2023 (*Source* Chen et al. [2024c])

Table 1 Utilization Rate of C&I BESS in Australia under one-hour charging scenarios

	NSW	QLD	SA	TAS	VIC
Max	$289.60	$313.21	$236.50	$69.54	$169.20
Min	$ 36.42	$ 8.12	$ -4.29	$31.33	$ -3.73
Dif	$253.17	$305.10	$240.79	$38.21	$172.93
2nd Min	$ 81.48	$ 79.23	$ 64.06	$49.89	$ 46.60
2nd Max	$126.04	$128.46	$154.41	$67.93	$ 87.13
2nd Diff	$ 44.57	$ 49.23	$ 90.35	$18.04	$ 40.53
Diff1+Diff2	$297.74	$354.33	$331.15	$56.25	$213.46
Utilization	118%	116%	138%	147%	123%

Source Chen et al. (2024c)

charging occurs at noon, followed by discharging during the evening peak, then the revenue per megawatt-hour in Queensland could reach AUD 660.71, nearly doubling the income compared to the scenario with two charge and discharge cycles of one hour each. Considering that the cost of a two-hour

Table 2 Charging strategy for two-hour two-charge cycles

HOUR	NSW	QLD	SA	TAS	VIC
0	$ 99.47	$ 96.47	$100.39	$ 56.88	$ 67.02
1	$ 89.77	$ 86.69	$ 84.51	$ 53.15	$ 56.64
2	$ 83.82	$ 80.03	$ 74.53	$ 52.45	$ 48.21
3	$ 81.48	$ 79.23	$ 64.06	$ 49.89	$ 46.60
4	$ 86.03	$ 84.69	$ 66.64	$ 53.70	$ 51.21
5	$ 98.48	$ 97.27	$ 81.88	$ 59.77	$ 64.49
6	$126.04	$128.46	$133.91	$ 67.93	$ 87.13
7	$ 95.31	$ 77.84	$154.41	$ 63.92	$ 75.65
8	$ 64.44	$ 34.03	$102.18	$ 56.55	$ 49.82
9	$ 52.96	$ 20.68	$ 37.02	$ 48.98	$ 29.19
10	$ 40.75	$ 8.46	$ 19.17	$ 38.97	$ 10.63
11	$ 36.42	$ 8.12	$ 2.32	$ 31.33	$ -0.19
12	$ 38.55	$ 12.92	$ -4.29	$ 31.64	$ -3.73
13	$ 48.32	$ 24.21	$ 1.92	$ 31.43	$ 1.09
14	$ 64.98	$ 39.87	$ 14.54	$ 41.92	$ 11.66
15	$ 74.37	$ 61.15	$ 38.65	$ 51.94	$ 33.39
16	$115.86	$108.97	$ 89.52	$ 61.53	$ 81.81
17	$289.60	$313.21	$183.90	$ 69.54	$139.34
18	$268.10	$297.59	$236.50	$ 68.54	$169.20
19	$138.19	$144.36	$211.04	$ 65.33	$116.55
20	$123.92	$127.37	$161.32	$ 64.52	$101.49
21	$111.24	$110.38	$113.04	$ 62.12	$ 86.68
22	$110.31	$108.96	$102.77	$ 59.10	$ 77.24
23	$104.31	$101.39	$102.89	$ 58.63	$ 75.51

Source Chen et al. (2024c)

battery does not increase proportionally compared to a one-hour battery, and that additional equipment such as inverters is not required, this strategy is evidently more advantageous (Table 3).

2. **Eight Countries in Europe**

We have also compiled the average hourly day-ahead market prices for 2023 in eight Western and Southern European countries, including Belgium, France, Germany, Italy, the United Kingdom, the Netherlands, Portugal, and Spain, as illustrated in the chart below (Fig. 3).

Similarly, we can adopt the strategy of two charge and discharge cycles, with each charging session lasting two hours. A comparison reveals that the Netherlands offers the highest revenue at €241.78 per megawatt-hour; the five Western European countries and Italy show similar revenues, ranging from €200 to €240; while Portugal has the lowest at €152.84 per megawatt-hour, and Spain follows closely at €161.58. Thus, under comparable conditions, investing in commercial and industrial energy storage projects in Western Europe and Italy will yield higher returns (Table 4 and 5).

Table 3 Revenue of C&I BESS in Australia under two-hour two-charge cycles

	NSW	QLD	SA	TAS	VIC
Max	$289.60	$313.21	$236.50	$ 69.54	$169.20
Min	$ 36.42	$ 8.12	$ -4.29	$ 31.33	$ -3.73
Dif1	$253.17	$305.10	$240.79	$ 38.21	$172.93
Max2	$268.10	$297.59	$211.04	$ 68.54	$169.20
Min2	$ 38.55	$ 8.46	$ 1.92	$ 31.64	$ -0.19
Diff2	$229.55	$289.14	$209.12	$ 36.90	$169.39
2nd Max	$126.04	$128.46	$154.41	$ 67.93	$ 87.13
2nd Min	$ 81.48	$ 79.23	$ 64.06	$ 49.89	$ 46.60
Diff3	$ 44.57	$ 49.23	$ 90.35	$ 18.04	$ 40.53
2nd Max2	$ 98.48	$ 97.27	$133.91	$ 63.92	$ 75.65
2nd Min2	$ 83.82	$ 80.03	$ 66.64	$ 52.45	$ 48.21
Diff4	$ 14.65	$ 17.25	$ 67.27	$ 11.47	$ 27.44
Diff1+2+3+4	$541.94	$660.71	$607.53	$104.62	$410.29
Diff1+2	$482.72	$594.23	$449.91	$ 75.11	$342.32
Diff1+3	$297.74	$354.33	$331.15	$ 56.25	$213.46

Source Chen et al. (2024c)

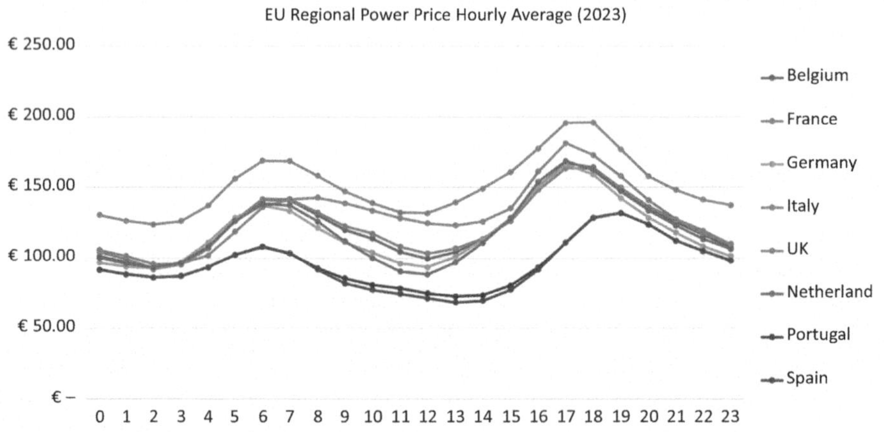

Fig. 3 The United Kingdom and selected EU countries hourly average power price in 2023 (*Source* Chen et al. [2024c])

Table 4 Charging strategy for two-hour two-charge cycles in the United Kingdom and selected EU countries

HOUR	Belgium	France	Germany	Italy	UK	Netherland	Portugal	Spain
0	€ 101.43	€ 104.36	€ 96.56	€ 130.54	€ 105.83	€ 100.02	€ 91.54	€ 91.49
1	€ 96.67	€ 98.88	€ 93.69	€ 126.29	€ 101.32	€ 95.88	€ 88.30	€ 88.30
2	€ 91.97	€ 92.38	€ 92.44	€ 123.72	€ 95.52	€ 92.98	€ 85.97	€ 85.97
3	€ 95.20	€ 95.34	€ 96.68	€ 126.11	€ 95.59	€ 96.38	€ 86.93	€ 86.90
4	€ 106.96	€ 107.07	€ 111.03	€ 137.15	€ 101.98	€ 108.10	€ 93.45	€ 93.41
5	€ 126.35	€ 126.64	€ 128.49	€ 156.21	€ 118.62	€ 126.09	€ 102.32	€ 102.34
6	€ 140.92	€ 141.65	€ 137.15	€ 168.88	€ 136.10	€ 138.33	€ 107.90	€ 108.08
7	€ 140.55	€ 141.46	€ 133.24	€ 168.52	€ 141.51	€ 137.12	€ 103.15	€ 103.43
8	€ 130.29	€ 132.10	€ 121.23	€ 158.12	€ 142.65	€ 125.84	€ 92.71	€ 91.67
9	€ 120.04	€ 122.56	€ 111.34	€ 147.32	€ 138.85	€ 112.11	€ 85.39	€ 81.95
10	€ 113.81	€ 117.30	€ 103.94	€ 139.01	€ 133.70	€ 100.08	€ 80.93	€ 77.32
11	€ 104.35	€ 108.05	€ 96.00	€ 132.18	€ 128.16	€ 90.34	€ 78.23	€ 74.38
12	€ 99.41	€ 103.16	€ 93.45	€ 131.72	€ 124.60	€ 88.26	€ 74.81	€ 71.22
13	€ 104.09	€ 106.89	€ 100.99	€ 139.31	€ 123.19	€ 96.97	€ 72.78	€ 68.50
14	€ 112.87	€ 113.76	€ 112.58	€ 149.14	€ 125.86	€ 110.69	€ 73.53	€ 69.55
15	€ 127.31	€ 126.19	€ 128.56	€ 160.98	€ 135.30	€ 128.20	€ 80.41	€ 77.44
16	€ 150.62	€ 148.23	€ 150.78	€ 177.59	€ 161.10	€ 153.85	€ 93.46	€ 91.77
17	€ 167.15	€ 163.46	€ 166.08	€ 195.68	€ 181.18	€ 168.65	€ 110.97	€ 111.21
18	€ 163.97	€ 163.21	€ 159.13	€ 195.94	€ 172.75	€ 162.24	€ 128.33	€ 128.36
19	€ 149.03	€ 149.76	€ 142.16	€ 176.86	€ 157.81	€ 147.12	€ 131.70	€ 131.70
20	€ 134.59	€ 136.27	€ 128.53	€ 157.78	€ 140.76	€ 133.59	€ 123.70	€ 123.70
21	€ 125.16	€ 127.30	€ 117.95	€ 148.20	€ 127.36	€ 122.89	€ 112.24	€ 112.22
22	€ 116.44	€ 119.19	€ 108.12	€ 141.19	€ 117.19	€ 113.26	€ 104.87	€ 104.88
23	€ 107.51	€ 109.88	€ 101.42	€ 137.38	€ 109.82	€ 106.39	€ 98.16	€ 98.09

Source Chen et al. (2024c)

Table 5 Revenue of C&I BESS in the United Kingdom and selected EU countries under two-hour two-charge cycles

	Belgium	France	Germany	Italy	UK	Netherland	Portugal	Spain
Max	€ 167.15	€ 163.46	€ 166.08	€ 195.94	€ 181.18	€ 168.65	€ 131.70	€ 131.70
Min	€ 99.41	€ 103.16	€ 93.45	€ 131.72	€ 123.19	€ 88.26	€ 72.78	€ 68.50
Diff1	€ 67.74	€ 60.30	€ 72.63	€ 64.21	€ 57.99	€ 80.40	€ 58.92	€ 63.20
Max2	€ 163.97	€ 163.21	€ 159.13	€ 195.68	€ 172.75	€ 162.24	€ 128.33	€ 128.36
Min2	€ 104.09	€ 106.89	€ 96.00	€ 132.18	€ 124.60	€ 90.34	€ 73.53	€ 69.55
Diff2	$ 59.88	$ 56.32	$ 63.13	$ 63.49	$ 48.14	$ 71.89	$ 54.80	$ 58.81
2nd Max	€ 140.92	€ 141.65	€ 137.15	€ 168.88	€ 142.65	€ 138.33	€ 107.90	€ 108.08
2nd Min	€ 91.97	€ 92.38	€ 92.44	€ 123.72	€ 95.52	€ 92.98	€ 85.97	€ 85.97
Diff3	€ 48.95	€ 49.27	€ 44.71	€ 45.16	€ 47.13	€ 45.35	€ 21.94	€ 22.11
2nd Max2	€ 140.55	€ 141.46	€ 133.24	€ 168.52	€ 141.51	€ 137.12	€ 103.15	€ 103.43
2nd Min2	€ 95.20	€ 95.34	€ 93.69	€ 123.72	€ 95.52	€ 92.98	€ 85.97	€ 85.97
Diff4	€ 45.35	€ 46.12	€ 39.54	€ 44.80	€ 46.00	€ 44.14	€ 17.19	€ 17.46
Diff1+2+3+4	€ 221.92	€ 212.01	€ 220.01	€ 217.66	€ 199.26	€ 241.78	€ 152.84	€ 161.58
Diff1+2	€ 127.62	€ 116.62	€ 135.76	€ 127.70	€ 106.13	€ 152.29	€ 113.72	€ 122.01
Diff1+3	€ 116.68	€ 109.57	€ 117.34	€ 109.37	€ 105.12	€ 125.75	€ 80.86	€ 85.30
Utilization	174%	182%	162%	170%	188%	159%	134%	132%

Source Chen et al. (2024c)

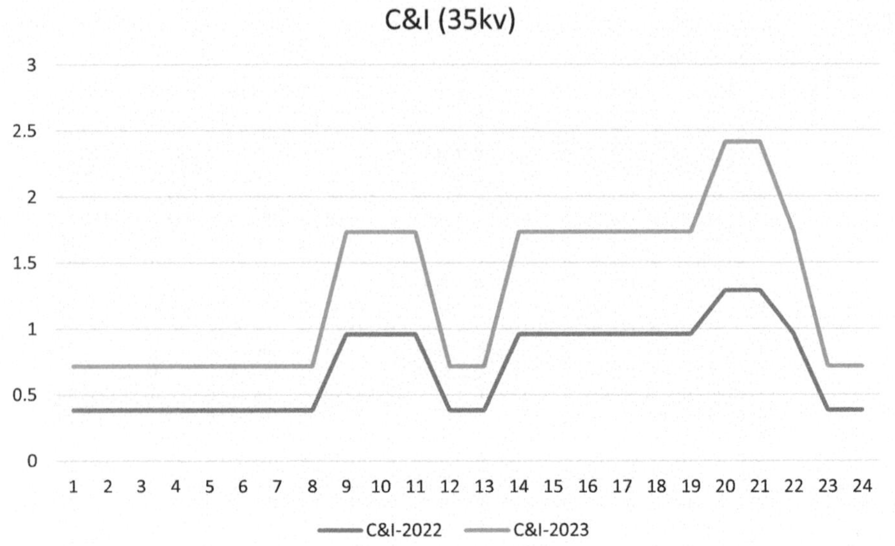

Fig. 4 Zhejiang, China C&I (35kv) hourly power price in 2022 vs. 2023 (*Source* Chen et al. [2024c])

3. **Mainland China (Selected Provinces)**

Mainland China employs time-of-use pricing for commercial and industrial sectors, differentiated by voltage and time periods. The following chart displays the commercial and industrial electricity prices for 220 kV and 35 kV in Zhejiang Province and Shandong Province for December 2022 and December 2023. The curves are very similar to the day-ahead market electricity price curves of the aforementioned countries in Australia and Europe, allowing for the assessment of the profitability of commercial and industrial energy storage facilities (Figs. 4 and 5).

4.2.2 *Investment Analysis of C&I BESS—A Case Study of the Financing Lease Market*

The leasing model for commercial and industrial energy storage has emerged in recent years as an innovative financial and operational approach that allows companies to install and utilize energy storage systems without substantial capital investment. The following are the main characteristics of this model:

1. **Overview of the Model**

- No large upfront investment required: Companies do not need to pay expensive initial purchase costs to install energy storage systems. Instead, they can use these systems through leasing agreements with fixed monthly rental fees.

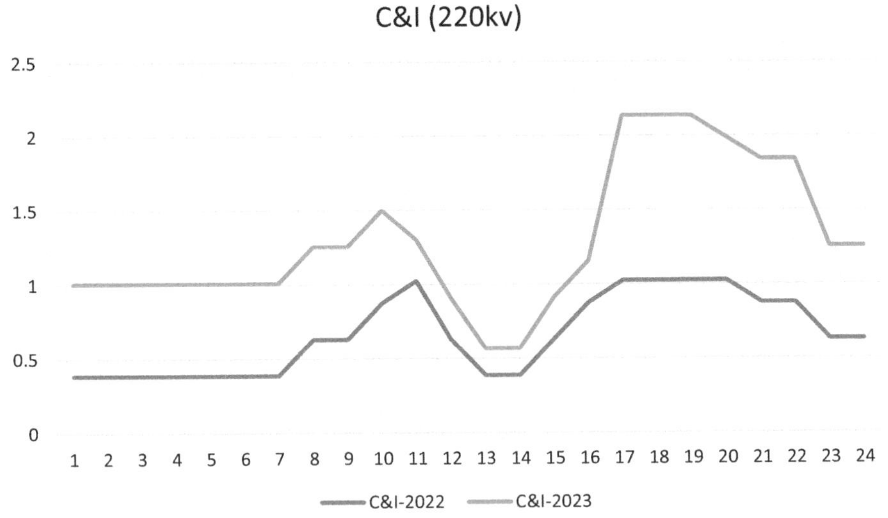

Fig. 5 Shandong, China C&I (220kv) hourly power price in 2022 vs. 2023 (*Source* Chen et al. [2024c])

- Flexible contract terms: Leasing contracts typically have flexible durations set according to the company's needs and financial situation.

2. **Cost Benefits**
   - Operational cost savings: Energy storage systems reduce operational costs for companies by optimizing energy use and participating in electricity market activities (such as demand response and price arbitrage).
   - Predictable financial planning: The leasing model provides a stable payment structure, making it easier for companies to engage in long-term financial planning and budget management.

3. **Equipment Maintenance and Upgrades**
   - Maintenance services: Leasing agreements typically include maintenance and repair services, alleviating the maintenance burden on companies.
   - Technology upgrades: As technology advances, the leasing model enables companies to upgrade to more advanced energy storage systems without worrying about the depreciation and obsolescence of existing equipment.

4. **Risk Management**

    - Reduced technology risk: The leasing model lowers the technical and performance risks that companies face when purchasing and installing energy storage systems.
    - Adaptability to market changes: The flexibility of leasing agreements allows companies to adapt more quickly to changes in the energy market and policies.

5. **Compliance and Incentives**

    - Policy compliance: The leasing model helps companies comply with local energy efficiency and renewable energy regulations.
    - Utilizing government incentives: Companies can take advantage of government tax breaks and energy subsidies, which sometimes also apply to leased energy storage equipment.

6. **Innovation in Business Models**

    - Service-oriented model: This model is similar to the concept of Energy-as-a-Service, providing a way to transform energy infrastructure into a service.

The leasing model for commercial and industrial energy storage offers companies a cost-effective and low-risk way to deploy and utilize energy storage technology. It not only alleviates the financial and operational burdens on companies but also allows them to flexibly adapt to technological advancements and market changes, making it an effective way to promote the widespread adoption of sustainable energy solutions. As energy storage technology develops and costs continue to decrease, this model has the potential to be applied more broadly in the commercial and industrial markets (Fig. 6).

Participants in C&I BESS leasing and their objectives

Equipment Seller: Equipment Sales Profit

In the leasing model, equipment manufacturers face multiple decision variables that directly impact the feasibility and profitability of their business model. The following is a detailed explanation of these key decision variables:

1. **Equipment Costs**

    - Procurement or manufacturing costs: The direct costs of the equipment, including raw materials, manufacturing, transportation, and installation costs.

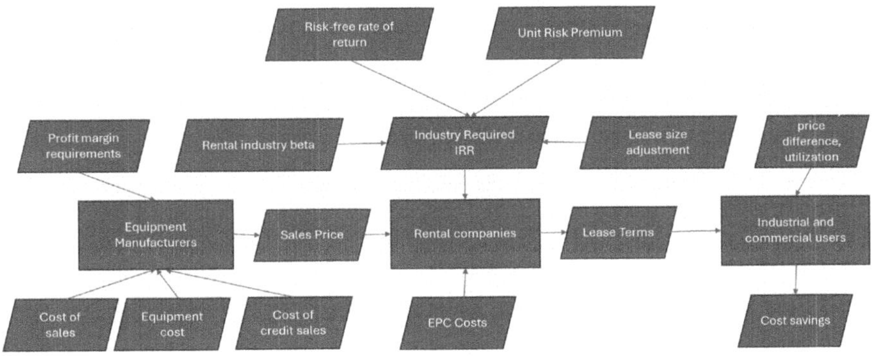

Fig. 6 Participants in C&I BESS leasing and their objectives (*Source* Chen et al. [2024c])

- R&D costs: The costs associated with developing new technologies or improving existing technologies.
- Decision considerations: Cost control is crucial for maintaining competitiveness and achieving profitability. Equipment manufacturers need to evaluate how to reduce costs through economies of scale, technological innovation, or supply chain management.

2. **Sales Costs**

- Marketing expenses: The costs associated with sales and marketing activities.
- Customer acquisition costs: The expenses required to attract and acquire new customers.
- Decision considerations: Manufacturers must weigh the costs of promotional activities against potential benefits to ensure the cost-effectiveness of their marketing strategies.

3. **Sales Prices**

- Pricing strategy: Setting leasing prices to cover costs and achieve profits while remaining competitive in the market.
- Price elasticity: Considering the market's sensitivity to price changes.
- Decision considerations: Manufacturers need to analyze market demand, competitor pricing, and their own cost structure to establish reasonable sales prices.

4. **Sales Payment Terms**

- Payment terms: Determining the schedule and method for customers to pay rent.
- Credit policy: Establishing customer credit evaluation and control policies.

- Decision considerations: Appropriate payment terms can attract customers, but excessively long terms may affect cash flow and financial health.

5. **Financing Costs of Accounts Receivable**
    - Financing costs: The cost of funds required to provide credit sales services.
    - Risk assessment: Considering the credit risks and default risks associated with credit sales.
    - Decision considerations: Manufacturers need to assess the feasibility and costs of providing credit sales, ensuring risk control and funding efficiency.
6. **Gross and Net Profit Margins**
    - Gross profit margin: The proportion of the difference between sales revenue and sales costs.
    - Net profit margin: The proportion of profit after deducting all operating expenses, financing costs, and taxes from sales revenue.
    - Decision considerations: Profit margins are key indicators of business success. Manufacturers need to optimize profit margins through effective cost control and pricing strategies.

Equipment manufacturers need to consider these decision variables comprehensively when implementing the leasing model to ensure the sustainability and profitability of their business. These decisions involve detailed considerations of cost control, market positioning, risk management, and financial planning, which are crucial for ensuring long-term success.

Financing Lease Company: Capital Returns

Financing lease companies need to consider multiple key variables when making business decisions, as these variables directly affect the company's profitability and market competitiveness. The following is a detailed explanation of these decision variables:

1. **Equipment Costs**
    - Purchase price: The acquisition cost of the equipment is one of the main expenses for financing lease companies. Companies must carefully evaluate the purchase price to ensure cost-effectiveness.
    - Equipment lifespan and maintenance: Considering the durability of the equipment and maintenance costs. Equipment with a long lifespan and low maintenance costs can reduce long-term operating expenses.

2. **EPC Costs**

    - Engineering and construction costs: EPC (Engineering, Procurement, Construction) costs include all expenses required to install leased equipment. This typically applies to large equipment or complex projects.
    - Project management and execution: The efficiency of managing and executing EPC projects directly affects project costs and timelines.

3. **Leasing Terms**

    - Lease duration: Determining the duration of the leasing contract, which affects rental pricing and the equipment's residual value.
    - Rental fees: Rental pricing needs to consider market competitiveness, equipment costs, and expected returns.
    - Residual value and buyback: Residual value assessment is crucial for the final handling of the equipment. Some contracts may include buyback options, allowing customers to purchase the equipment after the lease term expires.

4. **Cost of Capital**

    - Borrowing rates: Financing lease companies typically need to borrow funds to purchase equipment, so borrowing rates directly affect capital costs.
    - Fundraising: In addition to traditional loans, companies may also raise funds through issuing bonds, equity financing, or other financial instruments.

5. **Leasing Industry IRR (Internal Rate of Return)**

    - Market return rates: IRR is a key indicator for evaluating investment effectiveness. Financing lease companies need to assess the IRR of different market segments to determine the most profitable markets or types of equipment.
    - Market and economic trends: Market demand, economic conditions, and industry trends all impact IRR. Companies need to continuously monitor and analyze these factors.

The decision-making of financing lease companies involves a comprehensive consideration of multiple variables, from equipment procurement to capital management, market positioning, and return rate evaluation. To ensure business success and sustainability, companies need to conduct detailed market analysis, financial planning, and risk management. By optimizing these decision variables, financing lease companies can enhance their position and profitability in a highly competitive market.

Commercial and Industrial Energy Storage Users: Cost Savings

Commercial and industrial users must consider multiple key factors when deciding whether to adopt energy storage systems to ensure the economic viability and efficiency of their investment. The following is a detailed discussion of these key decision variables:

1. **Electricity Price Difference Between Peak and Off-Peak**
   - Cost-saving potential: The price difference between peak and off-peak electricity in the market is a key factor in determining the economic viability of energy storage systems. Commercial and industrial users can charge during off-peak hours when electricity prices are low and use or sell electricity during peak hours to save costs.
   - Market analysis: Users need to analyze the electricity market structure and pricing mechanisms in their region, predicting trends in electricity price fluctuations.
2. **Charging and Discharging Cycles**
   - System design: Choosing the appropriate energy storage system requires considering the required charging and discharging cycles. Different types of storage technologies (such as lithium batteries and flow batteries) are suitable for different charging and discharging needs.
   - Economic assessment: The frequency and duration of charging and discharging will affect the system's efficiency and lifespan, thereby impacting overall economic viability.
3. **Equipment Leasing Costs**
   - Direct costs: Equipment leasing costs include rental fees, maintenance, and potential upgrade costs.
   - Cost comparison: Commercial and industrial users need to compare the long-term costs of purchasing versus leasing equipment, considering cash flow and financial flexibility.
4. **Equipment Utilization Efficiency**
   - Performance parameters: Considering performance parameters such as energy density, charging and discharging efficiency, and lifespan to ensure efficient operation.
   - Operational strategy: The way the equipment is used (such as the timing and frequency of charging and discharging) will directly

affect its efficiency and lifespan, requiring careful planning to maximize investment returns.

When deciding to invest in energy storage systems, commercial and industrial users need to comprehensively consider price fluctuations in the electricity market, the charging and discharging characteristics of the equipment, leasing costs, and overall equipment utilization efficiency. Through careful analysis and assessment of these variables, users can ensure that the chosen energy storage solution is both economical and efficient, aligning with their energy needs and financial goals. In the ever-changing energy market, this comprehensive decision-making approach is crucial for maintaining competitiveness and achieving long-term energy-saving objectives.

4.2.3 Return Calculation for C&I BESS Financing Leasing

Based on the above analysis, we have designed a simple calculation model for commercial and industrial energy storage leasing returns, which can be calculated based on the following three-party assumptions:

- Asset side: Cost of energy storage equipment (including batteries, inverters, etc.), EPC costs, battery capacity, subsidy amount;
- Leasing side: Leasing duration, required leasing IRR, residual value estimate;
- User side: Daily arbitrage income, operational costs, operational efficiency;

Additionally, inflation assumptions during the lease term need to be estimated (Fig. 7).

The calculation can estimate the following cash flow forecast outputs:

- Residual value and its present value
- Operating income
- Lease payments (financial costs)
- Operating costs
- Net cash flow

Based on these outputs, the project's net cash flow and net present value can be calculated, allowing for the approval of leasing results. In the following three examples, we can see that in Belgium, with a subsidy of 50% and a required return rate of 12%, the project is feasible (Fig. 8, Tables 6, 7, 8).

For Spain, however, the subsidy needs to be increased to 70% to meet the requirement of a 12% return rate.

In the calculations for Zhejiang Province, it was found that with a subsidy of 10%, the requirement for a 13% return rate can be met.

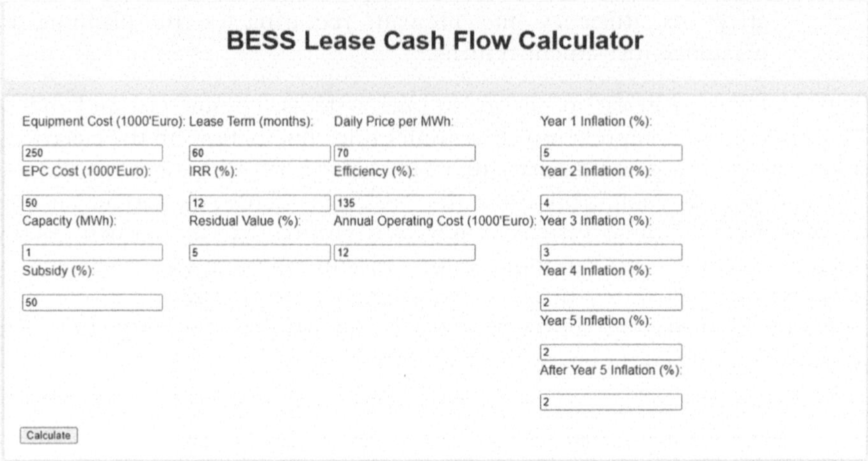

Fig. 7 A simple BESS lease cash flow model (*Source* Chen et al. [2024c])

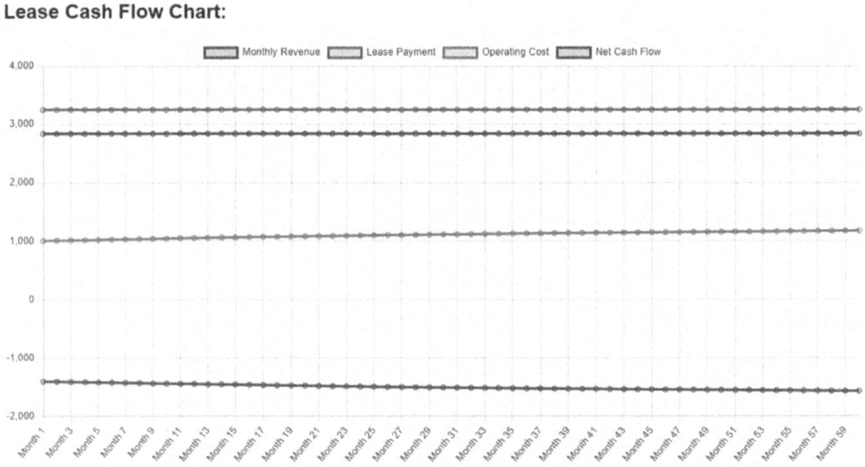

Fig. 8 BESS lease cash flow output (*Source* Chen et al. [2024c])

Table 6 Return analysis for Belgium C&I BESS under various scenarios

Scenario Description: Belgium										
Scenario#	Equipment Cost	EPC Cost	Subsidy	Final Cost	Residual Value	IRR	Efficiency	Daily Rent	Daily Saving	Feasible?
Unit	1000'EUR	1000'EUR		1000'EUR				EUR	EUR	
1	€ 463.76	€ 92.75	0%	€ 556.52	0%	13%	100%	€ 422.08	€ 221.92	FALSE
2	€ 463.76	€ 92.75	10%	€ 500.87	0%	13%	100%	€ 379.87	€ 221.92	FALSE
3	€ 463.76	€ 92.75	20%	€ 445.21	0%	13%	100%	€ 337.67	€ 221.92	FALSE
4	€ 463.76	€ 92.75	30%	€ 389.56	0%	13%	100%	€ 295.46	€ 221.92	FALSE
5	€ 463.76	€ 92.75	40%	€ 333.91	0%	12%	100%	€ 247.59	€ 221.92	FALSE
6	€ 463.76	€ 92.75	50%	€ 278.26	0%	12%	100%	€ 206.32	€ 221.92	TRUE
7	€ 463.76	€ 92.75	60%	€ 222.61	0%	12%	100%	€ 165.06	€ 221.92	TRUE
8	€ 463.76	€ 92.75	70%	€ 166.96	0%	12%	100%	€ 123.79	€ 221.92	TRUE
9	€ 463.76	€ 92.75	80%	€ 111.30	0%	12%	100%	€ 82.53	€ 221.92	TRUE

Source Chen et al. (2024c)

Table 7 Return analysis for Spain C&I BESS under various scenarios

Scenario Description: Spain											
Scenario#	Equipment Cost	EPC Cost	Subsidy	Final Cost	Residual Value	IRR	Efficiency	Daily Rent	Daily Saving	Feasible?
Unit	1000'EUR	1000'EUR		1000'EUR				EUR	EUR	
1	€ 463.76	€ 92.75	0%	€ 556.52	0%	13%	100%	€ 422.08	€ 161.58	FALSE
2	€ 463.76	€ 92.75	10%	€ 500.87	0%	13%	100%	€ 379.87	€ 161.58	FALSE
3	€ 463.76	€ 92.75	20%	€ 445.21	0%	13%	100%	€ 337.67	€ 161.58	FALSE
4	€ 463.76	€ 92.75	30%	€ 389.56	0%	13%	100%	€ 295.46	€ 161.58	FALSE
5	€ 463.76	€ 92.75	40%	€ 333.91	0%	12%	100%	€ 247.59	€ 161.58	FALSE
6	€ 463.76	€ 92.75	50%	€ 278.26	0%	12%	100%	€ 206.32	€ 161.58	FALSE
7	€ 463.76	€ 92.75	60%	€ 222.61	0%	12%	100%	€ 165.06	€ 161.58	FALSE
8	€ 463.76	€ 92.75	70%	€ 166.96	0%	12%	100%	€ 123.79	€ 161.58	TRUE
9	€ 463.76	€ 92.75	80%	€ 111.30	0%	12%	100%	€ 82.53	€ 161.58	TRUE

Source Chen et al. (2024c)

Table 8 Return analysis for Zhejiang, China C&I BESS under various scenarios

Scenario Description: Zhejiang										
Scenario#	Equipment Cost	EPC Cost	Subsidy	Final Cost	Residual Value	IRR	Efficiency	Daily Rent	Daily Saving	Feasible?
Unit	1000'EUR	1000'EUR		1000'EUR				EUR	EUR	
1	€ 463.76	€ 92.75	0%	€ 556.52	0%	13%	100%	€ 422.08	€ 402.18	FALSE
2	€ 463.76	€ 92.75	10%	€ 500.87	0%	13%	100%	€ 379.87	€ 402.18	TRUE
3	€ 463.76	€ 92.75	20%	€ 445.21	0%	13%	100%	€ 337.67	€ 402.18	TRUE
4	€ 463.76	€ 92.75	30%	€ 389.56	0%	13%	100%	€ 295.46	€ 402.18	TRUE
5	€ 463.76	€ 92.75	40%	€ 333.91	0%	12%	100%	€ 247.59	€ 402.18	TRUE
6	€ 463.76	€ 92.75	50%	€ 278.26	0%	12%	100%	€ 206.32	€ 402.18	TRUE
7	€ 463.76	€ 92.75	60%	€ 222.61	0%	12%	100%	€ 165.06	€ 402.18	TRUE
8	€ 463.76	€ 92.75	70%	€ 166.96	0%	12%	100%	€ 123.79	€ 402.18	TRUE
9	€ 463.76	€ 92.75	80%	€ 111.30	0%	12%	100%	€ 82.53	€ 402.18	TRUE

Source Chen et al. (2024c)

Additionally, considering that the cost of domestic energy storage systems is generally lower than in Europe, the return rate for commercial and industrial energy storage in Zhejiang Province may be higher than the above calculation results.

In summary, we briefly introduced the investment logic and return calculations for commercial and industrial energy storage projects. In the next section, we will discuss the more complex investment analysis of large-scale energy storage systems.

4.3 *Utility-Scale BESS Investment Analysis*

In this section, we will primarily discuss the investment analysis of Front-of-the-Meter (FTM) energy storage systems, commonly referred to as large-scale energy storage systems, or simply large storage.

4.3.1 Features of Utility-Scale BESS

Front-of-the-Meter (FTM) energy storage systems are those installed in front of the electricity meter of power users, meaning they are located on the generation side, transmission side, or distribution side of the power system. These systems are typically owned and operated by utility companies, independent system operators, or specialized energy storage service companies, serving the entire grid rather than individual end users. The characteristics of FTM energy storage systems include:

Large Storage Capacity.

- Large scale: FTM energy storage systems usually have significant capacity, capable of providing tens to hundreds of megawatt-hours (MWh) of electricity storage to meet the large-scale demands of the grid.
- High power: These systems are designed to deliver high power output, supporting grid stability and load management.

Business Model

Corresponding to the large capacity of FTM (Front-of-the-Meter) energy storage systems, their business model is also more complex:

- Diversified Revenue Sources: FTM energy storage systems can generate revenue through various means, including frequency regulation, electricity market arbitrage, providing backup capacity, demand response services, and deferring grid upgrades.
- Participation in Electricity Markets: FTM energy storage systems can directly participate in wholesale electricity markets, profiting by buying and selling electricity and providing grid services.
- Partnerships: Operators may establish partnerships with utilities, grid operators, or third-party energy service companies to jointly develop and manage FTM energy storage projects.

With a more complex business model comes a more intricate revenue structure. Taking Australia's large-scale storage market as an example, its revenue sources differ significantly from those of commercial and industrial storage, with most revenue coming from frequency control ancillary services (FCAS) and energy arbitrage—charging batteries when prices are low and discharging during high-price periods. Historically, although the market is considered relatively small, the former has provided the larger share of profits for grid-scale BESS before Q4 2023. (Fig. 9).

FCAS is used to maintain the frequency of the electrical system close to 50 cycles per second at any given moment. There are eight independent FCAS delivery markets in the National Electricity Market of Australia, with response times ranging from 6 seconds to 5 minutes and frequency deviation levels varying from 50 Hz. Before 2021, 80% of the total revenue in Australia's large battery market came solely from FCAS services. This proportion dropped to 49% in the first two quarters of 2023. From Q2 2022 onwards, we see a steady increase in the proportion of revenue derived from FCAS. This suggests that batteries are increasingly being utilized to provide essential grid stability services, such as regulating frequency and voltage.

Balanced portfolio by late 2024: By Q3 2024, the revenue split is more balanced, with FCAS contributing around 40–60% depending on the quarter. This demonstrates a more diversified revenue model for battery operators.

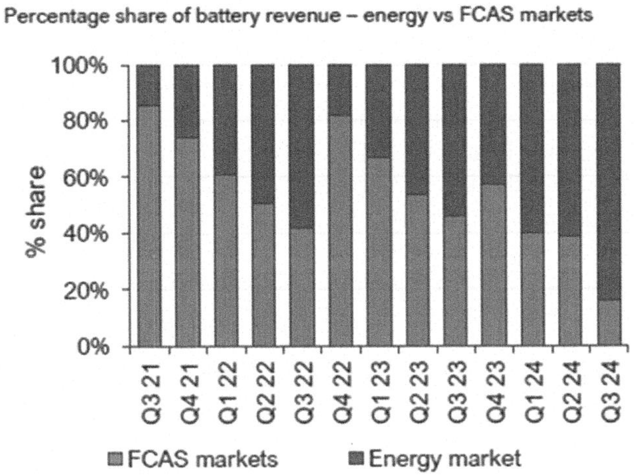

Fig. 9 BESS revenue share: energy arbitrage vs. FCAS (*Source* AEMO [2024])

In contrast, the revenue model of the United Kingdom's large-scale storage market is more complex. For instance, the 2022 revenue of the large-scale storage investment fund GRID primarily came from four categories:

- Capacity Market (CM)
- Firm Frequency Response (FFR)
- Dynamic Frequency Response (DFR)
- Energy Trading (Fig. 10)

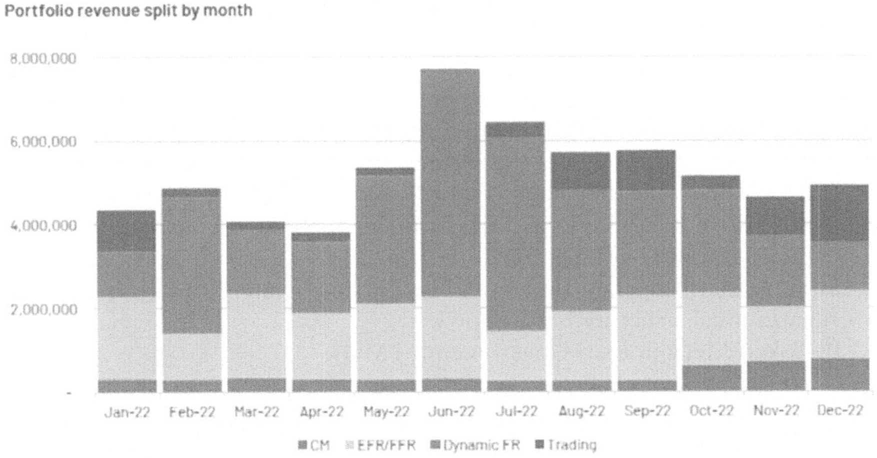

Fig. 10 UK BESS fund GRID revenue breakdown in 2022 (*Source* GRID [2023])

In 2023, GRID's revenue became more diversified, including EFR/FFR, DC/DM/DR dynamic services, energy trading, and capacity market.

For the six months ending June 30, 2023, GRID's asset revenue was £20.5 million, a 31.9% decrease from the first half of 2022 (£30.1 million). Revenue from Firm Frequency Response (FFR) dropped from £7.7 million in the first half of 2022 to £4 million in the first half of 2023, as the National Grid ESO began phasing out this service in favor of dynamic services.

As more batteries come online in the United Kingdom, revenue from Dynamic Containment (DC) fell from £15.9 million in the first half of 2022 to £6 million in the first half of 2023, suppressing prices in the ancillary services market. In contrast, revenues from the smaller services of Dynamic Moderation (DM) and Dynamic Regulation (DR), launched in March, 2022, increased as the services matured and procurement expanded.

As the portfolio strategy shifted from ancillary services, trading revenue rose from £1.8 million to £4.6 million. Low price volatility and low utilization in the BM (Balancing Mechanism) reduced trading opportunities in the first half of 2023, resulting in trading revenue falling short of expectations.

Capacity market revenue increased from £1.8 million to £4.6 million. With new capacity market contracts coming online, capacity market revenue is expected to continue increasing, which is confirmed in GRID (2024a,2024b) (Fig. 11).

Compared to GRID, another large-scale storage investment fund in the United Kingdom, GSF has a more international market. In 2022, GSF's revenue primarily came from the United Kingdom (55.48%) and Ireland (41.35%), with a small portion from Germany (2.14%) and the United States (1.03%). In the United Kingdom, revenue was concentrated in FFR and DC, accounting for nearly 90% of the UK portion. In contrast, GRID's revenue came entirely from the United Kingdom, with the top 10 assets contributing over 50% of total revenue, of which FFR and DC accounted for 76% (Fig. 12).

Perhaps considering GSF's international operational characteristics, the Tokyo Metropolitan Government recently selected GSF and Itochu Corporation to launch Japan's first energy storage fund. This fund will finance the deployment of energy storage systems across Japan, helping to stabilize the grid and promote the integration of renewable energy. This initiative is expected to drive Japan's energy transition and facilitate the broader adoption of storage solutions (Itochu, 2023).

The project will operate under a PPP (Public–Private Partnership) model. Its organizational structure is as follows:

LP: Tokyo Metropolitan Government (TMG).

- Aims to establish a financing model for grid batteries, aiding the introduction and expansion of renewable energy.

GP: "Local Company" + "New Energy Fund".

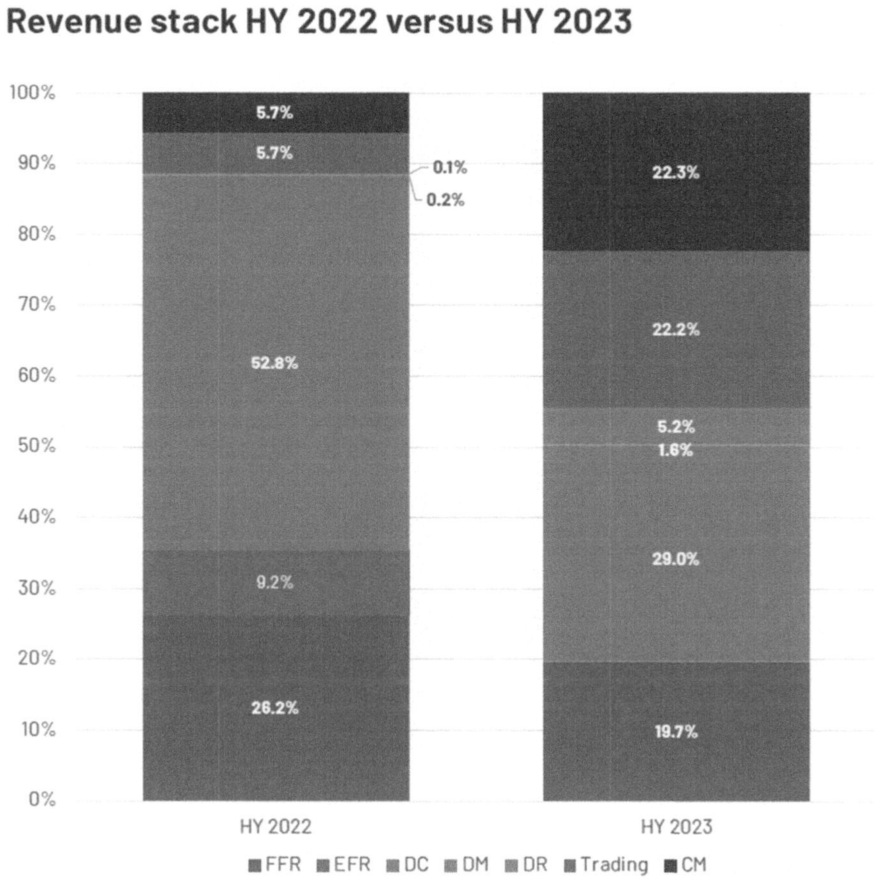

Fig. 11 UK BESS fund GRID revenue stack HY 2022 vs. HY 2023 (*Source* GRID [2023])

- Itochu Corporation: Provides its expertise and network in the Japanese market to drive the fund's success.
- Gore Street Capital (GSF): Has extensive experience in renewable energy and storage investments (Fig. 13).

Operational Characteristics

Large-scale energy storage projects have unique operational characteristics that make them indispensable components of the power system. They not only provide scheduling flexibility but also significantly enhance the resilience of the grid. The following discusses these operational characteristics in detail:

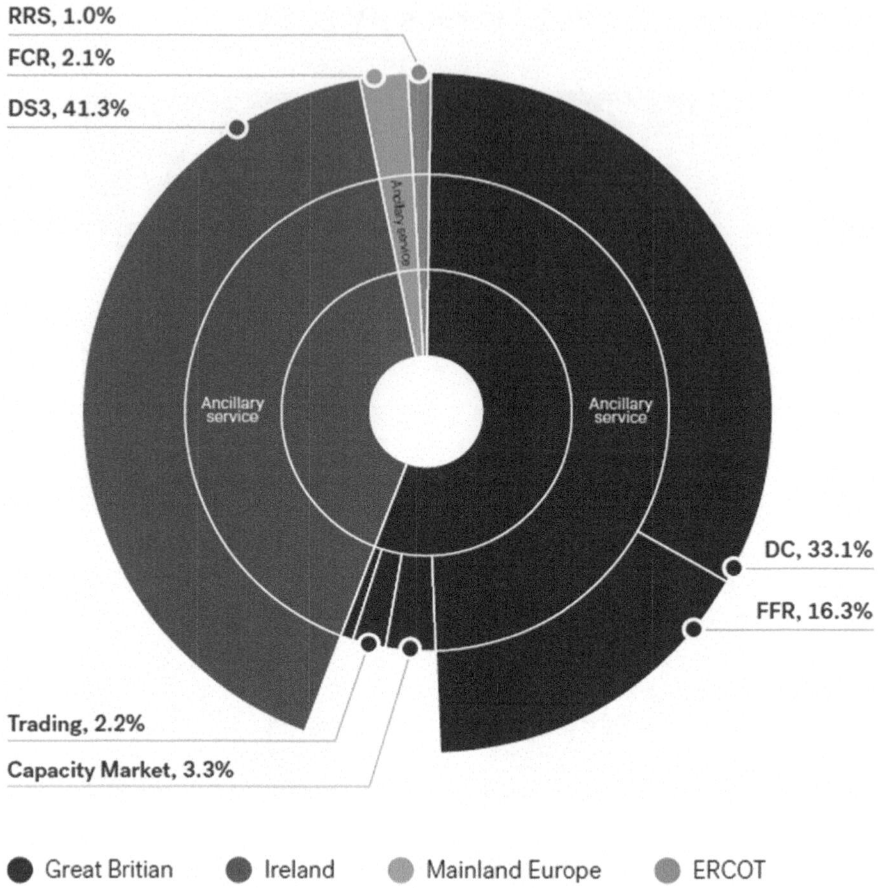

Fig. 12 UK BESS fund GSF revenue breakdown in 2022 Annual Report (*Source* GSF [2022])

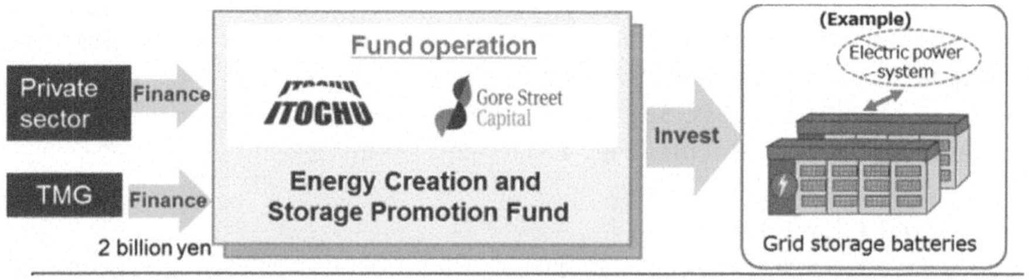

Fig. 13 Scheme of the utility-scale energy storage with the TMG (*Source* ITOCHU Corporation [2023])

Scheduling Flexibility

- Rapid Response: Large FTM energy storage systems can quickly respond from a complete standstill within seconds or minutes, providing or absorbing electricity. This rapid response capability is crucial for managing grid frequency, providing emergency power support, and addressing instantaneous demand peaks.
- Versatility: FTM storage projects can not only provide basic electricity storage and release functions but also perform various grid services, including frequency regulation, voltage support, power quality management, and supply–demand balancing.
- Optimizing Renewable Energy: By storing excess renewable energy and releasing it when needed, FTM energy storage systems help optimize the use of renewable energy, reducing the amount of renewable generation that must be curtailed due to oversupply.

Enhancing Grid Resilience

- Backup Power and Black Start Capability: In the event of a large-scale grid failure, FTM energy storage systems can serve as critical backup power sources, quickly providing electricity to help restore grid operations. Some storage systems also have black start capability, meaning they can autonomously start and restore partial grid operations in the event of a complete power outage.
- Alleviating Grid Congestion: Through localized electricity storage and release, FTM storage projects help alleviate grid congestion, especially during high load periods. This not only improves the efficiency of electricity transmission but also reduces the need for new transmission line construction.
- Improving System Stability: FTM storage projects help maintain grid stability by balancing electricity supply and demand, preventing voltage and frequency fluctuations from exceeding safe limits. This is crucial for preventing grid failures and enhancing overall grid reliability.

Policy and Regulatory Environment

The policy and regulatory environment for large-scale energy storage projects plays a decisive role in their development. Policies, regulations, and incentive measures in different countries and regions directly impact the commercialization and large-scale deployment of storage technologies. The following are some key considerations related to the policy and regulatory environment faced by FTM storage projects, along with relevant examples:

1. **Policy Support and Incentives**

- Subsidies and Tax Incentives: Many governments offer direct subsidies or tax incentives for storage projects to reduce initial investment costs. For example, the Investment Tax Credit (ITC) in the United States provides significant financial support for solar projects that include storage facilities.
- Renewable Energy Quotas and Credit Systems: Some regions implement Renewable Portfolio Standards (RPS) or green certificate trading mechanisms, allowing storage projects to contribute to achieving renewable energy goals, further incentivizing the development of storage projects.

2. **Electricity Market Access and Rules**

- Market Access: Regulatory agencies need to establish clear rules that allow storage systems to participate in electricity markets, including wholesale and ancillary service markets. For instance, the Federal Energy Regulatory Commission (FERC) Order 841 requires electricity market operators to modify their rules to enable storage resources to compete.
- Pricing and Settlement Mechanisms: The economic viability of storage projects largely depends on the pricing and settlement mechanisms of the electricity market, including how ancillary services are priced.

3. **Technical Standards and Interconnection Requirements**

- Safety and Performance Standards: To ensure the safety and reliability of systems, storage projects must comply with national and international technical standards, such as safety standards for batteries and performance testing standards.
- Interconnection Requirements: Grid interconnection standards specify the technical requirements for connecting storage systems to the grid, ensuring stable and safe operation of the systems.

4. **Examples**

- California: As a pioneer in the storage field, California has passed multiple legislative and regulatory measures to promote the development of storage technologies. This includes setting specific storage deployment targets (such as SB 100) and providing financial incentives for storage projects (such as the Self-Generation Incentive Program, SGIP).
- European Union: The EU has established a series of measures to promote energy transition through its "Clean Energy" package, which includes support for the deployment of storage technologies.

Additionally, the European Network of Transmission System Operators for Electricity (ENTSO-E) is developing technical standards applicable to storage systems.

Large-scale energy storage systems, with their significant scale, high power, and diversified business models, have become indispensable components of the power system. By providing grid services and participating in electricity markets, FTM energy storage systems contribute significantly to improving the efficiency, reliability, and flexibility of the grid. With technological advancements and decreasing costs, FTM energy storage systems are expected to see broader application worldwide.

4.3.2 Investment Analysis of Large-Scale Energy Storage Projects

In this section, we discuss the investment analysis of large-scale energy storage projects, focusing primarily on revenue forecasting, cost forecasting, and discount rates.

1. **Long-Term Revenue Forecasting**

Large-scale energy storage projects typically have long cycles, generally exceeding 20 years, making revenue forecasting a crucial aspect of investment analysis. As mentioned in the previous section, unlike the price arbitrage model of commercial and industrial energy storage, the revenue model for large storage systems is more complex, with common components including frequency regulation services and capacity markets.

(1) **Price Arbitrage**

In Sect. 9.13.3 of this book, "**Long-Term Electricity Price Expectations,**" we discussed the long-term expectations of electricity prices, which are critical for the revenue of renewable energy, especially concerning price arbitrage income. For example, for large storage projects in the United States, we can refer to the long-term electricity price forecast provided by the US Energy Information Administration (EIA) as shown in Fig. 9.16 Long-term electricity price forecast by EIA.

Once electricity prices can be predicted, we can also forecast the daily peak and trough price differences based on historical data. The table below illustrates a regression model predicting peak and trough prices based on average daily prices, demonstrating a clear positive correlation among the three variables (Table 9).

Building on this, we can use the long-term electricity prices and the daily peak-trough price model to forecast long-term peak-trough price differences (Fig. 14).

Table 9 Daily max and min electricity price regression results for the United Kingdom and selected EU countries

Country	Intercept	Slope	R-squared
Belgium	31.07	1.20	92.9%
France	25.31	1.21	94.5%
Germany	38.83	1.18	87.6%
Italy	23.09	1.21	95.0%
Netherlands	41.58	1.19	87.3%
Portugal	47.72	0.93	70.7%
Spain	51.34	0.91	69.2%
United Kingdom	-36.52	1.73	78.0%

Country	Intercept	Slope	R-squared
Belgium	-27.43	0.80	83%
France	-21.70	0.78	85%
Germany	-32.23	0.82	75%
Italy	1.49	0.71	82%
Netherlands	-53.75	0.94	71%
Portugal	-38.22	1.05	82%
Spain	-41.44	1.07	81%
United Kingdom	-6.51	0.70	76%

Source Chen et al. (2024d)

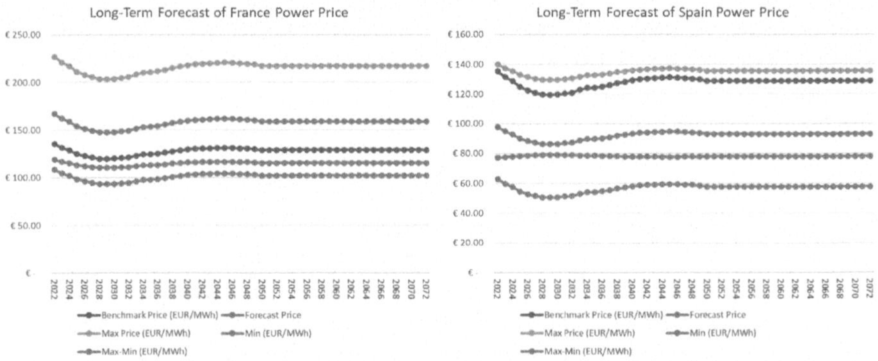

Fig. 14 Long-term power price forecast for France and Spain (*Source* Chen et al. [2024d])

In Sect. 9 of the book, **"C&I BESS Investment Analysis,"** we analyzed how to predict energy storage system revenue from price arbitrage based on daily peak-trough price differences. This will not be reiterated in this section.

(2) **Frequency Regulation Services**

Forecasting revenue from frequency regulation services (FCAS) is even more challenging. Taking the Australian market as an example, the chart below shows that the proportion of FCAS revenue fluctuated significantly between 2022 and 2023. For instance, in Q3 2022, the revenue accounted for only 30%, but in Q4 of the same year, it rebounded to nearly 80%.

Currently, there is no particularly accurate measurement model for predicting revenue from frequency regulation services. For the Australian market, we tentatively extrapolate based on recent revenue proportions (45%–55%), as illustrated in Fig. 10. BESS Revenue Share: Energy Arbitrage vs. FCAS.

(3) **Capacity Market**

The Australian government has recognized that relying solely on highly unstable price arbitrage and frequency regulation services is detrimental to the development of large storage projects. This is because highly unstable revenue cash flows make it difficult, if not impossible, to secure long-term low-cost debt financing, thereby complicating project financing for such large-scale projects, which can only rely on more expensive equity financing.

For this reason, the Australian government has vigorously promoted the Capacity Investment Scheme (CIS) starting in 2023, aiming to establish a minimum revenue expectation for large storage projects through stable capacity market revenues, thus encouraging private capital investment.

The CIS involves competitive bidding for renewable energy and clean dispatchable capacity projects sought by the Australian government to:

- Add 32 GW of new capacity by 2030;
- Fill the expected reliability gap as aging coal-fired power plants retire;
- Achieve the Australian government's goal of 82% renewable electricity by 2030.

The Australian government will provide income guarantees for successful CIS bidding projects, stipulating "minimum" and "maximum" income levels. This will create a long-term income safety net, reducing financial risks for investors and encouraging more investments at the required times and locations.

On November 23, 2023, the Australian government announced the expansion of the capacity market investment plan, targeting a total of 32 GW of new capacity nationwide, which includes:

- 23 GW of renewable energy generation capacity, equivalent to an investment of $52 billion;
- 9 GW of clean dispatchable capacity, equivalent to an investment of $15 billion (adding 7.9 GW on top of the 1.1 GW already completed in the first phase).

The expanded CIS will be launched from 2024 to 2027, with competitive bidding held approximately every six months starting in April/May 2024.

The payment mechanism for the CIS is illustrated in the chart below. When income falls below the minimum threshold, the government will provide a guaranteed income; when income exceeds the maximum threshold, large storage projects must return the excess income to the government (Fig. 15).

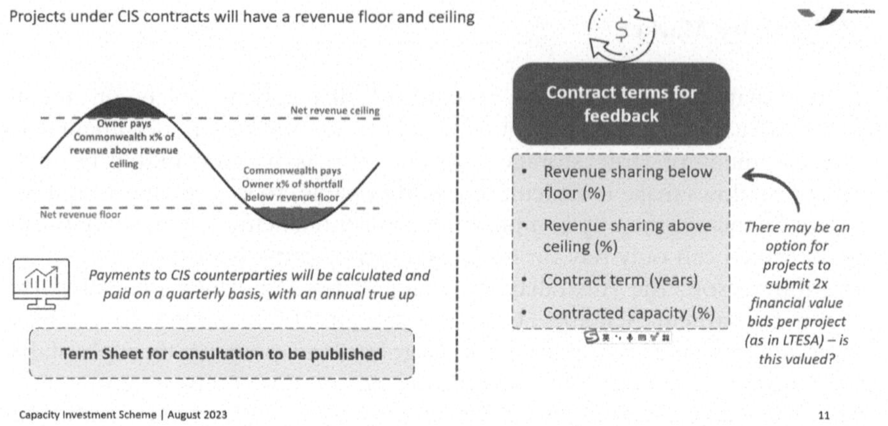

Fig. 15 CIS Payment Scheme (*Source* Australian Government DCCEEW (2023); Chen et al. [2024d])

In the next section, we will discuss the forecasting of these three types of revenue (price arbitrage, frequency regulation services, and capacity market) within the investment analysis model for large-scale energy storage projects.

2. Long-Term Cost Forecasting

To establish a comprehensive long-term cash flow forecast for large storage projects, it is necessary to predict not only long-term revenues but also long-term costs, including operational costs and financing costs (if long-term debt financing is used).

Operational and Maintenance (Inflation-driven):

Long-term operational and maintenance costs are primarily determined by the long-term inflation rate. Currently, in the capital markets, the long-term inflation rate can be derived from comparing the yields of Treasury Inflation Protected Securities (TIPS) and normal Treasury bonds to obtain a long-term unbiased estimate of the Breakeven Inflation Rates (BEIR). For example, the following chart shows the long-term inflation rate estimates in the United States for periods ranging from 5 to 30 years (Fig. 16).

The next chart presents the long-term inflation rate estimates in Germany for periods from 2.5 to 22.5 years (Fig. 17).

Considering that short-term inflation rates can be directly observed from the market, we can combine both short-term and long-term inflation rates to establish a curve. The following chart illustrates the 30-year inflation expectations based on bond market data and published inflation rates as of September 1, 2023.

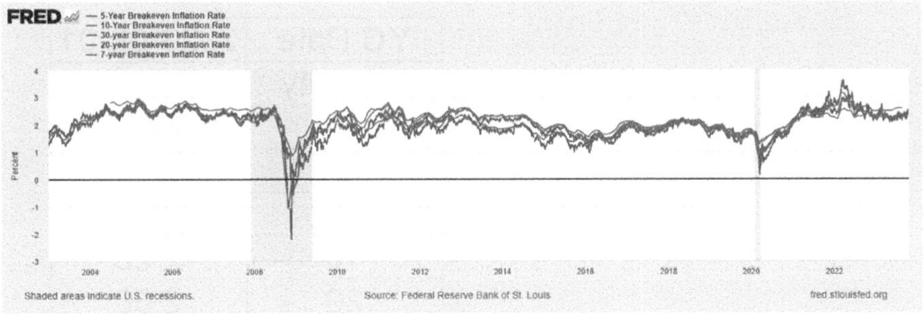

Fig. 16 US breakeven inflation rate (*Source* Federal Reserve Bank of St. Louis,[1] Chen et al. [2024d])

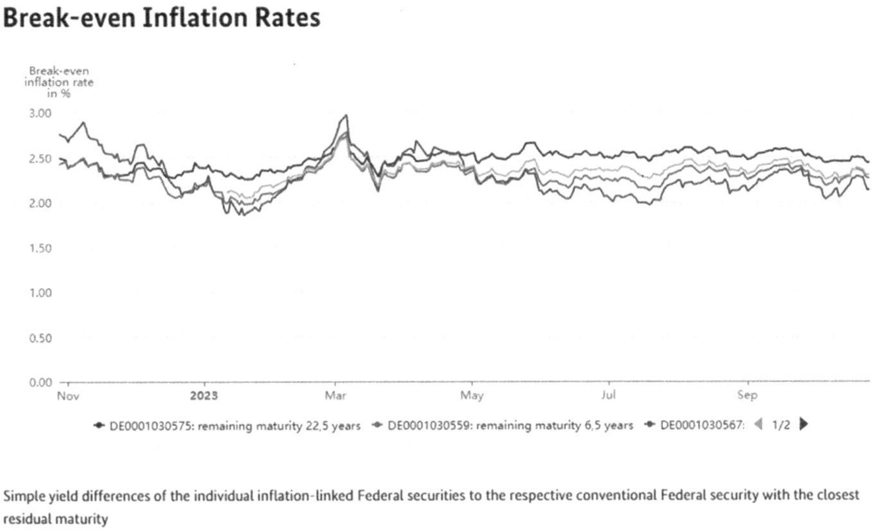

Fig. 17 Germany breakeven inflation rate (*Source* Federal Republic of Germany Finance Agency,[2] Chen et al. [2024d])

[1] https://fred.stlouisfed.org/series/T5YIE.

[2] https://www.deutsche-finanzagentur.de/en/federal-securities/types-of-federal-securities/inflation-linked-federal-securities.

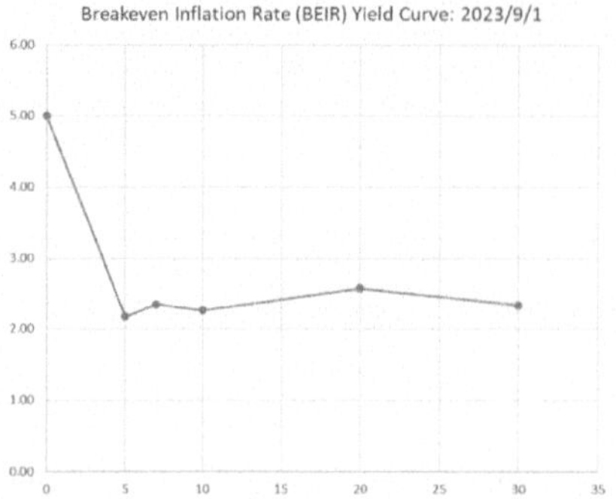

YC Date	2023-09-01
Maturity	BEIR
0	5.00
5	2.17
7	2.35
10	2.26
20	2.58
30	2.34

With this foundation, we can forecast long-term operational and maintenance costs. For example, the following chart shows the operational cost forecast for large storage projects based on the long-term inflation rate in the United States (Fig. 18).

3. Selection of Long-Term Financing and Discount Rates

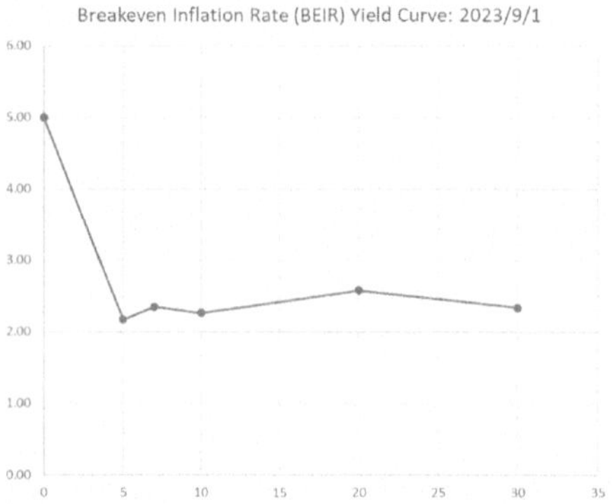

YC Date	2023-09-01
Maturity	BEIR
0	5.00
5	2.17
7	2.35
10	2.26
20	2.58
30	2.34

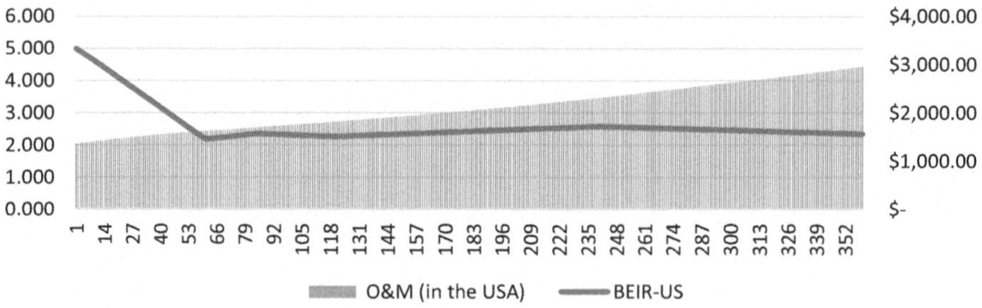

Fig. 18 Inflation adjusted O&M costs (*Source* Chen et al. [2024d])

The costs of long-term debt financing and equity financing, as well as the selection of discount rates, were discussed in Sect. 9.13.3 of this book, **"Long-Term Electricity Price Expectations,"** and will not be reiterated here.

4.3.3 Investment Analysis Model for Large Storage Projects

In this section, we discuss some results from our self-developed investment analysis model for large storage projects, focusing on investment opportunities in representative global markets.

1. **Australian Market**

For large storage projects in Australia, we can derive average income from price arbitrage based on long-term electricity price forecasts. Additionally, we can predict FCAS income based on the revenue proportion from FCAS and recently announced CIS investment plans to estimate capacity market income. The following chart presents a 50-year income forecast for a large storage project of 200 MW/400MWh in New South Wales, Australia (Fig. 19).

By combining capital expenditure (CAPEX) and operational costs (OPEX), we can determine the net cash flow and the project's internal rate of return (IRR), which is 17.32% (Fig. 20).

For other states covered by the Australian NEM market, Queensland has the highest IRR at 22.68%, followed by South Australia at 20.22%. Victoria's IRR is 11.87%, while Tasmania has the lowest at -5.03%.

Therefore, based on the above assumptions, if investing in large storage projects in Australia, one should prioritize Queensland and South Australia, while avoiding Tasmania as much as possible.

2. **European Market**

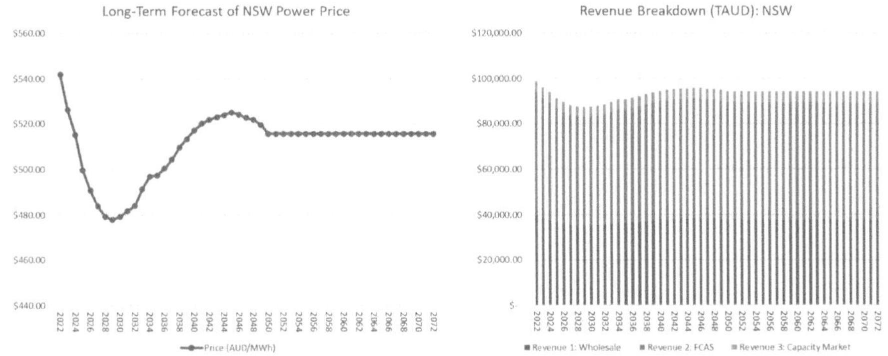

Fig. 19 AUS NSW utility-scale BESS analysis: price and revenue (*Source* Chen et al. [2024d])

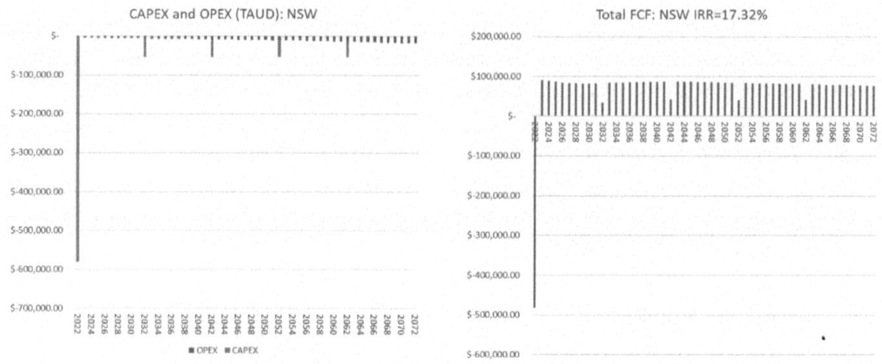

Fig. 20 AUS NSW utility-scale BESS analysis: CAPEX/OPEX and FCF/IRR (*Source* Chen et al. [2024d])

See Fig. 21.

Using the same principles, we can conduct investment analysis for large storage projects in the eight European countries discussed in the previous article of this series. Based on model assumptions regarding price arbitrage, frequency regulation services, capacity market income, and operational costs, we forecast the 50-year income for a similarly sized large storage project of 200 MW/ 400MWh and calculate its internal rate of return.

The results indicate that the Netherlands has the highest IRR at around 27%, while the other four countries (Belgium, France, Germany, and Italy) have IRRs around 23.5%. The United Kingdom has a lower IRR of about 20% (Fig. 22).

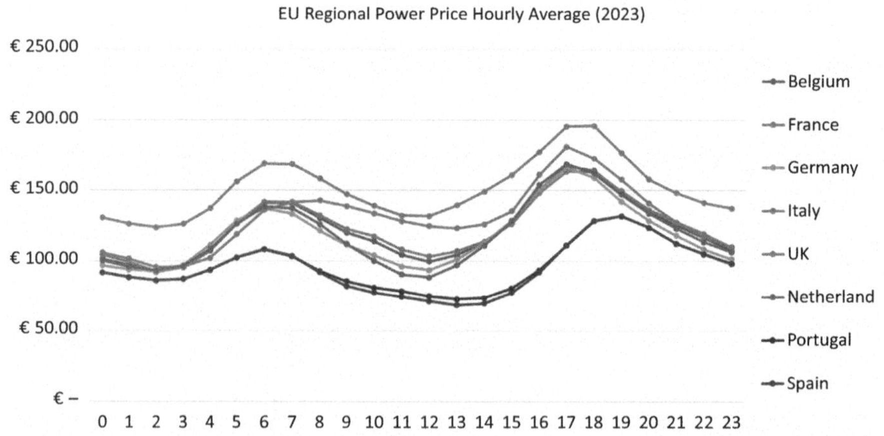

Fig. 21 Average hourly power prices in 2023: The United Kingdom and selected EU countries (*Source* Chen et al. [2024d])

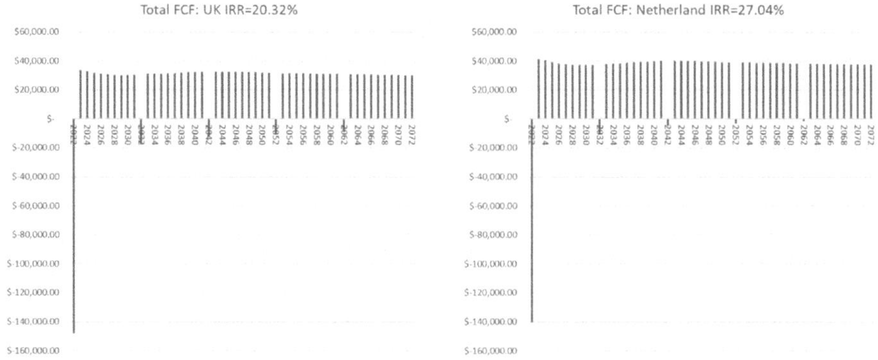

Fig. 22 The United Kingdom vs. Netherlands utility-scale BESS analysis: FCF/IRR (*Source* Chen et al. [2024d])

Spain and Portugal have the lowest IRRs, ranging from 13.7% to 14.9% (Fig. 23).

Based on this analysis, when investing in large storage projects in Europe, we should prioritize the Netherlands and the other three Western European countries, as well as Italy, while considering Spain and Portugal last. Observant readers may note that this order aligns closely with the rankings for commercial and industrial storage in the previous article. This is due to the model's assumption that frequency regulation income is proportional to price arbitrage income, which may not hold true across different countries' electricity markets.

Preparation is key to success. Conducting investment analysis for large storage projects is of utmost importance, primarily reflected in the following aspects:

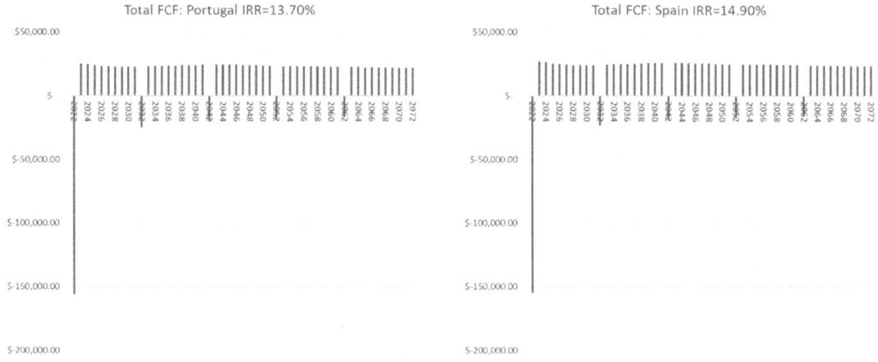

Fig. 23 Spain vs. Portugal utility-scale BESS analysis: FCF/IRR (*Source* Chen et al. [2024d])

1. **Assessing the Economic Feasibility of the Project**

Investment analysis aids investors and project developers in evaluating the economic feasibility of large storage projects, including cost–benefit analysis, revenue forecasting, and return rate calculations. By comprehensively assessing the project's initial investment costs, operational maintenance costs, expected revenues, and risk factors, investment analysis ensures that the project is economically sound and can deliver the anticipated financial returns.

2. **Determining Funding Needs and Financing Strategies**

Accurate investment analysis helps identify the funding requirements for the project, including start-up capital and operating capital, and provides a basis for the project's financing strategy. This includes assessing the costs and feasibility of different financing channels, such as debt financing, equity financing, or government subsidies, as well as developing an appropriate capital structure.

3. **Understanding the Market and Policy Environment**

Investment analysis also involves evaluating market trends, competitive dynamics, and the policy environment, which are crucial for predicting the project's long-term profitability potential. Understanding factors such as market demand, electricity price fluctuations, policy incentives, and regulatory requirements helps investors make more informed decisions.

4. **Risk Assessment and Management**

Large storage projects face various risks, including technological risks, market risks, and policy and legal risks. Investment analysis identifies and assesses these potential risks, providing support for risk management and mitigation strategies, thereby protecting investments and ensuring successful project implementation.

5. **Promoting Sustainable Development**

Investment analysis of large storage projects also includes evaluating the project's impact on environmental, social, and governance (ESG) factors. This helps ensure that the project aligns with sustainable development goals, promotes the use of clean energy, reduces carbon emissions, and delivers positive socioeconomic benefits to the community.

6. **Optimizing Project Design and Operation**

Through investment analysis, project developers can optimize the design and operational strategies of the project, improving the efficiency and performance of the storage system. This may involve selecting the most suitable storage technology, adjusting project scale and configuration, and formulating effective market participation strategies.

Conducting comprehensive investment analysis is crucial for ensuring the success of large storage projects. It not only helps assess the financial feasibility and risks of the project but also promotes more informed decision-making, optimizes project design and operation, and supports the sustainable transition of energy systems. As global energy markets and policy environments continue to evolve, in-depth investment analysis of large storage projects will be key to ensuring their long-term success.

5 Investment Opportunities and Challenges

The energy storage market is a dynamic and rapidly evolving landscape, presenting both significant investment opportunities and challenges that investors need to carefully consider. NZA (2021) model five US decarbonization pathways, analyzing infrastructure needs and socio-economic impacts.

Battery Technology Advancements and Costs

The energy storage market is being driven by significant advancements in battery technology, particularly in lithium-ion batteries, which are becoming more efficient, longer-lasting, and less expensive.

Ongoing research and development in battery technologies are leading to:

- **Higher Energy Density:** Batteries are becoming more compact and lightweight, able to store more energy in a smaller space.
- **Improved Lifespan:** Batteries are lasting longer, reducing the need for frequent replacements and lowering the overall cost of ownership.
- **Enhanced Safety:** Safety features are being integrated into battery designs to mitigate the risks of overheating, fires, and explosions.

These advancements are driving down the cost of battery storage, making it increasingly competitive with other energy storage technologies and traditional fossil fuel-based power generation.

Policy Support and Regulatory Frameworks

Government policies, subsidies, and regulations play a crucial role in shaping the energy storage market and creating a supportive environment for investment.

Key policy considerations include:

- **Market Design:** Electricity markets need to be designed to properly value the services provided by energy storage, such as frequency regulation, peak shaving, and voltage support.
- **Permitting and Siting:** Streamlining the permitting process for energy storage projects can reduce development costs and timelines.
- **Grid Integration Standards:** Clear standards for the interconnection of energy storage systems to the grid are essential to ensure safety, reliability, and interoperability.

Market Development and Investment Models

The energy storage market is attracting investment from a range of players, including utilities, independent power producers, project developers, battery manufacturers, and venture capitalists. Different business models and investment opportunities are emerging:

- **Standalone Energy Storage Projects:** These projects are dedicated solely to providing energy storage services, typically selling these services to grid operators or to large electricity consumers.
- **Co-located Storage with Renewable Energy:** Integrating energy storage with renewable energy projects, such as solar or wind farms, can enhance their value by making them more dispatchable and reliable.
- **Energy Storage as a Service:** This model involves providing energy storage services on a subscription basis, enabling companies or individuals to access the benefits of energy storage without making large upfront investments.

6 Conclusion: A Key Component of a Clean Energy Future

Energy storage is an essential enabler of the transition to a clean, reliable, and affordable energy future. By addressing the intermittency challenges of renewable energy sources, enhancing grid stability, and creating new opportunities for flexible and efficient energy management, energy storage is transforming the way we generate, distribute, and consume electricity.

The energy storage market is experiencing rapid growth, driven by falling technology costs, supportive government policies, and the increasing need for grid flexibility and resilience. Continued investment in research and development, innovation in business models, and a supportive policy environment are crucial to unlock the full potential of energy storage and accelerate the transition to a sustainable energy system.

References

Australian Energy Market Operator (AEMO). (2024). *Quarterly energy dynamics Q3 2024.* https://aemo.com.au/-/media/files/major-publications/qed/2024/qed-q3-2024.pdf

Australian Government Department of Climate Change, Energy, the Environment and Water (DCCEEW). (2023). *Capacity investment scheme.* https://www.dcceew.gov.au/energy/renewable/capacity-investment-scheme

Bloomberg New Energy Finance (BloombergNEF). (2021). *Battery pack prices cited below 100/kWh for the first time in 2020, while market average sits at 137/kWh.* https://about.bnef.com/blog/battery-pack-prices-cited-below-100-kwh-for-the-first-time-in-2020-while-market-average-sits-at-137-kwh/

Chen, J. et al. (2024a). *Why the performance of new energy assets is dismal: Breaking new ground in new energy investment (Part I).* Caixin Column Article. https://opinion.caixin.com/2024-01-12/102155632.html

Chen, J. et al. (2024b). *Stabilizing long-term expectations: Breaking new ground in new energy investment (Part II).* Caixin Column Article. https://opinion.caixin.com/2024-01-15/102156495.html

Chen, J. et al. (2024c). *Exploring commercial and industrial energy storage models: Breaking new ground in new energy investment (Part III).* Caixin Column Article. https://opinion.caixin.com/2024-01-23/102159486.html

Chen, J. et al. (2024d). *How to invest in large-scale energy storage systems: Breaking new ground in new energy investment (Part IV).* Caixin Column Article. https://opinion.caixin.com/2024-01-30/102161886.html

Department of Energy (DOE). (2020). *Energy storage grand challenge roadmap.* https://www.energy.gov/energy-storage-grand-challenge/downloads/energy-storage-grand-challenge-roadmap

Gresham House Energy Storage Fund plc (GRID). (2023). *Powering the renewable energy transition: Interim report and accounts as at 30 June 2023.* https://greshamhouse.com/wp-content/uploads/2023/09/GRID-Interim-Report-30-June-2023-FINAL-PUBLISHED.pdf

GRID. (2024a). *Powering the renewable energy transition: Annual report and financial statements for the year ended 31 December 2023.* https://greshamhouse.com/wp-content/uploads/2024/04/GRID-Annual-Report-2023-Signed.pdf

GRID. (2024b). *Gresham House Energy Storage Fund plc (GRID): Interim results presentation for period ending 30 June 2024.* https://greshamhouse.com/wp-content/uploads/2024/10/Gresham-House-Energy-Storage-Fund-plc-Interim-2024.pdf

Gore Street Energy Storage Fund plc (GSF). (2022). *Annual report of gore street energy storage fund Plc For the year ended 31 March 2022.* https://www.gsenergystoragefund.com/docs/librariesprovider22/archive/reports/annual-report-2022.pdf

Gudmunds, D., Nyholm, E., Taljegard, M., & Odenberger, M. (2020). Self-consumption and self-sufficiency for household solar producers when introducing an electric vehicle. *Renewable Energy, 148*, 1200–1215. https://doi.org/10.1016/j.renene.2019.10.030

International Renewable Energy Agency (IRENA). (2020). *Electricity storage valuation framework: Assessing system value and ensuring project viability*. Accessed 8 March 2025. From https://www.irena.org/publications/2020/Mar/Electricity-Storage-Valuation-Framework-2020

IRENA. (2024). *Renewable power generation costs in 2023*. International Renewable Energy Agency, Abu Dhabi. From https://www.irena.org/-/media/Files/IRENA/Agency/Publication/2024/Sep/IRENA_Renewable_power_generation_costs_in_2023.pdf

Itochu. (2023). *Establishment of a fund exclusively for utility scale energy storage for the first time in japan promoting energy generation and storage through government-industry collaboration with the Tokyo metropolitan government*. https://www.itochu.co.jp/en/news/press/2023/231204_2.html

Jülch, V. (2016). Comparison of electricity storage options using levelized cost of storage (LCOS) method. *Applied Energy, 183*, 1594–1606. From https://www.sciencedirect.com/science/article/pii/S0306261916312740

McKinsey. (2023). *Enabling renewable energy with battery energy storage systems*. https://www.mckinsey.com/industries/automotive-and-assembly/our-insights/enabling-renewable-energy-with-battery-energy-storage-systems/

Net-zero America (NZA). (2021). *Net-zero America: Potential pathways, infrastructure, and impacts*. https://netzeroamerica.princeton.edu/

Ziegler, M. S., Mueller, J. M., Pereira, G. D., Song, J., Ferrara, M., Chiang, Y. M., & Trancik, J. E. (2019). Storage requirements and costs of shaping renewable energy toward grid decarbonization. *Joule, 3*(9), 2134–2153. https://www.sciencedirect.com/science/article/pii/S2542435119303009

Case Reference

Bizeray, A. (2024). *AI is a critical differentiator for energy storage system success*. Energy Storage News. Accessed 1 January 2024. From https://www.energy-storage.news/ai-is-a-critical-differentiator-for-energy-storage-system-success/

Business Wire. (2023). *NineDot energy selects stem's athena AI platform for New York city site*. Accessed 1 January 2024. https://www.businesswire.com/news/home/20231024890570/en/NineDot-Energy-Selects-Stem%E2%80%99s-Athena-AI-Platform-for-New-York-City-Site

Murray, C. (2023). *ERCOT and CAISO market changes increase need for AI-driven optimisation, says stem inc CEO*. Energy Storage News. https://www.energy-storage.news/ercot-and-caiso-market-changes-increase-need-for-ai-driven-optimisation-says-stem-inc-ceo/

Podorozhko, Y. (2025). *AI energy storage—The future of energy solutions*. MadAppGang. https://madappgang.com/blog/ai-energy-storages/

Rocky Mountain Institute (RMI). (2015). *The economics of battery energy storage*. Accessed 23 January 2025. From https://rmi.org/insight/economics-battery-energy-storage/

Tesla. (2025). *Tesla virtual power plant*. Accessed 1 January 2024. https://www.tesla.com/virtual-power-plant

Whitney, R. (2023). *IoT + AI, or how to reduce energy costs*. Firmbee. https://firmbee.com/iot-ai-or-how-to-reduce-energy-costs

CHAPTER 11

Decarbonizing Hard-to-Abate Sectors: Innovations for a Net-Zero Future

1 Introduction: The Challenge of Deep Decarbonization

The world is on a critical mission to achieve net-zero emissions by mid-century, a goal essential for averting the worst impacts of climate change. While significant strides have been made in decarbonizing the power sector through the rapid deployment of renewable energy technologies, some sectors of the economy present particularly stubborn challenges. These "hard-to-abate" sectors, characterized by high energy intensity, process emissions, and limited availability of low-carbon alternatives, are proving to be the toughest nuts to crack on the road to a sustainable future (Figs. 1, 2, and 3).

The IRENA (2024) concentrates on five specific hard-to-abate sectors: heavy-duty trucks, shipping, aviation, iron and steel, and chemicals and petrochemicals.

The combined emissions from these five sectors constitute roughly **a fifth of total global CO_2 emissions**. In absolute terms, this is equivalent to **37 $GtCO_2$** annually, as of 2022. They also account for approximately **a quarter of the world's energy consumption** (411 EJ), underscoring their reliance on energy. The 2022 sector breakdown look like the following:

- **Heavy-Duty Trucks:** Responsible for 1.8 Gt CO_2, or about 5% of global CO_2 emissions.
- **Shipping:** 0.86 Gt CO_2, which is about 10% of transport-related emissions or roughly 2–3% of global CO_2.
- **Aviation:** 0.8 Gt CO_2, which is also about 10% of all transport-related emissions or roughly 2–3% of global CO_2.

J. Chen, *Climate Finance*,
https://doi.org/10.1007/978-981-96-7975-1_11

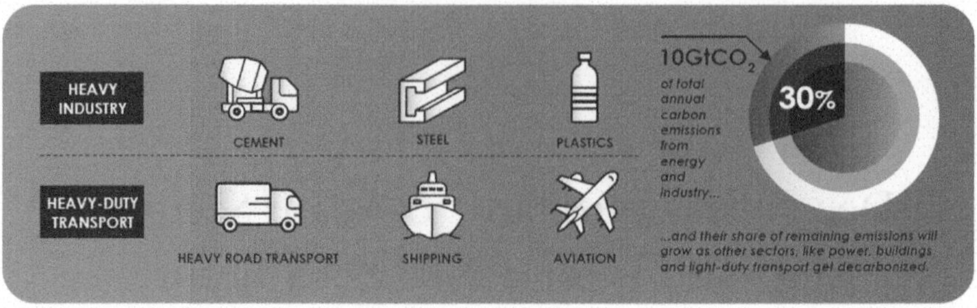

Fig. 1 Hard-to-abate sectors 2018 *Source* ETC (2018)

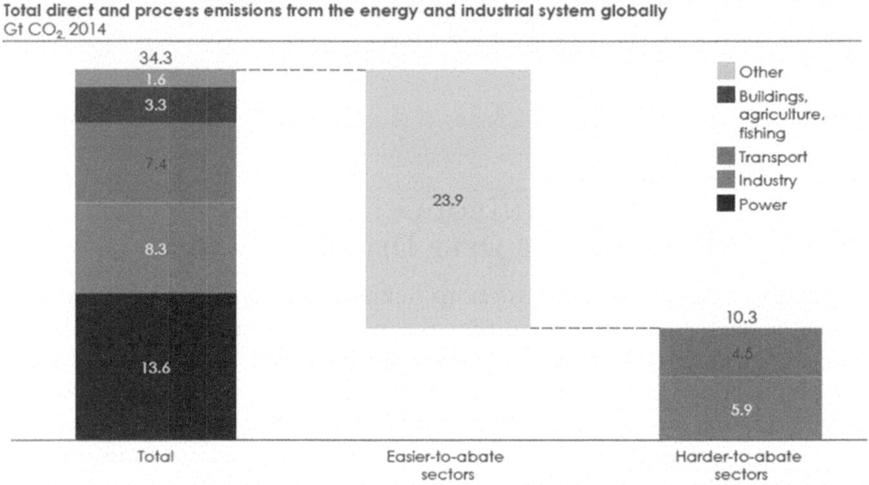

Fig. 2 Emissions from easier-to-abate vs. hard-to-abate sectors, 2014 *Note* Easier-to-abate sectors include rail and light-duty road transport, pulp and paper, aluminum and other industries, power, buildings, agriculture, fishing, and others *Source* ETC (2018) and IEA (2017)

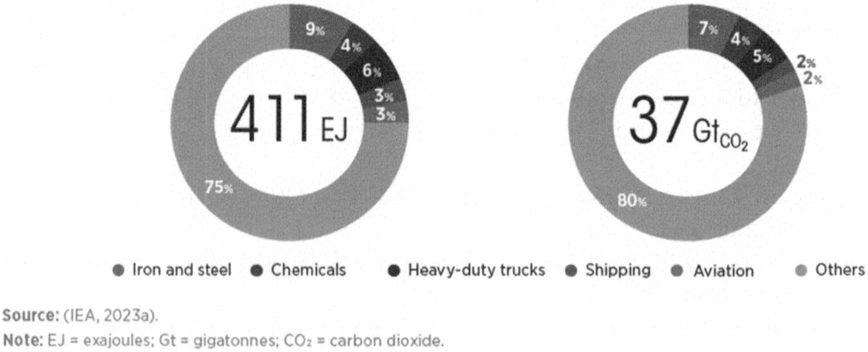

Fig. 3 Energy consumption and CO_2 emissions for selected hard-to-abate sectors, 2022 *Source* IEA (2023a) and IRENA (2024)

- **Iron and Steel:** This sector is by far the largest emitting sector, being responsible for 2.8 Gt CO_2.
- **Chemicals and Petrochemicals:** A further 1.3 Gt CO_2 is attributable to this sector.

Compared with the ETC (2018) report, which states that these harder-to-abate sectors account for **10Gt (30%) of total global CO_2 emissions annually**, combined with easier-to-abate sectors making up **34.3 Gt of CO_2 emissions in 2014**, it is clear that while some progress has been made in recent years, the current pace of decarbonization is too slow, and emissions are likely to increase without greater action.

Decarbonizing these industries is not simply a matter of replacing fossil fuel-based energy sources with renewable alternatives. The very nature of their production processes often involves inherent emissions. For example, the chemical reactions involved in steelmaking and cement production release carbon dioxide (CO_2) as a byproduct, regardless of the energy source used.

Addressing the emissions from these hard-to-abate sectors requires a combination of innovative technologies, supportive policies, and substantial investments. We need to develop and deploy breakthrough technologies, such as carbon capture, utilization, and storage (CCUS), explore the potential for electrification and hydrogen as alternative energy carriers, and implement process efficiency improvements to minimize emissions.

This chapter delves into the unique challenges posed by hard-to-abate sectors, explores the promising technologies and pathways for decarbonization, and examines the investment landscape and opportunities for driving innovation and scaling up solutions. By understanding the complexities of these sectors and the potential solutions emerging, we can chart a course toward a net-zero future where even the most challenging industries contribute to a sustainable and prosperous world.

2 Key Hard-to-Abate Sectors

Hard-to-abate sectors encompass a diverse range of industries that share common characteristics: high energy consumption, emissions inherent to their production processes, and limited availability of cost-effective and scalable low-carbon alternatives.

Many agencies have proposed roadmaps for decarbonization of those hard-to abate sectors. IEA (2021) charts a 2050 net-zero roadmap focusing on rapid renewable deployment and energy efficiency. Europe-based Energy Transitions Commission (ETC, 2018) argues that it is technically and economically feasible to achieve net-zero-carbon emissions from "harder-to-abate" sectors (heavy industry and long-distance transport) by mid-century (around 2050), which can be achieved without resorting to controversial approaches or sacrificing economic growth. In a follow-up report, ETC (2020) emphasizes clean electrification, hydrogen, and CCUS are critical for net-zero by 2050/2060.

Table 1 Summary table of US DOE, ETC, IRENA industrial decarbonization roadmap

Feature	*DOE industrial decarbonization roadmap*	*IRENA: Decarbonizing hard-to-abate sectors with renewables*	*ETC mission possible*
Primary geographic focus	The united states	G7 Countries	Global
Sectors covered	Iron & steel, chemicals, food & beverage, refining, cement	Heavy-duty trucks, shipping, aviation, iron & steel, chemicals/petrochemicals	Heavy industry & long-distance transport
Main emphasis	Detailed RD&D needs and technology pathways	Policy recommendations for renewable energy deployment	Technical and economic feasibility with global strategies
Approach	Technical, with in-depth analysis	Policy-oriented, highlighting role of renewables	Global, systems focused, multi-stakeholder
Scope of analysis	Deep dives into five US subsectors with specific pathways	More broad, with focus on enabling conditions	High level, addressing complex systemic issues

Source US DOE (2022), ETC (2018), and IRENA (2024)

US DOE (2022) outlines a strategy to achieve near-zero greenhouse gas (GHG) emissions in the US industrial sector by 2050, while maintaining competitiveness and ensuring equity. IRENA (2024) provides recommendations for the G7 to accelerate the decarbonization of five "hard-to-abate" sectors: heavy-duty trucks, shipping, aviation, iron and steel, and chemicals/petrochemicals (Table 1).

These reports provide a comprehensive look at the challenges, opportunities, and necessary steps to decarbonize hard-to-abate sectors, each with its own unique perspective and recommendations. While each report has distinct priorities and focus areas, there is a great deal of overlap in terms of the key technologies and changes that will be needed to meet climate goals. They all underscore that the scale of transformation needed is massive, but also achievable with decisive action (Fig. 4).

In the following sections, we will discuss the five major hard-to-abate sectors as outlined in the above chart from IRENA (2024).

2.1 Heavy Industry

Heavy industry is a major contributor to global greenhouse gas emissions, accounting for about 15–20% of global CO_2 emissions. Decarbonizing this

2022	Heavy-duty tracks	Shipping	Aviation	Iron and steel	Chemicals and petrochemicals
Activity	30 trillion tkm	110 trillion tkm	6 trillion pkm 220 billion tkm	1.8 billion tonnes	719 million tonnes
Energy consumption [EJ/year]	26.8	11.2	11	35	16
CO_2 emissions [Gt]	1.8	0.86	0.8	2.8	1.3

Source: (ICAO, 2023a; IEA, 2023a, 2023b; UNCTAD, 2022).
Note: EJ = exajoules; Gt = gigatonnes; tkm = tonne kilometre; pkm = passenger kilometre.

Fig. 4 Activity metrics for selected hard-to-abate sectors, 2022 *Source* ICAO (2023), IEA (2023a, b), UNCTAD (2022), and IRENA (2024)

sector is crucial for achieving climate goals but presents significant challenges. Bataille et al. (2018) review decarbonization pathways for energy-intensive industries.

Iron and Steel: Steelmaking, a foundational industry for infrastructure, construction, and manufacturing, is highly energy-intensive and relies heavily on fossil fuels, particularly coal, which is used to produce coke, a key ingredient in the blast furnace process. The chemical reactions involved in converting iron ore to steel also release significant amounts of CO_2. The iron and steel sector is responsible for about 8% of global CO_2 emissions, primarily due to reliance on fossil fuels in production processes. Current production methods are energy-intensive and carbon-heavy. Here are some probable solutions:

- Direct Electrification: Using renewable electricity for electric arc furnaces can significantly reduce emissions.
- Hydrogen-Based Production: Transitioning to hydrogen-based direct reduction processes is a promising pathway.

There is a growing pipeline of low-carbon steel production projects, with significant commitments from major steel producers to reduce emissions. However, the transition is still in its early stages.

Chemicals: The chemical industry is vast and diverse, encompassing the production of a wide range of products, from fertilizers and plastics to pharmaceuticals and paints. Many chemical processes rely on fossil fuels as feedstocks or for energy, and some chemical reactions inherently release greenhouse gases.

Material Economics (2019) analyzes net-zero pathways for EU heavy industry by 2050. The sector relies heavily on fossil fuels for energy and feedstocks, contributing significantly to global emissions. The circular economy principles are not yet widely implemented, limiting recycling and reuse. Some solutions:

- Energy Efficiency: Improving process efficiency and adopting renewable feedstocks can help reduce emissions.
- CCUS Technologies: Implementing carbon capture, utilization, and storage (CCUS) can mitigate emissions from existing processes.

Some companies are setting ambitious decarbonization targets, and there is increasing interest in bio-based alternatives. However, the sector still faces significant barriers to widespread adoption of sustainable practices.

2.2 Transportation

The transportation sector is responsible for about 16% of global CO_2 emissions, and decarbonizing certain modes of transportation is particularly challenging due to energy density requirements and the lack of readily available low-carbon alternatives.

Aviation: Air travel relies on jet fuel, a highly energy-dense fuel derived from petroleum. While biofuels offer a potential alternative, their production is currently limited, and they are more expensive than conventional jet fuel. Electric aircraft are emerging but face challenges related to battery weight and range, limiting their applicability to short-haul flights. McKinsey (2023) finds SAF crucial for aviation decarbonization, though scaling production and cost remain challenges. Aviation is a significant contributor to global CO_2 emissions, with fossil fuels dominating energy consumption. Sustainable aviation fuels (SAF) currently represent only a small fraction of total fuel use. Probable solutions include:

- Technological Improvements: Continued advancements in fuel efficiency and the adoption of SAF are critical.
- Electric Propulsion: Exploring electric and hybrid aircraft for short-haul flights can help reduce emissions.

The ICAO (2023) has set a long-term goal for net-zero emissions by 2050, with increasing production facilities for SAF. However, the sector still relies heavily on carbon offsetting rather than direct emissions reductions.

Shipping: The shipping industry, which transports goods globally, relies heavily on heavy fuel oil, a highly polluting and carbon-intensive fuel. Transitioning to low-carbon fuels, such as liquefied natural gas (LNG) or biofuels, or adopting alternative propulsion systems, such as hydrogen fuel cells or battery-powered ships, faces technical and economic challenges, particularly for long-distance voyages. Bouman et al. (2017) review emission reduction technologies in shipping, finding potential for 50–60% cuts by 2050. The shipping sector is heavily dependent on low-grade fossil fuels, contributing significantly to global emissions. Regulatory changes, such as the IMO's sulfur cap, have prompted shifts but have not yet led to substantial decarbonization. Here are some potential solutions:

- Alternative Fuels: Transitioning to low-carbon biofuels and green e-fuels is essential, though they come at a higher cost.
- Energy Efficiency: Implementing energy-efficient technologies and operational measures can yield immediate emissions reductions.

The IMO has set ambitious targets for emissions reductions, aiming for a 20–30% decrease by 2030 and net-zero by 2050 (IRENA, 2024). Collaborative initiatives, such as green shipping corridors, are being established to facilitate the transition.

Heavy-Duty trucks: Long-haul trucking, which transports goods over long distances, relies on diesel fuel, a fossil fuel with high energy density. Electric trucks are emerging but currently face limitations in range and payload capacity, making them more suitable for shorter routes and lighter loads. Hydrogen fuel cell trucks are another potential solution but face challenges related to infrastructure development and fuel costs. Heavy-duty trucks account for about 25% of transport-related CO_2 emissions, primarily relying on diesel and natural gas. The sector's activity is expected to double by mid-century, potentially increasing emissions significantly if no action is taken. Probable solutions include:

- Efficiency Standards: Implementing stringent efficiency standards can reduce emissions in the short term.
- Electrification: Battery electric trucks are emerging as a viable solution, with significant cost reductions in battery technology making them competitive.
- Biofuels: Sustainable biomass-based diesel substitutes can reduce emissions from existing internal combustion engine (ICE) vehicles.

The adoption of electric trucks is growing, with over 116 models available (IRENA, 2024). However, the current pace is insufficient to meet climate targets, necessitating rapid infrastructure development for charging.

2.3 Other Sectors

- **Agriculture:** Agriculture contributes to greenhouse gas emissions through livestock (e.g., methane from cattle), fertilizer production, and land-use change (e.g., deforestation). Reducing emissions from agriculture requires a combination of practices, such as improving livestock management, developing more efficient fertilizers, and promoting sustainable land use.

- **Buildings:** The construction and operation of buildings account for a significant portion of global energy consumption and emissions. Reducing emissions from buildings involves improving energy efficiency, using low-carbon building materials, and electrifying heating and cooling systems.
- **Waste Management:** Landfills emit methane, a potent greenhouse gas, as organic waste decomposes. Reducing methane emissions from waste management requires diverting organic waste from landfills through composting, anaerobic digestion, and waste reduction efforts.

3 Decarbonization Pathways and Technologies

Addressing the emissions from hard-to-abate sectors requires a portfolio of innovative technologies, process improvements, and policy solutions. This section explores some of the most promising pathways and technologies for decarbonizing these challenging industries (Fig. 5).

ETC (2020) argues that there are three steps providing a simplified framework for thinking about the complex task of transforming our economies to reach net-zero GHG emissions by mid-century.

Here's a breakdown of each step:

Step 1: Use Less Energy

- **Concept:** This first step emphasizes the need to drastically reduce the overall demand for energy in the economy. It recognizes that, no matter how clean our energy sources are, using less energy in the first place makes the transition easier, less costly, and more achievable.

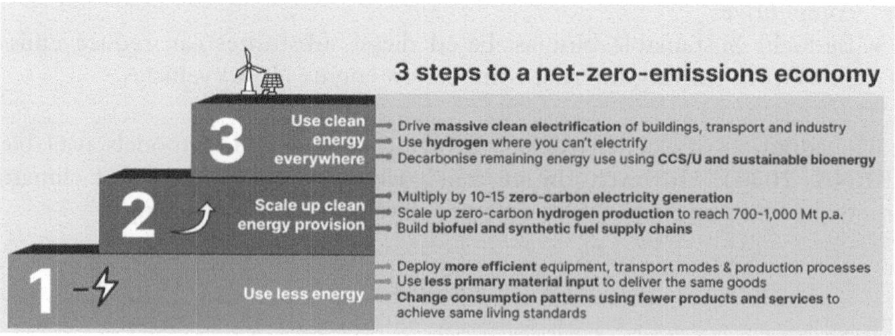

Fig. 5 Steps for industrial decarbonization *Source* ETC (2020)

- **Key Strategies:**
  - Deploy more efficient equipment: This includes things like developing better engines, more efficient turbines, smart grids and appliances and more energy-efficient industrial equipment.
  - **Improve transport modes:** Reducing overall distances and volumes of travel through modal shift (e.g., switching from road transport to rail), better planning and public transport.

- **Changes to Production Processes**: Process intensification, heat recovery and optimized production processes to minimize waste.
- * **Change Consumption Patterns:** Reducing the consumption of carbon-intensive products and services in favor of sustainable options. This entails a focus on greater material efficiency, less over-consumption, more sharing, reuse, and recycling of products and infrastructure.
- * **Reduce Primary Material Input:** Shifting from a linear economy toward a circular one, by increasing the use of secondary materials and limiting use of primary resources.
- **Importance:** By actively reducing demand, we can decrease the scale of the challenge that must be met by clean energy supply and associated infrastructure, as well as reduce waste in the system. As a result of this, the level of investments required as well as the pace of transition needed would be reduced. This step reduces energy consumption and material use, and thereby lowers CO_2 emissions as well as other negative impacts of our economy.

Step 2: Scale Up Clean Energy Provision

- **Concept:** This step focuses on the need to rapidly increase the production and supply of clean, zero-carbon energy sources. This encompasses replacing fossil fuels with sources that do not generate GHG emissions.
- **Key Strategies:**
  - **Massive Electrification**: Transitioning many energy uses from fossil fuel-based energy to electricity, including transportation, building heating, and industry.

- **Scale-Up of Renewables:** Generating electricity through solar, wind, hydro, and nuclear sources. This includes also development of more advanced technology such as floating solar and offshore wind farms.
- * **Scale-up of green hydrogen production:** Investing heavily to develop electrolysis technology and infrastructure so as to generate clean hydrogen that can be used in transport, industry, and to balance power markets.

- **Scale Up Bioenergy Production**: Sustainably produced low-carbon biofuels and bioenergy must be scaled up to address those sectors that cannot be electrified.
- **Importance:** This step provides the clean energy source that will be the backbone of the decarbonized economy. It requires significant investment, innovation, and deployment on a massive scale, but is vital to replace the current fossil fuel-based energy system.

Step 3: Use Clean Energy Everywhere

- **Concept:** This final step concerns how we deploy the clean energy that is being produced. Once we have increased the supply of low-carbon energy, we then need to use it effectively and transition entire sectors toward using this clean energy supply, and reduce dependence on fossil fuel-based technologies.
- **Key Strategies:**
  - **Direct electrification:** Where appropriate, end-use applications currently powered by fossil fuels must be switched to electrification, where feasible.
  - **Utilize hydrogen:** Where direct electrification is not feasible or efficient (such as long-distance transportation and some industrial processes), hydrogen (produced via electrolysis) can be used.
  - **Use sustainable bioenergy**: In those sectors that are difficult to electrify or decarbonize using hydrogen, alternative low-carbon fuels that are produced from sustainable bioenergy are essential.
  - **Address Residual Emissions:** Where all else fails, CCS/U must be deployed.
- **Importance:** This step underscores that decarbonization involves more than just switching to clean energy production. It means actively choosing to use clean energy for powering vehicles, industrial equipment, buildings, and appliances. It requires a shift from fossil-based energy sources to sustainable and low-carbon alternatives, including clean hydrogen, biofuels, and bio-feedstocks

Overall Significance of the Three Steps

- **Interconnectedness:** The three steps are not independent; they are interconnected and need to be pursued simultaneously and in parallel. Reductions in energy demand, for example, can reduce the scale of the challenge for ramping-up clean energy provision.
- **Emphasis on System Thinking:** The three steps show a need for system thinking that considers the interaction between supply, demand, and usage.

- **Clear Goals:** These three steps help break down the challenge of decarbonization into concrete and manageable actions that can guide policymakers, businesses, and individuals.

In essence, the three steps provide a framework for a transition to net-zero emissions, which requires us to (1) reduce our total energy consumption, (2) provide clean energy supply, and (3) use that clean energy everywhere, with a focus on electrification. The order of these actions is important, because if we do not address the demand side first, and improve energy efficiency at every level, we could end up making the challenge larger and more expensive than it needs to be.

In the Fig. 6, IRENA (2024) summarizes the key technological pathways and their readiness assessments for five hard-to-abate sectors: heavy-duty trucks, shipping, aviation, iron and steel, and chemicals and petrochemicals. Here's a synthesis of the pathways and their relevance to each sector:

Key Technological Pathways

1. **Reduced Demand and Improved Energy Efficiency**
   - **Relevance:** High
   - **Readiness:** High
   - **Description:** This pathway focuses on reducing energy and material demand through efficiency improvements, behavioral changes, and the principles of the circular economy.
2. **Direct Use of Clean Electricity**
   - **Relevance:** High
   - **Readiness:** High
   - **Description:** This involves replacing fossil fuel-based technologies with those powered directly by renewable electricity, enhancing process efficiency.
3. **Indirect Use of Clean Electricity via Synthetic Fuels and Feedstocks**
   - **Relevance:** High
   - **Readiness:** Moderate
   - **Description:** This pathway includes sourcing energy and feedstocks from hydrogen and its derivatives produced using renewable electricity and sustainable carbon sources.
4. **Direct Use of Renewable Heat and Biomass**
   - **Relevance:** Moderate
   - **Readiness:** Moderate

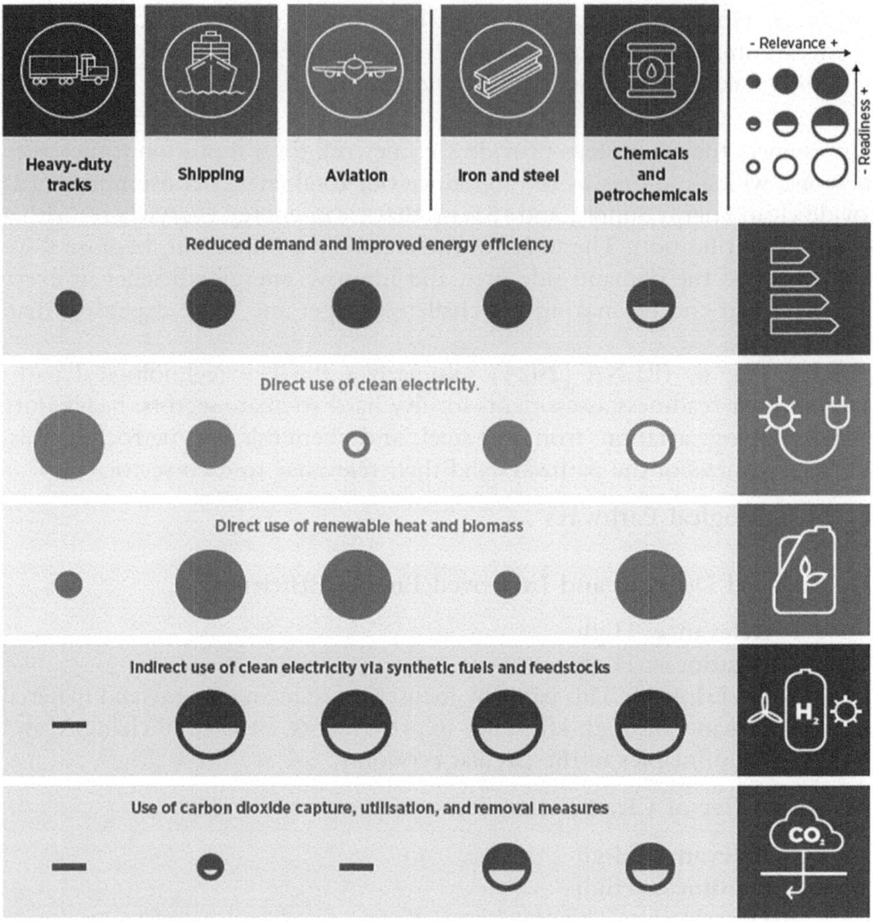

Fig. 6 Key technological pathways and readiness assessment for selected sectors *Source* IRENA (2024)

- **Description:** This pathway focuses on satisfying heat requirements with renewable heat sources and directly replacing fossil fuels with biofuels where electrification is not feasible.

5. **Use of Carbon Dioxide Capture, Utilization, and Removal Measures (CCUS)**
   - **Relevance:** Moderate
   - **Readiness:** Low
   - **Description:** This pathway involves capturing CO_2 emissions from processes where emissions cannot be fully eliminated, storing them permanently, or utilizing them in ways that prevent their release.

Sector-Specific Insights

- **Heavy-Duty Trucks:** The direct use of clean electricity (electric trucks) and improved energy efficiency are crucial for decarbonization. The readiness for battery electric trucks is high, while hydrogen trucks are still developing.
- **Shipping:** The sector can benefit from both direct electrification (for short routes) and the use of biofuels or synthetic fuels. Energy efficiency improvements can provide immediate emissions reductions.
- **Aviation:** The use of sustainable aviation fuels (SAF) and improvements in energy efficiency are key. Direct electrification is still in the early stages for larger aircraft, but advancements in battery technology may change this.
- **Iron and Steel:** Direct electrification through electric arc furnaces and the use of hydrogen for iron reduction are promising pathways. The readiness for these technologies is increasing, but widespread adoption is still developing.
- **Chemicals and Petrochemicals:** The sector can leverage bio-based feedstocks and renewable hydrogen. CCUS technologies are less mature but are critical for reducing emissions from fossil fuel-based processes.

The pathways outlined in Figure S2 highlight the importance of a multifaceted approach to decarbonization across these sectors. While some technologies are ready for deployment, others require further development and investment to achieve significant emissions reductions. The report emphasizes that a combination of these pathways will be necessary to meet net-zero targets by mid-century.

3.1 Carbon Capture, Utilization, and Storage (CCUS)

CCUS encompasses a suite of technologies designed to capture CO_2 emissions from industrial processes or directly from the atmosphere (Direct Air Capture), offering a potential solution for mitigating emissions from sectors where avoiding emissions is difficult or impossible. Global CCS Institute (2020): CCS crucial for net-zero by 2050, analyzing facilities, policy, and storage. Global CCS Institute (2023): CCS needs massive scaling up to meet climate goals, details regional progress.

The CCUS process involves three main steps:

1. **Capture:** CO_2 is captured from flue gases at power plants or industrial facilities using a variety of methods, such as:
   - **Post-Combustion Capture:** Capturing CO_2 from the exhaust gas after combustion has occurred.

- **Pre-Combustion Capture:** Removing CO_2 from the fuel before combustion.
- **Oxy-Fuel Combustion:** Burning fuel in pure oxygen, producing a flue gas that is primarily CO_2 and water vapor, making CO_2 capture easier.

2. **Utilization:** Captured CO_2 can be used as a feedstock for producing valuable products, such as:
   - **Fuels:** CO_2 can be combined with hydrogen to produce synthetic fuels, such as methane or methanol.
   - **Chemicals:** CO_2 can be used to produce chemicals, such as urea (used in fertilizers) and polymers (used in plastics).
   - **Building Materials:** CO_2 can be used to create building materials, such as concrete and aggregates, offering a way to permanently store carbon.
3. **Storage:** Captured CO_2 that is not utilized can be transported and permanently stored underground in geological formations, such as depleted oil and gas reservoirs, saline aquifers, or unmineable coal seams.

CCUS offers a potential pathway for decarbonizing industries that have inherent process emissions, such as steelmaking and cement production. However, CCUS faces several challenges, including high costs, the need for large-scale infrastructure development (pipelines, storage sites), and the potential for CO_2 leakage from storage sites.

Case Study 1: The Sleipner CCS Project in Norway

Focus: Highlight a Long-Running and Successful CCS Project Demonstrating the Feasibility of Capturing and Storing CO_2 Emissions from Natural Gas Production

The Sleipner Carbon Capture and Storage (CCS) project in Norway is one of the world's longest-running and most successful CCS initiatives. This case study explores how Equinor has been capturing and storing $CO_2$from the Sleipner natural gas field in the North Sea since 1996, preventing over one million tons of CO_2 from entering the atmosphere annually. It highlights the geological factors that make the Sleipner site suitable for CO_2 storage, the cost-effectiveness of CCS in the context of natural gas production, and the importance of long-term monitoring to ensure the integrity of CO_2 storage sites.

Illustration: How Equinor Captures and Stores CO_2 at Sleipner

The Sleipner CCS Project:
The Sleipner CCS project, operated by Equinor, captures CO_2 from natural gas production at the Sleipner field in the North Sea. The

captured CO_2 is then transported and injected into a deep saline aquifer, the Utsira Formation, located beneath the seabed. This project has been operational since 1996 and has successfully stored over 20 million tons of CO_2 to date.

Preventing CO_2 Emissions:
The Sleipner project captures approximately one million tons of CO_2 annually from the natural gas processing operations. This CO_2 is a byproduct of the natural gas extraction process and would otherwise be released into the atmosphere. By capturing and storing this CO_2, the project significantly reduces greenhouse gas emissions.

Discussion: Geological Factors, Cost-Effectiveness, and Long-Term Monitoring

1. **Geological Factors for CO_2 Storage:**
   The Utsira Formation, where the CO_2 is stored, is a deep saline aquifer with ideal geological characteristics for CO_2 storage. It has a thick, permeable sandstone layer that can hold large volumes of CO_2, and it is capped by an impermeable shale layer that prevents the CO_2 from escaping. These geological factors make the Sleipner site highly suitable for long-term CO_2 storage.
2. **Cost-Effectiveness of CCS in Natural Gas Production:**
   The Sleipner project demonstrates the cost-effectiveness of CCS in the context of natural gas production. By capturing CO_2 at the source, the project avoids the costs associated with retrofitting existing infrastructure. Additionally, the Norwegian carbon tax on offshore oil and gas operations provides a financial incentive for CO_2 capture and storage, making the project economically viable.
3. **Importance of Long-Term Monitoring:**
   Long-term monitoring is crucial to ensure the integrity and safety of CO_2 storage sites. At Sleipner, a comprehensive monitoring program is in place, including seismic surveys, pressure measurements, and geochemical analysis. These monitoring activities help detect any potential CO_2 leakage and ensure that the stored CO_2 remains securely trapped in the geological formation.

Conclusion

The Sleipner CCS project in Norway is a pioneering example of the feasibility and effectiveness of capturing and storing CO_2 emissions from natural gas production. By preventing over one million tons of CO_2 from entering the atmosphere annually, the project significantly contributes to reducing greenhouse gas emissions.

The geological factors that make the Sleipner site suitable for CO_2 storage, such as the permeable sandstone layer and impermeable shale cap, are critical to the project's success. The cost-effectiveness of CCS in the context of natural gas production is enhanced by financial incentives like the Norwegian carbon tax. Long-term monitoring ensures the integrity and safety of the CO_2 storage site, providing confidence in the project's sustainability.

Understanding the methodologies and strategies employed by the Sleipner CCS project can provide valuable insights for other regions and industries seeking to implement CCS technologies and contribute to global efforts to mitigate climate change.

3.2 *Electrification*

Electrification involves replacing fossil fuel-based processes with electric-powered alternatives, reducing emissions if the electricity is generated from low-carbon sources such as renewables. Electrification offers a promising pathway for decarbonizing certain industrial processes and transportation modes.

Examples of electrification in hard-to-abate sectors include:

- **Electric Arc Furnaces (EAFs) for Steelmaking:** EAFs use electricity to melt scrap steel, offering a lower-emission alternative to traditional blast furnaces that rely on coal.
- **Electric Vehicles (EVs):** EVs are replacing gasoline and diesel vehicles, reducing transportation emissions if the electricity used to charge them comes from clean sources.

Electrification faces challenges related to:

- **Process Suitability:** Not all industrial processes can be easily electrified, as some require high temperatures or specific chemical reactions that are difficult to achieve with electricity.
- **Electricity Grid Capacity and Cleanliness:** Electrification requires access to sufficient electricity generation capacity, and the emissions reductions achieved depend on the carbon intensity of the electricity grid. While electrification offers a pathway to decarbonization, hydrogen is also emerging as a key solution, especially for hard-to-electrify sectors. Green hydrogen, produced via electrolysis using renewable energy, could become cost-competitive by 2030 (IRENA, 2020). Furthermore, renewable hydrogen production costs are projected to decline significantly, further enhancing its competitiveness (Hydrogen Council, 2021).

Case Study 2: The Electrification of Public Transportation in Shenzhen, China

Focus: Showcase the Large-Scale Electrification of a City's Bus Fleet, Demonstrating the Potential for Reducing Emissions from Urban Transportation

Shenzhen, China, has achieved a remarkable milestone by transitioning its entire bus fleet to electric buses, making it the first city in the world to do so. This case study explores how Shenzhen's electrification of its bus fleet has resulted in significant reductions in air pollution and greenhouse gas emissions. It highlights the benefits of electrifying public transportation systems, the need for charging infrastructure investments, and the role of government policies in incentivizing the adoption of electric vehicles.

Illustration: How Shenzhen Transitioned Its Entire Bus Fleet to Electric Buses

1. **The Electrification Journey:**
   Shenzhen began adopting electric buses in 2009 as part of a national electric vehicle demonstration program. By the end of 2017, the city had fully electrified its urban transit fleet, comprising 16,359 electric buses. This transition was supported by strong government policies, substantial subsidies, and coordinated efforts between public and private stakeholders.
2. **Significant Reductions in Air Pollution and Emissions:**
   The electrification of Shenzhen's bus fleet has led to substantial environmental benefits. The city has reduced CO_2 emissions by approximately 1.35 million tons annually and conserved 160,000 tons of coal per year. Additionally, the transition has significantly reduced pollutants such as nitrogen oxides, non-methane hydrocarbons, and particulate matter, improving air quality and public health (C40 Cities, 2016; Murdie, 2023).

Discussion: Benefits, Infrastructure Investments, and Government Policies

1. **Benefits of Electrifying Public Transportation Systems:**

Electrifying public transportation systems offers numerous benefits, including:

- **Reduced Emissions:** Electric buses produce zero tailpipe emissions, significantly reducing greenhouse gas emissions and improving air quality.
- **Lower Operating Costs:** Electric buses have lower operating and maintenance costs compared to diesel buses, resulting in long-term cost savings.
- **Enhanced Public Health:** Reduced air pollution leads to improved public health outcomes, decreasing respiratory and cardiovascular diseases (Berlin et al., 2020; Holland et al., 2021).

- **Need for Charging Infrastructure Investments:**
- The successful deployment of electric buses requires substantial investments in charging infrastructure. Shenzhen has built more than 500 bus charging stations and 5,100 bus charging points to support its electric bus fleet. These investments ensure that buses can be charged efficiently and reliably, minimizing downtime and maximizing operational efficiency (Cahyaani, 2020; IAA Mobility, 2023).
- **Role of Government Policies in Incentivizing the Adoption of Electric Vehicles:**

These include:

- **Subsidies:** Both national and local governments provided substantial subsidies to offset the high upfront costs of electric buses.
- **Regulatory Support:** Policies mandating the electrification of public transportation and supporting infrastructure development facilitated the transition.
- **Public–Private Partnerships:** Collaboration between government agencies, bus operators, and manufacturers ensured the successful implementation of the electrification project.

Conclusion

The electrification of Shenzhen's bus fleet demonstrates the significant potential for reducing emissions from urban transportation through the adoption of electric vehicles. By transitioning its entire bus fleet to electric buses, Shenzhen has achieved substantial reductions in air pollution and greenhouse gas emissions, improved public health, and set a global example for sustainable urban transportation.

The success of Shenzhen's electrification project highlights the importance of investing in charging infrastructure and the critical role of government policies and incentives in facilitating the adoption of electric vehicles. By providing financial support, regulatory frameworks, and fostering public-private partnerships, governments can accelerate the transition to clean and sustainable transportation systems.

Understanding the methodologies and strategies employed by Shenzhen can provide valuable insights for other cities and regions seeking to electrify their public transportation systems and contribute to global efforts to mitigate climate change.

3.3 Hydrogen

Hydrogen is a versatile energy carrier that can be produced from a variety of sources, including renewable energy, natural gas, and nuclear power. When produced from low-carbon sources, hydrogen offers a promising pathway for decarbonizing hard-to-abate sectors, particularly those where electrification is challenging.

Hydrogen Production:

- **Electrolysis:** Using electricity to split water molecules into hydrogen and oxygen. When renewable electricity is used, this process produces "green" hydrogen with zero emissions.
- **Steam Methane Reforming (SMR) with Carbon Capture:** SMR is a common method for producing hydrogen from natural gas. Adding carbon capture technology to the process can significantly reduce emissions, producing "blue" hydrogen.

Applications in Hard-to-Abate Sectors:

- **Steelmaking:** Hydrogen can be used as a reducing agent to replace coal in the steelmaking process, significantly reducing emissions.
- **Heavy-Duty Transportation:** Hydrogen fuel cells can power heavy-duty trucks, buses, ships, and potentially even aircraft, offering a zero-emission alternative to diesel and jet fuel.
- **Chemicals and Refining:** Hydrogen is already used as a feedstock in many chemical processes, and its use can be expanded with the availability of low-carbon hydrogen.

Challenges for Hydrogen Deployment:

- **Production Costs:** Producing green hydrogen through electrolysis is currently more expensive than producing hydrogen from fossil fuels.
- **Infrastructure Development:** A significant buildout of hydrogen production, storage, and transportation infrastructure is needed to support widespread adoption.
- **Safety Considerations:** Hydrogen is flammable and requires careful handling and storage.

3.4 Process Efficiency Improvements

Improving the efficiency of industrial processes can significantly reduce energy consumption and emissions, even without switching to entirely new technologies.

Examples of process efficiency improvements include:

- **Improving Cement Kiln Efficiency:** Using alternative fuels (e.g., biomass, waste materials), optimizing kiln operations to reduce heat loss,

and adopting new clinker materials can reduce energy consumption and emissions in cement production.
- **Lightweighting Materials:** Designing lighter-weight vehicles, aircraft, and other products using advanced materials can reduce fuel consumption and emissions throughout the product's life cycle.
- **Waste Heat Recovery:** Capturing and reusing waste heat from industrial processes can improve energy efficiency and reduce fuel consumption.

3.5 Circular Economy Approaches

Circular economy principles, which emphasize reducing material consumption, reusing products, and recycling materials, can contribute to decarbonizing hard-to-abate sectors by reducing the demand for energy-intensive production processes. Material Economics (2018) finds circular economy practices could reduce EU industrial emissions by 56% by 2050.

Examples of circular economy solutions include:

- **Steel Recycling:** Recycling steel scrap reduces the need to produce new steel from iron ore, significantly lowering emissions.
- **Cement Alternatives:** Using alternative materials, such as fly ash (a byproduct of coal combustion) or slag (a byproduct of steelmaking), as partial replacements for cement in concrete production can reduce the demand for new cement and lower emissions.
- **Plastic Recycling and Reuse:** Reducing plastic waste through recycling and reuse can lower the demand for new plastic production, which is energy-intensive and relies on fossil fuels as feedstocks.

Case Study 3: The Ellen MacArthur Foundation's Circular Economy for Plastics

Focus: Highlight the Potential for a Circular Economy Approach to Reduce Plastic Waste and Lower Emissions Associated with Plastic Production

The Ellen MacArthur Foundation has been a leading advocate for the circular economy, particularly in the context of plastics. This case study explores the Foundation's efforts to promote a circular economy for plastics, emphasizing the potential to reduce plastic waste and lower emissions associated with plastic production. It highlights how the Foundation is advocating for reducing plastic consumption, reusing packaging, and improving recycling rates to minimize the need for virgin plastic production. It also discusses the challenges of transitioning to a circular economy, the need for collaboration across the plastics value chain, and the potential for circular economy models to create new business opportunities and reduce environmental impacts.

Illustration: How the Ellen MacArthur Foundation is Promoting a Circular Economy for Plastics

1. **The New Plastics Economy Initiative:**
   The Ellen MacArthur Foundation launched the New Plastics Economy initiative to build momentum toward a circular economy for plastics. The initiative brings together key stakeholders, including businesses, governments, and NGOs, to rethink and redesign the future of plastics (Ellen MacArthur Foundation, 2025).
2. **Reducing Plastic Consumption:**
   The Foundation advocates for reducing plastic consumption by encouraging the design of products and packaging that use less plastic. This includes promoting reusable packaging solutions and encouraging businesses to eliminate unnecessary plastic items (Ellen MacArthur Foundation, 2019a).
3. **Reusing Packaging:**
   The Foundation promotes the reuse of packaging as a key strategy to reduce plastic waste. This involves designing packaging that can be reused multiple times, creating systems for collecting and refilling reusable packaging, and encouraging consumers to adopt reusable options (Ellen MacArthur Foundation, 2019a).
4. **Improving Recycling Rates:**
   Improving recycling rates is another critical component of the circular economy for plastics. The Foundation works to enhance recycling infrastructure, promote the use of recycled materials in new products, and support innovations in recycling technologies (Ellen MacArthur Foundation, 2023).

Discussion: Challenges, Collaboration, and Benefits of Circular Economy Models

1. **Challenges of Transitioning to a Circular Economy:**

Transitioning to a circular economy for plastics presents several challenges:

- **Technical Challenges:** Developing and scaling up new materials and recycling technologies.
- **Economic Barriers:** Ensuring that circular economy practices are economically viable and competitive with traditional linear models.
- **Behavioral Change:** Encouraging consumers and businesses to adopt new practices and behaviors that support a circular economy.

(Ellen MacArthur Foundation, 2019b; McKinsey Sustainability, 2016).

2. **Need for Collaboration Across the Plastics Value Chain:**

Achieving a circular economy for plastics requires collaboration across the entire value chain (Ellen MacArthur Foundation, 2023), including:

- **Manufacturers:** Designing products and packaging for reuse and recyclability.
- **Retailers:** Offering and promoting reusable packaging options.
- **Consumers:** Adopting reusable and recyclable products.
- **Governments:** Implementing policies and regulations that support circular economy practices.
- **Potential for Circular Economy Models to Create New Business Opportunities and Reduce Environmental Impacts:**

Circular economy models offer significant potential to create new business opportunities and reduce environmental impacts (Ellen MacArthur Foundation, 2019c). Benefits include:

- **Economic Growth:** New business models, such as product-as-a-service and reverse logistics, can drive economic growth and innovation.
- **Resource Efficiency:** Circular economy practices reduce the need for virgin materials, conserving natural resources and reducing environmental degradation.
- **Emission Reductions:** By minimizing the production of new plastics and enhancing recycling, circular economy models can significantly reduce greenhouse gas emissions.

Conclusion

The Ellen MacArthur Foundation's efforts to promote a circular economy for plastics demonstrate the significant potential for reducing plastic waste and lowering emissions associated with plastic production. By advocating for reducing plastic consumption, reusing packaging, and improving recycling rates, the Foundation is driving a shift toward more sustainable practices in the plastics industry.

Transitioning to a circular economy presents challenges, including technical, economic, and behavioral barriers. However, collaboration across the entire plastics value chain is essential to overcome these challenges and achieve a circular economy. Circular economy models offer substantial benefits, including economic growth, resource efficiency, and emission reductions.

Understanding the methodologies and strategies employed by the Ellen MacArthur Foundation can provide valuable insights for other organizations and stakeholders seeking to adopt circular economy practices and contribute to global efforts to reduce plastic waste and environmental impacts.

4 Investment Opportunities and Challenges

Decarbonizing hard-to-abate sectors presents a significant investment opportunity, with the potential to create new markets, drive innovation, and generate economic growth while addressing the urgent need to reduce emissions. However, scaling up investment in these sectors faces a unique set of challenges.

4.1 *The Investment Landscape*

The investment landscape for decarbonization technologies in hard-to-abate sectors is rapidly evolving, attracting capital from a range of sources, including:

- **Venture Capital and Private Equity:** Early-stage companies developing innovative decarbonization technologies are attracting significant venture capital and private equity investment.
- **Corporate Investment:** Major companies in hard-to-abate sectors are investing in research and development, pilot projects, and partnerships to explore and deploy low-carbon solutions.
- **Government Funding:** Governments are providing grants, subsidies, and other financial incentives to support the development and demonstration of decarbonization technologies.
- **Debt Financing:** Banks and other financial institutions are increasingly providing debt financing for large-scale decarbonization projects, particularly those with proven technologies and strong revenue streams.

The market for decarbonization solutions is expected to grow significantly in the coming years. For example, the global market for CCUS is projected to reach $150 billion by 2030, and the market for green hydrogen is expected to grow to over $2.5 trillion by 2050.

4.2 *Challenges to Scaling Up Investments*

Several key challenges are hindering the large-scale deployment of decarbonization technologies:

- **Technological Maturity:** Many technologies are still in early stages of development, with uncertainties about their performance, scalability, and costs.
- **High Capital Costs:** Decarbonization technologies often require substantial upfront capital investments, making them risky for investors and companies, especially in the absence of strong policy support or a clear carbon price signal.
- **Policy and Regulatory Gaps:** Supportive policies and regulations are essential for creating a level playing field for low-carbon technologies,

incentivizing their adoption, and driving market demand. Key policy needs include:

  - **Carbon Pricing:** Putting a price on carbon emissions creates a financial incentive for companies to reduce their emissions and invest in cleaner technologies.
  - **Technology Incentives:** Providing tax credits, subsidies, or other financial incentives can help to reduce the upfront costs of decarbonization technologies and accelerate their deployment.
  - **Infrastructure Investments:** Investing in infrastructure, such as pipelines for transporting hydrogen or CO_2 and storage facilities for captured carbon, is essential for supporting the large-scale deployment of certain technologies.

- **Infrastructure Constraints:** The deployment of some technologies, such as hydrogen and CCUS, requires significant infrastructure development, which can be costly and time-consuming. For example, building a network of hydrogen pipelines or developing large-scale CO_2 storage facilities requires careful planning, permitting, and community engagement.

5 Conclusion: Innovation for a Net-Zero Future

Decarbonizing hard-to-abate sectors is essential for achieving global climate goals, but it presents a unique set of challenges. These industries require innovative solutions, supportive policies, and substantial investments to overcome technological hurdles, address cost barriers, and create a level playing field for low-carbon alternatives.

The good news is that the pace of innovation in these sectors is accelerating. Breakthrough technologies like CCUS and green hydrogen are gaining traction, electrification is expanding, and process efficiency improvements are yielding significant emissions reductions. Governments, businesses, and investors are increasingly recognizing the economic opportunities and environmental imperative of decarbonizing these industries.

While the challenges are substantial, the transition to a net-zero future is within reach if we act decisively and collaboratively. By fostering innovation, scaling up investments, and implementing smart policies, we can transform hard-to-abate sectors from climate laggards into climate leaders, creating a more sustainable and prosperous world for all.

References

Bataille, C. et al. (2018). A review of technology and policy deep decarbonization pathway options for making energy-intensive industry production consistent with the Paris agreement. *Journal of Cleaner Production, 187*, 960–973. https://www.sciencedirect.com/science/article/pii/S0959652618307686

Bouman, E. A., Lindstad, E., Rialland, A. I., & Strømman, A.H. (2017). State-of-the-art technologies, measures, and potential for reducing GHG emissions from shipping—A review. *Transportation Research Part D: Transport and Environment, 52*, 408–421. https://www.sciencedirect.com/science/article/pii/S1361920916307015

Energy Transitions Commission (ETC). (2018). *Mission possible: Reaching net zero carbon emissions from harder-to-abate sectors by mid-century*. https://www.energy-transitions.org/wp-content/uploads/2020/08/ETC_MissionPossible_FullReport.pdf

ETC. (2020). *Making mission possible: Delivering a net-zero economy. Energy transitions commission*. https://www.energy-transitions.org/publications/making-mission-possible/

Global Carbon Capture and Storage Institute (Global CCS Institute). (2020). *Global status of CCS 2020*. https://www.globalccsinstitute.com/resources/publications-reports-research/global-status-of-ccs-report-2020/

Global CCS Institute. (2023). *Global status of CCS 2023*. https://www.globalccsinstitute.com/resources/publications-reports-research/global-status-of-ccs-2023-executive-summary/

Hydrogen Council. (2021). *Hydrogen* insights: A perspective on hydrogen investment, market development and cost competitiveness. https://hydrogencouncil.com/en/hydrogen-insights-2021/

International Energy Agency (IEA). (2017). *Energy technology perspectives 2017*. https://www.iea.org/reports/energy-technology-perspectives-2017

IEA. (2021). *Net zero by 2050: a roadmap for the global energy sector*. https://www.iea.org/reports/net-zero-by-2050

IEA. (2023a). *World energy outlook 2023*. https://www.iea.org/reports/world-energy-outlook-2023

IEA. (2023b). *Primary chemicals–net zero emissions guide*. https://www.iea.org/reports/primary-chemicals

International Civil Aviation Organisation (ICAO). (2023). *Presentation of 2022 Air Transport Statistical Results*. https://www.icao.int/sustainability/WorldofAirTransport/Documents/ARC_2022_Tables_final_12032024.pdf

International Renewable Energy Agency (IRENA). (2020). "*Green hydrogen cost reduction: Scaling up electrolysers to meet the 1.5^{0}c climate goal*." https://www.irena.org/publications/2020/Dec/Green-hydrogen-cost-reduction

IRENA. (2024). *Decarbonising hard-to-abate sectors with renewables perspectives for the G7*. https://www.irena.org/-/media/Files/IRENA/Agency/Publication/2024/Apr/IRENA_G7_Decarbonising_hard_to_abate_sectors_2024.pdf

Material Economics. (2018). *The circular economy—A powerful force for climate mitigation*. https://materialeconomics.com/node/14

Material Economics. (2019). *Industrial transformation 2050—Pathways to net-zero emissions from EU heavy industry*. https://materialeconomics.com/sites/default/files/2024-06/material-economics-industrial-transformation-2050.pdf

McKinsey. (2023). *Decarbonizing aviation: Executing on net-zero goals*. https://www.mckinsey.com/industries/aerospace-and-defense/our-insights/decarbonizing-aviation-executing-on-net-zero-goals

United Nations Conference on Trade and Development (UNCTAD). (2022). In *Review of Maritime Transport 2022, United Nations Conference on Trade and Development, Geneva*. https://unctad.org/rmt2022

United States Department of Energy (U.S. DOE). (2022). *Industrial decarbonization roadmap*. https://www.energy.gov/sites/default/files/2022-09/Industrial%20Decarbonization%20Roadmap.pdf

Case Reference

Berlin, A., Zhang, X., & Chen Y. (2020). *Electric buses in Shenzhen, China*. https://iea.blob.core.windows.net/assets/db408b53-276c-47d6-8b05-52e53b1208e1/e-bus-case-study-Shenzhen.pdf

C40 Cities. (2016). *Shenzhen—New energy vehicles* (including electric buses). https://www.c40.org/case-studies/c40-good-practice-guides-shenzhen-new-energy-vehicles-including-electric-buses/

Cahyaani, A. (2020). *Shenzhen's electric mobility. Circle economy foundation. Circle economy*. Accessed 1 January 2024. https://knowledge-hub.circle-economy.com/article/5218

Ellen MacArthur Foundation. (2019a). *Reuse: Rethinking packaging*. https://www.ellenmacarthurfoundation.org/assets/downloads/Reuse.pdf)

Ellen MacArthur Foundation. (2019b). *The circular economy: Challenges and opportunities*. https://www.ellenmacarthurfoundation.org/explore/the-circular-economy-in-detail

Ellen MacArthur Foundation. (2019c). *The circular economy: An economic opportunity*. https://www.ellenmacarthurfoundation.org/explore/the-circular-economy-in-detail

Ellen MacArthur Foundation. (2023). *The global commitment 2023 progress report*. https://www.ellenmacarthurfoundation.org/global-commitment-2023/overview

Ellen MacArthur Foundation. (2025*). New Plastics Economy*. https://www.ellenmacarthurfoundation.org/our-work/activities/new-plastics-economy

Holland, S. P., Mansur, E. T., Muller, N. Z., & Yates, A. J. (2021). The environmental benefits of transportation electrification: Urban buses. *Energy Policy, 148*, 111–921. https://doi.org/10.1016/j.enpol.2020.111921

IAA Mobility. (2023). *Shenzen: The city of green future*. https://www.iaa-mobility.com/en/newsroom/news/sustainability/shenzen-the-city-of-green-future

McKinsey Sustainability. (2016). *The circular economy: moving from theory to practice*. https://www.mckinsey.com/business-functions/sustainability/our-insights/the-circular-economy-moving-from-theory-to-practice

Murdie, M. (2023). *Shenzhen's shift to an electric mobility system. Circle-economy.com*. https://knowledge-hub.circle-economy.com/article/22912

World Bank. (2021). *Electrification of public transport: A case study of the shenzhen bus group*. Accessed 23 January 2025. From https://documents1.worldbank.org/curated/en/708531625052490238/pdf/Electrification-of-Public-Transport-A-Case-Study-of-the-Shenzhen-Bus-Group.pdf

CHAPTER 12

Investing in Nature-Based Solutions and Climate Adaptation: Building Resilience for a Changing World

1 Introduction: Harnessing Nature's Power

Humanity faces an unprecedented challenge: climate change. We've engineered remarkable technological advancements, yet we often overlook a powerful ally in the fight against this global threat—nature itself. Nature is not merely a passive victim of climate change; it's a dynamic force capable of both mitigating climate change and helping us adapt to its inevitable impacts.

Nature-based solutions (NbS) offer a compelling approach to addressing climate change, working in harmony with ecosystems to build resilience and create a more sustainable future. From vast forests that act as carbon sinks to coastal wetlands that buffer storm surges, nature provides a wealth of services that are essential for human well-being and planetary health.

This chapter explores the crucial role of nature-based solutions and climate adaptation in building a more resilient world. We'll delve into the diverse ways nature can help us mitigate climate change and adapt to its impacts, highlighting the importance of investing in these solutions to create a more sustainable and equitable future.

Defining Key Concepts:

- **Nature-Based Solutions (NbS):** Actions to protect, sustainably manage, and restore natural or modified ecosystems that address societal challenges effectively and adaptively, simultaneously providing human well-being and biodiversity benefits. In the context of climate change, NbS focus on harnessing the power of nature to mitigate greenhouse gas emissions (e.g., through carbon sequestration) and adapt to climate impacts (e.g., by reducing flood risks or enhancing water security).

J. Chen, *Climate Finance*,
https://doi.org/10.1007/978-981-96-7975-1_12

- **Climate Adaptation:** The process of adjustment to actual or expected climate change and its effects. Adaptation seeks to moderate harm or exploit beneficial opportunities. It involves making changes to systems, processes, and infrastructure to cope with the impacts of a changing climate, whether they are gradual shifts or extreme events.

The Synergistic Power of NbS and Adaptation:

NbS and climate adaptation are intertwined, often working in concert to create a more holistic and effective approach to addressing climate change. For example, restoring a coastal mangrove forest not only sequesters carbon (mitigation) but also provides a natural barrier against storm surges, reducing flood risks for coastal communities (adaptation).

UNEP (2025) discusses the critical role of nature-based solutions in addressing the climate emergency and promoting biodiversity, highlighting the dual need for protection and sustainable management of natural resources. It emphasizes that by harnessing nature's potential, emissions can significantly decline, supporting global climate goals. Furthermore, the document calls for increased investment in nature-based initiatives, suggesting that greater financial resources could unlock the full benefits of ecosystems as the world transitions toward more sustainable practices. It is estimated that by 2030, nature-based solutions could reduce emissions by **up to 11.7 gigatons** of carbon dioxide equivalent annually, **over 40 percent** of what is needed for limiting global warming. Currently, approximately **US$133 billion** per year is allocated to nature-based solutions, with the majority coming from public funds.

UNEP (2020) conducts economic analyses, suggesting that while NbS can yield significant benefits, they often involve complex trade-offs, diminishing returns, and challenges in valuation, necessitating clear objectives, effective policy frameworks, and adaptive management strategies to maximize their efficacy and societal equity.

Table 1 from UNEP (2020) illustrates how nature-based solutions can be strategically implemented across different systems to yield significant ecological and societal benefits. Each ecosystem presents unique challenges and opportunities, and the report emphasizes that successful NbS leverage natural processes to foster resilience against climate change while promoting biodiversity. This integrated approach can enhance community well-being, boost local economies, and create sustainable environments effectively. By recognizing the interconnectedness of ecosystems and societal needs, stakeholders can better align conservation and development efforts for holistic land management.

Table 1 NbS, ecosystems, and societal benefits

System	Extent of Modification	Nature-based solution	Societal benefit
Forest		Preservation	Carbon sequestration in biomass in vegetation and soils; biodiversity protection; flooding, drought, and erosion protection, recreation and tourism, water infiltration and storage
		Restoration	
		Enhanced management for woodfuel harvest	Carbon sequestration in biomass in vegetation and soils; provision of fuel and forest products to local users; flooding, drought, and erosion protection
		Production	Carbon sequestration in standing biomass and harvested products; sustainable income; water infiltration and storage; reduced pressure on natural forests
Grassland / Savanna		Preservation	Carbon sequestration in biomass in vegetation and soils; biodiversity protection; slope stabilization
		Restoration	
		Grazing management	Carbon sequestration in biomass in vegetation and soils; slope stabilization
Coastal/ riparian		Preservation	Protecting lives and property from storms and flooding; carbon sequestration; enhancement of biodiversity and fisheries production
		Restoration	
		Maintenance of slope vegetation	Reduced erosion and slope stabilization
		Maintenance of coastal, floodplain and riverine vegetation	Protecting lives and property from storms and flooding; carbon sequestration
Agriculture		Agroforestry	Carbon sequestration in soils and biomass; reduced erosion; maintenance of soil fertility; pollinator habitat; storm protection; shading
		Reduce tillage and carbon restoration practices	Carbon sequestration in soils; maintenance of soil fertility
		Agricultural intensification	Enhanced food security; reduced pressure for conversion of other areas.
Urban		Urban forests and green spaces	Carbon sequestration in biomass in vegetation; shading; stormwater disposal and flood protection; recreation
		Green roofs	Cooling; stormwater control; pollution reduction; carbon sequestration

Source UNEP (2020)

2 The Importance of Nature-Based Solutions

Nature's role in regulating the climate and providing essential services for human societies is undeniable. Investing in the protection, restoration, and sustainable management of ecosystems is not just an environmental imperative; it's a strategic investment in our own resilience and well-being. Nature-based solutions (NbS) offer climate mitigation and adaptation benefits while supporting biodiversity (Seddon et al., 2020). The IUCN (2020) Global Standard provides a framework for effective NbS design and implementation.

2.1 Carbon Sequestration

Nature is a master of carbon management. Through photosynthesis, plants and trees absorb carbon dioxide (CO_2) from the atmosphere and store it in their biomass and soils, acting as natural carbon sinks. Protecting and restoring these natural carbon sinks is crucial for mitigating climate change. Griscom et al. (2017) find natural climate solutions (NCS) can provide 37% of needed mitigation by 2030.

- **Forests:** Forests are the Earth's primary terrestrial carbon sinks, playing a vital role in regulating the global carbon cycle. Trees absorb CO_2 as they grow, storing carbon in their wood, leaves, roots, and the surrounding soil. Deforestation, on the other hand, releases stored carbon back into the atmosphere, contributing to climate change. Protecting existing forests, promoting sustainable forestry practices, and restoring degraded forests are essential for maximizing carbon sequestration.
- **Other Ecosystems:** While forests are the most prominent carbon sinks, other ecosystems also contribute significantly to carbon sequestration:
    - **Wetlands:** Wetlands, such as marshes, swamps, and peatlands, store vast amounts of carbon in their waterlogged soils. Protecting and restoring wetlands is crucial for preventing the release of this stored carbon.
    - **Grasslands:** Grasslands store carbon in their soils, although to a lesser extent than forests. Sustainable grazing practices and avoiding the conversion of grasslands to other land uses can help to maintain their carbon storage capacity.
    - **Coastal Ecosystems:** Mangrove forests, seagrass beds, and salt marshes sequester and store significant amounts of carbon, often referred to as "blue carbon." Protecting and restoring these coastal ecosystems is essential for climate change mitigation. Taillardat et al. (2018) suggest blue carbon strategies are most effective for mitigation at a national level.

2.2 *Climate Resilience*

Nature-based solutions not only mitigate climate change by sequestering carbon but also enhance our resilience to the impacts of a changing climate. Healthy, well-functioning ecosystems provide a range of services that protect communities, infrastructure, and economies from climate-related risks.

- **Flood Mitigation:** Natural ecosystems play a vital role in regulating water flows and reducing flood risks:
    - **Forests:** Forests act as natural sponges, absorbing rainfall, slowing runoff, and reducing the peak flow of water into rivers and streams. Deforestation can increase flood risks by reducing the water-holding capacity of landscapes.
    - **Wetlands:** Wetlands act as natural buffers, absorbing excess water during heavy rainfall and releasing it slowly, reducing flood peaks and protecting downstream areas.

  - **Coastal Ecosystems:** Mangrove forests, salt marshes, and seagrass beds provide natural coastal defenses, reducing the impact of storm surges and coastal erosion.
- **Drought Resilience:** Sustainable land management practices that promote healthy soils and vegetation cover can enhance drought resilience:
  - **Agroforestry:** Integrating trees into agricultural landscapes can improve soil health, increase water infiltration, and provide shade for crops, making them more resilient to drought.
  - **Soil Conservation:** Practices such as no-till farming, cover cropping, and contour plowing can reduce soil erosion, improve water retention, and enhance the ability of soils to withstand drought conditions.
- **Heat Island Mitigation:** Urban green spaces, such as parks, street trees, and green roofs, can help to mitigate the urban heat island effect, making cities more livable during heat waves:
  - **Shade and Evapotranspiration:** Trees and other vegetation provide shade and cool the air through evapotranspiration (the process of water evaporating from leaves), reducing temperatures in urban areas.
  - **Reduced Heat Absorption:** Green spaces absorb less heat than concrete and asphalt surfaces, further mitigating the urban heat island effect.
- **Biodiversity Conservation:** Maintaining biodiversity is essential for ecosystem resilience to climate change impacts. Diverse ecosystems are better equipped to adapt to changing conditions, providing a wider range of services that support human well-being.

Case Study 1: Mangrove Restoration in Vietnam

Focus: Showcase the Protective Benefits of Coastal Ecosystems and the Role of Community-Based Mangrove Restoration in Reducing Coastal Erosion and Enhancing Resilience to Storms

Mangrove restoration in Vietnam exemplifies the significant protective benefits of coastal ecosystems and the role of community-based efforts in reducing coastal erosion and enhancing resilience to storms. This case study explores how communities in Vietnam are working to restore degraded mangrove forests, providing natural coastal defenses against typhoons and storm surges, enhancing biodiversity, and providing livelihoods for local people. It highlights the importance of integrating traditional ecological knowledge with scientific approaches in nature-based solutions (NbS) projects, the role of community-based organizations in driving restoration efforts, and the multiple benefits of healthy coastal ecosystems.

Illustration: How Communities in Vietnam are Restoring Mangrove Forests

1. **Community-Based Mangrove Restoration:**
   In Vietnam, community-based organizations and local communities are actively involved in restoring degraded mangrove forests. These efforts include planting mangrove seedlings, protecting existing mangrove areas, and educating local populations about the importance of mangroves for coastal protection and biodiversity.
2. **Providing Natural Coastal Defenses:**
   Mangroves act as natural barriers against coastal erosion, typhoons, and storm surges. Their complex root systems stabilize the shoreline, reduce wave energy, and trap sediments. These protective benefits are crucial for coastal communities in Vietnam, which are frequently affected by extreme weather events.
3. **Enhancing Biodiversity and Providing Livelihoods:**
   Restored mangrove forests enhance biodiversity by providing habitats for various marine and terrestrial species. They also support local livelihoods through sustainable practices such as fishing, aquaculture, and eco-tourism. These activities generate income for communities and promote the sustainable use of natural resources.

Discussion: Integrating Knowledge, Community Engagement, and Benefits of Healthy Coastal Ecosystems

1. **Integrating Traditional Ecological Knowledge with Scientific Approaches:**
   Integrating traditional ecological knowledge with scientific approaches is essential for the success of mangrove restoration projects. Local communities possess valuable knowledge about their environment, which can complement scientific methods and enhance the effectiveness of restoration efforts.
2. **Role of Community-Based Organizations in Driving Restoration Efforts:**
   Community-based organizations play a crucial role in driving mangrove restoration efforts. They mobilize local resources, coordinate planting and protection activities, and engage with stakeholders to ensure the sustainability of restoration projects. Their involvement fosters a sense of ownership and responsibility among community members.
3. **Multiple Benefits of Healthy Coastal Ecosystems:**
   Healthy coastal ecosystems, such as mangrove forests, provide multiple benefits, including:

- **Climate Mitigation:** Mangroves sequester significant amounts of carbon, contributing to climate change mitigation.
- **Biodiversity Conservation:** Mangroves support diverse marine and terrestrial species, enhancing ecosystem resilience.
- **Economic Opportunities:** Sustainable practices associated with mangroves, such as fishing and eco-tourism, generate income for local communities.

Conclusion

Mangrove restoration in Vietnam showcases the significant protective benefits of coastal ecosystems and the crucial role of community-based efforts in reducing coastal erosion and enhancing resilience to storms. By restoring degraded mangrove forests, communities in Vietnam are providing natural coastal defenses, enhancing biodiversity, and supporting local livelihoods.

Integrating traditional ecological knowledge with scientific approaches is essential for the success of nature-based solutions (NbS) projects. Community-based organizations play a vital role in driving restoration efforts, ensuring local ownership and sustainability. Healthy coastal ecosystems offer multiple benefits, including climate mitigation, biodiversity conservation, and economic opportunities.

Understanding the methodologies and strategies employed in mangrove restoration projects can provide valuable insights for other regions and stakeholders seeking to adopt similar approaches and contribute to global efforts to combat climate change and promote sustainable development.

3 Investing in Climate Adaptation

Adapting to the impacts of climate change is no longer a choice; it's a necessity. Investing in climate adaptation measures is crucial for reducing vulnerability, protecting lives and livelihoods, and building a more resilient future.

3.1 Infrastructure Resilience

Climate change poses significant risks to infrastructure, including transportation systems, energy grids, water infrastructure, and buildings. Investing in climate-resilient infrastructure is essential for ensuring the continued functionality of these systems and reducing the economic costs of climate-related damages. OECD (2018) emphasizes the need for climate-resilient infrastructure and aligning financial resources to achieve environmental goals.

- **Climate-Proofing Infrastructure:** New infrastructure should be designed and built to withstand the projected impacts of climate change. This involves incorporating climate projections into engineering designs, using climate-resilient materials, and considering the long-term impacts of sea-level rise, extreme weather events, and temperature extremes.

- **Retrofitting Existing Infrastructure:** Much of the infrastructure already in place is vulnerable to climate change impacts. Retrofitting existing infrastructure to enhance its resilience can involve elevating roads and bridges, strengthening structures to withstand higher wind loads, improving drainage systems to handle increased rainfall, and installing flood barriers to protect coastal communities. Hallegatte et al. (2019) highlight the importance of resilient infrastructure, especially in developing countries, and offer recommendations for enhancing it.

3.2 Water Resource Management

Climate change is altering precipitation patterns, intensifying droughts in some regions and increasing flood risks in others. Adapting to these changes requires a holistic approach to water resource management. Water scarcity, worsened by climate change, threatens economic growth (World Bank, 2016).

- **Water Conservation:** Conserving water resources is essential for reducing vulnerability to drought. This can involve implementing efficient irrigation systems, promoting water-wise landscaping, encouraging water-efficient appliances, and raising awareness about water conservation practices among households and businesses.
- **Water Infrastructure:** Investing in water infrastructure is crucial for ensuring a reliable supply of water in a changing climate. Source water protection offers multifaceted benefits, including improved water quality and climate resilience (Abell et al., 2017). This includes building new dams and reservoirs to store water during periods of abundance, upgrading water treatment plants to handle changing water quality, and developing drought-resistant water supply systems.

Case Study 2: Water Harvesting and Conservation in Rajasthan, India

Focus: Highlight Traditional and Innovative Techniques for Managing Water Resources in Arid and Semi-Arid Regions Facing Increasing Water Scarcity Due to Climate Change

Water scarcity is a significant challenge in Rajasthan, India, one of the driest regions in the country. This case study explores how communities in Rajasthan have revived ancient water harvesting structures, such as johads (earthen dams) and tanks, to capture rainwater and recharge groundwater aquifers. These efforts enhance water security for agriculture and domestic use, demonstrating the potential of blending traditional knowledge with modern technologies in water management. The study highlights the role of community participation in maintaining and managing water resources and the potential for rainwater harvesting to enhance resilience to drought.

Illustration: How Communities in Rajasthan Are Reviving Ancient Water Harvesting Structures

1. **Traditional Water Harvesting Techniques:**
   In Rajasthan, traditional water harvesting structures like johads, baoris (step wells), and tanks have been used for centuries to capture and store rainwater. These structures are designed to collect runoff during the monsoon season, allowing water to percolate into the ground and recharge aquifers. Johads, in particular, are small earthen dams constructed across seasonal streams to capture rainwater (CEEW, 2025).
2. **Enhancing Water Security:**
   Reviving and maintaining these traditional structures has significantly improved water security in Rajasthan. By capturing rainwater and recharging groundwater, these systems provide a reliable source of water for agriculture and domestic use, even during dry periods. This has helped communities withstand droughts and reduce their dependence on external water sources.

Discussion: Integrating Knowledge, Community Participation, and Benefits of Rainwater Harvesting

1. **Integrating Traditional Knowledge with Modern Technologies:**
   Combining traditional ecological knowledge with modern technologies enhances the effectiveness of water management strategies. Traditional methods, such as johads and tanks, are complemented by modern techniques like check dams, contour trenching, and the use of geospatial technologies for mapping and monitoring water resources. This integrated approach ensures sustainable water management practices (International Water Management Institute (IWMI, 2024).
2. **Role of Community Participation in Water Management:**
   Community participation is crucial for the success of water harvesting and conservation efforts. Local communities are involved in the construction, maintenance, and management of water harvesting structures. This participatory approach fosters a sense of ownership and responsibility, ensuring the long-term sustainability of water resources (CEEW, 2025).
3. **Multiple Benefits of Rainwater Harvesting:**
   Rainwater harvesting provides multiple benefits, including:

- **Enhanced Water Security:** By capturing and storing rainwater, communities have a reliable source of water for agriculture and domestic use.

- **Groundwater Recharge:** Water harvesting structures help recharge groundwater aquifers, improving the availability of water during dry periods.
- **Biodiversity Conservation:** Restored water bodies support local biodiversity, providing habitats for various species.
- **Economic Opportunities:** Improved water availability supports agriculture and other livelihoods, contributing to economic development.

Conclusion

Water harvesting and conservation efforts in Rajasthan, India, demonstrate the significant potential of traditional and innovative techniques for managing water resources in arid and semi-arid regions. By reviving ancient water harvesting structures such as johads and tanks, communities in Rajasthan have enhanced water security, improved groundwater recharge, and created economic opportunities.

Integrating traditional ecological knowledge with modern technologies is crucial for effective water management. Community participation plays a vital role in maintaining and managing water resources, ensuring the sustainability of these efforts. Rainwater harvesting provides multiple benefits, including enhanced water security, groundwater recharge, biodiversity conservation, and economic development.

Understanding the methodologies and strategies employed in water harvesting and conservation projects in Rajasthan can provide valuable insights for other regions and stakeholders seeking to adopt similar approaches and enhance resilience to drought and water scarcity.

3.3 Disaster Preparedness and Early Warning Systems

Extreme weather events, such as hurricanes, floods, heat waves, and wildfires, are becoming more frequent and intense due to climate change. Investing in disaster preparedness and early warning systems is crucial for reducing the human and economic costs of these events. UNDRR (2020) provides standardized hazard definitions to support the Sendai Framework, SDGs, and Paris Agreement.

- **Early Warning Systems:** Early warning systems use a combination of monitoring, forecasting, and communication technologies to provide timely alerts about impending hazards. These systems can give communities time to prepare, evacuate if necessary, and take steps to protect their property and livelihoods. Investing in early warning systems for a range of climate-related hazards, such as floods, droughts, heat waves, and storms, is essential for reducing the vulnerability of communities.

- **Disaster Risk Reduction:** Disaster risk reduction encompasses a range of strategies aimed at reducing the potential impacts of disasters. This includes:
    - **Building Codes and Standards:** Implementing building codes that require structures to withstand extreme weather events, such as high winds, heavy rainfall, and seismic activity, can significantly reduce damage and save lives.
    - **Land-Use Planning:** Restricting development in high-risk areas, such as floodplains or wildfire-prone zones, can minimize exposure to hazards.
    - **Community Preparedness Programs:** Educating communities about disaster risks, developing evacuation plans, and conducting drills can help to ensure a more effective response to emergencies.

Case Study 3: The Cyclone Preparedness Program in Bangladesh

Focus: Showcase a Successful Early Warning System and Community-Based Disaster Preparedness Program That Has Significantly Reduced Cyclone-Related Deaths in a Highly Vulnerable Country

The Cyclone Preparedness Program (CPP) in Bangladesh is a highly effective initiative that has significantly reduced cyclone-related deaths through a comprehensive early warning system and community-based disaster preparedness. This case study explores how Bangladesh has developed a comprehensive cyclone preparedness program, including early warning systems, cyclone shelters, evacuation plans, and community-based volunteer networks. It highlights the crucial role of early warning systems in saving lives, the importance of community participation and education in disaster preparedness, and the need for continuous investment in strengthening these systems as climate change intensifies cyclones.

Illustration: How Bangladesh Developed a Comprehensive Cyclone Preparedness Program

1. **The Cyclone Preparedness Program (CPP):**
   The CPP was established in 1972 as a joint initiative between the Government of Bangladesh and the Bangladesh Red Crescent Society (BDRCS). The program aims to minimize the loss of lives and property by strengthening disaster management capacities in coastal areas. It integrates early warning systems, evacuation plans, cyclone shelters, first aid, search and rescue, relief distribution, and rehabilitation activities (BDRCS, 2025).
2. **Early Warning Systems:**
   The CPP operates an extensive telecommunication network with HF and VHF radio sets that link the CPP headquarters with coastal areas. The Bangladesh Meteorological Department (BMD) provides cyclone

forecasts and warnings, which are disseminated through this network to community volunteers. These volunteers then relay the warnings to residents using megaphones, sirens, and other means, ensuring timely evacuation and preparedness.

3. **Cyclone Shelters and Evacuation Plans:**
   The CPP has established numerous cyclone shelters in coastal areas, providing safe refuge for residents during cyclones. These shelters are equipped with basic amenities and are strategically located to ensure accessibility. The program also includes detailed evacuation plans, with volunteers assisting in the transportation of people and livestock to shelters (Relief Web, 2023).
4. **Community-Based Volunteer Networks:**
   The CPP relies on a vast network of approximately 76,020 volunteers who are trained in disaster preparedness and response. These volunteers play a critical role in disseminating warnings, assisting with evacuations, providing first aid, and conducting search and rescue operations. Their local knowledge and presence ensure effective community engagement and response.

Discussion: Early Warning Systems, Community Participation, and Continuous Investment

1. **The Crucial Role of Early Warning Systems in Saving Lives:**
   Early warning systems are essential for reducing the impact of cyclones. Timely and accurate warnings allow communities to evacuate and take necessary precautions, significantly reducing casualties and damage. The CPP's robust early warning system, combined with effective communication channels, ensures that residents receive warnings well in advance of a cyclone's landfall.
2. **Importance of Community Participation and Education in Disaster Preparedness:**
   Community participation and education are vital for the success of disaster preparedness programs. The CPP engages local communities through training and awareness programs, empowering them to take proactive measures during cyclones. Community-based volunteer networks ensure that preparedness efforts are localized and culturally relevant, enhancing their effectiveness.
3. **Need for Continuous Investment in Strengthening Systems:**
   Continuous investment in strengthening early warning systems, infrastructure, and community capacity is essential as climate change intensifies cyclones. This includes upgrading technology, expanding the network of cyclone shelters, and enhancing volunteer training programs. Sustained funding and support from government and international partners are crucial for maintaining and improving these systems (Relief Web, 2023).

Conclusion

The Cyclone Preparedness Program (CPP) in Bangladesh is a successful model of early warning systems and community-based disaster preparedness that has significantly reduced cyclone-related deaths. By integrating early warning systems, cyclone shelters, evacuation plans, and community-based volunteer networks, the CPP ensures effective and timely responses to cyclones.

The crucial role of early warning systems in saving lives cannot be overstated. Community participation and education are essential for developing resilient solutions, while continuous investment in strengthening these systems is necessary to address the increasing intensity of cyclones due to climate change.

Understanding the methodologies and strategies employed by the CPP can provide valuable insights for other regions and stakeholders seeking to enhance disaster preparedness and resilience through comprehensive and community-based approaches.

3.4 Community Resilience

Building community resilience to climate change involves empowering communities to adapt to changing conditions and recover from climate-related shocks.

- **Empowering Communities:** Local communities are on the frontlines of climate change impacts. Engaging them in adaptation planning, decision-making, and project implementation is crucial for ensuring that solutions are tailored to their specific needs and priorities. This includes providing communities with access to information, resources, and training, and supporting community-led initiatives. IIED (2019) proposes a framework for delivering climate finance to local actors, addressing poverty, resource degradation, and climate change.
- **Social Safety Nets:** Social safety nets play a vital role in helping communities cope with the impacts of climate change, particularly for vulnerable populations. This includes:
    - **Insurance Programs:** Insurance can provide financial protection against climate-related losses, such as crop failures, property damage, or business interruption.
    - **Disaster Relief Funds:** Funds can provide immediate assistance to communities affected by disasters, helping to meet basic needs such as food, water, shelter, and medical care.
    - **Social Protection Programs:** Social protection programs, such as cash transfers, food assistance, and employment programs, can help to reduce vulnerability to climate shocks and support livelihoods during times of crisis.

4 Financing Mechanisms for Nature-Based Solutions and Climate Adaptation

Scaling up investments in nature-based solutions and climate adaptation requires a combination of public funding, private investment, and innovative financing mechanisms. GCA (2019) urges leadership for climate resilience across sectors, emphasizing financial systems. IPCC (2022) assesses climate impacts, adaptation, and vulnerabilities across ecosystems and human communities. Deutz et al. (2020) find that $598–824 billion is needed annually by 2030 to address the biodiversity crisis. CPI (2021) reports $632 billion in climate finance for 2019/20, far short of needs, with adaptation finance lagging.

4.1 Public Funding

Governments play a crucial role in providing financial support for NbS and adaptation projects through:

- **Government Grants and Subsidies:** Grants and subsidies can provide direct funding for projects, reducing the financial burden on communities and incentivizing investment in NbS and adaptation. For example, governments can offer subsidies for reforestation projects, grants for farmers to implement soil conservation practices, or funding for coastal communities to restore protective mangrove forests.
- **Public–Private Partnerships:** Public–private partnerships (PPPs) can leverage public funding to attract private investment in NbS and adaptation projects. For example, a government might provide a loan guarantee to a private company investing in a large-scale reforestation project, reducing the risk for the private investor, and encouraging greater participation.

4.2 Private Investment

The private sector is playing an increasingly important role in financing NbS and adaptation, driven by both financial returns and a growing recognition of the risks and opportunities associated with climate change.

- **Impact Investing:** Impact investors seek to generate both financial returns and measurable positive social or environmental impact. NbS and adaptation projects offer attractive opportunities for impact investors, as they can provide quantifiable benefits, such as carbon sequestration, flood risk reduction, or improved water security.
- **Green Bonds:** Green bonds are debt securities issued to raise capital specifically for projects with environmental benefits, including NbS and

adaptation initiatives. The green bond market has grown rapidly in recent years, providing a significant source of funding for projects such as reforestation, sustainable agriculture, and climate-resilient infrastructure.

- **Corporate Sustainability Investments:** Companies are increasingly recognizing that investing in NbS and adaptation can benefit their operations, supply chains, and reputation. For example, a company that sources raw materials from agricultural regions might invest in water conservation projects or drought-resistant crops to ensure the long-term viability of its supply chain.

4.3 Innovative Financing Mechanisms

A range of innovative financing mechanisms are being developed to unlock new sources of funding for NbS and adaptation.

- **Carbon Markets:** Carbon markets, such as emissions trading schemes or carbon offset programs, can provide financial incentives for projects that reduce greenhouse gas emissions or sequester carbon. For example, companies could purchase carbon credits from reforestation projects to offset their emissions.
- **Insurance and Risk Transfer:** Insurance products and risk transfer mechanisms can help to manage climate risks and incentivize adaptation investments. For example, parametric insurance, which pays out based on predefined weather triggers (e.g., rainfall levels, wind speeds), can provide rapid financial assistance to communities after extreme weather events, helping them to recover more quickly.
- **Blended Finance:** Blended finance structures combine public and private capital to de-risk investments and attract greater private sector participation. For example, a development finance institution might provide a concessional loan to a community-led mangrove restoration project, making the project more financially viable and encouraging private investors to participate.

5 Conclusion: Investing in a Resilient Future

Nature-based solutions and climate adaptation are essential investments in a resilient future. By harnessing the power of nature, adapting our infrastructure and systems to changing climate conditions, and empowering communities to build resilience, we can mitigate the risks of climate change, protect lives and livelihoods, and create a more sustainable world.

Scaling up these investments requires a collaborative effort, engaging governments, businesses, investors, and communities in a shared commitment to building a climate-resilient future. By prioritizing nature-based solutions and climate adaptation, we can not only address the urgent challenges of climate change but also create a more equitable, prosperous, and sustainable world for all.

References

Abell, R. et al. (2017). *Beyond the source: The environmental, economic and community benefits of source water protection*. https://www.nature.org/content/dam/tnc/nature/en/documents/Beyond_The_Source_Full_Report_FinalV4.pdf. Accessed 8 March 2025.

Council on Energy, Environment and Water (CEEW). (2025). Framework for India's Sustainable Agriculture Initiatives. https://www.ceew.in/sustainable-agriculture-initiatives/tarun-bharat-sangh-johad-water-conservation-harvesting-and-revitalisation

Climate Policy Initiative (CPI). (2021). *Global landscape of climate finance 2021*. CPI. https://www.climatepolicyinitiative.org/publication/global-landscape-of-climate-finance-2021/

Deutz, A. et al. (2020). *Financing nature: Closing the global biodiversity financing gap*. From https://www.paulsoninstitute.org/wp-content/uploads/2020/09/FINANCING-NATURE_Full-Report_Final-Version_091520.pdf. Accessed 3 March 2025.

Global Center on Adaptation (GCA). (2019). *Adapt now: A global call for leadership on climate resilience*. https://gca.org/reports/adapt-now-a-global-call-for-leadership-on-climate-resilience/

Griscom, B. W. et al. (2017). Natural climate solutions. *Proceedings of the National Academy of Sciences, 114*(44), 11645–11650. https://www.pnas.org/content/114/44/11645

Hallegatte, S., Rentschler, J., & Rozenberg, J. (2019). *Lifelines: The resilient infrastructure opportunity*. https://openknowledge.worldbank.org/handle/10986/31805

International Institute for Environment and Development (IIED). (2019). *Money where it matters: Designing funds for the frontier*. https://www.iied.org/10199iied. Accessed 8 March 2025.

Intergovernmental Panel on Climate Change (IPCC). (2022). *Climate change 2022: Impacts, adaptation and vulnerability*. https://www.ipcc.ch/report/ar6/wg2/

International Union for Conservation of Nature (IUCN). (2020). *Global standard for nature-based solutions*. https://portals.iucn.org/library/sites/library/files/documents/2020-020-En.pdf

International Water Management Institute (IWMI). (2024). The gender dynamics, community strategies, and vulnerabilities in South Punjab's hill torrent floods. https://www.iwmi.org/blogs/rising-above-the-torrents/

Organisation for Economic Co-operation and Development (OECD). (2018). *Climate-resilient infrastructure*. https://www.oecd.org/environment/cc/policy-perspectives-climate-resilient-infrastructure.pdf

Seddon, N. et al. (2020). Understanding the value and limits of nature-based solutions to climate change and other global challenges. *Philosophical Transactions of the Royal Society B: Biological Sciences, 375*(1794), 20190120. https://doi.org/10.1098/rstb.2019.0120

Taillardat, P., Friess, D. A., & Lupascu, M. (2018). *Mangrove blue carbon strategies for climate change mitigation are most effective at the national scale. Biology Letters, 14*(10). https://doi.org/10.1098/rsbl.2018.0251

United Nations Environment Programme (UNEP). (2020). *The economics of nature-based solutions: Current status and future priorities*. https://www.un.org/sites/un2.un.org/files/2021/04/nature-based-solutions-20110426.pdf

United Nations Office for Disaster Risk Reduction (UNDRR). (2020). Hazard definition and classification review. https://www.undrr.org/media/47681/download?startDownload=20250730

UNEP. (2025). *UNEP and nature-based solutions*. https://www.unep.org/unep-and-nature-based-solutions

World Bank. (2016). *High and dry: Climate change, water, and the economy*. https://www.worldbank.org/en/topic/water/publication/high-and-dry-climate-change-water-and-the-economy

Case References

Bangladesh Red Crescent Society (BDRCS). (2025). *Cyclone preparedness programm* (CPP). https://bdrcs.org/cyclone-preparedness-programm-cpp/

Relief Web. (2023). *Cyclone mocha flash appeal Bangladesh*. https://reliefweb.int/report/bangladesh/cyclone-mocha-flash-appeal-bangladesh-may-december-2023

CHAPTER 13

Innovative Financing Mechanisms for Climate Action: Unlocking Capital for a Sustainable Future

1 Introduction: Bridging the Finance Gap

The world stands at a pivotal moment. The urgency of addressing climate change is undeniable, the scientific evidence is overwhelming, and the costs of inaction are mounting. Yet, a significant obstacle stands in our path: the need for trillions of dollars in investment to transition to a low-carbon and climate-resilient future. While public funding is essential, it's not enough. Unlocking the vast resources of the private sector is crucial for achieving the scale of investment needed to meet this global challenge.

The good news is that the financial world is responding with innovation. A new wave of financing mechanisms is emerging, designed to attract private capital, de-risk investments, and accelerate the flow of funds toward climate solutions. UNFCCC (2021) outlines the framework for climate finance under the UNFCCC, including the goal of USD 100 billion annually by 2025.These innovative approaches go beyond traditional grants and conventional loans, offering creative solutions to mobilize capital, incentivize sustainable practices, and generate both financial returns and positive impact.

This chapter will explore a toolkit of innovative financing mechanisms for climate action, including blended finance, concessional capital, green bonds, sustainability-linked loans, and impact investing. By understanding these mechanisms and their potential applications, we can bridge the financing gap, unlock the capital needed for a sustainable future, and accelerate the transition to a low-carbon and climate-resilient world.

J. Chen, *Climate Finance*,
https://doi.org/10.1007/978-981-96-7975-1_13

2 Blended Finance: Catalyzing Private Investment

Blended finance is a powerful tool for mobilizing private capital for projects that have high social and environmental impact but may face challenges attracting traditional investment due to perceived risks or lower financial returns. It involves strategically using public or philanthropic funds to de-risk projects, improve their risk-return profiles, and create a more attractive investment proposition for private investors.

2.1 *The Concept of Blended Finance*

Convergence (2024) defines blended finance as the following:

> "The use of catalytic capital from public or philanthropic sources to increase private sector investment in developing countries to realize the Sustainable Development Goals (SDGs). Blended finance is a structuring approach, not an investment approach."

Imagine a renewable energy project in a developing country struggling to secure financing from commercial banks due to the perceived risks associated with an emerging market. Or a sustainable agriculture project that offers significant environmental benefits but struggles to generate the high financial returns typically sought by private investors. This is where blended finance comes in.

Blended finance acts as a catalyst, using a combination of public or philanthropic funds and private capital to bridge the financing gap. It's not about replacing private investment but rather about using public or philanthropic funds strategically to unlock larger flows of private capital.

2.2 *Key Features of Blended Finance*

Blended finance structures typically incorporate several key features:

- **Risk Mitigation:** The use of concessional capital, such as grants, guarantees, or concessional loans, from public or philanthropic sources, can help to reduce risks for private investors. For example, a government might provide a loan guarantee for a renewable energy project, ensuring that the private lender will be repaid even if the project faces financial difficulties. OECD (2021) emphasizes risk transfer mechanisms in blended finance for sustainable development.
- **Leverage:** Blended finance aims to leverage small amounts of public or philanthropic funds to attract much larger amounts of private capital. The idea is to use public funds strategically to "crowd in" private investment, maximizing the impact of limited public resources.

- **Catalytic Effect:** Blended finance can play a catalytic role in demonstrating the viability of new markets or technologies, building investor confidence, and paving the way for greater private sector participation in the future. By proving the concept and mitigating initial risks, blended finance can help to create a pipeline of bankable projects that can attract commercial investment.

2.3 Structures of Blended Finance

According to Convergence,[1] the global network for blended finance, there are four major structures of blended finance. Convergence (2021) analyzes the blended finance market and scaling opportunities (Fig. 1).

The above chart outlines four key structures of blended finance, each designed to leverage capital in unique ways to enhance investment in climate-related projects. Besides the normal commercial debt/equity structure,

1. **Concessional Capital**
   - **Description**: This structure involves contributions from public or philanthropic investors who provide funding at below-market rates within

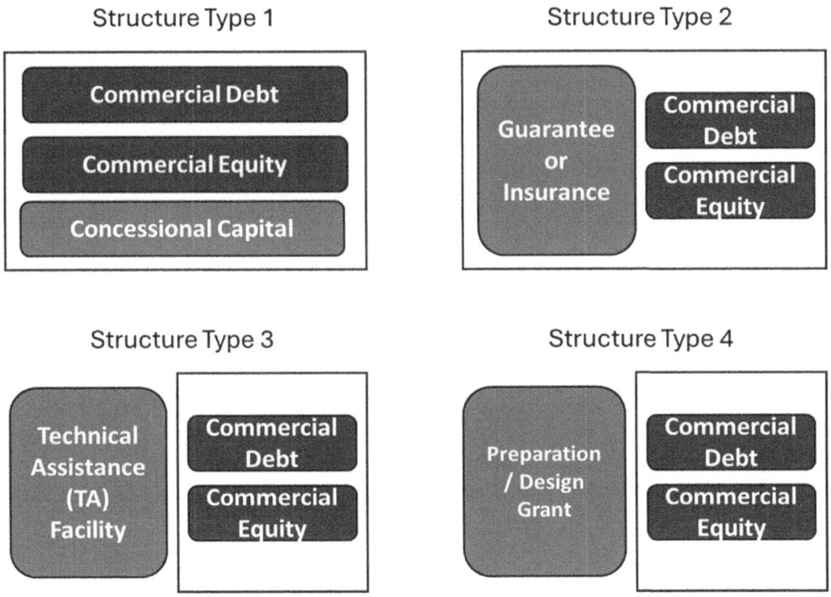

Fig. 1 Four major types of blended finance *Source* Convergence's blended finance primer

[1] Convergence's blended finance primer. https://www.convergence.finance/blended-finance.

the capital structure. Concessional capital refers to the financial deposits made under favorable terms to encourage private investment.
- **Purpose**: It offers an additional layer of protection by providing financial incentives or risk mitigation for private investors, thereby lowering their investment risks and promoting greater participation in climate financing, making them more attractive to private investors. This support encourages private investment by improving the financial viability of the projects.

2. **Guarantee/Insurance**
- **Description**: In this structure, public or philanthropic investors provide credit enhancements, such as guarantees or insurance on financial instruments at below-market terms.
- **Purpose**: This reduces investment risks for private investors by ensuring that their capital is protected against potential losses. It can help unlock additional private capital by providing reassurance.

3. **Technical Assistance (TA) Facility**
- **Description**: This structure involves a grant-funded technical assistance facility that can be deployed pre- or post-investment.
- **Purpose**: It aims to assist projects in strengthening their commercial viability and developmental impact, providing valuable support beyond just financial investment.

4. **Preparation/Design Grant**
- **Description**: This structure is associated with funding for transaction design or preparation, such as grants for project preparation or design-stage activities.
- **Purpose**: It helps in the early stages of project development, ensuring that projects are well-designed and ready for implementation, which can increase their chances of success in attracting further investment.

These structures represent different strategies within blended finance that can be employed to bridge financing gaps and enhance investment for sustainable development initiatives.

2.4 Current Status of Blended Finance

The Convergence (2024) "State of Blended Finance 2024: Climate Edition" report gives the most recent status of the newly created finance field, and there are the key findings from the report:

1. **Record Growth in Climate-Blended Finance**: The climate-blended finance market rebounded significantly in 2023, achieving its highest annual financing total of **$18.3 billion**, a **120% increase** from the previous year. Climate-related investments accounted for **80%** of the total blended finance market.

2. **Increased Private Sector Participation**: Private sector investment surged by nearly **200%** in 2023, indicating a strong recovery and growing interest in climate initiatives. This shift is largely attributed to improved market conditions and the effectiveness of blended finance structures in attracting institutional investors.
3. **Concessional Capital and Guarantees**: The use of concessional guarantees and risk insurance has increased, demonstrating their effectiveness in mobilizing private capital. These instruments can mobilize **6 to 25 times** more financing compared to traditional debt.
4. **Geographical and Sectoral Disparities**: There are persistent geographical imbalances in funding, particularly affecting lower-middle-income countries. While **33%** of blended adaptation financing came from private sources, adaptation finance remains underfunded compared to mitigation efforts.
5. **Focus on Gender-Responsive Climate Finance**: The share of gender-responsive climate-blended deals increased to **22%** in 2023. This suggests a growing recognition of the importance of integrating gender considerations into climate finance.
6. **Challenges in Adaptation Financing**: The report highlights significant barriers to scaling private investment in adaptation projects, with public sector financing still dominating this space. The need for innovative financial instruments and better data transparency is critical for attracting private capital.
7. **Role of Nationally Determined Contributions (NDCs)**: The report emphasizes the importance of aligning blended finance with countries' NDCs, which are crucial for achieving climate goals. Effective integration of blended finance within NDC frameworks can enhance investment opportunities and attract private sector involvement.
8. **Recommendations for Future Action**: The report outlines several strategic recommendations, including:
    - Expanding the use of concessional guarantees and risk insurance.
    - Enhancing support for blended finance in low-income countries.
    - Increasing focus on cross-cutting climate initiatives that address both mitigation and adaptation.
9. **Need for Standardization and Data Transparency**: Greater structural standardization of blended finance deals and improved data transparency are essential for bridging financing gaps and catalyzing transformative change in climate action.
10. **Emerging Market Opportunities**: Emerging Markets and Developing Economies (EMDEs) are seen as critical areas for blended finance, with many countries demonstrating strong commitments to climate action and investment opportunities in renewable energy and sustainable infrastructure.

The report underscores the evolving landscape of climate-blended finance, highlighting both significant progress and ongoing challenges. It calls for enhanced collaboration between public and private sectors, innovative financing solutions, and a focus on gender-responsive initiatives to effectively mobilize capital for climate action.

Case Study 1: The Global Energy Efficiency and Renewable Energy Fund (GEEREF)

Focus: Demonstrate How Blended Finance Can Mobilize Private Investment in Renewable Energy and Energy Efficiency Projects in Emerging Markets

The Global Energy Efficiency and Renewable Energy Fund (GEEREF) is an innovative initiative that uses blended finance to mobilize private investment in renewable energy and energy efficiency projects in emerging markets. This case study explores how GEEREF, managed by the European Investment Bank (EIB), leverages public funds from donor countries and private capital from institutional investors to provide debt and equity financing for renewable energy and energy efficiency projects in developing and transition economies. It highlights the challenges of attracting private investment to emerging markets, the role of concessional capital in de-risking projects, and the impact of GEEREF in scaling up renewable energy and energy efficiency deployments.

Illustration: How GEEREF Mobilizes Investment

1. The GEEREF Structure

   GEEREF is a Fund-of-Funds that invests in specialized renewable energy and energy efficiency private equity funds in emerging markets. Launched in 2008 with funding from the European Union, Germany, and Norway, GEEREF combines public funds with private capital to support small and medium-sized projects. The fund's investments aim to achieve a triple bottom line: providing access to sustainable energy (people), combating climate change (planet), and delivering financial returns (profit) (European Investment Bank (EIB), 2025; GEEREF, 2025).
2. Leveraging Public and Private Capital

   GEEREF uses a blended finance approach to attract private investment by leveraging public funds to de-risk projects. Public funds from donor countries provide the initial capital, which is used to attract private sector investors. This combination of concessional finance and private capital enables GEEREF to offer debt and equity financing for renewable energy and energy efficiency projects, making them more attractive to private investors (European Investment Bank (EIB), 2025; GEEREF, 2025).
3. Impact of GEEREF

By the end of 2021, GEEREF had invested in 14 funds across Africa, Asia, Latin America, and the Caribbean, supporting a total of 188 renewable energy and energy efficiency projects. These projects have provided clean energy access, reduced greenhouse gas emissions, and generated financial returns for investors. GEEREF's investments have contributed to environmental sustainability and economic development in emerging markets (European Investment Bank (EIB), 2021 & 2025).

Discussion: Challenges, Concessional Capital, and Impact

1. **Challenges of Attracting Private Investment to Emerging Markets**

Attracting private investment to renewable energy and energy efficiency projects in emerging markets involves several challenges (Tonkonogy et al., 2018; World Bank, 2021a):

- **Perceived Risks:** Investors often perceive higher risks in emerging markets due to political instability, regulatory uncertainties, and currency fluctuations.
- **Lack of Infrastructure:** Limited infrastructure and access to financing can hinder project development and implementation.
- **Market Barriers:** Emerging markets may lack the regulatory frameworks and market conditions necessary to support large-scale renewable energy projects.
- **Role of Concessional Capital in De-Risking Projects**
- Concessional capital plays a crucial role in de-risking projects and attracting private investment. By providing below-market-rate finance, guarantees, and other risk mitigation instruments, concessional capital can lower the perceived risks and improve the financial viability of projects. This approach helps bridge the gap between public and private sector funding, enabling the scaling up of renewable energy and energy efficiency projects in emerging markets (International Energy Agency, 2025; World Bank, 2021a).
- **Impact of GEEREF in Scaling Up Renewable Energy and Energy Efficiency Deployments**
- GEEREF's blended finance model has successfully mobilized private investment and scaled up renewable energy and energy efficiency deployments in emerging markets. The fund's investments have provided access to sustainable energy, reduced greenhouse gas emissions, and contributed to economic development. By leveraging public funds to attract private capital, GEEREF has demonstrated the effectiveness of blended finance in addressing global climate and energy challenges (European Investment Bank (EIB), 2021, 2025).

Conclusion

The Global Energy Efficiency and Renewable Energy Fund (GEEREF) exemplifies how blended finance can mobilize private investment in renewable energy and energy efficiency projects in emerging markets. By leveraging public funds to de-risk projects and attract private capital, GEEREF has successfully supported the development and implementation of numerous clean energy projects, contributing to environmental sustainability and economic development.

Attracting private investment to emerging markets involves significant challenges, including perceived risks, lack of infrastructure, and market barriers. Concessional capital plays a crucial role in addressing these challenges by providing risk mitigation and improving the financial viability of projects.

Understanding the methodologies and strategies employed by GEEREF can provide valuable insights for other regions and stakeholders seeking to mobilize private investment and scale up renewable energy and energy efficiency deployments through blended finance approaches.

3 Concessional Capital: Unlocking Public Funding

Concessional capital is the most common type of blended finance, and plays a vital role in climate finance, particularly for supporting projects in developing countries that face higher risks and may not be commercially viable without some form of public support. It refers to funding provided on more favorable terms than commercial loans, such as lower interest rates, longer grace periods, or grant components.

Convergence (2024) defines concessional capital as the following:

> "Funds provided on below-market terms within the capital structure of a transaction to reduce the overall cost of capital for the borrower and/or provide additional downside protection to senior investors (e.g., in a first-loss position). Concessional capital can be provided through various instruments, including debt, equity, grants, and mezzanine capital."

3.1 The Role of Concessional Capital

Concessional capital is essential for:

- **Addressing Market Failures:** In many cases, the private sector alone is unable or unwilling to invest in projects that have significant social and environmental benefits but may not generate high financial returns. Concessional capital can help to bridge this gap, addressing market failures and promoting investments that align with broader societal goals.

- **Supporting Early-Stage Technologies:** Emerging climate-friendly technologies often face higher risks and uncertainties, making it difficult to attract private investment. Concessional capital can provide crucial support for demonstration projects, pilot programs, and early-stage deployments, helping to de-risk these technologies and pave the way for commercialization.
- **Promoting Equity and Justice:** Developing countries are often disproportionately impacted by climate change but have limited resources to invest in mitigation and adaptation. Concessional capital can help to level the playing field, providing developing countries with access to the finance they need to address climate change and pursue sustainable development pathways.

3.2 *Sources of Concessional Capital*

The primary sources of concessional capital for climate finance include:

- **Development Finance Institutions (DFIs):** DFIs are specialized financial institutions, often government-backed, that provide financing for development projects in developing countries. Many DFIs have a strong focus on climate change, offering concessional loans, grants, and guarantees to support climate-related projects. Examples of major DFIs include the World Bank, the Asian Development Bank, the African Development Bank, and the European Investment Bank. World Bank (2020) proposes a transformative approach to climate finance, emphasizing maximizing impact through eight levers of climate action.
- **Government Agencies:** Government agencies in developed countries often provide bilateral aid for developing countries, including funding for climate change mitigation and adaptation. For example, the US Agency for International Development (USAID) and the UK's Foreign, Commonwealth & Development Office (FCDO) have dedicated programs for climate finance.

3.3 *Applications of Concessional Capital*

Concessional capital is being used to support a wide range of climate-related activities in developing countries:

- **Renewable Energy:** Financing solar, wind, geothermal, and hydropower projects, particularly in countries with limited access to electricity or high reliance on fossil fuels.

- **Energy Efficiency:** Supporting energy efficiency upgrades in buildings, industries, and transportation systems, helping to reduce energy consumption and emissions.
- **Climate-Smart Agriculture:** Investing in sustainable agricultural practices, such as agroforestry, drought-resistant crops, and water conservation, to enhance food security and build resilience to climate change impacts.
- **Forest Conservation and Restoration:** Supporting projects to protect existing forests, prevent deforestation, and restore degraded landscapes, contributing to carbon sequestration and biodiversity conservation.
- **Climate Adaptation and Resilience:** Funding projects to build climate resilience, such as early warning systems for extreme weather events, flood defenses, drought-resistant infrastructure, and climate-resilient healthcare systems. GCF (2021) analyzes its adaptation portfolio, highlighting private sector engagement and challenges in adaptation planning and outcome measurement.

3.4 *Challenges and Considerations*

While concessional capital is crucial for climate finance, its effective deployment requires careful consideration of several challenges:

- **Limited Availability:** The demand for concessional capital often exceeds the supply, leading to competition for funding and requiring prioritization of projects.
- **Bureaucracy and Conditionality:** Accessing concessional funding can involve complex application processes, strict reporting requirements, and conditions imposed by donors.
- **Sustainability and Ownership:** It's essential to ensure that projects funded with concessional capital are sustainable in the long term and that recipient countries have ownership over the projects, rather than becoming dependent on external aid.
- **Debt Sustainability:** While concessional loans offer more favorable terms than commercial loans, it's crucial to avoid creating unsustainable debt burdens for developing countries.

Navigating these challenges requires collaboration between donor countries, recipient countries, and development finance institutions, ensuring that concessional capital is used strategically, effectively, and equitably to support climate action and sustainable development. The World Economic Forum (WEF, 2020) highlights the growing challenges of economic stagnation and accelerating climate change impacts, compounded by social unrest and widening inequality, demanding urgent collective action.

4 Green Bonds: Tapping the Debt Market

The green bond market has emerged as a powerful force in climate finance, channeling billions of dollars into projects that promote environmental sustainability. These bonds, which function like traditional bonds but are specifically earmarked for green initiatives, offer investors a way to align their portfolios with their sustainability goals while also generating financial returns.

4.1 *The Green Bond Market*

The green bond market has experienced explosive growth in recent years. In 2014, global green bond issuance totaled just $36.6 billion. By 2021, that figure had soared to over $500 billion, demonstrating the surging investor appetite for these sustainable investments. Climate Bonds Initiative (2024a) mentions that sustainable debt reached USD 5.1 trillion by June 2024. This growth is driven by several factors, including:

- **Increased Investor Demand:** Investors, particularly institutional investors like pension funds and insurance companies, are increasingly seeking to incorporate environmental, social, and governance (ESG) factors into their portfolios. Green bonds offer a way to invest in projects with measurable environmental benefits.
- **Corporate Sustainability Commitments:** Companies are increasingly setting ambitious sustainability targets, including commitments to reduce their carbon footprints and transition to cleaner energy sources. Green bonds provide a way for companies to finance these initiatives and demonstrate their commitment to sustainability.
- **Government Support:** Governments are playing a supportive role by issuing sovereign green bonds, developing policy frameworks that encourage green bond issuance, and providing incentives for investors.

4.2 *Types of Green Bonds*

Green bonds come in various forms, catering to different investor preferences and project needs. The two most common types are:

- **Use of Proceeds Bonds:** These bonds are the most prevalent type of green bond. The proceeds from the bond issuance are specifically earmarked for financing eligible green projects, such as renewable energy installations, energy-efficient buildings, sustainable transportation infrastructure, or water management projects. The bond issuer is typically required to provide detailed information about the projects being financed, demonstrating their alignment with recognized green bond standards.

- **Sustainability-Linked Bonds (SLBs):** SLBs link the financial terms of the bond, such as the interest rate, to the issuer's achievement of predefined sustainability performance targets (SPTs). If the issuer fails to meet the SPTs, the interest rate may increase, creating a financial incentive for the issuer to improve its sustainability performance. SPTs can be related to a variety of environmental or social metrics, such as greenhouse gas emissions reductions, water usage efficiency, or improvements in workplace safety.

4.3 Issuance Process and Standards

The issuance process for green bonds typically involves several key steps:

- **Project Selection and Eligibility:** The issuer must identify projects that meet recognized green bond standards and align with the bond's environmental objectives. This involves assessing the environmental benefits of the projects, ensuring that they contribute to climate change mitigation or adaptation, and verifying that they comply with relevant environmental regulations.
- **Independent Verification:** To ensure transparency and credibility, issuers often seek independent verification of the green credentials of their projects. Third-party verifiers, such as specialized environmental consulting firms or certification bodies, assess the projects against established green bond standards and provide assurance to investors that the bonds are genuinely green.
- **Framework Development:** Issuers typically develop a Green Bond Framework, a document that outlines the criteria for project selection, the process for allocating bond proceeds, the metrics for measuring environmental impact, and the reporting requirements for investors.
- **Bond Issuance and Marketing:** The issuer works with investment banks to structure the bond, determine the financial terms, and market the bond to investors.
- **Reporting and Transparency:** Throughout the life of the bond, the issuer is typically required to provide investors with regular reports on the use of proceeds, the progress of the financed projects, and the environmental impact achieved.

Key standards and principles that guide the green bond market include:

- **Green Bond Principles (GBP):** The GBP, developed by the International Capital Market Association (ICMA), are voluntary process guidelines that recommend transparency and disclosure, promoting integrity in the green bond market. ICMA (2021): Green Bond Principles promote transparency and integrity in the green bond market.

- **Climate Bonds Standard:** The Climate Bonds Initiative (CBI) provides a science-based certification scheme for green bonds, ensuring that projects align with climate goals and meet specific sector criteria. The most recent CBI (2024b) updated Standard now includes general-purpose assets and sustainability-linked debt instruments, allowing for broader certification coverage. By establishing rigorous, science-based criteria and providing independent assessments, this certification fosters investor confidence and promotes climate integrity in green finance.
  - The Climate Bonds Standard offers a credible labeling scheme for investments aimed at combating climate change, launched in 2012.
  - More than USD 270 billion of green bonds have been certified since the scheme's inception.
  - The updated Standard includes certification for a wider range of debt instruments, including general-purpose assets and sustainability-linked debt.
  - Certification assesses alignment with published criteria and is validated by independent Climate Bonds Approved Verifiers.
  - Two levels of certification are available: "Aligned" for those meeting climate criteria at certification and "Transition" for those reaching alignment by 2030.
  - Certified investments adhere to the ICMA Green Bond Principles, enhancing credibility and visibility to investors.
  - The scheme aims to drive global financial markets toward climate-consistent investments aligned with the Paris Climate Agreement goals.

4.4 *Current Status of Green Bonds*

The CBI (2024a) "Sustainable Debt Market Summary for H1 2024" highlights significant growth in the issuance of green, social, sustainability, and sustainability-linked (GSS +) bonds, totaling USD 554 billion, a 7% increase from the previous year. Green bonds prominently led this market, contributing 70% of the total aligned volume, while sovereign issuances reached a record of USD 104 billion, indicating heightened governmental engagement in sustainable finance. Notably, Europe dominated aligned GSS + volumes, showcasing its commitment to sustainable investments amid a backdrop of rising global interest rates. The following are the key findings of the report:

- As of June 30, 2024, cumulative GSS + bonds reached USD 5.1 trillion, with H1 2024 alone accounting for USD 554 billion in new issuances.
- The volume of aligned GSS + bonds in H1 2024 marked a 7% increase compared to H1 2023, with green bonds comprising 70% of this figure at USD 385.1 billion.

- Europe was the leading region for GSS + issuances, capturing USD 291.1 billion (53%) of the total aligned volume in H1 2024.
- Sovereign GSS + bonds achieved a record high of USD 104 billion in H1 2024, representing a 12% increase from the previous year.
- Non-financial corporate issuers made a significant contribution to the GSS + market, totaling USD 145.1 billion, led by companies like Pattern Energy.
- Aligned sustainability-linked bonds (SLBs) experienced a sharp decline in issuance, with H1 2024 volume at USD 4.6 billion, down 45% from the previous year.
- The USA emerged as a major contributor to aligned green bond volume, increasing its issuance by 57% year-on-year to USD 47.6 billion.

Case Study 2: The IFC's First Green Bond Issuance

Focus: Highlight a Landmark Green Bond Issuance That Helped to Establish the Market and Demonstrate the Potential for Green Bonds to Mobilize Capital for Sustainable Projects

The International Finance Corporation (IFC), a member of the World Bank Group, issued its first green bond in 2008, marking a significant milestone in the development of the green bond market. This landmark issuance raised $165 million to finance renewable energy and energy efficiency projects in developing countries. This case study explores how the IFC's first green bond helped to establish the market and demonstrate the potential for green bonds to mobilize capital for sustainable projects. It highlights the role of multilateral development banks in pioneering new financial instruments, the importance of developing clear standards and guidelines for green bonds, and the catalytic effect of early issuances in building market confidence.

Illustration: How IFC Issued the First Green Bond

1. **The First Green Bond Issuance:**
   In 2008, the IFC issued its inaugural green bond, raising $165 million to finance renewable energy and energy efficiency projects in developing countries. This issuance was a response to growing investor demand for climate-related investments and aimed to demonstrate the viability of green bonds as a tool for mobilizing capital for sustainable projects. The funds raised were allocated to projects that met specific environmental criteria, ensuring that the proceeds were used to support climate-friendly initiatives (World Bank, 2021b).
2. **Leveraging Concessional Capital and Private Investment:**
   The IFC's green bond issuance combined public funds with private capital to support renewable energy and energy efficiency projects. By providing a fixed-income investment with a clear environmental benefit,

the IFC attracted institutional investors who were interested in sustainable investments. This blended finance approach helped to de-risk the projects and mobilize additional private sector funding, demonstrating the potential for green bonds to attract capital for sustainable development.

3. **Impact of IFC's Green Bond:**
   The issuance of the first green bond by the IFC had a significant impact on the development of the green bond market. It set a precedent for future issuances and established a model for transparency and accountability in the use of proceeds. The success of this issuance demonstrated the financial viability of green bonds and encouraged other issuers to enter the market. As a result, the green bond market has grown rapidly, with annual issuances exceeding $1 trillion by 2023 (World Bank, 2019).

Discussion: Role of Multilateral Development Banks, Standards and Guidelines, and Market Confidence

1. **Role of Multilateral Development Banks in Pioneering New Financial Instruments:**
   Multilateral Development Banks (MDBs) like the IFC play a crucial role in pioneering new financial instruments such as green bonds. By leveraging their financial expertise and credibility, MDBs can de-risk investments and attract private capital to sustainable projects. Their involvement provides assurance to investors about the environmental impact and financial viability of the projects, helping to build market confidence and encourage further investment (Asian Development Bank, 2023; Zucker-Marques & Gallagher, 2023).
2. **Importance of Developing Clear Standards and Guidelines for Green Bonds:**
   The development of clear standards and guidelines for green bonds is essential to ensure transparency, accountability, and credibility in the market. The Green Bond Principles (GBP), coordinated by the International Capital Market Association (ICMA), provide a framework for the issuance of green bonds, including criteria for project eligibility, use of proceeds, and impact reporting. These guidelines help to prevent greenwashing and ensure that green bonds deliver genuine environmental benefits (International Capital Market Association (ICMA) 2021; Ministry of the Environment of Japan, 2022).
3. **Catalytic Effect of Early Issuances in Building Market Confidence:**
   Early issuances of green bonds, such as the IFC's first green bond, have a catalytic effect in building market confidence and encouraging further investment. These early issuances demonstrate the financial viability and environmental impact of green bonds, attracting more

issuers and investors to the market. As the market grows, it becomes more robust and diversified, with a wider range of projects and issuers participating, further enhancing its credibility and impact (World Bank, 2019).

Conclusion

The IFC's first green bond issuance in 2008 marked a significant milestone in the development of the green bond market, demonstrating the potential for green bonds to mobilize capital for sustainable projects. By leveraging concessional capital and private investment, the IFC set a precedent for future issuances and established a model for transparency and accountability in the use of proceeds.

Multilateral development banks play a crucial role in pioneering new financial instruments, providing assurance to investors and building market confidence. The development of clear standards and guidelines for green bonds is essential to ensure their credibility and prevent greenwashing. Early issuances have a catalytic effect, encouraging further investment and contributing to the growth and diversification of the green bond market.

Understanding the methodologies and strategies employed by the IFC in its first green bond issuance can provide valuable insights for other regions and stakeholders seeking to mobilize capital for sustainable projects and support the development of the green bond market.

5 Sustainability-Linked Loans: Incentivizing Sustainability Performance

Sustainability-Linked Loans (SLLs) represent a relatively new and innovative financing mechanism that ties the financial terms of a loan to a borrower's sustainability performance. This creates a direct link between a company's sustainability efforts and its cost of capital, incentivizing companies to improve their environmental, social, and governance (ESG) performance. S&P Global (2021) reports SLLs outpacing green bonds and loans, particularly in the United States, driven by corporate interest in flexible financing tied to sustainability.

5.1 Linking Finance to Sustainability

Imagine a company seeking a loan to expand its operations. Instead of a traditional loan with a fixed interest rate, the company opts for a sustainability-linked loan. The interest rate on the loan is not fixed; it's linked to the company's achievement of predefined sustainability performance targets (SPTs). If the company achieves its targets, it benefits from a lower interest rate, reducing its financing costs. However, if it fails to meet the targets, the interest rate may increase, creating a financial incentive for the company to improve its sustainability performance.

5.2 *Key Features and Benefits*

Key features of SLLs include:

- **Flexibility:** SPTs can be tailored to a wide range of sustainability metrics, allowing companies to focus on areas that are most relevant to their business and industry. Targets might be related to greenhouse gas emissions reductions, energy efficiency improvements, water conservation, waste reduction, or social impact goals.
- **Incentivization:** The financial incentives built into SLLs provide a clear and tangible motivation for companies to improve their ESG performance, going beyond voluntary commitments and linking sustainability to their financial bottom line.
- **Transparency:** SLLs typically require companies to report regularly on their progress toward their SPTs, enhancing transparency and accountability. LMA (2021, 2023) defines SLLP framework, focusing on KPI selection, SPTs, and ESG integration.

5.3 *Challenges and Considerations*

While SLLs offer significant potential for driving sustainability improvements, several challenges and considerations need to be addressed:

- **Setting Ambitious Targets:** It's crucial to ensure that SPTs are ambitious and meaningful, representing a genuine commitment to improving sustainability performance rather than simply reflecting "business-as-usual" practices.
- **Measuring and Reporting:** Developing robust and transparent methodologies for measuring and reporting on sustainability performance is essential for ensuring the credibility of SLLs and avoiding accusations of greenwashing.
- **Greenwashing Concerns:** The potential for greenwashing, where companies make misleading claims about their sustainability performance to secure more favorable loan terms, is a valid concern. Strong verification and reporting standards are needed to mitigate this risk.

The Reorg (2023) report analyzes trends in sustainability-linked loans (SLLs). Key findings include a decline in the overall share of SLLs in the European leveraged loan market, primarily due to a prevalence of amend-and-extend transactions (A&Es) where existing loan terms are recycled. Excluding A&Es, SLLs comprise nearly half the market, consistent with previous years.

The range of margin adjustments for missed ESG targets narrowed, with plus/minus 7.5 bps being most common. Transparency improved with increased reporting requirements, including sustainability reports and external verification. SLLs predominantly focused on environmental KPIs, particularly climate change, while social KPIs related to health and safety also appeared. Notably, governance KPIs were absent. The report also highlights market and regulatory developments aimed at enhancing transparency and standardization in the ESG market, including new standards from the IFRS Foundation and proposed EU regulations. These developments, alongside increasing lender demand for robust ESG reporting, are expected to further shape the SLL market.

Case Study 3: Enel's Sustainability-Linked Revolving Credit Facility

Focus: Illustrate How a Major Utility Company Is Using a Sustainability-Linked Loan (SLL) to Incentivize Its Transition to Renewable Energy and Reduce Its Carbon Footprint

Enel, a multinational energy company, secured a €10 billion sustainability-linked revolving credit facility (SLL) in 2019, with interest rates linked to the company's progress in increasing its renewable energy capacity and reducing its carbon emissions intensity. This case study explores how Enel is using this SLL to incentivize its transition to renewable energy and reduce its carbon footprint. It highlights the role of SLLs in aligning corporate financing with sustainability goals, the challenges of setting ambitious and measurable sustainability performance targets, and the importance of independent verification to ensure transparency and credibility.

Illustration: How Enel Secured the Sustainability-Linked Revolving Credit Facility

1. **The Sustainability-Linked Revolving Credit Facility:**
   In 2019, Enel secured a €10 billion sustainability-linked revolving credit facility, which was later increased to €13.5 billion in 2022. This facility is unique because the interest rates are linked to Enel's performance in achieving specific sustainability targets. These targets include increasing the percentage of renewable energy capacity in Enel's portfolio and reducing the company's carbon emissions intensity. If Enel meets its sustainability targets, it benefits from lower interest rates on the credit facility. Conversely, if it fails to meet these targets, the interest rates increase (Enel Group, 2022 & 2023a).
2. **Leveraging Concessional Capital and Private Investment:**
   The sustainability-linked revolving credit facility (SLL) leverages concessional capital by linking financial terms to Enel's sustainability performance. This innovative financing mechanism incentivizes Enel to achieve its environmental goals, thereby aligning its financial interests with its sustainability objectives. The facility's structure demonstrates

how financial instruments can be designed to promote corporate responsibility and environmental stewardship (Enel Group, 2023b).

3. **Impact of Enel's Sustainability-Linked Loan:**
   Enel's use of the SLL has had a significant impact on its sustainability initiatives. By linking the cost of capital to environmental performance, Enel has a strong financial incentive to increase its renewable energy capacity and reduce carbon emissions. This approach not only supports Enel's transition to a more sustainable energy mix but also sets a precedent for other companies to follow, demonstrating the potential of SLLs to drive corporate sustainability (Enel Group, 2023a & 2023b).

Discussion: Role of SLLs, Setting Sustainability Targets, and Independent Verification

1. **Role of SLLs in Aligning Corporate Financing with Sustainability Goals:**
   Sustainability-linked loans (SLLs) play a crucial role in aligning corporate financing with sustainability goals. By tying financial terms to the achievement of specific environmental, social, and governance (ESG) targets, SLLs incentivize companies to improve their sustainability performance. This alignment helps companies integrate sustainability into their core business strategies and demonstrates their commitment to responsible corporate practices (Enel Group, 2023a; ICMA, 2021).
2. **Challenges of Setting Ambitious and Measurable Sustainability Performance Targets:**
   Setting ambitious and measurable sustainability performance targets is essential for the success of SLLs but presents several challenges (Eikelenboom et al., 2022; Enel Group, 2023a):

- **Defining Clear Metrics:** Companies must define clear, quantifiable metrics that accurately reflect their sustainability goals.
- **Ensuring Feasibility:** Targets must be ambitious yet achievable, considering the company's current capabilities and market conditions.
- **Maintaining Flexibility:** Companies need to adapt targets as circumstances change, ensuring they remain relevant and attainable.

3. **Importance of Independent Verification to Ensure Transparency and Credibility:**
   Independent verification is crucial for ensuring the transparency and credibility of sustainability-linked loans. Third-party verification provides assurance that the company is meeting its sustainability targets and that the reported outcomes are accurate. This process enhances investor confidence and supports the integrity of the SLL market (ICMA, 2021; Sucofindo, 2024).

Conclusion

Enel's €10 billion sustainability-linked revolving credit facility (SLL) exemplifies how major utility companies can use innovative financial instruments to incentivize their transition to renewable energy and reduce their carbon footprint. By linking interest rates to the achievement of specific sustainability targets, Enel has aligned its financial interests with its environmental goals, demonstrating the potential of SLLs to drive corporate sustainability.

SLLs play a crucial role in aligning corporate financing with sustainability goals, but setting ambitious and measurable targets presents challenges. Independent verification is essential for ensuring transparency and credibility, providing assurance to investors and supporting the integrity of the SLL market.

Understanding the methodologies and strategies employed by Enel in securing and utilizing its SLL can provide valuable insights for other companies and stakeholders seeking to leverage financial instruments to support their sustainability initiatives and contribute to global climate goals.

6 Impact Investing: Generating Financial Returns and Measurable Impact

Impact investing represents a growing movement in finance that seeks to generate both financial returns and measurable, beneficial social and environmental impact. Impact investors are intentionally seeking investments that contribute to positive change while also generating a financial profit.

6.1 The Impact Investing Landscape

The impact investing market has grown rapidly in recent years, attracting investors who are seeking to align their portfolios with their values and contribute to a more sustainable and equitable world. A 2020 report by the Global Impact Investing Network (GIIN) estimated that the global impact investing market had reached $715 billion in assets under management, demonstrating the growing interest in this approach to investing.

The "State of the Market 2024" report from the Global Impact Investing Network (GIIN, 2024a) highlights the continued growth and maturation of the impact investing sector, showcasing a compound annual growth rate (CAGR) of 14% in assets under management (AUM) over the past five years. The report discusses significant trends such as the rising popularity of equity-like debt and diversification into public asset classes, despite challenges like fragmented measurement frameworks and regulatory complexities. Additionally, investor satisfaction remains high for both financial performance and impact, although many do not meet their initial targets, signaling a need for improved data-sharing practices and accountability within the industry.

- The impact investing market has experienced a steady growth trajectory, with AUM increasing at a 14% CAGR over the past five years.
- There is a notable rise in equity-like debt and emerging asset classes, reflecting a strategic shift among investors in how they allocate capital.
- Despite high satisfaction rates regarding performance, many investors are not achieving their expected financial or impact returns, highlighting a disconnect between expectations and actual results.
- Fragmentation in impact measurement frameworks poses a significant challenge, with 92% of investors indicating it complicates their ability to compare performance.
- Most impact investors target risk-adjusted, market-rate returns, with 86% reporting their financial investments performing in line with or exceeding expectations.
- The integration of artificial intelligence in investment processes is gaining attention, although 47% of investors have no immediate plans to adopt it.
- Only 62% of investors codify impact metrics into legal documents, indicating a need for stronger accountability measures within impact investing practices.

The report "Sizing the Impact Investing Market 2024" by the Global Impact Investing Network (GIIN, 2024b) reveals that the global impact investing market has reached $1.571 trillion USD, driven by increasing institutional participation and a variety of investors seeking positive social and environmental impact alongside financial returns. The research highlights significant growth trends, particularly among larger organizations, and emphasizes the critical role of government policies that shape investment landscapes. As the urgency for addressing global challenges escalates, the report calls for broader engagement from diverse investors to meet Sustainable Development Goals.

- The impact investing market size is estimated at $1.571 trillion USD, showcasing significant growth over the years.
- The research involved a comprehensive analysis of data from 1,593 organizations to calculate this market size accurately.
- Approximately 59% of the investing organizations in the sample were identified as investment managers, focusing on diverse impact strategies.
- Institutional investors, particularly pension funds, hold substantial influence in the market, representing a growing segment of capital flow.
- Despite growth, the allocation of impact investing in emerging markets remains disproportionately low compared to developed markets.
- The analysis shows that 94% of impact investors reported that their financial and impact performance met or exceeded expectations.

- Continuous educational initiatives and structured frameworks by organizations like GIIN are pivotal for fostering investment growth and engagement.

The GIIN reports collectively underscore the dynamic nature of the impact investing market, highlighting significant growth, diverse participation, and the importance of addressing geographic disparities and measurement challenges. As the sector matures, the focus on aligning financial returns with social and environmental impact will be essential for attracting broader investor engagement and achieving the SDGs.

6.2 Climate-Focused Impact Investing

Climate-focused impact investing is a type of impact investing strategy dedicated to generating positive environmental impacts specifically related to climate change while also yielding financial returns. It encompasses both **mitigation** and **adaptation** efforts aimed at addressing the multifaceted challenges posed by climate change.

- **Mitigation** refers to efforts aimed at reducing or preventing the emission of greenhouse gases. The goal is to limit the severity of climate change by transitioning to a low-carbon economy. Key areas of focus include renewable energy, energy efficiency, sustainable transportation, and sustainable agriculture.
- **Adaptation** involves adjusting practices, processes, and structures to minimize the damage caused by climate change. This may include building climate-resilient infrastructure, developing drought-resistant crops, and enhancing water management systems.

Areas of Investment

A. **Mitigation Investments**

1. **Renewable Energy**: Investments in solar, wind, geothermal, and hydroelectric projects contribute to reducing reliance on fossil fuels. Crowd-funded solar installations and private equity in wind farms are common examples.
2. **Energy Efficiency**: Financing technologies and retrofits that improve energy efficiency in homes, buildings, and industrial plants. This may involve smart grids, LED lighting, and energy management systems.
3. **Sustainable Transportation**: Investments in electric vehicles (EVs), public transportation, and infrastructure supporting non-motorized transport, such as bike lanes. This sector aims to reduce emissions from one of the largest contributors to greenhouse gases, the transportation industry.

4. **Carbon Capture and Storage (CCS)**: Supporting technological developments in capturing carbon emissions from industrial processes or directly from the atmosphere and storing them underground.
5. **Sustainable Agriculture**: Financing practices that promote soil health, reduce fertilizer usage, and improve crop resilience to climate impacts. This includes investments in organic farming, agroforestry, and permaculture.

B. **Adaptation Investments**

1. **Climate-Resilient Infrastructure**: Funding construction of infrastructure that can withstand the effects of climate change, such as rising sea levels, extreme weather, and flooding. Examples include flood defenses, improved drainage systems, and resilient transport networks.
2. **Water Management**: Investments in technologies and projects that improve water conservation, irrigation efficiency, and management of water resources in the face of climate variability.
3. **Disaster Risk Reduction**: Financing projects that enhance community resilience to natural disasters through early warning systems, emergency preparedness, and community-based adaptation strategies.
4. **Ecosystem Restoration**: Supporting the rehabilitation of natural ecosystems (e.g., wetlands, forests, and mangroves) that play crucial roles in climate adaptation, such as providing natural buffers against storms and floods.
5. **Agricultural Adaptation**: Investments in developing climate-resilient crop varieties, promoting sustainable land management practices, and implementing practices to conserve biodiversity.

The Role of Policy and Regulation

Government policies significantly influence climate-focused impact investing. Supportive frameworks, tax incentives, and regulations that favor low-carbon technologies can stimulate investments. Conversely, fossil fuel subsidies and lack of clear regulations may hinder growth in this sector. Policymakers can enhance investments by:

- Creating stable regulatory environments for renewable energy projects.
- Implementing carbon pricing mechanisms to internalize climate costs.
- Encouraging green bonds and other financial instruments to raise capital for climate initiatives.

Climate-focused impact investing is crucial for addressing the global climate crisis through both mitigation and adaptation efforts. By directing capital toward innovative solutions that reduce greenhouse gas emissions and enhance resilience to climate change, investors can play a vital role in creating a sustainable future. Coordinated actions from investors, policymakers, and communities can maximize the impact of these investments, ultimately contributing to a more resilient global economy and environment. As climate challenges evolve, so too must the strategies employed in impact investing to ensure they effectively address the pressing issues at hand.

6.3 Measuring and Managing Impact

A key principle of impact investing is the measurement and management of impact. Impact investors are not only seeking financial returns; they also want to understand the positive social or environmental outcomes that their investments are generating.

Measuring impact involves:

- **Defining Impact Goals:** Clearly articulating the specific social or environmental outcomes that the investment aims to achieve.
- **Developing Metrics:** Identifying appropriate metrics to track progress toward impact goals. For climate-related investments, these metrics might include greenhouse gas emissions reductions, renewable energy generation capacity, or the number of people benefiting from climate adaptation projects.
- **Collecting Data:** Gathering data to track the performance of the investment and its impact on the intended beneficiaries or environmental outcomes.
- **Reporting and Transparency:** Communicating the impact results to investors and stakeholders, providing transparency and accountability.

Challenges in impact measurement include:

- **Attribution:** Determining the extent to which an investment has contributed to a particular outcome, especially when multiple factors may be involved.
- **Additionality:** Ensuring that an investment has led to an outcome that would not have occurred otherwise, demonstrating that the investment has made a real difference.

Despite these challenges, the field of impact measurement is evolving rapidly, with a growing number of frameworks, methodologies, and tools available to support impact investors in tracking and managing the impact of their investments.

Impact investing is a powerful force for mobilizing private capital for climate action, aligning financial returns with positive social and environmental outcomes, and building a more sustainable and equitable world.

7 Conclusion: A Toolkit for Climate Action

The climate crisis demands urgent and ambitious action. Traditional financing approaches alone are insufficient to mobilize the trillions of dollars needed to transition to a low-carbon and climate-resilient future. The good news is that a wave of innovation is sweeping through the financial world, creating a diverse toolkit of financing mechanisms to unlock capital for climate solutions.

This chapter has explored a range of these innovative mechanisms:

- **Blended Finance:** Strategically using public or philanthropic funds to de-risk investments and attract private capital.
- **Concessional Capital:** Providing funding on favorable terms to support climate action in developing countries.
- **Green Bonds:** Tapping the debt market to raise capital specifically for green projects.
- **Sustainability-Linked Loans:** Incentivizing companies to improve their sustainability performance by linking financial terms to ESG targets.
- **Impact Investing:** Generating both financial returns and measurable positive social and environmental impact.

These mechanisms are not mutually exclusive; they can be used in combination to create tailored financing solutions for a wide range of climate-related projects. The key is to understand the strengths and limitations of each mechanism, the contexts in which they are most effective, and the importance of transparency, accountability, and robust impact measurement.

As the climate finance landscape continues to evolve, we can expect to see further innovation in financing mechanisms, driven by the urgency of the climate crisis, the growing recognition of the financial risks and opportunities associated with climate change, and the increasing demand for investments that align with sustainability goals.

The challenge now is to scale up the use of these innovative mechanisms, accelerate the flow of capital toward climate solutions, and build a financial system that supports a just and equitable transition to a sustainable future for all.

References

Climate Bonds Initiative (CBI). (2024a). *Sustainable debt market summary H1 2024*. https://www.climatebonds.net/resources/reports/sustainable-debt-market-summary-h1-2024

CBI. (2024b). *Climate bonds standard V4.2: Expanding standard: Agri-food entity and future asset certification*. https://www.climatebonds.net/climate-bonds-standard-v42

Convergence. (2021). *The state of blended finance 2021*. https://www.convergence.finance/resource/the-state-of-blended-finance-2021/view

Convergence. (2024). *State of blended finance 2024: Climate edition*. https://www.convergence.finance/resource/state-of-blended-finance-2024-climate-edition/view

Green Climate Fund (GCF). (2021). *Adaptation Portfolio & Approach of the GCF | Readiness Knowledge Bank. Readiness Knowledge Bank*. https://knowledge.greenclimate.fund/readiness/research/adaptation-portfolio-and-approach-of-the-gcf/. Accessed 1 January 2025.

Global Impact Investing Network (GIIN). (2020). *2020 Annual impact investor survey. The GIIN*. https://thegiin.org/research/publication/impinv-survey-2020

GIIN. (2024a). "State of the Market 2024: Trends, Performance and Allocations." https://thegiin.org/publication/research/state-of-the-market-2024-trends-performance-and-allocations/

GIIN. (2024b). "Sizing the Impact Investing Market 2024." https://thegiin.org/publication/research/sizing-the-impact-investing-market-2024/

International Capital Market Association (ICMA). (2021). *Green bond principles. International capital market association*. https://www.icmagroup.org/sustainable-finance/the-principles-guidelines-and-handbooks/green-bond-principles-gbp/

Loan Market Association (LMA). (2021). *Sustainability linked loan principles*. https://www.lma.eu.com/application/files/8416/2210/4806/Sustainability_Linked_Loan_Principles.pdf

LMA. (2023). *Sustainability linked loan principles*. https://www.lsta.org/content/sustainability-linked-loan-principles-sllp/

OECD. (2021). *Making blended finance work for sustainable development*. https://www.oecd.org/en/publications/making-blended-finance-work-for-sustainable-development_52138dbb-en.html

Reorg. (2023). *H1 2023 European sustainability-linked bonds wrap*. https://go.reorg-research.com/european-sustainability-linked-bonds-wrap

S&P Global. (2021). *Sustainability-linked loan supply outpaces green bonds and loans amid US surge*. https://www.spglobal.com/marketintelligence/en/news-insights/latest-news-headlines/sustainability-linked-loan-supply-outpaces-green-bonds-and-loans-amid-us-surge-65569374

United Nations Framework Convention on Climate Change (UNFCCC). (2021). *Climate finance in the negotiations*. https://unfccc.int/topics/climate-finance/the-big-picture/climate-finance-in-the-negotiations

World Economic Forum (WEF). (2020). *The global risks report 2020*. https://www.weforum.org/reports/the-global-risks-report-2020

World Bank. (2020). *Transformative climate finance: A new approach for climate finance to achieve low-carbon resilient development in developing countries*. https://openknowledge.worldbank.org/handle/10986/33917

Case References

Asian Development Bank (ADB). (2023). *Greening financial systems and the role of multilateral development banks*. https://www.adb.org/news/events/greening-financial-systems-and-role-multilateral-development-banks

Eikelenboom, M., Stella, C., & Decadri, S. (2022). *Overcoming the challenges to sustainability*. https://www.adlittle.com/en/insights/report/overcoming-challenges-sustainability

Enel Group. (2022). *Sustainability-linked revolving credit facility increased to 13.5 billion euros*. https://www.enel.com/media/explore/search-press-releases/press/2022/05/enel-sustainability-linked-revolving-credit-facility-increased-to-135-billion-euros. Accessed 1 January 2024.

Enel Group. (2023a). *Sustainability report 2023*. https://www.enel.com/content/dam/enel-com/documenti/investitori/sostenibilita/2023/sustainability-report_2023.pdf

Enel Group. (2023b). *Sustainability-linked finance*. https://www.enel.com/investors/investing/sustainable-finance/sustainability-linked-finance

European Investment Bank (EIB). (2021). *Impact report 2021*. https://geeref.com/assets/documents/2021%20GEEREF%20Impact%20Report.pdf. Accessed 1 January 2024.

EIB. (2025). *Global energy efficiency and renewable energy* (GEEREF). https://www.eib.org/en/products/equity/funds/geeref. Accessed 1 January 2024.

Global Energy Efficiency and Renewable Energy Fund (GEEREF). (2025). *About GEEREF*. https://geeref.com. Accessed 1 January 2024.

International Energy Agency (IEA). (2025). *Emerging and developing economy context*. https://www.iea.org/reports/scaling-up-private-finance-for-clean-energy-in-emerging-and-developing-economies/key-findings. Accessed 23 January 2025.

International Capital Market Association (ICMA). (2021). *Guidelines for green, social, sustainability and sustainability—Linked bonds external reviews*. https://www.icmagroup.org/assets/documents/Sustainable-finance/Guidelines-for-GreenSocialSustainability-and-Sustainability-Linked-Bonds-External-Reviews-February-2021-170221.pdf

Ministry of the Environment of Japan. (2022). *Green bond and sustainability-linked bond guidelines*. greenfinanceportal.env.go.jp. https://greenfinanceportal.env.go.jp/en/bond/guideline/guideline.html

Sucofindo. (2024). *The role of third parties in greenhouse gas verification: Reinforcing integrity and credibility of emission reports*. https://www.sucofindo.co.id/en/articles/the-role-of-third-parties-in-greenhouse-gas-verification-reinforcing-integrity-and-credibility-of-emission-reports/. Accessed 1 January 2024.

Tonkonogy, B. et al. (2018). *Blended finance in clean energy: Experiences and opportunities*. Climate Policy Initiative. https://www.convergence.finance/api/file/5308a4a56fa095ac994e393d07b572aa:610f8a04e0569a1650b0fe4e84e9740a73005d00d66f4707af94c44cf0b1de9c79c802f6526e51161d177f1383289e85edce0140c654a176fdec022321a36c955784131f0bf500b95c6c1eab2b763ba30da63d12ff6786382b0392520af3149d57b8ed2a90fe300616fe41cb73a6171e9cc2c0f5ba1aee24617c3c933f6d8fa3bd76c7a76c6d75f8c9c667bdb919866f3670490f61791157aecbe729a90266d2

World Bank. (2019). *10 years of green bonds: Creating the blueprint for sustainability across capital markets*. https://www.worldbank.org/en/news/immersive-story/2019/03/18/10-years-of-green-bonds-creating-the-blueprint-for-sustainability-across-capital-markets. Accessed 23 January 2025.

World Bank. (2021a). *What you need to know about concessional finance for climate action*. https://www.worldbank.org/en/news/feature/2021/09/16/what-you-need-to-know-about-concessional-finance-for-climate-action

World Bank. (2021b). *What you need to know about IFC's green bonds*. https://www.worldbank.org/en/news/feature/2021/12/08/what-you-need-to-know-about-ifc-s-green-bonds. Accessed 23 January 2025.

Zucker-Marques, M., & Gallagher, K. P. (2023). Sustainable future bonds: Boosting multilateral development banks lending and improving the global reserve system. *Global Policy, 15*(1), 166–182. https://doi.org/10.1111/1758-5899.13307

CHAPTER 14

Navigating the Challenges: Greenwashing and Impact Measurement in Climate Finance

1 Introduction: Ensuring Integrity and Accountability

The global momentum behind climate finance is undeniable. Trillions of dollars are flowing into investments aimed at mitigating climate change, transitioning to cleaner energy sources, and building resilience to climate impacts. This surge in climate-aligned capital holds immense promise for creating a more sustainable future. However, alongside this surge come growing concerns about greenwashing—the practice of making misleading or exaggerated claims about environmental benefits—and the need for robust impact measurement to ensure that investments deliver tangible results. Granoff et al. (2024) emphasize the importance of climate solutions investing, including technologies and nature-based solutions, for achieving a net-zero economy.

Maintaining integrity and accountability is paramount for the credibility and effectiveness of climate finance. Without transparency, reliable data, and a commitment to measuring real-world impact, the potential for greenwashing to mislead investors and misallocate capital is significant.

The consequences of failing to address these challenges are severe:

- **Eroding Investor Confidence:** Greenwashing can lead to skepticism and mistrust among investors, making them hesitant to commit capital to climate-related projects and potentially hindering the flow of finance needed to achieve global climate goals.
- **Misallocating Capital:** If investments are not genuinely sustainable or fail to deliver promised environmental and social benefits, capital is diverted away from truly impactful solutions, delaying progress on climate action.

J. Chen, *Climate Finance*,
https://doi.org/10.1007/978-981-96-7975-1_14

- **Damaging Reputations:** Companies and financial institutions engaging in greenwashing risk reputational damage, consumer backlash, and regulatory scrutiny, ultimately undermining their long-term success and sustainability.

This chapter will delve into the challenges of greenwashing and impact measurement in climate finance, providing a framework for understanding these issues, offering practical guidance for identifying and mitigating risks, and highlighting the importance of transparency, accountability, and a commitment to measuring real-world outcomes.

2 Greenwashing: Unmasking Misleading Claims

Greenwashing is a pervasive problem, affecting a wide range of industries and sectors. In the context of climate finance, greenwashing involves making misleading or exaggerated claims about the environmental benefits of investments, projects, or financial products, often with the intention of attracting capital from investors seeking sustainable options.

2.1 Defining Greenwashing

Greenwashing can take many forms, but it generally involves creating a false impression of environmental responsibility. It's about making a company or investment appear more sustainable than it actually is, often through clever marketing, selective disclosure of information, or the use of vague and unsubstantiated claims. UN defines greenwashing as the following[1]:

> "By misleading the public to believe that a company or other entity is doing more to protect the environment than it is, greenwashing promotes false solutions to the climate crisis that distract from and delay concrete and credible action."

Greenwashing involves various deceptive tactics that companies use to mislead consumers about their environmental practices. Here are some common tactics:

1. **Vague Claims**: Companies make broad statements about sustainability without providing specific details or evidence, making it hard for consumers to verify the claims.
2. **Misleading Labels**: Using terms like "green" or "eco-friendly" without standard definitions can confuse consumers, as these labels may not reflect actual environmental benefits.

[1] United Nations. "Greenwashing – the deceptive tactics behind environmental claims". https://www.un.org/en/climatechange/science/climate-issues/greenwashing.

3. **Exaggeration of Impact**: Companies may promote minor improvements as significant achievements or suggest that meeting minimum regulatory standards is a major advancement.
4. **Selective Disclosure**: Highlighting one positive environmental attribute of a product while ignoring other negative impacts, such as pollution from production processes.
5. **Irrelevant Claims**: Companies might claim to avoid illegal practices that do not relate to the product's overall environmental impact, diverting attention from more significant issues.
6. **Isolation of Sustainability Attributes**: Communicating sustainability features of a product without considering the overall environmental impact of the company's operations, such as a garment made from recycled materials produced in a polluting factory.

These tactics undermine genuine sustainability efforts and can mislead consumers, investors, and the public, ultimately hindering effective climate action.

2.2 Types of Greenwashing

In the realm of climate finance, greenwashing can manifest in various ways:

- **Project-Level Greenwashing:** Misrepresenting the environmental benefits of specific climate-related projects. For example, a renewable energy project might be promoted as "carbon neutral" while failing to account for the emissions associated with the manufacturing of solar panels or wind turbines.
- **Corporate Greenwashing:** Making misleading claims about a company's overall sustainability performance or its contributions to climate action. A company might highlight its investments in renewable energy while overlooking its continued reliance on fossil fuels in other parts of its operations.
- **Financial Product Greenwashing:** Exaggerating the environmental credentials of investment funds, green bonds, or other financial products. A fund labeled as "green" or "sustainable" might include investments in companies with significant environmental footprints or a weak track record on climate action.

2.3 Identifying Greenwashing

Identifying greenwashing requires a critical eye and a willingness to look beyond superficial claims. Leveraging AI and data analysis can assist in this process (Thanyawatpornkul, 2024; WEF, 2024). Here are some tips for investors, consumers, and other stakeholders to unmask misleading environmental claims: Gatti et al. (2019) reviewed greenwashing research, finding that voluntary CSR creates grey zones enabling misleading claims.

- **Scrutinize Claims:** Don't take vague or unsubstantiated claims at face value. Look for specific, measurable, and verifiable data to support any environmental claims made by a company or about an investment product. Ask questions about the methodologies used to assess environmental impact, the sources of data, and the assumptions made.
- **Examine the Bigger Picture:** Consider a company's overall environmental footprint, not just a single initiative or product. Look for evidence of a comprehensive and integrated approach to sustainability, addressing all aspects of the company's operations, supply chain, and products.
- **Seek Independent Verification:** Look for third-party certifications or verifications of sustainability claims. Independent audits, certifications from reputable organizations, and ESG ratings from independent agencies can provide more objective assessments of a company's environmental performance. ESMA (2024) found NCAs face resource and data challenges in greenwashing supervision.
- **Use Reputable Resources:** Consult trusted sources of information on corporate sustainability, such as ESG ratings agencies, environmental NGOs, and independent research organizations. Cross-check information from different sources to get a more balanced perspective.

Case Study 1: Investigation into Deutsche Bank's DWS Unit for Greenwashing (2022)

Focus: Highlight Greenwashing Concerns in the Financial Sector, Specifically Focusing on Exaggerated or Misleading Claims about the Sustainability of Investment Funds

The investigation into Deutsche Bank's asset management division, DWS, in 2022, serves as a significant example of greenwashing concerns in the financial sector. This case study explores how DWS faced investigations and regulatory scrutiny for allegedly overstating the sustainability credentials of some of its funds, raising concerns about greenwashing in the ESG (Environmental, Social, and Governance) investing market. It highlights the challenges of defining and measuring "green" or "sustainable" investments, the need for clear and consistent standards, and the role of regulators in preventing greenwashing and protecting investors.

Illustration: How DWS Faced Criticism and Regulatory Scrutiny

1. **Allegations of Greenwashing:**
   In 2022, DWS, a subsidiary of Deutsche Bank, faced allegations of greenwashing when it was accused of overstating the sustainability

credentials of some of its investment funds. Investigations revealed that DWS had invested significant amounts from its so-called "green" funds into fossil fuel companies, while simultaneously marketing these funds as environmentally friendly. This discrepancy raised concerns about the authenticity of DWS's ESG claims (Reuters, 2023; Wehrmann, 2023).

2. **Regulatory Investigations and Legal Actions:**

   The allegations led to investigations by regulatory authorities, including the US Securities and Exchange Commission (SEC) and Germany's financial supervisory authority, BaFin. These investigations focused on whether DWS had misled investors about the sustainability of its funds. The scrutiny resulted in significant management changes at DWS, including the resignation of its CEO (Kowsmann et al., 2021; Reuters, 2022).

3. **Financial and Reputational Consequences:**

   The exposure of DWS's greenwashing practices led to significant financial and reputational consequences. The company faced legal challenges, consumer backlash, and increased scrutiny from regulators and advocacy groups. The controversy damaged DWS's reputation as a leader in sustainable investing and highlighted the risks associated with making misleading environmental claims (Gendre, 2024; Wehrmann, 2023).

Discussion: Challenges of Defining and Measuring Sustainable Investments, Role of Consumer Awareness, and Need for Regulatory Oversight

1. **Challenges of Defining and Measuring "Green" or "Sustainable" Investments:**

   Defining and measuring "green" or "sustainable" investments is challenging due to the lack of standardized criteria and the complexity of ESG factors. The financial sector lacks universally accepted definitions and metrics for sustainability, making it difficult to verify the authenticity of ESG claims. This ambiguity allows for varying interpretations and potential misuse of the "sustainable" label, as seen in the DWS case (International Capital Market Association (ICMA), 2021).

2. **Role of Consumer Awareness and Activism in Holding Companies Accountable:**

   Consumer awareness and activism play a crucial role in holding companies accountable for greenwashing. In the case of DWS, consumer advocacy and investigative journalism brought attention to the discrepancies between the company's marketing claims and actual practices. Increased consumer demand for transparency and genuine sustainability has pressured financial institutions to improve their ESG performance and reporting (Igini, 2022).

3. **Need for Clear and Consistent Standards and Regulatory Oversight:**

Clear and consistent standards for defining and measuring sustainable investments are essential to prevent greenwashing and protect investors. Regulatory oversight plays a critical role in ensuring that financial institutions adhere to these standards and provide accurate and transparent information about their ESG practices. The DWS scandal underscores the importance of robust regulatory frameworks and third-party verification to maintain the integrity of the ESG investing market (International Capital Market Association (ICMA), 2021).

Conclusion

The investigation into Deutsche Bank's DWS unit for greenwashing in 2022 highlights significant concerns about misleading claims in the financial sector regarding the sustainability of investment funds. By overstating the sustainability credentials of its funds, DWS faced severe financial and reputational consequences, including regulatory investigations and legal actions.

The challenges of defining and measuring "green" or "sustainable" investments underscore the need for clear and consistent standards in the financial sector. Consumer awareness and activism play a crucial role in holding companies accountable for greenwashing, while robust regulatory oversight is essential to ensure transparency and protect investors.

Understanding the methodologies and strategies employed in the DWS controversy can provide valuable insights for other financial institutions and stakeholders seeking to promote genuine sustainability efforts and avoid the pitfalls of greenwashing.

3 Impact Measurement: Tracking Real-World Outcomes

Investing in a sustainable future requires more than just good intentions. It demands a commitment to measuring the real-world impact of investments, ensuring that capital is flowing toward solutions that deliver tangible environmental and social benefits. Impact measurement is the process of tracking and quantifying the positive outcomes generated by an investment, going beyond financial returns to assess its contribution to a more sustainable world.

3.1 The Importance of Impact Measurement

Impact measurement is essential for several reasons:

- **Ensuring Accountability:** It holds investors and companies accountable for their claims about the environmental and social benefits of their investments, preventing greenwashing and promoting transparency.

- **Informing Decision-Making:** Impact data can inform investment decisions, helping investors identify projects and companies that are generating the most significant positive impact.
- **Driving Continuous Improvement:** By tracking impact over time, investors and companies can identify areas for improvement, refine their strategies, and maximize the positive outcomes of their investments.
- **Building a Case for Investment:** Demonstrating the positive impact of climate-related investments can help to attract more capital from investors who are seeking both financial returns and social and environmental benefits.

3.2 *Levels of Impact Measurement*

Impact can be measured at different levels, ranging from the immediate outputs of an investment to its broader, long-term outcomes:

- **Output Level:** Measuring the direct outputs of a project or investment. For example, the number of renewable energy installations financed, the hectares of forest restored, or the tons of CO_2 emissions reduced. Output-level metrics are often relatively easy to quantify but may not fully capture the broader impact of the investment.
- **Outcome Level:** Assessing the broader environmental or social outcomes that result from the investment. For example, the improvement in air quality due to reduced emissions, the increased access to clean energy in rural communities, or the enhanced biodiversity resulting from habitat restoration. Outcome-level metrics are more challenging to measure but provide a more comprehensive picture of the impact.

3.3 *Frameworks and Methodologies*

A variety of frameworks and methodologies have been developed to guide impact measurement, providing investors and companies with tools for tracking and reporting on the social and environmental performance of their investments.

Some widely used frameworks include:

- Impact Frontier (2023): Norms for managing investment impact, covering positive/negative effects and investor contribution strategies.
- **Impact Reporting and Investment Standards (IRIS +):** Developed by the Global Impact Investing Network (GIIN), IRIS + provides a common language and standardized metrics for measuring and reporting

on the social, environmental, and financial performance of impact investments. It covers a wide range of sectors and impact themes, including climate change.

- **Global Impact Investing Network (GIIN) Impact Measurement & Management (IMM):** The GIIN's IMM guidance provides a step-by-step framework for impact investors to develop and implement impact measurement and management (IMM) systems. It emphasizes the importance of integrating IMM into all stages of the investment process, from due diligence to portfolio management to reporting.
- **Sustainability Accounting Standards Board (SASB):** SASB standards provide industry-specific guidance for disclosing material sustainability information, including metrics related to climate change impacts. SASB (2023): IFRS Foundation's data privacy and communication subscription policies, especially for sustainability updates. These standards are designed to help companies communicate their sustainability performance to investors in a consistent and comparable way.

3.4 *Challenges of Impact Measurement*

While impact measurement is crucial for climate finance, it's not without its challenges. Accurately and reliably measuring the real-world impact of complex investments, particularly those with long-term horizons, can be difficult.

Key challenges include:

- **Attribution:** Isolating the specific contribution of an investment to a particular outcome can be challenging, especially when multiple factors are at play. For example, if a company reduces its emissions after receiving an investment from a climate fund, it can be difficult to determine the precise extent to which the investment drove those reductions, as opposed to other factors, such as government regulations or changing market conditions.
- **Additionality:** Demonstrating that an investment has led to an outcome that would not have occurred otherwise—known as additionality—is crucial for proving the impact of the investment. For example, if a renewable energy project would have been built regardless of receiving an investment from a climate fund, the fund's impact is questionable.

Data Availability and Quality:

- Collecting accurate and reliable data to track impact can be difficult, especially for long-term outcomes. Data may be scattered across different sources, inconsistent in format, or unreliable in quality.
- **Standardization:** The lack of widely adopted standardized impact metrics and reporting methods can make it challenging to compare the

impact of different investments and assess the overall effectiveness of climate finance.

3.5 *Best Practices for Impact Measurement*

Despite these challenges, effective impact measurement is possible with careful planning, a commitment to transparency, and the adoption of best practices. Here are some key steps that investors and companies can take to improve their impact measurement practices:

- **Define Clear Impact Goals:** Start by clearly articulating the specific social or environmental outcomes that the investment aims to achieve. These goals should be specific, measurable, achievable, relevant, and time-bound (SMART).
- **Select Appropriate Metrics:** Choose metrics that are directly relevant to the intended impact, aligned with industry standards or recognized frameworks (e.g., IRIS +), and feasible to collect. It's important to strike a balance between using standardized metrics that allow for comparison and incorporating metrics that are specific to the context of the investment.
- **Establish Baselines and Counterfactuals:** Defining a baseline against which to measure progress is crucial for understanding the impact of the investment. Consider what would have happened without the investment (the counterfactual scenario) to assess the added value created by the investment.
- **Track and Report:** Collect data regularly, analyze the results, and report transparently on the impact performance of the investment. Make impact data accessible to stakeholders, using clear language, visualizations, and narratives to communicate the findings effectively.
- **Seek Independent Verification:** Engaging third-party organizations to verify impact data and provide assurance to investors and other stakeholders can enhance the credibility and reliability of impact measurement.

Case Study 2: The Acumen Fund's Approach to Impact Measurement

Focus: Highlight a Leading Impact Investing Firm's Approach to Measuring the Social and Environmental Impact of Its Investments, Emphasizing the Importance of a Rigorous and Transparent Methodology

The Acumen Fund, a non-profit impact investing firm, has developed a comprehensive approach to measuring the social and environmental impact of its investments. This case study explores how Acumen uses a rigorous and transparent impact measurement framework that tracks both financial and social returns, incorporating metrics aligned with the United Nations Sustainable Development Goals (SDGs). It highlights the importance of defining clear impact goals, selecting appropriate metrics, collecting reliable data, and communicating impact results transparently.

Illustration: How Acumen Measures the Impact of Its Investments

1. **The Acumen Impact Measurement Framework:**
   Acumen employs a comprehensive impact measurement framework that focuses on three pillars: poverty focus, breadth, and depth. This framework helps Acumen track the social and environmental impact of its investments across various dimensions, ensuring that its portfolio companies deliver meaningful and measurable benefits to underserved communities (Acumen, 2023; Acumen Academy, 2025).
2. **Metrics Aligned with the United Nations Sustainable Development Goals (SDGs):**
   Acumen's impact metrics are aligned with the SDGs, ensuring that its investments contribute to global sustainability goals. For example, metrics related to climate resilience, affordable housing, and SME development are used to assess the impact of investments on specific SDGs. This alignment helps Acumen demonstrate its commitment to addressing pressing global challenges (Acumen, 2023; Acumen Academy, 2025).
3. **Collecting and Analyzing Impact Data:**
   Acumen uses a variety of tools and methodologies to collect and analyze impact data. One of the key approaches is Lean Data, which leverages mobile technology to gather high-quality data directly from customers and beneficiaries. This customer-centric approach ensures that the data collected is relevant, timely, and actionable. Acumen's impact measurement also includes qualitative and quantitative metrics to capture the full range of social and environmental impacts (Acumen, 2023; Field, 2019).

Discussion: Importance of Defining Impact Goals, Selecting Metrics, Collecting Data, and Communicating Results

1. **Importance of Defining Clear Impact Goals:**
   Defining clear impact goals is essential for guiding investment decisions and ensuring that investments align with the organization's mission and values. Acumen sets specific, measurable goals for each investment, focusing on areas such as poverty alleviation, climate resilience, and gender inclusion. These goals provide a clear framework for assessing the impact of investments and tracking progress over time (Acumen, 2023; Acumen Academy, 2025).
2. **Selecting Appropriate Metrics:**

Selecting appropriate metrics is crucial for accurately measuring the impact of investments. Acumen uses standardized metrics, such as those provided by the Impact Reporting and Investment Standards (IRIS), to ensure consistency and comparability across its portfolio. These metrics cover a range of impact areas, including financial inclusion, health, education, and environmental sustainability (Acumen, 2023; Han, 2022).

3. **Collecting Reliable Data:**

   Collecting reliable data is essential for making informed decisions and demonstrating the impact of investments. Acumen's Lean Data approach uses mobile technology to gather data directly from customers, ensuring that the data is accurate and reflects the lived experiences of beneficiaries. This approach allows Acumen to collect data efficiently and cost-effectively, providing valuable insights into the impact of its investments (Acumen, 2023; Acumen Academy, 2025).

4. **Communicating Impact Results Transparently:**

   Transparent communication of impact results is crucial for building trust with stakeholders and demonstrating accountability. Acumen publishes detailed impact reports that provide insights into the social and environmental performance of its portfolio companies. These reports include both quantitative data and qualitative narratives, offering a comprehensive view of the impact achieved (Acumen, 2023; Acumen Academy, 2025).

Conclusion

The Acumen Fund's approach to impact measurement exemplifies the importance of a rigorous and transparent methodology in assessing the social and environmental impact of investments. By using a comprehensive impact measurement framework aligned with the United Nations Sustainable Development Goals (SDGs), Acumen ensures that its investments deliver meaningful and measurable benefits to underserved communities.

Defining clear impact goals, selecting appropriate metrics, collecting reliable data, and communicating impact results transparently are essential components of effective impact measurement. Acumen's use of the Lean Data approach and its commitment to transparency provide valuable insights for other impact investors and stakeholders seeking to measure and report their social and environmental performance effectively.

Understanding the methodologies and strategies employed by Acumen in its impact measurement can provide valuable guidance for other organizations seeking to maximize the impact of their investments and contribute to sustainable development.

4 Ensuring Transparency and Accountability

Transparency and accountability are essential for building trust and confidence in the climate finance system. When investors, policymakers, and the public have access to clear and reliable information about climate-related investments, they can make more informed decisions, hold companies and financial institutions accountable for their actions, and track the effectiveness of climate finance in driving real-world change.

4.1 The Importance of Transparency

Transparency in climate finance serves several crucial purposes:

- **Enabling Informed Decision-Making:** Investors need access to accurate and comparable information about the environmental and social impacts of different investment options to make informed decisions that align with their values and sustainability goals.
- **Building Trust and Credibility:** Transparency helps to build trust between investors, companies, and other stakeholders, fostering a more collaborative and effective climate finance ecosystem.
- **Preventing Greenwashing:** By shining a light on investment practices and environmental performance, transparency makes it more difficult for companies and financial institutions to engage in greenwashing and make misleading claims about their sustainability efforts.
- **Driving Accountability:** Transparency allows stakeholders to hold companies and investors accountable for their climate commitments, their environmental performance, and the impact of their investments. SEC (2022) mandates enhanced ESG disclosures for investment advisors and companies.

4.2 Disclosure Frameworks and Standards

A number of frameworks and standards have emerged to promote transparency in climate-related investments, providing guidance for companies and financial institutions on how to disclose relevant information to investors and other stakeholders.

Key frameworks include:

- **Task Force on Climate-Related Financial Disclosures (TCFD):** The TCFD, established by the Financial Stability Board (FSB), provides recommendations for climate-related financial disclosures, focusing on four key areas: governance, strategy, risk management, and metrics and targets. The TCFD recommendations aim to enhance transparency around climate risks and opportunities, enabling investors to make more informed decisions and promoting a more resilient financial system. TCFD (2023) reports increased climate disclosures but notes challenges in data gathering, especially for asset managers and owners.

- **Sustainability Accounting Standards Board (SASB):** SASB develops industry-specific sustainability accounting standards, including metrics related to climate change impacts. These standards provide guidance for companies on how to disclose material sustainability information that is likely to affect their financial performance, helping investors to assess the ESG risks and opportunities associated with different companies.
- **Global Reporting Initiative (GRI):** The GRI Standards are a widely used framework for sustainability reporting, providing a comprehensive set of guidelines for companies to disclose their economic, environmental, and social performance. The GRI Standards cover a range of topics, including climate change, water management, biodiversity, and human rights. Emerging standards like ISO 14097 (ISO, 2021) provide frameworks for assessing and reporting climate-related investments, further enhancing transparency and enabling informed decision-making. Initiatives such as the Science-Based Targets initiative (SBTi, 2023) are developing criteria to guide financial institutions in setting emission reduction targets aligned with the 1.5 °C goal.

4.3 The Role of Verification and Certification

Third-party verification and certification play a crucial role in enhancing the credibility of sustainability claims and providing assurance to investors and other stakeholders. Independent verification involves an assessment of a company's sustainability performance, a project's environmental impact, or the alignment of a financial product with recognized standards, conducted by a qualified and impartial organization.

Common types of verification and certification include:

- **Green Bond Verification:** Specialized organizations verify that green bonds meet recognized standards, such as the Green Bond Principles (GBP) or the Climate Bonds Standard, providing assurance to investors that the bond proceeds are being used for eligible green projects.
- **ESG Ratings:** ESG rating agencies assess companies' performance on a range of environmental, social, and governance factors, providing scores or rankings that investors can use to evaluate companies' sustainability performance. CDP (2019) found companies identify $970 billion in climate risks and $2.1 trillion in opportunities, but focus narrowly on operational risks.
- **Sustainability Certifications:** Various certification schemes exist to verify the sustainability of products, services, or processes against specific

criteria. For example, the Fair Trade certification ensures that products are sourced ethically and sustainably, while the Forest Stewardship Council (FSC) certification verifies that wood products come from responsibly managed forests.

Verification and certification provide an additional layer of transparency and accountability, giving investors and other stakeholders greater confidence in the sustainability claims made by companies and the environmental benefits of climate-related investments.

Case Study 3: The Development of Sustainability-Linked Loan Principles (SLLP)

Focus: Examine the Development of Industry Guidelines for Sustainability-Linked Loans (SLLs) and the Role of These Principles in Promoting Integrity and Mitigating Greenwashing Risks

The Sustainability-Linked Loan Principles (SLLP) were developed to provide a framework for structuring sustainability-linked loans (SLLs), setting ambitious sustainability performance targets, and ensuring transparency in reporting. This case study explores how leading banks and financial institutions collaborated to create these principles, highlighting their role in promoting integrity and mitigating greenwashing risks in the financial sector.

Illustration: How the SLLP Provide a Framework for SLLs

1. **The Development of the SLLP:**
   The SLLP were developed by an experienced working party consisting of representatives from leading financial institutions active in the global syndicated loan markets. The principles aim to support environmentally and socially sustainable economic activity and growth by providing guidelines that capture the fundamental characteristics of SLLs. The SLLP are voluntary guidelines to be applied by market participants on a deal-by-deal basis, depending on the underlying characteristics of the transaction (LSTA, 2023; Loan Market Association, 2022).
2. **Framework for Structuring SLLs:**

The SLLP provide a comprehensive framework for structuring SLLs, focusing on five core components(Loan Market Association, 2022; LSTA, 2023):

- **Selection of Key Performance Indicators (KPIs):** Borrowers must select relevant and material KPIs that reflect their sustainability performance.
- **Calibration of Sustainability Performance Targets (SPTs):** SPTs must be ambitious and meaningful, tied to the borrower's sustainability strategy.

- **Loan Characteristics:** The loan terms, including interest rates, are linked to the borrower's performance against the SPTs.
- **Reporting:** Borrowers must regularly report on their progress toward achieving the SPTs.
- **Verification:** Independent verification of the borrower's performance against the SPTs is encouraged to ensure transparency and credibility.
- **Impact on Promoting Integrity and Mitigating Greenwashing Risks:**
- The SLLP play a crucial role in promoting integrity and mitigating greenwashing risks by providing clear guidelines for structuring and reporting on SLLs. By setting ambitious SPTs and requiring regular reporting and independent verification, the principles ensure that SLLs genuinely contribute to sustainability goals and are not merely used for marketing purposes. This transparency helps build trust among investors and stakeholders, supporting the growth of the sustainable finance market (FCA, 2023; LSTA, 2023).

Discussion: Importance of Industry Collaboration, Need for Clear Standards, and Benefits of SLLs

1. **Importance of Industry Collaboration in Developing Best Practices:**
   The development of the SLLP highlights the importance of industry collaboration in establishing best practices for sustainable finance. By bringing together leading financial institutions, the working party was able to leverage diverse expertise and perspectives to create a robust framework that addresses the complexities of sustainability-linked lending. This collaborative approach ensures that the principles are widely accepted and implemented across the industry (Loan Market Association, 2022; LSTA, 2023).
2. **Need for Clear Standards to Prevent Greenwashing:**
   Clear and consistent standards are essential to prevent greenwashing and ensure the credibility of sustainability-linked loans. The SLLP provide a structured approach to selecting KPIs, setting SPTs, and reporting progress, which helps prevent the misuse of sustainability claims. By adhering to these standards, borrowers and lenders can demonstrate their commitment to genuine sustainability efforts, enhancing the integrity of the market (FCA, 2023).
3. **Benefits of SLLs in Incentivizing Companies to Improve Sustainability Performance:**
   SLLs incentivize companies to improve their sustainability performance by linking loan terms to the achievement of specific SPTs. This alignment of financial and sustainability goals encourages companies to adopt more sustainable practices and invest in initiatives that reduce their environmental impact. Additionally, SLLs can enhance a company's reputation, attract sustainability-focused investors, and contribute

to long-term financial stability (Loan Market Association, 2022; LSTA, 2023).

Conclusion

The development of the Sustainability-Linked Loan Principles (SLLP) represents a significant step in promoting integrity and mitigating greenwashing risks in the financial sector. By providing a clear framework for structuring SLLs, setting ambitious sustainability performance targets, and ensuring transparency in reporting, the SLLP support environmentally and socially sustainable economic activity.

Industry collaboration was crucial in establishing these best practices, ensuring that the principles are widely accepted and implemented. Clear and consistent standards are essential to prevent greenwashing and maintain the credibility of sustainability-linked loans. The benefits of SLLs include incentivizing companies to improve their sustainability performance, enhancing their reputation, and attracting sustainability-focused investors.

Understanding the methodologies and strategies employed in the development of the SLLP can provide valuable insights for other financial institutions and stakeholders seeking to promote sustainable finance and support the transition to a low-carbon economy.

5 Conclusion: Building a Credible and Effective Climate Finance System

The urgency of the climate crisis demands a rapid and significant increase in climate finance. However, simply pouring money into climate-related projects is not enough. We must ensure that climate finance is being used effectively, transparently, and accountably to drive real-world change and support a just and equitable transition to a sustainable future.

This chapter has highlighted the crucial importance of addressing two major challenges in climate finance: greenwashing and impact measurement. We've explored the various forms that greenwashing can take, the need for investors and consumers to be vigilant in scrutinizing sustainability claims, and the importance of independent verification to ensure credibility. We've also delved into the complexities of impact measurement, the challenges of tracking real-world outcomes, and the best practices for ensuring that investments deliver tangible environmental and social benefits.

Building a credible and effective climate finance system requires a collective effort. Investors, companies, policymakers, and civil society all have a role to play in promoting transparency, demanding accountability, and ensuring that capital is directed toward solutions that truly make a difference.

We must:

- **Advocate for Stronger Disclosure Requirements:** Policymakers should implement mandatory disclosure requirements for climate-related financial risks and opportunities, aligned with robust frameworks like the TCFD recommendations. NGFS (2020) reports increasing adoption of SRI practices by central banks, but challenges remain in data and standardization.
- **Support the Adoption of Robust Standards:** Encourage the widespread adoption of standards and certifications that provide clear guidelines for green investments, such as the Green Bond Principles, the Climate Bonds Standard, and credible ESG rating methodologies.
- **Demand Greater Transparency from Companies and Financial Institutions:** Investors and consumers should demand clear, specific, and verifiable information about the environmental and social impacts of companies and investment products.
- **Encourage the Use of Standardized Impact Measurement Frameworks:** Investors and companies should embrace standardized impact measurement frameworks, such as IRIS + , to track and report on the outcomes of their investments in a consistent and comparable way. UNEP FI (2021) maps climate-related financial risk assessment methodologies, aiding institutions in navigating risk assessment tools.
- **Support the Development of Better Impact Metrics:** Continued research and innovation are needed to develop more robust and reliable impact metrics that capture the complexities of climate change mitigation and adaptation.
- **Hold Investors Accountable for Delivering on Their Impact Promises:** Investors should be held accountable for achieving the social and environmental outcomes they promise, and mechanisms for tracking and reporting on impact should be strengthened.

The growing awareness of the challenges of greenwashing and impact measurement is a positive sign. The momentum behind developing solutions is building. By working together, we can create a climate finance system that is transparent, accountable, and truly effective in driving the transition to a sustainable future.

References

Carbon Disclosure Project (CDP). (2019). *Major risk or rosy opportunity are companies ready for climate change?* https://cdn.cdp.net/cdp-production/cms/reports/documents/000/004/588/original/CDP_Climate_Change_report_2019.pdf. Accessed 1 January 2025.

European Securities and Markets Authority (ESMA). (2024). *Final report on greenwashing response to the European commission's request for input on "greenwashing risks and the supervision of sustainable finance policies."* https://www.esma.europa.eu/sites/default/files/2024-06/ESMA36-287652198-2699_Final_Report_on_Greenwashing.pdf

Gatti, L., Seele, P., & Rademacher, L. (2019). Grey zone in—Greenwash out. A review of greenwashing research and implications for the voluntary-mandatory transition of CSR. *International Journal of Corporate Social Responsibility, 4*(1). https://doi.org/10.1186/s40991-019-0044-9

Granoff, D., Granoff, I., & Rolfe, E. (2024). *Climate solutions investing in review: An analysis of key issues and recommendations for an investment framework*. The GIIN. https://thegiin.org/publication/research/climate-solutions-investing-in-review/. Accessed 1 January 2025.

International Organization for Standardization (ISO). (2021). *Greenhouse gas management and related activitie—Framework including principles and requirements for assessing and reporting investments and financing activities related to climate change*. https://www.iso.org/standard/72433.html

Network for Greening the Financial System (NGFS). (2020). *Network for Greening the Financial System Technical document Progress report on the implementation of sustainable and responsible investment practices in central banks' portfolio management*. https://www.ngfs.net/sites/default/files/medias/documents/sri_progress_report_2020.pdf. . Accessed 1 January 2025.

Sustainability Accounting Standards Board (SASB). (2023). Climate risk—Technical bulletin. https://www.sasb.org/knowledge-hub/climate-risk-technical-bulletin/

Science Based Targets initiative (SBTi). (2023). *Financial institutions near-term criteria version 2.0 pilot test participant terms of reference*. https://sciencebasedtargets.org/resources/files/FI-NT-Criteria-Pilot-Test-Participants-Terms-of-Reference.pdf. Accessed 1 January 2025.

Securities and Exchange Commission (SEC). (2022). *Enhanced disclosures by certain investment advisers and investment companies about environmental, social, and governance investment practices*. https://www.sec.gov/rules-regulations/2022/10/s7-17-22

Task Force on Climate-Related Financial Disclosures (TCFD). (2023). *2023 TCFD status report: Task force on climate-related financial disclosures*. https://www.fsb.org/2023/10/2023-tcfd-status-report-task-force-on-climate-related-financial-disclosures/

Thanyawatpornkul, R. (2024). Harnessing artificial intelligence for sustainable development in emerging markets: Exploring opportunities and challenges in Thailand. *European Journal of Sustainable Development Research, 8*(4). https://doi.org/10.29333/ejosdr/15435

World Economic Forum (WEF). (2024). *AI will accelerate sustainability—But is no silver bullet*. https://www.weforum.org/stories/2024/09/ai-accelerator-sustainability-silver-bullet-sdim/

Case References

Acumen. (2023). *Impact*. https://acumen.org/impact/

Acumen Academy. (2025). *Lean data approaches to measure social impact*. https://acumenacademy.org/course/lean-data-approaches-measure-social-impact. Accessed 1 January 2024.

Field, A. (2019). *Acumen spins off its impact measurement method into a separate startup*. Forbes. https://www.forbes.com/sites/annefield/2019/06/25/acumen-spins-off-its-impact-measurement-method-into-a-separate-startup/

Financial Conduct Authority (FCA). (2023). *FCA outlines concerns about sustainability-linked loans market*. https://www.fca.org.uk/news/news-stories/fca-outlines-concerns-about-sustainability-linked-loans-market

Gendre, I. (2024). *Lessons learned from the "deutsche bank" affair. Greenly*. https://greenly.earth/en-us/blog/ecology-news/greenwashing-what-mistake-did-deutsche-bank-make

Han, E. (2022). *What is impact measurement? Harvard business school online*. https://online.hbs.edu/blog/post/what-is-impact-measurement

Igini, M. (2022). *5 fast-fashion brands called out for greenwashing*. Earth.Org. https://earth.org/fast-fashion-brands-greenwashing/

Impact Frontier. (2023). Norms for Managing Investment Impact. https://impactfrontier.org

International Capital Market Association (ICMA). (2021). *Guidelines for green, social, sustainability and sustainability—Linked bonds external reviews*. https://www.icmagroup.org/assets/documents/Sustainable-finance/Guidelines-for-GreenSocialSustainability-and-Sustainability-Linked-Bonds-External-Reviews-February-2021-170221.pdf

Kowsmann, P., Ramey, C., & Michaels, D. (2021). U.S. authorities probing deutsche bank's DWS over sustainability claims. *Wall Street Journal*.https://www.wsj.com/articles/u-s-authorities-probing-deutsche-banks-dws-over-sustainability-claims-11629923018

Loan Market Association (LMA). (2022). *Sustainability-linked loan principles*. https://www.env.go.jp/content/900495735.pdf

Loan Syndications and Trading Association (LSTA). (2023). *Sustainability linked loan principles (SLLP)*. https://www.lsta.org/content/sustainability-linked-loan-principles-sllp/

Reuters. (2022). *Deutsche bank's DWS sued by consumer group over alleged greenwashing*. Reuters. https://www.reuters.com/business/finance/deutsche-banks-dws-sued-by-consumer-group-over-alleged-greenwashing-2022-10-24/

Reuters. (2023). *Deutsche bank's DWS and allegations of "greenwashing."* https://www.reuters.com/business/finance/deutsche-banks-dws-allegations-greenwashing-2022-06-09/

United Nations Environment Programme Finance Initiative (UNEP FI). (2021). The Climate Risk Landscape: Mapping Climate-related Financial Risk Assessment Methodologies. https://www.unepfi.org/themes/climate-change/the-climate-risk-landscape/

Wehrmann, B. (2023). *Deutsche bank unit DWS faces new greenwashing accusations over fossil fuel investments*. Clean Energy Wire. https://www.cleanenergywire.org/news/deutsche-bank-unit-dws-faces-new-greenwashing-accusations-over-fossil-fuel-investments

PART IV

Climate Finance Tools and Applications: Navigating Risks, Driving Action

The world of climate finance is complex and dynamic, requiring specialized tools, frameworks, and methodologies to assess risks, inform investment decisions, and drive meaningful action. This part delves into the practical applications of climate finance, equipping readers with the knowledge and skills to effectively navigate this evolving landscape.

We'll explore the tools and techniques used to assess both physical and transition risks, providing a comprehensive overview of the climate risk assessment landscape. We'll examine the key disclosure frameworks that are driving transparency and accountability in climate-related investments, offering guidance on how to navigate these standards and communicate climate risks and opportunities effectively. And we'll delve into the strategies and tools used to build climate-aligned investment portfolios, highlighting how investors are integrating climate considerations into their decision-making processes.

Chapter 15: Climate Risk Assessment: Tools, Frameworks, and Applications

This chapter provides a practical guide to climate risk assessment, exploring the diverse tools and frameworks used to quantify and manage the financial risks associated with climate change. We'll examine different types of climate risk assessment tools, their strengths and limitations, and key considerations for selecting and using these tools effectively. We'll also explore emerging trends in climate risk assessment, highlighting the role of technology and data innovation in advancing the field.

Chapter 16: Climate-Related Disclosure: Standards, Best Practices, and Implementation

Transparency and accountability are paramount in climate finance. This chapter focuses on climate-related disclosure, exploring the key frameworks and standards that are driving greater disclosure of climate risks and opportunities. We'll provide a step-by-step guide to implementing climate risk disclosures, discuss the evolving regulatory landscape, and examine best practices for communicating climate-related information effectively to investors and other stakeholders.

Chapter 17: Climate-Aligned Portfolio Management: Strategies and Tools
This chapter explores how investors are integrating climate considerations into their portfolio management decisions. We'll examine the key strategies for building climate-aligned investment portfolios, including approaches to assessing climate risks, identifying investment opportunities in climate solutions, and aligning portfolios with net-zero emissions targets. We'll also discuss the tools and techniques used to manage climate risks and enhance portfolio resilience.

Chapter 18: Challenges of Integrating Climate Considerations
Integrating climate change considerations into financial decision-making is not without its challenges. This chapter examines the key obstacles, including data gaps, model limitations, the complexity of communicating climate risks, and the need for organizational capacity building. We'll explore strategies for navigating these challenges, emphasizing the importance of transparency, collaboration, and a commitment to continuous improvement.

By mastering the tools and strategies presented in this part, readers will be equipped to navigate the complexities of climate finance, make more informed decisions, and contribute to a more sustainable and resilient future.

CHAPTER 15

Climate Risk Assessment: Tools, Frameworks, and Applications

1 Introduction: The Evolving Landscape of Climate Risk Assessment

Climate risk is financial risk. This simple yet profound statement is increasingly resonating across boardrooms, investment committees, and regulatory agencies worldwide. As the impacts of climate change become more evident and the transition to a low-carbon economy accelerates, understanding and managing climate-related financial risks is no longer optional; it's essential for long-term success and sustainability.

Climate risk poses unique challenges that traditional financial risk management approaches are ill-equipped to handle. Unlike conventional financial risks, which tend to be short term and cyclical, climate change impacts unfold over decades and centuries, requiring a longer-term perspective and a more nuanced understanding of complex, interconnected systems. Climate models and projections involve inherent uncertainties, and the financial implications of climate change can manifest in unexpected ways, potentially triggering cascading effects throughout the global economy.

Fortunately, the tools and frameworks for assessing climate risk are rapidly evolving, empowering decision-makers to navigate a changing world and build greater resilience into their strategies and operations. A growing array of sophisticated tools and methodologies are available, drawing on advances in climate science, data analytics, and financial modeling to provide a more comprehensive and granular understanding of climate-related financial risks.

This chapter will explore the diverse landscape of climate risk assessment tools, providing a practical guide to their applications, strengths, and limitations. We'll examine the key considerations for selecting and using these tools

J. Chen, *Climate Finance*,
https://doi.org/10.1007/978-981-96-7975-1_15

effectively and highlight the emerging trends that are shaping the future of climate risk assessment.

UNEP FI has provided a series of climate risk landscape reports (UNEP FI, 2021, 2023a, 2024a) and technical supplements (UNEP FI,) to help banks, insurers, and investors looking to enhance their capabilities in climate risk management and facilitate the global transition toward sustainability.

The UNEP FI reports trace a clear progression in understanding and managing climate-related financial risks, with a growing focus on the tools available to financial institutions.

1. **Foundational Reports (Setting the Stage):**
    - **UNEP FI (2020) "Charting a New Climate: TCFD Banking Programme Report":** This report marks the beginning of UNEP FI's deep dive into climate risk tools. Its primary importance lies in establishing the context of TCFD recommendations and emphasizing the need for financial institutions to assess and disclose climate-related risks, particularly *physical risks*. This report laid the groundwork for subsequent work on tools and methodologies.
    - **UNEP** FI (2021) **"The Climate Risk Landscape: Mapping Climate-related Financial Risk Assessment Methodologies":** This report significantly expands the scope by providing a *mapping of different methodologies* used for climate-related financial risk assessment. It helps financial institutions understand the various approaches available and begins to compare and contrast their strengths and weaknesses. This marked a crucial step toward providing clarity in a then-nascent field.
2. **Tool-Focused Reports (Deepening the Analysis):**
    - **UNEP** FI (2022) **"The Climate Risk Tool Landscape: 2022 Supplement":** This supplement builds directly on the 2021 report by providing a more *concrete analysis of specific climate risk tools*. It showcases *case studies* and offers insights into how different vendors approach various aspects of climate risk assessment. This practical, tool-focused approach was a significant step toward helping institutions choose and utilize the right tools.
    - **UNEP** FI (2023a) **"The 2023 Climate Risk Landscape" & (2023b) "Technical Supplement":** These reports provide an *updated overview of the climate risk tool market*, acknowledging its dynamic and rapidly evolving nature. The main report focuses on trends and the technical supplement goes deeper into methodologies and vendor comparisons (using a dummy portfolio). This iteration introduces a greater focus on economic value outputs and metrics like CVaR and CTVaR.

3. **Action-Oriented Reports (Focusing on Implementation):**
   - **UNEP** FI (2024a) **"The 2024 Climate Risk Landscape":** This report continues to track the evolution of the climate risk tool landscape, emphasizing *practical application* and integration into decision-making processes. It highlights emerging trends, like the increasing use of AI, and provides guidance on how financial institutions can best utilize these tools. The launch (and subsequent updates) of the *Climate Risk Tool Dashboard* in 2023–2024 is a direct outcome of this focus on practical utility.

     - **UNEP** FI (2024b) **"Managing Physical Climate-Related Risks in Loan Portfolios"** & (2024c) **"Assessing Climate Transition Risk":** These supplements provide *sector-specific guidance*, focusing on how physical and transition risks manifest in different types of loan portfolios and offering specific strategies for managing those risks. They demonstrate a more mature understanding of how climate risk tools can be applied to specific business contexts.

4. **Data-Focused Report:**
   - **UNEP** FI (2024d) **"The Climate Data Challenge":** This report addresses a critical challenge in the field: *access to reliable and readily available climate data*. It advocates for the use of open-source and neutral data platforms to address data gaps and improve the quality of risk assessments. This highlights the growing recognition that data availability and quality are fundamental to effective climate risk management.

5. **The Climate Risk Tool Dashboard** (2024e)**:** The dashboard is a *live, interactive resource* that accompanies these reports. Its importance is in providing a searchable, regularly updated database of climate risk tools, allowing financial institutions to easily compare and contrast different offerings based on their specific needs.

These reports, along with the dashboard, are essential reading for any financial institution seeking to understand and manage climate-related financial risks. They provide a comprehensive overview of the market, offer practical guidance on tool selection and implementation, and highlight emerging trends and challenges. The progression from initial context-setting to focused guidance and practical tools demonstrates UNEP FI's commitment to equipping the financial sector with the resources it needs to navigate the complexities of climate change.

2 Types of Climate Risk Tools and Their Applications

Climate risk assessment tools encompass a wide range of approaches and methodologies, each designed to address specific aspects of climate risk. This section provides an overview of the most common types of tools and their applications.

2.1 Transition Risk Assessment Tools

Transition risks stem from the economic and financial shifts associated with the transition to a low-carbon economy. UNEP FI (2024a) highlights the building sector's role in climate goals, linking real estate value to energy efficiency and retrofitting opportunities. These risks can arise from policy changes, technological advancements, shifting market dynamics, and evolving social expectations. Caldecott et al. (2023) provides a framework for investors to support a just transition, integrating social aspects into climate investment.

Transition risk assessment tools help to quantify these risks, providing insights into how different companies, sectors, and investments might be affected by the low-carbon transition. IEA (2024) analyzes global energy trends, focusing on energy security, clean tech investments, and electricity demand growth under various scenarios.

Examples of Transition Risk Assessment Tools:

- **Carbon Pricing Models:** These models simulate the impact of carbon pricing policies, such as carbon taxes or emissions trading schemes, on company profits, asset valuations, and investment portfolios. They use data on companies' carbon emissions, production processes, and financial performance to estimate the potential costs of carbon pricing and the financial implications for different sectors and investment strategies.
- **Stranded Asset Models:** Stranded asset models assess the risk of assets becoming uneconomical or unusable due to the transition to a low-carbon economy. They consider factors such as future energy demand, the pace of technological innovation, and the stringency of climate policies to identify assets that are at high risk of becoming stranded. For example, a stranded asset model might assess the risk of coal-fired power plants becoming uneconomical as renewable energy costs decline and carbon pricing policies are implemented.
- **Scenario Analysis Tools:** Scenario analysis tools help companies and investors explore the financial implications of different transition pathways. They use a range of scenarios, such as an "orderly transition" with gradual policy changes and smooth technological advancements or a "disorderly transition" with abrupt policy shifts and rapid technological disruption, to assess the potential risks and opportunities under different future conditions.

Applications of Transition Risk Assessment Tools:

- **Investment Decision-Making:** Investors use transition risk tools to assess the climate resilience of their portfolios, identify companies or sectors that are well-positioned for the low-carbon transition, and avoid investments in assets at high risk of becoming stranded.
- **Corporate Strategy:** Companies use these tools to assess their exposure to transition risks, develop adaptation strategies, make informed decisions about capital investments, adjust their product development plans, and manage their carbon footprint.
- **Policy Analysis:** Governments and regulators use transition risk models to evaluate the potential economic and financial impacts of different climate policies, such as carbon pricing mechanisms or renewable energy mandates, helping to design effective and efficient regulations.

UNEP FI (2023a) assesses 16 providers of transition risk tools (12 are integrated climate risk tool providers with both transition and physical risk, 4 are only transition risk providers). Here's a comparison, focusing on supported scenarios (Table 1).

The above table is incomplete, as the full comparison is considering other factors like policy changes, technological advancements, and shifting market dynamics. Many align with TCFD recommendations and use IPCC, NGFS, or IEA scenarios. They offer metrics like carbon footprinting, temperature scores, stranded asset analysis, and financial impact assessments (e.g., Climate Value-at-Risk). Some tools take a top-down approach (macroeconomic modeling), while others use a bottom-up approach (company-level analysis).

MSCI Inc.'s Value-at-Risk provides climate-adjusted metrics, including Implied Temperature Rise (ITR), enabling portfolio-level analysis and stress-testing capabilities. The following table provides the full transition risk metrics for MSCI's Climate Value-at-Risk tool (Table 2).

2.1.1 Case Study 15.1: MSCI's Climate Value-at-Risk (VaR) Model

Focus: Showcase a Leading Investment Research and Data Provider, MSCI, and Its Approach to Assessing the Financial Risks of Climate Change for Investment Portfolios

MSCI, a prominent investment research and data provider, has developed the Climate Value-at-Risk (Climate VaR) model to assess the financial risks of climate change for investment portfolios. This case study explores how MSCI's Climate VaR model uses climate scenarios and company data to estimate the potential impact of climate change on the value of investments, considering both physical and transition risks. Investors use this model to assess the climate resilience of their portfolios, identify high-risk holdings, and make more informed investment decisions.

Table 1 Selected transition risk provider

	Risk type	*Scenarios*					
Transition Risk Tool Provider	P = Physical risk, T = Transition Risk, and I = Integrated	Scenario Basis	< 2.0 °C (RCP 2.6)	2.0 °C (RCP 4.5)	3.0 °C (RCP 6.0)	> 4.0 °C (RCP 8.B)	Disorderly?
BlackRock—BlackRock's Aladdin® platform	I	standard & customized scenarios	✓ (NGFS Net Zero and Delayed Transition)		✓ (NGFS Current Policy)		✓ (NGFS Delayed Transition)
CLIMAFIN—Climate Risk Assessment Platform	I	✓	✓	✓	✓	✓	✓
Entelligent—T-Risk	T		✓	✓ (coming soon)	✓(coming soon)	✓	✓ (coming soon)
ICE—Climate Transition Analytics Platform	T	✓	✓	✓	✓	✓	✓
ISS ESG—Transition Value at Risk	I	✓	✓				
McKinsey/ Planetrics—Planetrics' PlanetView Platform	I	✓	✓	✓	✓	✓	✓
Moody's/RMS—Climate Solutions	I	✓ NGFS scenarios & a worst-case scenario	✓	✓	✓	✓	✓
Morningstar Sustainalytics—Low Carbon Transition Rating	I	✓	✓				

	Risk type	*Scenarios*					
MSCI Inc.—Climate Value-at-Risk	I	✓	✓	✓	✓	✓	✓ (Orderly & Disorderly)
Oliver Wyman and S&P—Climate Credit Analytics (CCA)	T	✓	✓	✓	✓	✓	✓
Ortec Finance—Climate MAPS in partnership with Cambridge Econometrics	I	✓ baseline & customized scenarios	✓ Net-zero (by 2050) Orderly scenarioo	✓	✓ Limited Action scenario	✓ Failed Transition scenario	✓ Net zero (by 2050) financial crisis
PricewaterhouseCoopers GmbH—Climate Excellence Transition Risk	T	✓	✓	✓	✓	✓	✓
S&P (The Climate Service)—Climanomics	I		✓	✓	✓	✓	✓
SAS—Climate Risk Offering	I	✓	✓	✓	✓	✓	✓
Willis Towers Watson—WTW Climate Transition Value at Risk	I	✓	✓ Well below 2DS, or 1.5C		✓ Business as usual		✓ delayed transition
1in1000 Initiative 2°Investing Initiative and the Oxford Sustainable Finance Group at the University of Oxford PRISK module	I	✓	✓	✓	✓		✓ (Degree of disorderly shock can be set flexibly)

Source UNEPFI (2023a)

Table 2 Transition risk metrics for MSCI's climate value-at-risk tool

1st Level Risk Metric	*2nd Level Risk Metric*	*3rd Level Risk Metric*	*MSCI Inc.—Climate Value-at-Risk*
Risk type	P = Physical risk, T = Transition Risk,and I = Integrated		I
	Description		Climate Value-at-Risk (Climate VaR) is designed to provide a forward-looking and return-based valuation assessment to measure climate related risks and opportunities in an investment portfolio. The fully quantitative model offers deep insights into how climate change could affect company valuations
Scenarios	Scenario Basis		✓
	< 2.0 °C (RCP 2.6)		✓
	2.0 °C (RCP 4.5)		✓
	3.0 °C (RCP 6.0)		✓
	> 4.0 °C (RCP 8.5)		✓
	Disorderly?		✓ (Orderly & Disorderly)
Time horizons	Short-term (2025–2040)		✓
	Mid-term (2050)		✓
	Long-term (2100)		✓
Transition Hazards	Policy		✓
	Technology		✓
Risk analysis	Level of analysis	Asset	✓
		Firm	✓
		Sector	✓
		Country	✓
	Impact Channel	Macroenvironment	✓
		Supply chain	✓
		Operations and assets	✓
		Markets and customers	✓
	Depth	Exposure	✓
		Sensitivity	✓
		Adaptive Capacity	✓ (Climate Value-at-Risk: Technology Opportunities)

(continued)

Table 2 (continued)

1st Level Risk Metric	*2nd Level Risk Metric*	*3rd Level Risk Metric*	*MSCI Inc.—Climate Value-at-Risk*
	Approach	Top-Down	✓
		Bottom-Up	✓
Asset classes	Equity		✓
	Bonds, Corporate		✓
	Bonds, Government		✓
	Loans, Corporate		✓ (Financed emissions: in Total Portfolio Footprint solution; ✓)
	Loans, Project		✓ (Financed emissions: in Total Portfolio Footprint solution; ✓)
	Mortgages		✓ (MSCI Real Estate Climate Solution)
	Real Estate/Real Assets		✓ (MSCI Real Estate Climate Solution)
User inputs	Counterparty name		✓ (ISIN)
	Location		✓ (Financed emissions: in Total Portfolio Footprint solution; ✓)
	Value of asset		✓ (Financed emissions: in Total Portfolio Footprint solution; ✓)
Validity	Open-source		(-)
	Peer-reviewed		(-)
	Source references		✓
Outputs	Quantitative		✓
	Semi-quantitative		✓
	Non-financial metrics		✓ (Scores)
	Financial metrics		✓
	Temperature Alignment		✓ (MSCI ESG Climate: Implied Temperature Rise Metric)
Geography	Global		✓
	North America		✓
	South America		✓
	United Kingdom		✓
	European Union		✓
	Rest of Europe		✓
	APAC		✓
	Africa		✓

Source UNEPFI (2023a)

Illustration: How MSCI's Climate VaR Model Works

1. **The Climate Value-at-Risk (Climate VaR) Model:**

MSCI's Climate VaR model provides a forward-looking valuation assessment to measure climate-related risks and opportunities. The model evaluates both physical risks (e.g., extreme weather events, sea-level rise) and transition risks (e.g., policy changes, technological advancements) to estimate the potential impact of climate change on the value of investments. The model incorporates various climate scenarios to provide a comprehensive view of potential future outcomes (MSCI, 2020).

2. **Incorporating Climate Scenarios and Company Data:**

The Climate VaR model uses a range of climate scenarios to assess the potential financial impact of climate change on companies. These scenarios include different temperature pathways (e.g., 1.5 °C, 2 °C, 3 °C) and consider both physical and transition risks. The model integrates company-specific data, such as greenhouse gas emissions, revenue from low-carbon technologies, and exposure to climate-related hazards, to provide a detailed assessment of each company's climate risk profile (MSCI, 2020).

3. **Application by Investors:**

Investors use MSCI's Climate VaR model to assess the climate resilience of their portfolios, identify high-risk holdings, and make more informed investment decisions. The model helps investors quantify the potential financial impact of climate risks on their portfolios, enabling them to adjust their asset allocation, engage with companies on climate performance, and develop strategies to mitigate climate-related risks (MSCI, 2025).

Discussion: Incorporating Long-Term Climate Risks, Using Climate Scenarios, and Influencing Asset Allocation

1. **Challenges of Incorporating Long-Term Climate Risks into Short-Term Investment Horizons:**

Incorporating long-term climate risks into short-term investment horizons presents several challenges (MSCI, 2025):

- **Data Uncertainty:** Long-term climate projections involve significant uncertainties, making it difficult to predict precise financial impacts.
- **Time Horizon Mismatch:** Investors often focus on short-term returns, while climate risks may manifest over longer periods.

- **Complexity:** Assessing the financial impact of climate risks requires complex modeling and scenario analysis, which can be resource-intensive.
- **Importance of Using a Range of Climate Scenarios:**

Using a range of climate scenarios is crucial for providing a comprehensive assessment of climate risks. Different scenarios capture various potential future outcomes, helping investors understand the range of possible impacts on their portfolios. This approach allows investors to assess the resilience of their investments under different climate conditions and develop strategies to mitigate risks (MSCI, 2025).

3. **Potential for Climate VaR Models to Influence Asset Allocation Decisions:**

Climate VaR models can significantly influence asset allocation decisions by providing insights into the potential financial impacts of climate risks. Investors can use these models to identify high-risk holdings, adjust their portfolios to reduce exposure to climate risks, and allocate capital to more resilient and sustainable investments. This proactive approach can enhance portfolio resilience and support the transition to a low-carbon economy (MSCI, 2020).

Conclusion

MSCI's Climate Value-at-Risk (Climate VaR) model exemplifies a sophisticated approach to assessing the financial risks of climate change for investment portfolios. By incorporating climate scenarios and company data, the model provides a comprehensive assessment of both physical and transition risks, enabling investors to make more informed decisions.

Incorporating long-term climate risks into short-term investment horizons presents challenges, but using a range of climate scenarios helps provide a comprehensive view of potential future outcomes. Climate VaR models can significantly influence asset allocation decisions, encouraging investors to reduce exposure to climate risks and allocate capital to more resilient and sustainable investments.

Understanding the methodologies and strategies employed by MSCI in developing and applying the Climate VaR model can provide valuable insights for other financial institutions and stakeholders seeking to enhance their climate risk assessment processes and support sustainable investment practices.

2.2 Physical Risk Assessment Tools

Physical risks arise from the direct impacts of climate change, such as sea-level rise, extreme weather events (e.g., floods, droughts, heat waves, wildfires), and changes in temperature and precipitation patterns. Physical risk assessment tools help to quantify these risks, providing insights into the potential for damage, disruption, and financial losses. UNDRR (2023) emphasizes building resilience against increasing disasters impacting global development.

Examples of Physical Risk Assessment Tools:

- **Catastrophe (CAT) Models:** Traditionally used by insurance companies to assess the risks of natural disasters, CAT models are being adapted to incorporate climate change projections. These models use data on historical hazard events, asset exposures (e.g., location and value of properties), and vulnerability factors (e.g., building construction types) to estimate the potential financial losses from future climate-related hazards.
- **Geospatial Analysis Tools:** Geospatial analysis tools, such as Geographic Information Systems (GIS), are used to map and assess physical climate risks. By combining climate hazard data (e.g., flood maps, sea-level rise projections) with asset exposure data (e.g., location of buildings, infrastructure networks), these tools can identify areas that are most vulnerable to climate impacts. EEA (2023) assesses climate adaptation and disaster risk reduction practices in Europe.
- **Infrastructure Vulnerability Models:** These models assess the resilience of specific infrastructure assets, such as roads, bridges, power grids, and water systems, to climate-related hazards. They consider factors such as the design and age of the infrastructure, the projected changes in climate variables (e.g., temperature, precipitation), and the potential for cascading failures to estimate the likelihood and severity of damage or disruption.

Applications of Physical Risk Assessment Tools:

- **Insurance and Reinsurance:** Insurance companies use physical risk models to set premiums that reflect the changing risk landscape due to climate change. They can also use these models to develop new insurance products that address specific climate risks, such as parametric insurance policies that pay out based on predefined weather triggers.
- **Real Estate:** Real estate investors and developers use physical risk assessment tools to evaluate the vulnerability of properties to climate hazards, informing their investment decisions and setting insurance premiums. These tools can also be used by homeowners to assess the risks to their properties and take steps to improve resilience.
- **Infrastructure Planning:** Governments and infrastructure operators use physical risk assessment tools to guide investments in climate-resilient infrastructure, prioritize adaptation measures, and develop long-term plans that consider the impacts of climate change. UNEPFI (2024) offers guidance for retail banks on managing physical climate risks in loan portfolios.

The UNEP FI (2023a) Climate Risk Landscape report also assesses 19 providers of physical climate risk tools, 12 are integrated risk providers, while the rest 7 are only physical risk providers. Here's a comparison of the providers mentioned, focusing on their supported climate scenarios (Table 3).

Again, the above table is incomplete, the full physical risk metrics include risk metrics on different hazards (floods, extreme heat, wildfire, etc.), time horizons (short, mid, long-term), and asset classes (real estate, mortgages, etc.). Many align with TCFD recommendations and incorporate scenario analysis using IPCC or NGFS climate scenarios. Key metrics include risk scores, financial impact assessments, and vulnerability indicators. Some tools offer bottom-up approaches (asset-level analysis) while others use top-down methods.

Moody's/RMS Climate Solutions provides a broad spectrum of climate solutions and insights, ranging from entity-level to macro-level analytics, spanning risk identification, quantification, and climate readiness. Incorporates a large natural catastrophe database (NatCatSERVICE). The following table provides the full physical risk metrics for Moody's/RMS Climate Solutions tool (Table 4).

2.2.1 Case Study 15.2: Moody's Climate Risk Scores and Their Impact on Credit Ratings

Focus: Highlight How a Major Credit Rating Agency, Moody's, Is Incorporating Climate Risks into Its Credit Rating Methodologies, Influencing Corporate Financing Costs and Investment Decisions

Moody's, a leading credit rating agency, has developed climate risk scores that assess companies' exposure to physical and transition risks, incorporating these scores into its credit rating assessments. This case study explores how Moody's climate risk scores influence corporate financing costs and investment decisions. It highlights the implications of integrating climate risks into credit ratings for businesses, investors, and the financial system, as well as the challenges of quantifying climate risks and the potential for credit ratings to incentivize companies to improve their climate performance.

Illustration: How Moody's Developed Climate Risk Scores

1. **Moody's Climate Risk Scores:**

Moody's has developed a comprehensive approach to assessing climate-related risks, using climate risk scores to evaluate companies' exposure to both physical and transition risks. Physical risks include the potential damage and disruption caused by acute events like hurricanes and chronic changes like sea-level rise, while transition risks encompass the financial impacts of shifting to a low-carbon economy, such as policy changes and technological advancements (Moody's, 2025).

Table 3 Selected physical risk provider

	Risk Type	*Scenarios*			
Transition Risk Tool Provider	P = Physical risk, T = Transition Risk, and I = Integrated	< 2.0 °C (RCP 2.6)	2.0 °C (RCP 4.5)	3.0 °C (RCP 6.0)	> 4.0 °C (RCP 8.5)
BlackRock—BlackRock's Aladdin® platform	I	✓	✓	✓	✓ (inc. tail end risk)
Carbon Tracker—2 Degrees of Separation	P	✓	✓ (NZE/SDS/APS)	✓	✓ (STEPS)
CLIMAFIN—Climate Risk Assessment Platform	I	✓	✓	✓	✓
ISS ESG—Physical Risk Solution	I		✓		✓
JBA Risk Management—Climate Change Flood Model	P	Not off-the-shelf but automated to allow creation	✓ (Worldwide)	Not off-the-shelf but automated to allow creation	✓ (Worldwide)
McKinsey/Planetrics—Planetrics' PlanetView Platform	I	✓	✓	✓	✓
Moody's/RMS—Climate Solutions	I	✓	✓	✓	✓
Morningstar Sustainalytics—Physical Climate Risk Metrics	I	✓			✓
MSCI Inc.—Climate Value-at-risk	I	✓	✓	✓	✓
Munich Re-Location Risk Intelligence	P	✓ SSP for chronical risks currently in develop-ment	✓ SSP for chronical risks currently in develop-ment	✓SSP for chronical risks currently in develop-ment	✓ SSP for chronical risks currently in development
Ortec Finance—Climate PREDICT	I	✓	✓	✓	✓
PricewaterhouseCoopers GmbH -Climate Excellence Physical Risk	P	✓	✓		✓

(continued)

Table 3 (continued)

	Risk Type	*Scenarios*			
S&P (The Climate Service)—Climanomics	I	✓	✓	✓	✓
SAS—Climate Risk Offering	I	✓ (any scenarios executable from the Central Scenario Manager)	✓	✓	✓
South Pole—Climate risk deep-dive assessment	P	✓		✓	✓
Sust Global—Climate Explorer	P	✓	✓		✓
Willis Towers Watson—Bespoke Physical Risk Analytics	I	✓	✓		✓
XDI Systems—XDI Hub	P	✓	✓	✓	✓
1in1000 Initiative 2°Investing Initiative and the Oxford Sustainable Finance Group at the University of Oxford PRISK module	I	✓	✓	✓	✓

Source UNEPFI (2023a)

2. **Incorporating Climate Risk Scores into Credit Ratings:**

Moody's integrates climate risk scores into its credit rating methodologies, affecting the overall credit assessments of companies. Companies with higher climate risk scores, indicating greater exposure to climate-related risks, may face higher borrowing costs due to perceived higher credit risk. Conversely, companies with lower climate risk scores, indicating better management of climate risks, may benefit from lower costs of capital (Moody's, 2025).

3. **Application by Investors:**

Investors use Moody's climate risk scores to screen investments, engage with companies, and manage portfolio risk. By incorporating climate risk assessments into their decision-making processes, investors can better understand the potential financial impacts of climate-related risks on their portfolios and make more informed investment decisions (Moody's, 2025).

Table 4 Physical risk metrics for Moody's/RMS climate solutions tool

1st Level Risk Metric	*2nd Level Risk Metric*	*3rd Level Risk Metric*	*Moody's/RMS - Climate Solutions*
Risk Type	P = Physical risk, T = Transition Risk, and I = Integrated		I
	Description		Offer a broad spectrum of climate solutions and insights, ranging from entity level information to macro level analytics; spanning identification and quantification of climate risk and readiness
Scenarios	< 2.0 °C (RCP 2.6)		✓
	2.0 °C (RCP 4.5)		✓
	3.0 °C (RCP 6.0)		✓
	> 4.0 °C (RCP 8.5)		✓
Time horizons	Baseline/historical		✓
	Short-term (2025–2040)		✓
	Mid-term (2050)		✓
	Long-term (2100)		✓
Transition Risks	Chronic		✓
	Acute		✓
Risk analysis	Level of analysis	Asset	✓
		Firm	✓
		Sector	✓
		Country	✓
		Portfolio	✓
	Impact Channel	Macroenvironment	✓
		Supply chain	✓
		Operations and assets	✓
		Markets and customers	✓
	Method	Physical Exposure	✓
		Vulnerability indicators	✓
		Physical impact modelling	✓
		Financial modelling	✓
Physical Hazard Type	Flood, coast		✓

(continued)

Table 4 (continued)

1st Level Risk Metric	*2nd Level Risk Metric*	*3rd Level Risk Metric*	*Moody's/RMS - Climate Solutions*
	Flood, inland		✓
	Extreme weather		✓
	Extreme heat		✓
	Extreme precipitation		✓
	Landslide		✓
	Drought		✓
	Water scarcity		✓
	Wildfire		✓
Asset classes	Equity		✓
	Bonds, Corporate		✓
	Bonds, Government		✓
	Loans, Corporate		✓
	Loans, Project		✓
	Mortgages		✓
	Real Estate/Real Assets		✓
User inputs	Counterparty name		
	Location		✓
	Value of asset		✓
	Characteristics of asset		✓
Validity	Open-source		✓
	Peer-reviewed		✓
	Source references		✓
Outputs	Quantitative		✓
	Semi-quantitative		✓
	Non-financial metrics		✓
	Financial metrics		✓
Geography	Global		✓
	North America		✓
	South America		✓
	United Kingdom		✓
	European Union		✓
	Rest of Europe		✓
	APAC		✓
	Africa		✓

Source UNEPFI (2023a)

Discussion: Implications of Integrating Climate Risks into Credit Ratings

1. **Implications for Businesses:**

Integrating climate risks into credit ratings has significant implications for businesses. Companies with high climate risk scores may face higher borrowing costs, making it more expensive to raise capital. This financial pressure can incentivize companies to improve their climate risk management practices and reduce their exposure to climate-related risks. Additionally, transparent climate risk assessments can enhance a company's reputation and attract sustainability-focused investors (Moody's, 2025).

2. **Implications for Investors:**

For investors, integrating climate risks into credit ratings provides valuable insights into the potential financial impacts of climate change on their investments. This information helps investors assess the long-term viability of their portfolios and make more informed decisions. By considering climate risks, investors can better manage their exposure to potential financial losses and support the transition to a low-carbon economy (Moody's, 2025).

3. **Implications for the Financial System:**

Integrating climate risks into credit ratings can enhance the resilience of the financial system by promoting better risk management practices. By identifying and addressing climate-related risks, financial institutions can reduce their vulnerability to climate shocks and support the stability of the financial system. Additionally, transparent climate risk assessments can improve market efficiency by enabling better pricing of climate-related risks (Moody's, 2025).

Challenges of Quantifying Climate Risks

1. **Data Availability and Quality:**

One of the primary challenges of quantifying climate risks is the availability and quality of data. Accurate climate risk assessments require comprehensive and reliable data on physical and transition risks, which can be difficult to obtain. Additionally, data quality can vary significantly across different regions and sectors, complicating the assessment process (Moody's, 2025).

2. **Standardizing Metrics:**

Standardizing metrics for climate risk assessment is another challenge. Different industries and regions may have varying definitions and metrics for assessing climate risks, making it difficult to compare and aggregate data. Developing standardized metrics and methodologies is essential for ensuring consistency and comparability in climate risk assessments (Moody's, 2025).

3. **Long-Term Projections:**

Climate risks often have long-term implications that can be difficult to quantify. Assessing the potential financial impacts of climate risks requires long-term projections and scenario analysis, which involve significant uncertainties. Developing robust models and methodologies for long-term climate risk assessment is crucial for providing accurate and actionable insights (Moody's, 2025).

Conclusion

Moody's incorporation of climate risk scores into its credit rating methodologies represents a significant step in integrating climate-related risks into financial assessments. By evaluating companies' exposure to physical and transition risks, Moody's provides valuable insights that influence corporate financing costs and investment decisions.

The implications of integrating climate risks into credit ratings are far-reaching, affecting businesses, investors, and the financial system. While there are challenges in quantifying climate risks, such as data availability, standardizing metrics, and long-term projections, the benefits of improved risk management and enhanced market efficiency are substantial.

Understanding the methodologies and strategies employed by Moody's in developing and applying climate risk scores can provide valuable insights for other financial institutions and stakeholders seeking to integrate climate risks into their credit assessments and support sustainable investment practices.

2.3 Portfolio Alignment Tools

Portfolio alignment tools assess the alignment of investment portfolios with climate goals, such as the Paris Agreement targets or net-zero emissions commitments. These tools help investors understand the climate implications of their investment decisions and identify opportunities to shift capital toward a more sustainable future. SBTi (2024) offers guidance for financial institutions to set science-based emissions reduction targets.

Examples of Portfolio Alignment Tools:

- **Carbon Footprint Analysis Tools:** These tools calculate the carbon emissions associated with a portfolio of investments, providing a measure of the portfolio's contribution to climate change. They use data on companies' greenhouse gas emissions, energy consumption, and production processes to estimate the carbon footprint of different investments.

PCAF (2024) provides a standardized framework for GHG accounting and reporting in the financial industry.

- **Implied Temperature Rise (ITR) Tools:** ITR tools estimate the temperature increase implied by a portfolio's emissions trajectory. They assess whether the portfolio is aligned with a specific climate goal, such as limiting warming to 1.5 °C or 2 °C above pre-industrial levels.
- **Climate Scenario Analysis Tools:** These tools assess the performance of a portfolio under different climate scenarios, such as an orderly transition to a low-carbon economy or a scenario with more severe physical climate impacts. They help investors understand how their portfolios might perform under different future climate conditions and identify potential risks and opportunities. PACTA (2022) introduces a climate scenario analysis tool for investment portfolio alignment.

Applications of Portfolio Alignment Tools:

- **Investment Management:** Portfolio managers use alignment tools to guide their asset allocation decisions, reduce their exposure to climate risks, and increase their investments in climate solutions.
- **Reporting and Disclosure:** Investors use these tools to communicate the climate alignment of their portfolios to clients, beneficiaries, and other stakeholders, demonstrating their commitment to sustainable investing.
- **Engagement and Stewardship:** Investors use portfolio alignment tools to engage with companies on their climate performance, advocating for improved practices, and supporting efforts to reduce emissions and enhance climate resilience.

2.4 *Scenario Analysis and Stress Testing Tools*

Climate change presents a future filled with uncertainties. We cannot predict with absolute certainty how the climate will change, how societies will respond, or what the precise economic and financial impacts will be. Scenario analysis and stress testing tools provide a framework for exploring these uncertainties, helping organizations to assess their vulnerability to different potential futures and develop more resilient strategies.

- **Scenario Analysis:** Scenario analysis involves developing a set of plausible and diverse future scenarios, each based on different assumptions about key drivers of change, such as greenhouse gas emissions trajectories, technological advancements, economic growth, and policy responses. By analyzing how their business, investments, or portfolio might perform under different scenarios, organizations can identify potential risks and opportunities, challenge their assumptions, and develop strategies that are robust to a range of possible outcomes.

- **Climate Stress Testing:** Climate stress tests are a specific type of scenario analysis used by financial institutions and regulators to assess the resilience of the financial system to climate risks. These tests involve simulating the impact of different climate scenarios on the balance sheets, profitability, and capital adequacy of banks, insurers, and other financial institutions. Stress testing helps to identify vulnerabilities, assess the potential for systemic risks, and inform supervisory actions to enhance the resilience of the financial system. Bank of England (2022): CBES assessed climate-related financial risks for banks and insurers under different scenarios.

Examples of Scenario Analysis and Stress Testing Tools:

- **Network for Greening the Financial System (NGFS) Scenarios:** The NGFS, a global network of central banks and supervisors, has developed a set of climate scenarios specifically for use in financial risk assessments. These scenarios cover a range of possible climate pathways, including orderly and disorderly transitions to a low-carbon economy, and provide a common framework for stress testing and scenario analysis in the financial sector.
- **International Energy Agency (IEA) Scenarios:** The IEA develops energy-focused scenarios that explore different pathways for the global energy system, considering factors such as energy demand, technology development, and policy choices. These scenarios can be used to assess the implications of different energy transitions for various sectors, including finance, energy, and transportation.
- **Proprietary Scenario Analysis Tools:** Many consulting firms, research institutions, and software providers offer proprietary scenario analysis tools that allow organizations to customize scenarios, incorporate their own data and assumptions, and explore the implications for their specific business or investment portfolio.

Benefits of Scenario Analysis and Stress Testing:

- **Enhanced Risk Awareness:** Exploring a range of potential futures raises awareness of climate-related risks and opportunities, challenging assumptions and encouraging a more forward-looking perspective. ECB (2020): Guide outlines supervisory expectations for banks to manage and disclose climate-related risks.
- **Improved Strategic Planning:** Scenario analysis can help organizations develop more robust strategies that are adaptable to different possible climate outcomes, reducing their vulnerability to unexpected events.
- **Informed Decision-Making:** By understanding the potential impacts of different climate scenarios, decision-makers can make more informed

choices about investments, risk mitigation strategies, and capital allocation.

- **Strengthened Resilience:** Stress testing helps financial institutions identify vulnerabilities and take early action to mitigate risks, enhancing the resilience of the financial system to climate shocks.

2.5 Disclosure Reporting Tools

As the demand for transparency in climate-related financial risks and opportunities grows, companies and financial institutions are increasingly expected to disclose their climate-related information to investors, regulators, and other stakeholders. Disclosure reporting tools provide guidance, templates, and software solutions to streamline the reporting process, ensure data accuracy, and align disclosures with recognized frameworks and standards.

Examples of Disclosure Reporting Tools:

- **TCFD Reporting Software:** Several software platforms have been developed specifically to help companies align their disclosures with the recommendations of the Task Force on Climate-Related Financial Disclosures (TCFD). These tools provide guidance on the TCFD framework, templates for reporting different elements of the recommendations, and features for data management and analysis.
- **SASB Reporting Tools:** Software and resources are available to assist companies in reporting sustainability data aligned with the Sustainability Accounting Standards Board (SASB) standards. SASB (2023) provides guidance on climate risk reporting. These tools provide sector-specific guidance, data collection templates, and reporting templates to streamline the process and ensure consistency.
- **GRI Reporting Software:** Software solutions facilitate reporting in accordance with the Global Reporting Initiative (GRI) Standards, a widely used framework for sustainability reporting. GRI (2025) released updated Universal Standards for sustainability reporting. These tools provide templates, guidance, and data management features to simplify the reporting process and ensure compliance with GRI requirements.

Benefits of Using Disclosure Reporting Tools:

- **Streamlined Reporting Process:** These tools can simplify and automate many aspects of the reporting process, saving time and reducing the burden on internal teams.
- **Improved Data Accuracy:** Specialized software can help ensure data accuracy, consistency, and completeness, reducing the risk of errors and enhancing the credibility of disclosures.
- **Alignment with Standards:** Reporting tools that are specifically designed for recognized frameworks like the TCFD or SASB can help

companies align their disclosures with best practices and ensure compliance with evolving regulatory requirements.

- **Enhanced Transparency and Comparability:** Using standardized reporting tools and frameworks can make climate-related disclosures more transparent and comparable across different companies, facilitating informed decision-making by investors and other stakeholders.

3 Key Considerations for Selecting and Using Climate Risk Assessment Tools

The landscape of climate risk assessment tools is rapidly evolving, with a growing number of providers offering a diverse array of products and services. Choosing the right tools for a specific purpose requires careful consideration of several factors:

3.1 Data Quality, Accuracy, and Comprehensiveness

The foundation of any climate risk assessment is data. The accuracy, reliability, and completeness of the data inputs directly influence the quality and usefulness of the model outputs. When selecting climate risk assessment tools, it's essential to evaluate the data sources they use, the methodologies for processing and validating the data, and the comprehensiveness of the datasets.

Key questions to consider include:

- **What are the sources of climate hazard data used by the tool?** Are they based on reputable scientific sources, such as the Intergovernmental Panel on Climate Change (IPCC) reports or outputs from recognized climate models?
- **How is the data downscaled to regional or local scales?** Does the tool use appropriate downscaling techniques to provide relevant information for the specific geographic location of interest?
- **How is the data validated and quality-checked?** What measures are in place to ensure the accuracy and reliability of the data?
- **How comprehensive are the datasets?** Does the tool cover a wide range of climate hazards, including both physical and transition risks? Does it provide data on relevant exposure and vulnerability factors, such as population density, infrastructure assets, and building types?
- **How frequently is the data updated?** Climate science is constantly evolving, and new data is becoming available regularly. It's essential to use tools that rely on up-to-date data.

3.2 Model Transparency and Validation

Climate risk models can be complex, involving numerous variables, assumptions, and mathematical equations. Understanding the underlying methodologies, assumptions, and limitations of these models is crucial for interpreting the results appropriately and avoiding overconfidence in the outputs.

Key questions to consider:

- **Is the model methodology clearly documented and explained?** Can you understand the logic behind the model and the assumptions it makes?
- **Has the model been validated against historical data?** Has it been tested to see how well it predicts past events?
- **What are the key limitations of the model?** What are the potential sources of error or uncertainty in the results?
- **Has the model been peer-reviewed or independently verified?** Has it been subjected to scrutiny by other experts in the field?

Transparency in model methodologies and assumptions is essential for building trust in the results and enabling users to make informed decisions based on a clear understanding of the model's strengths and limitations.

3.3 Usability and Ease of Integration

Climate risk assessment tools should be user-friendly, accessible to non-experts, and easy to integrate into existing workflows and systems.

Key considerations:

- **User Interface:** Is the tool's interface intuitive and easy to navigate? Does it provide clear instructions and guidance?
- **Data Input and Output:** Is it easy to import data into the tool and export the results in a usable format?
- **Integration with Existing Systems:** Can the tool be integrated with existing risk management systems, data platforms, or reporting tools?
- **Training and Support:** Does the tool provider offer training and support to help users understand and utilize the tool effectively?

Choosing tools that are user-friendly and can be seamlessly integrated into existing workflows will encourage wider adoption and facilitate more effective climate risk management.

3.4 Cost and Value for Money

Climate risk assessment tools can range in price from free, open-source tools to sophisticated commercial platforms that require significant investment. It's crucial to carefully evaluate the costs and benefits of different tools to ensure that they provide a positive return on investment.

Key factors to consider:

- **Subscription Fees:** Many commercial tools require ongoing subscription fees, which can vary widely depending on the features and functionality offered.
- **Data Costs:** Some tools require users to purchase additional data, such as climate hazard data or asset exposure data, which can add to the overall cost.
- **Consulting Services:** Implementing and using complex climate risk assessment tools often require specialized expertise, which may involve hiring consultants to provide training, support, or custom model development.

It's essential to weigh these costs against the potential benefits of using the tool, such as:

- **Reduced Financial Losses:** By identifying and managing climate risks, companies can potentially avoid or reduce financial losses associated with climate change impacts or the low-carbon transition.
- **Improved Investment Decisions:** Using climate risk assessment tools can help investors make more informed decisions, allocating capital to more resilient assets and avoiding investments that are at high risk.
- **Enhanced Reputation and Brand Value:** Demonstrating a proactive approach to climate risk management can enhance a company's reputation among investors, customers, and other stakeholders.
- **Improved Regulatory Compliance:** Using tools that align with recognized frameworks and standards can help companies meet evolving regulatory requirements for climate risk disclosure.

3.4.1 Compliance with Regulatory Requirements

The regulatory landscape for climate risk disclosure is rapidly evolving. Several jurisdictions, including the European Union, the United Kingdom, and several US states, are implementing mandatory climate risk reporting requirements, particularly for publicly listed companies and financial institutions.

When selecting climate risk assessment tools, it's essential to ensure that they align with relevant regulations and can support the production of compliant disclosures.

Key considerations:

- **Alignment with Disclosure Frameworks:** Does the tool provide outputs that can be used to meet the requirements of recognized disclosure frameworks, such as the Task Force on Climate-Related Financial

Disclosures (TCFD) recommendations or the Sustainability Accounting Standards Board (SASB) standards?
- **Data Accuracy and Reliability:** Regulators are increasingly demanding higher levels of data accuracy and reliability in climate risk disclosures. Tools should use credible data sources and employ rigorous validation methods to ensure that the information reported is trustworthy.
- **Auditability and Traceability:** Companies may be required to provide evidence to support their climate risk disclosures. Tools should provide auditable trails of data sources, assumptions, and model outputs to demonstrate transparency and accountability.

As the regulatory landscape for climate risk disclosure continues to evolve, it's crucial for companies and financial institutions to stay informed about the latest requirements and select tools that can support their compliance efforts.

4 Emerging Trends: AI, ML, and Data Innovation

The field of climate risk assessment is rapidly advancing, driven by technological innovations that are enhancing the accuracy, granularity, and usability of climate risk models. Artificial intelligence (AI), machine learning (ML), and new data sources are playing a key role in this transformation, enabling more sophisticated and insightful risk assessments.

4.1 The Role of Technology

AI and ML are revolutionizing how we analyze vast amounts of data, identify patterns, and make predictions. In the context of climate risk assessment, these technologies are being applied to:

- **Enhance Data Analysis:** AI algorithms can sift through massive datasets of climate data, identifying trends, anomalies, and correlations that might not be apparent to human analysts. This enables more accurate projections of future climate impacts and a better understanding of the complex interactions within the climate system.
- **Improve Model Accuracy:** ML algorithms can be trained on historical climate data and used to improve the accuracy of climate models, reducing uncertainties and providing more reliable projections of future climate conditions (Rolnick et al., 2022).

4.2 AI and ML Applications

Here are some specific applications of AI and ML in climate risk modeling (WEF, 2024):

- **Downscaling Climate Models:** Global climate models (GCMs) provide projections at a relatively coarse spatial resolution, making it challenging to assess risks at local scales. ML techniques are being used to downscale GCM outputs to finer resolutions, providing more detailed and localized climate data for risk assessments.
- **Predictive Analytics:** AI and ML can be used to develop predictive models that assess the likelihood and severity of future climate impacts, such as floods, droughts, or heatwaves, based on historical data, current climate conditions, and future projections.
- **Automated Risk Assessments:** AI can automate certain aspects of the risk assessment process, such as data collection, analysis, and report generation, increasing efficiency and reducing costs.
- **Identifying Climate-Resilient Investments:** AI and ML can be used to analyze large datasets of company information, financial data, and climate projections to identify investments that are well-positioned to thrive in a low-carbon economy and are resilient to climate risks.

4.3 Data Innovation

New data sources and technologies are also expanding the horizons of climate risk assessment, providing richer and more timely information for informing decisions.

Key innovations include:

- **Satellite Data:** Satellite imagery and remote sensing data are providing valuable insights into environmental changes, such as deforestation rates, sea-level rise, and the spread of wildfires. This data can be integrated into climate risk models to improve the accuracy of projections and provide a more granular understanding of localized risks. ESA (2023) offers satellite-derived climate data records via its Open Data Portal.
- **Internet of Things (IoT) Sensors:** The deployment of IoT sensors is enabling the collection of real-time data on climate variables, such as temperature, precipitation, wind speed, and soil moisture. This real-time data can be fed into climate risk models to provide more dynamic and responsive assessments of current and future risks.
- **Open Data Platforms:** Open data platforms, which make climate data freely accessible to researchers and practitioners, are fostering collaboration and innovation in climate risk modeling. By sharing data and models, the climate risk community can collectively improve the quality and accessibility of risk assessment tools. Climate Trace (2024) details 2023 global emissions, with power generation as the largest source.

5 Conclusion: Navigating a Changing Risk Landscape

Climate risk assessment is an essential practice for any organization seeking to navigate the complexities of a changing climate. The tools and frameworks available for assessing these risks are rapidly evolving, driven by advancements in climate science, data analytics, and technology. By understanding the different types of climate risk assessment tools, their strengths and limitations, and the key considerations for selecting and using them effectively, organizations can gain valuable insights into their exposure to climate risks, make more informed decisions, and build greater resilience into their operations and strategies.

The journey of climate risk assessment is a continuous one. As climate change unfolds and our understanding of its impacts deepens, we can expect to see further innovation and refinement of these tools. By embracing a forward-looking approach, engaging with the latest scientific knowledge, and utilizing the best available tools and frameworks, we can navigate the changing risk landscape and contribute to building a more sustainable and resilient future for all.

References

Bank of England. (2022). Results of the 2021 climate biennial exploratory scenario (CBES). Retrieved 8 March, 2025, from https://www.bankofengland.co.uk/stress-testing/2022/results-of-the-2021-climate-biennial-exploratory-scenario

Climate Trace. (2024). Country inventory. Retrieved 8 March, 2025, from https://climatetrace.org/inventory

European Central Bank (ECB). (2020). Guide on climate-related and environmental risks Supervisory expectations relating to risk management and disclosure. Retrieved 8 March, 2025, from https://www.bankingsupervision.europa.eu/ecb/pub/pdf/ssm.202011finalguideonclimate-relatedandenvironmentalrisks~58213f6564.en.pdf

European Environment Agency (EEA). (2023). Climate change adaptation and disaster risk reduction in Europe: Enhancing coherence of the knowledge base, policies and practices. Retrieved from https://www.eea.europa.eu/publications/climate-change-adaptation-and-disaster

European Space Agency (ESA). (2023). Climate change initiative: Open data portal. Retrieved 8 March, 2025, from https://climate.esa.int/en/data/

Global Reporting Initiative (GRI). (2025). Universal standards. Retrieved 8 March, 2025, from https://www.globalreporting.org/standards/standards-development/universal-standards/

International Energy Agency (IEA). (2024). World energy outlook 2024—Analysis. Iea. Retrieved 8 March, 2025, from https://www.iea.org/reports/world-energy-outlook-2024

Paris Agreement Capital Transition Assessment (PACTA). (2022). PACTA for investors methodology document climate scenario analysis for investment portfolios. Retrieved 8 March, 2025, from https://www.transitionmonitor.com/wp-content/uploads/2023/02/PACTA-for-Investors-Methodology-document_Final.1.pdf

Partnership for Carbon Accounting Financials (PCAF). (2024). The global GHG accounting and reporting standard for the financial industry. Retrieved 8 March, 2025, from https://carbonaccountingfinancials.com/standard

Rolnick, D. et al. (2022). Tackling climate change with machine learning. *ACM Comput Surv, 55*(2), 42:1–42:96. Retrieved from https://doi.org/10.1145/3485128

Sustainability Accounting Standards Board (SASB). (2023). Climate risk—Technical bulletin. Sasb. Retrieved 8 March, 2025, from https://sasb.ifrs.org/knowledge-hub/climate-risk-technical-bulletin/

United Nations Environment Programme Finance Initiative (UNEP FI). (2020). Charting a new climate: TCFD banking programme report. Retrieved from https://www.unepfi.org/industries/banking/charting-a-new-climate/

UNEP FI. (2021). The climate risk landscape: Mapping climate-related financial risk assessment methodologies. Retrieved from https://www.unepfi.org/themes/climate-change/the-climate-risk-landscape/

UNEP FI. (2022). The climate risk tool landscape: 2022 supplement. Retrieved from https://www.unepfi.org/publications/the-climate-risk-tool-landscape-2022-supplement/

UNEP FI. (2023a). The 2023 climate risk landscape. Retrieved 8 March, 2025, from https://www.unepfi.org/themes/climate-change/2023-climate-risk-landscape/

UNEP FI. (2023b). The 2023 climate risk landscape: Technical supplement. Retrieved from https://www.unepfi.org/wordpress/wp-content/uploads/2023/05/2023-Climate-Risk-Landscape-Technical-supplement.pdf

UNEP FI. (2024a). The 2024 climate risk landscape. Retrieved from https://www.unepfi.org/themes/climate-change/2024-climate-risk-landscape/

UNEP FI. (2024b). Managing physical climate-related risks in loan portfolios. Retrieved from https://www.unepfi.org/themes/climate-change/managing-physical-climate-related-risks-in-loan-portfolios/

UNEP FI. (2024c). Assessing climate transition risk: methodologies and roles for financial institutions. Retrieved from https://www.unepfi.org/themes/climate-change/assessing-climate-transition-risk-methodologies-and-roles-for-financial-institutions/

UNEP FI. (2024d). The climate data challenge: The critical role of open-source and neutral data platforms. Retrieved from https://www.unepfi.org/themes/climate-change/the-climate-data-challenge-the-critical-role-of-open-source-and-neutral-data-platforms/

UNEP FI. (2024e). Database: The climate risk dashboard. Retrieved from https://www.unepfi.org/themes/climate-change/the-climate-risk-dashboard/

United Nations Office for Disaster Risk Reduction (UNDRR). (2023). GAR special report 2023: mapping resilience for the sustainable development goals. Retrieved 8 March, 2025, from https://www.undrr.org/gar/gar2023-special-report

World Economic Forum (WEF). (2024). 9 ways AI is helping tackle climate change. World Economic Forum. Retrieved 8 March, 2025, from https://www.weforum.org/stories/2024/02/ai-combat-climate-change/

Case Reference

Moody's. (2025). Climate risk. www.moodys.com. Retrieved from https://www.moodys.com/web/en/us/capabilities/climate-risk.html

Morgan Stanley Capital International (MSCI). (2020). Climate value-at-risk. Retrieved from https://www.msci.com/documents/1296102/16985724/MSCI-ClimateVaR-Introduction-Feb2020.pdf

MSCI. (2025). Climate and net-zero solutions. Retrieved from https://www.msci.com/our-solutions/climate-and-net-zero

CHAPTER 16

Climate-Related Disclosure: Standards, Best Practices, and Implementation

1 Introduction: The Transparency Imperative

In the fight against climate change, information is power. Transparency about climate-related risks and opportunities is essential for mobilizing capital toward sustainable solutions, holding companies and investors accountable for their actions, and building a more resilient financial system and economy. As climate change becomes an increasingly prominent factor in financial decision-making, the demand for clear, consistent, and comparable climate-related disclosures is growing rapidly. FSB (2024) reports progress on consistent climate disclosures, highlighting ISSB's role and challenges like regulatory inconsistencies and SME capacity building. TCFD (2023) notes increased climate disclosure adoption but identifies data sourcing challenges, particularly for investee companies. IFRS (2023) highlights progress in aligning corporate reporting with ISSB Standards, with growing adoption across jurisdictions representing over 57% of global GDP.

Disclosure is not merely a box-ticking exercise; it's a strategic imperative. By openly communicating their climate-related risks and opportunities, companies and financial institutions can:

- **Empower Investors to Make Informed Decisions:** Investors need reliable and comprehensive information on climate risks and opportunities to assess the potential impact on their portfolios and make investment decisions that align with their sustainability goals. CFA Institute (2020) emphasizes the integration of climate change analysis in investment processes, highlighting the need for transparent carbon pricing and enhanced disclosures. BlackRock (2022) emphasizes the growing

J. Chen, *Climate Finance*,
https://doi.org/10.1007/978-981-96-7975-1_16

importance of sustainability and decarbonization for long-term company success.

- **Build Trust and Credibility:** Transparency fosters trust and credibility with investors, customers, employees, and other stakeholders, demonstrating a commitment to responsible business practices and climate action.
- **Drive Efficient Capital Allocation:** Clear and consistent disclosures enable investors to compare the climate performance of different companies and investment options, leading to a more efficient allocation of capital toward sustainable solutions.
- **Enhance Risk Management and Resilience:** The process of disclosing climate-related information encourages companies to identify, assess, and manage their climate risks, strengthening their resilience to climate impacts and the low-carbon transition.

This chapter will explore the key frameworks and standards that are driving climate-related disclosure, providing a practical guide to implementing these disclosures and communicating climate risks and opportunities effectively.

2 Key Disclosure Frameworks

The most recent disclosure report, "Achieving Consistent and Comparable Climate-related Disclosures 2024 Progress report," by the Financial Stability Board (FSB, 2024) highlights significant advancements in global climate-related financial disclosures, primarily driven by the adoption of the International Sustainability Standards Board (ISSB) standards. Notable achievements include enhanced interoperability between diverse disclosure frameworks, increased jurisdictional commitment to mandatory reporting, and the establishment of robust assurance and ethics frameworks to enhance the reliability of climate disclosures. Despite progress, challenges remain for small- and medium-sized enterprises and emerging markets due to regulatory uncertainties.

Key Points

- High-quality, consistent climate-related disclosures are vital for managing sustainability-related financial risks and increasing transparency.
- The ISSB published its inaugural disclosure standards in 2023, marking a significant milestone in establishing a global disclosure framework.
- Jurisdictions have increasingly incorporated ISSB standards into their regulations, with over three-fourths of FSB member jurisdictions proposing climate-related disclosure requirements.
- Implementation challenges persist, particularly for small and medium enterprises due to data gaps and the perceived high cost of compliance.

- The FSB and ISSB are prioritizing capacity building to aid jurisdictions and organizations in adopting the new standards effectively.
- The Basel Committee on Banking Supervision is finalizing guidelines to enhance consistency in climate-related financial risk disclosures for banks.
- The ongoing evolution of compliance frameworks is leading to gradual alignment between different regional and international standards, fostering greater interoperability.

As can be seen from the report, several frameworks and standards have emerged to guide climate-related disclosure, providing a common language and a set of best practices for companies and financial institutions to communicate relevant information to their stakeholders.

What Are TCFD, SASB, GRI, ISSB?

The TCFD (Task Force on Climate-related Financial Disclosures), ISSB (International Sustainability Standards Board), SASB (Sustainability Accounting Standards Board), and GRI (Global Reporting Initiative) are key frameworks and organizations focused on enhancing climate and sustainability disclosures in the financial and corporate sectors. Here's a breakdown of their relationships and functions:

TCFD (Task Force on Climate-Related Financial Disclosures)

- **Purpose**: TCFD provides recommendations for companies to disclose climate-related financial risks and opportunities in their annual financial filings.
- **Focus**: It emphasizes governance, strategy, risk management, metrics, and targets as crucial components of climate-related disclosures.
- **Influence**: TCFD has influenced multiple regulatory frameworks worldwide and has formed the foundation for many other disclosure standards, including ISSB's work.
- **Note**: TCFD has released the following statement[1]: "Concurrent with the release of its 2023 status report on October 12, 2023, the **TCFD has fulfilled its remit and disbanded.** The FSB has asked the IFRS Foundation to take over the monitoring of the progress of companies' climate-related disclosures."

SASB (Sustainability Accounting Standards Board)

- **Purpose**: SASB develops industry-specific standards for sustainability disclosures that address the financial impacts of sustainability issues on a company's performance.

[1] https://www.fsb-tcfd.org/.

- **Relationship with ISSB**: SASB's standards are being integrated into ISSB's work to offer detailed, industry-relevant metrics that complement broader ESG reporting. The ISSB has absorbed SASB's standards, recognizing their utility in providing granular sustainability information.
- **Complementary Focus**: While SASB concentrates on financial impacts relevant to investors, it aligns with TCFD's risk-focused approach.

GRI (Global Reporting Initiative)

- **Purpose**: GRI is aimed at broader sustainability reporting beyond financial impacts, including social and environmental dimensions. Its standards guide organizations in reporting on their economic, environmental, and social impacts.
- **Comprehensive Approach**: GRI emphasizes stakeholder inclusiveness, sustainability context, and completeness in disclosures, which differs somewhat from the financial materiality focus of TCFD and ISSB.
- **Alignment Efforts**: Recently, GRI has initiated efforts to align with ISSB standards, acknowledging the importance of both financial and broader sustainability disclosures.

ISSB (International Sustainability Standards Board)

- **Purpose**: ISSB was established to create and maintain a comprehensive global baseline of sustainability disclosure standards that provide investors and other capital market participants with information about a company's sustainability-related risks and opportunities. ISSB operates under the IFRS (International Financial Reporting Standards) Foundation's oversight, taking on the responsibility for developing sustainability disclosure standards, particularly in the wake of the TCFD's disbandment.
- **Integration with TCFD**: The ISSB's inaugural standards are informed by TCFD recommendations, and they aim to provide more transparent and comparable sustainability reporting that includes climate-related disclosures.
- **Global Framework**: By focusing on interoperability and broad acceptance, ISSB seeks to unify various global reporting frameworks under one set of standards.

Relationships

- **Interoperability and Integration**: ISSB aims to provide a cohesive framework that integrates the specific climate-risk focus of TCFD, the industry-specific guidance of SASB, and the broader sustainability reporting principles of GRI.

- **Increasing Consistency**: As regulatory bodies and jurisdictions begin to include ISSB standards, it fosters a unified approach to climate-related disclosures, enhancing reliability and comparability across different sectors and regions.
- **Challenges and Support**: Despite progress, challenges remain, particularly for small- and medium-sized enterprises regarding compliance costs and data availability. Organizations like the FSB, ISSB, and others are prioritizing capacity-building efforts to support these entities in adapting to new standards effectively.

Together, these organizations represent a concerted move toward improved transparency and accountability in corporate sustainability and climate-related financial reporting.

AtlasZero (2024) discusses the transition from the Task Force on Climate-related Financial Disclosures (TCFD) to the International Sustainability Standards Board (ISSB) as companies move toward mandatory climate reporting. It highlights that while the ISSB standards build on TCFD recommendations, they introduce additional requirements aimed at enhancing transparency and financial stability. As the IFRS Foundation oversees the ISSB, it reinforces the importance of comprehensive climate-related disclosures without replacing the TCFD framework itself.

Although ISSB is becoming the most recent global disclosure standards, it still is heavily influenced by TCFD framework and SASB standards, and complemented by GRI. So we will discuss the TCFD, SASA, GRI, respectively, in the following sections.

2.1 Task Force on Climate-Related Financial Disclosures (TCFD)

The Task Force on Climate-Related Financial Disclosures (TCFD), established by the Financial Stability Board (FSB) in 2015, has become the leading global framework for climate-related disclosures. The TCFD's recommendations are designed to help companies and financial institutions provide investors with clear, consistent, and comparable information about their climate-related risks and opportunities.

The TCFD recommendations are structured around four core elements:

- **Governance:** Disclosures on the organization's governance around climate-related risks and opportunities. This includes the board's oversight of climate-related issues, the role of management in assessing and managing risks, and the integration of climate considerations into the organization's overall strategy.
- **Strategy:** Disclosures on the actual and potential impacts of climate-related risks and opportunities on the organization's businesses, strategy, and financial planning. This includes identifying the most significant

climate-related risks and opportunities, assessing their potential financial impacts, and explaining how the organization is adapting its strategy to address these challenges and capitalize on opportunities.

- **Risk Management:** Disclosures on the processes used by the organization to identify, assess, and manage climate-related risks. This includes describing the organization's risk management framework, the methodologies used to assess risks, and the processes for integrating climate risks into existing risk management processes.
- **Metrics and Targets:** Disclosures on the metrics and targets used by the organization to assess and manage climate-related risks and opportunities. This includes disclosing the key metrics used to track climate-related performance (e.g., greenhouse gas emissions, energy consumption, water usage), the organization's targets for reducing emissions or improving resilience, and the progress made toward achieving these targets.

The TCFD recommendations are voluntary, but they have gained widespread support from investors, companies, and regulators worldwide. PRI (2024) provides a framework for investors to report climate-related investment activities, aligning with TCFD and GFANZ. Aligning disclosures with the TCFD framework provides several benefits, including:

- **Improved Risk Management:** The process of developing TCFD-aligned disclosures encourages companies to systematically assess their climate risks, leading to more effective risk management practices.
- **Enhanced Investor Confidence:** Transparent and consistent disclosures build investor confidence, demonstrating a commitment to managing climate risks and opportunities.
- **Reduced Cost of Capital:** Companies that demonstrate strong climate risk management practices and provide transparent disclosures may benefit from a lower cost of capital, as investors perceive them as less risky.

2.1.1 Case Study 16.1: The Impact of TCFD Disclosures on the Financial Sector

Focus: Examine the Broader Impact of TCFD Adoption on the Financial Sector, Exploring How Disclosures Are Influencing Investment Decisions and Risk Management Practices

The Task Force on Climate-related Financial Disclosures (TCFD) has had a significant impact on the financial sector by influencing investment decisions and risk management practices. This case study explores how financial institutions, including banks, insurance companies, and asset managers, are increasingly using TCFD-aligned disclosures from companies to assess climate-related financial risks, inform investment decisions, and engage with companies on their climate performance.

Illustration: How Financial Institutions Use TCFD-Aligned Disclosures

1. **Assessing Climate-Related Financial Risks:**

Financial institutions use TCFD-aligned disclosures to assess the climate-related financial risks of their investments. These disclosures provide detailed information on companies' governance, strategy, risk management, and metrics related to climate risks. By analyzing this information, financial institutions can identify potential risks, such as exposure to physical risks (e.g., extreme weather events) and transition risks (e.g., regulatory changes), and incorporate these risks into their risk management frameworks.

2. **Informing Investment Decisions:**

TCFD-aligned disclosures help investors make more informed investment decisions by providing insights into companies' climate strategies and their preparedness for the low-carbon transition. Investors can use this information to identify companies that are well-positioned to manage climate risks and capitalize on opportunities, as well as those that may face significant challenges. This enables investors to allocate capital more effectively and support companies that demonstrate strong climate performance.

3. **Engaging with Companies on Climate Performance:**

Financial institutions use TCFD-aligned disclosures to engage with companies on their climate performance. By analyzing the disclosed information, investors can identify areas where companies need to improve their climate strategies and risk management practices. This engagement can drive positive change, encouraging companies to adopt more robust climate policies, set ambitious targets, and enhance their transparency.

Discussion: Challenges, Standardization, and Role of Regulators

1. **Challenges of Comparing Disclosures Across Different Companies:**

Comparing TCFD-aligned disclosures across different companies presents several challenges:

- **Data Consistency:** Companies may use different methodologies and assumptions in their disclosures, making it difficult to compare data consistently (FSOC, 2022; Chapter 2: Understanding Climate Risks, 2023).

- **Scope and Detail:** The level of detail and scope of disclosures can vary significantly, with some companies providing comprehensive information and others offering more limited insights.
- **Evolving Standards:** As the field of climate risk disclosure evolves, standards and best practices are continuously being updated, leading to variations in how companies report their climate risks.
- **Need for Standardized Methodologies and Data:**

Standardized methodologies and data are essential for ensuring the consistency and comparability of TCFD-aligned disclosures. Standardization helps investors and other stakeholders accurately assess and compare the climate risks and opportunities of different companies. Efforts to develop standardized frameworks, such as the TCFD recommendations and the work of the Financial Stability Board (FSB), are crucial for promoting consistency and reliability in climate risk reporting.

3. **Role of Regulators in Promoting Consistency and Comparability:**

Regulators play a critical role in promoting consistency and comparability in TCFD reporting. By setting clear guidelines and standards for climate risk disclosures, regulators can ensure that companies provide high-quality, comparable information. Initiatives such as the SEC's proposed rules to enhance and standardize climate-related disclosures and the efforts of the Financial Stability Oversight Council (FSOC) to coordinate climate risk assessment and disclosure are essential for fostering transparency and accountability in the financial sector.

Conclusion

The adoption of TCFD-aligned disclosures has had a significant impact on the financial sector by influencing investment decisions and risk management practices. Financial institutions use these disclosures to assess climate-related financial risks, inform investment decisions, and engage with companies on their climate performance. However, challenges remain in comparing disclosures across different companies, highlighting the need for standardized methodologies and data.

Regulators play a crucial role in promoting consistency and comparability in TCFD reporting, ensuring that companies provide high-quality, comparable information. The benefits of TCFD-aligned disclosures include enhanced investor confidence, improved risk management, and a strengthened commitment to climate action.

Understanding the methodologies and strategies employed by financial institutions in using TCFD-aligned disclosures can provide valuable insights for other stakeholders seeking to enhance their climate risk assessment processes and support the transition to a low-carbon economy.

2.2 *Sustainability Accounting Standards Board (SASB)*

The Sustainability Accounting Standards Board (SASB) develops industry-specific sustainability accounting standards, including metrics related to climate change. Unlike the TCFD recommendations, which are designed to be broadly applicable across all sectors, SASB standards are tailored to the specific risks and opportunities associated with different industries.

SASB's focus is on disclosing financially material sustainability information—information that is likely to affect a company's financial performance and is therefore relevant to investors. The standards identify the most important sustainability topics for each industry, including climate change, and provide guidance on the metrics that companies should disclose to communicate their performance on these issues.

For example, SASB standards for the oil and gas industry include metrics related to greenhouse gas emissions, methane emissions, water management, and the transition to a low-carbon economy. Standards for the electric utility industry cover topics such as renewable energy generation, energy efficiency, and climate change adaptation.

Aligning disclosures with SASB standards provides several benefits:

- **Improved Investor Communication:** SASB standards provide a clear and consistent framework for communicating material sustainability information to investors, enabling them to make more informed decisions.
- **Enhanced Risk Management:** The process of identifying and disclosing material sustainability issues encourages companies to focus on the most significant ESG risks and opportunities, leading to more effective risk management practices.
- **Reduced Cost of Capital:** Companies that demonstrate strong sustainability performance and provide transparent disclosures may benefit from a lower cost of capital, as investors perceive them as being better managed and less exposed to ESG risks.

2.2.1 *Case Study 16.2: The Use of SASB Standards in the Electric Utility Sector*

Focus: Examine How Companies in the Electric Utility Sector Are Using SASB Standards to Disclose Their Climate-Related Performance and Compare Their Progress

The electric utility sector is increasingly using the Sustainability Accounting Standards Board (SASB) standards to disclose climate-related performance, focusing on greenhouse gas emissions, renewable energy generation capacity, energy efficiency programs, and climate adaptation plans. This case study explores how electric utility companies are leveraging SASB's industry-specific standards to enhance transparency and accountability in their transition to a cleaner energy system.

Illustration: How Electric Utility Companies Use SASB Standards

1. **Disclosing Greenhouse Gas Emissions:**

Electric utility companies use SASB standards to disclose their greenhouse gas (GHG) emissions, including Scope 1, 2, and 3 emissions. By providing detailed data on GHG emissions, companies can demonstrate their progress in reducing carbon footprints and complying with regulatory requirements. For example, J-POWER, a Japanese electric utility company, discloses its gross global Scope 1 emissions and the percentage of emissions under regulatory limits using SASB metrics (J-Power, 2025).

2. **Renewable Energy Generation Capacity:**

SASB standards guide electric utility companies in disclosing their renewable energy generation capacity. This includes reporting the percentage of total energy generated from renewable sources, such as wind, solar, and hydroelectric power. By tracking and reporting this data, companies can showcase their commitment to transitioning to renewable energy and reducing reliance on fossil fuels (IFRS Foundation, 2022).

3. **Energy Efficiency Programs:**

Electric utility companies disclose their energy efficiency programs using SASB standards, including metrics on customer electricity savings from efficiency measures. These disclosures help stakeholders understand the impact of energy efficiency initiatives on reducing overall energy consumption and GHG emissions. For example, companies may report the percentage of electric load served by smart grid technology and the savings achieved through energy efficiency programs (KPMG, 2023).

4. **Climate Adaptation Plans:**

SASB standards also guide electric utility companies in disclosing their climate adaptation plans. These plans outline the strategies and measures companies are implementing to enhance the resilience of their infrastructure and operations to climate-related risks, such as extreme weather events and sea-level rise. By providing detailed information on climate adaptation efforts, companies can demonstrate their proactive approach to managing climate risks (Accenture, 2021).

Discussion: Benefits, Challenges, and Potential of SASB Disclosures

1. **Benefits of Using a Standardized Framework for Disclosure:**

Using SASB standards provides several benefits for electric utility companies:

- **Enhanced Comparability:** Standardized disclosures enable stakeholders to compare climate performance across companies and sectors consistently.
- **Increased Transparency:** Detailed and consistent reporting enhances transparency, building trust with investors, regulators, and other stakeholders.
- **Improved Decision-Making:** Access to standardized data helps investors and other stakeholders make informed decisions about the company's climate strategy and performance (KPMG, 2023).

2. **Challenges of Data Collection and Reporting for Complex Infrastructure Assets:**

Disclosing climate-related performance for complex infrastructure assets presents several challenges (Accenture, 2021; KPMG, 2023):

- **Data Availability:** Collecting accurate and comprehensive data on GHG emissions, energy use, and other metrics can be challenging, especially for large, geographically dispersed operations.
- **Reporting Consistency:** Ensuring consistency in data reporting across different business units and regions requires robust data management systems and processes.
- **Regulatory Compliance:** Navigating different regulatory requirements and standards across jurisdictions adds complexity to the reporting process.

3. **Potential for SASB Disclosures to Drive Greater Transparency and Accountability:**

SASB disclosures have the potential to drive greater transparency and accountability in the electric utility sector's transition to a cleaner energy system (KPMG, 2023):

- **Investor Confidence:** Transparent and standardized disclosures build investor confidence in the company's ability to manage climate risks and opportunities.
- **Regulatory Compliance:** Detailed disclosures help companies comply with regulatory requirements and demonstrate their commitment to sustainability.

- **Stakeholder Engagement:** Clear and comprehensive reporting fosters engagement with stakeholders, including investors, customers, and regulators, enhancing the company's reputation and credibility.

Conclusion

The use of SASB standards in the electric utility sector exemplifies the importance of standardized climate-related disclosures in enhancing transparency and accountability. By disclosing greenhouse gas emissions, renewable energy generation capacity, energy efficiency programs, and climate adaptation plans, electric utility companies can provide stakeholders with valuable insights into their climate performance and strategy.

The benefits of using a standardized framework for disclosure include enhanced comparability, increased transparency, and improved decision-making. However, challenges such as data availability, reporting consistency, and regulatory compliance must be addressed to ensure effective disclosure. SASB disclosures have the potential to drive greater transparency and accountability, building investor confidence and supporting the transition to a cleaner energy system.

Understanding the methodologies and strategies employed by electric utility companies in using SASB standards can provide valuable insights for other sectors and stakeholders seeking to enhance their climate risk assessment processes and support the transition to a low-carbon economy.

2.3 Global Reporting Initiative (GRI)

The Global Reporting Initiative (GRI) provides a comprehensive framework for sustainability reporting, covering a wide range of environmental, social, and governance (ESG) topics, including climate change. The GRI Standards are designed to be universally applicable, meaning that organizations of all sizes, sectors, and locations can use them to report on their sustainability performance.

The GRI Standards cover a wide range of topics, including:

- **Economic:** Economic performance, market presence, indirect economic impacts, procurement practices.
- **Environmental:** Materials, energy, water, biodiversity, emissions, effluents and waste, environmental compliance, supplier environmental assessment.
- **Social:** Employment, labor/management relations, occupational health and safety, training and education, diversity and equal opportunity, non-discrimination, freedom of association and collective bargaining, child labor, forced or compulsory labor, security practices, indigenous

rights, human rights assessment, local communities, supplier social assessment, public policy, customer health and safety, marketing and labeling, customer privacy, socioeconomic compliance.

Within each topic area, the GRI Standards provide specific disclosure indicators that companies can use to report on their performance.

The benefits of using the GRI Standards include:

- **Enhanced Stakeholder Engagement:** The GRI framework encourages companies to engage with a wide range of stakeholders, including investors, employees, customers, communities, and NGOs, to understand their expectations and concerns related to sustainability.
- **Improved Reputation:** Transparent and comprehensive sustainability reporting can enhance a company's reputation, demonstrating its commitment to responsible business practices and stakeholder engagement.
- **Increased Transparency:** The GRI Standards promote transparency by providing a standardized framework for disclosure, enabling stakeholders to compare the sustainability performance of different organizations.

3 Implementing Climate Risk Disclosures: A Step-by-Step Guide

Implementing climate-related disclosures can seem daunting, especially for companies that are new to this process. However, a structured approach can simplify the task and ensure that disclosures are effective, meaningful, and aligned with best practices.

3.1 Understanding the Requirements

The first step is to carefully review the specific requirements of the chosen disclosure framework. Whether a company chooses to align with the TCFD recommendations, SASB standards, the GRI Standards, or a combination of frameworks, it's essential to understand the key elements of the framework, the specific metrics and indicators that need to be disclosed, and the reporting guidelines.

It's also important to consider the target audience for the disclosures. While investors are a primary audience, other stakeholders, such as customers, employees, communities, and regulators, may also be interested in the company's climate-related information. IFRS (2024) compares IFRS S2 with TCFD, noting S2's more detailed requirements.

3.2 Assessing Climate Risks and Opportunities

The core of climate-related disclosure is a comprehensive assessment of the company's climate risks and opportunities. This assessment should consider both physical and transition risks, as well as the potential for climate change to create new business opportunities.

The assessment process can be broken down into three main steps:

- **Step 1: Governance and Strategy:**
  - **Governance:** Begin by assessing the company's governance structures and processes related to climate change.

    Key Questions:

    Does the board of directors have oversight of climate-related risks and opportunities?

    Does management have clear responsibility for climate-related issues?

    Are climate considerations integrated into the company's overall strategy and risk management framework?
  - **Strategy:** Identify and evaluate the potential impacts of climate change on the company's businesses, strategy, and financial planning.

    Key Questions:

    What are the most significant climate-related risks and opportunities facing the company?

    How could climate change impact the company's revenues, costs, and profitability?

    How is the company adapting its strategy to address climate risks and capitalize on opportunities?
- **Step 2: Risk Management:**

  Risk Assessment: Conduct a thorough assessment of the company's climate-related risks, considering both physical risks (e.g., extreme weather events, sea-level rise) and transition risks (e.g., policy changes, technological advancements, market shifts).

  Key Questions:

  What are the specific climate hazards that could impact the company's operations or assets?

  How vulnerable is the company to these hazards?

  What are the potential financial implications of these risks?

  Risk Management: Describe the processes used to manage climate-related risks.

  Key Questions:

  How are climate risks integrated into the company's existing risk management framework?

What specific measures are being taken to mitigate climate risks?

How is the company monitoring and reviewing its climate risk management processes?

Scenario Analysis and Stress Testing: Utilize scenario analysis and stress testing to evaluate the potential impacts of different climate scenarios on the company's financial performance and resilience.

Key Questions:

How would the company's business be affected by different levels of global warming?

What are the financial implications of a rapid transition to a low-carbon economy?

How resilient is the company to extreme weather events or other climate shocks?

- **Step 3: Metrics and Targets:**

Metrics: Select appropriate metrics to track the company's climate-related performance.

Key Questions:

What are the key metrics for measuring the company's greenhouse gas emissions, energy consumption, water usage, and other relevant factors?

Are these metrics aligned with industry standards and best practices?

Targets: Set targets and goals for climate action, demonstrating the company's commitment to reducing its environmental footprint and contributing to a low-carbon future.

Key Questions:

Does the company have targets for reducing its greenhouse gas emissions?

Does it have plans to transition to renewable energy sources or improve its energy efficiency?

Is it investing in climate adaptation measures to enhance its resilience?

Progress Tracking: Track progress toward achieving these targets and report on the outcomes.

Key Questions:

How is the company measuring its progress toward its climate targets?

What challenges or barriers has the company encountered?

What lessons has the company learned from its climate action efforts?

3.3 *Collecting and Analyzing Relevant Data*

Effective climate risk disclosure requires reliable and accurate data. Companies need to gather data from a variety of sources, both internal and external, to assess their climate risks and opportunities comprehensively.

Key data sources include:

- **Internal Data:**
- **Operational Data:** Data on the company's energy consumption, greenhouse gas emissions, water usage, waste generation, and other relevant environmental metrics.
- **Financial Data:** Data on the company's revenues, costs, and profitability, as well as its exposure to climate-sensitive assets or markets.
- **Risk Management Data:** Information on the company's risk management framework, its assessment of climate risks, and its mitigation and adaptation strategies.
- **External Data:**
- **Climate Models and Projections:** Data from global climate models (GCMs), downscaled to regional or local scales, providing projections of future climate change, such as temperature increases, sea-level rise, and changes in precipitation patterns.
- **Scientific Reports and Assessments:** Reports from the Intergovernmental Panel on Climate Change (IPCC), national climate assessments, and other scientific organizations that provide insights into climate change impacts, risks, and vulnerabilities.
- **Industry Data:** Data on industry trends, benchmarks, and best practices related to climate change mitigation and adaptation.
- **Regulatory Data:** Information on current and future climate-related regulations, policies, and incentives.

Once data has been collected, it needs to be analyzed to identify key trends, assess potential risks and opportunities, and inform the company's disclosure strategy. This analysis can involve:

- **Quantitative Analysis:** Using statistical methods to analyze data, calculate key metrics (e.g., carbon footprint, implied temperature rise), and project future impacts.
- **Qualitative Analysis:** Conducting research, reviewing industry reports, and engaging with experts to gather insights into emerging trends, best practices, and the potential implications of climate change for the company's business.

3.4 *Communicating Climate Risks and Opportunities Effectively*

Effective communication is crucial for making climate-related disclosures meaningful and impactful. Disclosures should be clear, concise, transparent, and tailored to the target audience.

Key principles for effective communication:

- **Clarity and Conciseness:** Use plain language, avoid technical jargon, and focus on the most material information.
- **Transparency:** Clearly explain the methodologies used to assess climate risks and opportunities, the data sources, and the assumptions made.
- **Balance:** Present a balanced view of both risks and opportunities, avoiding overly optimistic or pessimistic portrayals.
- **Materiality:** Focus on disclosing information that is relevant and material to investors and other stakeholders, prioritizing issues that are likely to have a significant impact on the company's financial performance or long-term sustainability.
- **Visualizations:** Use charts, graphs, maps, and other visuals to present complex data in a clear and accessible way, enhancing comprehension and engagement.
- **Storytelling and Narrative:** Frame climate-related information within relatable narratives that connect with the audience's values and interests. Use real-world examples and case studies to illustrate the potential impacts of climate change and the company's response.
- **Target Audience:** Tailor the language, level of detail, and communication channels to the specific target audience. Investors, regulators, customers, and employees may have different information needs and preferences.

4 Evolving Regulatory Landscape and Mandatory Disclosure

The landscape of climate-related disclosure is rapidly shifting from voluntary guidelines to mandatory requirements. As the urgency of addressing climate change grows and the financial risks become more apparent, governments and regulators worldwide are recognizing the need for standardized and comparable climate-related information to guide investment decisions, promote transparency, and mitigate systemic risks.

4.1 *The Shift Toward Mandatory Disclosure*

Several jurisdictions have already implemented or are considering mandatory climate risk disclosure regulations, including:

- **European Union:** The EU's Corporate Sustainability Reporting Directive (CSRD) will require companies to disclose a wide range of sustainability information, including climate-related data, aligned with the European Sustainability Reporting Standards (ESRS). The CSRD will apply to all large companies, listed SMEs, and non-EU companies with significant activity in the EU. CSRD mandates enhanced ESG disclosures for EU companies (European Commission, 2024).
- **United Kingdom:** The UK government has mandated TCFD-aligned disclosures for large companies and financial institutions, requiring them to report on their governance, strategy, risk management, and metrics and targets related to climate change.
- **New Zealand:** New Zealand was the first country to introduce mandatory climate-related disclosures, requiring financial institutions and large listed companies to report in line with the TCFD recommendations.
- **United States:** The US Securities and Exchange Commission (SEC) has proposed a rule on climate-related disclosures that would require publicly traded companies to disclose their greenhouse gas emissions and climate-related risks in their registration statements and periodic reports. SEC (2024) requires climate risk disclosures from US registrants.

4.2 Key Regulatory Developments

CDSB (2022) explains its consolidation into IFRS Foundation and the formation of ISSB to create global sustainability disclosure standards.

- **European Union's CSRD:** The CSRD significantly expands the scope of sustainability reporting requirements in the EU, introducing more detailed and standardized disclosure standards. The ESRS, which are being developed by the European Financial Reporting Advisory Group (EFRAG), will cover a wide range of sustainability topics, including climate change, biodiversity, and social responsibility.
- **United States' SEC Proposed Rule:** The SEC's proposed rule, if adopted, would mark a major shift in climate disclosure requirements in the United States. It would require companies to disclose their direct and indirect greenhouse gas emissions (Scope 1 and Scope 2) and, in some cases, emissions from their value chain (Scope 3). Companies would also be required to disclose climate-related risks that are reasonably likely to have a material impact on their business, their strategy for managing those risks, and the impact of climate change on their financial statements.

4.3 Implications for Companies and Investors

The shift toward mandatory climate-related disclosure has significant implications for both companies and investors:

- **Companies:**
  - **Increased Compliance Burden:** Companies will need to invest in systems and processes to collect, analyze, and report climate-related data, which can be a significant undertaking, particularly for companies with complex operations or global supply chains.
  - **Enhanced Scrutiny:** Companies can expect greater scrutiny from investors, regulators, and other stakeholders regarding their climate performance. This scrutiny will likely intensify as more standardized and comparable data becomes available.
  - **Potential Litigation Risks:** Companies that fail to disclose material climate risks or make misleading claims in their disclosures could face legal challenges from investors or regulators.
- **Investors:**
  - **Improved Access to Information:** Mandatory disclosure will provide investors with access to more standardized, comparable, and reliable climate-related information, enabling them to make more informed investment decisions and assess the climate performance of different companies.
  - **Enhanced Engagement Opportunities:** Investors will have more leverage to engage with companies on their climate performance, advocate for improved practices, and hold companies accountable for their climate commitments.

The move toward mandatory climate risk disclosure is a significant step forward in building a more transparent, accountable, and resilient financial system. By providing investors with the information they need to assess climate risks and opportunities, these regulations can help to accelerate the flow of capital toward sustainable solutions and support the transition to a low-carbon economy.

4.3.1 Case Study 16.3: The SEC's Proposed Rule on Climate Disclosures and Its Potential Impacts on US Companies

Focus: Analyze the Potential Impacts of the SEC's Proposed Rule on Climate-Related Disclosures for Publicly Traded Companies in the United States

The Securities and Exchange Commission (SEC) has proposed a rule to enhance and standardize climate-related disclosures for publicly traded companies in the United States. This case study examines the potential impacts of the SEC's proposed rule on corporate disclosure practices, focusing on how companies are preparing for the rule's implementation, assessing their climate risks, developing emissions accounting methodologies, and considering the implications for financial reporting and investor relations.

Illustration: How Companies Are Preparing for the SEC's Proposed Rule

1. **Assessing Climate Risks:**

Companies are conducting detailed assessments of their climate-related risks to comply with the SEC's proposed rule. This involves identifying physical risks (e.g., extreme weather events, sea-level rise) and transition risks (e.g., regulatory changes, market shifts) that could impact their operations, financial performance, and strategic planning. Companies are using scenario analysis to evaluate the potential impacts of different climate scenarios on their business (U.S. Securities and Exchange Commission, 2024; PwC, 2024).

2. **Developing Emissions Accounting Methodologies:**

To comply with the SEC's proposed rule, companies are developing robust methodologies for accounting and reporting their greenhouse gas (GHG) emissions. This includes measuring Scope 1 (direct emissions), Scope 2 (indirect emissions from purchased energy), and, in some cases, Scope 3 (other indirect emissions) emissions. Companies are leveraging established frameworks such as the Greenhouse Gas Protocol to ensure accurate and consistent emissions reporting (U.S. Securities and Exchange Commission, 2024; White & Case LLP, 2024).

3. **Considering Implications for Financial Reporting and Investor Relations:**

Companies are evaluating the implications of the SEC's proposed rule for their financial reporting and investor relations. This includes assessing how climate-related risks and opportunities could impact their financial statements, such as through asset impairments, changes in operating costs, and potential liabilities. Companies are also enhancing their communication with investors to provide transparent and decision-useful climate-related information (U.S. Securities and Exchange Commission, 2024; PwC, 2024).

Discussion: Benefits, Challenges, and Ongoing Debate

1. **Benefits of the SEC's Proposed Rule:**

The SEC's proposed rule offers several benefits:

- **Enhanced Transparency:** Standardized climate-related disclosures provide investors with consistent and comparable information, improving transparency.
- **Informed Decision-Making:** Reliable climate-related data helps investors assess the potential financial impacts of climate risks and opportunities, facilitating better investment decisions.
- **Market Efficiency:** By enabling better pricing of climate-related risks, the rule can enhance market efficiency and stability (U.S. Securities and Exchange Commission, 2024; PwC, 2024).

2. **Challenges of Implementing the Rule's Requirements:**

Implementing the SEC's proposed rule presents several challenges:

- **Data Collection and Verification:** Collecting accurate and comprehensive climate-related data can be difficult, especially for companies with complex supply chains.
- **Resource Allocation:** Smaller companies or those with limited resources may struggle to meet the new reporting requirements.
- **Alignment with Existing Frameworks:** Companies already reporting under different frameworks (e.g., TCFD, SASB) may face challenges in aligning their practices with the new SEC requirements (White & Case LLP, 2024; Balsanek et al., 2024).

3. **Ongoing Debate About the Scope and Stringency of Climate Disclosure Regulations:**

The SEC's proposed rule has sparked a debate about the scope and stringency of climate disclosure regulations:

- **Scope of Disclosures:** Some stakeholders argue for more comprehensive disclosures, including Scope 3 emissions, while others advocate for a more focused approach.
- **Regulatory Burden:** Critics of the rule express concerns about the regulatory burden on companies, particularly smaller firms, and the potential costs of compliance.
- **Legal Challenges:** The rule has faced legal challenges, with opponents questioning the SEC's authority to mandate such disclosures and raising concerns about potential First Amendment violations (U.S. Securities and Exchange Commission, 2024; Balsanek et al., 2024).

Conclusion

The SEC's proposed rule on climate-related disclosures is poised to significantly impact corporate disclosure practices in the United States. By assessing their climate risks, developing emissions accounting methodologies, and considering the implications for financial reporting and investor relations, companies are preparing for the potential implementation of the rule.

The benefits of the rule include enhanced transparency, improved investor decision-making, and greater market efficiency. However, challenges such as data collection, resource allocation, and alignment with existing frameworks must be addressed. The ongoing debate about the scope and stringency of climate disclosure regulations highlights the complexities of implementing such a rule.

Understanding the methodologies and strategies employed by companies in adapting to the SEC's proposed rule can provide valuable insights for other organizations and stakeholders seeking to enhance their climate risk assessment processes and support the transition to a net-zero economy.

5 Conclusion: Transparency as a Catalyst for Action

Climate-related disclosure is no longer a niche practice; it's becoming a mainstream expectation for companies and financial institutions. As the urgency of addressing climate change grows, the demand for transparency, accountability, and reliable information on climate-related risks and opportunities will only intensify.

This chapter has explored the key frameworks and standards that are shaping climate-related disclosure, providing a practical guide to implementing disclosures, communicating effectively, and navigating the evolving regulatory landscape.

By embracing transparency, adopting recognized disclosure frameworks, and engaging proactively with investors and other stakeholders, companies and financial institutions can demonstrate their commitment to climate action, build trust and credibility, and contribute to a more sustainable future.

As climate change reshapes the global economy, transparency will be a crucial catalyst for driving the transition to a low-carbon and climate-resilient world.

References

AtlasZero. (2025). Does IFRS replace TCFD? Atlaszero.earth. TCFD. Retrieved 1 January, 2025, from https://www.atlaszero.earth/blog/article/does-ifrs-replace-tcfd

BlackRock. (2022). Larry fink's annual 2022 letter to CEOs: The Power of Capitalism. BlackRock. Retrieved from https://www.blackrock.com/corporate/investor-relations/larry-fink-ceo-letter

Climate Disclosure Standards Board (CDSB). (2022). Climate disclosure standards board. Retrieved from https://www.cdsb.net/climate-guidance
Chartered Financial Analyst Institute (CFA Institute). (2020). Climate change analysis in the investment process. Retrieved from https://rpc.cfainstitute.org/-/media/documents/article/industry-research/climate-change-analyis.pdf
European Commission. (2024). Corporate sustainability reporting. European Commission. Retrieved from https://ec.europa.eu/info/business-economy-euro/company-reporting-and-auditing/company-reporting/corporate-sustainability-reporting_en
Financial Stability Board (FSB). (2024). Achieving consistent and comparable climate-related disclosures. Retrieved from https://www.fsb.org/uploads/P121124.pdf
International Financial Reporting Standards (IFRS). (2023). IFRS - General Sustainability-related Disclosures. Retrieved from https://www.ifrs.org/projects/completed-projects/2023/general-sustainability-related-disclosures/
IFRS. (2024). Comparison IFRS S2 climate-related disclosures with the TCFD recommendations. Retrieved from https://www.ifrs.org/content/dam/ifrs/supporting-implementation/ifrs-s2/ifrs-s2-comparison-tcfd.pdf
Principles for Responsible Investment (PRI). (2024). PRI 2024 reporting framework. Retrieved from https://dwtyzx6upklss.cloudfront.net/Uploads/g/v/v/aguidetoinvestorclimatereporting_2024rf_8900.pdf
Securities and Exchange Commission (SEC). (2024). The enhancement and standardization of climate-related disclosures for investors. Retrieved from https://www.sec.gov/rules-regulations/2024/03/s7-10-22
Task Force on Climate-Related Financial Disclosures (TCFD). (2023). 2023 TCFD status report: Task force on climate-related financial disclosures. Financial Stability Board. Retrieved 8 March, 2025, from https://www.fsb.org/2023/10/2023-tcfd-status-report-task-force-on-climate-related-financial-disclosures/
Tango. (2023). 2023 sustainability reporting frameworks update: SASB, GRESB, and CDP. Retrieved from https://watchwire.ai/2023-sustainability-reporting-frameworks-update-sasb-gresb-and-cdd/

Case Reference

Accenture. (2021). Challenges in ESG data gathering. Retrieved from https://www.accenture.com/content/dam/accenture/final/a-com-migration/pdf/pdf-170/accenture-esg-data-challenges-brochure-digital.pdf
Balsanek, K. et al. (2024). SEC stays climate rules: an overview of ongoing legal challenges. DLA Piper. Retrieved from https://www.dlapiper.com/en/insights/publications/2024/04/sec-stays-climate-rules-an-overview-of-ongoing-legal-challenges
International Financial Reporting Standards Foundation (IFRS Foundation). (2022). Renewable energy in electric utilities & power generators industry. Retrieved 1 January, 2024, from https://sasb.ifrs.org/standards/process/projects/renewable-energy-in-electric-utilities-power-generators-industry/
J-Power. (2025). SASB index. Retrieved 1 January, 2024, from https://www.jpower.co.jp/english/sustainability/esg_data/sasb/
Klynveld Peat Marwick Goerdeler (KPMG). (2023). Utilities and ESG. Retrieved from https://kpmg.com/us/en/articles/2023/utilities-esg-reporting-strategic-advantage.html

PricewaterhouseCoopers (PwC). (2024). SEC adopts climate-related disclosure rules. Retrieved from https://viewpoint.pwc.com/dt/us/en/pwc/in_briefs/2024/2024-in-brief/ib202402.html

U.S. Securities and Exchange Commission. (2024). The enhancement and standardization of climate-related disclosures for investors. Retrieved from https://www.sec.gov/rules-regulations/2024/03/s7-10-22

White & Case LLP. (2024). SEC adopts climate change disclosure rules; court imposes temporary stay. Retrieved from https://www.whitecase.com/insight-alert/sec-adopts-climate-change-disclosure-rules-court-imposes-temporary-stay

CHAPTER 17

Climate-Aligned Portfolio Management: Strategies and Tools

1 Introduction: Investing in a Changing Climate

The investment landscape is undergoing a profound transformation. Climate change, once considered a distant environmental concern, is now recognized as a significant financial risk and a defining factor in long-term investment success. Investors who ignore climate change do so at their own peril, exposing their portfolios to potential losses, missed opportunities, and a growing disconnect from the values and expectations of their clients and beneficiaries.

Navigating the complexities of climate change presents a unique set of challenges for investors:

- **Long-Term Risks vs. Short-Term Horizons:** The impacts of climate change often unfold over decades, while many investors operate on shorter time horizons, focused on quarterly earnings reports and annual performance benchmarks. This mismatch in timeframes can make it challenging to fully grasp the long-term implications of climate change for investment portfolios.
- **Uncertainty and Complexity:** Climate models and projections, while providing valuable insights, involve inherent uncertainties. The precise magnitude and timing of climate impacts can be difficult to predict, and the interactions between the climate system, human societies, and the economy are complex and multifaceted.
- **Data Gaps and Inconsistent Disclosure:** Accessing reliable and comparable climate-related data on companies can be a challenge. While disclosure practices are improving, data gaps persist, particularly for Scope 3 emissions (emissions from a company's value chain), and inconsistencies

J. Chen, *Climate Finance*,
https://doi.org/10.1007/978-981-96-7975-1_17

in reporting methodologies can make it difficult to compare the climate performance of different companies.

Despite these challenges, the investment community is increasingly recognizing the imperative of addressing climate change. A growing number of investors are seeking to align their portfolios with climate goals, driven by a combination of factors:

- **Fiduciary Duty:** Investors have a fiduciary duty to act in the best interests of their clients or beneficiaries. This includes considering the financial risks posed by climate change, which can impact asset values, disrupt operations, and affect long-term returns.
- **Investor Demand:** Clients, beneficiaries, and the public are increasingly demanding more sustainable investment options. Investors are facing growing pressure to align their portfolios with environmental and social values, including addressing climate change.
- **Regulatory Requirements:** Evolving regulations, such as mandatory climate risk disclosure rules and requirements for pension funds to consider ESG factors, are pushing investors to incorporate climate considerations more explicitly into their decision-making processes.

PRI (2020) emphasizes integrating climate factors into investment strategies. Boehm et al. (2023) highlights the need for increased and equitable climate finance. WEF (2023) identifies converging crises exacerbated by geopolitical tensions, emphasizing future volatility and emerging threats. PRI's "PRI Strategy 2024–27" (PRI, 2024) outlines the organization's mission to advance responsible investment (RI) globally by supporting signatories in integrating ESG issues into their investment practices. The strategy focuses on four key areas: driving signatory progression, strengthening regional RI ecosystems, amplifying signatory impact through collaborative initiatives, and influencing policy and market practices to create an enabling environment for RI. The plan emphasizes the importance of a sustainable global financial system, long-term value creation, and addressing systemic risks such as climate change and inequality. The PRI aims to achieve these goals through tailored support, streamlined reporting, and enhanced collaboration with signatories and stakeholders worldwide.

A very recent article, "2025: A reset moment for responsible investment," (PRI, 2025) discusses the critical state of responsible investment (RI) in light of the political upheavals and compounding global crises evidenced in 2024, which compel the RI community to adapt and reinforce its relevance. The author highlights the need for RI practitioners to strengthen their investment case and integrate environmental, social, and governance (ESG) considerations into mainstream practices amid increasing political volatility and economic challenges. Ultimately, the post conveys that the commitment to sustainable financial systems is essential, urging the RI community to remain resilient and proactive in countering division and isolation. It outlines the challenges faced by the RI community:

- Over 70 countries held elections in 2024, indicating a strong public demand for political change amid rising global crises.
- Historical climate events in 2024, including wildfires and significant economic losses, underline the urgent need for responsible investment initiatives.
- Economic inequality and humanitarian crises persist, with projections suggesting it will take over 250 years to close the gender pay gap.
- The responsible investment sector must adapt to ongoing political cycles, emphasizing long-term viability in changing conditions.
- A significant effort is needed to enhance the integration of responsible investing into mainstream investment processes.
- The RI community must improve its evidence base to counter misconceptions and reinforce the importance of ESG in investment practices.

According to a recent article (Financial Times, 2025), BlackRock, the world's largest money manager, has withdrawn from the Net-Zero Asset Managers (NZAM) initiative, citing confusion over its practices and legal inquiries from public officials. This move follows similar exits by major US banks (including JPMorgan, Citigroup, Bank of America, Morgan Stanley, Wells Fargo, and Goldman Sachs) from climate-focused groups, amid increasing pressure from conservative politicians and regulatory scrutiny. **Obviously 2025 is at the critical juncture for responsible investment (RI), demanding the need for adaptation amidst a politically fragmented and volatile global landscape.**

This chapter explores the emerging field of climate-aligned investing, providing a roadmap for investors seeking to navigate the complexities of climate change, mitigate risks, identify opportunities, and build portfolios that are positioned for long-term success in a world transitioning to a low-carbon economy. GSIA (2023) reports that global sustainable investment assets have reached US$30.3 trillion. IEA (2024) analyzes global energy trends amid rising geopolitical risks, highlighting the urgency of clean energy transitions.

2 Integrating Climate Risks into Investment Decision-Making

Effective climate-aligned investing begins with a thorough understanding of climate risks and their potential impact on investment portfolios. Investors need to move beyond simplistic views of climate change as a purely environmental issue and recognize that climate risks are fundamentally financial risks.

NGFS (2020) provides guidance for supervisors on integrating climate-related and environmental risks into prudential supervision.

2.1 Understanding Climate Risks

Climate risks manifest in two primary forms:

- **Physical Risks:** These risks arise from the direct impacts of climate change, such as:
  - **Extreme Weather Events:** Hurricanes, floods, droughts, heatwaves, and wildfires can damage property, disrupt operations, and lead to significant financial losses for companies in various sectors.
  - **Sea-Level Rise:** Rising sea levels threaten coastal communities, infrastructure, and real estate assets, leading to increased flood risks, property damage, and potentially large-scale displacement of populations.
  - **Changes in Temperature and Precipitation Patterns:** Shifting temperature and precipitation patterns can impact agricultural yields, water availability, and human health, with consequences for food security, economic productivity, and social stability.

Example: The insurance industry is on the frontlines of physical climate risks. In 2017, hurricanes Harvey, Irma, and Maria caused an estimated $265 billion in insured losses in the United States and the Caribbean, highlighting the vulnerability of insurance companies to extreme weather events.

- **Transition Risks:** These risks arise from the economic and financial shifts associated with the transition to a low-carbon economy. They can include:
  - **Policy and Regulatory Changes:** Governments are implementing policies to reduce greenhouse gas emissions, such as carbon pricing, renewable energy mandates, and fuel efficiency standards. These policies can impact the profitability of companies in carbon-intensive sectors, create stranded assets, and lead to shifts in investment flows. BlackRock (2024) analyzes the capital reallocation during the transition to a low-carbon economy and introduces its Transition Scenario.
  - **Technological Advancements:** Rapid innovation in clean technologies, such as renewable energy, energy storage, and electric vehicles, is disrupting existing industries and creating new market opportunities. Companies that fail to adapt to these technological advancements risk falling behind competitors and losing market share.
  - **Shifting Market Dynamics:** Consumer preferences are evolving, with growing demand for sustainable products and services.

Investors are also increasingly incorporating climate considerations into their decisions, putting pressure on companies to improve their environmental performance. These market shifts can impact company valuations, create new investment opportunities, and lead to a reassessment of traditional investment strategies.

Example: The coal industry has been significantly impacted by transition risks. The rise of renewable energy, declining costs of solar and wind power, and policies aimed at phasing out coal-fired power plants have led to a sharp decline in the value of coal companies and a wave of bankruptcies in the sector.

2.2 Assessing Climate Risk Exposure

Once investors understand the nature of climate risks, the next step is to assess their portfolio's exposure to these risks. This involves examining both the overall portfolio and individual holdings.

- **Portfolio-Level Assessment:** Evaluating the aggregate climate risk exposure of the portfolio considering factors such as:
  - **Geographic Location:** Certain regions are more vulnerable to specific climate hazards. For example, coastal regions are exposed to sea-level rise and storm surges, while arid and semi-arid regions face increased drought risks.
  - **Sector Allocation:** Some sectors, such as energy, transportation, and agriculture, are more exposed to climate risks than others. A portfolio heavily weighted toward fossil fuels, for example, would be more vulnerable to transition risks.
  - **Specific Holdings:** Analyzing the climate risk exposure of individual companies within the portfolio, considering their carbon footprints, reliance on climate-sensitive resources, and their strategies for managing climate risks.
- **Company-Level Assessment:** Conducting a more detailed assessment of the climate risks facing individual companies:
  - **Carbon Footprint:** Measuring the company's greenhouse gas emissions, both direct and indirect, to assess its contribution to climate change and its potential exposure to carbon pricing regulations.
  - **Climate-Sensitive Assets:** Identifying assets that are vulnerable to physical climate hazards or transition risks, such as facilities located in flood-prone areas, infrastructure assets exposed to extreme weather events, or investments in fossil fuel reserves that could become stranded.
  - **Climate Risk Management:** Evaluating the company's strategies for managing climate risks, including its policies on emissions

reductions, its investments in climate adaptation measures, and its disclosure of climate-related information.

Practical Guidance for Climate Risk Assessments:

- **Gather Data:** Collect data from multiple sources, including company reports, sustainability disclosures, ESG ratings agencies, climate data providers, and industry research.
- **Utilize Tools:** Employ climate risk assessment tools, such as those discussed in Chapter 15, to quantify risks, model potential impacts, and compare the performance of different companies or sectors.
- **Engage with Companies:** Reach out to companies directly to request additional information on their climate risks, their strategies, and their performance on key metrics.
- **Consult with Experts:** Seek advice from climate risk specialists or consultants who can provide insights, guidance, and customized assessments.

Challenges in Climate Risk Assessment:

- **Data Availability and Quality:** Accessing reliable and comparable data on companies' climate risks can be challenging, as disclosure practices vary widely, and data gaps exist, particularly for Scope 3 emissions.
- **Inconsistent Methodologies:** Different climate risk assessment tools and frameworks may use varying methodologies and assumptions, making it difficult to compare results across different assessments.
- **Uncertainty and Complexity:** Climate projections involve inherent uncertainties, and the interplay between climate change, economic factors, and social factors can be complex.

2.2.1 Case Study 17.1: The Norwegian Sovereign Wealth Fund's Partial Divestment from Fossil Fuels

Focus: Examine a Nuanced Approach to Fossil Fuel Divestment by a Large Sovereign Wealth Fund, Balancing Financial Considerations with Climate Risks and Ethical Concerns

The Norwegian Sovereign Wealth Fund, also known as the Government Pension Fund Global (GPFG), has taken a nuanced approach to fossil fuel divestment. This case study explores how the GPFG, one of the world's largest investment funds, decided to divest from some fossil fuel companies, particularly those focused on coal, while maintaining investments in certain oil and gas companies that are transitioning to cleaner energy sources. It highlights the challenges of defining "green" or "sustainable" energy companies, the role of engagement with companies to encourage emissions reductions, and the debate over the effectiveness of partial divestment strategies.

Illustration: How the Norwegian Sovereign Wealth Fund Implemented Partial Divestment

1. Decision to Divest from Coal and Certain Oil Companies:

In 2019, the Norwegian Sovereign Wealth Fund announced it would divest from companies involved in coal and certain oil and gas exploration activities. The decision was driven by both financial and ethical considerations, aiming to reduce the fund's exposure to climate-related risks and align with global efforts to combat climate change. The fund divested from companies that derive more than 30% of their revenue from coal or produce more than 20 million tons of thermal coal annually (The Bloomberg, 2021; Guardian, 2019a).

2. Retaining Investments in Transitioning Oil and Gas Companies:

While divesting from coal and certain oil companies, the GPFG retained investments in oil and gas companies that are actively transitioning to cleaner energy sources. This included companies like BP and Shell, which have significant investments in renewable energy technologies. The fund's strategy aimed to support companies that are making tangible efforts to reduce their carbon footprint and contribute to the energy transition (Arvin, 2021; The Guardian, 2019b).

3. Impact and Implementation:

The GPFG's divestment plan involved selling shares in 134 companies engaged primarily in oil and gas exploration, amounting to an estimated \$6 billion in investments. The fund also set a mandate to invest up to \$20 billion in renewable energy projects, focusing on wind and solar power. This strategic shift aimed to balance financial returns with sustainability goals, reducing the fund's exposure to volatile fossil fuel markets while supporting the growth of renewable energy (The Guardian, 2019a; Norges Bank Investment Management, 2025).

Discussion: Challenges, Engagement, and Effectiveness of Partial Divestment

1. **Challenges of Defining "Green" or "Sustainable" Energy Companies:**

Defining what constitutes a "green" or "sustainable" energy company presents several challenges (The Arvin, 2021; Guardian, 2019a):

- **Evolving Standards:** The criteria for sustainability are continuously evolving, making it difficult to establish consistent benchmarks.

- **Mixed Portfolios:** Many companies have mixed portfolios that include both fossil fuel and renewable energy investments, complicating the assessment of their overall sustainability.
- **Transparency:** Ensuring transparency and accuracy in companies' sustainability claims is essential but challenging, given the potential for greenwashing.

2. **Role of Engagement with Companies to Encourage Emissions Reductions:**

Engagement with companies plays a crucial role in encouraging emissions reductions and promoting sustainability (Norges Bank Investment Management, 2025; The Guardian, 2019a):

- **Active Ownership:** By maintaining investments in transitioning companies, the GPFG can leverage its influence as a major shareholder to advocate for stronger climate actions.
- **Dialogue and Collaboration:** Engaging in dialogue with company management and collaborating on sustainability initiatives can drive meaningful change and accelerate the transition to cleaner energy.
- **Monitoring Progress:** Continuous monitoring of companies' progress toward their climate goals ensures accountability and transparency.

3. **Debate Over the Effectiveness of Partial Divestment Strategies:**

The effectiveness of partial divestment strategies is a subject of debate (Johansmeyer, 2022; Plantinga & Scholtens, 2024):

- **Financial Impact:** Partial divestment allows funds to reduce exposure to high-risk fossil fuel assets while maintaining financial returns from companies transitioning to renewable energy.
- **Market Signal:** Divesting from certain fossil fuel companies sends a strong market signal about the financial risks associated with unsustainable practices.
- **Comprehensive Approach:** Critics argue that partial divestment may not be sufficient to drive the systemic change needed to address climate change and advocate for more comprehensive divestment strategies.

Conclusion

The Norwegian Sovereign Wealth Fund's partial divestment from fossil fuels represents a nuanced approach to balancing financial considerations with climate risks and ethical concerns. By divesting from coal and certain oil companies while retaining investments in transitioning oil and gas companies, the GPFG aims to reduce its exposure to climate-related risks and support the transition to a low-carbon energy system.

The challenges of defining "green" or "sustainable" energy companies, the importance of engagement with companies to encourage emissions reductions, and the debate over the effectiveness of partial divestment strategies highlight the complexities of implementing such an approach. The GPFG's strategy demonstrates that partial divestment can be a pragmatic and impactful way to address climate risks while maintaining financial returns.

Understanding the methodologies and strategies employed by the Norwegian Sovereign Wealth Fund in its partial divestment decision can provide valuable insights for other institutional investors and stakeholders seeking to align their investments with sustainability goals and support the transition to a low-carbon economy.

3 Setting Climate-Aligned Investment Strategies

Once investors understand the climate risks facing their portfolios, they can develop investment strategies that align with their climate goals, mitigate risks, and capitalize on opportunities in the transition to a low-carbon economy.

3.1 Defining Climate Goals

The first step is to define clear and measurable climate goals for the investment portfolio. This might involve:

- **Aligning with the Paris Agreement:** Setting a goal to align the portfolio with the Paris Agreement targets of limiting global warming to well below 2 degrees Celsius, preferably to 1.5 degrees Celsius, compared to pre-industrial levels.
- **Achieving Net-Zero Emissions:** Committing to achieving net-zero emissions for the portfolio by a specific date, meaning that the portfolio's investments are no longer contributing to the increase in greenhouse gas concentrations in the atmosphere.
- **Supporting the Sustainable Development Goals (SDGs):** Aligning investments with the SDGs, which include goals related to climate action, affordable and clean energy, sustainable cities and communities, and responsible consumption and production.

Specific targets can be set within these broader goals, such as:

- **Sector-Based Targets:** Setting emissions reduction targets for specific sectors within the portfolio. For example, aiming for a 50% reduction in emissions from the energy sector by 2030.

- **Engagement Targets:** Setting targets for engaging with companies on climate action. For example, aiming to engage with 75% of the companies in the portfolio on their climate policies and emissions reduction targets.
- **Impact Targets:** Setting targets for investing in climate solutions that generate positive environmental or social impact. For example, aiming to invest 10% of the portfolio in renewable energy projects.

The specific climate goals and targets should be tailored to the investor's values, mission, risk tolerance, and investment horizon.

3.2 Strategies for Portfolio Alignment

CPI (2023) finds climate finance flows reached \$1.3 T in 2021/22, but a five-fold increase is needed by 2030. CPI (2024) reports climate finance grew to \$1.46 T in 2022, still far below the \$7.4 T needed annually. Once climate goals are established, investors can employ a range of strategies to align their portfolios:

- **Negative Screening:** This approach involves excluding companies or sectors with high-carbon footprints or poor environmental practices from the portfolio
  - **Fossil Fuel Divestment:** A common example of negative screening is divesting from fossil fuel companies, particularly those involved in the extraction and production of coal, oil, and gas. This strategy sends a strong signal to the market about the investor's commitment to climate action and reduces exposure to assets that are at risk of becoming stranded.
  - **Other Exclusion Criteria:** Investors may also choose to exclude companies involved in deforestation, those with poor environmental records, or those that fail to meet certain sustainability criteria.

Considerations:

- **Scope and Criteria:** Clearly defining the scope of the exclusions and the criteria used to identify companies to be excluded.
- **Financial Implications:** Assessing the potential financial impact of divestment, considering the size of the excluded sector or companies, the availability of alternative investments, and the potential for divestment to affect returns.
- **Engagement vs. Divestment:** Weighing the potential benefits of engaging with companies to improve their practices versus divesting entirely.

  - **Positive Screening:** This strategy involves identifying and investing in companies that are actively contributing to climate solutions or are well-positioned for the transition to a low-carbon economy.

- **Clean Technology Investments:** Investing in companies that are developing or deploying clean technologies, such as renewable energy, energy efficiency, sustainable transportation, and carbon capture, utilization, and storage (CCUS).
- **Climate-Resilient Companies:** Identifying companies that are taking proactive steps to adapt to climate change and build resilience into their operations, such as those investing in water conservation, climate-smart agriculture, or disaster preparedness.
- **ESG Leaders:** Investing in companies with strong environmental, social, and governance (ESG) performance, as these companies are often better positioned to manage climate risks and capitalize on opportunities in the transition to a sustainable economy.

Considerations:

- **Due Diligence:** Conducting thorough due diligence to assess the credibility of companies' climate claims, their technological viability, and their financial performance.
- **Impact Measurement:** Tracking and measuring the environmental and social impact of investments to ensure that they are delivering on their sustainability promises.
- **Valuation:** Carefully evaluating the valuation of climate-focused companies, as their growth prospects and risk profiles may differ from those of traditional companies.

  - **Engagement and Active Ownership:** This strategy involves leveraging an investor's ownership stake in companies to influence their behavior on climate change. TCFD (2017) recommends integrating climate risks and opportunities into governance, strategy, and risk management.

- **Engagement:** Engaging in dialogue with companies to understand their climate policies, advocate for improvements, and encourage them to set ambitious targets for emissions reductions and climate resilience.
- **Proxy Voting:** Voting on shareholder resolutions related to climate change, supporting proposals that align with the investor's climate goals and holding companies accountable for their actions.
- **Collaborative Engagement:** Working with other investors through initiatives such as Climate Action 100 + , which coordinates engagement with the world's largest greenhouse gas emitters, to amplify investor voice and drive systemic change. As of 2023, Climate Action 100 + (2024)

reports that 77% of their focus companies have committed to net-zero targets by 2050 or sooner.

Considerations:

- **Engagement Strategy:** Developing a clear and focused engagement strategy, identifying priority companies and issues, and setting realistic expectations for outcomes.
- **Resources and Expertise:** Investing in the resources and expertise needed to conduct effective engagement, including building relationships with company management, understanding complex climate issues, and developing persuasive arguments.
- **Measuring Impact:** Tracking the outcomes of engagement efforts to assess their effectiveness and identify areas for improvement.
  - **Impact Investing:** Impact investing goes beyond simply considering ESG factors in investment decisions; it seeks to generate measurable, beneficial social or environmental impact alongside a financial return.
- **Climate Focus:** Impact investors targeting climate change might invest in renewable energy projects, energy efficiency solutions, sustainable agriculture initiatives, or companies developing climate adaptation technologies.
- **Dual Objectives:** Impact investors are driven by both financial and impact objectives, seeking investments that align with their values and generate a positive contribution to solving pressing social and environmental challenges.

Considerations:

- **Impact Measurement:** Developing robust methodologies for measuring and managing the impact of investments, ensuring that capital is flowing toward solutions that deliver tangible results. Impact Frontiers (2024): Norms aid impact management by classifying enterprise impact and investor strategies. GIIN (2024): IRIS + helps translate impact intentions into measurable results for impact investors.
- **Financial Returns:** Balancing the pursuit of positive impact with the need to generate financial returns that meet the investor's financial objectives.
- **Additionality:** Ensuring that investments are truly driving positive change that would not have occurred without the investment (i.e., demonstrating additionality).

The choice of strategies and their combination will depend on the investor's specific climate goals, risk tolerance, investment horizon, and resources.

3.2.1 Case Study 17.2: Generation Investment Management's Sustainable Investment Strategy

Focus: Showcase a Leading Investment Firm That Has Fully Integrated Sustainability and Climate Considerations into Its Investment Philosophy and Portfolio Management

Generation Investment Management, co-founded by former US Vice President Al Gore, has fully integrated sustainability and climate considerations into its investment philosophy and portfolio management. This case study explores how Generation Investment Management focuses on investing in companies that contribute to a sustainable future, including those in renewable energy, energy efficiency, sustainable agriculture, and circular economy sectors. It highlights the rationale behind Generation's long-term, sustainable investment approach, its track record of financial performance, and its influence on other investors.

Illustration: How Generation Investment Management Implements Its Sustainable Investment Strategy

1. Investment Philosophy and Approach:

Generation Investment Management's investment philosophy is based on the conviction that sustainability factors directly affect long-term business profitability. The firm integrates sustainability analysis into every investment decision, using environmental, social, and governance (ESG) factors as tools to evaluate the quality of businesses and management teams. This approach aims to identify companies that are well-positioned for long-term secular trends and are part of the solution to material sustainability issues in their sector (Generation Investment Management, 2022, 2025a).

2. Focus on Sustainable Sectors:

Generation Investment Management focuses on investing in companies that contribute to a sustainable future. This includes sectors such as renewable energy, energy efficiency, sustainable agriculture, and circular economy. The firm seeks out companies with proven technology and commercial traction, run by talented, mission-driven management teams. By investing in these sectors, Generation aims to support the transition to a low-carbon economy and create long-term value for its clients (Generation Investment Management, 2025b).

3. Track Record of Financial Performance:

Generation Investment Management has demonstrated a strong track record of financial performance. For example, its flagship Global Equity Fund outperformed its benchmark index by over 500 basis points per year over a ten-year period. This success has proven to skeptics that sustainable investing can deliver superior financial returns while addressing critical environmental and social issues (Generation Investment Management, 2025a, 2025c; Reichelstein & Bebb, 2016).

Discussion: Rationale, Financial Performance, and Influence on Other Investors

1. Rationale Behind Generation's Long-Term, Sustainable Investment Approach:

The rationale behind Generation's sustainable investment approach is based on the belief that sustainability factors are critical to long-term business success. By integrating ESG factors into investment decisions, Generation aims to identify companies that are well-managed, forward-thinking, and capable of navigating the challenges and opportunities of a transitioning economy. This approach is rooted in the conviction that sustainable businesses are better positioned to deliver long-term, attractive, risk-adjusted returns (Generation Investment Management, 2022, 2025a).

2. Track Record of Financial Performance:

Generation Investment Management has a proven track record of financial performance, demonstrating that sustainable investing can yield competitive returns. The firm's flagship Global Equity Fund, for instance, has consistently outperformed its benchmark, showcasing the effectiveness of integrating sustainability into the investment process. This performance has helped to validate the business case for sustainable investing and attract a growing number of investors (Generation Investment Management, 2023; Reichelstein & Bebb, 2016).

3. Influence on Other Investors:

Generation Investment Management has had a significant influence on other investors by demonstrating that sustainable investing can be both profitable and impactful. The firm's success has encouraged other investment firms to integrate ESG factors into their investment processes and consider sustainability as a key driver of long-term value. Generation's advocacy for sustainable investing has also contributed to the broader adoption of ESG principles across the financial industry (Generation Investment Management, 2022, 2025c).

Conclusion

Generation Investment Management's sustainable investment strategy exemplifies the integration of sustainability and climate considerations into investment philosophy and portfolio management. By focusing on companies that contribute to a sustainable future, Generation aims to deliver long-term, attractive, risk-adjusted returns while addressing critical environmental and social issues.

The rationale behind Generation's approach is rooted in the belief that sustainability factors are essential to long-term business success. The firm's strong track record of financial performance has demonstrated the viability of sustainable investing and influenced other investors to adopt similar practices. Generation's commitment to sustainable investing has helped to drive the broader adoption of ESG principles across the financial industry.

Understanding the methodologies and strategies employed by Generation Investment Management can provide valuable insights for other investment firms and stakeholders seeking to enhance their sustainability practices and support the transition to a net-zero economy.

4 Tools and Techniques for Portfolio Alignment

A growing array of tools and techniques are available to help investors align their portfolios with climate goals, measure their progress, and manage climate-related risks. These tools can provide valuable insights and support more effective decision-making.

4.1 Carbon Footprint Analysis

Carbon footprint analysis is a fundamental tool for assessing the climate impact of an investment portfolio. It involves quantifying the greenhouse gas (GHG) emissions associated with the portfolio's holdings, providing a baseline for setting emissions reduction targets and tracking progress over time.

- **Methodologies:** Several methodologies exist for calculating carbon footprints, including:
  - **Equity Ownership Approach:** This approach attributes emissions to investors based on their ownership stake in companies. For example, if an investor owns 1% of a company's shares, they are attributed with 1% of the company's emissions.
  - **Market-Based Approach:** This approach allocates emissions based on the revenue generated from different sectors or activities. For example, if a company derives 50% of its revenue from renewable energy and 50% from fossil fuels, the investor would be attributed with emissions proportional to their investment in each sector.
- **Scope 3 Emissions:** A major challenge in carbon footprint analysis is accounting for Scope 3 emissions, which are emissions that occur

throughout a company's value chain, including upstream emissions from suppliers and downstream emissions from the use of the company's products. Scope 3 emissions can be difficult to measure accurately, but they are often a significant portion of a company's overall footprint.

- **Data Availability:** The quality and availability of emissions data vary widely across companies and sectors. Some companies provide detailed and audited emissions data, while others provide limited or estimated data. PCAF (2025) offers a standard for measuring and reporting financed emissions.

4.2 Implied Temperature Rise (ITR)

Implied Temperature Rise (ITR) is a metric that estimates the temperature increase implied by a portfolio's emissions trajectory. It assesses whether the portfolio's holdings are aligned with a specific climate goal, such as limiting global warming to 1.5 °C or 2 °C above pre-industrial levels.

- **Methodology:** ITR calculations use emissions data from a portfolio's holdings, project those emissions into the future based on different scenarios, and then estimate the temperature increase that would result from those emissions. SBTi (2024) provides guidance for financial institutions to set science-based GHG reduction targets.
- **Time Horizons:** ITR calculations can be conducted over different time horizons, such as 2030, 2050, or 2100. The choice of time horizon will influence the results, as longer time horizons will generally result in higher projected temperature increases.
- **Emission Scenarios:** ITR calculations can also incorporate different emissions scenarios, such as those developed by the Intergovernmental Panel on Climate Change (IPCC), to assess the portfolio's alignment with climate goals under different possible futures.

4.3 Climate Scenario Analysis

Climate scenario analysis is a powerful tool for understanding how a portfolio might perform under different climate pathways. It involves using climate models and economic scenarios to project future climate impacts and assess their potential financial implications.

- **Types of Scenarios:** A variety of climate scenarios are available, including:
  - **Orderly Transition Scenarios:** These scenarios assume that governments take early and ambitious action to reduce emissions, leading to a smooth transition to a low-carbon economy.

  - **Disorderly Transition Scenarios:** These scenarios assume that climate action is delayed or less ambitious, leading to more abrupt policy changes, rapid technological disruptions, and potentially greater economic and financial volatility.
  - **Hot House World Scenarios:** These scenarios assume that emissions continue to rise unabated, leading to severe climate change impacts and potentially catastrophic consequences.

- **Scenario Narratives:** Climate scenarios often include detailed narratives that describe the socioeconomic and technological context of the scenario, providing a richer understanding of the potential implications.

4.4 ESG Data and Ratings

Environmental, social, and governance (ESG) data providers and rating agencies play an increasingly important role in climate-aligned investing. They provide investors with data and assessments of companies' performance on a range of sustainability factors, including climate change.

- **ESG Data:** ESG data providers collect information on companies' environmental impacts (e.g., greenhouse gas emissions, water usage, waste management), social practices (e.g., labor standards, human rights, community relations), and governance structures (e.g., board diversity, executive compensation, anti-corruption policies).
- **ESG Ratings:** ESG rating agencies use this data to assess companies' sustainability performance, providing scores or rankings that investors can use to compare companies and identify those with strong ESG practices.

Investors can use ESG data and ratings to:

- **Identify ESG Leaders:** Invest in companies with high ESG ratings, indicating that they are managing their environmental and social impacts effectively and have strong governance structures.
- **Manage Risks:** Avoid companies with low ESG ratings or those facing significant controversies related to their environmental or social practices.
- **Engage with Companies:** Use ESG data and ratings to inform their engagement with companies, encouraging them to improve their sustainability performance and address areas of concern.

4.5 Engagement Platforms and Tools

Collaboration among investors is essential for driving corporate action on climate change. Investor engagement platforms and tools facilitate this collaboration, providing resources for:

- **Sharing Information:** Platforms allow investors to share information about companies' climate performance, engagement strategies, and voting records.
- **Coordinating Engagement:** Tools enable investors to coordinate their engagement efforts, developing joint letters to companies, filing shareholder resolutions, and amplifying their collective voice.
- **Tracking Progress:** Platforms can track corporate progress on climate action, providing investors with data and insights to inform their engagement strategies.

Examples of investor engagement initiatives include:

- **Climate Action 100 + :** A global investor initiative engaging with the world's largest greenhouse gas emitters to encourage them to take ambitious action on climate change.
- **CDP (formerly the Carbon Disclosure Project):** A non-profit organization that runs a global disclosure system for companies to report their environmental data, including climate change-related information.
- **The Investor Agenda:** A collaborative platform that provides investors with resources and guidance on climate action, including engagement tools, policy advocacy, and investment strategies.

4.6 PACTA as Comprehensive Climate-Aligned Portfolio Management Tool

PACTA (Paris Agreement Capital Transition Assessment) tool is a comprehensive climate-aligned portfolio management solution. PACTA enables financial institutions to assess their investment portfolios' alignment with climate scenarios, thereby addressing climate risks while pursuing sustainable investment strategies. PATCA (2022a; 2022b) describes the PACTA methodology for investors, and banks, respectively. Here are the **Key Features of PACTA for investors:**

- **Scenario Analysis:** PACTA compares portfolio holdings against various climate scenarios (e.g., IEA, IPCC) to determine alignment with decarbonization pathways. It's "scenario agnostic," meaning any scenario with production targets can be used.
- **Granular Data:** Uses asset-based, company-level data (e.g., production plans of power plants) for a detailed, forward-looking analysis (5-year horizon). The online tool uses Asset Impact data.
- **Sector Focus:** Covers eight key climate-critical sectors: Power, Oil & Gas, Coal, Automotive, Steel, Cement, and Aviation, representing over 70% of global CO_2 emissions.

- **Metrics:** Employs different metrics depending on the sector and data availability:
  - *Production Volume Trajectory:* Measures alignment of production volumes with scenario targets. Used for sectors with clear decarbonization pathways (Power, Fossil Fuels, Automotive).
  - *Technology/Fuel Mix:* Analyzes the proportion of investments in high- vs. low-carbon technologies within a sector. Also used for sectors with clear pathways.
  - *Emission Intensity:* Compares the portfolio's emission intensity to scenario targets. Used for sectors without well-defined technology pathways (Steel, Cement, Aviation).
- **Accounting Principles:** Offers two ways to attribute company production to financial assets:
  - *Ownership Weight Approach:* Based on the percentage of outstanding shares owned (for equity portfolios).
  - *Portfolio Weight Approach:* Based on the weighting of each position within the portfolio (for both equity and bond portfolios).
- **Market-Share Approach:** Allocates scenario targets to companies based on their market share within a sector.
- **Open Source and Free:** PACTA is a free, open-source tool, allowing for transparency and wider adoption.

Limitations:

- **Data Reliance:** Relies on self-reported portfolio data from financial institutions.
- **Scenario Simplification:** Climate scenarios are simplified representations of complex systems.
- **Data Accuracy:** Potential for errors in company-level data.
- **Scope:** Doesn't cover all sectors (e.g., agriculture) or asset classes (e.g., sovereign debt, private equity).

The following are the **Key Aspects of PACTA for Banks:**

- **Goal:** To help banks understand their contribution to climate change through lending activities and enable them to define effective climate strategies. It assesses alignment with climate scenarios, not direct emissions reduction.
- **Focus:** Assesses a loan book's alignment with different climate scenarios by linking loans to physical assets of client companies in climate-critical sectors. It provides forward-looking projections based on company production plans.

- **Sectors:** Covers five key sectors: Power, Fossil Fuels, Automotive, Steel, and Cement. Plans to incorporate Heavy-Duty Vehicles, Aviation, and Shipping are underway.
- **Metrics:** Uses three core metrics:
  - *Technology/Fuel Mix:* Assesses the mix of high- vs. low-carbon technologies financed by the loan book, both currently and projected into the future.
  - *Production Volume Trajectory:* Measures the alignment of projected production volumes (of specific technologies) with climate scenario targets.
  - *Emission Intensity:* Compares the financed emissions intensity of a sector within the loan book to scenario targets (primarily used for Steel and Cement).
- **Data:** Uses granular, asset-level data (e.g., power plant capacity). The methodology is data-agnostic; banks can use various data sources. The free online tool incorporates an Asset Impact dataset.
- **Methodology:**
  - *Scenario Allocation:* Uses a market-share approach to allocate decarbonization efforts to companies proportionally to their market share.
  - *Asset Allocation:* Employs a portfolio-weight approach, allocating physical assets based on the loan amount relative to the total portfolio. Also offers an unweighted approach for client-level analysis.
  - *Consolidation:* Aggregates asset-level data up the corporate ownership chain using Financial Control consolidation, considering majority-owned subsidiaries. An Equity Ownership approach is also explained.
- **Time Horizon:** Analyzes alignment at present and over a 5-year horizon.
- **Benchmarks:** Allows comparison with a corporate economy benchmark (all companies in the dataset) and scenario benchmarks.
- **Open Source and Free:** PACTA is a free, open-source tool and methodology. A software package in R and supporting documentation are available.

Limitations:

- **Data Quality:** Relies on accurate loan book and company data, which can be challenging, especially for non-listed companies or general-purpose loans. Segmentation of loans for diversified companies is not fully addressed yet.
- **Scenario Simplification:** Climate scenarios are simplified models and may not capture all complexities.

- **Focus on Production:** Primarily analyzes production-side changes and doesn't fully capture demand-side dynamics.
- **No Financial Risk Quantification:** Doesn't model actual financial losses, though it can inform risk assessment.
- **Limited Sector Coverage:** Doesn't cover all relevant sectors yet.

Implementation of PACTA for Portfolio Analysis:

PACTA provides a structured methodology for analyzing the alignment of investment portfolios with climate goals. Financial institutions can upload their portfolios into the PACTA tool, which uses granular, asset-based data to evaluate exposure to high-carbon sectors and assess alignment with various climate scenarios, such as those outlined in the Paris Agreement.

Key Metrics Utilized by PACTA:

- **Technology Mix:** This metric evaluates the distribution of technologies within a portfolio, indicating how investments should evolve to align with climate goals.
- **Production Volume Trajectory:** This metric measures the expected production changes over the next five years against climate scenario targets, helping investors understand whether their portfolios are on track to meet necessary reductions in emissions.
- **Emission Intensity:** For sectors without clear decarbonization pathways, this metric assesses the emissions produced per unit of output, providing insights into the carbon efficiency of investments.

Case Application:

We are able to run a sample bank loan portfolio in R package, and an sample investor portfolio on PACTA online platform. The following figures illustrate the tool output in different climate metrics, including technology mix, alignment of emission intensities, alignment of production trajectories, etc. (Figs. 1, 2, 3, 4 and 5).

In the next case study, we will show how a financial institution using PACTA might analyze its equity and corporate bond portfolios, discovering that a significant portion is invested in fossil fuel companies. By leveraging PACTA's metrics, the institution can identify opportunities for engagement with these companies to encourage them to adopt more sustainable practices or consider divesting from those that are not transitioning effectively.

4.6.1 Case Study 17.3: A Latin American Pension Fund's Journey Toward Paris Alignment with PACTA

Focus: Examine the application of PACTA by a Latin American pension fund to assess and improve the Paris Agreement alignment of its listed equity portfolio, balancing financial considerations with climate risks and ethical concerns, while navigating data and market-specific challenges (PACTA, 2023).

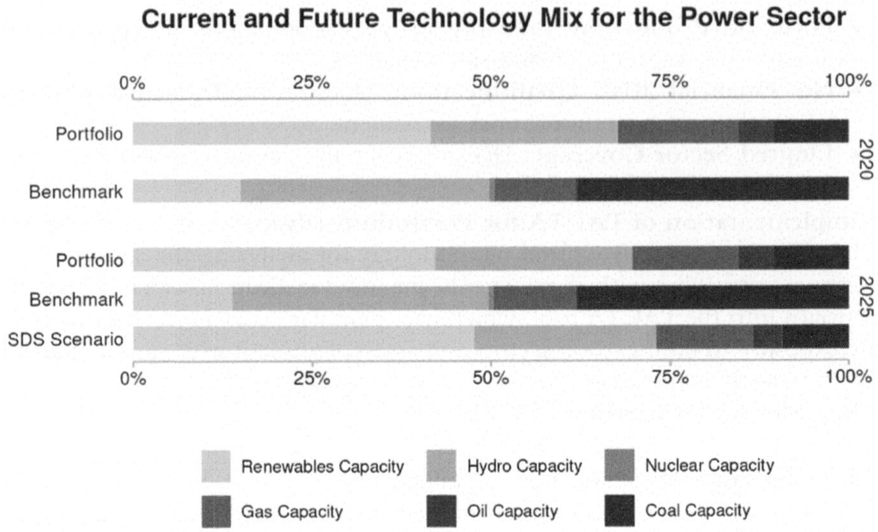

Fig. 1 Current and future technology mix for the power sector in the sample bank loan portfolio. *Source* PACTA Tool Generated Image

Illustration: How a Latin American Pension Fund Used PACTA to Develop a Paris-Aligned Investment Strategy.

1. **Initial Assessment with PACTA:** The pension fund, concerned about climate-related financial risks and its commitment to responsible investment, used PACTA to analyze its existing equity portfolio. The analysis covered key sectors such as power, oil and gas, and automotive, utilizing a 5-year forward-looking dataset of company capital expenditure plans. The assessment revealed significant misalignment with Paris Agreement targets, particularly in power generation and fossil fuel production. The portfolio held a high proportion of companies with limited capital allocated toward renewable energy technologies. It also revealed data gaps for several portfolio companies, hindering a complete assessment.
2. **Portfolio Rebalancing Informed by PACTA:** Based on the PACTA results, the pension fund implemented a phased approach to portfolio rebalancing. It increased allocations to companies demonstrating strong alignment, such as those investing heavily in renewable energy, electric vehicles, and sustainable solutions. For companies showing some level of transition planning—evidenced by setting science-based targets or making demonstrable reductions in emission intensity—the fund maintained its positions and prioritized engagement. The fund also incorporated tier 3 companies in non-PACTA sectors to maintain diversification and market relevance.

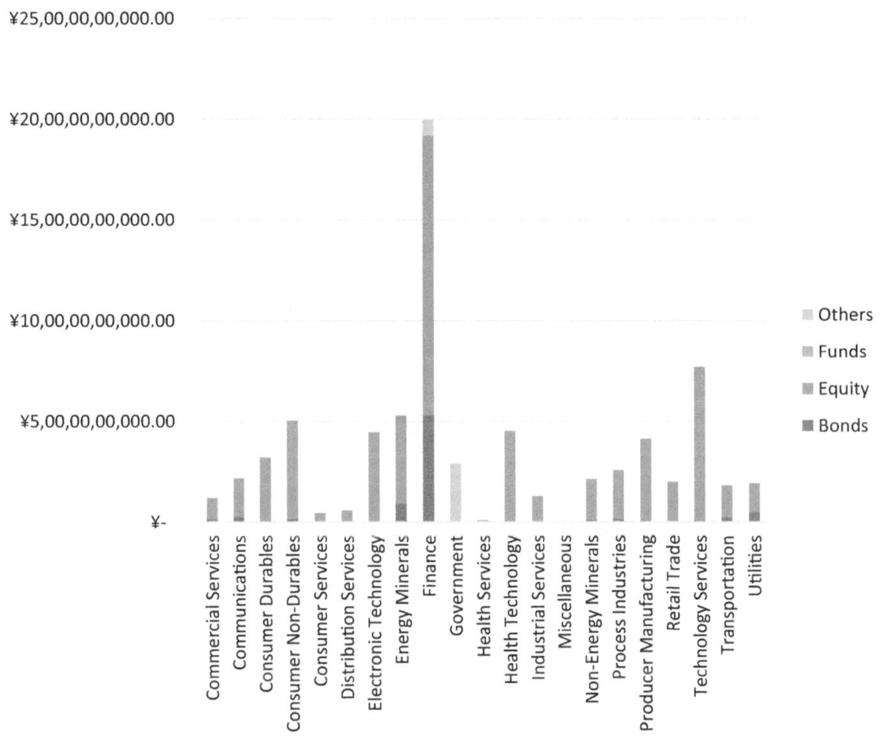

Fig. 2 Investor portfolio composition in the sample investor portfolio. *Source* PACTA Tool Generated Image

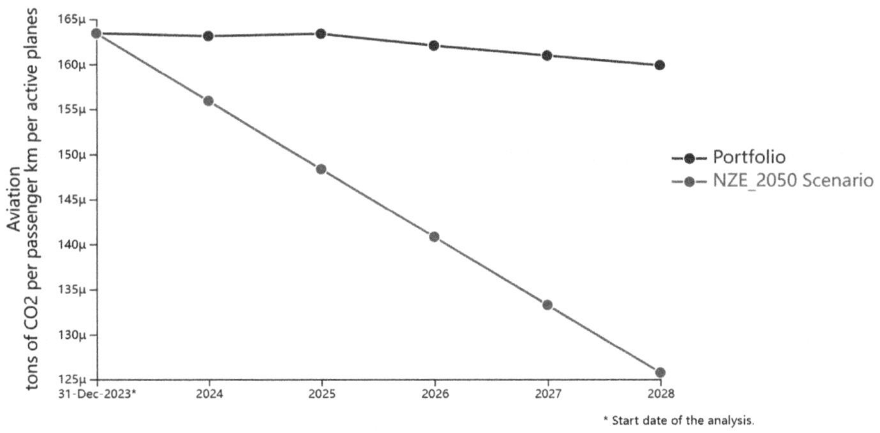

Fig. 3 Alignment of emission intensities in the aample investor portfolio. *Source* PACTA Tool Generated Image

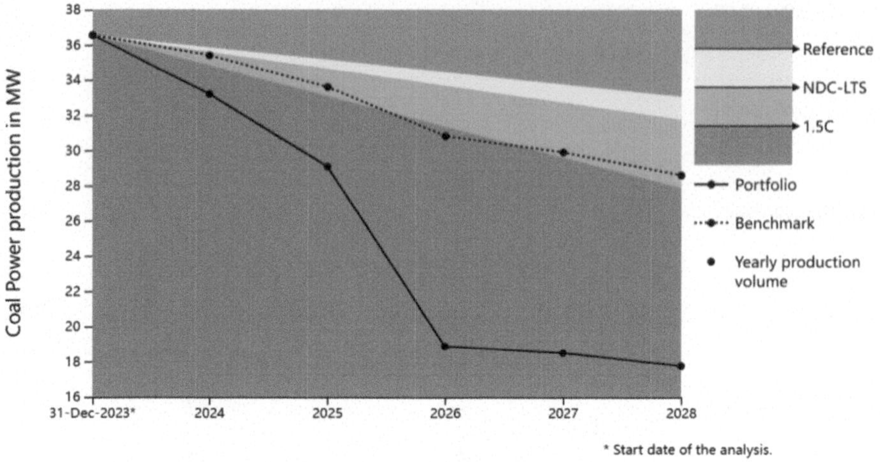

Fig. 4 Alignment of production trajectories in the sample investor portfolio. *Source* PACTA Tool Generated Image

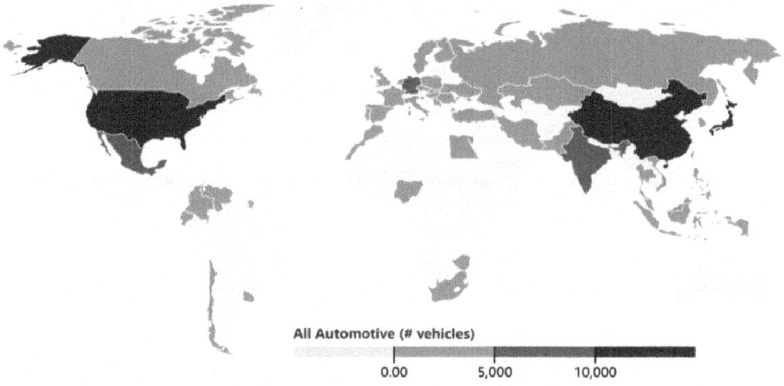

Fig. 5 Geographic exposure of listed equity in the sample investor portfolio. *Source* PACTA Tool Generated Image

3. **Engagement Strategy Based on PACTA and Transition Plans:** The pension fund developed a robust engagement strategy informed by PACTA results and company transition plans. It prioritized engagement with companies in its portfolio demonstrating high transition risk exposure or low alignment scores, particularly in carbon-intensive sectors. The engagement focused on requesting improvements to their climate performance, advocating for more ambitious decarbonization targets, and encouraging the development and implementation of robust transition plans.
4. **Impact Measurement and Reporting:** The pension fund used PACTA to track the climate performance of its portfolio companies annually,

monitoring changes in alignment and the effectiveness of its engagement efforts. It integrated these findings into its impact reporting, demonstrating its commitment to Paris alignment and responsible investment principles to its stakeholders.

Discussion: Challenges, Engagement, and Measurement in Emerging Markets

1. **Data Availability and Quality:** The pension fund faced challenges related to data availability and quality, particularly for companies in non-PACTA sectors or those with less developed sustainability reporting practices. This reinforced the need to promote greater transparency and standardized disclosure in the region.
2. **Engagement Effectiveness in Emerging Markets:** The effectiveness of engagement strategies in emerging markets requires further analysis, considering local market dynamics, corporate governance structures, and shareholder activism practices. Collaborative engagement with other investors and stakeholders was considered crucial to maximize influence.
3. **Forward-Looking Alignment vs. Current Performance:** Using forward-looking alignment metrics based on projected company plans provided the pension fund with greater insight into potential future performance and allowed for more strategic engagement. This contrasted with relying solely on past performance or lagging indicators.
4. **Portfolio Diversification and Financial Performance:** The fund's experience highlighted the challenge of balancing portfolio diversification with climate objectives. It demonstrated that by including tier 3 companies a Paris aligned transition strategy does not necessarily lead to underperformance of a portfolio and that financial returns could be maintained.

Conclusion

The Latin American pension fund's experience demonstrates that the application of PACTA can be instrumental in assessing and improving the Paris alignment of investment portfolios in emerging markets. By using PACTA in combination with a robust engagement strategy, investors can contribute to real economy emission reductions and encourage the transition to a low-carbon economy, while managing climate-related financial risks and fulfilling their responsibilities as long-term investors. The case also reinforces the need for improved data availability, quality and disclosure practices in emerging markets to support more comprehensive climate-aligned investment strategies.

5 Engaging with Clients and Stakeholders

Effective climate-aligned portfolio management requires clear and transparent communication with clients and other stakeholders. Investors need to explain their climate strategies, address concerns, and build support for their approach to integrating climate considerations into investment decisions.

Communicating Climate Strategies

SBTi (2024) provides guidance for financial institutions to set science-based GHG reduction targets. Key elements of a communication strategy for climate-aligned investing include:

- **Rationale:** Clearly explaining the rationale for integrating climate considerations into investment decisions, emphasizing the financial risks of ignoring climate change and the opportunities associated with investing in a low-carbon future.
- **Strategies:** Describing the specific strategies being used to align the portfolio with climate goals, such as negative screening, positive screening, engagement, and impact investing.
- **Performance:** Reporting on the portfolio's climate performance, using metrics such as carbon footprint, implied temperature rise, and the percentage of investments allocated to climate solutions.
- **Transparency:** Being open and honest about the challenges and uncertainties associated with climate-aligned investing and disclosing any limitations in data or methodologies.

Addressing Client Concerns

Clients may have various concerns about climate-aligned investing, such as:

- **Potential for Lower Returns:** Some clients may worry that incorporating climate considerations into investment decisions could lead to lower returns.
- **Increased Risk:** Clients may perceive climate-aligned investments as being riskier than traditional investments.

Addressing these concerns effectively requires:

- **Evidence-Based Communication:** Providing data and evidence to show that climate-aligned investing can generate competitive returns, especially over the long term.
- **Highlighting Long-Term Risks:** Emphasizing that ignoring climate change poses significant financial risks that could ultimately lead to lower returns and greater volatility.

- **Focusing on Opportunities:** Showcasing the investment opportunities associated with the transition to a low-carbon economy, such as renewable energy, energy efficiency, and sustainable transportation.
- **Transparency and Trust:** Building trust with clients through transparent communication, clear explanations of the investment strategy, and regular reporting on performance and impact.

Collaborating with Other Investors

Collaboration among investors can amplify their voice, increase their leverage with companies, and accelerate the shift toward a more sustainable economy.

Investors can collaborate by:

- **Joining Investor Initiatives:** Participating in initiatives like Climate Action 100 + or the Investor Agenda to engage with companies on climate change and advocate for policy changes.
- **Sharing Knowledge and Best Practices:** Participating in conferences, webinars, and online forums to learn from other investors and share experiences.
- **Developing Joint Statements and Letters:** Working together to draft joint statements or letters to companies, expressing their expectations on climate action and urging them to improve their practices.
- **Filing Shareholder Resolutions:** Collaborating on shareholder resolutions to push companies to take specific actions on climate change, such as setting emissions reduction targets or disclosing their climate risks.

By working together, investors can play a powerful role in shaping corporate behavior, influencing policy decisions, and driving the transition to a low-carbon and climate-resilient future.

6 Conclusion: The Future of Climate-Aligned Investing

The investment world is awakening to the realities of climate change. Investors are increasingly recognizing that climate risks and opportunities are not just environmental concerns; they are financial imperatives that demand attention and action. The field of climate-aligned investing is rapidly evolving, driven by growing investor demand, evolving regulations, and the increasing availability of tools and data to support more informed decision-making.

As the transition to a low-carbon economy accelerates, climate-aligned investing will become increasingly mainstream. Investors who fail to integrate climate considerations into their strategies risk being left behind, facing higher risks, missing out on opportunities, and losing the trust of their clients and beneficiaries.

The future of climate-aligned investing will be shaped by several key trends:

- **Increased Data Availability and Transparency:** The quality, availability, and comparability of climate-related data will continue to improve, driven by advances in technology, standardized reporting frameworks, and evolving regulations.
- **More Sophisticated Tools and Analytics:** The development of more sophisticated climate risk assessment tools, portfolio alignment tools, and impact measurement methodologies will enable investors to make more informed and nuanced decisions.
- **Greater Investor Collaboration:** Collaboration among investors will intensify, as they work together to engage with companies, advocate for policy changes, and pool their resources to drive systemic change.

Investors have a crucial role to play in addressing climate change. By embracing climate-aligned investment strategies, embracing transparency, and collaborating with other stakeholders, they can contribute to a more sustainable and resilient future for all.

References

BlackRock. (2024). Transition to a low-carbon economy. BlackRock. Retrieved from https://www.blackrock.com/corporate/insights/blackrock-investment-institute/publications/mega-forces/low-carbon-transition

Boehm, S. et al. (2023). State of climate action 2023. www.wri.org. Retrieved from https://www.wri.org/research/state-climate-action-2023

Climate Action 100+. (2024). 2024 Progress Report. Retrieved 10 March, 2025, from https://www.climateaction100.org/wp-content/uploads/2024/01/Climate-Action-100-Progress-Update-2023.pdf

Financial Times (FT). (2025). BlackRock quits climate change group in latest green climbdown. Retrieved from http://www.chineseft.com/interactive/187932/en?exclusive

Global Impact Investing Network (GIIN). (2024). Welcome to IRIS+ system | the generally accepted system for impact investors to measure, manage, and optimize their impact. Retrieved from https://iris.thegiin.org/

Global Sustainable Investment Alliance (GSIA). (2023). Global sustainable investment review 2022. Retrieved from https://www.gsi-alliance.org/members-resources/gsir2022/

Impact Frontiers. (2024). Impact management norms. Impact Frontiers. Retrieved from https://impactfrontiers.org/norms/

Network for Greening the Financial System (NGFS). (2020). Guide for supervisors: Integrating climate-related and environmental risks into prudential supervision. Banque de France. Retrieved from https://www.ngfs.net/en/guide-supervisors-integrating-climate-related-and-environmental-risks-prudential-supervision

Partnership for Carbon Accounting Financials (PCAF). (2025). The global GHG accounting and reporting standard for the financial industry. Retrieved from https://carbonaccountingfinancials.com/standard

Paris Agreement Capital Transition Assessment (PACTA). (2022a). PACTA for investors methodology document. Retrieved from https://pacta.rmi.org/wp-content/uploads/2024/04/PACTA-for-Investors-Methodology-document_v1.0_202404.pdf

PACTA. (2022b). PACTA for banks supporting documents. Retrieved from https://pacta.rmi.org/wp-content/uploads/2024/05/PACTA-for-Banks-Methodology-document_v1.2.3_030524.pdf

Principles for Responsible Investment (PRI). (2020). Climate change for asset owners. Retrieved from https://www.PRI.org/introductory-guides-to-responsible-investment/an-introduction-to-responsible-investment-climate-change-for-asset-owners/5981.article

PRI. (2024). PRI strategy 2024–27. Retrieved from https://www.unpri.org/about-us/pri-2024-27-strategy

PRI. (2025). 2025: A reset moment for responsible investment. Retrieved from https://www.unpri.org/pri-blog/2025-a-reset-moment-for-responsible-investment/12987.article

Science Based Targets initiative (SBTi). (2024). Financial sector science-based targets guidance. Retrieved from https://sciencebasedtargets.org/resources/files/Financial-Sector-Science-Based-Targets-Guidance.pdf

Task Force on Climate-Related Financial Disclosures (TCFD). (2017). Implementing the recommendations of the task force on climate-related financial disclosures. Retrieved from https://assets.bbhub.io/company/sites/60/2020/10/FINAL-TCFD-Annex-Amended-121517.pdf

World Economic Forum (WEF). (2023). Global risks report 2023. World Economic Forum. Retrieved from https://www.weforum.org/reports/global-risks-report-2023/

Case References

Arvin, J. (2021). Norway's trillion-dollar wealth fund sold the last of its investments in fossil fuel companies. Vox. Retrieved from https://www.vox.com/22256192/norway-oil-gas-investments-fossil-fuel

Bloomberg. (2021). Norway's $1.4 trillion wealth fund set to get strict CO2 mandate. Pensions & Investments. Retrieved from https://www.pionline.com/sovereign-wealth-funds/norways-14-trillion-wealth-fund-set-get-strict-co2-mandate

Generation Investment Management (GIM). (2022). Sustainability in the investment process. [PDF] https://www.generationim.com/media/st1db1im/sustainability-in-the-investment-process.pdf

GIM. (2023). Global equity quarterly investor letter. Retrieved from https://www.generationim.com/media/mwilx00x/generation-im-q3-2023-global-equity-investor-letter-website.pdf)

GIM. (2025a). Sustainable investing at generation investment management. Retrieved from https://www.generationim.com/our-firm/

GIM. (2025b). Our strategies. Retrieved from https://www.generationim.com/our-strategies/

GIM. (2025c). Our firm. Retrieved from https://www.generationim.com/our-firm/

Johansmeyer, T. (2022). How fossil fuel divestment falls short. Harvard Business Review. Retrieved from https://hbr.org/2022/11/how-fossil-fuel-divestment-falls-short

Norges Bank Investment Management (NBIM). (2025). Responsible investment. Retrieved from https://www.nbim.no/en/responsible-investment/

PACTA. (2023). Making the climate transition bloom. Retrieved 23 January, 2025, from https://pacta.rmi.org/wp-content/uploads/2023/06/making_the_climate_transition_bloom.pdf

Plantinga, A., & Scholtens, B. (2024). The finance perspective on fossil fuel divestment. *Current Opinion in Environmental Sustainability, 66*, 101394–101394. Retrieved from https://doi.org/10.1016/j.cosust.2023.101394

Reichelstein, S., & Bebb, D. (2016). Sustainable investing at generation investment management. Stanford Graduate School of Business. Retrieved 1 January, 2024, from https://www.gsb.stanford.edu/faculty-research/case-studies/sustainable-investing-generation-investment-management

The Guardian. (2019a). World's biggest sovereign wealth fund to ditch fossil fuels. Retrieved from https://www.theguardian.com/business/2019/jun/12/worlds-biggest-sovereign-wealth-fund-to-ditch-fossil-fuels

The Guardian. (2019b). Norway's $1tn wealth fund to divest from oil and gas exploration. Retrieved from https://www.theguardian.com/world/2019/mar/08/norways-1tn-wealth-fund-to-divest-from-oil-and-gas-exploration

CHAPTER 18

Challenges of Integrating Climate Considerations: Overcoming Barriers to Action

1 Introduction: From Awareness to Action

The world is waking up to the realities of climate change. Businesses, investors, and governments are increasingly recognizing the urgent need to mitigate emissions, adapt to a changing climate, and build a more sustainable future. Yet, translating this growing awareness into concrete action can be a daunting task. While the imperative is clear, the path forward is often complex, paved with challenges and obstacles that can hinder progress. Global risks are interconnected, including climate change and economic instability (World Economic Forum, 2023).

The UNEP FI (2023), "Climate Risk Landscape" report, has outlined 4 most recent risk assessment tool trends.

1. **Integrated Risk Assessment:** Recognizing that climate risks are interconnected, tool providers are increasingly offering integrated solutions that assess both physical and transition risks within a single platform. This shift is driven by user demand for a more holistic view of climate-related financial impacts. However, modeling the complex interactions between these risks, such as tipping points, remains a work in progress.
2. **Net-Zero Focus and Updated Scenarios:** With the global push toward net-zero emissions, climate risk tools have incorporated more detailed 1.5 °C scenarios and updated existing scenarios to reflect the latest climate science, policy commitments, and technological advancements. This includes updates from sources like the IPCC, IEA, and NGFS. Tools now provide greater granularity in sectoral decarbonization pathways and offer more sophisticated analysis of transition risks under various net-zero scenarios.

J. Chen, *Climate Finance*,
https://doi.org/10.1007/978-981-96-7975-1_18

3. **Enhanced Data and Transparency:** Data availability and transparency have improved significantly. Many tools now account for all three emission scopes (Scope 1, 2, and 3), offering more comprehensive coverage. Tool providers are also placing a greater emphasis on transparency by providing more detailed documentation of their methodologies and assumptions, boosting user confidence, and facilitating better interpretation of results. Open-source data and initiatives from organizations like the IEA and NGFS further contribute to this trend.
4. **User-Friendly Tools and Disclosure Focus:** Driven by rising regulatory demands for climate-related disclosures (e.g., TCFD, ISSB), tool providers are developing more user-friendly and purpose-built tools. These tools often feature automated reporting capabilities aligned with specific disclosure frameworks, simplifying the reporting process and ensuring compliance. There's also a trend toward greater use of visualization and interactive dashboards, making the outputs more digestible and actionable.

As we can see, the risk assessment integration, data availability and transparency, model interpretation have been the centerpieces of the most recent climate assessment tool development. However, the "implementation gap"—the disconnect between acknowledging the importance of climate change and taking concrete steps to address it—is still a pervasive problem. Organizations may understand the risks, set ambitious goals, and even invest in sophisticated tools and frameworks, but they often struggle to effectively integrate climate considerations into their core decision-making processes, operations, and strategies. Climate risk modeling faces challenges in data and methodology (Jackman, 2023). Central banks are increasingly integrating sustainable investment, but face data challenges (NGFS, 2020).

Addressing these challenges is not just about avoiding potential pitfalls; it's about unlocking opportunities. By actively confronting the barriers to climate action, organizations can:

- **Enhance Risk Management:** Identifying and addressing data gaps, model limitations, and communication challenges leads to more accurate risk assessments and more effective risk management strategies.
- **Improve Decision-Making:** Overcoming communication barriers, building organizational capacity, and fostering a culture of climate awareness enables more informed and strategic decision-making about climate-related investments, policies, and operations.
- **Build Credibility and Trust:** Being transparent about the challenges and limitations of climate risk assessments and disclosures enhances credibility with investors, customers, and other stakeholders, fostering trust and collaboration.

This chapter will explore the key challenges organizations face when integrating climate considerations into their practices, offering practical guidance for overcoming these obstacles and building a more resilient and sustainable future.

2 Data Challenges and Model Limitations

Data is the foundation of climate risk assessment and decision-making. However, accessing reliable, accurate, and relevant data can be a significant challenge. Furthermore, the models used to analyze this data and project future climate impacts have inherent limitations that must be carefully considered.

2.1 Data Availability and Quality

Several factors contribute to the data challenges in climate risk assessment:

- **Historical Data Limitations:** Climate change is altering the frequency and intensity of hazards, making the past an imperfect guide to the future. Historical data may not fully capture the risks associated with more extreme events or gradual shifts in climate patterns. For example, relying solely on historical flood data to assess future flood risks in a region experiencing increased rainfall due to climate change could lead to an underestimation of the risks.
- **Regional and Local Data Scarcity:** Global climate models (GCMs), which provide projections of future climate change, often have a coarse spatial resolution, typically representing climate conditions over grid cells that are tens or hundreds of kilometers in size. This coarse resolution makes it difficult to assess risks at the local scales where adaptation decisions are made. Downscaling techniques can help to translate global projections to regional scales, but data limitations at local levels, such as detailed topographical data, land-use patterns, or localized weather patterns, can still hinder accurate risk assessments.
- **Data Quality Issues:** Inconsistent data collection methods, incomplete datasets, errors in data entry, and a lack of standardized data formats can all compromise the quality of climate risk assessments. For example, if different organizations use different methodologies to measure greenhouse gas emissions or assess the vulnerability of infrastructure to climate hazards, it can be difficult to compare results and make informed decisions.
- **Data Accessibility:** Even when data is available, it may not be easily accessible or readily shared between different organizations or sectors. Data may be held in proprietary databases, lack standardized formats that allow for easy integration, or be subject to confidentiality restrictions.

This lack of data sharing can hinder collaboration and impede the development of comprehensive risk assessments. UNEP FI (2024) emphasizes open-source climate data platforms for robust risk assessments.

Addressing these data challenges requires a multi-pronged approach:

- **Investing in Data Collection:** Governments, research institutions, and private companies need to invest in collecting more high-quality climate data, particularly at regional and local scales. This includes expanding weather monitoring networks, supporting remote sensing technologies, and conducting ground-based surveys to gather data on climate hazards, asset exposures, and vulnerabilities.
- **Supporting Open Data Initiatives:** Promoting open data platforms and policies that make climate data freely accessible to researchers, policymakers, and practitioners can encourage innovation, collaboration, and more accurate risk assessments.
- **Promoting Data Standardization Efforts:** Developing standardized data formats, protocols, and methodologies for collecting and reporting climate-related information can enhance data comparability and facilitate data sharing. FSB (2020) analyzes climate change's impact on financial stability, focusing on physical and transition risks and data gaps.

UNEP FI (2024) highlights the urgent need for accessible, reliable, and comparably standardized climate data due to growing climate change impacts and increasing regulatory demands. It emphasizes the potential of open-source, neutral data platforms like Dataland to bridge critical gaps in climate data availability and quality, thereby enhancing risk assessments and decision-making for financial institutions and other stakeholders. It argues that open-source and neutral data platforms are critical for assessing climate risk for several reasons:

1. **Enhanced Data Reliability and Comparability:** These platforms can improve data reliability and comparability by collecting and presenting company-specific *raw* data in standardized formats according to established data frameworks. This reduces bias introduced by data transformations or processing performed by third-party providers who may have vested interests or use different methodologies, leading to inconsistencies. Standardized data also facilitates more accurate comparisons across companies, sectors, and regions.
2. **Increased Transparency:** Open-source platforms promote transparency by providing access to the underlying data and methodologies used for risk assessments. This allows users to understand the assumptions and potential biases that may influence the analysis, fostering greater trust and

accountability. Users can also scrutinize the data and offer corrections or improvements, leading to a more robust and reliable dataset.

3. **Improved Accessibility and Reduced Costs:** Free and open-source platforms remove the financial barriers associated with accessing climate data, making it available to a wider range of stakeholders, including smaller financial institutions, academics, researchers, NGOs, and policymakers who may not have the resources to purchase expensive commercial data. This democratizes access to critical information and promotes broader participation in climate risk assessment.
4. **Faster Innovation and Collaboration:** Open-source platforms foster faster innovation and collaboration by enabling users to build upon existing tools and frameworks, share best practices, and contribute to the development of new methodologies. This accelerates the development of more sophisticated and tailored climate risk assessment tools and solutions.
5. **Empowerment of Users:** By providing access to raw, unbiased data, these platforms empower users to conduct their own independent analyses and draw their own conclusions without relying on the interpretations of third-party providers. This gives users greater control over the assessment process and allows them to tailor the analysis to their specific needs and circumstances.

However, the effectiveness of open-source and neutral data platforms hinges on several factors:

- **Achieving Critical Mass:** The platform needs to attract a sufficient number of users and data providers to ensure comprehensive coverage and usefulness. A "network effect" is needed, where increased participation enhances the value of the platform for all.
- **Data Quality Control:** While raw data can reduce certain biases, robust quality control mechanisms are still crucial to ensure accuracy and consistency.
- **Maintaining Neutrality:** Governance structures must be designed to ensure the platform remains neutral and free from undue influence by any particular stakeholder group.
- **Technical Expertise and Support:** User-friendly interfaces and technical support are essential, especially for users with less technical expertise.

By addressing these challenges, open-source and neutral data platforms can become powerful tools for driving informed decision-making and effective action on climate change.

2.1.1 *Case Study 18.1: The California Department of Water Resources (DWR) and Climate Data Challenges*

Overview

The California Department of Water Resources (DWR) is responsible for managing water resources in a state increasingly affected by drought and water scarcity due to climate change. This case study highlights the ongoing challenges faced by the DWR in addressing data gaps and limitations, assessing future water availability, modeling climate change impacts on snowpack and runoff, and planning for water shortages.

Challenges Faced by DWR

Data Gaps and Limitations:

- **Incomplete Data:** The DWR grapples with incomplete and inaccessible data, which hinders effective water management. Critical data on groundwater levels, snowpack, and river flows are often missing or outdated, complicating the assessment of water availability and climate impacts (California Water Data Consortium, 2023).
- **Modeling Uncertainties:** Climate models used to predict future water scenarios have inherent uncertainties. These models must account for variables such as temperature increases, changing precipitation patterns, and variations in runoff timing and magnitude, all of which are influenced by climate change (Lettenmaier & Lund, 2020; Mirchi et al., 2013).

Climate Change Impacts:

- **Reduced Snowpack:** Warmer temperatures drive the snow line higher, reducing snowpack and consequently diminishing a critical water storage source. This shift results in less water availability during the dry season (California Department of Water Resources (DWR), 2015).
- **Increased Flood Risks:** More precipitation falling as rain instead of snow exacerbates flood risks and creates additional challenges for water supply reliability (California Department of Water Resources, 2025).
- **Drought Frequency:** Droughts are becoming more frequent and persistent, further straining water resources and requiring more sophisticated management strategies (California Department of Water Resources (DWR), 2015).

Efforts to Improve Data Collection and Collaboration

Improving Data Collection:

- **Weather Generator Tool:** The DWR has developed a "Weather Generator" tool to help hydrologists and water resource managers better understand and prepare for climate impacts. This tool simulates increased temperature effects on droughts and floods, aiding in stress-testing water systems to identify vulnerabilities (California Department of Water Resources, 2025).

- **Automated Data Collection:** Recommendations from the California Water Data Consortium include automating data collection and reporting critical water datasets to improve data quality and accessibility (California Water Data Consortium, 2023).

Collaborations with Research Institutions:

- **Partnerships:** The DWR collaborates with various research institutions to enhance climate data and modeling capabilities. These partnerships support the development of more accurate and comprehensive climate models, which are essential for informed water management decisions (California Department of Water Resources, 2025).
- **Technical Reports:** Collaborations have led to the publication of technical reports and policy briefs that outline strategies for improving water data infrastructure and cross-agency collaboration (California Water Data Consortium, 2023).

Using Climate Models and Scenarios
Climate Action Plan:

- **Phased Approach:** The DWR's Climate Action Plan guides the department's response to climate change through a phased approach. This includes developing a Greenhouse Gas Emissions Reduction Plan, standardizing climate change analysis tools, and assessing the vulnerabilities of water assets to climate impacts (California Department of Water Resources, 2025).

Scenario Planning:

- **Multiple Models:** The DWR uses a range of climate models and scenarios to predict future water availability and plan for potential shortages. These models consider various climate variables and their potential impacts on water resources, helping to inform adaptive management strategies (California Department of Water Resources (DWR), 2015).
- **Stress Testing:** Tools like the Weather Generator are used to stress-test water resource systems against extreme climate events, ensuring that the infrastructure can handle unprecedented conditions (California Department of Water Resources, 2025).

Conclusion

The California Department of Water Resources faces significant challenges in managing water resources amid increasing drought and water scarcity due to climate change. Data gaps and modeling uncertainties complicate efforts to assess future water availability and plan for shortages. However, the DWR is actively working to improve data collection, collaborate with research institutions, and utilize a range of climate models and scenarios to inform its water management strategies. These efforts are crucial for building resilience and ensuring a reliable water supply for California's future.

2.2 *Model Limitations*

Climate risk models, while powerful tools, are simplifications of a complex reality and have inherent limitations that must be acknowledged and addressed. ECB (2020) guides financial institutions to manage and disclose climate-related risks.

Key model limitations include:

Model Complexity: Climate risk models, particularly those that integrate both physical and transition risks, can be highly complex, involving numerous variables, assumptions, and interdependencies. This complexity can make it challenging for users to understand the underlying logic of the models, interpret the results, and communicate the findings to decision-makers.

Addressing Complexity: Model developers should strive for transparency in their methodologies and assumptions, providing clear documentation and user-friendly interfaces that make the models more accessible to non-experts. Sensitivity analysis, which involves testing how model outputs change when key input parameters are varied, can help to understand the influence of different assumptions and the robustness of the results.

Uncertainty in Climate Projections: Climate models provide a range of possible future scenarios, not precise predictions. This uncertainty stems from the inherent complexity of the climate system, the limitations of scientific understanding, and the unpredictability of human behavior, which influences future greenhouse gas emissions.

Managing Uncertainty: Modelers should communicate uncertainty transparently, using ranges of potential outcomes and probabilities rather than presenting a single "most likely" scenario. Decision-makers need to understand that climate risk assessments are not about predicting the future with certainty but rather about providing a framework for understanding potential risks and opportunities and making informed choices in the face of uncertainty.

3 Model Interpretation and Communication

Even the most sophisticated climate risk models are only as useful as our ability to understand and communicate their results. Bridging the gap between complex scientific outputs and actionable insights for decision-makers is a crucial challenge.

3.1 *Bridging the Technical Divide*

Communicating complex technical information from climate models to non-expert audiences, such as business leaders, policymakers, and the public, can be fraught with difficulties. Technical jargon, statistical concepts, and the inherent uncertainties of climate projections can create confusion and hinder understanding. Poortvliet et al. (2020) analyze IPCC's communication of climate risks, finding a focus on threats but less on efficacy and concrete examples. Roberts et al. (2021) offer a handbook for communicating climate risk, stressing intuitive thinking, and understanding policymakers' perspectives.

To bridge this technical divide, effective communication is essential. This involves:

- **Using Clear and Concise Language:** Avoid technical jargon and use plain language that is accessible to a broad audience. Explain complex concepts in simple terms, using analogies or metaphors to make the information more relatable.
- **Employing Visuals:** Charts, graphs, maps, and other visual aids can make data more engaging and understandable. Use color-coding, clear labels, and intuitive designs to highlight key findings and trends.
- **Framing Information:** Present climate risk information in a way that is relevant to the audience's interests and concerns. For example, when communicating with business leaders, focus on the potential financial impacts of climate change and the opportunities for building resilience or developing new products and services. When communicating with policymakers, highlight the implications for public health, infrastructure, or economic development.
- **Using Storytelling and Narratives:** Stories and narratives can make climate risk information more compelling and memorable. Use real-world examples, case studies, or personal anecdotes to illustrate the potential impacts of climate change and the benefits of taking action.

3.2 *Communicating Uncertainty*

Communicating uncertainty in a way that is both accurate and understandable is a significant challenge. Oversimplifying uncertainty can mislead decision-makers, while dwelling on it can lead to paralysis or inaction. Kopp et al. (2023) discuss challenges in communicating sea-level rise uncertainty and advocate for clear communication and adaptive management.

Key principles for effective communication of uncertainty:

- **Use Clear Language:** Explain uncertainty using plain language, avoiding technical terms like "confidence intervals" or "probability distributions." For example, instead of saying "there is a 90% probability that sea levels will rise by at least one meter by 2100," you could say "scientists are very confident that sea levels will rise by at least one meter by 2100."

- **Present a Range of Outcomes:** Show a range of possible outcomes, rather than focusing on a single "most likely" scenario. Use visuals, such as fan charts or maps showing different levels of risk, to illustrate the potential variability in future impacts.
- **Focus on the Implications:** Rather than dwelling on the technical details of uncertainty, emphasize the implications for decision-making. Explain how different scenarios might affect the organization's operations, investments, or strategies, and what actions can be taken to prepare for a range of possible outcomes.
- **Emphasize Adaptive Management:** Highlight the importance of adaptive management—an iterative approach to decision-making that acknowledges uncertainty, monitors outcomes, and adjusts strategies as needed. Explain that uncertainty is not a reason for inaction but rather a call for flexibility and ongoing learning.

3.3 Addressing the "Black Box" Problem

Some climate risk models, particularly those developed by commercial providers, use proprietary algorithms or data, making it difficult for users to understand how the models work and assess their reliability. This lack of transparency, often referred to as the "black box" problem, can erode trust in the models and hinder their adoption.

To address this challenge:

- **Promote Open-Source Models:** Encourage the development and use of open-source climate risk models, where the underlying code and data are transparent and accessible for scrutiny by the scientific community.
- **Demand Data Transparency:** Investors and other users of climate risk models should demand transparency from model providers about the data sources, methodologies, and assumptions used in their models.
- **Support Independent Verification:** Independent verification of climate risk models by third-party experts can provide assurance about their accuracy and reliability, enhancing trust in the results.

4 Organizational Capacity Building

Integrating climate considerations effectively into an organization's practices requires more than just adopting new tools and frameworks. It demands a fundamental shift in mindset, a commitment to building internal expertise, and a willingness to embed climate awareness into the organization's culture and decision-making processes. IMF (2023) emphasizes capacity building in financial sectors to address climate risks through training, specialized units, and international cooperation.

4.1 Developing Internal Expertise

Building internal expertise in climate change is essential for organizations to effectively assess and manage climate risks, navigate the complexities of disclosure frameworks, and make informed decisions about climate-aligned investments and operations.

Key steps to building internal capacity:

- **Training and Education:** Provide training programs for staff on climate science, risk assessment methodologies, disclosure frameworks, and investment strategies. Training can range from introductory courses on climate change basics to more specialized workshops on specific topics, such as scenario analysis, carbon footprinting, or ESG integration.
- **Hiring Specialists:** Hiring climate risk experts, data scientists, or sustainability professionals can bring in-house expertise and provide dedicated support for climate-related initiatives. These specialists can help to conduct climate risk assessments, develop disclosure reports, integrate climate considerations into investment strategies, and advise on sustainability best practices.
- **Engaging External Consultants:** For organizations that lack the internal resources or expertise to address climate change comprehensively, working with external consultants or advisors can be valuable. Consultants can provide specialized knowledge, conduct tailored risk assessments, develop disclosure strategies, or support the implementation of climate-related initiatives.

4.2 Integrating Climate Considerations into Existing Processes

Integrating climate risk management into existing business processes is crucial for ensuring that climate considerations are not treated as a separate, siloed activity but rather become an integral part of the organization's decision-making at all levels. SASB (2024) provides a framework for identifying, measuring, and managing climate-related financial risks and emphasizes industry-specific disclosures.

Key areas for integration:

- **Risk Management Frameworks:** Incorporate climate risks into the organization's enterprise risk management (ERM) system. This involves identifying, assessing, and managing climate risks alongside other financial, operational, and strategic risks.

- **Investment Policies:** Update investment policies to explicitly include climate considerations and align with ESG goals. This may involve setting climate-related investment criteria, adopting negative screening policies, or incorporating impact measurement into investment decision-making processes.
- **Strategic Planning:** Integrate climate risks and opportunities into long-term strategic planning processes. This involves considering how climate change might affect the organization's markets, operations, supply chains, and competitive landscape, and developing strategies to mitigate risks and capitalize on opportunities.
- **Operational Decision-Making:** Consider climate factors in day-to-day operational decisions, such as supply chain management, resource allocation, product development, and marketing. For example, a company might choose to source materials from suppliers with lower-carbon footprints, invest in energy-efficient equipment, or develop products that appeal to environmentally conscious consumers. ESMA (2021) provides guidance on Article 8 of the Taxonomy Regulation, focusing on KPI definitions, methodologies, and cost implications.

4.3 *Establishing a Robust Governance Framework*

A clear governance structure is essential for overseeing climate-related issues, ensuring accountability, and driving progress on climate action within the organization.

Key elements of a strong climate governance framework:

- **Board-Level Oversight:** The board of directors should have adequate knowledge of climate risks and opportunities and provide oversight of the organization's climate strategy. This may involve establishing a dedicated sustainability committee or incorporating climate considerations into the responsibilities of existing board committees.
- **Management Accountability:** Clear responsibilities for climate risk management, disclosure, and investment decision-making should be assigned to specific individuals or teams within the organization. These individuals or teams should have the authority, resources, and expertise to carry out their responsibilities effectively.
- **Integration with Existing Governance Structures:** Climate governance should be integrated with existing corporate governance structures, such as risk management committees, audit committees, and executive compensation plans. This ensures that climate considerations are embedded into the organization's decision-making processes at all levels.

4.3.1 Case Study 18.2: Bank of America's Sustainable Finance Team

Overview

Bank of America has made significant strides in addressing climate change, managing climate risks, and developing sustainable finance solutions. This case study showcases how the bank has built its internal capacity through the establishment of a dedicated Sustainable Finance team, hiring climate risk experts, and developing internal training programs for staff on climate change, ESG investing, and green finance products.

Building Internal Capacity

Establishment of the Sustainable Finance Team:

- **Dedicated Team:** Bank of America has created a dedicated Sustainable Finance team led by Karen Fang, the Global Head of Sustainable Finance. This team focuses on integrating climate considerations into the bank's financial activities and supporting the transition to a low-carbon economy (Gombar, 2022).
- **Global Presence:** The team has expanded to 35 members, spread across developed and emerging markets, to fulfill its role as a catalyst for new technologies and sustainable projects (Gombar, 2022).

Hiring Climate Risk Experts:

- **Expertise:** The bank has hired climate risk experts to enhance its understanding of climate-related financial risks and opportunities. These experts help develop strategies to mitigate risks and capitalize on sustainable finance opportunities.
- **Training Programs:** Bank of America has implemented internal training programs to educate staff on climate change, ESG investing, and green finance products. These programs ensure that employees are equipped with the knowledge and skills needed to support the bank's sustainability goals (Bank of America, 2025a).

Developing Sustainable Finance Solutions

Sustainable Finance Initiatives:

- **Commitment to Sustainable Finance:** Bank of America has committed to mobilizing $1.5 trillion in sustainable finance by 2030, including $1 trillion for climate projects and $500 billion for social development (Bank of America, 2025a; Segal, 2022). This commitment supports projects that address climate change, promote social equity, and contribute to the United Nations Sustainable Development Goals (SDGs).
- **Green Bonds:** The bank is a leading underwriter of green bonds, having supported over 225 clients in raising more than $300 billion through ESG-themed bond offerings (Segal, 2022). These bonds finance projects

related to renewable energy, energy efficiency, clean transportation, and other sustainable initiatives.

Innovative Financing Solutions:

- **Equality Progress Sustainability Bonds:** Bank of America has introduced first-of-their-kind Equality Progress Sustainability Bonds, providing new options for fixed-income investors and capital for businesses and communities (Bank of America, 2025a).
- **Breakthrough Energy Catalyst:** The bank is an investor in the Breakthrough Energy Catalyst program, which focuses on innovative technologies such as direct air capture, green hydrogen, long-duration energy storage, and sustainable aviation fuel (Gombar, 2022).

Importance of Building Internal Expertise
Leadership Commitment:

- **Top-Down Support:** The commitment from senior leadership, including Vice Chair Paul Donofrio and Global Head of Sustainable Finance Karen Fang, has been crucial in driving the bank's sustainable finance strategy (Segal, 2022). Leadership support ensures that sustainability is integrated into the bank's core business functions.
- **Strategic Alignment:** The bank's sustainable finance strategy aligns with its broader goals of responsible growth and achieving net-zero greenhouse gas emissions by 2050 (Bank of America, 2025b).

Benefits of Integrating Climate Considerations:

- **Risk Management:** Integrating climate considerations into financial decision-making helps the bank manage climate-related risks and avoid potential stranded assets. This proactive approach enhances the bank's resilience to climate impacts.
- **Market Opportunities:** By focusing on sustainable finance, Bank of America can capitalize on emerging market opportunities in renewable energy, energy efficiency, and other low-carbon technologies. This positions the bank as a leader in the transition to a sustainable economy.

Conclusion

Bank of America's Sustainable Finance team exemplifies how a major financial institution can build internal capacity to address climate change, manage climate risks, and develop sustainable finance solutions. Through the establishment of a dedicated team, hiring climate risk experts, and implementing training programs, the bank has integrated climate considerations into its core business functions. Leadership commitment and strategic alignment have been critical in driving these efforts, resulting in significant contributions to sustainable finance and the transition to a low-carbon economy.

5 Navigating Uncertainty and Building Resilience

Climate change presents a future fraught with uncertainties. The precise magnitude, timing, and impacts of climate change are difficult to predict with absolute certainty. This uncertainty can be paralyzing, leading to inaction or a reluctance to make long-term commitments. However, effectively integrating climate considerations requires embracing uncertainty, adapting to changing conditions, and building resilience into strategies and operations.

5.1 Embracing Uncertainty

Rather than seeking perfect information or waiting for definitive answers, organizations need to adopt an adaptive management approach that acknowledges uncertainty and allows for flexibility in decision-making. TCFD (2020) provides guidance on scenario analysis for climate-related risks and opportunities. This involves:

- **Iterative Planning:** Developing strategies and plans that are not static but can be adjusted and refined as new information becomes available, risks evolve, and opportunities emerge.
- **Scenario Planning:** Using scenario analysis to explore a range of possible future climate outcomes, considering both optimistic and pessimistic scenarios, and developing contingency plans to respond to different eventualities.
- **Monitoring and Evaluation:** Continuously monitoring the effectiveness of climate-related actions, tracking progress toward goals, and adjusting strategies based on lessons learned and changing conditions.

5.1.1 Building a Culture of Climate Awareness

Integrating climate considerations effectively requires a shift in organizational culture. It's not enough for a few individuals or departments to champion climate action; the entire organization needs to embrace a culture that values sustainability, recognizes the importance of climate change, and supports the integration of climate considerations into decision-making at all levels. WBCSD (2020) emphasizes building long-term resilience through ESG integration and risk management.

Fostering a culture of climate awareness can involve:

- **Leadership Commitment:** Strong leadership commitment from the top is essential for demonstrating the importance of climate action and setting the tone for the entire organization.
- **Employee Engagement:** Engaging employees in climate-related initiatives, providing training and development opportunities, and creating channels for feedback and ideas can foster a sense of ownership and shared responsibility.
- **Communication and Education:** Regularly communicating about climate change, sharing information about the organization's climate strategy, and providing educational resources can help to raise awareness and build knowledge among employees.
- **Incentives and Recognition:** Recognizing and rewarding employees for their contributions to climate action can reinforce positive behaviors and encourage greater participation.

5.1.2 *Case Study 18.3: The Dutch Delta Program*

Overview

The Netherlands, a country highly vulnerable to sea-level rise, has implemented the Delta Program, a long-term strategy for managing water risks. This case study showcases how the Delta Program adopts a flexible and adaptive approach to manage the risks of sea-level rise and flooding, emphasizing the importance of continuous learning and integrating scientific knowledge into decision-making (National Delta Programme, 2024a, b, 2025).

Development and Implementation of the Delta Program

Historical Context:

- **Flood Disasters:** The Netherlands has a history of devastating floods, such as the 1953 flood disaster that resulted in over 1,800 deaths and significant economic losses. These events highlighted the need for robust flood protection measures.
- **Delta Works:** In response to past floods, the Netherlands implemented the Delta Works, a series of civil engineering projects designed to protect the country from the sea. This included the construction of storm surge barriers and dikes.

Adaptive Strategy:

- **Delta Act and Delta Fund:** The Delta Program was formalized through the Delta Act in 2011, which established the Delta Fund with an annual budget of €1 billion. This ensures consistent funding for flood protection, freshwater supply, and spatial adaptation measures.
- **Delta Commissioner:** The Delta Commissioner oversees the implementation of the Delta Program, ensuring that it is updated annually based on new scientific insights and climate data.

Key Components:

- **Flood Protection:** Strengthening dikes, creating floodplains, and implementing storm surge barriers to protect against sea-level rise and extreme weather events.
- **Freshwater Supply:** Ensuring sufficient freshwater availability through measures such as water storage, efficient water use, and managing saltwater intrusion.
- **Spatial Adaptation:** Integrating climate resilience into urban planning and infrastructure development to mitigate the impacts of flooding, heat, and drought.

Flexible and Adaptive Planning
Long-term Horizon:

- **Scenario Planning:** The Delta Program uses scenario planning to account for uncertainties in climate change, demographic shifts, and economic developments. This approach helps identify tipping points and adapt strategies accordingly.
- **Monitoring and Recalibration:** The program is regularly reviewed and updated based on new scientific knowledge and observed climate impacts. This continuous learning process ensures that the program remains effective in the face of changing conditions.

Integrated Approach:

- **Collaboration:** The Delta Program involves a wide range of stakeholders, including central and local governments, water authorities, research institutions, and the private sector. This collaborative approach ensures that diverse perspectives and expertise are incorporated into decision-making.
- **Science-Based Decision-Making:** The program relies on scientific research and data from institutions like Deltares and the Royal Netherlands Meteorological Institute (KNMI). This ensures that policies and measures are grounded in the latest climate science.

Challenges and Benefits
Challenges:

- **Uncertainty:** Managing the uncertainty inherent in long-term climate projections and their impacts on sea-level rise and flooding is a significant challenge. The Delta Program addresses this through adaptive strategies and scenario planning.
- **Political and Financial Commitment:** Sustaining long-term political and financial commitment is essential for the success of the Delta

Program. The establishment of the Delta Fund and the role of the Delta Commissioner help ensure consistent support and funding.

Benefits:

- **Resilience:** The adaptive and flexible approach of the Delta Program enhances the resilience of the Netherlands to climate change impacts. By continuously updating strategies based on new knowledge, the program can effectively respond to emerging risks.
- **Integrated Solutions:** The program's integrated approach to flood protection, freshwater supply, and spatial planning ensures that climate resilience is embedded in all aspects of development. This holistic strategy supports sustainable and resilient growth.

Conclusion

The Dutch Delta Program exemplifies a long-term, adaptive approach to managing the risks of sea-level rise and flooding. By incorporating flexible planning, continuous learning, and scientific knowledge into decision-making, the Netherlands has developed a robust strategy to protect its citizens and infrastructure from climate change impacts. The program's success highlights the importance of sustained political and financial commitment, collaborative efforts, and the integration of climate resilience into all aspects of planning and development.

6 Conclusion: A Continuous Journey of Improvement

Integrating climate considerations into organizational practices is not a one-time event; it's an ongoing journey of learning, adaptation, and improvement. The challenges are real and complex, but they are not insurmountable.

By embracing transparency, fostering collaboration, investing in capacity building, and engaging stakeholders in a meaningful way, organizations can overcome the barriers to action, enhance their resilience to climate change, and contribute to a more sustainable future.

As the climate crisis unfolds and our understanding of its implications deepens, the need for continuous improvement in climate risk assessment, disclosure, and investment decision-making will only intensify. By embracing this challenge and viewing it as an opportunity for innovation and transformation, organizations can position themselves for long-term success in a world that is increasingly shaped by the realities of climate change.

References

European Securities and Markets Authority (ESMA). (2021). Final Report Advice on Article 8 of the Taxonomy Regulation. Retrieved from https://www.esma.europa.eu/sites/default/files/library/esma30-379-471_final_report_-_advice_on_article_8_of_the_taxonomy_regulation.pdf

Financial Stability Board (FSB). (2020). The implications of climate change for financial stability. Retrieved from https://www.fsb.org/2020/11/the-implications-of-climate-change-for-financial-stability/

International Monetary Fund (IMF). (2023). Capacity building in the financial sector—From climate risk analysis to CBDCs. Retrieved from https://www.imf.org/en/News/Articles/2023/03/14/sp-capacity-building-financial-sector-climate-risk-analysis-cbdc

Jackman, A. (2023). The challenge of climate risk modelling in financial institutions—Overview, critique and guidance. UK Centre for Greening Finance and Investment (CGFI). Retrieved from https://www.cgfi.ac.uk/2023/12/the-challenge-of-climate-risk-modelling-in-financial-institutions-overview-critique-and-guidance/

Kopp, R. E. et al. (2023). Communicating future sea-level rise uncertainty and ambiguity to assessment users. *Nature Climate Change, 13*(7), 648–660. Retrieved from https://doi.org/10.1038/s41558-023-01691-8

Network for Greening the Financial System (NGFS). (2020). Progress report on the implementation of sustainable and responsible investment practices in central banks' portfolio management. Retrieved from https://www.ngfs.net/en/publications-and-statistics/publications/progress-report-implementation-sustainable-and-responsible-investment-practices-central-banks

Poortvliet, P. M. et al. (2020). Communicating climate change risk: A content analysis of IPCC's summary for policymakers. *Sustainability, 12*(12), 48–61. Retrieved from https://doi.org/10.3390/su12124861

Roberts, F. E., Meyer, K. D., & Hubble-Rose, L. (2021). Communicating climate risk: A handbook. Climate Action Unit, University College London. London, United Kingdom. Retrieved 8 March, 2025, from https://www.ucl.ac.uk/climate-action-unit/sites/climate_action_unit/files/communicating_climate_risk_-_a_handbook.pdf

Task Force on Climate-Related Financial Disclosures (TCFD). (2020). Task force on climate-related financial disclosures guidance on scenario analysis for non-financial companies. Retrieved from https://assets.bbhub.io/company/sites/60/2020/09/2020-TCFD_Guidance-Scenario-Analysis-Guidance.pdf

United Nations Environment Programme Finance Initiative (UNEP FI). (2023). United nations environment programme finance initiative. Retrieved from https://www.unepfi.org/themes/climate-change/2023-climate-risk-landscape/

UNEP FI. (2024). The climate data challenge technical supplement to the 2024 climate risk landscape report. Retrieved from https://www.unepfi.org/wordpress/wp-content/uploads/2024/05/Dataland-Final-Report-The-Climate-Data-Challenge-1.pdf

World Business Council for Sustainable Development (WBCSD). (2020). Building long term business resilience. WBCSD. Retrieved 1 January, 2025, from https://www.wbcsd.org/resources/building-long-term-business-resilience/

World Economic Forum (WEF). (2023). Global risks report 2023. World Economic Forum. Retrieved from https://www.weforum.org/reports/global-risks-report-2023/

Case References

Bank of America. (2025a). How sustainable finance can work for you. Retrieved from https://about.bankofamerica.com/en/making-an-impact/sustainable-finance

Bank Of America. (2025b). Environmental sustainability. Retrieved from https://about.bankofamerica.com/en/making-an-impact/environmental-sustainability

California Department of Water Resources (DWR). (2015). California climate science and data for water resources management. Retrieved 1 January, 2024, from https://cawaterlibrary.net/document/california-climate-science-and-data-for-water-resources-management/

DWR. (2025). Climate change program. Retrieved from https://water.ca.gov/programs/all-programs/climate-change-program

California Water Data Consortium. (2023). New report: Putting data to work. Retrieved 1 January, 2024, from https://cawaterdata.org/news/new-report-putting-data-to-work/

Gombar, V. (2022). BofA's $1.5 trillion sustainable funding to focus on 'impact.' Bloomberg NEF. Retrieved from https://about.bnef.com/blog/bofas-1-5-trillion-sustainable-funding-to-focus-on-impact/

Lettenmaier, D. P., & Lund, J. R. (2020). How will climate change affect California's water resources? Retrieved from https://www.nae.edu/228946/How-Will-Climate-Change-Affect-Californias-Water-Resources

Mirchi, A. et al. (2013). Climate change impacts on California's water resources, pp. 301–319. Retrieved from https://www.researchgate.net/publication/273378884_Climate_Change_Impacts_on_California's_Water_Resources

National Delta Programme (NDP). (2024a). Outlines delta programme 2025. Retrieved 24 January, 2025, from https://english.deltaprogramma.nl/documents/publications/2024/09/17/dp-2025-outlines

NDP. (2024b). Sea-level rise in the Netherlands. Retrieved 24 January, 2025, from https://english.deltaprogramma.nl/documents/publications/2023/09/19/sea-level-rise-in-the-netherlands

NDP. (2025). What is the national delta programme? Retrieved from 24 January, 2025, from https://english.deltaprogramma.nl/delta-programme/what-is-the-delta-programme

Segal, M. (2022). BofA more than doubles sustainable finance activity, mobilizing $250 billion in 2021. ESG Today. Retrieved 1 January, 2024, from https://www.esgtoday.com/bofa-more-than-doubles-sustainable-finance-activity-mobilizing-250-billion-in-2021/

PART V

Moving Forward: Shaping the Future of Climate Finance

We've explored the science of climate change, the financial risks it poses, and the innovative tools and strategies emerging to address these challenges. Now, we turn our attention to the path ahead—the future of climate finance and the collective action needed to build a more sustainable and resilient world.

This part examines the crucial role of governments in creating an enabling environment for climate finance, the complexities and opportunities of international climate finance, and the practical steps individuals and organizations can take to integrate climate considerations into their practices. We'll also explore the emerging trends that are shaping the future of climate finance, from the transformative potential of technology to the evolving regulatory landscape and the growing importance of global cooperation.

Chapter 19: The Role of Governments and Policy: Creating an Enabling Environment

Governments play a pivotal role in shaping the climate finance landscape. This chapter explores the policy instruments governments can use to mobilize climate finance, from carbon pricing mechanisms and renewable energy targets to innovative financial instruments and public-private partnerships. We'll also examine the critical role of international climate agreements and frameworks, such as the Paris Agreement, in setting global goals and fostering collaboration. Finally, we'll delve into the Green Climate Fund (GCF) and other multilateral mechanisms that are channeling finance to developing countries to support their climate action efforts.

Chapter 20: International Climate Finance: Flows, Challenges, and Innovations
Addressing climate change requires a global response, and international climate finance is crucial for supporting developing countries in their mitigation and adaptation efforts. This chapter examines the complex landscape of international climate finance, exploring the various actors, funding mechanisms, and challenges involved in mobilizing and delivering climate finance across borders. We'll also highlight the innovations and emerging trends that are shaping the future of international climate finance, such as blended finance, green bonds, and the use of blockchain technology to enhance transparency and efficiency.

Chapter 21: A Roadmap for Climate Finance: Integrating Climate Considerations into Practice
This chapter provides a practical roadmap for individuals and organizations seeking to integrate climate considerations into their financial decision-making and operations. We'll start by outlining the steps involved in defining a climate finance strategy, assessing risks and opportunities, and setting clear objectives. We'll then delve into the selection and implementation of climate risk assessment tools, providing guidance on choosing the right tools for specific needs and integrating them effectively into existing workflows. We'll also explore the importance of stakeholder engagement, emphasizing the need for clear communication, collaboration, and capacity building. Finally, we'll discuss the crucial role of measuring and reporting on climate impact, highlighting best practices for tracking progress, ensuring transparency, and holding organizations accountable for their actions.

Chapter 22: The Future of Climate Finance: Trends, Opportunities, and a Call to Action
The climate finance landscape is constantly evolving, driven by technological advancements, shifting market dynamics, evolving regulations, and the growing urgency of addressing climate change. This chapter explores the emerging trends and opportunities that are shaping the future of climate finance. We'll examine the transformative potential of technologies like artificial intelligence (AI), blockchain, and big data in enhancing climate risk assessment, facilitating green investments, and improving transparency. We'll discuss the evolving regulatory landscape, including the growing momentum behind mandatory climate risk disclosure requirements. And we'll highlight the need for greater global cooperation, innovation, and a collective commitment to action to unlock the full potential of climate finance and build a more sustainable future for all.

This final part of the book offers a forward-looking perspective on the evolving landscape of climate finance, providing a roadmap for action and a call to embrace the challenges and opportunities of this critical endeavor. By working together, governments, businesses, investors, and individuals can harness the power of finance to drive the transition to a low-carbon and climate-resilient world.

CHAPTER 19

The Role of Governments and Policy: Creating an Enabling Environment for Climate Action

1 Introduction: The Power of Policy

The climate crisis demands a global response, but markets alone cannot solve this monumental challenge. While voluntary initiatives by businesses and investors are important, they are insufficient to achieve the scale and urgency required to address this global threat. Strong and effective government policies are essential to create a level playing field, incentivize investment in climate solutions, and ensure a just and equitable transition to a low-carbon and climate-resilient future.

Governments hold the key to unlocking the trillions of dollars needed to finance this transformation. They are not just bystanders in this critical endeavor; they are active players, with the power to shape market signals, incentivize innovation, reduce risk, and foster collaboration. Developed countries exceeded the USD 100 billion climate finance goal for the first time in 2022, primarily through public finance (OECD, 2024), as shown in the Fig. 1.

The Fig. 2 shows the trends in public climate finance activities reported between 2016 and 2022, categorized by climate theme: mitigation, cross-cutting (addressing both mitigation and adaptation), and adaptation. The figure presents the number of activities reported, not the financial value of the finance.

Key observations from the figure include:

- **Adaptation Activities Grew Rapidly, Especially After 2019:** There's a marked upward trend in the number of reported adaptation activities. While there was a slight dip in 2021, the number increased significantly over the period, indicating a growing focus on adaptation projects. This

J. Chen, *Climate Finance*,
https://doi.org/10.1007/978-981-96-7975-1_19

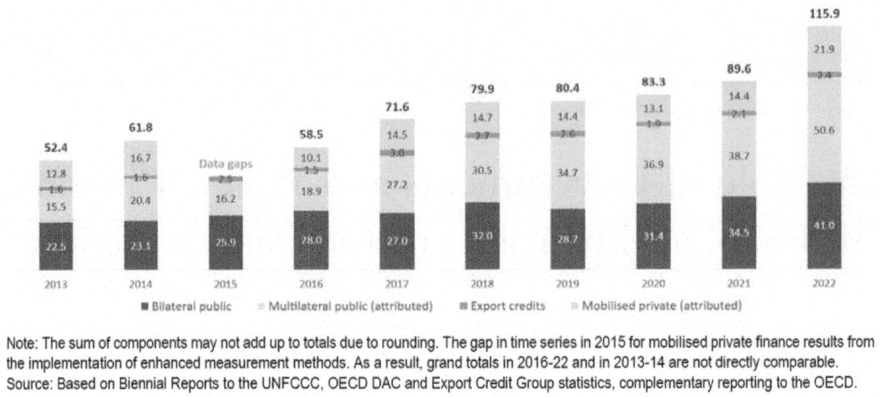

Fig. 1 Climate finance provided and mobilized in 2013–2022 (USD billion) (*Source* OECD [2024])

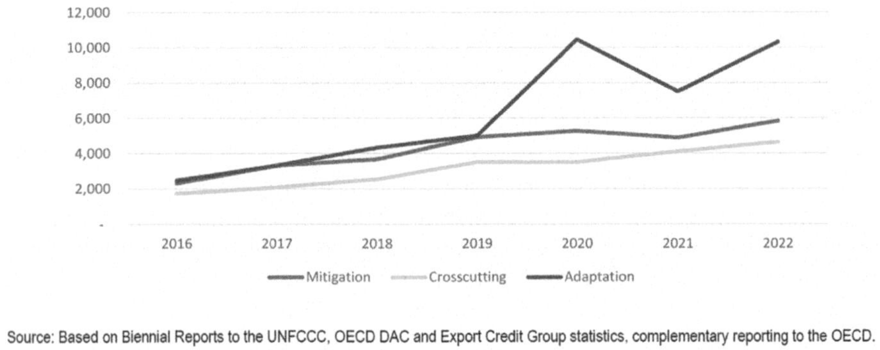

Fig. 2 Public climate finance provided in 2016–2022 by climate theme, per number of activities (*Source* OECD [2024])

rapid increase suggests a significant shift in the focus of public climate finance toward adaptation.

- **Mitigation Activities Saw Slower but Steady Growth:** The number of mitigation activities increased steadily between 2016 and 2022. While there were some variations year-to-year, the overall trend is upward. However, the growth is considerably less pronounced compared to adaptation, reflecting perhaps the relative maturity of the mitigation finance landscape.
- **Cross-Cutting Activity Numbers Remained Relatively Stable:** The number of cross-cutting activities also increased slightly over the period, but with a slower growth trajectory compared to both mitigation and adaptation. The trend here suggests consistent but not significantly increasing attention to projects that address both mitigation and adaptation simultaneously.

- **Adaptation Surpassed Mitigation in Number of Activities in 2020:** Around 2020, the number of reported adaptation activities overtook mitigation activities, and this trend continued through 2022. This crossover is a visually striking indication of the increasing emphasis on adaptation within public climate finance.

Apparently, governments play a multifaceted role in climate finance, acting as:

- **Regulator:** Setting standards, enforcing regulations, and creating a level playing field for businesses and investors, promoting transparency, and preventing market distortions. Carbon pricing mechanisms generated USD 104 billion in 2023, but broader implementation is needed (World Bank, 2024a).
- **Investor:** Providing public funding for climate-related projects, leveraging private investment, and supporting the development of new technologies and solutions.
- **Catalyst:** Creating incentives, reducing risk, and fostering collaboration to drive private sector investment in climate action. Governments can play a crucial role in de-risking projects, offering guarantees, and creating market signals that attract private capital.
- **International Actor:** Engaging in international agreements, mobilizing climate finance for developing countries, and promoting global cooperation.

This chapter explores the key policy instruments governments can use to mobilize climate finance, examine the critical role of international agreements, and discuss the challenges and opportunities of public funding and multilateral finance mechanisms.

2 Policy Instruments for Mobilizing Climate Finance

Governments have a wide range of policy instruments at their disposal to encourage investment in climate solutions and create an enabling environment for climate finance.

2.1 Carbon Pricing Mechanisms

A cornerstone of effective climate policy is putting a price on carbon emissions, creating a financial incentive for companies to reduce their emissions and invest in cleaner technologies. This "carbon price" can be implemented through two primary mechanisms: carbon taxes and emissions trading schemes (ETS). IMF (2019) highlights carbon pricing's effectiveness.

- **Carbon Taxes:** A carbon tax is a direct tax levied on the carbon content of fossil fuels or on the greenhouse gas emissions produced by companies. The tax is typically imposed at the point of production or importation of fossil fuels. The price of the tax reflects the social cost of carbon emissions, encouraging companies to reduce emissions and invest in cleaner alternatives.
- **Emissions Trading Schemes (ETS):** An ETS is a market-based approach to regulating emissions. The government sets a cap on the total amount of emissions allowed in a particular sector or region. Companies are allocated or can purchase permits to emit greenhouse gases. The permits can be traded on a market, creating a price signal that reflects the relative scarcity of emissions allowances. Companies that reduce their emissions below their allocated levels can sell their excess permits, generating revenue. Companies that emit more than their allowance must purchase additional permits, incurring a cost.

Successful Carbon Pricing Policies:

- **The European Union Emissions Trading System (EU ETS):** The EU ETS is the world's largest carbon market, covering over 10,000 power plants and industrial installations. The ETS has significantly reduced emissions in covered sectors, but the carbon price has been volatile, and the system has faced challenges in addressing carbon leakage (emissions shifting to other countries).
- **The Carbon Tax in British Columbia, Canada:** British Columbia implemented a carbon tax in 2008, which has been credited with reducing emissions and generating revenue for the province. The carbon tax has also been shown to have a positive impact on innovation, encouraging investment in clean energy and energy efficiency.

Challenges of Implementing Carbon Pricing:

- **Political Opposition:** Carbon pricing policies often face political opposition from fossil fuel industries and consumers concerned about higher energy prices.
- **Economic Competitiveness:** Concerns about the competitiveness of industries that face higher costs due to carbon pricing, leading to calls for border adjustments or other measures to ensure a level playing field. Carbon Pricing Leadership Coalition (2019) emphasizes carbon pricing as effective for emission reduction and addressing competitiveness concerns with policy solutions.
- **Revenue Recycling:** How carbon pricing revenues are used can impact the effectiveness and fairness of the policy. Revenues can be used to

offset the impact of the tax on businesses or consumers, fund investments in clean energy, or reduce other taxes. IMF (2019) highlights the need for holistic policy design, and international cooperation for climate mitigation.

World Bank (2024a) report of "State and Trends of Carbon Pricing 2024" analyzes the latest developments in carbon pricing initiatives globally. The Fig. 3 shows the carbon pricing policy ecosystem and report scope, covered by the report.

World Bank (2024a) report find that:

- **Adoption Slow but Steady:** While the adoption of new carbon pricing instruments has been limited in the past year, the total number now stands at 75 globally (39 carbon taxes and 36 Emissions Trading Systems (ETSs)). There's been progress in middle-income countries like Brazil, India, and Türkiye, indicating future uptake. Subnational initiatives are also increasing.
- **Prices Insufficient:** Despite a decade of growth, carbon prices remain too low to drive the transformative change needed to meet the Paris Agreement goals. Many existing instruments, including some established ETSs, experienced price decreases in the past year. Prices fall short of both the High-Level Commission's recommended range and the IPCC's estimated marginal abatement costs for limiting warming to 1.5 °C.
- **Record Revenues:** Carbon pricing revenue reached a record high of USD 104 billion in 2023, exceeding USD 100 billion for the first time. This was driven by high prices in the EU ETS and other factors. ETSs generated the majority of the revenue. More than half of the revenue was used to finance climate and nature-related programs.

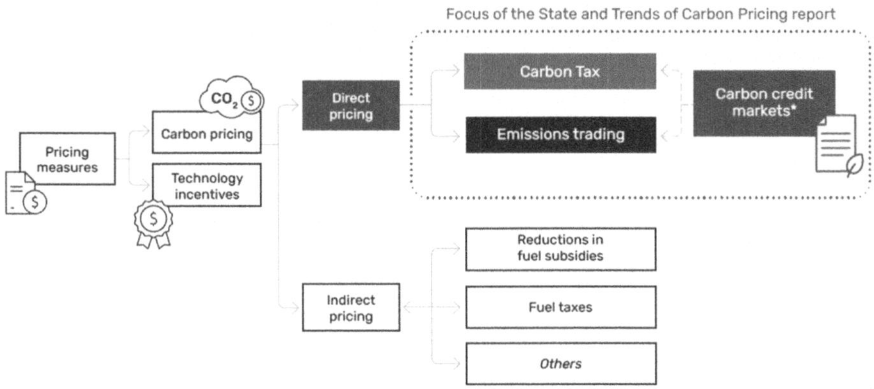

Fig. 3 Carbon pricing policy ecosystem and report scope (*Source* World Bank [2024a])

- **Carbon Credit Markets Mixed:** Carbon credit issuances declined for the second consecutive year, mainly due to reduced issuances from nature-based projects and renewable energy projects. Retirements remained below issuances, resulting in a growing pool of non-retired credits. Prices for most carbon credits decreased, except for those from carbon removal projects, which showed greater resilience. However, credits with specific attributes (co-benefits, corresponding adjustments, recent vintages) traded at a premium.
- **Integrity Crucial:** Concerns about the quality and integrity of carbon credits persist and underscore the importance of initiatives like the Integrity Council for the Voluntary Carbon Market (ICVCM), which is developing a quality benchmark. Its first approved credits are expected in 2024.
- **Article 6 Progress Despite Setbacks:** Implementation of Article 6 of the Paris Agreement (international carbon markets) continues, with a growing number of bilateral agreements. 2023 saw the first trade of Internationally Transferred Mitigation Outcomes (ITMOs). However, COP28 did not finalize rules for the Article 6.4 mechanism, creating uncertainty about its operationalization timeline.
- **Flexible Approaches Emerging:** Governments increasingly use multiple carbon pricing instruments to expand coverage, price levels, and flexibility. Carbon pricing is also being explored for sectors beyond power and industry, such as maritime transport and waste. The EU's Carbon Border Adjustment Mechanism (CBAM) came into effect, requiring reporting of embedded emissions, which is expected to incentivize carbon pricing adoption in exporting countries.
- **World Bank Support Continues:** The World Bank remains committed to supporting carbon pricing initiatives through various programs, providing data and analysis, technical assistance, and capacity building. They emphasize the need for stronger political commitment and global cooperation to fully unlock the potential of carbon pricing and drive the transition to a low-carbon economy.

Next, we will introduce the European Union emissions trading system in Case Study 1

Case Study 1: The European Union Emissions Trading System (EU ETS)

Overview

The European Union Emissions Trading System (EU ETS) is a major example of a carbon market in operation, designed to reduce greenhouse gas emissions cost-effectively. This case study highlights how the EU ETS has established a price for carbon emissions, encouraging companies to reduce their emissions and invest in cleaner technologies (European Commission,

2025). Covering over 10,000 power plants and industrial installations, the EU ETS is a cornerstone of the EU's climate policy.

Development and Implementation of the EU ETS

Cap-and-Trade System:

- **Mechanism:** The EU ETS operates on a cap-and-trade principle, where a cap is set on the total amount of greenhouse gases that can be emitted by installations covered by the system. Companies receive or buy emission allowances, which they can trade with one another as needed. Each allowance represents the right to emit one ton of CO_2 or its equivalent(Appunn & Wettengel, 2024).
- **Phases:** The system has evolved through several phases. The first phase (2005–2007) was a learning period. The second phase (2008–2012) coincided with the first commitment period of the Kyoto Protocol. The third phase (2013–2020) introduced significant changes, including a shift toward auctioning allowances rather than free allocation. The fourth phase (2021–2030) continues to tighten the cap on emissions and includes more sectors and gases (Environmental Protection Agency, 2025).

Coverage:

- **Sectors:** The EU ETS covers around 45% of the EU's greenhouse gas emissions, including CO_2 from power stations, industrial plants, and civil aviation within the European Economic Area (EEA). From 2027, a new system (EU ETS2) will cover fuel distribution for road transport and buildings.
- **Geographic Reach:** The system includes all 27 EU member states plus Iceland, Norway, and Liechtenstein.

Impact on Emissions Reduction and Investment

Emissions Reduction:

- **Achievements:** The EU ETS has significantly reduced emissions in the sectors it covers. Between 2005 and 2023, emissions from these sectors decreased by about 47%. The system has helped the EU meet its 2020 target of reducing greenhouse gas emissions by 20% compared to 1990 levels.
- **Market Stability Reserve:** To address the surplus of allowances and stabilize the market, the EU introduced the Market Stability Reserve (MSR) in 2019. The MSR adjusts the supply of allowances based on

the number of permits in circulation, helping to maintain a stable carbon price.

Investment in Cleaner Technologies:

- **Economic Incentives:** By putting a price on carbon, the EU ETS makes it economically attractive for companies to invest in emissions reduction technologies. This includes renewable energy, energy efficiency measures, and other low-carbon innovations.
- **Innovation Fund:** Revenues from the auctioning of allowances support the EU's Innovation Fund, which finances the development of innovative low-carbon technologies and projects (GOV.UK, 2013).

Challenges and Successes

Challenges:

- **Carbon Leakage:** One of the main challenges is carbon leakage, where companies relocate production to countries with less stringent climate policies, undermining the effectiveness of the EU ETS. To mitigate this, certain sectors receive free allowances to maintain competitiveness.
- **Price Volatility:** The carbon price has experienced volatility, influenced by economic conditions and policy changes. Ensuring a stable and predictable carbon price is crucial for long-term investment decisions.

Successes:

- **Policy Integration:** The EU ETS is integrated with other EU climate policies, such as the Renewable Energy Directive and the Energy Efficiency Directive, creating a comprehensive framework for emissions reduction (European Commission, 2025).
- **Global Influence:** As the world's first and largest international emissions trading system, the EU ETS has influenced the development of similar schemes worldwide, contributing to global climate action.

Future Prospects

Strengthening and Expansion:

- **Reforms:** The EU continues to reform and strengthen the ETS to ensure it meets its climate goals. This includes tightening the cap on emissions, expanding coverage to more sectors, and enhancing the MSR.

- **ETS2:** The introduction of ETS2 for road transport and buildings represents a significant expansion of the system, aiming to address emissions from sectors previously outside the scope of the original ETS.

Government Policy Support:

- **Regulatory Framework:** Strong government policy support is essential for the success of the EU ETS. This includes setting ambitious emissions reduction targets, ensuring compliance, and providing financial support for innovation and transition.

Conclusion

The European Union Emissions Trading System (EU ETS) is a major example of a carbon market in operation, demonstrating a significant impact on emissions reduction and investment in cleaner technologies. Despite challenges such as carbon leakage and price volatility, the EU ETS has achieved substantial emissions reductions and influenced global climate policy. Continuous reforms and government policy support are crucial for strengthening and expanding the system, ensuring it remains a key tool in the EU's efforts to combat climate change.

2.2 Renewable Energy Targets and Incentives

Governments can play a crucial role in accelerating the deployment of renewable energy through the use of targets and incentives. Renewable energy targets set specific goals for the percentage of energy generated from renewable sources. These targets can create a predictable market signal for investors, driving investment in solar, wind, hydropower, and other clean energy technologies. IRENA (2023, 2024) provide data on renewable energy finance flows, capacity, and technology trends.

- **Renewable Energy Targets:** Countries have set a wide range of renewable energy targets, from ambitious targets of 100% renewable electricity by mid-century to more modest goals of increasing the share of renewable energy in the electricity mix. Examples of countries with ambitious renewable energy targets include:
  - **Germany:** Germany has a target of achieving 100% renewable electricity by 2035.
  - **Denmark:** Denmark aims to achieve 100% renewable energy consumption by 2050.
  - **China:** China has ambitious targets for renewable energy deployment, aiming to generate nearly 60% of its electricity from renewable sources by 2030.

- **Renewable Energy Incentives:** Governments offer a range of financial incentives to encourage private sector investment in renewable energy projects. REN21 (2024) offers a global overview of renewable energy status, including policy and investment trends.
  - **Feed-in Tariffs (FITs):** A feed-in tariff is a guaranteed price paid to renewable energy producers for the electricity they generate, providing long-term revenue stability and reducing the financial risks associated with renewable energy investments. FITs can help to attract investors and accelerate the deployment of renewable energy projects.
  - **Renewable Portfolio Standards (RPS):** Renewable portfolio standards mandate that utilities generate a certain percentage of their electricity from renewable sources. RPS programs create a market demand for renewable energy, incentivizing utilities to invest in renewable energy projects.
  - **Renewable Energy Tax Credits:** Tax credits can provide financial incentives to businesses that invest in renewable energy systems, reducing the upfront costs and making these investments more attractive.
  - **Auctions:** Many governments hold auctions for renewable energy projects, awarding contracts to the lowest-cost bidders. Auctions can help to drive down the costs of renewable energy and incentivize technological innovation.

Case Study 2: China's Renewable Energy Investment Boom

Overview

China's renewable energy investment boom is a prime example of how government investment and policy can drive the rapid expansion of renewable energy capacity in a major emerging economy. This case study highlights how China, through ambitious renewable energy targets, subsidies, and financing programs, has become a global leader in renewable energy investment and deployment.

Promotion of Renewable Energy Sources

Ambitious Targets and Policies:

- **Renewable Energy Targets:** In 2020, China committed to achieving 1,200 GW of renewable energy capacity by 2030. The country is on track to meet this goal five years early, with projections indicating it could have as much as 1,000 GW of solar power alone by the end of 2026 (Howe, 2023).
- **Five-Year Plans:** China's renewable energy policies are driven by its Five-Year Plans. The 13th Five-Year Plan set targets for non-fossil energy

consumption and renewable power capacity, while the 14th Five-Year Plan emphasizes extensive expansion of renewable energy sources and integration into the energy system (Chinese Climate Policy, 2025).

Key Policy Instruments:

- **Feed-in Tariffs (FITs):** Generous FITs have been a cornerstone of China's renewable energy policy, providing financial incentives for the generation of renewable energy. This policy has significantly boosted the deployment of solar and wind power.
- **Subsidies and Financing Programs:** Access to capital from government policy banks and other financial incentives have supported the growth of renewable energy projects. Subsidies have been provided for various technologies, including solar, wind, and energy storage (Chinese Climate Policy, 2025).
- **Clean Energy Bases:** Initiatives such as the "whole-county distributed solar" and "clean energy base" programs have driven increased volumes of solar installations across the country (Myllyvirta, 2024).

Impact on Emissions, Revenue Generation, and Economic Performance

Emissions Reduction:

- **Significant Decrease:** China's renewable energy investments have contributed to a substantial reduction in greenhouse gas emissions. The country has rapidly expanded its solar and wind capacity, reducing its reliance on fossil fuels (Howe, 2023).
- **Global Leadership:** China is the world's largest producer of renewable energy, with significant contributions from solar and wind power. In 2023, China commissioned as much solar PV as the entire world did in 2022 (International Energy Agency, 2024).

Economic Performance:

- **Economic Growth:** Renewable energy has been a major driver of China's economic growth. In 2023, clean energy investments accounted for all of the growth in investment, highlighting the sector's importance to the economy (Myllyvirta, 2024).
- **Job Creation and Technological Innovation:** The renewable energy sector has created numerous jobs and spurred technological innovation. China dominates the global market for renewable energy technologies, particularly in solar manufacturing (Howe, 2023).

Challenges and Successes

Challenges:

- **Grid Integration:** The rapid expansion of renewable energy has stressed China's power grid, leading to issues with integrating variable renewable power. Technical challenges include managing supply and demand mismatches and ensuring stable grid operation (Siqi, 2024).
- **Continued Fossil Fuel Use:** Despite significant investments in renewables, China still relies heavily on coal for power generation. Balancing the transition to renewables with energy security concerns remains a challenge (International Energy Agency, 2024).

Successes:

- **Policy Support:** Consistent government support through policies, subsidies, and financial incentives has been crucial for the success of China's renewable energy boom. The government's commitment to carbon neutrality by 2060 has provided a powerful political signal favoring renewable investments (Howe, 2023).
- **Global Influence:** China's leadership in renewable energy has had a global impact, driving down the costs of renewable technologies and influencing other countries to adopt similar policies (Howe, 2023).

Importance of Technological Innovation

Innovation in Renewable Technologies:

- **Solar and Wind Power:** China's investments in solar and wind technologies have led to significant advancements and cost reductions. The country added substantial new capacities in both sectors in 2023, with solar installations reaching unprecedented levels (Myllyvirta, 2024).
- **Energy Storage:** China is rapidly scaling up its electricity storage capacity, including pumped hydro and battery storage. This is crucial for integrating larger amounts of variable renewable power into the grid and reducing reliance on fossil fuels (Myllyvirta, 2024).

Role in Global Climate Efforts:

- **Export of Technologies:** China is the world's top supplier of renewable energy technologies, with a dominant position in the solar panel supply chain. This has helped drive global renewable energy deployment and reduce costs (Howe, 2023).

Contribution to Global Goals:

- China's renewable energy investments are critical for meeting global climate targets, including the goals of the Paris Agreement. The country's progress in renewable energy is essential for global efforts to combat climate change (Howe, 2023).

Conclusion

China's renewable energy investment boom showcases the transformative impact of government investment and policy on the rapid expansion of renewable energy capacity. Through ambitious targets, subsidies, and financing programs, China has become a global leader in renewable energy deployment. The successes of the renewable energy industry, including significant emissions reductions and economic growth, highlight the importance of long-term policy stability and technological innovation. However, challenges such as grid integration and continued reliance on fossil fuels must be addressed to ensure a sustainable energy transition. China's experience provides valuable lessons for other jurisdictions aiming to achieve similar goals in the global fight against climate change.

2.3 *Energy Efficiency Standards and Policies*

Energy efficiency standards and policies are another critical tool for reducing energy consumption and greenhouse gas emissions. These policies mandate minimum energy performance levels for buildings, appliances, and vehicles, encouraging the development and adoption of more efficient technologies and promoting energy conservation. IEA (2024) forecasts weak energy efficiency progress, emphasizing the need for increased policy action and investments, particularly in electrification.

- **Building Codes:** Building codes can mandate energy efficiency standards for new construction and renovations. These codes might require energy-efficient windows, insulation, HVAC systems, or lighting, reducing the energy consumption and emissions associated with buildings throughout their life cycle.
- **Appliance Standards:** Appliance standards set minimum energy efficiency levels for appliances, such as refrigerators, washing machines, dishwashers, and air conditioners. These standards, often expressed as Energy Star ratings, encourage manufacturers to produce more efficient appliances and give consumers incentives to choose energy-efficient options.
- **Fuel Economy Standards:** Fuel economy standards mandate minimum fuel efficiency levels for passenger vehicles, trucks, and other vehicles. These standards can reduce gasoline consumption, lower transportation emissions, and drive innovation in fuel-efficient technologies, rank countries' energy efficiency. IEA (2023) reports slowing energy intensity

progress but highlights increased efficiency investments and the potential of doubling efficiency efforts.

2.4 Green Finance Instruments and Policies

Governments can also play a significant role in mobilizing private sector investment in climate-friendly projects through the use of financial instruments and policies.

- **Green Bonds:** Governments can issue sovereign green bonds, demonstrating their commitment to climate action and signaling to investors that they consider climate-related investments to be a priority. Governments can also develop regulatory frameworks that encourage private sector green bond issuances, providing clarity for investors and reducing the cost of capital for green bond projects. Climate Bonds Initiative (2024) reports USD 5.4 trillion cumulative GSS + debt, with green bonds dominating at 62%.
- **Sustainability-Linked Loans:** Governments can develop guidelines and incentives for sustainability-linked loans (SLLs), which tie loan terms (e.g., interest rates) to a borrower's achievement of predefined sustainability performance targets. These loans can incentivize companies to improve their environmental, social, and governance (ESG) performance, reducing their borrowing costs as they make progress on their sustainability goals.
- **Green Banks:** Governments can establish specialized green banks or financial institutions that provide financing for clean energy projects and other sustainable investments. Green banks can de-risk projects, provide technical assistance, and help to mobilize private capital for climate action.

2.5 Public–Private Partnerships (PPPs)

Public–private partnerships (PPPs) are a mechanism for leveraging public funding to attract private investment in infrastructure projects. In a PPP, the government typically provides some form of financial support, such as grants, loans, or guarantees, to de-risk the project and make it more attractive to private investors. The private partner then designs, builds, finances, and often operates the infrastructure project. World Bank (2024b) highlights climate-smart PPPs for resilient infrastructure, especially in vulnerable nations.

PPPs can be particularly useful for financing large-scale climate-related infrastructure projects, such as renewable energy plants, energy-efficient buildings, and public transportation systems.

Advantages of PPPs:

- **Access to Private Capital:** PPPs can unlock private sector capital for projects that might not be feasible through traditional public funding alone.
- **Leveraging Private Sector Expertise:** PPPs bring in private sector expertise in project design, construction, operation, and management, bringing efficiency and innovation to infrastructure development.
- **Risk Sharing:** PPPs can allow for a sharing of risks between the public and private sectors, potentially reducing the financial burden on governments.

Challenges of PPPs:

- **Complex Structures:** Structuring effective PPPs can be complex, requiring careful negotiation and contract drafting to ensure a balance between public and private interests.
- **Value for Money:** Ensuring that PPPs provide value for money for taxpayers is essential, especially for large-scale projects. Careful analysis of the costs and benefits is critical.
- **Risk Management:** PPP contracts need to effectively allocate and manage risks between the public and private partners, addressing potential issues such as construction delays, cost overruns, or operational challenges. OECD (2024) emphasizes scaling up private climate finance in developing countries to meet Paris Agreement goals.

3 International Climate Agreements and Frameworks

Addressing climate change requires a global response. International agreements and frameworks play a crucial role in setting global goals, fostering cooperation, and mobilizing climate finance to support developing countries in their efforts to reduce emissions and adapt to a changing climate.

3.1 The Paris Agreement: A Global Framework for Climate Action

The Paris Agreement, adopted in 2015, is a landmark international agreement aimed at limiting global warming to well below 2 degrees Celsius, preferably to 1.5 degrees Celsius, compared to pre-industrial levels. It represents a historic commitment by nearly every country in the world to address climate change and create a more sustainable future.

Key Elements of the Paris Agreement:

- **Nationally Determined Contributions (NDCs):** Each country sets its own emissions reduction targets and plans for achieving them. These

NDCs are not legally binding, but they represent the country's commitment to climate action.

- **Transparency and Accountability:** Countries are required to report on their emissions and progress toward their targets, providing transparency and accountability for climate action.
- **Finance:** Developed countries have committed to mobilizing $100 billion per year in climate finance by 2020 to support developing countries in their mitigation and adaptation efforts. The Paris Agreement emphasizes the need to increase the flow of climate finance to developing countries to help them achieve their climate goals. UNFCCC (2024) synthesizes NDCs under the Paris Agreement.
- **Adaptation:** The Agreement recognizes the importance of adapting to the impacts of climate change and encourages countries to develop adaptation plans to reduce vulnerability to climate-related risks. IPCC (2023) reports on the urgency of climate action and the need for emissions reductions.

Case Study 3: The Paris Agreement and Its Impact on National Climate Policies

Overview

The Paris Agreement, adopted in 2015, has significantly influenced the development and strengthening of national climate policies around the world. This legally binding international treaty aims to limit global warming to well below 2 °C, preferably to 1.5 °C, compared to pre-industrial levels. Countries have committed to this goal by submitting Nationally Determined Contributions (NDCs), outlining their emissions reduction targets and climate action plans.

Development and Implementation of Nationally Determined Contributions (NDCs)

National Commitments:

- **NDCs:** Under the Paris Agreement, each country must submit NDCs, which detail their plans to reduce national emissions and adapt to the impacts of climate change. These commitments are updated every five years to reflect increased ambition and progress.
- **Global Stocktake:** The agreement includes a global stocktake every five years to assess collective progress toward achieving its long-term goals. The first global stocktake in 2023 highlighted the need for more ambitious actions to limit warming to 1.5 °C (Maizland & Fong, 2025; United Nations Framework Convention on Climate Change, 2025a).

Examples of National Policies:

- **European Union:** The EU has committed to reducing greenhouse gas emissions by at least 55% by 2030 compared to 1990 levels. This target is part of the European Green Deal, which aims to make the EU climate-neutral by 2050.
- **United States:** The United States has pledged to reduce emissions by 50–52% below 2005 levels by 2030. This commitment was reaffirmed under the Biden administration, which rejoined the Paris Agreement after a brief withdrawal under the previous administration.
- **China:** China aims to peak carbon emissions before 2030 and achieve carbon neutrality by 2060. The country has also set targets for increasing the share of non-fossil fuels in primary energy consumption.

Challenges and Successes

Challenges:

- **Ambition Gap:** Despite the commitments made, there is a significant gap between current NDCs and the emission reductions needed to meet the Paris Agreement goals. Many countries' pledges are not ambitious enough and lack the necessary policies for full implementation (Victor et al., 2022).
- **Implementation and Enforcement:** The non-binding nature of NDCs means there is no legal enforcement mechanism to ensure countries meet their targets. This reliance on voluntary compliance poses challenges for accountability and effectiveness.

Successes:

- **Increased Ambition:** The Paris Agreement has prompted many countries to enhance their climate commitments over time. For example, several countries have set net-zero targets, reflecting a long-term vision for decarbonization.
- **International Collaboration:** The agreement has fostered international collaboration and peer pressure, encouraging countries to take more ambitious actions. Annual COP meetings provide a platform for countries to share progress, learn from each other, and negotiate further commitments (Stallard & Poynting, 2025).

Importance of International Collaboration and Peer Pressure

Role of International Cooperation:

- **Technology Transfer:** The Paris Agreement emphasizes the importance of international cooperation on climate-safe technology development and transfer. This helps developing countries access the technologies needed to reduce emissions and adapt to climate impacts (United Nations Framework Convention on Climate Change, 2025b).
- **Climate Finance:** Developed countries have committed to providing $100 billion annually to support climate action in developing countries. This financial support is crucial for enabling ambitious climate policies and addressing equity concerns (Stallard & Poynting, 2025).

Peer Pressure and Diplomacy:

- **Diplomatic Efforts:** The agreement's framework encourages countries to set ambitious targets and demonstrate leadership in climate action. Diplomatic efforts and peer pressure play a vital role in motivating countries to enhance their commitments.
- **Global Stocktake:** The global stocktake process provides an opportunity to assess collective progress and apply pressure on lagging countries to increase their ambition. This process is essential for maintaining momentum and accountability (Roelfsema et al., 2020).

Monitoring and Reporting Progress

Transparency and Accountability:

- **Reporting Requirements:** The Paris Agreement includes robust transparency and reporting mechanisms. Countries must regularly report on their emissions and progress toward their NDCs, ensuring accountability and transparency (United Nations Framework Convention on Climate Change, 2025c).
- **Independent Assessments:** Independent organizations, such as the Climate Action Tracker, evaluate countries' progress and the adequacy of their commitments. These assessments help identify gaps and areas for improvement (Stallard & Poynting, 2025).

Continuous Improvement:

- **Regular Updates:** Countries are required to update their NDCs every five years, reflecting increased ambition and incorporating new scientific knowledge. This iterative process ensures that national policies remain aligned with the long-term goals of the Paris Agreement (United Nations Framework Convention on Climate Change, 2025c).

- **Adaptive Policies:** National policies must be flexible and adaptive to respond to emerging challenges and opportunities. Continuous monitoring and evaluation are essential for making necessary adjustments and ensuring effective implementation.

Conclusion

The Paris Agreement has significantly influenced national climate policies, driving countries to set ambitious emissions reduction targets and develop comprehensive climate action plans. Despite challenges such as the ambition gap and implementation issues, the agreement has fostered international collaboration and peer pressure, encouraging countries to enhance their commitments. Robust monitoring and reporting mechanisms are crucial for ensuring transparency and accountability. The Paris Agreement's impact demonstrates the importance of international cooperation and continuous improvement in global efforts to combat climate change.

3.2 The United Nations Framework Convention on Climate Change (UNFCCC)

The United Nations Framework Convention on Climate Change (UNFCCC), adopted in 1992, is the primary international treaty for addressing climate change. The UNFCCC serves as the overarching framework for global climate action, providing a forum for countries to negotiate agreements, share information, and support each other in their efforts to mitigate and adapt to climate change.

Key Institutions and Mechanisms of the UNFCCC:

- **The Conference of the Parties (COP):** The annual meeting of all countries that are parties to the UNFCCC, where key decisions are made on climate action. The COP is the highest decision-making body of the UNFCCC.
- **The Kyoto Protocol:** The Kyoto Protocol, adopted in 1997, is an international agreement that commits developed countries to binding emissions reduction targets. While the Kyoto Protocol has been a significant step forward in international climate action, it has been criticized for not doing enough to address climate change and for excluding major developing countries from legally binding emissions targets.

3.3 Other International Initiatives and Collaborations

Beyond the Paris Agreement and the UNFCCC, a range of other international initiatives and collaborations are promoting climate action and mobilizing climate finance:

- **Mission Innovation:** A global initiative launched in 2015 to accelerate clean energy innovation and reduce the cost of clean energy technologies. Participating countries have pledged to increase their public investments in clean energy research and development.
- **Powering Past Coal Alliance:** A coalition of countries and organizations committed to phasing out coal-fired power generation and transitioning to cleaner energy sources.
- **International Solar Alliance:** An alliance of countries with high solar potential, promoting the deployment of solar energy through technology transfer, capacity building, and investment.

4 The Green Climate Fund (GCF) and Other Multilateral Mechanisms

4.1 *The Green Climate Fund (GCF)*

The Green Climate Fund (GCF), established in 2010 under the United Nations Framework Convention on Climate Change (UNFCCC), is a major multilateral mechanism for mobilizing and channeling climate finance to developing countries. The GCF aims to support developing countries in their efforts to mitigate and adapt to climate change, promoting a transition to low-emission and climate-resilient development pathways. GCF (2024) reports a record replenishment of $12.8B, reaching $13.5B committed across 243 projects.

Key features of the GCF:

Funding Mechanisms:

- The GCF receives contributions from developed countries and other donors, providing grants, loans, equity investments, and guarantees for climate-related projects.
- **Project Eligibility:** The GCF prioritizes projects that contribute to the Paris Agreement goals, promoting climate change mitigation, adaptation, and climate-resilient development.
- **Country Ownership and Partnership:** The GCF emphasizes country ownership, ensuring that projects are aligned with national priorities, and promotes partnerships between developed and developing countries to share knowledge and expertise.

The GCF is a critical source of funding for climate action in developing countries, supporting projects across a wide range of sectors, including:

- **Renewable Energy:** Financing renewable energy projects, such as solar, wind, geothermal, and hydropower, to reduce reliance on fossil fuels and enhance energy security.
- **Energy Efficiency:** Supporting projects that improve energy efficiency in buildings, industries, and transportation systems, reducing energy consumption and emissions.
- **Climate-Smart Agriculture:** Investing in sustainable agricultural practices, such as agroforestry, drought-resistant crops, and water conservation, to enhance food security, build resilience to climate impacts, and promote sustainable land management.
- **Adaptation and Resilience:** Funding projects to build resilience to climate change impacts, such as early warning systems for extreme weather events, flood defenses, drought-resistant infrastructure, and climate-resilient healthcare systems.

Challenges facing the GCF:

- **Meeting Funding Goals:** The GCF is facing challenges in meeting its target of mobilizing $100 billion per year in climate finance, which is crucial for supporting ambitious climate action in developing countries.
- **Project Approval Process:** The GCF's project approval process can be lengthy and complex, potentially delaying the flow of funds to projects that are urgently needed.
- **Transparency and Accountability:** The GCF is working to enhance its transparency and accountability, ensuring that funds are used effectively and that results are clearly communicated to donors and stakeholders. GCF faces challenges in mobilizing funds, project approvals, and transparency, but plays a key role in adaptation finance (UNEP FI, 2023).

Beyond the GCF, other multilateral climate finance mechanisms are playing a critical role in supporting developing countries. UNEP FI (2023) reports a widening adaptation finance gap (US$194-366B yearly), decreased flows, and slow implementation despite increased planning. These include:

- **The Climate Investment Funds (CIF):** The CIF is a multi-donor trust fund that provides financing for climate-related investments in developing countries, particularly for large-scale projects. CIF (2024) celebrates 15 years, mobilizing $12B for ~400 climate projects in developing countries.
- **The Adaptation Fund:** The Adaptation Fund provides grants to developing countries to support climate adaptation projects, focusing on activities that benefit the most vulnerable populations.

- **The Least Developed Countries Fund (LDCF):** The LDCF is a dedicated fund to support climate action in the world's least developed countries, providing concessional financing for projects related to mitigation, adaptation, and technology development.

5 Conclusion: Creating an Enabling Environment

Governments play a crucial role in shaping the landscape of climate finance. Through a combination of policy instruments, international agreements, and financial mechanisms, governments can create an enabling environment that incentivizes investment in climate solutions, reduces risk, promotes innovation, and ensures a just and equitable transition to a low-carbon future. IEA (2024) analyzes global energy trends, highlighting clean energy growth, geopolitical tensions, and climate challenges. Boehm et al. (2023) assesses progress on climate mitigation, finding insufficient progress but some positive trends.

The challenges are real, but so are the opportunities. By implementing robust policies, engaging in international cooperation, and supporting multilateral financing mechanisms, governments can drive a global shift toward a more sustainable and resilient world.

References

Boehm, S., et al. (2023). *State of climate action 2023*. www.wri.org. https://www.wri.org/research/state-climate-action-2023

Carbon Pricing Leadership Coalition (CPLS). (2019). *The high-level commission on carbon pricing and competitiveness*. https://www.carbonpricingleadership.org/highlevel-commission-on-carbon-pricing-and-competitiveness

Climate Investment Funds (CIF). (2024). *CIF annual report 2023: Bolder ambitions, more urgency, unflinching determination*. https://www.cif.org/knowledge-documents/cif-annual-report-2023-bolder-ambitions-more-urgency-unflinching-determination. Accessed 1 January 2025.

Climate Bonds Initiative (CBI). (2024). *Sustainable debt market summary Q3 2024*. https://www.climatebonds.net/resources/reports/sustainable-debt-market-summary-q3-2024. Accessed 1 January 2025.

Green Climate Fund (GCF). (2024). *Annual report 2023*. https://www.greenclimate.fund/document/annual-report-2023

International Energy Agency (IEA). (2023). *Energy efficiency 2023*. https://www.iea.org/reports/energy-efficiency-2023

IEA. (2024). *Energy efficiency 2024*. https://www.iea.org/reports/energy-efficiency-2024

International Monetary Fund (IMF). (2019). *Fiscal monitor: How to mitigate climate change*. https://www.imf.org/en/Publications/FM/Issues/2019/09/12/fiscal-monitor-october-2019

Intergovernmental Panel on Climate Change (IPCC). (2023). *AR6 synthesis report: Climate change 2023*. https://www.ipcc.ch/report/sixth-assessment-report-cycle/

International Renewable Energy Agency (IRENA). (2023). *Renewable energy statistics 2023*. https://www.irena.org/-/media/Files/IRENA/Agency/Publication/2023/Jul/IRENA_Renewable_energy_statistics_2023.pdf

IRENA. (2024). *Renewable energy statistics 2024*. https://www.irena.org/-/media/Files/IRENA/Agency/Publication/2024/Jul/IRENA_Renewable_Energy_Statistics_2024.pdf

Organisation for Economic Co-operation and Development (OECD). (2024). *Climate finance provided and mobilised by developed countries in 2013–2022*. Climate Finance and the USD 100 Billion Goal. OECD Publishing. https://doi.org/10.1787/19150727-en.

United Nations Environment Programme Finance Initiative (UNEP FI). (2023). *Adaptation gap report 2023*. https://www.unep.org/resources/adaptation-gap-report-2023

United Nations Framework Convention on Climate Change (UNFCCC). (2024). *2024 NDC synthesis report*. https://unfccc.int/process-and-meetings/the-paris-agreement/nationally-determined-contributions-ndcs/2024-ndc-synthesis-report

World Bank. (2024a). *Publication: State and trends of carbon pricing 2024*. https://hdl.handle.net/10986/41544. Accessed 9 March 2025.

World Bank. (2024b). *Climate-smart PPPs*. https://ppp.worldbank.org/public-private-partnership/energy-and-power/climate-smart-ppps

Case References

Appunn, K., & Wettengel, J. (2024). *Understanding the European Union's emissions trading systems (EU ETS)*. Clean Energy Wire. https://www.cleanenergywire.org/factsheets/understanding-european-unions-emissions-trading-system. Accessed 25 January 2025.

Chinese Climate Policy (CCC). (2025). *6: Renewable power*. https://chineseclimatepolicy.oxfordenergy.org/book-content/domestic-policies/renewable-power/

Environmental Protection Agency (EPA). (2025). *EU emissions trading system*. https://www.epa.ie/our-services/licensing/climate-change/eu-emissions-trading-system-/

European Commission (EC). (2025). *EU emissions trading system (EU ETS)*. https://climate.ec.europa.eu/eu-action/eu-emissions-trading-system-eu-ets_en

GOV.UK. (2013). *EU ETS: Carbon markets*. https://www.gov.uk/guidance/eu-ets-carbon-markets

Howe, C. (2023). *Explainer: The numbers behind china's renewable energy boom*. . Reuters. https://www.reuters.com/sustainability/climate-energy/numbers-behind-chinas-renewable-energy-boom-2023-11-15/

International Energy Agency (IEA). (2024). *World energy investment 2024*. https://www.iea.org/reports/world-energy-investment-2024/china

Maizland, L., & Fong, C. (2025). *Global climate agreements: Successes and failures*. Council on Foreign Relations. https://www.cfr.org/backgrounder/paris-global-climate-change-agreements

Myllyvirta, L. (2024). *Analysis: Clean energy was top driver of China's economic growth in 2023*. Carbon Brief. https://www.carbonbrief.org/analysis-clean-energy-was-top-driver-of-chinas-economic-growth-in-2023/

REN21 (2024). Renewables 2024 Global Status Report. https://www.ren21.net/reports/global-status-report/

Roelfsema, M., van Soest, H. L., & Harmsen, M. et al. (2020). Taking stock of national climate policies to evaluate implementation of the Paris Agreement. *Nature Communications, 11*, 2096. https://doi.org/10.1038/s41467-020-15414-6
Siqi, J. (2024). *China's green energy boom is stressing the grid—And sparking new currents in power reform*. https://www.scmp.com/economy/china-economy/article/3268893/chinas-green-energy-boom-stressing-grid-and-sparking-new-currents-power-reform
Stallard, E., & Poynting, M. (2025). *What is the Paris climate agreement and why has Trump withdrawn?* https://www.bbc.com/news/science-environment-35073297. BBC News Climate & Science
United Nations Framework Convention on Climate Change (UNFCCC). (2025a). *The Paris agreement*. https://unfccc.int/process-and-meetings/the-paris-agreement
UNFCCC. (2025b). *Key aspects of the Paris agreement*. https://unfccc.int/most-requested/key-aspects-of-the-paris-agreement
UNFCCC. (2025c). *Nationally determined contributions (NDCs)*. https://unfccc.int/process-and-meetings/the-paris-agreement/nationally-determined-contributions-ndcs
Victor, D.G. et al. (2022). *Success of the Paris agreement hinges on the credibility of national climate goals*. Brookings Institution. https://www.brookings.edu/articles/success-of-the-paris-agreement-hinges-on-the-credibility-of-national-climate-goals/
Wikipedia. (2025). *European Union emissions trading system*. https://en.wikipedia.org/wiki/European_Union_Emissions_Trading_System

CHAPTER 20

International Climate Finance: Flows, Challenges, and Innovations

1 Introduction: The Global Imperative of Climate Finance

Climate change is a global challenge that demands a global response. Greenhouse gas emissions from any country contribute to the warming of the planet, affecting every corner of the world. Yet, the impacts of climate change are not evenly distributed. Developing countries, despite contributing the least to global emissions historically, are often the most vulnerable to the devastating effects of a changing climate.

This inequity is at the heart of the international climate finance debate. UNDP (2017) highlights women's vulnerability to climate change and the role of climate finance in promoting gender equality. The principle of "common but differentiated responsibilities" recognizes that while climate change is a shared problem, developed countries have a greater responsibility to address it, not only by reducing their own emissions but also by providing financial support to developing countries to help them mitigate climate change, adapt to its impacts, and pursue sustainable development pathways.

International climate finance encompasses both public and private financial flows from developed countries to developing countries to support climate action. This finance is essential for:

- **Enabling a Just Transition:** Ensuring that developing countries are not unfairly burdened with the costs of addressing a problem they did not primarily create.
- **Scaling Up Climate Action:** Providing the financial resources needed to implement ambitious mitigation and adaptation measures in developing

J. Chen, *Climate Finance*,
https://doi.org/10.1007/978-981-96-7975-1_20

countries, which are often home to the most vulnerable populations and ecosystems.
- **Unlocking Sustainable Development Opportunities:** Supporting the transition to low-carbon and climate-resilient economies in developing countries, creating new jobs, promoting economic growth, and improving quality of life.

UNFCCC (2024) reports a rise in climate finance flows, particularly for mitigation, with adaptation finance lagging. The Climate Policy Initiative (CPI, 2024) report, "Global Landscape of Climate Finance 2024," indicates that current finance is far below the required amount to limit warming to 1.5 °C. The CPI report has done an important work to map the global climate finance flow in 2021/2022, as shown in the Fig. 1.

The finance flow chart is averaging data from both years to smooth out fluctuations. It breaks down the landscape by sources and intermediaries, financial instruments, usage (adaptation/mitigation/dual benefits), and destination region. Here's a summary:

1. **Sources and Intermediaries:**

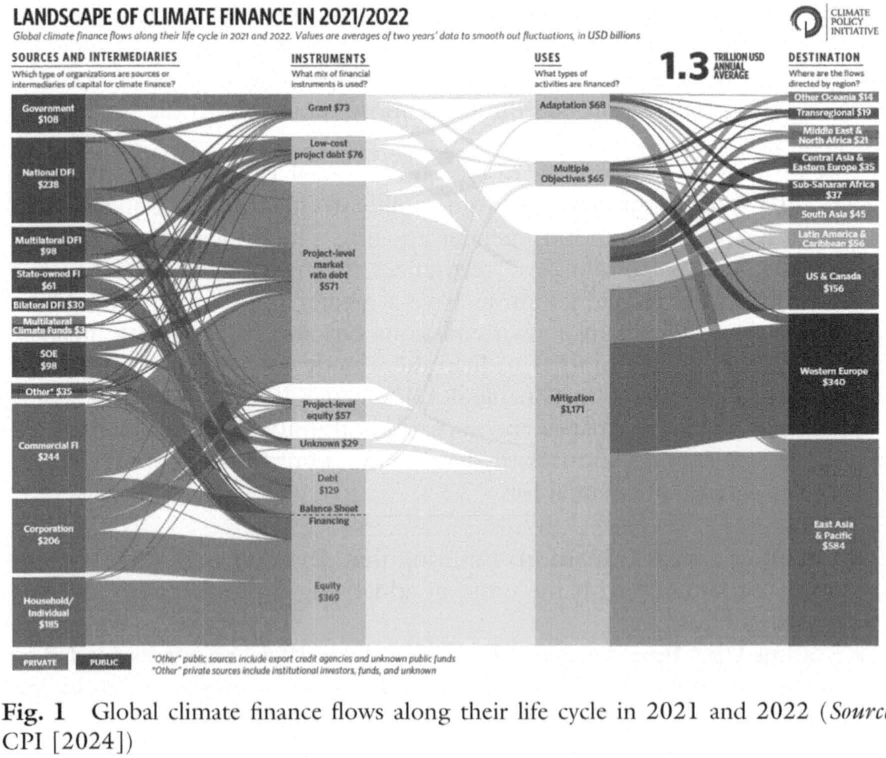

Fig. 1 Global climate finance flows along their life cycle in 2021 and 2022 (*Source* CPI [2024])

- **Public Sources:** Governments, National DFIs,[1] Multilateral DFIs, Bilateral DFIs, Multilateral Climate Funds, State-Owned Enterprises (SOEs), and other public institutions (like export credit agencies) are primary sources. National DFIs play a significant role, channeling $238 billion.
- **Private Sources:** Commercial FIs, Corporations, Households/ Individuals, and other private actors (institutional investors, funds) contribute. Commercial FIs are the largest private intermediary at $244 billion.

2. **Financial Instruments:**

- **Debt:** Represents the largest instrument class ($741 billion), including low-cost project debt and project-level market-rate debt. Market-rate debt makes up the lion's share of debt financing.
- **Equity:** At $426 billion, this includes project-level equity and balance-sheet financing, showing a substantial amount of direct investment.
- **Grants:** $73 billion in grant funding, largely from public sources, plays a vital role, particularly for adaptation projects where returns are less easily quantifiable.

3. **Climate Finance Usage:**

- **Mitigation:** The vast majority ($1,171 billion) of climate finance is directed toward mitigation, addressing the reduction of greenhouse gas emissions.
- **Adaptation:** A much smaller portion ($68 billion) is allocated for adaptation, focusing on building resilience to the impacts of climate change. This highlights a critical funding gap given the growing impacts of climate change.
- **Dual Benefits:** Projects offering both mitigation and adaptation benefits received $65 billion, growing faster than the other categories.

4. **Destination (by Region):**

- **East Asia & Pacific:** Received the largest share of climate finance ($584 billion), largely driven by flows to China and, to a lesser extent, developing economies in the region.
- **Western Europe:** Attracted $340 billion, showing significant investment within developed economies.
- **US & Canada:** Received $156 billion, a substantial amount but less than Western Europe or East Asia & Pacific as a percentage of total climate finance.

[1] Development Finance Institutes.

- **Other Regions:** Funding to other regions like Latin America & Caribbean, South Asia, Sub-Saharan Africa, Middle East & North Africa, and other areas is significantly lower, emphasizing the concentration of climate finance in specific regions. The smallest flows are directed toward LDCs, highlighting a concerning disparity in access to climate finance.

There are several key takeaways from the flow chart:

Imbalance Between Mitigation and Adaptation: The overwhelming focus on mitigation compared to adaptation reveals a major concern, as both are crucial for addressing climate change.
Concentration of Finance: The distribution heavily favors advanced economies and China, leaving other developing and vulnerable regions significantly underfunded.
Debt Dependence: The reliance on debt instruments, even for adaptation, raises concerns about debt sustainability for developing countries.
Importance of DFIs: National and multilateral DFIs play a crucial role in channeling climate finance, especially to developing countries.

This chapter delves into the complex landscape of international climate finance, exploring the various actors, funding mechanisms, and challenges involved. We'll also examine the innovations and emerging trends that are shaping the future of climate finance, highlighting the opportunities for greater efficiency, transparency, and impact.

2 The Landscape of International Climate Finance: Actors and Mechanisms

The world of international climate finance involves a diverse array of actors, institutions, and financial mechanisms. Understanding this complex landscape is essential for navigating the flows of climate finance, identifying opportunities for engagement, and advocating for more effective and equitable solutions.

2.1 Public Climate Finance

Public climate finance refers to funding provided by governments and public institutions in developed countries to support climate action in developing countries. This finance can flow through various channels:

- **Bilateral Channels:** Developed countries often provide climate finance directly to developing countries through their bilateral aid agencies and development programs. These agencies work directly with governments, organizations, and communities in developing countries to support specific projects or programs. Some of the major bilateral donors of climate finance include:

- **The United States:** The US Agency for International Development (USAID) is a key channel for US climate finance, providing funding for projects in areas such as renewable energy, sustainable agriculture, and climate adaptation.
- **Germany:** Germany's Federal Ministry for Economic Cooperation and Development (BMZ) has a strong focus on climate change, supporting a range of initiatives in developing countries, including renewable energy deployment, forest conservation, and climate-resilient infrastructure.
- **Japan:** The Japan International Cooperation Agency (JICA) provides loans, grants, and technical assistance to developing countries, with a growing portfolio of climate-related projects.
- **The United Kingdom:** The UK's Foreign, Commonwealth & Development Office (FCDO) has a dedicated climate and environment program, supporting projects in areas such as clean energy, sustainable agriculture, and climate resilience.

- **Multilateral Channels:** Multilateral Development Banks (MDBs) are international financial institutions that provide loans, grants, and other forms of financing to developing countries. MDBs play a significant role in mobilizing climate finance, often working in partnership with governments and other donors to support large-scale infrastructure projects and programs. Key MDBs involved in climate finance include:

  - **The World Bank:** The World Bank is the largest multilateral development bank, providing a range of financial instruments, including concessional loans, grants, and guarantees, to support climate-related projects in developing countries. World Bank (2021): Action Plan (2021–2025) targets 35% climate co-benefits.
  - **The Asian Development Bank (ADB):** The ADB has a strong focus on climate change, with a dedicated Climate Change Fund and a commitment to aligning its operations with the Paris Agreement goals. ADB (2024) stresses Asia's high emissions, increasing climate risks, high public support for climate action, and financing gaps for adaptation.
  - **The African Development Bank (AfDB):** The AfDB has made climate change a top priority, with a goal of allocating 40% of its financing to climate-related projects by 2025. AfDB (2023) emphasizes Africa's natural capital decline, limited private climate finance, and innovative financing opportunities.
  - **The European Investment Bank (EIB):** The EIB, the lending arm of the European Union, is a major provider of climate finance,

supporting projects in renewable energy, energy efficiency, and climate adaptation.

- **Climate Funds:** Dedicated climate funds, established under the UNFCCC or through other international agreements, are specifically designed to channel finance to developing countries for climate action. These funds often have specific mandates, focusing on particular sectors or activities, and may offer a variety of financing instruments, including grants, concessional loans, and equity investments. Key climate funds include:
  - **The Green Climate Fund (GCF):** The GCF is the largest multilateral climate fund, aiming to support developing countries in both mitigation and adaptation efforts. It emphasizes country ownership, ensuring that projects are aligned with national priorities, and promotes partnerships between developed and developing countries.
  - **The Adaptation Fund:** The Adaptation Fund focuses specifically on supporting adaptation projects in developing countries that are particularly vulnerable to the impacts of climate change. It provides grants to developing countries to finance projects that build resilience to climate risks, such as sea-level rise, extreme weather events, and water scarcity. Adaptation Fund's, 2024 report highlights growth, approving $163.4M for 21 new projects, benefiting 45.75M people (Adaptation Fund, 2024).
  - **The Least Developed Countries Fund (LDCF):** The LDCF is a dedicated fund to support climate action in the world's least developed countries (LDCs), which are among the most vulnerable to climate change impacts. The LDCF provides grants for projects related to mitigation, adaptation, and technology transfer.

CPI (2024) reports multilateral DFIs provided an average of $88 billion in 2021/2022 annually, while bilateral DFIs provided $30 billion, and multilateral climate funds provided $3 billion. OECD (2023) reports that developed countries reached the $100 billion climate finance goal in 2022, and majority of that is public finance.

2.2 *Private Climate Finance*

While public climate finance plays a critical role, mobilizing private capital is essential for scaling up climate action to the levels needed to address the climate crisis. Private climate finance encompasses investments from businesses, financial institutions, and individual investors that flow from developed countries to developing countries to support climate-friendly projects and activities. Blended finance, a growing market, leverages public funds to attract private investment for sustainable development (Blended Finance Taskforce, 2017).

Key channels for private climate finance include:

- **Foreign Direct Investment (FDI):** Foreign direct investment (FDI) involves companies investing in businesses or projects in other countries. FDI can play a significant role in supporting the development of climate-friendly industries and technologies in developing countries. For example, a company might invest in building a renewable energy project in a developing country, contributing to both economic development and emissions reductions.
- **Commercial Loans:** Commercial banks and other financial institutions provide loans for a wide range of projects, including those related to climate change. These loans can support the financing of renewable energy projects, energy efficiency upgrades, sustainable transportation infrastructure, and climate adaptation measures.
- **Impact Investing:** Impact investors seek to generate both financial returns and measurable positive social or environmental impact. Impact investing is a rapidly growing field, and climate change is a major focus area for many impact investors. They are investing in companies and projects that are contributing to climate solutions, such as renewable energy, sustainable agriculture, and climate-resilient infrastructure, while also aiming to generate competitive financial returns. Impact investing market reached $1.571 trillion, but more capital is needed for SDGs (GIIN, 2024).

Challenges of Mobilizing Private Climate Finance in Developing Countries

Attracting private climate finance to developing countries can be challenging due to several factors:

- **Perceived Risks:** Investors may perceive higher risks associated with investing in developing countries, including political instability, regulatory uncertainty, currency fluctuations, and a lack of reliable data on project performance.
- **Policy Uncertainty:** Inconsistent or unpredictable government policies, such as sudden changes in feed-in tariffs for renewable energy or a lack of clear carbon pricing mechanisms, can create uncertainty for investors and discourage long-term investments.
- **Lack of Bankable Projects:** Many climate-friendly projects in developing countries may not be considered "bankable"—meaning they lack the financial track record, robust business plans, or risk mitigation measures that would make them attractive to commercial investors.
- **Limited Access to Capital:** Many businesses and project developers in developing countries may face limited access to capital, particularly

for large-scale infrastructure projects that require significant upfront investment.

The Fig. 2 presents the growth in climate finance from 2018 to 2022, comparing the absolute values in 2018 (USD billions) with the relative growth over the period (indexed to 2018 = 1). It breaks this information down by country groupings: Advanced economies, China, EMDEs[2] (excluding LDCs and China), LDCs,[3] and SIDS.[4] EMDEs (excluding LDCs and China) have the least growth of the five country groups, and still have a long way to catch up.

Strategies for Enhancing Private Climate Finance:

Governments and development finance institutions can play a crucial role in addressing these challenges and creating a more enabling environment for private climate finance:

- **De-risking Investments:** Governments can use public funds to de-risk investments through mechanisms such as loan guarantees, risk insurance, or concessional finance, reducing the perceived risks for private investors.
- **Creating Policy Certainty:** Establishing clear, consistent, and long-term policies, such as stable renewable energy incentives, predictable carbon

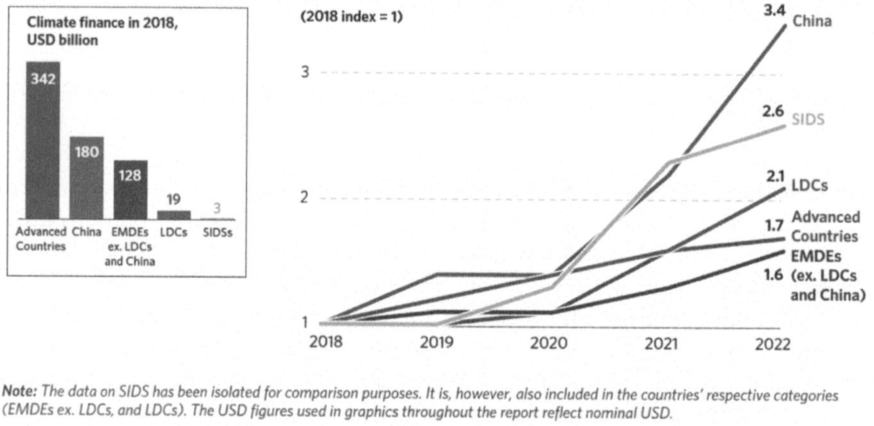

Fig. 2 Growth in climate finance compared to 2018 absolute values (*Source* CPI [2024])

[2] Emerging Markets and Developing Economies.

[3] Least Developed Countries.

[4] Small Island Developing States and associate overseas islands territories.

pricing mechanisms, and transparent regulatory frameworks, can build investor confidence and encourage long-term investments.

- **Developing Bankable Projects:** Providing technical assistance, capacity building, and project development support can help to create a pipeline of bankable climate-friendly projects that are attractive to private investors.
- **Improving Access to Finance:** Facilitating access to finance for businesses and project developers in developing countries, through mechanisms such as green banks, loan guarantee programs, or partnerships with international financial institutions, can unlock private capital for climate action. WEDO (2024) advocates for Gender Just Climate Solutions, emphasizing community-led and feminist approaches.

By working together, governments, development finance institutions, and private investors can mobilize the capital needed to scale up climate action in developing countries and create a more sustainable and equitable future for all.

Case Study 1: BlackRock's Investment in Renewable Energy in India

Overview

BlackRock, the world's largest asset manager, has significantly invested in renewable energy projects in India, recognizing the growth potential of the Indian renewable energy market and the importance of decarbonizing the energy sector. This case study highlights the growing role of institutional investors in financing renewable energy projects in developing countries, driven by both financial returns and a desire to address climate change (Proctor, 2022).

Support for Renewable Energy Projects

Key Initiatives:

- **Investment in Tata Power Renewables:** In 2022, BlackRock, along with Mubadala Investment Company, invested $525 million to acquire an 11.43% stake in Tata Power Renewable Energy Limited (TPREL). This investment supports Tata Power's plans to expand its renewable energy capacity significantly (Joshi, 2022; Mubadala, 2022).
- **Project Focus:** The investment aims to support the development of a broad-based portfolio of renewable energy assets, including solar and wind farms, which are critical for India's energy transition (Proctor, 2022).

Examples of Supported Projects:

- **Solar and Wind Farms:** TPREL, a subsidiary of Tata Power, focuses on generating power through renewable sources. With this investment, Tata Power plans to scale its generation capacity to over 30 GW by 2027, up from the current 13.5 GW, with a target to increase its clean energy portfolio from 34 to 80% by 2030 (Joshi, 2022).

Challenges and Opportunities for Institutional Investors in Emerging Markets Challenges:

- **Policy Stability and Regulatory Certainty:** One of the primary challenges for institutional investors in emerging markets is the need for stable and predictable policy frameworks. Regulatory uncertainty can deter investment and affect the long-term viability of projects.
- **Infrastructure and Grid Integration:** Developing countries often face challenges related to infrastructure and grid integration. Ensuring that the grid can handle increased renewable energy capacity and addressing bottlenecks in permitting and construction are critical for project success.

Opportunities:

- **High Growth Potential:** Emerging markets like India present significant growth opportunities for renewable energy investments. The increasing demand for electricity, driven by economic growth and urbanization, creates a substantial market for clean energy solutions.
- **Government Support:** The Indian government has set ambitious renewable energy targets and provides various incentives, such as tax benefits and subsidies, to attract investment in the sector (Proctor, 2022). This supportive policy environment enhances the attractiveness of the market for institutional investors.

Importance of Policy Stability and Regulatory Certainty

Stable Policy Framework:

- **Long-Term Commitments:** Stable and long-term policy commitments from the government are essential for attracting institutional investment. Policies that support renewable energy development, such as feed-in tariffs, renewable purchase obligations, and tax incentives, provide the necessary confidence for investors.
- **Regulatory Clarity:** Clear and consistent regulatory guidelines help streamline project development and reduce risks associated with compliance and approvals. This clarity is crucial for ensuring that projects can be executed efficiently and within budget.

Risk Mitigation:

- **Power Purchase Agreements (PPAs):** Long-term PPAs with fixed prices provide revenue certainty and reduce market risks for renewable energy projects. These agreements are vital for securing financing from institutional investors.
- **Government Guarantees:** In some cases, government guarantees or support mechanisms can help mitigate risks associated with project financing and operations, making investments more attractive to institutional investors.

Potential for Large-Scale Investments to Accelerate the Transition to a Clean Energy Economy

Scalability and Impact:

- **Large-Scale Projects:** Institutional investors like BlackRock have the financial capacity to support large-scale renewable energy projects, which can significantly accelerate the transition to a clean energy economy. These projects contribute to substantial emissions reductions and enhance energy security (Proctor, 2022).
- **Catalytic Effect:** Investments by major institutional investors can have a catalytic effect, attracting additional capital from other investors and financial institutions. This multiplier effect can amplify the impact of initial investments and drive further growth in the renewable energy sector.

Sustainable Development Goals (SDGs):

- **Alignment with SDGs:** Investments in renewable energy align with multiple SDGs, including affordable and clean energy (SDG 7), climate action (SDG 13), and sustainable cities and communities (SDG 11). By supporting clean energy projects, institutional investors contribute to broader sustainable development objectives.

Conclusion

BlackRock's investment in renewable energy projects in India exemplifies the growing role of institutional investors in financing the transition to a clean energy economy in developing countries. By investing in solar and wind farms through partnerships with companies like Tata Power, BlackRock not only seeks financial returns but also aims to address climate change and promote sustainable development. Despite challenges such as policy stability and regulatory certainty, the opportunities for high growth and government support make emerging markets like India attractive for large-scale renewable energy investments. Institutional investors' involvement is crucial for accelerating the transition to a low-carbon future and achieving global climate goals (Proctor, 2022).

3 Challenges in Mobilizing and Delivering Climate Finance

While international climate finance has grown in recent years, significant challenges remain in mobilizing the necessary resources and ensuring that these funds are used effectively, transparently, and equitably to support climate action in developing countries.

3.1 Meeting the $100 Billion Climate Finance Goal

In 2009, at the COP15 climate summit in Copenhagen, developed countries pledged to mobilize $100 billion per year in climate finance by 2020 to support developing countries in their mitigation and adaptation efforts. This pledge was reaffirmed in the Paris Agreement in 2015. The $100 billion goal has become a symbolic target, representing the commitment of developed countries to support climate action in developing countries and a key element of international climate negotiations.

However, reaching this target has proved challenging. While climate finance flows from developed to developing countries have increased, they have consistently fallen short of the $100 billion goal. Estimates of climate finance flows vary depending on methodologies and definitions, but most analyses indicate that the goal has not been met. Zagema et al. (2023) report climate finance falls short of the $100 billion goal, with only $21–24.5 billion as genuine support.

The composition of climate finance also raises concerns:

- **Mitigation vs. Adaptation:** A significant portion of climate finance has been directed toward mitigation projects, such as renewable energy and energy efficiency. Adaptation finance, which supports projects to build resilience to climate change impacts, has received significantly less funding, despite the urgent needs of developing countries facing the effects of climate change.
- **Public vs. Private Finance:** While the goal includes both public and private finance, the majority of climate finance has come from public sources. Mobilizing private capital at scale remains a challenge, particularly for adaptation projects, which often have longer payback periods and less clear revenue streams.

The $100 billion goal itself has also been criticized as being insufficient to meet the needs of developing countries, which face escalating costs from climate change impacts and the need to invest in low-carbon development pathways.

3.2 *Ensuring Transparency and Accountability*

Tracking and reporting climate finance flows accurately and transparently is essential for ensuring accountability, building trust between developed and developing countries, and assessing the effectiveness of climate finance in driving real-world change. However, achieving this transparency is fraught with challenges:

- **Definitions and Methodologies:** Different countries and institutions use varying definitions and methodologies for accounting for climate finance. This lack of consistency makes it difficult to compare figures from different sources and assess overall progress toward the $100 billion goal. For example, some countries may include export credits or concessional loans in their climate finance figures, while others may not.
- **Data Availability:** Data on private climate finance flows can be particularly difficult to track, as private companies are not subject to the same reporting requirements as governments or multilateral institutions.
- **Attribution and Additionality:** Determining the extent to which a particular investment can be attributed to climate finance and whether it represents additional funding beyond existing development assistance can be challenging. For example, if a development project has both climate and non-climate objectives, it can be difficult to determine how much of the funding should be counted as climate finance.

Efforts are underway to improve transparency and accountability in climate finance:

- **UNFCCC Standing Committee on Finance:** This committee provides guidance on methodologies for measuring, reporting, and verifying climate finance flows.
- **OECD Development Assistance Committee (DAC) Rio Markers:** The DAC Rio Markers are a set of indicators used to track climate-related development finance. They allow donors to classify their aid flows according to their climate objectives (mitigation or adaptation).

3.3 *Addressing the Needs of Developing Countries*

Developing countries have diverse needs for climate finance, reflecting their varying levels of development, vulnerability to climate change impacts, and national priorities. WRI (2017) calls for reform of multilateral climate funds to improve efficiency and equitable allocation.

Key areas where climate finance is needed include:

- **Mitigation:** Supporting the transition to low-carbon energy systems, reducing deforestation, promoting sustainable agriculture, and investing in climate-smart technologies.
- **Adaptation:** Building resilience to climate impacts, such as sea-level rise, extreme weather events, and water scarcity, through investments in infrastructure, early warning systems, and capacity building.
- **Technology Transfer:** Facilitating the transfer of clean technologies and knowledge from developed to developing countries to accelerate the adoption of climate solutions.
- **Capacity Building:** Strengthening the institutional and technical capacity of developing countries to plan, implement, and manage climate action projects.

CPI (2024) reports climate finance flows in EMDEs heavily favors mitigation finance (89% of total climate finance flow), compared with adaption finance (USD 196 billion between 2018 and 2022). Within transition finance flows, energy sector and transport sector are the most important sectors heavily invested:

- **Energy Systems Dominance:** Mitigation finance to EMDEs ex. LDCs overwhelmingly favored energy systems, receiving 55% of the total finance volume. This focus led to significant growth in renewable energy capacity, especially in China, where the share of renewables in the electricity mix increased dramatically. Other EMDEs also saw growth in renewables, but at a more modest pace, and with significant regional variations (e.g., Brazil with a high renewable share vs. Egypt with a much lower one). The increase in private funding for energy systems also contributed to the dominance of the private sector in providing over half of the mitigation finance in several regions.
- **Transport as a Key Sector:** The transport sector received the second largest share (31%) of mitigation funding. Outside of China, this sector was primarily financed by public sources. Key investments included infrastructure development for mass transit and the adoption of zero- and low-emission vehicles. China's transport sector, on the other hand, saw substantial private investment, particularly in battery electric vehicles (BEVs).
- **Underfunding of Other Sectors:** Despite their significant mitigation potential, other sectors received very little funding:
  - **Buildings and Infrastructure:** While experiencing growth, this sector only accounted for 7% of total mitigation finance. Private

investment played an increasing role, signaling growing commercial viability.

- **Agriculture, Forestry, and Other Land Uses (AFOLU), Industry, Waste, and Wastewater:** These sectors, crucial for addressing both CO2 and non-CO2 greenhouse gas emissions, were starkly underfunded. The report highlights the need for significantly increased investment in these areas, along with supportive policy environments and research and development. Adaptation finance showed a different sectoral distribution. Water and wastewater management received the largest share (51%), followed by cross-sectoral projects (33%, encompassing policy support, capacity building, and disaster risk management), and AFOLU (9%). This reflects the prioritization of adapting to immediate climate risks, such as water stress and extreme weather events.

It's crucial that climate finance is allocated effectively and equitably to address these diverse needs. This requires:

- **Country Ownership:** Ensuring that developing countries have ownership over the projects and programs that are financed, aligning investments with national priorities and development plans.
- **Vulnerability Focus:** Prioritizing finance for countries and communities that are most vulnerable to the impacts of climate change, recognizing that those who have contributed the least to the problem are often the most affected.
- **Needs-Based Allocation:** Allocating finance based on the specific needs of different countries and sectors, rather than a one-size-fits-all approach.

The Fig. 3 shows that while the overall growth in climate finance to EMDEs (ex. LDCs and China) is positive, it's unevenly distributed. Some regions show stronger and more consistent growth than others, highlighting varying needs and investment opportunities.

Case Study 2: The Asian Development Bank's (ADB) Support for Sustainable Transportation in Southeast Asia

Overview

The Asian Development Bank (ADB) plays a crucial role in promoting sustainable transportation systems and reducing emissions from the transport sector in Southeast Asia (ADB, 2025a). This case study highlights how ADB finances investments in public transportation, electric vehicle charging infrastructure, and sustainable urban mobility solutions to reduce congestion, air pollution, and greenhouse gas emissions in the region (UN, 2010).

Support for Sustainable Transportation Projects

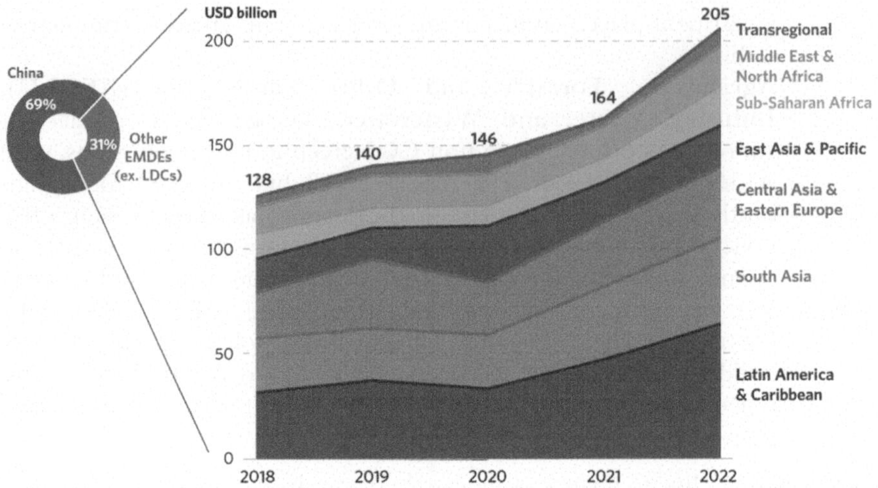

Fig. 3 Climate finance growth in EMDEs (ex. LDCs and China) (*Source* CPI [2024])

Key Initiatives:

- **Public Transportation:** ADB supports the development of efficient and clean public transportation systems, including metro rail, bus rapid transit (BRT), and electric buses. These projects aim to reduce reliance on private vehicles, alleviate traffic congestion, and lower emissions.
- **Electric Vehicle Charging Infrastructure:** Investments in electric vehicle (EV) charging infrastructure are crucial for promoting the adoption of EVs. ADB funds projects that establish charging networks to support the transition to electric mobility.
- **Sustainable Urban Mobility:** ADB promotes integrated urban mobility solutions, such as non-motorized transport (walking and cycling), transit-oriented development, and smart traffic management systems. These initiatives enhance the livability of cities and reduce the environmental impact of transportation.

Examples of Supported Projects:

- **Metro Manila BRT System:** ADB is financing the development of a BRT system in Metro Manila, Philippines, to improve public transport efficiency and reduce emissions.
- **Indonesia Sustainable Urban Transport Program:** This program includes investments in electric buses, non-motorized transport infrastructure, and smart traffic management systems in Indonesian cities.

- **EV Charging Network in Thailand:** ADB supports the establishment of a comprehensive EV charging network in Thailand to facilitate the adoption of electric vehicles and reduce transport-related emissions.

Challenges of Developing Sustainable Transportation Systems

Unique Challenges:

- **Rapid Urbanization:** Southeast Asia is experiencing rapid urbanization, leading to increased demand for transportation infrastructure. Developing sustainable transport systems in this context requires careful planning and significant investment.
- **Financial Constraints:** Developing countries often face financial constraints that limit their ability to invest in large-scale sustainable transportation projects. Access to concessional finance and risk mitigation instruments is essential to overcome these barriers.
- **Technical and Institutional Capacity:** Many countries in the region lack the technical and institutional capacity to design, implement, and manage complex transportation projects (ADB, 2025b). Capacity building and technical assistance are crucial for successful project execution.

Importance of Integrated Planning and Policy Coordination:

- **Holistic Approach:** Sustainable transportation requires an integrated approach that considers land-use planning, economic development, and environmental sustainability. Coordination among various government agencies and stakeholders is essential for effective implementation.
- **Policy Support:** Supportive policies, such as incentives for clean vehicles, regulations for emissions standards, and urban planning guidelines, are necessary to create an enabling environment for sustainable transportation.

Role of ADB in Providing Technical Assistance and Capacity Building

Capacity Building:

- **Training and Education:** ADB provides training and educational programs to build the capacity of local institutions, government agencies, and communities. This includes workshops, technical training, and knowledge-sharing platforms.
- **Institutional Strengthening:** Strengthening local institutions is crucial for sustainable transportation. ADB supports the development of institutional frameworks, governance structures, and policy-making processes that enhance transport planning and management.

Technical Assistance:

- **Project Preparation:** ADB offers technical assistance for project preparation, including feasibility studies, environmental and social impact assessments, and financial modeling. This ensures that projects are well-designed and ready for implementation.
- **Implementation Support:** ADB provides ongoing support during project implementation, including procurement, contract management, and monitoring and evaluation. This helps ensure that projects are completed on time and within budget.

Conclusion

The Asian Development Bank's support for sustainable transportation in Southeast Asia demonstrates the vital role of multilateral development banks in promoting clean and efficient transport systems. By financing investments in public transportation, electric vehicle charging infrastructure, and sustainable urban mobility solutions, ADB helps reduce congestion, air pollution, and greenhouse gas emissions in the region. Despite challenges such as rapid urbanization, financial constraints, and capacity limitations, ADB's integrated planning approach, policy coordination, and technical assistance are key to the success of these initiatives. ADB's efforts highlight the importance of sustainable transportation in achieving inclusive and environmentally sustainable development in Southeast Asia.

4 Innovations and Emerging Trends

The landscape of climate finance is constantly evolving, driven by technological advancements, shifting market dynamics, and the growing recognition of the urgent need to scale up climate action. This section explores some of the most promising innovations and emerging trends in international climate finance.

Blended Finance

Blended finance, as discussed in Chapter 13, is an approach that combines public and private capital to make climate-related investments more attractive to private investors. It involves using public funds strategically to de-risk projects, improve their risk-return profiles, and leverage larger amounts of private investment.

In the context of international climate finance, blended finance is particularly important for mobilizing private capital for projects in developing countries. This is because private investors often perceive higher risks associated with investing in emerging markets, and blended finance can help to mitigate these risks.

Common blended finance structures in climate finance include:

- **Concessional Loans and Grants:** Development finance institutions (DFIs) and government agencies can provide concessional loans or grants to project developers, reducing the cost of capital and making projects more financially viable.
- **Guarantees and Risk Mitigation Instruments:** Public funds can be used to provide guarantees for loans or other risk mitigation instruments, such as political risk insurance, to protect private investors from potential losses.

Green Bonds

Green bonds, also explored in Chapter 13, are debt securities issued to raise capital specifically for projects with environmental benefits, including climate change mitigation and adaptation. The green bond market has experienced rapid growth in recent years, providing a significant source of funding for climate-friendly projects worldwide.

Green bonds are increasingly being used to finance climate-related projects in developing countries. This is driven by several factors:

- **Growing Investor Demand:** Investors are increasingly seeking to align their portfolios with sustainability goals and are looking for investment opportunities that generate both financial returns and positive environmental impact.
- **Supportive Policy Frameworks:** Governments in developing countries are developing policy frameworks that encourage green bond issuances, such as tax incentives, regulatory clarity, and green bond labeling schemes.
- **Multilateral Development Bank Support:** MDBs are playing a key role in developing the green bond market in developing countries, providing technical assistance, capacity building, and credit enhancement to support green bond issuances.

Technology and Innovation

IRENA (2023) finds 2022 energy transition investment reached USD 1.3 trillion but needs quadrupling to meet climate goals. Renewable energy investment, at USD 0.5 trillion, is insufficient, especially for off-grid solutions. Technology is playing an increasingly important role in enhancing the efficiency, transparency, and impact of climate finance. New technologies and innovative approaches are being used to:

- **Track Climate Finance Flows:** Blockchain technology can be used to track climate finance flows from source to beneficiary, enhancing transparency, reducing transaction costs, and improving accountability. Blockchain-based platforms can create a secure and tamper-proof record of transactions, making it easier to monitor the use of funds and ensure that they are reaching their intended beneficiaries. Schulz and Feist (2020) suggest blockchain can enhance transparency and streamline climate finance flows under the GCF.
- **Identify Investment Opportunities:** Artificial intelligence (AI) and machine learning (ML) can be used to analyze vast amounts of data, such as climate projections, economic data, and company information, to identify promising climate-related investment opportunities. These technologies can help investors to identify projects that are both financially viable and environmentally impactful, accelerating the flow of capital toward climate solutions.
- **Mobilize Capital from New Sources:** Crowdfunding platforms and other digital tools can be used to connect investors with climate-related projects, mobilizing capital from a wider range of sources, including individual investors, philanthropic organizations, and impact investors.

5 Conclusion: Toward a More Effective and Equitable Climate Finance System

International climate finance is essential for enabling a just and equitable transition to a low-carbon and climate-resilient world. Developed countries have a moral and political obligation to fulfill their commitments to support climate action in developing countries, not only because these countries are often the most vulnerable to climate impacts but also because their participation is crucial for achieving global climate goals. WEF (2023) highlights interconnected global risks, including economic instability, climate change, and geopolitical tensions, impacting long-term progress. IEA (2024) analyzes the growth of clean energy, rising electricity demand, and regional variations in energy transitions amidst geopolitical factors.

While progress has been made in mobilizing climate finance, significant challenges remain. Meeting the $100 billion goal, ensuring transparency and accountability in funding flows, and addressing the diverse needs of developing countries require a concerted and collaborative effort from governments, multilateral institutions, and the private sector.

Fortunately, innovative solutions are emerging. Blended finance, green bonds, and technological advancements are creating new opportunities to unlock private capital, enhance transparency, and drive more impactful climate investments.

Moving forward, it's essential to:

- **Increase Ambition:** Developed countries need to significantly increase their climate finance commitments, going beyond the $100 billion goal and providing more predictable and long-term funding.
- **Promote Equity and Justice:** Climate finance should prioritize the needs of the most vulnerable countries and communities, ensuring that it contributes to a just and equitable transition.
- **Enhance Transparency and Accountability:** Improving methodologies, data collection, and reporting mechanisms is crucial for tracking climate finance flows, building trust, and ensuring that funds are being used effectively.
- **Embrace Innovation:** Supporting the development and deployment of innovative financing mechanisms and technologies can unlock new sources of capital and drive more efficient and impactful climate investments.

By working together, the global community can create a more effective and equitable climate finance system that supports ambitious climate action in developing countries and paves the way for a more sustainable and resilient future for all.

References

Adaptation Fund. (2024). *Annual performance report for the fiscal year 2024*. https://www.adaptation-fund.org/document/annual-performance-report-for-the-fiscal-year-2024/. Accessed 1 January 2025.

Asian Development Bank (ADB). (2024). *Asia-Pacific climate report: Catalyzing finance and policy solutions*. https://www.adb.org/climate-report/editions/2024

African Development Bank (AfDB). (2023). *African economic outlook 2023*. https://www.afdb.org/sites/default/files/documents/publications/afdb23-01_aeo_main_english_0602.pdf

Blended Finance Taskforce. (2017). *Better finance*, Better World. https://www.blendedfinance.earth/better-finance-better-world

The Climate Policy Initiative (CPI). (2024). Global landscape of climate finance. https://www.climatepolicyinitiative.org/publication/global-landscape-of-climate-finance-2024/

Global Impact Investing Network (GIIN). (2024). *Sizing the impact investing market 2024*. https://thegiin.org/publication/research/sizing-the-impact-investing-market-2024/

International Energy Agency (IEA). (2024). *World energy outlook 2024*. https://www.iea.org/reports/world-energy-outlook-2024

International Renewable Energy Agency (IRENA). (2023). *Global landscape of renewable energy finance 2023*. https://www.irena.org/Publications/2023/Feb/Global-landscape-of-renewable-energy-finance-2023

Organisation for Economic Co-operation and Development (OECD). (2023). *Climate finance provided and mobilised by developed countries*. https://www.oecd.org/content/dam/oecd/en/publications/reports/2024/05/climate-finance-provided-and-mobilised-by-developed-countries-in-2013-2022_8031029a/19150727-en.pdf

Schulz, K., & Feist, M. (2020). Leveraging blockchain technology for innovative climate finance under the Green Climate Fund. *Earth System Governance, 7*, Article 100084. https://doi.org/10.1016/j.esg.2020.100084

United Nations Development Programme (UNDP). (2017). *Gender and climate finance.* UNDP. https://www.undp.org/publications/gender-and-climate-finance

United Nations Climate Change Secretariat (UNFCCC). (2024). *UNFCCC standing committee on finance sixth biennial assessment and overview of climate finance flows summary and recommendations.* https://unfccc.int/sites/default/files/resource/UNFCCC_BA6_Summary_Web_Final.pdf

Women's Environment & Development Organization (WEDO). (2024). *Gender just climate solutions.* https://wedo.org/what-we-do/our-programs/gender-just-climate-solutions/

World Bank (2021). World Bank Group Climate Change Action Plan 2021–2025: Supporting green, resilient, and inclusive development. https://openknowledge.worldbank.org/entities/publication/ee8a5cd7-ed72-542d-918b-d72e07f96c79

World Economic Forum (WEF). (2023). *Global risks report 2023.* https://www.weforum.org/reports/global-risks-report-2023/

World Resource Institute (WRI). (2017). *The future of the funds exploring the architecture of multilateral climate finance.* https://files.wri.org/d8/s3fs-public/The_Future_of_the_Funds_0.pdf

Zagema, B. et al. (2023). *Assessing the delivery of the $100 billion commitment.* https://oxfamilibrary.openrepository.com/bitstream/handle/10546/621500/bp-climate-finance-shadow-report-050623-en.pdf

Case References

Asian Development Bank (ADB). (2025a). *Transport.* https://www.adb.org/what-we-do/topics/transport

ADB. (2025b). *Regional: Southeast Asia transport project preparatory facility phase 2.* https://www.adb.org/projects/52084-002/main. Accessed 1 January 2024.

Joshi, A. (2022). *BlackRock and Mubadala's acquisition of 11.43% stake in Tata power renewables approved.* Mercomindia. https://www.mercomindia.com/blackrock-mubadalas-acquisition-tata-power-renewables. Accessed 1 January 2024.

Mubadala. (2022). *BlackRock and Mubadala invests in India's Tata power renewables.* https://annual2022.mubadala.com/news/blackrock-and-mubadala-invests-in-indias-tata-power-renewables

Proctor, D. (2022). *BlackRock-led group invests $525M toward India renewable energy.* Power. https://www.powermag.com/blackrock-led-group-invests-525m-toward-india-renewable-energy/. Accessed 1 January 2024.

United Nations (UN). (2010). *Asian development bank and the partnership on sustainable low carbon transport.* Department of Economic and Social Affairs. https://sdgs.un.org/statements/asian-development-bank-and-partnership-sustainable-low-carbon-transport-8151. Accessed 1 January 2024.

CHAPTER 21

A Roadmap for Climate Finance: Integrating Climate Considerations into Practice

1 Introduction: Turning Knowledge into Action

The world is increasingly aware of the urgency of climate change and the crucial role that finance plays in driving solutions. We've explored the science, the financial risks, the investment opportunities, and the innovative financing mechanisms emerging to address this global challenge. But knowledge without action is futile. This chapter provides a practical roadmap for translating climate finance principles into tangible strategies and actions, empowering individuals and organizations to become active participants in the transition to a sustainable future.

The "knowing-doing gap" is a common challenge. Organizations may understand the importance of climate change, express support for sustainability goals, and even invest in climate risk assessment tools or disclosure frameworks. Yet, they often struggle to effectively integrate climate considerations into their core decision-making processes, operations, and strategies.

This roadmap is designed to bridge that gap, providing a clear and actionable guide for integrating climate considerations into practice. Whether you are an investor seeking to align your portfolio with climate goals, a business leader looking to manage climate risks and opportunities, or a policymaker designing regulations to support climate finance, this chapter offers practical steps and guidance to help you navigate this complex and evolving landscape.

J. Chen, *Climate Finance*,
https://doi.org/10.1007/978-981-96-7975-1_21

2 Defining a Climate Finance Strategy: Objectives, Risks, and Opportunities

The first step in integrating climate considerations into practice is to define a clear and comprehensive climate finance strategy. This strategy should align with the organization's values and mission, set specific goals, assess climate-related risks and opportunities, and guide decision-making across different functions. TCFD (2021) provides guidance on climate-related metrics, targets, and transition plans. UNEP FI (2023a) provides the following roadmap for a low-carbon bank of 2030.

Figure 1 shows the three zones of progressing from "in 2019" to "by 2030" and then "by 2050." It charts the transformation journey of a bank as it moves from a traditional "banking as usual" model to a position of "institutionalization" within the desired net-zero economy.

The three zones and their corresponding stages are:

1. **"Banking as usual zone" (in 2019):** This represents the initial state of a typical bank which is characterized by:
    - **Focus on Efficiency:** A focus on internal efficiency to achieve the status-quo and preventing it from changing.
    - **Passive Mindset:** A passive mindset that means they are waiting for others to move first.
    - **Reputational Matter:** Sustainability is viewed as only a reputational matter rather than a core element of the business model.

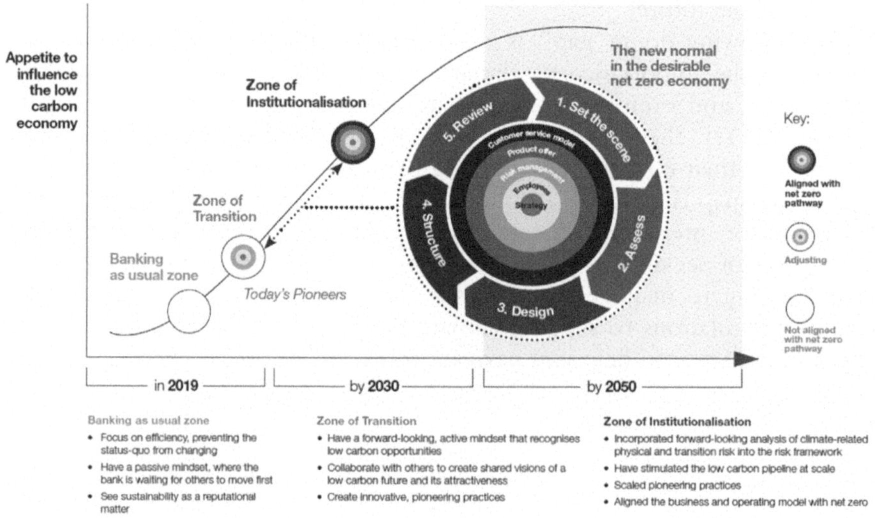

Fig. 1 The roadmap to a low-carbon bank of 2030 (*Source* UNEP FI [2023a] and CISL [2021])

This stage is marked by a circle not filled in, representing that the bank is not aligned with net-zero pathways at this point.

2. **"Zone of Transition" (by 2030):** This is a phase of transformation, where banks are labeled "Today's Pioneers" who are:
    - **Forward-Looking and Active:** Banks at this stage have adopted a forward-looking active mindset that recognizes low-carbon opportunities.
    - **Collaboration:** Banks will collaborate with others to create shared visions of a low-carbon future.
    - **Innovation:** There is a focus on creating innovative, pioneering practices.
    - This stage is marked by a circle with a fill, but also a red dot inside, showing that they are "adjusting" rather than aligned.
3. **"Zone of Institutionalization" (by 2050):** This is the desired end-state. Here, banks are fully integrated into the net-zero economy, and are characterized by:
    - **Integrated Climate Analysis:** A bank incorporates forward-looking analysis of climate-related physical and transition risk into the risk framework.
    - **Low-Carbon Pipeline:** They have stimulated the low-carbon pipeline at scale.
    - **Scaled Practices:** They have scaled the pioneering practices they established during the "Zone of Transition."
    - **Aligned Business Model:** They have aligned their business and operating model with net-zero requirements.
    - This stage is marked by a circle that is full, and a circle with a dark purple fill, to indicate they are fully aligned to net-zero pathways.

The transition stage is of vital importance and consists of five phases:

1. **Phase 1—Set the Scene**
    - This initial phase is about establishing a foundation for a productive dialogue between the bank and the client. This requires setting the client's current starting point, positioning the bank's role, and establishing communication.
    - **Tasks:** Develop a deeper understanding of climate-related risks and opportunities; Clarify how the bank can effectively support its client in their net-zero transition journey.
2. **Phase 2—Assess**
    - This phase involves a thorough evaluation of the client's current situation and ambitions. The aim is to understand where the client is currently and where they intend to go.

- **Tasks:** Both the bank and the client should understand their baseline position, as well as the current level of targeted decarbonization; Map forward-looking strategic and operational implications, alongside possible financing opportunities.

3. **Phase 3—Design**
   - The main focus of this stage is to develop a strategic plan for the transition. It is an iterative process that helps the client to formulate an action plan for reaching their net-zero goal.
   - **Tasks:** The client develops a robust, science-based net-zero decarbonisation plan with appropriate metrics and targets; Identify associated financing requirements and prioritize those requirements over the short, medium, and long term.
4. **Phase 4—Structure**
   - This phase shifts toward the implementation of the transition plan by structuring financial solutions. The goal here is to develop solutions that reflect the client's current needs.
   - **Tasks:** Create a tailored financial structure that is appropriate for the client's financing needs while also taking into account the client's longer-term strategy; The client and bank must agree on the financing structure, pricing, and sign off on a deal.
5. **Phase 5—Review**
   - **Description:** This final, but still ongoing phase, is about continuous monitoring and support. The goal is to evaluate the success of the structured solution and further advance the net-zero agenda.
   - **Tasks:** Successful deployment of financing strategies, and a client that invests to deliver agreed outcomes; Ongoing monitoring of progress and measurable impact, with a goal of supporting systemic change in low-carbon business models.

2.1 Setting Clear Objectives

A well-defined climate finance strategy starts with a clear articulation of the organization's objectives. These objectives should be grounded in the organization's core values and mission, ensuring that its climate-related actions are aligned with its overall purpose and identity. SBTi (2024) offers a framework for financial institutions to set science-based targets.

- **Alignment with Values and Mission:** For example, a university endowment fund with a mission to promote sustainability and social responsibility might set a goal of aligning its investments with the Paris Agreement targets, divesting from fossil fuel companies, and increasing its allocations to climate solutions. A bank with a commitment to serving local communities might prioritize lending to businesses that are reducing their environmental impact or supporting the transition to a clean energy economy.

- **Specific Climate Goals:** Once the organization's values and mission are clear, it's essential to set specific, measurable, achievable, relevant, and time-bound (SMART) goals for its climate finance activities. These goals will provide a roadmap for action, guide decision-making, and enable the organization to track its progress over time.

Examples of climate finance objectives:

- **Emissions Reduction Targets:** A manufacturing company might set a target to reduce its greenhouse gas emissions by 25% by 2030, aligning with science-based targets or industry benchmarks.
- **Investment Goals:** A pension fund might set a goal to allocate 10% of its portfolio to climate solutions by 2025, focusing on investments in renewable energy, energy efficiency, sustainable transportation, or climate adaptation technologies.
- **Impact Goals:** A non-profit organization might set a goal to mobilize $50 million in funding over the next five years to support community-based climate resilience projects in vulnerable regions.

2.2 *Assessing Climate Risks*

A crucial element of any climate finance strategy is a thorough assessment of climate-related risks. This assessment should encompass both physical and transition risks, considering the potential impacts on the organization's operations, assets, investments, and supply chains. NGFS (2020) provides guidance for supervisors on integrating climate-related and environmental risks into prudential supervision.

- **Physical Risks:** Physical risks arise from the direct impacts of climate change, such as more frequent and intense extreme weather events, sea-level rise, and changes in temperature and precipitation patterns. These risks can damage infrastructure, disrupt operations, impact supply chains, and affect the value of assets.
- **Transition Risks:** Transition risks stem from the economic and financial shifts associated with the transition to a low-carbon economy. These risks can arise from policy changes, such as carbon pricing or renewable energy mandates, technological advancements that disrupt existing industries, shifting consumer preferences for sustainable products, and evolving investor expectations around climate action.

The process of assessing climate risks can be complex, requiring the use of specialized tools and methodologies, as discussed in previous chapters. However, even a basic risk assessment can provide valuable insights into the organization's vulnerabilities and inform its climate finance strategy.

2.3 Identifying Opportunities

While climate change presents significant risks, it also creates opportunities for innovation, growth, and competitive advantage. WEF (2023) highlights climate adaptation failures as a key long-term global risk. Organizations that proactively embrace climate action can benefit from:

- **Investing in Clean Technologies:** The transition to a low-carbon economy is driving rapid growth in markets for clean technologies, such as renewable energy, energy efficiency, sustainable transportation, and carbon capture, utilization, and storage (CCUS). Investing in these technologies can generate financial returns, reduce operational costs, and enhance brand reputation. IEA (2024) emphasizes clean energy transition and grid investments for lower system costs and energy security.
- **Developing New Products and Services:** The growing demand for sustainable solutions is creating opportunities for companies to develop new products and services that meet the needs of environmentally conscious consumers. For example, companies can innovate in areas such as plant-based foods, sustainable fashion, eco-friendly packaging, or renewable energy services.
- **Building Climate Resilience:** Investing in adaptation measures to protect assets, operations, and supply chains from climate impacts can not only reduce risks but also create new business opportunities. For example, companies can invest in water-efficient technologies, drought-resistant crops, or climate-resilient infrastructure to enhance their resilience and gain a competitive advantage.

Identifying these opportunities requires a forward-looking perspective, a willingness to embrace innovation, and a commitment to integrating sustainability into core business strategies.

Case Study 1: ING's Terra Approach to Sustainable Finance

Overview

ING, a Dutch multinational banking and financial services corporation, has developed the Terra approach, a comprehensive and ambitious climate finance strategy. This strategy aligns ING's lending and investment activities with the goals of the Paris Agreement. The Terra approach involves setting targets for reducing the carbon footprint of its loan portfolio, increasing green financing, engaging with clients on climate action, and advocating for supportive policies (ING, 2025a, 2025b, 2025c).

Support for Climate-Related Projects

Key Initiatives:

- **Carbon Footprint Reduction:** ING aims to steer the most carbon-intensive parts of its portfolio toward net zero by 2050. This includes sectors such as power generation, oil & gas, automotive, shipping, aviation, steel, cement, residential mortgages, and commercial real estate.
- **Green Financing:** ING is committed to increasing its green financing activities, supporting projects that contribute to environmental sustainability and climate resilience (ING, 2025c).
- **Client Engagement:** ING actively engages with its clients to encourage and support their transition to more sustainable practices. This involves providing consulting services and setting intermediate goals for reducing carbon emissions by 2030.
- **Advocacy:** ING advocates for policies that support the transition to a low-carbon economy, collaborating with other financial institutions and stakeholders to drive systemic change (ING, 2025a, 2025b).

Examples of Supported Projects:

- **Renewable Energy Projects:** ING finances renewable energy projects, such as wind and solar farms, to reduce reliance on fossil fuels and lower greenhouse gas emissions.
- **Sustainable Real Estate:** ING provides financing for energy-efficient buildings and retrofitting projects to improve the sustainability of residential and commercial real estate.
- **Sustainable Transportation:** ING supports the development of low-emission transportation solutions, including electric vehicles and sustainable shipping practices.

Challenges of Measuring and Managing the Carbon Footprint

Complexity of Diverse Portfolios:

- **Sector-Specific Methodologies:** ING uses sector-specific methodologies to measure and steer its loan book toward net-zero emissions. This involves assessing the technology shifts needed across different sectors and comparing them with clients' current and planned technologies (2025b; ING, 2025a).
- **Data Collection:** Collecting accurate and comprehensive data on emissions across a diverse portfolio can be challenging. ING utilizes global

databases that track public and private companies to gather the necessary information without burdening clients with data provision.

Collaboration and Innovation:

- **PACTA for Banks:** ING co-created the Paris Agreement Capital Transition Assessment (PACTA) for Banks with the 2° Investing Initiative. This methodology helps measure the alignment of ING's lending activities with climate goals by analyzing the technology shifts required in various sectors. (Azoulay et al., 2022).
- **Client Data Integration:** ING integrates client data from global databases to assess the current mix of technologies and planned shifts, enabling targeted financing to support the transition.

Importance of Client Engagement and Collaboration

Client Support and Consulting:

- **Guidance and Consulting:** ING provides consulting services to its clients, helping them understand the importance of sustainability and guiding them through the transition process. This includes setting intermediate goals and offering financial products that support sustainable practices.
- **Collaborative Initiatives:** ING collaborates with other financial institutions and stakeholders to establish measurement methodologies, emissions data, and reporting frameworks. This collective effort enhances the ability of financial institutions to support the transition to net-zero emissions (ING, 2025c).

Strategic Partnerships:

- **Poseidon Principles:** ING is a founding signatory of the Poseidon Principles for the shipping sector, which set a framework for measuring and reporting the climate impact of shipping loans.
- **Sustainable STEEL Principles:** ING led the development of the Sustainable STEEL Principles, helping banks measure and report the emissions associated with their steel loan portfolios.

Role of Financial Institutions in Driving the Transition

Driving Systemic Change:

- **Advocacy and Policy Support:** ING advocates for supportive policies that facilitate the transition to a low-carbon economy. This includes engaging with regulators, policymakers, and industry groups to promote sustainable practices.

- **Financial Innovation:** ING develops innovative financial products and services that support sustainability, such as green bonds, sustainability-linked loans, and impact investing funds (ING, 2025c).

Scaling Impact:

- **Global Leadership:** As a leading global financial institution, ING's commitment to sustainability sets an example for other banks and financial institutions. By integrating sustainability into its core business strategy, ING demonstrates the potential for financial institutions to drive significant environmental and social impact.
- **Sustainable Development Goals (SDGs):** ING's Terra approach aligns with multiple SDGs, including affordable and clean energy (SDG 7), climate action (SDG 13), and sustainable cities and communities (SDG 11).

Conclusion

ING's Terra approach to sustainable finance exemplifies how a global financial institution can develop a comprehensive and ambitious climate finance strategy. By setting targets for reducing the carbon footprint of its loan portfolio, increasing green financing, engaging with clients on climate action, and advocating for supportive policies, ING is driving the transition to a low-carbon economy (Azoulay et al., 2022). Despite challenges in measuring and managing the carbon footprint of a diverse portfolio, ING's collaborative efforts and innovative methodologies demonstrate the critical role of financial institutions in promoting sustainability and achieving global climate goals.

3 Selecting and Implementing Climate Risk Tools

Once an organization has defined its climate finance strategy and assessed its risks and opportunities, it's essential to select and implement appropriate tools to support decision-making and track progress. The world of climate finance offers a diverse array of tools, ranging from simple carbon footprint calculators to sophisticated climate risk models and portfolio alignment platforms. UNEP FI (2021) provides an overview of climate risk assessment methodologies, emphasizing the need for standardized approaches and integration of physical and transition. UNEP FI (2023a, 2023b) also provides a detailed roadmap for financial institutions to select climate risk tools (Fig. 2).

The roadmap provides a step-by-step process to:

1. Determine **specific requirements** regarding assets and output metrics.

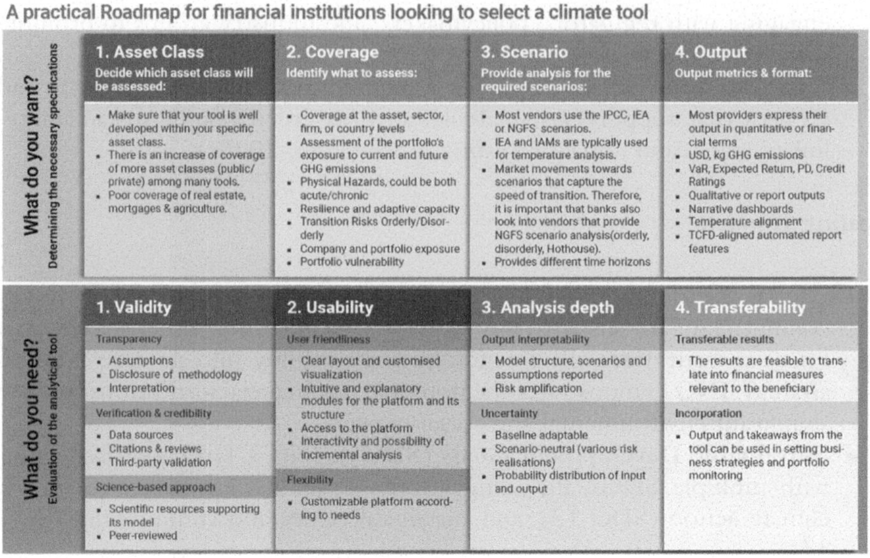

Fig. 2 The roadmap for FIs to select climate risk tools (*Source* UNEP FI [2023a, 2023b])

2. Evaluate the **analytical tool** itself for transparency, user-friendliness, and data quality.
3. Ensure the selected tool aligns with **strategic decisions** and **regulatory needs**.

In the following sections, we will discuss the steps in details.

3.1 Matching Tools to Needs

The key is to choose tools that align with the organization's specific objectives, size, sector, and level of expertise. There is no one-size-fits-all solution.

Here's a framework for selecting the most appropriate tools:

1. **Define Your Objectives:** What are you trying to achieve with climate risk assessment? Are you primarily focused on measuring your carbon footprint, assessing your vulnerability to physical or transition risks, aligning your investment portfolio with climate goals, or producing climate-related disclosures?
2. **Consider Your Scope:** What is the scope of your assessment? Are you focusing on your own organization's operations, your investment portfolio, or your supply chain?

3. **Assess Your Resources:** What resources are available for data collection, analysis, and tool implementation? Do you have in-house expertise, or will you need to rely on external consultants or data providers?
4. **Evaluate Tool Features:** Consider the key features of different tools, such as:

   - **Data Requirements:** What data inputs does the tool require? Do you have access to this data, or will you need to purchase it from a third-party provider?
   - **Model Complexity:** How complex is the model underlying the tool? Can you understand the methodology and interpret the results?
   - **Cost:** What are the costs associated with the tool, including subscription fees, data costs, and consulting services?
   - **Ease of Use:** Is the tool user-friendly and accessible to non-experts? Does it integrate well with your existing systems and workflows?

3.2 *Integration into Existing Workflows*

To maximize the effectiveness of climate risk assessment tools, it's crucial to integrate them seamlessly into existing workflows and processes. This ensures that climate considerations are not treated as a separate, siloed activity but rather become an integral part of the organization's decision-making across different functions. COSO and WBCSD (2018) provides guidance on integrating ESG risks, including climate-related risks, into existing ERM frameworks.

Here are some examples of how climate risk tools can be integrated:

- **Risk Management Frameworks:** Climate risks can be incorporated into the organization's enterprise risk management (ERM) system, alongside other financial, operational, and strategic risks. This involves identifying, assessing, and managing climate risks using the same processes and structures that are already in place for other types of risks.
- **Investment Policies and Due Diligence:** Climate risk assessment tools can be used to inform investment decisions, asset allocation strategies, and due diligence processes. Investors can use these tools to screen potential investments for climate risks, evaluate the carbon footprint of their portfolios, and identify companies that are taking proactive steps to address climate change.
- **Strategic Planning:** Scenario analysis and stress testing tools can help organizations evaluate the resilience of their strategic plans to climate change. By exploring a range of possible future climate scenarios, organizations can identify potential vulnerabilities, assess the impact of different climate policies, and develop strategies that are adaptable to changing conditions.

- **Sustainability Reporting:** Disclosure reporting tools can streamline the process of producing climate-related disclosures that align with recognized frameworks, such as the TCFD recommendations or the SASB standards. SASB (2023) highlights climate risks across industries and their financial implications, recommending industry-specific metrics for disclosures. These tools can help to ensure data accuracy, consistency, and comparability, enhancing the credibility and transparency of disclosures.

3.3 Data Consistency and Model Validation

The accuracy and reliability of climate risk assessments depend heavily on the quality of the data inputs and the robustness of the models used. It's crucial to ensure data consistency, validate model outputs, and understand the limitations of the tools being used. Arribas et al. (2022) stress the urgent need for improved climate risk assessments (CRA), highlighting the need for a broader scope and better stakeholder representation.

Key considerations:

- **Data Quality Checks:** Implement procedures to verify the accuracy and completeness of climate-related data, both from internal sources and external providers. This may involve cross-checking data against multiple sources, conducting data audits, or engaging with data providers to understand their methodologies. NGFS (2022) emphasizes the need for better climate data, especially to support sustainable finance and prevent greenwashing.
- **Model Validation:** Validate climate models and risk assessment tools against historical data to assess their accuracy and predictive power. This involves testing the model's ability to reproduce past events and evaluating its sensitivity to changes in key input parameters. Crisil (2023) highlights validation challenges for climate risk and ESG models, noting that traditional credit risk approaches are inadequate. Luo et al. (2023) present a framework for assessing physical climate risks, using publicly available data to quantify potential power generation losses.
- **Understanding Model Limitations:** Recognize that all models are simplifications of reality and have inherent limitations. Clearly communicate the assumptions, uncertainties, and potential biases associated with model outputs.

Case Study 2: Swiss Re's Use of Climate Models to Assess Catastrophe Risks

Overview

Swiss Re, a leading global reinsurer, utilizes sophisticated climate models to assess the increasing risks of extreme weather events and inform its underwriting and pricing decisions. By developing proprietary climate models and partnering with climate scientists, Swiss Re incorporates the latest climate projections into its risk assessments. This approach enables the company to estimate potential losses from hurricanes, floods, wildfires, and other climate-related disasters, adjust reinsurance premiums accordingly, and encourage clients to take steps to reduce their risks.

Support for Climate-Related Projects

Key Initiatives:

- **Proprietary Climate Models:** Swiss Re has developed its own climate models, which are continuously updated with the latest scientific data and projections. These models help the company assess the risks associated with various natural catastrophes (Bertogg, 2021).
- **Collaboration with Scientists:** By partnering with climate scientists and research institutions, Swiss Re ensures that its models incorporate cutting-edge climate science and reflect the most current understanding of climate change impacts (Swiss Re, 2025a).
- **Risk Assessment Tools:** Swiss Re offers a range of tools and services, such as the Climate Risk Scores and the Sustainability Compass platform, to help clients understand and mitigate their climate risks.

Examples of Supported Projects:

- **Climate Risk Scores:** Swiss Re developed 12 Climate Risk Scores based on IPCC AR6 science, showing trends of future hazard development over 5-year intervals from 2030 to the end of the century. These scores help clients plan risk mitigation measures.
- **Sustainability Compass:** This interactive online platform allows clients to visualize site and portfolio risks, facilitating informed decision-making and strategic planning (Swiss Re, 2025b).

Challenges of Climate Modeling

Complexity and Uncertainty:

- **Dynamic Risk Landscape:** The risk posed by both primary (e.g., hurricanes, earthquakes) and secondary perils (e.g., thunderstorms, wildfires) is not static. Climate change, urbanization, and other factors continuously alter the risk landscape, requiring models to be frequently updated and recalibrated (*Financial Times*, 2025).

- **Incorporating Uncertainty:** Accurately predicting the frequency and severity of extreme weather events involves significant uncertainty. Swiss Re's models incorporate a range of scenarios to account for this uncertainty and provide a comprehensive risk assessment.

Data Collection and Integration:

- **Comprehensive Datasets:** Collecting and integrating data from various sources, including historical loss data, climate projections, and real-time monitoring, is essential for accurate modeling. Swiss Re leverages global databases and collaborates with external experts to enhance its datasets (Araullo, 2024).

Importance of Incorporating Uncertainty into Risk Assessments

Scenario Analysis:

- **Multiple Scenarios:** Swiss Re's models analyze multiple scenarios, including different pathways for greenhouse gas emissions and socioeconomic developments. This approach helps capture a wide range of potential outcomes and provides a robust basis for decision-making.
- **Future Hazard Risk Categories:** By combining Climate Risk Scores with present risk exposure, Swiss Re presents Future Hazard Risk Categories that help clients anticipate and prepare for future climate risks.

Risk Management:

- **Adaptive Strategies:** Incorporating uncertainty into risk assessments allows Swiss Re and its clients to develop adaptive strategies that can be adjusted as new information becomes available. This enhances resilience and ensures that risk management practices remain effective over time (Swiss Re, 2025c).

Role of Reinsurance in Incentivizing Climate Adaptation

Incentivizing Risk Reduction:

- **Premium Adjustments:** Swiss Re adjusts reinsurance premiums based on the assessed risk levels. Clients who take proactive measures to reduce their climate risks, such as investing in resilient infrastructure or implementing disaster preparedness plans, may benefit from lower premiums.
- **Encouraging Best Practices:** By providing risk mitigation services and guidance, Swiss Re encourages clients to adopt best practices for climate

adaptation. This includes building resilient infrastructure, implementing early warning systems, and adopting sustainable land-use practices.

Supporting Climate Resilience:

- **Financial Resilience:** Reinsurance provides financial resilience by covering losses from extreme weather events. This enables communities and businesses to recover more quickly and reduces the economic impact of disasters.
- **Public–Private Partnerships:** Swiss Re collaborates with governments, NGOs, and other stakeholders to develop comprehensive adaptation and resilience strategies. These partnerships leverage Swiss Re's expertise and financial resources to maximize impact (Wagener, 2024).

Conclusion

Swiss Re's use of climate models to assess catastrophe risks demonstrates the critical role of sophisticated risk assessment tools in managing the increasing risks of extreme weather events. By developing proprietary models and collaborating with climate scientists, Swiss Re incorporates the latest climate projections into its underwriting and pricing decisions. Despite the complexities and uncertainties of climate modeling, Swiss Re's approach enhances transparency, reduces transaction costs, and improves accountability in climate finance. The company's efforts to incentivize climate adaptation and build resilience highlight the important role of reinsurance in driving climate action and supporting sustainable development (Wagener, 2024).

4 Engaging with Stakeholders: Communication, Collaboration, and Capacity Building

Climate finance is not a solitary endeavor. It requires collaboration, communication, and capacity building across different sectors, organizations, and individuals. Engaging with stakeholders is crucial for building trust, sharing knowledge, and amplifying the impact of climate action.

4.1 Communicating Climate Risks and Opportunities

Effective communication about climate risks and opportunities is essential for raising awareness, mobilizing support, and driving informed decision-making. This involves communicating with a variety of stakeholders, including investors, customers, employees, policymakers, and the public. CDSB (2024) provides guidance on climate-related disclosures, now consolidated within the ISSB framework.

Key principles for effective communication:

- **Clarity and Conciseness:** Use plain language, avoid technical jargon, and focus on the most material information. Explain complex concepts in simple terms, using analogies or metaphors to make the information more relatable.
- **Transparency:** Be open and honest about the organization's climate risks, its strategies for managing those risks, and the uncertainties involved. Clearly explain the methodologies used to assess risks and the limitations of the data or models used.
- **Relevance:** Tailor communication to the specific interests and concerns of different stakeholders. For example, when communicating with investors, focus on the financial implications of climate change and the organization's strategies for managing climate-related financial risks. When communicating with employees, emphasize the importance of sustainability for the long-term success of the organization and the role they can play in reducing the company's environmental impact.
- **Visualizations:** Use charts, graphs, maps, and other visuals to present data in a clear and engaging way. Visuals can help to make complex information more accessible and memorable.
- **Storytelling:** Use storytelling and narratives to make climate change more relatable and to connect with the audience's values and emotions. Real-world examples, case studies, and personal anecdotes can help to bring the issue to life.

4.2 Building Relationships with Key Stakeholders

Building strong relationships with key stakeholders in the climate finance landscape is essential for fostering collaboration, sharing knowledge, and advocating for supportive policies.

Key stakeholders to engage with:

- **Investors:** Engage with investors to understand their expectations regarding climate change, communicate the organization's climate strategy, and build confidence in its approach to managing climate risks and opportunities. CFA Institute (2020) emphasizes investor engagement on climate risks and opportunities.
- **Policymakers:** Work with policymakers to advocate for policies that support climate action, provide feedback on proposed regulations, and share insights from the private sector on the challenges and opportunities of integrating climate considerations into business practices.
- **NGOs and Civil Society:** Collaborate with NGOs and civil society organizations that are working on climate change, sharing knowledge, learning from best practices, and addressing community concerns.

- **Industry Peers:** Engage with other companies in the same industry to share best practices, learn from each other's experiences, and collaborate on initiatives to promote climate action.

4.3 Collaboration and Capacity Building

Collaboration is essential for accelerating climate action and mobilizing finance at the scale needed to address the climate crisis. Organizations can benefit from collaborating with:

- **Industry Initiatives:** Joining industry initiatives or coalitions that are focused on climate change, such as the We Mean Business Coalition, the RE100 initiative (companies committed to 100% renewable energy), or sector-specific sustainability groups. These initiatives provide a platform for sharing best practices, advocating for policy changes, and demonstrating collective leadership on climate action.
- **Working Groups and Task Forces:** Participating in working groups or task forces focused on specific aspects of climate finance, such as developing methodologies for climate risk assessment or exploring innovative financing mechanisms. WRI (2024) highlights the need for global financial system reform and increased collaboration to address climate change challenges.
- **Academic Institutions and Research Organizations:** Partnering with universities and research institutions to access cutting-edge knowledge, conduct joint research projects, and develop new tools and solutions.

Capacity building is also crucial for ensuring that organizations have the knowledge, skills, and resources needed to effectively integrate climate considerations into their practices. This involves:

- **Training Programs:** Investing in training programs for staff on climate science, risk assessment methodologies, disclosure frameworks, and investment strategies.
- **Knowledge Sharing:** Facilitating the sharing of knowledge and best practices through conferences, workshops, webinars, and online platforms.
- **Technical Assistance:** Providing technical assistance to developing countries to build their capacity to plan, implement, and manage climate-related projects.

5 Measuring and Reporting on Climate Impact: Metrics, Transparency, and Accountability

Measuring and reporting on the impact of climate finance activities is crucial for ensuring accountability, tracking progress, and demonstrating the value of investments in climate solutions. This involves going beyond financial returns to assess the environmental and social outcomes achieved. Impact measurement and management are critical for maximizing positive outcomes and minimizing negative ones (GIIN, 2024). Both positive and negative impacts, as well as investor contributions, should be evaluated (Impact Frontiers, 2024).

5.1 Developing Meaningful Metrics

Selecting appropriate metrics is essential for effective impact measurement. The choice of metrics will depend on the organization's objectives, the type of projects being financed, and the availability of data.

Key considerations:

- **Relevance:** Metrics should be directly relevant to the intended impact and aligned with the organization's climate goals.
- **Measurability:** Metrics should be quantifiable and measurable, allowing for objective assessment of progress.
- **Comparability:** Whenever possible, use standardized metrics that allow for comparison with other organizations or projects.
- **Data Availability:** Choose metrics for which data is readily available or can be collected reliably.

Examples of impact metrics for climate finance:

- **Greenhouse Gas Emissions Reductions:** The amount of greenhouse gas emissions avoided or reduced as a result of the investment.
- **Renewable Energy Generation Capacity:** The amount of renewable energy capacity installed or financed.
- **Energy Efficiency Improvements:** The amount of energy saved or the reduction in energy intensity.
- **Number of People Benefiting from Climate Adaptation Projects:** The number of people who have benefited from projects that enhance resilience to climate change impacts, such as flood defenses or drought-resistant agriculture.

5.2 *Transparency and Reporting*

Transparent and consistent reporting is crucial for building trust, demonstrating accountability, and enabling stakeholders to assess the impact of climate finance activities.

Key elements of effective reporting:

- **Clear Objectives and Methodology:** Clearly state the organization's climate goals and the methodology used to measure impact.
- **Data Sources and Quality:** Provide transparency about the data sources used, the quality of the data, and any limitations or assumptions made.
- **Quantitative and Qualitative Data:** Use a combination of quantitative data (e.g., emissions reductions, financial returns) and qualitative data (e.g., case studies, stakeholder testimonials) to provide a comprehensive picture of impact.
- **Visualizations and Storytelling:** Use charts, graphs, maps, and other visuals to present data in a clear and engaging way. Incorporate storytelling and narratives to bring the impact to life.

Reporting mechanisms can include:

- **Sustainability Reports:** Many organizations publish annual sustainability reports that include information on their climate-related activities, performance, and impact.
- **Impact Reports:** Some organizations produce dedicated impact reports that focus specifically on the social and environmental outcomes of their investments or projects.
- **Investor Communications:** Investors often provide regular updates to their clients or beneficiaries on the climate performance and impact of their portfolios.

5.3 *Accountability and Verification*

Accountability is essential for ensuring that climate finance is being used effectively and that organizations are delivering on their commitments. Several mechanisms can enhance accountability:

- **Internal Audits:** Organizations can conduct internal audits to assess the effectiveness of their climate risk management and impact measurement processes, identifying areas for improvement and ensuring that they are meeting their stated goals.
- **External Verification:** Seeking independent verification of climate-related data, impact assessments, and disclosures from third-party organizations can enhance credibility and provide assurance to stakeholders.

This verification can be conducted by specialized auditing firms, certification bodies, or sustainability rating agencies.

- **Stakeholder Feedback:** Gathering feedback from stakeholders, such as investors, beneficiaries, communities, and NGOs, can provide valuable insights into the perceived impact of climate finance activities and identify areas where the organization can improve its performance.

Case Study 3: The City of Copenhagen's Climate Plan Monitoring and Evaluation System

Overview

The City of Copenhagen has set an ambitious goal to become the world's first carbon neutral capital by 2025. To achieve this, the city has implemented a comprehensive monitoring and evaluation system that tracks its progress on key metrics, such as greenhouse gas emissions reductions, renewable energy deployment, and energy efficiency improvements. This system utilizes data dashboards, online platforms, and public reports to communicate progress to citizens and stakeholders.

Support for Climate-Related Projects

Key Initiatives:

- **CPH 2025 Climate Plan:** Adopted in 2012, the CPH 2025 Climate Plan is based on four pillars: Energy Consumption, Energy Production, Mobility, and City Administration Initiatives. Each pillar includes specific targets and actions to reduce CO_2 emissions and promote sustainability (UD, 2025).
- **Monitoring and Evaluation System:** The city uses a sophisticated system to track progress toward its climate goals. This includes collecting data on emissions, energy use, and other relevant metrics, which are then analyzed and reported through various platforms (C40 Knowledge, 2017).
- **Public Communication:** Copenhagen uses data dashboards, online platforms, and public reports to communicate its progress to citizens and stakeholders. This transparency helps build public trust and engagement in the city's climate initiatives.

Examples of Supported Projects:

- **Renewable Energy Deployment:** The city has invested in renewable energy projects, such as biomass-fueled combined heat and power plants and wind turbines, to replace fossil fuels and reduce emissions.

- **Energy Efficiency Improvements:** Partnerships with private building owners and businesses aim to enhance energy efficiency in buildings, which is one of the most cost-effective ways to cut emissions (Damsø et al., 2017).
- **Sustainable Mobility:** Initiatives to promote walking, cycling, and public transport aim to reduce emissions from road traffic. The goal is for at least 75% of all trips to be made by foot, bike, or public transport by 2025.

Challenges of Achieving Standardized and Comparable Climate Disclosures

Complexity and Data Quality:

- **Diverse Data Sources:** Collecting reliable data from diverse sources, including energy consumption, transportation, and waste management, is complex. Ensuring data quality and consistency is crucial for accurate monitoring (UNEPCCC, 2025).
- **Dynamic Environment:** The dynamic nature of urban environments means that data must be continuously updated and analyzed to reflect current conditions and progress.

Efforts to Standardize:

- **Integrated Reporting:** Copenhagen's monitoring system integrates data from various sectors to provide a comprehensive view of the city's climate performance. This helps ensure that all relevant factors are considered in the analysis (City of Copenhagen, 2025).
- **Collaboration with Experts:** The city collaborates with climate scientists, data analysts, and other experts to develop and refine its monitoring methodologies, ensuring that they are based on the latest scientific knowledge and best practices.

Importance of Investor Pressure in Driving Corporate Transparency

Transparency and Accountability:

- **Clear Targets:** Setting clear and measurable targets is essential for tracking progress and demonstrating accountability. Copenhagen's CPH 2025 Climate Plan includes specific goals for emissions reductions, renewable energy deployment, and energy efficiency improvements (City of Copenhagen, 2025).
- **Public Reporting:** Regular public reporting on progress helps build trust and engage citizens in the city's climate initiatives. It also provides a

basis for stakeholders to hold the city accountable for its commitments (Carbon Neutral Cities Alliance, 2025).

Engaging the Public:

- **Data Dashboards:** Interactive data dashboards allow citizens to track the city's progress in real-time. These dashboards provide detailed information on key metrics and highlight areas where further action is needed.
- **Online Platforms:** Copenhagen uses online platforms to share information about its climate initiatives and engage with the public. These platforms include interactive tools, educational resources, and opportunities for citizen participation.

Role of Coalitions in Promoting Leadership and Best Practices

Collaborative Networks:

- **Multi-Stakeholder Engagement:** Copenhagen collaborates with a wide range of stakeholders, including businesses, universities, and other cities, to share knowledge and best practices. This collaborative approach enhances the effectiveness of the city's climate initiatives.
- **International Partnerships:** The city is a member of the Carbon Neutral Cities Alliance (CNCA), which brings together cities committed to achieving carbon neutrality. This partnership provides a platform for sharing strategies and learning from other leading cities.

Leadership and Innovation:

- **Leading by Example:** Copenhagen's efforts to become carbon neutral serve as an inspiration for other cities and demonstrate that it is possible to combine economic growth with environmental sustainability.
- **Innovation and Experimentation:** The city encourages innovation and experimentation by providing opportunities for Danish and international operators to test new solutions and technologies in an urban setting (City of Copenhagen, 2025).

Conclusion

The City of Copenhagen's Climate Plan Monitoring and Evaluation System exemplifies how a city government can use data and technology to track progress toward ambitious climate goals and communicate achievements to citizens. By setting clear targets, collecting reliable data, and using transparent reporting mechanisms, Copenhagen demonstrates accountability, tracks progress, and engages the public in climate action. The city's collaborative approach and commitment to innovation highlight the importance of multi-stakeholder engagement and continuous improvement in achieving sustainability goals. Copenhagen's efforts serve as a model for other cities aiming to drive progress toward a more sustainable future.

6 Conclusion: A Collective Journey Toward a Sustainable Future

Integrating climate considerations into practice is a journey, not a destination. It requires a continuous commitment to learning, adaptation, and improvement. There will be challenges along the way, but the rewards of building a more sustainable and resilient future are immense.

By following the roadmap outlined in this chapter, organizations can take concrete steps to:

- **Develop a Clear Climate Finance Strategy:** Aligning their actions with their values, setting ambitious goals, and assessing risks and opportunities.
- **Select and Implement Appropriate Tools:** Utilizing the growing array of climate risk assessment tools, disclosure frameworks, and investment strategies to inform decision-making.
- **Engage with Stakeholders:** Building relationships, communicating transparently, and collaborating to amplify the impact of climate action.
- **Measure and Report on Impact:** Tracking progress, ensuring accountability, and demonstrating the value of investments in a sustainable future.

The transition to a low-carbon and climate-resilient world demands a collective effort. By embracing the principles of climate finance, organizations of all sizes and sectors can contribute to this transformation, creating a future where economic prosperity and environmental sustainability go hand in hand.

References

Arribas, A., et al. (2022). Climate risk assessment needs urgent improvement. *Nature Communications, 13*(1). https://doi.org/10.1038/s41467-022-31979-w

Climate Disclosure Standards Board (CDSB). (2024). *Climate Disclosure Standards Board*. https://www.cdsb.net/climate-guidance. Accessed 24 January 2025.

Chartered Financial Analyst Institute (CFAI). (2020). *Climate change analysis in the investment process*. https://rpc.cfainstitute.org/-/media/documents/article/industry-research/climate-change-analyis.pdf

Cambridge Institute for Sustainability Leadership (CISL). (2021). *Let's discuss climate: Achieveing net zero business 2050. The essential guide to bank-client engagement*. https://www.cisl.cam.ac.uk/system/files/documents/lets-discuss-climate-guide-to-bank-climate-engagement-cisl-may-2021.pdf. Accessed 9 March 2025.

Committee of the Sponsoring Organizations of the Treadway Commission & The World Business Council for Sustainable Development (COSO & WBCSD). (2018). *Applying enterprise risk management to environmental, social and governance-related risks*. https://www.wbcsd.org/resources/applying-enterprise-risk-management-to-environmental-social-and-governance-related-risks/

Crisil. (2023). *The validation challenge in climate risk and ESG models*. https://coalitiongreenwich.crisil.com/content/crisilcom/en/home/our-analysis/reports/2023/07/the-validation-challenge-in-climate-risk-and-ESG-models.html. Accessed 24 January 2025.

Global Impact Investing Network (GIIN). (2024). *The generally accepted system for impact investors to measure, manage, and optimize their impact*. https://iris.thegiin.org/

International Energy Agency (IEA). (2024). *World energy outlook 2024*. https://www.iea.org/reports/world-energy-outlook-2024

Impact Frontiers. (2024). *Impact management norms*. https://impactfrontiers.org/norms/

Luo, T., et al. (2023). A framework to assess multi-hazard physical climate risk for power generation projects from publicly-accessible sources. *Communications Earth & Environment, 4*(1), 1–13. https://doi.org/10.1038/s43247-023-00782-w

Network for Greening the Financial System (NGFS). (2020). *Network for greening the financial system technical document guide for supervisors integrating climate-related and environmental risks into prudential supervision*. https://www.ngfs.net/sites/default/files/medias/documents/ngfs_guide_for_supervisors.pdf

NGFS. (2022). *Final report on bridging data gaps*. https://www.ngfs.net/system/files/import/ngfs/medias/documents/final_report_on_bridging_data_gaps.pdf. Accessed 9 March 2025.

Sustainability Accounting Standards Board (SASB). (2023). *SASB standards climate risk technical bulletin 2023 update*. https://sasb.ifrs.org/wp-content/uploads/2023/11/SASB-Climate-Risk-Technical-Bulletin-2023-0823.pdf. Accessed 1 January 2025.

Science Based Targets initiative (SBTi). (2024). *Financial sector science-based targets guidance*. https://sciencebasedtargets.org/resources/files/Financial-Sector-Science-Based-Targets-Guidance.pdf

Task Force on Climate-Related Financial Disclosures (TCFD). (2021). *Task force on climate-related financial disclosures guidance on metrics, targets, and transition plans*. https://assets.bbhub.io/company/sites/60/2021/07/2021-Metrics_Targets_Guidance-1.pdf

United Nations Environment Programme Finance Initiative (UNEP FI). (2021). *Climate risk landscape: Mapping climate-related financial risk assessment methodologies*. https://www.unepfi.org/themes/climate-change/the-climate-risk-landscape/

UNEP FI. (2023a). *The 2023 climate risk landscape technical supplement*. https://www.unepfi.org/wordpress/wp-content/uploads/2023/05/2023-Climate-Risk-Landscape-Technical-supplement.pdf. Accessed 24 January 2025.

UNEP FI. (2023b). *The 2023 climate risk landscape*. https://www.unepfi.org/themes/climate-change/2023-climate-risk-landscape/. Accessed 24 January 2025.

World Economic Forum (WEF). (2023). *Global risks report 2023*. World Economic Forum. https://www.weforum.org/reports/global-risks-report-2023/

World Resource Institute (WRI). (2024). *How the climate finance puzzle fits into the global financial system*. https://www.wri.org/insights/climate-finance-and-the-global-financial-system. Accessed 24 January 2025.

Case References

Araullo, K. (2024). *Industry underestimated impact of natural disasters—Swiss Re. Insurance Business*. https://www.insurancebusinessmag.com/au/news/reinsurance/industry-underestimated-impact-of-natural-disasters--swiss-re-493378.aspx. Accessed 1 January 2024.

Azoulay, M., Casoli, A., & Kansy, T. (2022). *Managing financed emissions: How banks can support the net-zero transition*. McKinsey. https://www.mckinsey.com/industries/financial-services/our-insights/managing-financed-emissions-how-banks-can-support-the-net-zero-transition

Bertogg, M. (2021). *Tackling the here and now: Why we need to rethink our natural catastrophe risk models*. https://www.swissre.com/risk-knowledge/mitigating-climate-risk/rethinking-our-risk-models.html. Accessed 1 January 2024.

C40 Knowledge. (2017). *Copenhagen 2025 climate plan: Roadmap 2017–2020*. https://www.c40knowledgehub.org/s/article/Copenhagen-2025-Climate-Plan-Roadmap-2017-2020?language=en_US

Carbon Neutral Cities Alliance (CNCA). (2025). *Copenhagen*. https://carbonneutralcities.org/cities/copenhagen/

City of Copenhagen. (2025). *The CPH 2025 climate plan*. https://international.kk.dk/about-copenhagen/liveable-green-city/2025-climate-plan

Damsø, T., Kjær, T., & Christensen, T.B. (2017). Implementation of local climate action plans: Copenhagen—Towards a carbon-neutral capital. *Journal of Cleaner Production, 167*, 406–415. https://www.sciencedirect.com/science/article/pii/S0959652617318851

Financial Times (FT). (2025). Swiss Re says industry failed to estimate impact of extreme weather. https://www.ft.com/content/48b3e54a-771a-4a12-a412-527c34311ca9. Accessed 1 January 2024.

ING. (2025a). *Terra approach*. https://www.ing.com/Sustainability/Climate-action/Terra-approach.htm. Accessed 1 January 2024.

ING. (2025b). *Our Terra approach*. https://www.ing.com.tr/en/ing/sustainability/sustainability-sustainable-work/our-terra-approach. Accessed 1 January 2024.

ING. (2025c). *Sustainable finance*. https://www.ing.com.tr/en/ing/sustainability/sustainability-sustainable-work/sustainable-finance

Swiss Re. (2025a). *Natural hazard and climate risk management*. https://www.swissrefoundation.org/what-we-do/projects/natural-hazard-and-climate-risk-management.html. Accessed 1 January 2024.

Swiss Re. (2025b). *Climate risk services*. https://corporatesolutions.swissre.com/insurance-services/climate-risk-services.html

Swiss Re. (2025c). *Climate and natural catastrophe risk*. https://www.swissre.com/institute/research/topics-and-risk-dialogues/climate-and-natural-catastrophe-risk.html

United Nations Environment Programme Copenhagen Climate Centre (UNEPCCC). (2025). *UNEP Copenhagen climate centre*. https://unepccc.org

Urban Development (UD). (2025). *The CPH 2025 climate plan*. https://urbandevelopmentcph.kk.dk/climate

Wagener, D. (2024). *What reinsurers can do for climate adaptation and resilience*. United Nations. https://pacific.un.org/en/267537-what-reinsurers-can-do-climate-adaptation-and-resilience. Accessed 1 January 2024.

CHAPTER 22

The Future of Climate Finance: Trends, Opportunities, and a Call to Action

1 Introduction: Navigating a Transformative Landscape

The financial world is in the midst of a profound transformation. Climate change, once seen as a distant environmental concern, is now recognized as a defining force shaping markets, influencing investment decisions, and reshaping the very foundations of the global economy. The future of finance is inextricably linked to the future of the planet, and the way we mobilize and deploy capital will determine our ability to address the climate crisis and build a more sustainable and resilient world.

The climate finance landscape is dynamic and complex, driven by a convergence of powerful forces:

- **The Escalating Urgency of Climate Change:** The impacts of climate change are becoming increasingly evident and severe, from more frequent and intense extreme weather events to rising sea levels and disruptions to ecosystems and agriculture. The scientific consensus on the human causes of climate change is overwhelming, and the window for action is rapidly closing.
- **Breakthroughs in Technology and Innovation:** Rapid advancements in clean technologies, such as renewable energy, energy storage, and carbon capture, utilization, and storage (CCUS), are creating new possibilities for decarbonizing the economy and building resilience to climate impacts.
- **Shifting Investor Expectations:** Investors are increasingly recognizing the financial risks posed by climate change and seeking to align their portfolios with sustainability goals. The demand for climate-aligned

J. Chen, *Climate Finance*,
https://doi.org/10.1007/978-981-96-7975-1_22

investments is growing rapidly, driven by a combination of fiduciary duty, client demand, and evolving regulations.
- **A New Era of Regulation:** Governments worldwide are implementing policies and regulations to accelerate the transition to a low-carbon economy, including carbon pricing mechanisms, renewable energy mandates, and mandatory climate risk disclosure requirements. This evolving regulatory landscape is creating both challenges and opportunities for businesses, investors, and financial institutions.

This chapter will explore the key trends, opportunities, and challenges shaping the future of climate finance. We will examine the potential for technology to revolutionize the field, the implications of evolving regulations, and the crucial role of international cooperation in mobilizing capital for climate solutions on a global scale.

2 The Evolving Landscape of Climate Finance: Drivers of Change

The future of climate finance is not a predetermined path; it's a landscape of possibilities shaped by a confluence of powerful forces. Understanding these drivers of change is essential for navigating this dynamic terrain and identifying the opportunities and challenges that lie ahead.

2.1 The Urgency of Climate Action

The climate crisis is no longer a distant threat; it's a present reality with tangible and escalating consequences. This growing urgency is a primary driver of the transformation in climate finance.

- **Escalating Climate Impacts:** The impacts of climate change are becoming increasingly evident and severe. More frequent and intense extreme weather events are causing widespread damage to infrastructure, disrupting supply chains, and displacing communities. Rising sea levels threaten coastal cities and ecosystems, while droughts, heatwaves, and wildfires are causing agricultural losses, water scarcity, and health problems. These impacts are imposing significant economic costs, undermining development gains, and exacerbating social inequalities. WMO (2024) confirms 2023 as the warmest year on record (1.45 °C above pre-industrial levels), with record greenhouse gas levels.
- **Scientific Consensus:** The scientific community has reached an overwhelming consensus on the human causes of climate change and the urgent need to reduce greenhouse gas emissions to avoid catastrophic consequences. The Intergovernmental Panel on Climate Change (IPCC), the leading international body for assessing the science of climate change,

has warned that exceeding 1.5 degrees Celsius of warming above pre-industrial levels will lead to severe and irreversible impacts. IPCC (2023) finds human activity unequivocally caused global warming, exceeding 1.1 °C, with insufficient mitigation.

- **Growing Public Pressure:** Public awareness of climate change and its impacts is increasing, leading to growing pressure on governments, businesses, and investors to take action. Citizen movements, youth activism, and media attention are raising the profile of climate change, demanding more ambitious policies, and pushing for greater transparency and accountability from those in power.

2.2 Technological Advancements

Technological innovation is a powerful force for change, and advancements in clean technologies are creating new possibilities for mitigating climate change, adapting to its impacts, and building a more sustainable future. These breakthroughs are driving the transformation of climate finance by creating new investment opportunities, reducing the costs of climate solutions, and enhancing our ability to measure and manage climate risks.

Key areas of technological advancement driving climate finance:

- **Renewable Energy:** The cost of renewable energy technologies, such as solar photovoltaics and wind power, has plummeted in recent years, making them increasingly competitive with fossil fuels. IRENA (2024) reports decreasing renewable energy costs, notably solar and wind. Innovations in solar cell technology, wind turbine design, and energy storage are further driving down costs and improving the efficiency and reliability of renewable energy systems.
- **Energy Storage:** Addressing the intermittency of renewable energy sources like solar and wind power requires advancements in energy storage technologies. Innovations in battery technologies, such as lithium-ion, flow batteries, and solid-state batteries, are increasing storage capacity, improving lifespan, and reducing costs, making energy storage a more viable and scalable solution.
- **Carbon Capture, Utilization, and Storage (CCUS):** Capturing and storing carbon dioxide (CO_2) emissions from industrial processes and power plants is a crucial technology for decarbonizing hard-to-abate sectors, such as steel, cement, and aviation. Advancements in CCUS technologies, including improved capture methods, CO_2 transportation and storage infrastructure, and the utilization of captured CO_2 for producing valuable products, are making CCUS a more feasible and cost-effective option.
- **Digital Technologies:** Digital technologies, such as artificial intelligence (AI), blockchain, and the Internet of Things (IoT), are transforming the

way we assess and manage climate risks, invest in climate solutions, and track the impact of climate finance. BNEF (2024) emphasizes tripling renewables capacity by 2030 for net-zero.

- **AI** can analyze vast amounts of data, identify patterns, and improve the accuracy of climate risk assessments and investment decisions.
- **Blockchain** can enhance transparency and traceability in climate finance, facilitating secure and efficient transactions, and supporting the development of new market mechanisms, such as carbon trading platforms.
- **IoT sensors** can provide real-time data on environmental conditions, climate hazards, and the performance of climate-related projects, enhancing monitoring, evaluation, and decision-making.

2.3 *Shifting Investor Expectations*

Investors are no longer solely focused on financial returns; they are increasingly recognizing the importance of environmental, social, and governance (ESG) factors in their investment decisions. This shift in investor expectations is driving a fundamental change in how capital is allocated, creating a growing demand for climate-aligned investments and pushing companies to improve their sustainability performance. GSIA (2023) reports a global sustainable investment of $30.3T, with growth outside the United States, and highlights a shift toward corporate engagement.

Key trends in investor expectations:

- **ESG Integration:** ESG investing is becoming mainstream, with investors increasingly incorporating ESG factors into their investment analysis, portfolio construction, and engagement with companies. They are recognizing that companies with strong ESG performance are often better managed, more resilient to risks, and better positioned for long-term success in a world grappling with sustainability challenges.
- **Climate Risk as Financial Risk:** Investors are increasingly recognizing climate change as a material financial risk that can impact asset values, disrupt operations, and affect long-term returns. They are demanding more information from companies on their climate-related risks and opportunities, using this information to assess the resilience of their portfolios and guide their investment decisions.
- **Demand for Impact:** Investors are not only seeking to avoid negative impacts; they are also actively seeking investments that generate positive social and environmental outcomes. Impact investing, which aims to generate both financial returns and measurable impact, is growing rapidly, with climate change being a major focus area. PwC (2024) emphasizes AWM firms' need to adopt disruptive technologies to meet evolving investor expectations and drive growth.

2.4 *Evolving Regulatory Landscape*

Governments worldwide are recognizing the urgency of climate change and taking action to accelerate the transition to a low-carbon economy. This evolving regulatory landscape is creating a new playing field for climate finance, driving transparency, incentivizing investment in climate solutions, and pushing companies and financial institutions to take climate risks seriously. FSB (2020) highlights climate change implications for financial stability, focusing on physical and transition risks.

Key regulatory developments:

- **Mandatory Disclosure Requirements:** Several jurisdictions are implementing mandatory climate-related disclosure requirements for companies and financial institutions, recognizing the need for standardized and comparable information to inform investor decisions and promote market transparency. Examples include:
  - **The European Union's Corporate Sustainability Reporting Directive (CSRD):** This directive significantly expands the scope of sustainability reporting requirements, requiring companies to disclose information on a wider range of ESG topics, including climate change. The CSRD aims to provide investors with more comprehensive and comparable data, enhancing transparency and facilitating more sustainable investment decisions.
  - **The US Securities and Exchange Commission (SEC)'s Proposed Rule on Climate Disclosures:** This proposed rule would require publicly traded companies in the United States to disclose their greenhouse gas emissions and climate-related risks in their financial filings. If adopted, this rule would represent a major shift in climate disclosure requirements in the United States, providing investors with more consistent and comparable information on companies' climate performance.
- **Green Taxonomies:** Green taxonomies are classification systems that define which economic activities can be considered "green" or "sustainable." They provide clarity for investors seeking to align their portfolios with environmental goals and help to prevent greenwashing by establishing clear criteria for what qualifies as a green investment. Several jurisdictions are developing green taxonomies:
  - **The EU Taxonomy:** The EU Taxonomy is a comprehensive classification system that defines environmentally sustainable economic activities across various sectors. It aims to create a common language for green investments within the EU and guide the flow of capital toward activities that contribute to climate change mitigation and other environmental objectives.

  - **The Chinese Green Bond Endorsed Project Catalogue:** China has developed a taxonomy for green bond investments, defining eligible projects that align with national environmental goals.
- **Climate Stress Testing:** Financial regulators are increasingly using climate stress tests to assess the resilience of financial institutions to climate risks. NGFS (2024) provides guidance for supervisors on integrating climate-related and environmental risks into prudential supervision. These tests involve simulating the impact of different climate scenarios on banks, insurers, and other financial institutions, identifying potential vulnerabilities and informing supervisory actions to enhance the stability of the financial system.

The evolving regulatory landscape is creating both challenges and opportunities for the financial sector. Companies and financial institutions will need to adapt to new disclosure requirements, invest in data collection and analysis capabilities, and integrate climate considerations more deeply into their decision-making processes. However, this shift toward greater transparency and accountability can also drive innovation, unlock new investment opportunities, and contribute to a more sustainable and resilient financial system.

3 The Role of Technology: AI, Blockchain, and Data-Driven Solutions

Technology is rapidly transforming the landscape of climate finance, offering powerful tools to enhance efficiency, transparency, and impact. This section explores the key roles that artificial intelligence (AI), blockchain, and data-driven solutions are playing in shaping the future of climate finance.

3.1 Artificial Intelligence (AI)

AI algorithms, with their ability to analyze vast amounts of data, identify patterns, and make predictions, are becoming increasingly valuable in climate finance, enabling more accurate risk assessments, more informed investment decisions, and more efficient processes. Debnath et al. (2023) emphasize the need for less biased, transparent AI systems for climate action. Columbia University School (2024) assesses AI's potential in climate and nature, highlighting data gaps and ethical concerns.

- **Enhancing Climate Risk Assessment:** AI can analyze vast datasets of climate data, including historical climate records, weather patterns, satellite imagery, and socioeconomic data, to improve the accuracy and granularity of climate risk assessments. AI algorithms can identify trends, anomalies, and correlations that may not be apparent to human analysts, providing insights into the potential impacts of climate change on specific regions, assets, or sectors.

- **Optimizing Investment Decisions:** AI can help investors identify and evaluate climate-aligned investment opportunities by analyzing company data, financial information, climate projections, and other relevant factors. AI-powered tools can screen companies based on their carbon footprint, their exposure to climate risks, and their commitment to sustainability, helping investors to identify companies that are well-positioned for the transition to a low-carbon economy.
- **Automating Processes:** AI can automate tasks in climate finance, such as data collection, risk analysis, and reporting. This automation can improve efficiency, reduce costs, and free up human resources to focus on more strategic tasks, such as stakeholder engagement or policy advocacy.

Examples of AI applications in climate finance:

- **Climate Risk Modeling:** Companies like Jupiter Intelligence and Cervest are using AI to develop sophisticated climate risk models that provide detailed assessments of physical climate risks, such as flooding, drought, and extreme heat, for specific locations and assets.
- **Sustainable Investment Analysis:** Firms like Arabesque and Clarity AI are using AI to analyze ESG data and identify companies with strong sustainability performance, helping investors to make more informed and sustainable investment decisions.
- **Green Bond Verification:** AI can be used to automate the process of verifying the environmental credentials of green bond projects, ensuring that bond proceeds are being used for eligible green initiatives.

3.2 Blockchain

Blockchain technology, with its ability to create secure and transparent records of transactions, is emerging as a powerful tool for enhancing transparency, traceability, and efficiency in climate finance.

Key applications of blockchain in climate finance:

- **Tracking Climate Finance Flows:** Blockchain-based platforms can be used to track climate finance flows from source to beneficiary, creating a tamper-proof record of transactions and improving transparency and accountability. This can help to ensure that funds are being used for their intended purposes and that they are reaching the communities and projects that need them most.
- **Facilitating Green Investments:** Blockchain can facilitate green investments by connecting investors with climate-related projects, streamlining investment processes, and reducing transaction costs. For example,

blockchain-based platforms can be used to issue and trade green bonds, connect investors with renewable energy projects, or enable peer-to-peer lending for sustainable businesses.
- **Tokenization of Carbon Credits:** Blockchain can be used to create digital tokens that represent carbon credits, making it easier to track, trade, and verify these credits, potentially enhancing the efficiency and transparency of carbon markets. World Bank (2020) pilots blockchain for energy transitions and carbon markets in Chile, finding reduced costs and improved transparency.

Examples of blockchain initiatives in climate finance:

- **Climate Chain Coalition:** A global initiative that promotes the use of blockchain and other distributed ledger technologies to address climate change.
- **IBM's Climate Action Platform:** A blockchain-based platform that helps companies track their carbon emissions, manage carbon credits, and collaborate on sustainability initiatives.
- **Veridium:** A company that uses blockchain to tokenize carbon credits, making them more accessible and tradable for individuals and businesses.

3.3 Data-Driven Solutions

The increasing availability of climate-related data from various sources, including satellites, sensors, financial databases, and government agencies, is creating unprecedented opportunities for data-driven solutions in climate finance.

- **The Power of Big Data:** Big data analytics can be used to identify patterns, assess risks, and develop insights that would not be possible with smaller datasets. For example, by analyzing vast amounts of data on weather patterns, agricultural yields, and economic activity, researchers can develop more accurate models to assess the impact of climate change on different regions and sectors. Papadopoulos and Balta (2022) highlight the use of Big Data Analytics (BDA) to address climate change challenges and improve sustainability.
- **Data Visualization and Communication:** Data visualization tools can help to communicate complex climate-related information in a clear and compelling way, making it more accessible to investors, policymakers, and the public. Interactive maps, charts, graphs, and dashboards can be used to present data on climate risks, investment opportunities, and the impact of climate action projects.
- **Open Data Platforms:** Open data platforms that make climate data freely accessible to researchers, practitioners, and the public can accelerate

innovation and collaboration in climate finance. By sharing data, we can collectively improve the quality of climate risk assessments, develop more effective solutions, and track progress toward climate goals.

4 Evolving Regulatory Landscape and Global Cooperation

The regulatory landscape for climate finance is rapidly evolving, driven by a growing recognition of the urgency of climate change and the need for a more proactive and coordinated response. Governments worldwide are implementing policies and regulations to incentivize climate action, promote transparency, and mitigate systemic risks. International cooperation is also crucial for addressing this global challenge and ensuring that climate finance flows effectively to developing countries.

4.1 Mandatory Disclosure Requirements

Mandatory climate-related disclosure requirements are becoming increasingly common, as regulators recognize the need for standardized and comparable information to inform investor decisions and promote market transparency. These regulations require companies and financial institutions to disclose their climate-related risks and opportunities, their greenhouse gas emissions, and their strategies for managing climate change.

- **The EU's Corporate Sustainability Reporting Directive (CSRD):** The CSRD, which came into effect in January 2023, significantly expands the scope of sustainability reporting requirements in the EU. It requires companies to disclose information on a wide range of ESG topics, including climate change, aligned with the European Sustainability Reporting Standards (ESRS). The CSRD aims to provide investors with more comprehensive and comparable data, enhancing transparency and facilitating more sustainable investment decisions. The CSRD (European Commission, 2024) enhances ESG reporting, impacting EU and non-EU entities.
- **The US Securities and Exchange Commission (SEC)'s Proposed Rule on Climate Disclosures:** The SEC's proposed rule, released in March 2022, would require publicly traded companies in the United States to disclose their greenhouse gas emissions and climate-related risks in their registration statements and periodic reports. The proposed rule aims to provide investors with consistent, comparable, and decision-useful information about climate-related risks, helping them make more informed investment decisions.

These mandatory disclosure requirements are likely to have a significant impact on the climate finance landscape:

- **Increased Transparency:** Companies and financial institutions will be required to disclose more detailed and standardized information about their climate-related risks, opportunities, and performance.
- **Enhanced Investor Scrutiny:** Investors will have access to more comprehensive and comparable data, enabling them to better assess the climate performance of different companies and make more informed investment decisions.
- **Incentives for Climate Action:** Companies facing mandatory disclosure requirements will be incentivized to improve their climate risk management practices and accelerate their transition to a low-carbon economy.

4.2 *Green Taxonomies*

Green taxonomies are classification systems that define which economic activities can be considered "green" or "sustainable." They provide clarity for investors, policymakers, and businesses, guiding investment decisions, shaping policy incentives, and promoting the development of green financial products. IPSF (2022) introduces the Common Ground Taxonomy (CGT) for aligning green classifications

- **The EU Taxonomy:** The EU Taxonomy, a cornerstone of the EU's Sustainable Finance Action Plan, is a comprehensive classification system that defines environmentally sustainable economic activities across various sectors. It aims to create a common language for green investments within the EU, prevent greenwashing, and channel capital toward activities that contribute to environmental objectives, such as climate change mitigation and adaptation.
- **Other Taxonomies:** Other jurisdictions, including China, Canada, and ASEAN countries, are also developing their own green taxonomies, reflecting their specific environmental priorities and economic contexts. Climate Bonds Initiative (2024) analyzes global green taxonomy development and alignment.

4.3 *Global Cooperation*

Addressing climate change and mobilizing climate finance effectively requires international cooperation. No single country can solve this global challenge alone.

Key areas where global cooperation is essential:

- **Strengthening International Agreements:** The Paris Agreement provides a framework for global cooperation on climate action, but its success depends on countries fulfilling their commitments and ratcheting up their ambition over time. Continued negotiations and collaboration are essential to ensure that the Paris Agreement achieves its goals. UNFCCC (2024) synthesizes NDCs, finding a potential emissions peak before 2030 if commitments are met.
- **Enhancing Multilateral Climate Finance:** Multilateral institutions, such as the UNFCCC, the World Bank, and the Green Climate Fund (GCF), play a crucial role in channeling climate finance to developing countries, facilitating technology transfer, and promoting capacity building. Strengthening these institutions, increasing their funding, and ensuring that they operate transparently and effectively are essential for scaling up climate action globally. Boehm et al. (2023) report that global climate finance needs to increase significantly, to $1.31-$2.61 trillion annually by 2030.
- **Promoting Technology Transfer and Capacity Building:** Developing countries often lack the technology, expertise, and financial resources to implement ambitious climate action plans. Developed countries can support them by sharing knowledge, providing technical assistance, and facilitating the transfer of clean technologies.
- **Addressing Climate Justice:** Climate change disproportionately impacts developing countries, particularly the least developed countries and small island developing states, which have contributed the least to the problem. International climate finance should prioritize the needs of these vulnerable countries, ensuring that they receive adequate support to adapt to climate impacts and pursue sustainable development pathways. UNFCCC (2024) also highlights the need for enhanced financial resources to meet NDC commitments.

5 The Future of Climate-Aligned Investing: Trends and Opportunities

The investment landscape is changing rapidly as awareness of climate change grows and the transition to a low-carbon economy accelerates. Climate-aligned investing, which integrates climate considerations into investment decisions, is no longer a niche strategy; it's becoming a mainstream imperative.

5.1 Growing Investor Demand

Investor demand for sustainable and climate-aligned investments is surging, driven by several factors:

- **Heightened Awareness of Climate Risks:** Investors are increasingly recognizing the financial risks posed by climate change, from the physical impacts of extreme weather events to the transition risks associated with policy changes and technological disruptions.
- **Client and Beneficiary Pressure:** Investment funds and asset managers are facing growing pressure from their clients and beneficiaries to consider ESG factors, including climate change, in their investment decisions. Individuals and institutions are increasingly seeking to align their investments with their values and contribute to a more sustainable future.
- **Evolving Regulatory Landscape:** Mandatory climate risk disclosure requirements and other regulations are pushing investors to consider climate factors more explicitly in their investment processes and to disclose their climate-related risks and opportunities to stakeholders.

Evidence of this growing demand is apparent in:

- **The Growth of ESG-Focused Funds:** The number and size of investment funds that incorporate ESG factors into their investment strategies have grown significantly in recent years.
- **Surveys of Investor Attitudes:** Surveys of investors consistently show that a majority of investors consider climate change to be a material factor in their investment decisions.

5.2 Integration of Climate Factors into Mainstream Investing

Climate considerations are moving from the periphery to the mainstream of investment decision-making. Investors are increasingly integrating climate factors into their analysis across all asset classes and investment strategies, recognizing that climate change is relevant to every sector of the economy.

This shift is being driven by:

- **Improved Data Availability and Risk Assessment Tools:** The availability of more reliable and granular climate data, along with the development of sophisticated climate risk assessment tools, is making it easier for investors to quantify climate risks and opportunities and integrate them into their investment processes.
- **Growing Understanding of the Financial Materiality of Climate Change:** Investors are recognizing that climate change is not just an environmental issue but also a material financial issue that can impact asset values, corporate profitability, and economic growth.
- **Development of Standardized Metrics and Frameworks:** The emergence of standardized metrics and frameworks for assessing climate performance, such as the TCFD recommendations and SASB standards,

is making it easier for investors to compare companies and make informed decisions based on consistent and comparable data.

5.3 *New Investment Opportunities*

The transition to a low-carbon economy is creating a wealth of new investment opportunities, as investors seek to deploy capital in solutions that mitigate climate change, build resilience, and create a more sustainable future.

Key areas of opportunity:

- **Renewable Energy:** The renewable energy sector continues to grow rapidly, driven by falling costs, supportive policies, and increasing demand for clean electricity. Investment opportunities span a range of technologies, including solar, wind, geothermal, and hydropower, as well as energy storage and grid modernization.
- **Energy Efficiency:** Improving energy efficiency offers a cost-effective way to reduce emissions and enhance energy security. Investment opportunities include energy-efficient buildings, industrial processes, appliances, and transportation systems.
- **Green Hydrogen:** Hydrogen is emerging as a clean fuel source with the potential to decarbonize hard-to-abate sectors, such as heavy industry, long-haul transportation, and shipping. Investment opportunities include hydrogen production, storage, and distribution infrastructure, as well as companies developing hydrogen-based technologies.
- **Circular Economy:** A circular economy aims to minimize waste and resource consumption by keeping materials in use for as long as possible. Investment opportunities in this space include companies focused on recycling, remanufacturing, product design for circularity, and sharing economy platforms.
- **Climate Adaptation and Resilience:** The need to adapt to the impacts of climate change is creating investment opportunities in areas such as climate-resilient infrastructure, water management, drought-resistant agriculture, and disaster preparedness.

5.4 *Active Ownership and Engagement*

Investors are increasingly recognizing that they can play an active role in driving climate action by engaging with the companies they invest in and advocating for policies that support a low-carbon economy.

Active ownership and engagement strategies include:

- **Dialogue with Companies:** Investors can engage in direct dialogue with company management to discuss their climate policies, emissions reduction targets, and strategies for managing climate risks.
- **Shareholder Resolutions:** Investors can file shareholder resolutions that call on companies to take specific actions on climate change, such as setting science-based emissions reduction targets, disclosing their climate-related lobbying activities, or adopting more sustainable business practices.
- **Collaborative Engagement:** Investors can work together through initiatives such as Climate Action 100 + to amplify their voice and exert greater influence on companies.

Active ownership and engagement can be a powerful tool for:

- **Encouraging Corporate Climate Action:** Putting pressure on companies to take climate change seriously, set ambitious targets, and implement meaningful changes to reduce their environmental impact.
- **Improving Transparency and Accountability:** Encouraging companies to disclose more comprehensive and reliable information on their climate-related risks, opportunities, and performance.
- **Promoting Policy Change:** Advocating for government policies that support climate action, such as carbon pricing mechanisms, renewable energy incentives, and mandatory climate risk disclosure requirements.

6 A Call to Action: Collective Action for a Sustainable Future

The climate crisis is a defining challenge of our time, but it is also an opportunity to create a more sustainable, equitable, and prosperous future. Addressing this challenge requires a collective effort, with every segment of society—governments, businesses, investors, and individuals—playing a vital role.

The Need for Collective Action

Climate change is a complex, interconnected problem that cannot be solved by any single actor working in isolation.

- **Governments:** Must play a leading role by enacting ambitious climate policies, investing in research and development, and providing incentives for clean technologies and sustainable practices.
- **Businesses:** Need to reduce their emissions, adapt to climate impacts, and innovate to develop new solutions that contribute to a low-carbon economy.

- **Investors:** Have a crucial responsibility to align their portfolios with climate goals, engage with companies on climate action, and advocate for a more sustainable financial system.
- **Individuals:** Can make a difference through their consumption choices, their support for climate-friendly businesses, and their engagement in political and social movements demanding climate action.

The Opportunity for Leadership

Every stakeholder has an opportunity to demonstrate leadership on climate change.

- **Governments:** Can lead by example by setting ambitious national climate targets, implementing effective policies, and supporting international cooperation.
- **Businesses:** Can gain a competitive advantage by being early adopters of clean technologies, developing sustainable products and services, and building resilience to climate impacts.
- **Investors:** Can drive positive change by shifting capital toward climate solutions, engaging with companies on climate performance, and advocating for a more sustainable financial system.
- **Individuals:** Can be powerful advocates for climate action, influencing consumer demand, supporting policies that promote sustainability, and inspiring others to take action.

A Vision for a Sustainable Future

By working together, we can create a future where:

- **The Global Economy Is Powered by Clean Energy:** Reducing our dependence on fossil fuels, mitigating climate change, and improving air quality and public health.
- **Communities Are Resilient to Climate Impacts:** Adapting to changing conditions, protecting vulnerable populations, and ensuring that everyone has access to the resources they need to thrive.
- **Finance Is a Force for Good:** Driving innovation, creating jobs, and supporting a just and equitable transition to a low-carbon world.

The challenges are significant, but the opportunities are even greater. By embracing climate action as a collective imperative, we can shape a future where economic prosperity and environmental sustainability go hand in hand, leaving a healthy and resilient planet for generations to come.

References

Bloomberg New Energy Finance (BloombergNEF). (2024). *New energy outlook 2024*. https://about.bnef.com/new-energy-outlook/. Accessed 24 December 2024.

Boehm, S., et al. (2023). *State of climate action 2023*. https://www.wri.org/research/state-climate-action-2023

Climate Bonds Initiative (CBI). (2024). *Global green taxonomy development, alignment, and implementation 2024*. Climate Bonds Initiative. https://www.climatebonds.net/resources/reports/global-green-taxonomy-development-alignment-and-implementation-2024. Accessed 1 January 2024.

Columbia Climate School. (2024). *AI for climate and nature: Landscape assessment*. Columbia Climate School. https://www.climate.columbia.edu/ai-climate-nature-landscape-assessment. Accessed 24 January 2024.

Debnath, R., Creutzig, F., Sovacool, B. K., & Shuckburgh, E. (2023). Harnessing human and machine intelligence for planetary-level climate action. *NPJ Climate Action, 2*(1), 1–11. https://doi.org/10.1038/s44168-023-00056-3

European Commission. (2024). *Corporate sustainability reporting*. European Commission. https://ec.europa.eu/info/business-economy-euro/company-reporting-and-auditing/company-reporting/corporate-sustainability-reporting_en

Financial Stability Board (FSB). (2020). *The implications of climate change for financial stability*. https://www.fsb.org/2020/11/the-implications-of-climate-change-for-financial-stability/

Global Sustainable Investment Alliance (GSIA). (2023). *Global sustainable investment review 2022*. Global Sustainable Investment Alliance. https://www.gsi-alliance.org/members-resources/gsir2022/

Intergovernmental Panel on Climate Change (IPCC). (2023). *AR6 synthesis report: Climate change 2023*. IPCC. https://www.ipcc.ch/report/sixth-assessment-report-cycle/

International Platform on Sustainable Finance (IPSF). (2022). *International platform on sustainable finance common ground taxonomy—Climate change mitigation instruction report*. https://finance.ec.europa.eu/system/files/2022-06/220603-international-platform-sustainable-finance-common-ground-taxonomy-instruction-report_en.pdf. Accessed 24 January 2025.

International Renewable Energy Agency (IRENA). (2024). *Renewable power generation costs in 2023*. https://www.irena.org/Publications/2024/Sep/Renewable-Power-Generation-Costs-in-2023. Accessed 24 January 2025.

Network for Greening the Financial System (NGFS). (2024). *Guide for supervisors: integrating climate-related and environmental risks into prudential supervision*. Banque de France. https://www.ngfs.net/en/guide-supervisors-integrating-climate-related-and-environmental-risks-prudential-supervision. Accessed 1 January 2024.

Papadopoulos, T., & Balta, M. E. (2022). Climate change and big data analytics: Challenges and opportunities. *International Journal of Information Management, 63*, Article 102448. https://doi.org/10.1016/j.ijinfomgt.2021.102448

PwC. (2024). *Asset and wealth management revolution 2024*. PwC. https://www.pwc.com/gx/en/issues/transformation/asset-and-wealth-management-revolution.html. Accessed 24 January 2024.

United Nations Framework Convention on Climate Change (UNFCCC). (2024). *2024 NDC synthesis report*. https://unfccc.int/process-and-meetings/the-paris-agreement/nationally-determined-contributions-ndcs/2024-ndc-synthesis-report

World Meteorological Organization (WMO). (2024). State of the global climate 2023. From https://library.wmo.int/viewer/68835/download?file=1347_Global-statement-2023_en.pdf&type=pdf&navigator=1

World Bank. (2020). *Using blockchain to support the energy transition and climate markets: Results and lessons from a pilot project in Chile*. World Bank. https://documents.worldbank.org/en/publication/documents-reports/documentdetail/362831617169009719/using-blockchain-to-support-the-energy-transition-and-climate-markets-results-and-lessons-from-a-pilot-project-in-chile. Accessed 1 January 2024.

The manufacturer's authorised representative in the EU is Springer Nature Customer Service Centre GmbH, Europaplatz 3, 69115 Heidelberg, Germany. If you have any concerns regarding our products, please contact ProductSafety@springernature.com

Printed and bound by CPI Group (UK) Ltd, Croydon, CR0 4YY
08/10/2026
02229813-0002